THE BEDTRICK

D1363477

WORLDS Of DESIRE
THE CHICAGO SERIES ON SEXUALITY, GENDER, AND CULTURE
Edited by Gilbert Herdt

THE
BEDTRICK
Tales of Sex and Masquerade

Wendy Doniger

The University of Chicago Press

Chicago & London

Wendy Doniger (O'Flaherty) is the Mircea Eliade Professor of the History of Religions in the Divinity School and a professor in the Department of South Asian Languages and Civilizations and the Committee on Social Thought at the University of Chicago. She is the author of several books, including *Women, Androgynes, and Other Mythical Beasts* (1980), *Dreams, Illusion, and Other Realities* (1984), and *Splitting the Difference: Gender and Myth in Ancient Greece and India* (1999).

The University of Chicago Press, Chicago 60637
The University of Chicago Press, Ltd., London

© 2000 by The University of Chicago
All rights reserved. Published 2000
Printed in the United States of America

10 09 08 07 06 05 04 03 02 01 00   5 4 3 2 1

ISBN (cloth): 0-226-15642-7

Library of Congress Cataloging-in-Publication Data

Doniger, Wendy.
    The bedtrick : tales of sex and masquerade / Wendy Doniger.
        p.   cm. — (Worlds of desire)
    Includes bibliographical references and index.
    ISBN 0-226-15642-7 (alk. paper)
    1. Sex—Mythology—Comparative studies.   2. Deception.   I. Title.   II. Series.
BL325.S42 D64   2000
291.1'78357—dc21
                                                                                99-050887

⊗ The paper used in this publication meets the minimum requirements of the American National Standard for Information Sciences—Permanence of Paper for Printed Library Materials, ANSI Z39.48-1992.

*In memory of my father, Lester L. Doniger (1909–1971),
and for my son, Michael Lester O'Flaherty (b. 1971)*

CONTENTS

Now I remember how everything seemed possible when I was doing it, but as soon as I stopped, not, as if fucking itself were the origin of illusion.

Angela Carter, *Wise Children*

It's the illusion you fall in love with. And no matter how often it occurs, no matter how wise you are as to what the end will be, one more illusion is welcome—for only while it lasts do we catch a vision of our best selves.

Helen of Troy, quoted by John Erskine,
in *The Private Life of Helen of Troy*

Why a Book about a Bedtrick?

TEXTS AND APPROACHES

This is a book about the mythology of sex. More precisely, it is about the story of going to bed with someone whom you mistake for someone else. It is in some ways a companion volume to (a double or shadow of) my book entitled *Splitting the Difference: Gender and Myth in Ancient Greece and India.* Though each is self-contained, they are complementary; to use the Cinderella metaphor,[1] each book drops the other's second shoe. Where *Splitting the Difference* deals with men and women who split in two, fragmenting in situations that only occasionally involve either masquerades or sexual intimacy or both, *The Bedtrick* concentrates on precisely those two issues; that is, where *Splitting the Difference* is about gender, and about splitting the difference, *The Bedtrick* is about sex—more precisely, about lying about sex—and about telling the difference. And where *Splitting the Difference* deals, in a more or less classically philological way, with the historical development of texts within two specific and historically related traditions (ancient Greece and India, with a sideways glance at Victorian England and Hollywood), this book regards the entire world as its oyster and utilizes the irritating grains of sand consisting of a number of different methods to extract the string of narrative pearls. People who split or double in nonsexual ways (by being beheaded, for instance, or reified in mirrors) appear only in *Splitting the Difference,* but some of the people who split and double in order to play bedtricks overlap and appear in both books, double dipping as it were: some of the heroines of the first two chapters of *Splitting the Difference* (such as Saranyu/Samjna, Alcmena and Ahalya, and Eve White/Black) make a few cameo appearances in *The Bedtrick.* Each book, however, emphasizes a different aspect and different variants of those shared myths and considers them in the company of a different corpus of other myths.[2] This change of context[3] reveals a different set of meanings even in the same text (as

Borges demonstrated in his tale of Pierre Menard); texts on the same theme from other cultures offer a context in place of the historical context that most contemporary analyses of stories now attempt to supply.

To help the reader trace a theme or character through both books, I have employed a system of cross-references. A dagger (†) or a double dagger (‡) alerts the reader to the existence of other citations that constitute a context for the theme so marked, which can be located in the table of contents and/or in the index. A dagger refers to other citations in this book, and a double dagger to citations in both this book and *Splitting the Difference*. These three tools—the table of contents, the index, and the cross-references—are designed to help the reader use the book in a hypertextual way, to move from a particular instance of a theme to a place where it is more generally discussed. They are also intended to remind the reader that the theme in the particular text under discussion also appears elsewhere, often in another culture or a different age, and often with a different meaning, or that a concept briefly alluded to has been fully glossed elsewhere.

Aside from the obvious plan of arranging types of the bedtrick by culture and historical period, one might, ahistorically, arrange them according to the "schemes" or complexity of the plots, as William R. Bowden has done for the English Renaissance genre ("X, expecting to lie with A, is caused to lie with B instead through the conspiracy of A and B").[4] I have done a bit of that in chapter 1 (with the double-back, double-play, double-cross, double-back-cross, and double-back-cross-play) and chapter 8 (the double-cross-dress, double-back-cross-dress, double-back-cross-dress-play, and the double-cross-dress-back-play). I have also noted from time to time themes and plots that correspond to Stith Thompson's† periodic table of motifs and tale types (see appendix). But overall I have chosen to arrange the chapters according to the nature of the bedtrickster: rejected spouse, raped spouse, god or animal, ugly or beautiful woman, sexual rival, partner of a legal surrogate, politically disempowered victim, gender-crosser, incestuous relative, realistic plotter.

Each story can be read from the standpoint of the trickster (the person who plays the trick) or of the victim (by which I mean simply the dupe, the person who does not know that it is a trick, with none of the darker overtones of the word "victim"). Readers may find sympathies with either side—or, indeed, with both sides. Bedtricks have many different motives—people do it for love, for sex, for money, for revenge, to save their marriages, to protect themselves, to protect someone else, to gain information, to gain political power—the list could go on and on. But Marjorie Garber has argued convincingly that sex is always the bottom line in tricks of this sort (particularly cross-dressing tricks), even where other excuses are given, such as, "s/he did this in order to a) get a job, b) find a place in a man's world, and c) realize or fulfill some deep but acceptable need in terms of personal destiny." Garber remarks, "I regard such appropriations of transvestism in the service of a humanist 'progress narrative' as both unconvincing and highly problematic."[5] The progress narrative (a self-deceptive or hypocritical excuse for cross-dressing) is what Laurence Senelick calls (with reference to the film *Victor/Victoria*† [1982]) the device of "transvestite in spite of him/herself."[6] Other excuses (like the explanation given for Billy Tipton's real-life masquerade[7] or that of the fictional Tootsie†—that they did it to get a job) are just that, excuses.

My primary texts by definition involve a consummated sexual act, but in my commentaries on these texts I have invoked other texts in which the physical contact is less intimate (sometimes just a kiss) or frustrated (the trickster unmasked before consummation), so long as the issues of intimacy raised by the bedtrick are illuminated by the text in question. And I have also included some texts of unconsummated bedtricks that are consummated in later interpretations; thus, for instance, Edmond Rostand's play *Cyrano de Bergerac*† has no consummated bedtrick, but the kiss, as usual, stands for more, and the film version (*Roxanne*, 1987) connects the dots and consummates the act. So, too, the implicit bedtricks in Shakespeare's *The Comedy of Errors*† and *Twelfth Night*† were made explicit in contemporary productions[8] in which the twin brother or Sebastian staggers out, more or less naked, from the house of the bedtricked woman (Adriana or Olivia); a contemporary production of *Midsummer Night's Dream*,† too,[9] left no doubt in anyone's mind that Titania and Bottom became lovers. (Shakespeare also depicted explicit bedtricks in *All's Well That Ends Well*† and *Measure for Measure*† and a quasi bedtrick in *Much Ado about Nothing*.) The bedtrick is expressed by acts of different intensities according to different conventions in different cultures and periods.

Each of the ten chapters is divided into two parts. The first part presents the texts, generally beginning with an example taken from ancient Hindu mythology and then moving from India to the rest of the world, and from gods to humans. Where Saranyu/Samjna provided the seminal text (what Hindus call the *bija-mantra*) for *Splitting the Difference*, the pivot of this book is the story of Shiva, Parvati (Shiva's wife, here in the

form of Kali/Gauri), and the demon Adi, a myth that seems to have obsessed me even more than the tale of Samjna, perhaps because Shiva is
both my kind of god and my kind of guy: I touched upon this story in
my first book, *Siva: The Erotic Ascetic* (1973), translated it in *Hindu Myths*
(1975), and analyzed it in *Women, Androgynes, and Other Mythical Beasts*
(1980)—always, as here, using different variants and devising different
interpretations. In this book it provides a kind of thread, often involving
Shiva: Shiva's rejected wife must masquerade to seduce her husband
(chapter 1); the demon Adi masquerading as Parvati fools Shiva and becomes the raped mother (chapter 2); Shiva's sexual rival attempts to seduce Shiva's wife (chapter 5), who sends her servant in her place (chapter
6); the demon Adi becomes an animal (chapter 3) and a female (chapter
8), while Parvati reveals her fair (chapter 4) interior by sloughing her
black (chapter 7) outer sheath; she curses her son when he comes between
her and his father (chapter 9), and she is recognized by Shiva only during
the sexual act (chapter 10).

Each chapter then cross-culturally contextualizes the Hindu story with
variants of the theme from the Hebrew Bible, medieval courtly romances,
Shakespeare, operas, or contemporary literature, theater, and cinema. The
first part of each chapter emphasizes differences among variants of the
theme and different cultural aspects of each theme, noting other stories
of the same type in the same culture and dwelling upon some of the
striking details that make each variant unique, even within its own culture.
These sections do not have full conclusions; they present a body of materials, each piece analyzed in itself, but leave the broader interpretations for
the final part of each chapter, which I have called "Approaches."

The approaches present the shadow‡ of the text, the commentary, utilizing various disciplines: philosophy, psychology, zoology, feminism, theology, law, critical studies, queer theory, rhetoric, and structuralism. Although each set of ideas and questions is assigned to a chapter to which
it is particularly appropriate, all of the approaches are relevant to all ten
chapters, to all variants of the stories of the bedtrick, a wide range of
approaches to a wide range of genres, like Cyrano's† suggestion for various methodological critiques of his nose: aggressive, friendly, descriptive,
inquisitive, kindly, etc. In this way I have tried to create the textual and
methodological equivalent of the kind of "thick description" that Clifford
Geertz has prescribed for anthropological fieldwork. I have, for instance,
used structural analyses, Freudian terminology, and my own mild brand
of feminist consciousness throughout the book, though I have also explic-

itly discussed each of these methods in one of the ten discrete sections devoted to approaches.

These approaches, which embody ideas more than methods, are intended to raise the sorts of questions that might prove fruitful in drawing patterns of meanings from the stories in this book. Some of the questions are particularly associated with certain European or American disciplines, and some transcend or combine disciplines. But the ten approaches are not intended to summarize or even contribute to the disciplines upon which they draw. They ask the questions that the disciplines ask but do not give their answers, or cite all the scholars in those disciplines who have offered answers; they draw upon the more basic, classical formulations and leave it to interested readers to forage further in more sophisticated contemporary directions.[10] I claim no new insights into Lacan or Descartes; rather, I suggest that the texts of the bedtrick offer some answers to their questions, and I suggest some ways in which asking their questions enlarges our understanding of the bedtrick. I am poaching in these preserves, making commando raids to pick up any ideas I can find that shed light on the tricks played in the dark; I am using the theories that I know, the ones that I like, the ones that make sense to me for this problem. I am not trying to reconcile one discipline with the often warring methods of another, but I believe that it is possible to derive useful insights into a text from disciplines, or even schools within disciplines, that are not on speaking terms with one another. Nor do I mean to imply that my own disciplinary home, the history of religions, is necessarily more inclusive than the disciplines it draws upon, merely that some historians of religions, such as myself, find eclecticism a fruitful point of departure, or even of leverage.[11]

The questions will always take us back to the stories, which are greater than any of our ideas about them. I start with the stories, and leave them without final conclusions, to give the reader a chance to conceive her own ideas about them before hearing mine; and I have tried to arrange the stories in such a way as to let them speak for themselves while also telling the story that I want them to tell. Readers impatient with this agenda, and those who want to cut to the chase to find out why they should bother to read the stories at all, can always skip to the conclusion of each chapter, then to the sections on approaches, and finally to the summary conclusion of the book. Some people (I confess to being one of them) read academic books (and menus) backward, as if they were written in Hebrew: a glance first at the bibliography, to see, among other things, if their own works are cited[12] and what texts are used, so that if the book proves bankrupt of ideas, one can at least check out the assembled sources and develop one's own ideas about them. Such people will probably turn straight to the conclusion of this book right after finishing with the bibliography and the notes, and only then read the stories. As Count Orlofsky, patron of the bedtrick ball, sings in *Die Fledermaus,* in an aria that could be the school song for all the actors, tricksters, and victims in these stories about sex, "Chacun à son goût." Whenever I hear that aria, I feel that they're playing my song, methodologically speaking.

Texts as Contexts

In some cases, I have provided a nonnarrative context for the stories I tell: some of the Hindu myths, for instance, may be explained by certain assumptions encoded in the caste system, and some of the narratives of the Hebrew Bible by considerations of the position of the Jews in the ancient Near East; American films reflect the attitudes of the cold war; European fairy tales refract early modern ideas about embryology; and so forth.

But the meanings of these stories are not limited to their social contexts. I have tried to argue for the methodological assumptions underlying the broad comparative enterprise in a book, *The Implied Spider,* that began life as the introduction to this book, *The Bedtrick.* Let me apply the arguments in *The Implied Spider* to the problem posed by *The Bedtrick.*

Comparison takes a myth out of its historical context and supplies, instead, the context of other myths, often from other cultures. Frequently, the best way to understand a myth is by understanding how it differs from other myths in the same culture as well as from variants in other cultures. Such a supplementary context is needed because of the fragmentary nature of our understanding of myths, especially those embedded in ancient texts. When myths tell us what happened, they do not always tell us why the people in the story did what they did or how they felt about what happened to them. To this extent, they remain open and transparent and can be retold, within one culture or in several cultures, with several very different meanings. Although well-told myths always have plenty of details to give them life and reality, they do not always have *psychological* details. Laconic texts leave us in the dark, where one thing looks much like another.

In the Hebrew Bible story of Rachel and Leah,† for instance, if we ask how it was that Jacob was fooled, how he mistook Leah for Rachel, we find that the narrative background remains opaque and leaves us with insoluble riddles. Later Jewish commentaries raise and answer some of these questions, but we can also seek unofficial commentaries outside the tradition of the original text. Zwi Jagendorf, comparing the trick that Leah plays on Jacob with the bedtrick that Helena plays on her husband, Bertram (who thinks he's in bed with Diana), in *All's Well That Ends Well*,† agrees that "Shakespeare makes us understand in Helena's words what Leah might have thought in Jacob's arms."[13] And this is a two-way flow: questions about Shakespeare might be resolved by looking back at myths, "the same sort of myths out of which many of [Shakespeare's] plays develop."[14] Or by looking farther forward: Barbara Hodgdon compares the dynamics of *All's Well* with that of "the screwball film comedies of the late 1930's and early 1940's,"[15] as I will compare the tale of Rachel and Leah with the films that Bette Davis made in the 1940s and 1960s, in which she played her own evil twin.† I also think that Angela Carter's† story of twin sisters offers many wise answers to the questions left open by the Hebrew Bible story of Rachel and Leah, insights into the tension between sororal rivalry and solidarity, for example, answers that the rabbis did not choose to record (or did not think of), as well as different answers to questions that the rabbis did record. I have already suggested one way in which later productions can shed light on earlier texts, in resolving the question of the consummated or unconsummated bedtricks in *Cyrano, A Comedy of Errors,* and *Twelfth Night.*

The comparatist can use the speculations found in similar stories told in other cultures to fill in what is not said in the text under consideration. In this way we may use a Hollywood film or a modern British text to discipline our own imagination of what might have been in the minds of Rachel and Leah. And looking not only back but sideways, at India and Japan, further extends the parallax and hence the depth of our vision. In *Splitting the Difference* I called upon historical context to begin my analysis, but I also went on to argue, there and elsewhere, for the uses of cross-cultural, intertextual context (which Arjun Appadurai nicely characterizes as a "vertical takeoff, no taxiing on the [social contextual] runway")[16] in place of the historical, sociological context generally favored by contemporary trends in religious studies.[17] Terence Cave spells out the essential value of this method with regard to a bedtrick. Noting that people from the start compared the real Martin Guerre† with the fictional Amphitryon‡ (a man whom the god Zeus impersonated in order to seduce his wife, Alcmena), he remarks:

In this way, Martin Guerre immediately enters the intertextual labyrinth composed by the literary memory of Western civilization. His story cannot be recovered as a unique event, experienced by living individuals: it is shaped *ab initio* by existing narrative structures and interpretations. Amphitryon is one of his siblings, Odysseus another, perhaps Oedipus another again. Shakespeare's plays, the first of which were written during Martin's lifetime, flourish on the materials of which his story is made, and make it difficult to read that story as anything but an implausible but disturbing old tale.[18]

I would broaden the network of Cave's Western intertextual memory to include a different sort of memory that might be called infratextual; and I would enlarge the family to include more distant cousins of Martin Guerre, such as the Hindu gods Indra† and Shiva.†

But here a voice of caution is heard, raising questions about cultural constructions of the bedtrick. Did people at other times, and in other parts of the world, have the same ideas about sex and gender, desire and knowledge, that prevail in European and American society today? Would the author of the story of Rachel have felt like Angela Carter (let alone the directors of the Bette Davis films) about such things as sororal rivalry? And a related question: Did Freud† put our ideas about all of this into our heads (or, to use the currently hegemonic lingo, construct them)? Is the idea that the sexual act is both revelatory and concealing, for instance, just a modern European idea that we read back into ancient texts, or is it really present in those texts, too? If it is present in a muted form, how do we use the manifest content of contemporary texts to excavate the latent content of ancient texts? How do we know our questions are not projections (like the projections‡ of lust that facilitate the bedtrick)?

To some extent, of course, they are projections; we cannot know what was in the mind of an author. But projecting other texts, rather than, or in addition to, our own ideas, into the text in question at least makes the projection more subtle and argues for an imaginary line drawn not just between our heads and the Bible but between the heads of the auteurs of the Bette Davis films and the Bible. This method puts the texts themselves in conversation with one another,[19] sometimes even in the intimate pillow talk of textual intercourse. Ultimately, we cannot know if an earlier author thought like a later one; but what either of them thought is always a human possibility, and we who have the advantage of hindsight may now bring those later possibilities explicitly to our reading of the older texts, acknowledging what we are doing.

Can we generalize about the human meanings that flesh out the abstract armatures common to many, if not all, of these stories? William R. Bowden, speaking of Shakespeare, answered this question with a confident no: "Obviously, the bed trick is strictly a plot device. It cannot carry much universal significance."[20] But I venture a qualified yes, qualified in asserting cross-cultural, rather than universal, meanings for the bedtrick as well as for the concepts of sex, love, and knowledge that undergird it.[21] These meanings are in part essential and in part culturally constructed; that is, some basic meanings are inherent in the structure in all variants of the plot, while other meanings attach themselves to many variants, and still others serve rather to show how very differently any two retellings of the story may view the plot, inviting us to contrast these ideas with those of our own time and place.

Our stories range from lighthearted comedy and farce (such as Angela Carter's twins, the Telugu loincloth story, and *Some Like It Hot*) through moralizing texts (such as the Jain and Buddhist stories in chapters 1 and 4) to the *mise en abîme* of metaphysical and psychological confusion in the Japanese tale of *The Changelings*.† Other differences result from different cultural periods, different religious or secular contexts, different ideologies. The bedtrick in the Hebrew Bible is primarily about the paternal inheritance of elder and younger brothers and about negotiating the boundaries of incest, while in medieval Christianity, it is about the tension between marital and extramarital love. In Shakespeare it is used to overcome the tension between monogamy and promiscuity and to explore androgyny and sexual jealousy; in nineteenth-century Germany and Russia, it is about paranoia, particularly political paranoia; in nineteenth-century England, about the sexual threat of women and the terror of aging; and so forth. Intertextuality within each tradition allows each genre to reflect upon others and to intersect with them, producing potentially infinite crosscurrents and undertones. I leave it to each reader to pursue the streams of his or her own fancy further into whatever genres or contexts strike a note of sympathy or leave questions unanswered.

The key to the game of cross-cultural comparison lies in selecting the sorts of questions that might transcend any particular culture. Some people think that there are no such questions, but some think, as I do, that worthwhile cross-cultural questions can be asked. Marliss C. Desens assumes a commensurability in audience response to the bedtricks in Genesis and in Shakespeare: "It may be that some of our contemporary responses to the bed-trick belong to our own cultural context, and we should not ignore such responses [I would say, we should not assume that the first audiences shared them], but we might also pause to examine whether we have some common bond with those first audiences."[22]

This common bond is not necessarily a universal bond, but it is a cross-cultural bond. Though stories about bedtricks are told all over, some of the tricksters' motives, and many of their ways of getting caught and/or away with it, vary not just among cultures but among individuals. But comparison defamiliarizes what we take for granted. For example, this book will compare the story of Rachel and Leah in the Hebrew Bible (Genesis 28) with Angela Carter's story of Nora and Dora (in *Wise Children*). Both stories are about a woman whose sister takes her place in the bed of her husband or lover. By comparing them, I am asserting a degree of generality: some of the problems that confronted Rachel and Dora are also being faced by contemporary British and American women. My act of comparison inevitably brings a third element into the field of play: my voice in addition to those of the Hebrew Bible and Angela Carter. My selection of these stories rather than others, and my decision to highlight certain shared elements of them at the expense of other elements that are unique to each version, are particular to me, not merely to my time and place.

THE USES OF INSOMNIA

My agenda is multivalent: I am an old-fashioned philologist who finds Freud often relevant and sometimes persuasive, a feminist who finds structuralism the best starting point for the analysis of a myth, a heterosexual Jewish woman who was raised a Communist and has come to be more interested in the imagination than in what other people call "real life." The protagonist of e. e. cummings's *him* declares three props of his essence: "I am an Artist, I am a Man, I am a Failure."[23] My triad is "I am a Sanskritist,[24] I am a woman, I am an insomniac." I am by training an Indologist, by choice a mythologist,[25] and by nature interested in bedtricks.

I bring very different competencies to the different genres and cultures invoked in this book, beginning with my training as a Sanskritist and student of Indian literature. India, particularly Hinduism, is not only the culture that I know best, after my own (in some ways, better than my own), but the culture that I suspect of having the best stories; India has variations on mythological themes for which my own traditions do not even have themes.[26] I have presented the Indian texts in this book in much more detail than the European and American texts, in part because I know the Indian texts best and like them best but also because I assume that most of my readers know the European texts better and have better access to them.

But the meanings of the Indian stories extend into and are often clarified and deepened by European legends, novels, and films. My second qualification to write this book is my insomnia, which began at roughly the same time as my interest in storytelling and accounts for a good deal of my knowledge of English literature (particularly Shakespeare) and all of my knowledge of B movies. I am not a scholar of films; I don't study the old silent ones or many foreign films, nor do I keep up with the latest Hollywood trends in horror and mutilation; I am an American Movie Classic buff. I watch films but do not read much about them besides Leslie Halliwell and David Thomson; for me films are primary texts, and all I can contribute to the study of films is their classical mythological context. I earned the red badge of bloodshot eyes watching the *Late Late Late Show* with my mother, and I sometimes feel that I ought to win the literary equivalent of the Croix de Guerre for sitting through not only the many truly terrible films about bedtricks on "late Thursday/early Friday" television but the advertisements for used cars and phone sex (some of which also offer doubles) that punctuate them—until, at last, the coup de grâce is administered at dawn, to the appropriate military strains of "The Star Spangled Banner." (I also owe to my mother my love of opera,† whose plots share with B movies the dubious privilege of providing a happy retirement home for mythological kitsch.)

The sorts of films I have concentrated on are the lowbrow popular movies that provide a rich compost for myths to grow in, the B movies that are (along with *Star Trek*†)[27] the *reductio ad absurdum* of many myths, for Hollywood is as much a myth factory as it is a dream factory. It has even been stated as a kind of law of nature that the worse the film, the better the metaphysics.[28] B movies employ the technique of bricolage (the art of making new things out of the scraps of old things),[29] which lies at the heart of myths: to make money, films take what works and copy it, beginning with gross plots and titles (such as the various remakes of *The Prisoner of Zenda*†). This habit has become so notorious that when Alan Bennett's British play *The Madness of George III* was produced as a film for distribution in America, it was retitled *The Madness of King George* for fear that Americans would mistake the British title for the third in a series of which they had missed the first two installments. "A survey had

apparently shown that there were many filmgoers who came away from
Kenneth Branagh's film of *Henry V* wishing they had seen its four prede-
cessors."[30] Such repetitions catch up not just whole plots but the constit-
uent parts of the plots (the man, transformed into a woman, who gazes
in solipsistic lust at his own new breasts) and conventional images (the
swirling of the sky during a kiss) which abound in Indian TV and film
presentations of myths, too. These are the recycled pieces that we call
mythemes[31] when they occur in myths, clichés† when they occur in B
movies.[32] Terence Cave notes that the sense of cliché "is also the sense of
repetition, a compulsive returning to the 'same' place, a place already
known, as if one were discovering it for the first time."[33] Mircea Eliade
regarded this as the very essence of myth, "the eternal return,"[34] and it
is certainly the essence of a masquerade: to present something known in
such a way that people mistake it for something unknown (or the reverse).

The use of film clichés for the sexual act was wonderfully satirized in
an old Monty Python skit in which, as a couple starts to make love on
a bed, she sinks down backward and he bends over her as they fade out;
then you see waves crashing, a train rushing into a tunnel, a silo rising,
a silo falling, and so forth, until we see her sitting up angrily in bed saying
to him, as he sits there operating a movie projector, "Are you going to
show those films all night?" Films present unique aspects of the bedtrick
because where texts (even those that assume the primacy of vision) are
made of words, films (even "talkies") are made of images, inspiring new
takes on the problem of representing two visually "identical" people.

My basic comparison is between ancient India and contemporary
America, particularly Hollywood; the two worlds of Sanskrit texts and B
movies intersect in me. Like all of my other books, this is primarily a study
of stories from ancient India, seen through the ideas of a contemporary
American woman. It is intended to show what ideas about sex as truth
and/or lie are and are not shared by contemporary Americans and people
from other cultures, primarily ancient India.

The Hebrew Bible and Greek and Latin literature provide the third
circle of my texts. These three clusters of primary sources support the
platform on which this book stands, and each is represented by enough
texts to provide it with a literary, if not a social, context, a critical mass
of texts that illuminate one another. The fourth circle, still within my
own linguistic and cultural range, consists of German and French stories,
some of which I grew up with (Viennese mother, Russian father) and
others of which I sought for this project.

To indicate how yet other cultures have imagined yet other variations on the central theme, I have also drawn superficially upon myths from cultures I know less well. These other cultures are not always contextualized here at all, even by other texts. This fifth circle, a non-weight-bearing wall of my narrational edifice, constitutes the smallest fraction of this book but includes all the rest of the world. Like Bambi and his mother, I proceed with caution out of my safe Sanskrit-Hollywood-Hebrew-French/German thicket into this broader meadow of the wide world, a place where you can be shot down by a bad translation. (I inched out into this meadow at the very end of each chapter in *Splitting the Difference,* but I will stride boldly into it all the time here.) Here, like Blanche DuBois in Tennessee Williams's play *A Streetcar Named Desire,* I am "dependent upon the kindness of strangers" (upon their reliability, for translations and contextualizations).

Aside from stories from the Dravidian texts of South India and the Hebrew Bible, there is relatively little here from outside the language group known as Indo-European (Sanskrit, Greek, Norse, Celtic)—just a scattering of tales from Arabic, Inuit, Japanese, and Chinese texts, and an even thinner scattering from African, South American, Polynesian, Indonesian, and Native American sources (all in translation), narrative flotsam and jetsam from the ocean of my casual reading and viewing, carried to me by the strong current of my obsession. This uneven sampling reflects my weakness rather than any dearth of relevant stories; readers will surely be able to supply many other examples. Sometimes the meanings of the myths in these other cultures seem to agree with those of the cultures more broadly represented here, sometimes not; always we sense that we get only a portion of their meanings when we do not know the context. But to contextualize them would have made this long book infinitely long.[35]

APOLOGIA FOR THE LENGTH OF THIS BOOK

My mother bequeathed to me, along with the *Late Late Late Show* and opera, a passion for collecting things: paintings (for her) and stories (for me). My collection of bedtricks, made into the collage (or, if you will, bricolage) of this book, is certainly not exhaustive, merely a selection of some of my favorites. The goal of this promiscuously comparative book is not, primarily, to display my own obsession with stories about bedtricks but to display the human race's obsession with the theme. Since part of my argument is simply that there are variants of this myth all over the world, I have cited many, many stories. To say, "There are lots of stories about this," tells you something significant about the theme; actually to tell a lot of those stories tells you far more. I take as my motto the epigraph from Pier Paolo Pasolini's film *Il fiore delle Mille e una notte:* "Truth is not found in a single dream, but in many dreams."[36] This book was not destined to be a haiku.

The bedtrick turns out to be the sort of cannibalizing project that Maggie Kilgour calls "*The Text That Ate the World*," one of those themes that "set out to swallow reality in a single gulp . . . (*my* metaphor's bigger than *your* metaphor)," which she imagines as "a B-movie (written by Stephen King and directed by George Romero) about the 'encyclopedic impulse' to incorporate everything."[37] As my manuscript continued to grow, one potential publisher suggested that instead of publishing it in the old-fashioned way, on paper, I could simply put it on-line as a kind of Web site or chat bedroom and let people subscribe to the constant updates. Rejecting that option, I thought of subtitling it "The Silver Twig" (or, more arrogantly, "The Platinum Bough"), but if Sir James George Frazer has been an inspiration, he has not provided a methodological model. Then I thought of calling it "An Encyclopedia of Bedtricks" or "An Anthology of Bedtricks" or, in bad moments, "The Guinness Book of Bedtricks," for it ranges pretty widely, and I did try to arrange the stories systematically. But it would be presumptuous to claim that this book is an encyclopedia, for it is far too idiosyncratic in tone and taste to sustain the truth claims implicit in the title of "encyclopedia." My work to date was once described, by someone introducing me at a public event, as offering "a powerful anecdote" [*sic*] to certain lamentable trends in the field of the history of religions. This slip of the tongue is all the method to which I aspire here; I hope that *The Bedtrick* will indeed prove to be a powerful anecdote.

I have three primary goals in this book, in steeply declining order of importance. First is to delight and amuse; my criterion of selection has been primarily aesthetic rather than ideological: I have chosen the best stories I know, those rich in human insights and memorable images. Each chapter begins by telling some good stories, particularly stories not widely known in Europe and America, and by assembling clusters of vivid details. My second goal is to prove some points, such as the importance of the theme of the bedtrick, the fruitfulness of cross-cultural studies, the value of using many different approaches, and the existence of certain patterns in the ways that human beings have devised to deal with their sexual fantasies. This I have attempted to do by the sheer number of examples, as well as by analysis and arguments in the approach sections. Third, I hope to dazzle the reader with my peculiar erudition, by juxtaposing narratives that no one else would think of juxtaposing.

I certainly do not expect every, or perhaps even any, reader to read the book straight through. Terence Cave, writing on a similar topic, speaks for me:

> Few readers will have the patience to read this book from end to end. . . . The topic is many-sided and the angles of approach varied. On the other hand, this is not just a collection of essays. It was written as a whole and some parts are not easily understandable without reference to others, not so much because the argument follows a single direct line, but because themes and images . . . recur in different contexts, and without some knowledge of those contexts particular cases may seem arbitrary or fanciful.[38]

The fabric of the bedtrick is such that the threads keep unraveling and doubling back on themselves, like the themes in a fugue, the twists in a Möbius strip. The appearance of arbitrariness therefore threatens this book perhaps even more than it did Cave's, and to counteract it I have devised the system of cross-references described above. The division of the text into small subsections is also designed to make the text browser-friendly.

There were many more stories in earlier drafts, but I boiled them down, like the woman who prepared milk-rice for the Buddha when he ended his long meditation after achieving Enlightenment: she milked a thousand cows and fed the milk to five hundred cows; then she milked those five hundred cows and fed the milk to two hundred and fifty, and so on, until she fed the milk of sixteen cows to eight. She used the milk of those eight cows to prepare the milk-rice for the Buddha.[39] But I had to stop midway, at about two hundred and fifty, for unlike Schelling's (or Hegel s) ideological cows, which are all black at night[40] (like women and cats†), and more like the ancient Indian wishing-cow, which you can milk of whatever you desire,[41] narrative cows do not look alike or yield just one kind of milk. This book is my offering of milk-rice for the enlightened reader.

ACKNOWLEDGMENTS

Ordinarily, I thank individually the people who have helped me with a book, but I worked on this book for so long (thirteen years) that there are too many to list here: many colleagues, editors, audiences, and students during those years, to whom I owe so much, in so many ways. Over the long haul, I used earlier and, I hope, now unrecognizable versions of bits of this book as lectures and articles. Parts of chapter 1 were published in "The Criteria of Identity in a Telugu Myth of Sexual Masquerade," in *Syllables of Sky: Studies in South Indian Civilization in Honour of Velcheru Narayana Rao,* ed. David Shulman (Delhi: Oxford University Press, 1995), 103–32. Parts of chapter 3 appeared in "The Love That Dare Not Baa Its Name: Calf and Other Loves," review of Midas Dekkers, *Dearest Pet: On Bestiality,* in *London Review of Books* 16, no. 15 (Aug. 14, 1994): 3–4, 6; and in "The Mythology of Masquerading Animals, or, Bestiality," in *In the Company of Animals,* ed. Arien Mack, *Social Research* 62, no. 3 (fall 1995): 751–72. Parts of chapter 4 were published in "Myths and Methods in the Dark," *Journal of Religion* 76, no. 4 (Oct. 1996): 531–47. Parts of chapter 5 appeared in "Playing the Field: Adultery as Claim-Jumping," in *The Sense of Adharma,* by Ariel Glucklich (New York: Oxford University Press, 1994), 169–88; and, with Gregory Spinner, in "Misconceptions: Female Imaginations and Male Fantasies in Parental Imprinting," *Daedalus* 127, no. 1 (winter 1998): 97–130. Parts of chapter 6 were published in "Begetting on Margin: Adultery and Surrogate Pseudomarriage in Hinduism," in *From the Margins of Hindu Marriage: Essays on Gender, Religion, and Culture,* ed. Paul Courtright and Lindsey Harlan (New York: Oxford University Press, 1995), 160–83; and in "Sexual Doubles," in *Twins,* special issue of *Parabola* (summer 1994): 33–40. Parts of chapter 8 were published in "Double Cross-Dressing Chevalier, or, The Reluctant Transvestite," review of Gary Kates, *Monsieur d'Eon Is a Woman,* in *The Nation,* Oct. 16, 1995, 436–39; and in "Four in a Bed," review of Marjorie

Garber, *Vice Versa*, in *London Review of Books* 18, no. 3 (Feb. 8, 1996): 15–16. Parts of chapter 9 can be found in "Speaking in Tongues: Deceptive Stories about Sexual Deception," *Journal of Religion* 74, no. 3 (July 1994): 320–37; and in "Enigmas of Sexual Masquerade in Hindu Myths and Tales," in *Untying the Knot: On Riddles and Other Enigmatic Modes,* ed. David Shulman (New York: Oxford University Press, 1996), 208–27. Parts of chapter 10 were published in "What Did They Name the Dog?" review of Lawrence Wright, *Twins: Genes, Environment and the Mystery of Identity*, in *London Review of Books* 20, no. 10 (Mar. 19, 1998): 32; and in "Double Beds Hold at Least Four People," *University of Chicago Magazine* 82, no. 4 (summer 1990): 26–30. Parts of the conclusion appeared in "Sex, Lies, and Tall Tales," in *Truth-Telling, Lying, and Self-Deception,* in *Social Research* 63, no. 3 (fall 1996): 633–99.

Several chapters of this book were presented at public lectures, where both my hosts and the audience contributed precious pieces to the growing puzzle. I am grateful to those who invited me to give the Loy H. Witherspoon Lecture, University of North Carolina at Charlotte, 1990; the 1990 Tamblyn Lectures at Western Ontario University, London, Ontario; the 1991 Cole Lectures at Vanderbilt; the Mackay Lecture, St. Lawrence University, 1991; "Mythologie et sexualité: quelques masques, quelques déguisements," at a Conférence au Collège de France, 1992; the Whidden Lectures at McMaster University, 1993; the Orr Lecture at Dartmouth College, 1993; the Homer J. Armstrong Lectures at Kalamazoo College, 1993; the first J. Gonda Lecture, Koninklijke Nederlandse Akademie van Wetenschappen, Amsterdam, 1993; the Surjit Singh Lecture, Graduate Theological Union, 1994; the Ryerson Lecture, University of Chicago, 1995; the Berry Lectures, University of Hawaii, 1996; and the Wickenden Lectures, Miami University, Ohio, 1997.

But returning, like the rabbi from Cracow in the old story, to dig under my own stove,[1] I learned most of all from my own colleagues at the Divinity School (particularly Gary Ebersole, Michael Fishbane, Clark Gilpin, Paul Griffiths, Mark Krupnick, Bernie McGinn, Frank Reynolds, Martin Riesebrodt, and David Tracy) at the February 1991 Faculty Retreat. I am particularly indebted to Michael Fishbane for a conversation over lunch, one winter's day in 1990, that made me rethink the entire scope of the project. To David Shulman I owe so much, first of all for asking, as he drove me up the hill from Tel Aviv to Jerusalem in May 1996, when I told him what I was going to say about Saranyu, "You mean, like Rachel and Leah?" And then for doubling as my double during all those years in which we wrote such different articles about such similar subjects; and for his daily exhortations on email when I lost my way in the project. To Clark Gilpin I am so grateful, both for his continuing confidence in the book as, year after year, I failed to finish it and for allowing me to schedule my teaching in ways that gave me both time for writing and the benefit of priceless nourishing and inspiring input from my students. To Alan Thomas and Morris Philipson, for their indulgent encouragement and tactful suggestions over the years. To David Grene, for persuading me, relentlessly, that no one would read a 2,000-page book and insisting that I keep my eye on the ball(s). To Ann Grodzins Gold, Kirin Narayan, Marina Warner, Pamela Bruton, and Linda Hess, for their courage and generosity in reading monstrous drafts and their acumen and wisdom in helping me to fix some of the broken places. To Margaret Mahan and Warren Hassmer, for saving me days of work by devising the simplified system of cross-references. To Benjamin Sommer, for teaching me Hebrew and helping me to read the *midrashim*. And again I must thank Katherine Ulrich for her inspired, tireless sleuthing in the stacks, and my son, Michael Lester O'Flaherty, for hunting down many stories for me. Finally, the usual disclaimer, but with a twist: the flaws, particularly the excesses, of this book I wish to blame on David Tracy and Lorraine Daston, codependents in this obsessive quest, who indulged me by patiently listening to story after story and enabled me, *comme on dit*, by giving me things to read about bedtricks.

Sex, Text,
and Masquerade

※

BEDTRICKS

You go to bed with someone you think you know, and when you wake up you discover that it was someone else—another man or another woman, or a man instead of a woman, or a woman instead of a man, or a god, or a snake, or a foreigner or alien, or a complete stranger, or your own wife or husband, or your mother or father. This is what Shakespearean scholars call "the bedtrick"[1]—sex with a partner who pretends to be someone else.[2] The bedtrick contests the intimate relationship between sex and gender, power and identity, raising a number of questions: Why weren't you able to tell the difference in the dark? And why does it matter so much? Why is this story told over and over again? Why do we find it compelling? What deep human concerns does it respond to? How unique and unmistakable is one lover to another? Can you recognize your lover in the dark? Can true love always tell the difference? Is it the body that is desired, or the mind? How does sex change if we do or do not know who our partner actually is? And, at the bottom of it all, does sex tell the truth or lie?

The basic plot should make it onto anyone's list of the Ten Greatest Hits of World Mythology. There are Rachel and Leah, Tamar and Judah, and (I believe) Ruth and Naomi in the Hebrew Bible; Amphitryon in the Greek and Roman traditions; and, in medieval European literature, King Arthur begotten by a masquerading father and both Elaine and a false Guenever masquerading as Guenever.[3] There are the bedtricks in Boccaccio and in so many Shakespeare plays, especially *All's Well That Ends Well* and *Measure for Measure*. In opera we have Mozart's *The Marriage of Figaro* and *Così fan tutte*, Richard Strauss's *Rosenkavalier* and *Arabella*, Johann Strauss's *Fledermaus*, and Richard Wagner's *Tristan and Isolde* and *Götterdämmerung*. There are the transsexual and transvestite bedtricks in contemporary theater (*M. Butterfly, Prelude to a Kiss*) and cinema (*Some*

Like It Hot, The Crying Game). Moving outside the European tradition, we encounter an eleventh-century Japanese novel about a brother and sister who change places in their respective marital beds *(The Changelings)* and a modern Japanese novel about a bedtrick (Fumiko Enchi's *Masks*), as well as an infinite variety of bedtricks in the *Arabian Nights* and in the ancient Indian storytelling tradition. All of these texts are myths by my definition: stories that are believed to be true and that people continue to believe in the face of sometimes massive evidence that they are, in fact, lies;[4] much-retold narratives that are transparent to a variety of constructions of meaning, neutral structures that allow paradoxical meanings to be held in a charged tension.[5]

Scholars of high culture (particularly opera[6] and Shakespeare[7]) have tended to regard the bedtrick as a cheap trick—morally corrupt (the trickster who assumes another person's identity in bed is regarded as a kind of whore),[8] titillating, unrealistic, or simply farcical.[9] The fact that the bedtrick is both tragic and comic†—that the very word "tragicomedy" was first coined to describe a play about a bedtrick (Plautus's *Amphitryon*‡)—is a paradox that accounts in part for the confusion in its critical reception. Dr. Johnson, damning the bedtricks in *All's Well That Ends Well*† (in which Helena substitutes for Diana in Bertram's bed) and *Measure for Measure*† (in which Mariana substitutes for Isabella in Angelo's bed), remarks, "The story of Bertram and Diana had been told before of Mariana and Angelo, and, to confess the truth, scarcely merited to be heard a second time."[10] Even critics of popular culture tire of it; Terrence Rafferty, reviewing the film *Multiplicity*‡ (1996), calls "the hero's anxiety that one or more of his doppelgängers will sleep with his wife (who's unaware of their existence)" a "not very compelling issue . . . resolved in a protracted and mildly amusing farce climax."[11] Yet the bedtrick continues to compel audiences; though night-lights and pillow talk made the bedtrick harder and harder to take seriously after the seventeenth century, and though it strikes a contemporary reader as counterintuitive if not counterfactual,† "the irony of physical closeness and mental distance which underlies it persists in the modern understanding of sex."[12] Terence Cave encapsulates the paradox† with regard to recognition scenes in general (of which bedtrick recognitions are a subspecies) as he attempts "to account both for the extraordinary popularity of recognition scenes in all

†A dagger refers to a term or theme that occurs elsewhere in this book. A double dagger refers to a term or theme that occurs both elsewhere in this book and in the companion volume, *Splitting the Difference*. For a fuller explanation of this system of cross-references, see the preface.

types of literature and for the contempt and suspicion with which they are commonly regarded. The accusation of fraudulence is not simply an instance of cultural snobbism, although it may well take that form."[13]

There is a tension here between sex and text: though real people are often fooled with minor deceptions in bed, actual consummated bedtricks are rare in life but very common in texts. These stories seem to take place in a world in which many people literally do not know who they are in bed with—or, in the case of animals and gods, *what* they are in bed with. Why is there so much fantasy† about the bedtrick if it happens so seldom in reality? The answer consists in a range of good, human reasons, which are encoded in the stories in this book. These myths imagine a situation in which a man or woman goes to bed with someone s/he is crazy about and wakes up to discover the astonishing fact that the body in the bed belongs to someone entirely different, someone hated or alien or just *different*. Now, this is not just a myth. It happens to all of us, all the time, for that ol' black magic, sexual passion, is transformative, at least transformative of our perspective; it changes our view of our partner. Sometimes we go to bed with an animal and wake up with a god; that is, we go to bed relatively indifferent and wake up enchanted by sexual magic. On other occasions, we go to bed with a god and wake up with an animal; that is, we go to bed blinded by desire and wake up with our eyes relatively cleared by satiation. (My preliminary, unofficial opinion poll indicates that there is widespread disagreement about the prevalence of one model or the other.)

Many myths are simply the narrative embodiment, sometimes an exaggerated embodiment, of metaphors,[14] even clichés. English-speaking writers speak of something as "just a metaphor," but metaphor in India can be the strongest possible statement of causation.[15] The shock of violated intimacy in the bedtrick—the violation of the mind, often together with the rape† of the body—is a mythologized form of the everyday shock that makes people say, as the heroine of *Love Letters*† (1945) says to the man who is in fact a different person from the man she agreed to marry, "You're a stranger to me" or, as the confirmed bachelor in *Guys and Dolls* (1955) complains, "You marry a girl, and you wake up with somebody else." Perhaps the world's shortest switchback† bedtrick narrative appeared in the *New Yorker* on October 11, 1999, in the "Constabulary Notes from All Over" department: "[From the *Sudbury (Mass.) Town Crier*] 1:58 A.M. A Hudson Road resident reported a strange man in her bed, but then realized it was her husband" (p. 54). The casual joke that people make so often at their own expense—"I went to bed with X and woke up with Y"—implies that sex is revelatory, that in the morning you know the truth, that Y is the real person: "Behold!" as the Hebrew *hinneh* is usually translated (as in "Behold! It was Leah!"), for which the modern equivalent is probably "Oh wow!" or some blasphemous exclamation.

The mythology of the bedtrick unpacks the experience expressed in these and related clichés. Thus, the authors of *The Three Faces of Eve*‡ literalized a cliché to explain Eve White's split personality: "With a good deal of truth perhaps it may be stated that after her marriage, Mary Blank *changed*, that she became *another woman*."[16] And when Eve White (Lancaster) herself told her story a year later, she argued, "This isn't as far-fetched as it may sound at first. On the contrary, as an idea it's probably a cliché. . . . We say: The war *changed him*. Marriage made *a new woman* of her. He's a *different person* since he stopped drinking. He *found himself* in his new job. He isn't *the man he once was*."[17] But Mary Blank does not divorce her husband for sleeping with the "new woman," which is what Eve White wanted to do.[18] The myth of the bedtrick is about the violent disjunction that often takes place when we come up too quickly from the deep-sea dive of sexual intimacy into the cold light of the morning air and experience the emotional equivalent of the bends. Even in reaction to ordinary sexual betrayal, the betrayed partner may retroactively believe that the lover *was* someone else because the lover had been *with* someone else.

All sexual acts are bedtricks in the weakest sense: you never really know everything about your partner, and afterward, if you become estranged, the sudden distance, the total loss of intimacy, sometimes seem almost unbelievable, mythical. Similarly, the most basic bedtrick occurs, not when you mistake Joan for Susan (or Steve for Sam, not to mention Joan for Sam or Sam for Joan), but when you mistake lust for love; the shadow area between the two, lust and love,† is where the bedtrick happens, and why it matters. The myths in which the impostor is not *who* he or she seems to be is the strong form of the bedtrick, which dramatizes the weak form that occurs in more banal situations in which the impostor is not *how* he or she appears to be (ugly instead of beautiful,† unfaithful instead of faithful, out of love instead of in love, married instead of unmarried, and so on). Often a myth expresses the extreme case of a human situation; thus, the quandary of the copulating conjoined† twins expresses the extreme case of any two people whose bed is crowded by the phantoms† of other people, and the story of the French diplomat Boursicot,† who discovered that his lover of twenty years was not a woman but a man (the plot that was fictionalized in *M. Butterfly*†), expresses the extreme case of morning-after disappointment, regret, or surprise.

The bedtrick is not literally a universal theme, though it is demonstrably cross-cultural. I have found it in certain cultures at certain moments (ancient India, the Hebrew Bible, Renaissance England and Europe, Hollywood films), and different individuals in different cultures imagine different sorts of bedtricks to overcome different cultural barriers, from the great religious mythologies of the world to contemporary popular culture. Alexander Goldenweiser's "principle of limited possibilities" explains what he calls "dependent convergences" without recourse to a theory either of universal archetypes or of historical diffusion.[19] If we apply his theory of cultures to narratives, it suggests that the constraints of the traditional narrative form must somehow accommodate the constantly changing needs of the narrative community, and there is a limit to the number of *basic* plots that can be used.[20] Thus, something like a law of "irrational choice" operates to invoke bedtricks as so many dei ex machina in recurrent situations of sexual aporia. By asking profound questions about the interrelationships among sex and love, mind and body, identity and recognition, sameness and difference, illusion and reality, tales of the bedtrick offer a unique human probe into the ways in which these forces function in cultures, in stories, and in individual perceptions and individual lives.[21]

Telling the Difference

Contemporary Americans tend to assume that sexual intimacies, even intimacies exchanged in silence and in the dark, are as highly individualized as fingerprints, that bodies as well as faces have distinctive physiognomies,[22] that sex leads to an exploration of what is unique and distinctive about each partner. Yet many bedtrick stories seem at first to assume that if two people look alike, one cannot tell them apart (indeed, that in the dark one cannot tell *anyone* from anyone else). More than that: the stories often begin with the assumption that sex is an act in which the parties are interchangeable, that bodies can be changed without one's knowledge. But sometimes they go on to warn us that two people who appear to be identical are not in fact the same person, that we must strive to find other ways (the voice,† the scar,† memory,† the mind,† behavior†) to tell the two apart—and that sexual intimacy is the best way of all. On this deeper level, the face proves to be a false image of sameness, and the stories warn us that we must go deeper to find the mind and soul beneath the face.

Although many of the stories seem to begin by privileging vision, the fact that the reader or hearer always knows that people who look alike are not alike is a clue to the not-so-hidden agenda, which intersects with a primary agenda of our own time (particularly but not only as argued by feminists†): to deconstruct vision.† And some bedtricksters do not look exactly alike (except under cover of darkness): sisters, brothers, close friends, sons and fathers, mothers and daughters, servants and masters, and so forth. Thus, while some myths reaffirm sexual stereotypes, others challenge them. A gender asymmetry† is also at work here: men and women do not always feel the same about the power of sex to reveal either the distinct individualism or the sameness of partners in the dark.†

Bedtricksters are doublers: sometimes they become the doubles of other people (who may or may not exist), and sometimes they split themselves into an original and a double. But our double is not us: by definition, it is where we are not, and therefore things happen to it that do not happen to us. The idea of the substitute presupposes the idea of the unique, the authentic, the true form of which it is a false copy. What is it, then, that makes us say of a masquerading double, "It is the same"? The judgment that two different things are the same is, after all, our basic way of making sense out of the chaos of experience, the principle underlying all of our cognitive and scientific understandings, from the taxonomies of Linnaeus to the atomic periodic tables. When, therefore, we ask of doubles, "Is it the same? Is it the same person?" the answer is one of the many paradoxes† that make people tell this story over and over again: "It is the same and it is not the same." If we choose to use a less dichotomizing word than "same," such as "similar," we might construct a continuum (or, better yet, a Venn diagram: a set of categories that interlock like chain mail), with various degrees of resemblance or what Wittgenstein called "family likenesses,"[23] an appropriate image for actors in stories in which family resemblance† is often literally at issue.

But out of the infinite number of qualities that each person has, which features do we select in deciding whether two people are "similar"? Their appearance, the subverted criterion of myths? Their fingerprints? The noises they make in bed?[24] In any case, the basic problem of discrimination remains, albeit in a more relaxed form, even when we soften "the same" to "similar." Moreover, within the narratives, there is often a vital difference between yes and no: a choice must be made, something must be *done,* as a result of a decision that a person either is or is not "the same" as the person he or she pretends to be. The question of personal identity, within the texts, thus inspires a variant of the Passover question:[25] Why is this person different from all other people?

The texts in this book also inspire a related question: Why are sexual masquerades different from all other masquerades? This question requires us, from the very start, to stake out our turf. For the territory of the bedtrick is bounded on all sides by another territory, populated by people who masquerade as others in nonsexual situations: doppelgängers, mirror images, exact replicas, shadows, twins separated at birth, the creator who creates his double, clones, snatched bodies, possessions, Silent Sharers, surrogates, ghosts, tricksters, and so forth. These sorts of doubles sometimes appear as bedtricksters—Frankenstein's monster can replace him on the wedding night, brothers can replace one another in bed, and so forth—but many of them do not. Literary insights into these more general doubles may prove illuminating for the specific sexual themes as well, but I have limited the scope of this study to bedtricksters. That is, I am not setting out to solve the puzzle of personal identity posed by the broader literature of the double; rather, I hope to show that the concealment of one particular double, a sexual double, can prove more profoundly revealing than the masquerade of any other double.

Tales of the bedtrick do not solve the basic problem of identity, but they provide a vivid and captivating way to approach the problem through narrative. The bedtrick excludes from identity everything but sex, like the custom in some cultures of dressing the bride in a cloth that covers her entirely except the place where a hole is cut or left over her *pudendum* (here for once the Latin term seems more graphic than euphemistic), through which the groom is to extend his *membrum virile*.[26] The bedtrick offers a key to other masquerades. For though there are all sorts of reasons, sexual and nonsexual, for an individual to proliferate personalities, in the sexual act the opposite happens: two become one, as the double (the couple) coalesces into the one "beast with two backs," a simple truth noted even through the distorted lens of Shakespeare's Iago in a powerful tale of sexual (and racial†) jealousy† (*Othello* 1.1). The stories of the bedtrick represent this tension between the urge to diverge and the urge to merge, between the desire to masquerade, to assume the identity of another in addition to one's own, and the desire to lose one's own identity through intimate union with the other. As Terence Cave remarks, "Recognition plots are full of epistemophiliacs: the knowledge they seek has the character, whether explicit or implicit, of an impossible or incomprehensible sexual knowledge."[27]

Therefore, my tentative answer to the question "Why are sexual masquerades different from all other masquerades?" is that the sexual act is
in itself the most "doubling" and "undoubling" of acts. Where all other
doubles split into two, sexual doubles split and regroup into one. This
confluence of the masquerade and the sexual act was literally embodied
in David Ambrose's novel *The Man Who Turned into Himself*, about a
man who is drawn into a parallel world inside the mind of a man who
is very much like him in many ways, married to a woman almost exactly
like his wife. When the couple in the parallel world make love, the original
man is troubled to find himself "trapped inside the mind (if that's the
word) of this spineless, dumb, near-doppelganger of myself who's making
love to the equally near-doppelganger of my dead wife. *He's inside her
and I'm inside him.*"[28] A similar pun on "inside," again conflating the
ordinary sexual act and the magical bedtrick, is used in a film (*18 Again!*
[1988]) in which an eighteen-year-old boy, whose mind/soul has been
transposed into the body of an eighty-year-old man and back again, tries
to explain to a sexy older woman that his body has recently undergone
amazing changes, while she thinks he is just talking about adolescence;
when he then says, "Do you know what it feels like to be inside another
person's body?" she lowers her eyelashes and asks, "Do you?"

SEXUAL LIES AND SEXUAL TRUTH

One reason for the great number of stories about bedtricks is that people
are more deceptive about sex than about anything else. It could be argued
that all forms of love are deluding, including love of one's children or
country. But sexual love is, I think, the most deluding form of love. The
evidence, in both real life and imaginative texts, not just that people lie
about sex but that they often get away with it indicates that the victims
lie to themselves as much as the tricksters lie to them; the victims, who
fool themselves, are the ultimate tricksters. The lying of the trickster is
the obviously false element in a bedtrick, but the lying of the victim,
though less obvious, is often what sustains the mythology. Sexual fantasy†
is very real; seducers lie, but victims fantasize; sexual fantasy is the ghost
that gums up the machines of reason.

That the body could actually *be* a lie was argued by medieval European
authors such as Albertus, in the thirteenth century, who described hermaphrodites and effeminate males as "liars, whose bodies and behaviors
mislead."[29] Fear of sexual fraud and imposture led to the persecution even
of those hermaphrodites who were "not accused of sodomy or deliberate

deception."[30] They didn't have to *do* anything; what they *were* was a lie. In our day, Amy Bloom entitled her article on transsexuals, who believe they have been born with genitals that do not correspond to their true sexuality, "The Body Lies."

In uneasy alliance with the passages cited above, which tell us that the body lies, some stories seem to argue that the mind† or the soul or speech† or knowledge,† all in the service of true love,† supplies the touchstone of identity. Against this dual faction, however, more physiologically oriented stories argue that bodies don't lie, that there is a kind of naked, brutal honesty in the sexual moment of truth. In this view, though the outer trappings of the self may lie, at the eye of the sexual storm is another sort of eye that sees the truth, for some people their only truth. One might say that, at least in the era before pornographic films, the sexual act was the one area in which people were *forced* to be original, to be who they really were, if only for lack of some paradigm or stereotype to copy.

Many of these stories argue, echoing the familiar *in vino*† *veritas,* that there is surely *veritas in coitu.* The crude form of this assumption is that truth inheres in the physical act of sex; the more romantic† form of the same paradigm seeks the truth in the more spiritual act of falling in love.† Some of our texts argue that sexual love is the most reliable criterion of personal identity: the one you love and desire is the one you know, and the one you know is the real one; sexual love is not just a way of knowing who your lover is but also a way of knowing who *you* are, through the mirror† of the one you love and who loves you. Peter Steinfels may have had this in mind when he wisely remarked about sex, apropos of the 1998 Clinton scandals, "It puts the self at stake in a way that even death-defying activities like mountain climbing do not. Why else do people intuitively take betraying a spouse so seriously, and understand, even while reproving, why someone would lie about it?"[31] This line of thought supports monogamy†: it argues that if you want to stay who you are, you need to have—or at least to think you have—the same person in the bed beside you every night.

Some cultures emphasize the lies of sex, some the truth. The myths of Hollywood and of everyday Hinduism, for instance, tend on the whole to argue for the truth of sex. Shakespeare and Christianity, Buddhism and the ascetic traditions of Hinduism, argue, on the whole, that sex lies. But even in these cultures, and in many others, the two answers, yes and no, often coexist in tension within a single story. This, then, compounds the paradox of the double that is both us and non-us: the sexual act is simultaneously the most deceptive and the most truth-revealing, the most alienating and the most intimate, the most fantastic and the most real of human acts. I have always believed in both arms of this paradox and lived them in my conviction that sex was far more about truth than about power; and now I have written a book about them.

TEXTTRICKS

We might briefly consider the relationship between text and experience. What is the link between telling texts apart and telling lovers apart? How can we build a bridge between the experiences of the characters within the stories and the experiences of those who read or hear the stories? Besides being about the ways in which people in stories tell the difference between one person and another in bed, this book is about the ways in which storytellers tell the difference—tell *about* it in a story. The problem that is posed *within* the story (is this person the same as or different from the person he or she seems to be?) is mirrored on the methodological level by the problem posed by the analysis *of* the story (is this variant of the story the same as or different from the variant it seems to resemble?). Or the Passover question again: Why is this variant different from all other variants? The problem of the double *of* the story is both the same and not the same as the problem of the double *in* the story. The paradox "It is the same and it is not the same" is itself a double that lives in two worlds, the world inside the text, where the fictional victims must analyze the fictional tricksters, and the world outside the text, where the readers, ourselves, who frame and follow the plot, must compare and analyze texts. We can approach these two problems in similar ways, but not precisely the same way. That is, we may use stories that reveal the problems that arise when someone regards two individuals (in bed) as "the same" in order (perversely, perhaps, and certainly polymorphously) to demonstrate the advantages that arise when a scholar regards two different stories as both the same and not the same. We will discover again and again the profound difference, despite the apparent sameness, of certain stories that argue for the profound difference of people who appear to be the same. To assume that two stories with the same basic plot will make the same point about that plot is to fall victim to a texttrick.

Like the problem of the same and the different, truth and falsehood pose a problem for both narrative and method. Stories, particularly myths, about sexual masquerades are doubly powerful because both the story and the sexual act are masqueraders. The form and content, the myth and the masquerade, converge: both of them are both liars and truth-tellers, two-edged swords. Masqueraders pretend, and stories pretend, and yet their pretenses ultimately provide a kind of truth that is otherwise unattainable, compelling us beyond all other sorts of more falsifiable truths. Here is another paradox:† the story lies and tells the truth.

I have noted the role of certain clichés in myths, on the one hand, and in bedtrick stories, on the other. Terence Cave points out that the recognition scene is itself a cliché: "The sense of cliché is the sense of being cheated, of being brought to a moment of fullness only to find that it is empty."[32] But this is precisely what happens not just to the reader of a bedtrick, outside the frame of the story, but to the victim, inside it: the person he thought he was in bed with turns out, at the moment of fullness, to be empty of the desired identity. On the other hand, one could argue that it is precisely the known quantity of the cliché plot of the bedtrick that makes it satisfying, filling: when the victim of the bedtrick finally recognizes the trickster ("Oh, it's Mariana!" or "Behold, it was Leah!"), the reader of the story recognizes the plot ("Oh, it's a bedtrick!"). So we must consider both the ways in which, within the text, the trickster manipulates the ambiguity that hedges the truth or falsehood of the sexual act and the related ways, outside the text, in which the storyteller manipulates the ambiguity of the truth or falsehood of stories about the sexual act.

Some critics of the comparative method have satirized the view of scholars who emphasized the sameness of myths (and other human constructs) and have epitomized this view with the proverb "In the dark, all cows are black."[33] But what is said of scholars outside texts can also be said of characters within texts. This proverb also provides a metaphor for many myths of bedtricks; it is applied to women in early French and English sources and to ideas (like the idea of comparison) in later German sources—another instance of the parallelism between bedtricksters and stories. I have broached here the methodological problem of texts that look alike in the dark[34] and will deal in the rest of this book with the history of the idea that women, like cats or cows, look alike in the dark.

The concept of fragmentation,‡ too, is applied to both texts and characters within the texts. Since parts of the person masquerade as other parts, to fragment the sexual identity is to open the way to a liberating infinity of possibilities, of selves, rather than to a constricting totality.[35] To unmask by masquerading (what I will call the double-back,† masquerading as yourself) is to realize that we have no (one) sexual identity—a realization that reifies our infinite (though never total) identities. My texts, too, and in particular my uses of texts, are partial, fragmentary. My assumption that there is a text is pre- (or pre-post-) modern, but my assumption that there are multiple valid interpretations of that text, my use of texts from all levels of culture, and the fragmentary nature of my multiple approaches are postmodern. More precisely, my structuralist method of bricolage,[36] of putting myths together from the fragmentary rags and bones of the human imagination, is based upon my belief in an infinity of variants, in contrast with philosophical and psychological treatments that too often strive for, or claim, totality.

We cannot, I think, make many statements that will apply to *all* the stories, but we can isolate several patterns that do seem to occur in many of them, patterns that transgress the borders of culture to offer us several shared alternative views of the confluence of sex and deception. Even the cynical William Bowden concluded by suggesting: "We could use a major study of the bed trick throughout the history of literature, a study which would embrace such widely separated instances as the deception of Jacob by Laban and Leah (Genesis 29.15–30) and that night at the mill in Chaucer's Reeve's Tale. . . . In fact, there might be an interesting paper on the psychology of the bed trick in general. . . ."[37] I hope that there might even be an interesting book on the subject—this book.

ONE

How to Commit Adultery with Your Own Spouse

THE DOUBLE-BACK

Bedtricksters turn bedtricks to get into or out of someone's bed. That is, sometimes a person splits off a double in order *not to be* in the bed of someone who would force the bedtrickster to be there, but sometimes a person masquerades as a double in order *to be* in the bed of someone who would not want the bedtrickster to be there. If the wife of an unfaithful man imposes herself instead of some other surrogate between her man and the (real or fantasized) other woman, the two aspects of the trick—getting out of or into bed—collapse together, and the story turns into a double-back or switchback: the philanderer is tricked in such a way that he ends up in bed not merely with someone other than the intended erotic object but with the very person that he was trying *not* to sleep with, usually his wife. The two aspects become two episodes of one myth: the bedtrickster wants to be with one person and not to be with another, to disappear secretly from one bed in order to appear secretly in another. When the wife wishes to masquerade as her husband's mistress (or, rarely, the mistress as the wife), she wants to be with one man, but to be *a different woman* to that man.

I have written elsewhere about double-cross bedtricks designed to get people *out of* bed,‡ and we will encounter other examples of this pattern in chapter 6. Let us consider in this chapter a group of double-back tricks that get the trickster *into* bed. There are two more dichotomies that we might do best to consider from the very start. The first is the distinction between accidental and intended, or unknowing and knowing, bedtricks. Unknowing bedtricks occur when people who look alike are mistaken for one another without either of them intending this to happen. This is almost always a family matter; it happens to twins (as in Shakespeare's *Comedy of Errors*†) and to people fated to commit incest† (like Sophocles' Oedipus,† who did not know who his parents were and in ignorance killed his father and married his mother). Occasionally it happens in the backlash of an intended bedtrick, or a double-cross,† when the trickster inadvertently trips over his own traps. Sometimes both sorts of tricks occur in a single plot, as in Shakespeare's *Twelfth Night*,† when Viola knowingly pretends to be "Cesario" but does not at first know that her twin brother, Sebastian, has been, unknowingly, mistaken for "Cesario." We will encounter several unknowing bedtricks, but the focus of this book will be on the issue of knowledge,† hence on people who know that they are perpetrating bedtricks and on those who come to know that they did not know that they were knowingly tricked.

The second dichotomy to keep in mind is the distinction between surrogative and transformative bedtricks, or, to put it differently, between bedtricksters who pretend to be persons who do exist and those who pretend to be persons who do not. These, too, may exist side by side; thus, in *Twelfth Night* again, Viola pretends to be the nonexistent eunuch "Cesario," but then "Cesario" is mistaken for Viola's very real brother, Sebastian. Sometimes a woman substitutes herself for another woman whom her husband knows and desires, but sometimes she simply transforms herself into another form of herself, and he fails to recognize her as his own wife.

At issue here is the difference between, in the trick of surrogation, imitating someone else, replacing your personality with someone else's, which steals from that person and diminishes you, and, in the trick of transformation, extending who you are through your imagination of someone whose existence is your own creation. Natalie Zemon Davis sees the related contrast between imitating someone you do not know and someone you do know as "the difference between making another person's life your own and merely imitating him."[1] The key to this variation is not how many people are present but whether duality is masquerading as unity or unity is masquerading as duality. When the wife takes the place of another, real woman, duality is masquerading as unity: two women appear to be one. But when she pretends to be another, imaginary woman, unity is masquerading as duality: she appears to be two—or, better, she reveals that she *is* two, indeed often more than two.

Among transformative bedtricksters, who imitate nonexistent rivals, there is a subgenre of bedtricksters whose love is unrequited and who somehow learn all the qualities that their victims seek in a lover and pretend to have precisely those qualities, becoming not the trickster's double but the victim's imaginary partner. Salman Rushdie imagines a woman doing this: "What if the person you love did not really exist at all? . . . What if she created herself, out of her perception of your need—what if she falsely enacted the part of the person you could not resist, your dream-lover?"[2] Men play this trick more often than women, particularly in films. The hero constructs his own rival, finding out the necessary details through the repetition of the event over and over again (in *Groundhog Day* [1993]), by spying on psychoanalytic sessions (in *Everyone Says I Love You* [1997]), or by electronic surveillance (in *There's Something about Mary* [1998]). Usually the ideal lover is too good to be true, arousing the victim's suspicions; and then the usual double-bind† kicks in, and the trickster realizes that he or she wasn't the one the victim had begun to love. These films, in which the male trickster fails, are comedies; but when a woman tries the trick, and she succeeds, it can get nasty. In *Dream Lover* (1994), the trickster who constructs such an imaginary persona gets the man to marry her, but then she tries to destroy him, and he kills her in self-defense.

Some variants of this genre of the myth involve sexual partners who are not married, so that what is at stake is desire or, sometimes, love,† romantic identity.† But it is usually about marriage; most variants use marital terms (adultery, wife) and most examples confront issues of monogamy and legal progeny. The story of the man who mistakes his wife for his mistress is attested in many cultures.[3] The Möbius† strip logic of the double-back allows the rejected spouse to pretend to be precisely what he or she once was and is determined to become again: the chosen sexual partner.

As a story of a marriage, this variant of the bedtrick expresses a paradox: the husband is both horrified and delighted to find in bed someone different (from the woman he expected) and the same (as usual, his own wife). But the spouse who knowingly, and in disguise, tries to seduce a partner in order to test her or him is playing a dangerous game, no matter whether it fails or succeeds: if the bedtrickster is recognized, then the test of fidelity is invalidated, but if the bedtrickster is not recognized, and the spouse responds, the bedtrickster has destroyed the marriage—and, moreover, in societies where divorce is difficult or forbidden, may still be stuck in it. Indeed, even if the bedtrickster is not recognized and the spouse repels the advance, this is not proof that the spouse will not be unfaithful at some time in the future.

The switchback pattern occurs in both genders: a husband or wife may be tricked into committing adultery with a spouse mistaken for a lover.

One might think that this double-edged sword of a bedtrick played on
one's spouse would be equally dangerous for husbands and for wives, but
in the literature at large, far more bedtricks are engineered by wives than
by husbands. In part, this is an example of the broader fictional bias that
assumes that women fool men more often than they are fooled.‡ In part,
it results from the male authorship of most of our texts; Joel Fineman
remarks that the wit of the quasi bedtricks in *Twelfth Night*† and *As You
Like It*† is developed primarily from a masculine point of view, since there
is "no such thing, at least no *fun* in such a thing," as a woman with horns.[4]
But women may very well find fun, and wit, in the horns of a woman—
not to mention the horns of a man—and they may be heard laughing
behind the scenes of the tales of duped men.[5]

There are also other reasons why more women than men initiate acts
of self-cuckolding, such as that ol' devil the double standard† of social
consequences for male or female infidelity and hence the different consequences of a successful bedtrick played on a man or on a woman. The
double-back usually demonstrates the husband's infidelity and the wife's
fidelity; it is not supposed to demonstrate (and only very rarely does demonstrate) the husband's fidelity and the wife's infidelity. His trick, when
it fails, as it almost always does, proves her fidelity, while her trick, when
it succeeds, as it almost always does, proves his infidelity. The husband
who impersonates himself usually does it to test his wife's chastity, while
the wife does it to curtail her husband's adultery; since the women in our
stories already know that their husbands are unfaithful and simply want
to catch them at it, they lose nothing if they fail, and they can always try
again. But this same ploy puts husbands who try to bedtrick their own
wives into double jeopardy, as Marliss C. Desens points out: "[T]he husband's use of the bed-trick brings him face to face with his wife's sexuality
in connection with other men. It thus feeds his fear of cuckoldry instead
of alleviating it. [It] is based on jealousy and the fear of his wife's potential
infidelity, as well as on a keen awareness that his society will view any
infidelity on her part as reflecting on his ability to satisfy her sexually."[6]
In other words, men paint themselves into such a corner with their para-
noia† that they usually don't dare test their nightmare† fantasies of their
wives' infidelity; when they do dare, they know that they themselves will
be destroyed if they prove to be right. The trickster in Roald Dahl's "The
Great Switcheroo"† explicitly experiences precisely the slur "on his ability
to satisfy her sexually" that Desens has in mind, when he finds out more
about his wife than he wanted to know. Cervantes tells the story of a

man who gets his best friend to test his wife (without a bedtrick); though previously virtuous, she falls for him, and her husband dies of a broken heart.[7] And sometimes, as when Secundus† plays the trick upon his own mother, or when Cephalus† plays it upon his wife, Procris, it proves fatal.

Let us begin with the wife's trick and then go on to consider the husband's.

The God Who Committed Adultery with His Own Goddess

The goddess Parvati bedtricks her husband, the god Shiva, on numerous occasions when they quarrel, sometimes about a game of dice,† often about another woman—for Shiva is a notorious womanizer (or perhaps one should say goddessizer). Often she transforms herself into, or disguises herself as, a seductive foreign woman, a woman of low class, or an Outcaste woman.[8] These stories are told and retold both in vernacular texts and in a number of well-known medieval Sanskrit texts that assimilate the worship of the goddess to the worship of Shiva; there is considerable historical evidence that a dark,† independent goddess of South India was appropriated and made into Shiva's subservient wife in many texts of this sort. She disguises herself as a mountain woman, a Shabari, in a story told in a Sanskrit text composed in South India in the late medieval period, a story that begins, as many Hindu myths do, with a visit from the wandering sage, gossip, and troublemaker Narada:

Shiva and the Mountain Woman

One day Narada came to visit Shiva and Parvati on Kailasa and said, "You two would have even more pleasure playing dice than making love." They began to play dice, and Parvati, with a trick, took everything from Shiva, even his loincloth, and she laughed at him, and Shiva's entourage turned their faces away in modesty. Then Shiva said, "The sages and gods are laughing at this joke. How can you do this, you, a girl from a good family? If you have won, then at least give me back my loincloth." But she laughed and said, "Why do you need a loincloth, you hermit? You were naked enough when you went into the Pine Forest, begging and seducing the sages' wives, and the sages' curse cut off your 'loincloth.' That's why I took it from you in the game of dice." She said a lot of things like this to him, and he set his heart on going to a deserted spot in the forest.

But when Shiva had gone, Parvati was tormented by longing in separation. She went where Shiva was meditating, but she took the form of a magnificent mountain woman, dark and slender, with lips as scarlet and full as bimba fruits. He woke up and saw her and was overwhelmed by lust. He took her by the hand, but as soon as he touched her, she vanished, and when he couldn't see her, he was tormented by longing in separation, enveloped in a mistaken perception, though he himself was the destroyer of mistaken perceptions. But then he saw her again, and he asked whose she was, and she said, teasing him, "I am looking for a husband who is omniscient, independent, unwavering, and the best lord of the universe." He replied, "I, and I alone, am a suitable husband for you." She smiled and said, "You are indeed the husband that I seek. But you have no virtues. For a woman chose you before and won you by generating great ascetic heat, and you abandoned her in the wilderness." Shiva denied this and insisted that she marry him, and she said he must ask her father, the mountain Himalaya.

She took Shiva to her father, stood with him at the door, and said, "This is my father. Ask. Don't be ashamed. He will give me, there is no doubt about that. Don't hesitate." Shiva bowed to Himalaya and said, "Best of mountains, give your daughter to me today." Hearing this pitiful speech, Himalaya stood up and said to Shiva, "What kind of a joke is this? It isn't right for you to ask, since you are the one who gives everything in the universe." Just then Narada arrived, laughed, and said, "Whenever men have anything to do with women, they always end up deceived. You are the lord of the universe. You should speak as befits you." When Narada had enlightened him like this, Shiva woke up and laughed and said, "You spoke the truth, Narada. Having anything to do with a woman spells downfall for a man. Like a ghoul, she deluded me and brought me here. I won't stay near this mountain; I'll go to another part of the forest." Then Shiva vanished, but when they all praised him, he came back to Kailasa. Drums sounded, and all the gods, Indra and the others, sent a rain of flowers, and the great Shiva reigned there with Parvati.[9]

Shiva inherits many of the myths of Agni, the god of fire,[10] and we may see one of the sources of this myth of the mountain woman in the earlier myth in which Agni desires the wives of the Seven Sages, and Agni's wife, Svaha, takes the form of each of the wives in turn and receives the seed of her husband.‡[11] In the Shiva story, too, the woman has the agency: Parvati calls all the shots from the very start; she drives Shiva away, and although she is at first said to be "tormented by longing in separation," she turns the tables until he himself is "tormented by longing in separation." (In the many variants of this story, sometimes she, and sometimes he, is said to desire the other more, to have the sexual whip hand; this seems to vary according to the devotional stance of the text—she prevails in texts that worship the goddess, he in Shaiva devotional texts—but I have discovered no hard and fast rule about this.) She dwells with irony, which the author neglects no opportunity to hammer home with a heavy hand, on the fact that even Shiva, the lord of illusion and controller of the yogic power that cuts through illusion, is blind when it comes to sex. She teases Shiva with a series of puns† that turn upon her knowledge, and his ignorance, of the fact that she is his wife. Thus, when she says, "I am looking for a husband," she means both "a new husband" and "*my* husband" (i.e., you), and the woman "who chose you before" was Parvati herself, the speaker. When she accuses him of having, as a man, no virtues, no good qualities, she is also saying that, as God, he has no qualities at all, a common statement about his ineffability.

By forcing him to play what amounts to a game of strip poker (or strip dice), she satirizes the well-known myth of Shiva's castration‡ in the Pine Forest: once upon a time, Shiva, naked and ithyphallic, wandered into the Pine Forest, where sages were performing asceticism with their wives; when he seduced all the women, the sages, in retaliation, caused his erect penis (*linga*†) to fall off.[12] In her mockery of her husband, Parvati equates the loincloth† with the penis,† teasing him about the time the sages caused his "loincloth" (i.e., his *linga*) to fall off. Does this mean, therefore, that when she takes his loincloth she, too, castrates him? Shiva himself implicitly mocks and feminizes himself when he says that she acted like a ghoul, a reference to the fact that "marriage in the fashion of a ghoul" is the legal term for the rape of "a girl who is asleep, drunk, or out of her mind."[13] Shiva seems to be saying that he was out of his mind (presumably with a combination of ordinary lust and the extraordinary illusory powers of the goddess) when the mountain woman seduced him.

The dark skin† of the mountain woman introduces the familiar element of what we would call racial† prejudice and here is perhaps better described as caste prejudice. A version of the story recorded in Tulu in 1970 turns upon the blackness† of the skin of a Kadu Korpalu, a forest woman of low caste;[14] in this version also, Parvati appears to Shiva doubly disguised, as a human and as a low-caste person with a dark skin. Shiva dismisses both problems, lying by saying that he is a human (he is a god, as she immediately reminds him) and lying in the eyes of Hindu caste law by saying that all human beings are equal when it comes to sex. Parvati thus simultaneously deconstructs the power of a husband, the power of a god, and the power of caste.†

The theme lives on in North Indian folklore. A Hindi folk song reproduces the dialogue between Shiva and Parvati in disguise as a tribal woman, who is, in this version, married. At first she argues, "Five and seven are my brave brothers. They'll abuse you!" but when he persists, her repeated refrain goes, "Don't ask me about my caste. I'm just a tribal's wife!" And this is what he says:

> I'll get a beautiful skirt made (for you),
> and a glimmering blouse.
> I'll get the sun and moon to stand guard,
> and Indra will draw your water.
> I'll have Parvati sent back to her father's house;
> I'll make you my chief queen.[15]

No wonder Parvati delights in making a fool of him.

DOUBLE-BACKING HUSBANDS

Even when Shiva and Parvati are the subjects of the myth, they behave like humans in almost all respects, and the theme clearly applies not just to gods but to human beings. We have noted some of the reasons why men do not, generally, play double-backing bedtricks with their wives. But they can do it; just as Parvati becomes a low-caste woman to seduce Shiva, so Shiva sometimes disguises himself as an Outcaste or, on one occasion, as a Muslim sentry to seduce (or, perhaps, to rape) her.[16] On another occasion, he takes the form of one of his own worshipers, a hideous Skull-Bearer, to rape Parvati when she is incarnate as a human queen cursed to be raped by a Skull-Bearer.[17]

Some authors seem to reason that if one's spouse is going to commit adultery, it is better, at least, to keep it in the family, that self-cuckolding is better than being cuckolded by someone else. Marjorie Garber emphasizes the advantages of the successful bedtrick played by a husband against a wife in her analysis of a play by Ferenc Molnar in which a husband disguises himself as a guard and seduces his own wife, who, as both men and women often do, later claims false knowledge,† that is, claims to have seen through the deception from the beginning. But Garber asks, "With whom has she been unfaithful? . . . The only person he could bear to lose her to was himself."[18] In this reading, the husband is playing safe, having his cake and eating it, by offering himself up in place of another seducer.

In Thomas Middleton's *The Family of Love* (1602), the justice trying the case points out that the wife has technically committed no crime since a husband cannot cuckold himself.[19] But of course, he has just done precisely that. In George Chapman's *The Widow's Tears* (1612), the wife points out that she has watched her husband cuckold himself. In Richard Brinsley Sheridan's *The Rivals* (1775), the hero who masquerades as another man in order to woo the woman he loves finds himself as his own rival when he is forced to woo her in his original identity as well (an example of what I call the double-bind†).

Here is a paradox, a particularly strong form of the double-bind: since the man who tries to get his wife to commit adultery with him wants it both to succeed and not to succeed, both the wife's fidelity and her infidelity confirm his fantasies. The husband thus acts out his own divided wishes: on the one hand, that he should prove right in suspecting her and, on the other hand, that his suspicion should have no cause. Javier Marias tells the tale of a man who left his wife, Celia, and a few months later encountered and had sex with a prostitute who looked just like Celia, said her name was Victoria, and either was or was not Celia. His ambivalence is excruciating: "The face was Celia's face, which I knew so well, and at the same time it wasn't. . . . She still looked too much like Celia for me to feel distrustful or to decide that it wasn't her. Anyway, it was her, even if it wasn't. . . . Not daring to feel the certainty I now believe I feel out of jealousy, trying not to recognize the person I did recognize and at the same time not wanting to mistake my own ex-wife for an unknown prostitute. . . ."[20] When, later on that same night, he goes to Celia's home, his former home, and lets himself in with his key, he finds her in bed with another man, whose features he can't make out. At first he remarks, "It could have been me," and then he expresses his "relief that, although not alone, Celia was still alive and I would never know whether or not she was also Victoria."[21]

A vivid contemporary story of a man who manages to cuckold himself is Carin Clevidence's surreal tale (1994), which begins with an apt quote from Borges: "while we sleep here, we are awake elsewhere. . . . in this way every man is two men":

THE SOMNAMBULISTS

[The narrator, an elderly man who is alone, recalls how he had begun to suspect his wife of adultery one night when he had come home late and not gone to his bedroom but had discovered the next morning that someone had left the toilet seat up and used the hand towel in his bathroom. Then one night he saw a bruise on her breast.] I saw that it had been made by a mouth, a mouth had bitten her, bitten her here, and left a mark I never could have made. [For the next seven years, he never slept with her.] Night after night I dreamed of her arms, the curves of her warm body, the honey of her hair. But I would not let myself weaken, or sleep again in that tainted bed.

[When she becomes pregnant he throws her out, though she protests that he is the father of the child. Years later, he discovers a long line of ancestors who suffered from sleepwalking and were punished for crimes or misdemeanors that could have been, but were not at that time, explained by somnambulism. Thus, Gordon Emmett Faussignac, a minister, had been fished dead out of the river, wearing a red dress and a single clip-on earring, to the horror of his loyal parishioners. There were three documented cases of bigamy. And there was the devout Alice Faussignac.]

[Alice] shocked the community by not only becoming visibly pregnant, but swearing she was a virgin and had been visited by God. . . . Years later, . . . a man named Rodgers confessed. She had come into his room, he explained, and climbed into his bed in the middle of the night. . . . The affair had gone on for over a year. What surprised him most, he said, was her poise at all other times; she had never made the slightest allusion, by word or look, to the intimacy they shared. You, far cleverer than I, are not surprised. You had suspected long before that it would come to this, that, in my sleep, I had been cuckolding myself for years. . . . It never occurred to me until that moment that I might have been, myself, the cause of all that grim undoing.

Bigamy, transvestism,† a telltale scar,† a child fathered by a man other than the mother's husband—the truth about all of this masquerades beneath the surface of sleep,† in dream, in bed, in sex.

Amnesia tricks Wagner's Siegfried into inadvertently bedtricking his own wife, so that both are tricked, in a combination of a double-cross† and a double-back.[22] Amnesia makes possible a more sinister self-cuckolding in the 1991 film *Shattered*:

SHATTERED

A man who has been in a terrible automobile accident wakes up horribly disfigured, without a memory or a face. His wife, Judith, shows him (and the plastic surgeons) photos of his face and tells him who he is: her husband, Dan Merrick, a wealthy man who lives in San Francisco. The surgeons reconstruct his face according to the photos, and he begins to have memories of making love to Judith on a beach in Mexico. But when he finds photos of her making love to a man whose face is different from his, he becomes jealous and disturbed.

Ginny, his partner's wife, gets him alone and begins to strip, saying,

"We were lovers." But when she kisses him, asking, "Do you remember?" he says, "Stop it. I don't remember," and pushes her away. He learns from Ginny that he had treated Judith very badly, that she had been having an affair with a man named Jack Stanton, and that he had wanted a divorce. He thinks he has tracked Stanton down, but the person he is following turns out to be Judith in a man's wig and jacket, who says, "There is no Stanton; you shot him," and insists that she was playing the part of Stanton just now to convince people that Stanton was still alive, to protect him, Dan. Now he dreams of watching someone shoot a man who looks like himself, Dan, and when he wakes up he searches for Stanton's body until he finds a body that has been preserved in formaldehyde; it has his face, Dan's face. He realizes that, behind his reconstructed face, he is Jack Stanton.

Shocked, he falls and hits his head, and now again he remembers making love on the beach, but this time he sees his face, the face of Jack Stanton, and he hears her say, "Jack, I love you." As Jack, he remembers clearly that she shot Dan and tried to persuade him to run off with her. He had protested, "I'm out of your life," and in her furious resistance there had been a struggle in the car and an accident, in which she rolled free and he was disfigured and concussed. Now again there is a struggle in the car, but this time he is the one who rolls free; the car explodes, killing her.

At the end of the film we know that Jack will continue to masquerade as Dan in order to keep Dan's money. But throughout the film he has been masquerading, unknowingly, as his wife's lover masquerading as her husband. Not only has he committed adultery with (the woman he thinks is) his own wife, but he thinks he has murdered (the man he comes to realize is) his wife's husband; that is, he thinks that he is her husband and murdered her lover, but he learns that he is her lover and that the murdered man was her husband. Jack, thinking that he is Dan, searches obsessively for Jack, just as Oedipus† searched for the man who had caused the plague in Thebes, not knowing that he was that man, and as the heroine of *Love Letters*† (1945) offers to help her husband search for the woman he wrote to, not knowing that she is that woman. Jack is unknowingly masquerading as his own victim and his own prosecutor; as Judith complains, when she has finally told him that he is in fact Jack, "You hired somebody to find out that you're a murderer." Iocasta might easily have spoken these words to Oedipus.

"I don't get it," Dan keeps saying. "Why did she do all this?" Why indeed? If you don't have your face or your memories, who are you? What is there, besides the mind and the face, that she loves? Is it just the body? Or is it the idea that he is her lover, not her husband? Judith loves her lover so much that at one point she becomes him, masquerades as him; at that moment, she is committing adultery with herself. Dan has a lot of money, which furnishes, as usual in films of this genre, the primary motive. But sex plays its part, too; sex is what preserves Dan's memory.

The cinematic clue to the reality of Dan's memories of making love to Judith as Jack Stanton is the fact that they are in black-and-white. In *Shattered*, the contrast between color and black-and-white marks the boundary between the past and the present and also suggests that the intensity of sexual experience is what breaks through the color barrier to the memory of the black-and-white, "newsreal" past. (Stanley Kubrick used black-and-white in precisely the same way in *Eyes Wide Shut*, in 1999, for sexual flashbacks that were emotionally real, in contrast with the rest of the film, though only imagined.) The film convention of black-and-white used to represent reality, though not sex, is adapted from *The Wizard of Oz* (1939), which used color and black-and-white to distinguish dream (Oz, in color) from reality (a.k.a. Kansas, in black-and-white). Some black-and-white films before *Oz* had one or two special color scenes with no particular ontological significance, but subsequent films used the device to make other sorts of distinctions. At the end of *Portrait of Jenny* (1948, with the same cast and director as *Love Letters*,† 1945), the black-and-white shifts to full color for the portrait, unreal in the sense of art-in-contrast-with-life but in a deeper sense the only real thing in the film, like the color portrait at the end of the black-and-white *The Picture of Dorian Gray* (1945), another film about sexual doubles.‡ In the film *Pleasantville* (1998), color stands for the present, reality, and sex (what Stanley Kowalski in *A Streetcar Named Desire* [1951] called "all them colored lights"): the main sequences are in black-and-white, but gradually all the people who get laid start to see colors and to be seen as colored themselves, a testimony to sex as reality. In *Shattered*, color is what lies; truth, and sex, are in black-and-white. This symbolism has been well glossed by Marina Warner: "Absence of color is linked to the absence of the subject who was there in color before one's eyes when the image was made. It is as if black and white are the symbolic colors of loss, and hence of memory."[23] When Dan finally realizes that he is Jack, and now remembers making love to Judith *as Jack*, his memory is in color: the past and present are at last reconciled, and color tells the sexual truth.

Sexual memory is still an ambiguous clue, for both Dan and Jack had made love to Judith in Mexico (the foreign connection†), but the memory of sex on the beach, big wave and all, is all that remains of his previous life, his soul, if you will. Did he make love differently when he knew he was a lover than when he thinks he is a husband? Is that why the memories of the sexual past are more vivid than the present? Sex has already begun to assert its truth against other truth claims. In Jack's memories, Judith wears more makeup, has more glamorous hairstyles, is more vivid and more erotic and more evil, than she is in "Dan's" actual experience of her. After all, she was Jack's mistress but just Dan's wife.

Some of the implicit questions left unanswered in this film were explicitly posed, and partly answered, in the novel on which the film was based, *The Plastic Nightmare*, by Richard Neely (1969; designated on the cover as a "masterpiece of fifties high pulp"). Aside from minor differences in the detecting of the murder, in the format (Dan tells the novel in the first person), and in the names, there are significant variations that the filmmakers chose to make precisely in the area of the bedtrick. In the novel, Dan describes an exchange that takes place the first time he and Judith make love after the surgery: "She whispered, '*Now* do you remember?' I felt gutted and alone. '*Part* of me remembers,' I said, and realized my tactlessness. . . . 'I mean, does your *mind* remember?'"[24]

Judith in the novel explains to Jack (after he has figured out that he is in fact Jack) how she did it: after the crash, she saw some old photos of Dan: "They'd been taken seven or eight years ago, when Dan was a lot thinner. I thought how remarkably he resembled you. He was your height, was then about the same weight, had the same color eyes and hair and similar features. You could have been brothers. I don't wonder I found him attractive in those days."[25] It would therefore be easy to change his face, but how did she know he would have lost his memory? (As Dan says, "I had emerged from coma conveniently amnesiac.") And, even if we know how she did it, *why* did she do it? In the novel, she admits the stupidity, and the failure, of her plan: passion wears off fast, and they start sleeping in separate bedrooms. Finally she tells him, "It would never have worked anyway. . . . You began to remind me too much of *him*. I found I was *glad* when you moved into this room. Everything was breaking down all over again, just as it had with Dan."[26] The body corrupts the face, as it does in the enduring mythology of the transposed heads.‡ *Shattered* is an embodiment of two cynical clichés:† that sexual love never lasts, because lovers turn into spouses; and that an unfaithful lover turns the betrayed partner into a double of the person who replaces the partner, no longer his or her own self.

In the film, the sexual reality test† works not only positively, in Dan's subconscious identity as Jack, but negatively. He doesn't remember Ginny's kiss† because he isn't the man who was her lover (in which case, the film implies, he would have remembered), nor does she, apparently, recognize him then. Only later does she realize that he is not Dan from other clues: "Your smell, your hands, the lines on your palms." But in the novel, Ginny *does* know the difference, through the sexual act—which is consummated on the kitchen floor. Later, she tells him who he is and tells him how she knew: "I first began to wonder about you when I saw you smoking cigarettes. Dan never smoked them—only a pipe. . . . I didn't *really* begin to think about all those things until after that night . . . that night in the kitchen. It was *different.* I can't tell you exactly how or why—but afterwards I began to be sure you were not Dan."[27] Indeed, the fact that the mistress of the man he appears to be recognizes who he is not (and figures out who he must be) through the sexual act, *and tells him,* is a crucial point in the novel, in contrast with the film, in which Judith shoots Ginny before Ginny can tell "Dan" that she has finally figured it out (though she does give him vital information about Stanton), leaving him to work it all out by himself through his own sexual memory as the lover of the other man's wife. In the novel, only after Ginny has opened his eyes by seducing him does he remember seducing Judith in Mexico.

"Dan" knows, deep inside, who he is; his memory does survive, in his own body and in the body of his own mistress (a.k.a. his wife) and (in the novel) in the body of the mistress of the man he thinks he is. In the novel, Ginny knows who he is when he himself does not, reversing the usual genders in films like *Love Letters,*† where a man manipulates the memory of an amnesiac woman. In the film, too, it is a woman, Judith, who manipulates "Dan's" memory. *Shattered* is summed up in her reply to his quite reasonable question at the end, "Why didn't you tell me any of this before?": "I was trying to protect you from your own memory." (This could also sum up *Love Letters.*) But her efforts backfire: in the film, when she tries to destroy her husband's body with unspecified chemicals, she inadvertently preserves it with formaldehyde. And this becomes a metaphor for the soul, the memory that survives no matter how one tries to destroy it; for when Judith tries to destroy her lover's memory, she inadvertently preserves it, too—with the vividness of her own sexual presence and her desire for him. *Shattered* presents an extreme, and twisted, demonstration of the power of the sexual memory lodged in the body,‡ a power that is able to unmask even a bedtrick in which the trickster's most powerful ally is the victim's own mind.

The Double-Play, or Mixed Doubles

Two—which is to say four, two tricksters and two victims—can play at this game, when two tricksters perpetrate bedtricks in a double-play. Two men do this to their wives in Roald Dahl's "The Great Switcheroo"† and to their fiancées in Mozart and Da Ponte's opera *Così fan tutte*. A double-cross is added to a double-play in a film that is in many ways a double of *Double Indemnity* (1944) but owes even more to the story "The Great Switcheroo":† *Consenting Adults* (1992), in which a man named Richard, happily married to Priscilla, is persuaded by his neighbor Eddie, married to Kay, to participate in what Richard thinks is a double-play (wife-swapping without the knowledge of the wives). Eddie's argument follows the lines of that of the trickster in "The Great Switcheroo": "Do you ever wake up in the middle of the night and, you know, just sort of, do it? Like, half asleep. Would they know the difference? And would they mind? They want exactly what we want. In the heat of the moment, they'll love it. I'll bet you $1,000 we could pull it off. And who cares if we get caught? Big deal." As things transpire, however, Eddie has hired a woman who resembles Kay to get into the bed that night, and then, after Richard has made love to the look-alike, thinking that he was fooling Kay, and gone home, Eddie murders the look-alike, so that he (and, secretly, Kay) can collect the insurance money. Thus, Richard, the would-be bedtrickster, is framed for the murder of Kay. This double-play twists into a double-cross at the end to introduce a third bedtrick (in addition to the two that each husband is supposedly playing on his wife), to make it a kind of triple-play-cross.

The film *La règle du jeu* (*The Rules of the Game* [1939]) explicitly invokes the plot of *The Marriage of Figaro* in various inversions, but with a tragic ending in a double-play: both a man and a woman are mistaken for their servants, and the man is killed by the maid's jealous husband, who mistakes him for her lover. Another sort of double-play, involving two men and two women, takes place in a story that Joseph Roth composed in 1939, his *Tale of the 1002nd Night,* about a Viennese cavalryman who takes as his mistress a whore who is a dead ringer for a certain countess the cavalryman had seduced and then tired of. When the visiting shah of Persia desires the countess, the cavalryman sends him his own mistress, the ringer, and the shah can't tell the difference. The twist here is the fact that the trickster woman, the ringer, does not know that she is doubling for someone else, first with her lover (who knows she is a ringer) and then with another man (who doesn't know that he is a victim, any more than she knows that she is a trickster, or the countess knows that she is being impersonated).

In such modern versions of bedtricks, the cloak of darkness is rendered superfluous by a striking resemblance between two women. Sometimes it is a resemblance between a man's mistress and his wife (a not uncommon occurrence; we all know men who keep marrying the same woman, or their mother†). In a short story by Terry Southern, a woman named Grace, who has been cheating on her boring, faithful husband, has a change of heart and decides to revive their sex life by bleaching her hair and dressing sluttishly. Waiting for him in a half-lit room in their home, she discovers, to her chagrin, that she has inadvertently made herself resemble her husband's mistress, for he comes into the room and cries out, "*For Christ's fucking sake, Elaine, I told you never to come here!*"[28] No actual bedtrick is consummated, but one is intended; the wife openly changes into what she thinks to be a fantasy woman, not knowing that that woman is very real indeed and has already, through her own unknowing resemblance to the wife, taken her place in the husband's bed.

Stories in which the wife wants to sleep with her philandering husband sometimes also take into account the mistress's desires. The two women collude together, and the husband becomes the victim of both of them: not only does the wife get what she wants (to be the mistress), but the mistress gets what she wants (to be the wife). Olivia Goldsmith's novel *Switcheroo* begins from this premise—that the husband has taken a mistress who is a dead ringer for his wife, except for the blond hair. Goldsmith adds (without attribution) part of the premise, as well as most of the title, of Roald Dahl's "The Great Switcheroo"† but reverses the genders—the wife and mistress plot to change places. Reversing the genders, however, inevitably introduces other asymmetries,† such as the fact that the mistress looks like a *younger*† (and thinner) version of the wife; she is a New Age flake, certainly not a ringer for the *mind* of the wife, but what the hell, no one seems to care. The story becomes a complete double-play when a fourth player, the husband's best friend, John, gets into bed with the mistress, thinking he is in bed with the rejected wife. Indeed, there is even a suggestion that the husband is inadvertently doubling himself in his double-dealing adultery; he confesses to John, "It's not me going to that woman's house," to which John replies, "It's your evil twin?"[29] This undeveloped plot possibility (what Gary Saul Morson would call a sideshadow)[30] imagines that this wife's bedtrick is not only a double-cross in reaction to his betrayal (i.e., his adultery) but a double-cross-back in reaction to his betrayal (i.e., his fantasized bedtrick).

THE DOUBLE-CROSS

When a person betrays† a sexual partner in one sense of the word, by infidelity, that partner may stage a counter-betrayal, or double-cross, by engineering a retaliatory seduction. A wife double-crosses her husband in this way in the old Brighton joke retold by Angela Carter:†

> [A boy said to his father,] "I want to get married to the girl next door, Dad." His father replied, "I've got news for you, son. When I was your age, I used to get me leg over . . . the garden wall . . . and, cut a long story short, you can't marry the girl next door, son, on account of she's your sister." [The son kept finding other girls, but his dad said that he had fathered each girl. Finally the boy told his mother of his quandary,] and she said, "You just go ahead and marry who you like, son—'E's not your father!"[31]

Since the son, rather than a sexual partner, is the focal point where the two betrayals meet, the bedtrick is sidetracked into two sexual betrayals, one trickier than the other. This comic travesty of the tragedy of the Family Romance† (the tale of an adopted child who seeks his or her birth parents) pits the father's boastful infidelity against the mother's secret infidelity (or lie about a fantasized infidelity? false knowledge†?). The joke lies in the asymmetry† between the frivolity and openness of the man's act and the presumed shamefulness and secrecy of the woman's, as well as in her sense of revenge.

In a variant of the double-cross, when someone attempts to betray† a sexual partner either by infidelity or by pretending (through a bedtrick or a legal surrogation) to be someone else, the betrayed partner may retaliate by bedtricking the trickster, sending someone else in place of the desired object, perhaps someone diseased or demonic, or just of a lower class. In both the double-cross and the double-back, the bedtrickster's response is an attempt to undo what the victim (of this second trick) has done, tricking the trickster "measure for measure," according to the rabbinic rule that was specifically applied to the bedtricking of Judah by

Tamar† and that Shakespeare used for one of his two bedtricks.[32] But the double-back gets the counter-trickster into a desired bed, while the double-cross keeps the counter-trickster out of an undesired bed and puts someone else in instead. You fight fire with fire, lies with lies: and it is easier, as well as more fun, to bamboozle someone when you know that he or she is trying to bamboozle you. As in a judo throw, the intended victim utilizes the very conditions of secrecy and obscurantism that the trickster sets up, but uses them to make the trickster the victim of a second trick. As usual, the bedtrickster is subversive.

Double-backs often misfire when the double-backing trickster is confronted by another trickster engaged in a double-cross. Thus, in Boccaccio's *Decameron* (composed during the great Florentine plague, 1349–53), a man who is in love with a married woman convinces her that her husband is having an affair with another woman and that she should masquerade as that woman in the dark, in order to catch her husband in flagrante; but then he himself turns up in the dark and seduces her.[33] The wife thinks she is participating in a double-back, but her seducer adds one more double-cross. A double-cross is described in considerable psychological detail by Marguerite de Navarre (1492–1549), the sister of François I, who wrote her *Heptaméron* in response to Boccaccio's *Decameron*. "The Story of Bornet" tells of a man who makes an assignation with his maid and generously (and without her knowledge) shares her with his friend (a double-cross), not knowing that his clever wife had taken the place of the maid (a double-back).[34] In a variant on this theme, in Jean Giraudoux's telling of the Amphitryon‡ myth, the clever Alcmena, believing (wrongly, as it turns out) that Jupiter has secretly taken the place of her husband, Amphitryon, in her bed (in a double-cross), secretly sends Leda in her place (in another double-cross), thereby catapulting her husband into the very adultery from which she was trying to save herself. In Brome's *The Novella* (1632), the heroine comes to Venice, and although she disguises herself as a courtesan in order to find the man she loves, she tries to avoid actually sleeping with any of her suitors. On one occasion she substitutes for herself her Moorish servant, who is actually a disguised eunuch, though the customer discovers the trick before proceeding.[35] A thwarted droit du seigneur† involving a rather convoluted double-cross occurs in *The Queen of Corinth*, written by Fletcher, Field, and Massinger in 1616 or 1617 and inspired by *Controversia* 1.5 of the elder Seneca, the case of the man who raped two girls in one night. To allow for the tragicomic ending, the playwrights introduce "one radical change" into their material.[36] That change is the bedtrick, substituting the first victim for the intended second victim, which makes the villain merely *think* that he has raped two different women.

In real life (or at least in his posthumous memoirs, 1826–38, not quite the same thing), Giacomo Casanova (1725–98) *said* (which is not at all the same thing as proving) that he had engineered a double-cross in response to a woman's use of a bedtrick. Here, as so often, the double standard† twists the power plays so that Casanova sends his servant in his place, just as women do in combating the droit du seigneur,† while the woman initiates the sequence not through the use of political power (she has none) but merely through her own wits. Casanova tells us that, at Soleure, he had fallen in love with a beautiful young married woman whom he does not name (but we know to have been the baroness de Roll)[37] and that he had tricked another woman into helping him approach the baroness. This second woman he describes as "a widow, aged between thirty and forty years, of a jaundiced complexion, and a piercing and malicious aspect. In her efforts to hide the inequality of her legs, she walked with a stiff and awkward air." When she found out how she had been used, she told him, "I know all and I will be avenged."[38] Foolishly ignoring this threat, Casanova made an assignation with the baroness:

Casanova's Double-Cross

[Casanova crept into the room and made love for two hours, in darkness and silence, to the woman he found there. But the next morning, the baroness chided him for not coming to her in the night.] At last a dreadful suspicion came into my head that I had held within my arms for two hours the horrible monster whom I had foolishly received in my house. . . . I concluded, then, that I had spent two hours with this abominable monster; and what increased my anguish, and made me loathe and despise myself still more, was that I could not help confessing that I had been perfectly happy. It was an unpardonable mistake, as the two women differed as much as white does from black, and though the darkness forbade my seeing, and the silence my hearing, my sense of touch should have enlightened me—after the first set-to, at all events, but my imagination was in a state of ecstasy.[39]

Indeed, his amour propre was wounded; he remarked, "Her tender ecstasies equalled mine, and increased my bliss by making me believe (oh, fatal error!) that of all my conquests this was the one of which I had most reason to boast."[40] Presumably the constrictions of the occasion made it possible for the widow to conceal her telltale legs.‡

Then the widow wrote him a letter, adding insult to injury: "I leave your house, sir, well enough pleased, not that I have spent a couple of hours with you, for you are no better than any other man, but that I have revenged myself on the many open marks of contempt you have given me." She also told him that she had "a little ailment" (presumably syphilis) that he should take care not to pass on to his mistress (yet another way to stop him from sleeping with the other woman). But when Casanova discovered that his servant, Le Duc, had also contracted "a malady of a shameful character" at Soleure (from a milkmaid), he immediately engineered the myth of a double-cross, arguing (1) that he had not been fooled at all, and (2) that Le Duc had taken his place. The inspiration came from yet another woman friend (his housekeeper, soon to become his next lover), who asked him, "Tell me whether the widow could take her oath that she had spent the two hours on the sofa with you." "No, for she didn't see me, and I did not say a word."[41] And so Casanova wrote to the widow, saying that he had never left his room, never spent two hours with her, and that his servant had confessed that he had gone into her room in the dark, in all innocence, and had been seduced by her: "You plainly took him for someone else. . . . He left you without saying a word as soon as the day began to dawn, his motive being fear of recognition." She didn't believe Casanova and defied him to prove he wasn't there by proving that he had not been infected! Instead, Casanova sent Le Duc to her to show her *his* infection and to demand money to pay for his cure. She fell for this trick, and Casanova turned out to have, not syphilis, but just a mild dose of leukorrhea, from which he recovered quickly and on which his housekeeper congratulated him: "The only thing that can trouble you is the remembrance of the widow's foul embraces."[42] But it took far longer to recover from that remembrance and from the psychological effects of the widow's bedtrick.

The victory, such as it was, was won not in the bedroom but only on the staircase, as it were (in the *esprit de l'escallier,* the hindsight realization of what one *ought* to have done). It was not a double-cross in real life at all but merely the myth of a double-cross, a fiction like all the other (fictional) stories of double-crosses we have considered. Paul Zweig explains why Casanova was so devastated by this experience:

> Who would not be horrified at such a moment? But Casanova had perhaps more reason than most, for the very ground of his life had been challenged. As an erotic adventurer, he needed the paradisiac beauty of his beloved. Without her face, he could receive the pleasures of the body, but not the

grace of the emotions. . . . The bed-trick at Soleure forced him to see how fragile was the fantasy which he pursued, how much the world and his own male nature threatened the fable of innocence in which he needed to believe. Soleure is the first crack in the pure youthfulness which Casanova kept so remarkably intact until he was an old man.[43]

Casanova wrote of that episode, "Now that I am entering my dotage everything I foresee is black. . . . Accursed old age, fit to inhabit hell, where others have already placed it: *tristisque senectus* ('wretched old age')."[44] The trickster became the object rather than the subject of the trick when he grew old†—and fell victim to an *old* woman.† She claimed, in her letter, to have inoculated him against future illusions of the uniqueness of his sexual objects, but in fact she infected him not with syphilis (or leukorrhea) but with something far more lethal—old age.

Even more fictitious than the memoirs is a short story composed by Arthur Schnitzler (1862–1931) about Casanova's return to Venice, inspired by the episode at Soleure. Schnitzler calls it a *heimkehr*, "homecoming" (what Homer would have called a *nostos*), but given its connection with the earlier affair at Soleure I would call it

Casanova's Return

[While traveling home, Casanova encountered a woman, Amalia, whom he had seduced sixteen years ago. Now he was fifty-three and felt his age keenly. He smiled and was aware that the smile made him look younger. He was no longer interested in Amalia, though she still found him attractive and vowed, "In your arms I had my first taste of bliss, and I doubt not it is my destiny that my last bliss shall be shared with you!" She kissed his hands and said, "Tonight, I will kiss you on the lips." He, however, was fascinated by her young niece Marcolina, a highly intelligent young woman who argued with him about Voltaire but found him totally unattractive. He tried to enlist Amalia's aid, promising to sleep with her only if she got Marcolina to sleep with him, but Amalia could not persuade the girl. Casanova asked himself, "Am I really so repulsive?" and then reassured himself: "No, that is not the reason. Marcolina is not really a woman. She is a she-professor, a she-philosopher, one of the wonders of the world perhaps—but not a woman."

Then Casanova discovered that Marcolina was having an affair with Lieutenant Lorenzi, a young man who reminded Casanova of himself as he had been thirty years before. He bribed Lorenzi, who was desperately in need of money, to allow him, Casanova, to sleep with Marcolina in his place that night. Meanwhile, he plied Amalia's thirteen-year-old daughter with wine and raped her. That night, he and Lorenzi exchanged cloaks, and Casanova felt the sap of youth once more course through his veins. But then:] A ludicrous adventure now recurred to his mind. Twenty years ago he had spent a night with a middle-aged vixen in Soleure, when he had imagined himself to be possessing a beautiful young woman whom he adored. He recalled how next day, in a shameless letter, she had derided him for the mistake that she had so greatly desired him to make and that she had compassed with such infamous cunning. He shuddered at the thought and drove the detestable image from his mind.

[He went into Marcolina's room and bed in] impenetrable darkness. . . . From Marcolina's sigh of surrender, from the tears of happiness which he kissed from her cheeks, from the ever-renewed warmth with which she received his caresses, he felt sure that she shared his rapture; and to him this rapture seemed more intense than he had ever experienced. . . . Here at last was the reality which he had often falsely imagined himself to be on the point of attaining, and which had always eluded his grasp. . . . With the infallible conviction that he must be the bringer of delight even as he was the receiver, he felt prepared for the venture of disclosing his name. . . . Would not the ineffable bliss of this night transmute into truth what had been conceived in falsehood? His duped mistress, woman of women, had she not already an inkling that it was not Lorenzi, the stripling, but Casanova, the man, with whom she was mingling in these divine ardors? He began to deem it possible that he might be spared the so greatly desired and yet so intensely dreaded moment of revelation. He fancied that Marcolina, thrilling, entranced, transfigured, would spontaneously whisper his name. . . .

[He fell asleep, dreamed, and awoke to find the dawn light and Marcolina, in a nightdress, contemplating him] with unutterable horror, . . . shame and disgust. . . . He read the word which to him was the most dreadful of all words, since it passed a final judgment upon him—old man. [He fled and came upon Lorenzi, who challenged him to a duel. He killed Lorenzi and finished his journey to Venice.][45]

In Schnitzler's tale, Casanova remembers how he was tricked by a middle-aged woman, and he himself engineers a bedtrick to get a younger woman. We expect, from Amalia's hints ("I will kiss your lips tonight") and the reference to Soleure, that Amalia will act just like the older woman in Soleure and trick Casanova, this time as a counter-bedtrick for his intended bedtrick with Marcolina. Our loathing of Casanova—the rape of the child leaves no room for doubt as to Schnitzler's opinion—makes us hope that Amalia will puncture Casanova's delusions of youth and virility. This does not seem to happen, however, unless we are to understand that, while Casanova is asleep, Marcolina, whom he finds there at first light, replaces Amalia, with whom he spent the night. Schnitzler here is tricking the reader: our expectations take us there and back again, as if he sets us up for a trick and then tricks us out of it.

Isak Dinesen wrote a story, published in 1934, in which characters pair off in a kind of circle dance around a mysterious center that turns out to be a double-cross to avoid the droit du seigneur:

The Roads round Pisa

[A Danish nobleman named Augustus, who had left his wife because of her unbearable jealousy, met an old Italian noblewoman from Pisa (whom he mistook for a man at first, for she was bald without her wig) and learned her story: She had forced her granddaughter, Rosina, to marry an old, fat, and impotent man, Prince Pozentiani, though Rosina was in love with her cousin Mario. A month after the wedding, Rosina had successfully petitioned the pope for an annulment of her marriage on the ground that it had not been consummated. Prince Pozentiani had banished Mario from Pisa, but after the annulment Rosina had married Mario.

Augustus now encountered Rosina's best friend, Agnese (and mistook her, too, for a man, for she was wearing men's clothing and traveling in disguise); the old Prince Pozentiani; and his dashing young friend, Prince Nino—a man known for his spectacular success with woman, such that any woman who had him for a lover never took another lover. An argument arose, and Prince Nino challenged Prince Pozentiani to a duel. But before the duel began, Agnese told Pozentiani that, a year ago, Rosina had asked Agnese, a virgin like herself, to take her place in her bedroom for an hour, between midnight and 1 A.M., and something had happened to her in that hour that had blighted her life ever since. When the prince heard Agnese tell this, he said, "Always we fail because we are too small. I grudged the boy Mario that, in a petty grudge. And in my vanity I thought that I should prefer an heir to my name, if it was to be, out of a ducal house." He then begged Nino to forgive him, and he keeled over dead.

Nino then spoke to Agnese:] "I had left you," he said, speaking altogether like a person in a dream, "and was going away, but I turned back at the door. You were sitting up in the bed. Your face was in the shadow, but the lamp shone on your shoulders and your back. You were naked, for I had torn off your clothes. The bed had green and golden curtains, like my forests in the mountains, and you were like my picture of Daphne, who turns away and is changed into a laurel. And I was standing in the dark. Then the clock struck one. For a year, I have thought of nothing but that one moment." [At this Agnese walked out of the room and met Augustus.] She was changed, like a statue come to life, he thought. [She said to Augustus,] "I am free. . . . I am no more shut up within one hour. God!" she said with a sudden deep shudder, "I cannot remember it now if I try."[46]

Like the circular roads around Pisa, the stories wind in upon one another and come full circle, as characters discover that they are players in other peoples' stories.

Rosina, who does not want to sleep with the old prince, sends Agnese in her place, while the prince, being impotent, sends Nino in his place. But neither of the substitutes realizes the substitution of the other: the young girl's life is blighted because she believes she has been defiled by the horrid old man, and the young man's life is blighted because he believes that he has deflowered a woman in love with someone else ("For a year, I have thought of nothing but that one moment," he confesses; and it is for this reason that he challenges the old nobleman to a duel). When they exchange their stories, they realize that each of them had been tricked, but the trick is acceptable where the reality was intolerable. Each is freed from the lie of the past when they discover that their true stories are mirror images of one another.

Roald Dahl told a story (in 1965) about a notorious womanizer who is explicitly compared with Casanova,[47] and who may, or may not, be the victim of a double-cross that turns precisely on the distinction between an old woman and a young woman that plagued Casanova. The womanizer, traveling in Palestine, is given refuge and hospitality by a man who has an exquisitely beautiful wife and daughter. One of them—the traveler does not know which one—comes to his bed in the dark and demonstrates superb sexual technique:

THE VISITOR

All this [expertise in bed], you will probably say, indicated clearly that my visitor must have been the older woman. You would be wrong. It indicated nothing. True genius is a gift of birth. It has very little to do with age; and I can assure you I had no way of knowing for certain which of them it was in the darkness of that room. . . . Maddening it was not to know the true answer. It tantalized me. It also humbled me, for, after all, a connoisseur, a supreme connoisseur, should always be able to guess the vintage without seeing the label on the bottle.

[The next day, his host told him that he had another daughter in the house, who was concealed because she had leprosy. The guest realized in horror that his bedmate may have been neither the mother nor the lovely daughter he had met but, rather, the leprous girl. The host reassured his guest:] "Calm yourself down, Mr. Cornelius, calm yourself down! There's absolutely nothing in the world for you to worry about. It is not a very contagious disease. You have to have the most *intimate* contact with the person in order to catch it."[48]

The lovely lady† he thinks he has in his bed turns out to be loathly† in the extreme; the trickster is tricked by the man he thinks he has cuckolded (or whose daughter he thinks he has corrupted). His sexual pride is what blinds him. Apparently the mother and the first daughter (and the father?) collude together on the part of the other sister. But what if the father did *not* in fact substitute the leprous sister but merely intimated he had done so in order to destroy, retroactively, the pleasure of the man who had corrupted either his wife or his daughter? That is, what if he had lied about the bedtrick just as Casanova had lied at Soleure? The issue of age† substituting for youth is here doubled by the theme of ugliness substituting for beauty† to destroy a womanizer: after this, he hangs up his spurs.

THE DOUBLE-BACK-CROSS

In an episode in the Hindu corpus of divine marital squabbles, Shiva and Parvati trick one another into committing adultery with one another through two double-backs, first seriatim and then (in another variant of the myth) simultaneously. In a seventeenth-century Bengali variant of the myth with which we began this chapter, Parvati (here called Gauri or Chandi) takes the form of a *dom* (Outcaste) ferry woman:

SHIVA AND THE OUTCASTE WOMAN

Shiva came and asked the ferry woman to carry him across. He fell in love with the *dom* girl at first sight and proposed to enjoy her. Gauri vehemently protested on the ground that she was a woman of low origin, whereas Shiva was a great god, as he himself said. But finally Shiva purchased her beauty at the price of a diamond ring. After that Gauri revealed herself and berated Shiva for his licentious behavior.

Shiva made a plan to humiliate Gauri for thus humiliating him. He became a mouse and chewed her bodice. Then Shiva in the guise of an old itinerant tailor appeared in his own house, [darned the bodice], and then refused to be satisfied until Chandi had allowed herself to be enjoyed by him. Then Shiva threw off his disguise and berated Chandi as she had done him.[49]

The second double-back is specifically designed to counter the first, in a double-cross; cumulatively, this episode is a double-back-cross (two double-backs, one of which is also a double-cross). But sometimes both sexual partners are tricked in this way *at the same time.* They may or may not both be (as in the double-cross) intentional tricksters; each partner may have intended to bed someone else, not through a trick at all, but merely through common, or garden-variety, adultery. Such unwitting double-players are not tricksters tricked but deceivers deceived, mutual victims of an accidental double deception, in contrast with the double deception in the double-cross perpetrated by two people each of whom thinks he or she is the one plotting the trick. As usual, the results are asymmetrical;† often his double-back shows the husband that what he desires he already possesses, while hers shows the wife that she cannot possess what she desires.[50]

A double-back-cross, involving two deceivers and two intended victims, is depicted in a Sanskrit stanza by the seventh-century poet Amaru:

At night, a husband and a wife, each favoring a different lover, have separated in the meeting grove, only to meet together unaware in darkness. With hearts that melt in eagerness for bliss, both consummate their purpose; but what can we suppose they do when once they recognize each other?[51]

The *Gita Govinda,* composed in the twelfth or thirteenth century, borrows and reworks the Amaru stanza:

> Two lovers meeting in darkness
> Embrace and kiss
> And claw as desire rises
> To dizzying heights of love.
> When familiar voices reveal
> That they ventured into the dark
> To betray each other,
> The mood is mixed with shame.[52]

The voice† reveals the true identity of the lover mistaken for someone else in the dark.

There is also a Telugu version of this theme, composed in Madurai in the early eighteenth century, under the Nayaka dynasty, in a brief but highly concentrated stanza:

> A married woman failed to find
> the place of rendezvous;
> she was standing there, in the dark,
> when her husband came
> and embraced her, certain
> she was someone else.
> Great was their passion
> as they made love,
> each of them thrilling to a lover
> not there, while the God of Desire
> screamed with glee.[53]

This poem is used as an example of one of a number of rationalizations for the adultery of Ahalya;‡ this is number 3, "unconscious violation." As David Shulman comments, comparing this verse with Amaru's: "The Amaru verse allows the couple to recognize one another by their lovemaking, though they are too embarrassed to admit this; the Nayaka poet characteristically lets the violation in disguise succeed as such, without 'regressing' to a state of marital propriety. Violation is its own reward."[54] Shulman assumes that Amaru's couple reveal themselves in the sexual act, the moment of truth. I don't read that verse, or the *Gita Govinda* poem, quite that way; I think they only find out afterward. But in the Telugu poem they never find out at all; only the god (for Kama,† Eros, is explicitly a god in Hinduism, and the implicit god of the texts of Western eroticism) sees the truth, and laughs.

A double-back-cross takes place in the *Arabian Nights* story known as

THE WIFE'S DEVICE TO CHEAT HER HUSBAND

[When a certain woman's husband was out of town, a young man tried in vain to seduce her, enlisting the help of an old woman, who finally broke down the wife's resistance. The wife sent the old woman to find the lover, but when the old woman failed to find him, she decided to find another man, in order to get the gold the wife had promised her. She found] a pretty fellow, young and distinguished-looking, to whom the folk bowed and who bore in his face the traces of travel. [She went up to him and asked him if he would like some] meat and drink and a girl adorned and ready. [When he agreed, she brought him to his own house and knocked at the door. The wife] knew him and guessed how the case stood, [but she kept her wits about her and immediately saw how she could hoodwink him: she beat him with her slipper, accused him of violating the contract between them, and insisted that, when she heard that he was coming home, she had sent the old woman to test him. She concluded:] "I thought thee chaste and pure till I saw thee, with my own eyes, in this old woman's company and knew that thou didst frequent loose baggages." He swore to her, by Allah the Most High, that he had never in his life been untrue to her nor had done what she suspected him of.[55]

He was inadvertently heading for a double-back, sleeping with his wife when he meant to sleep with a whore; and she was, also inadvertently, heading for the same double-back, sleeping with her husband when she meant to sleep with a lover. They met in midstream, but she got the drop on him and pretended that her double-back had been intentional, designed only in response to his inadvertent one, that she *knew,* when he did not; this is the alibi of false knowledge.† This added twist makes this a doublecross as well, a double-back-cross.

THE DOUBLE-BACK-CROSS-PLAY

In the second of two versions of the story we are about to consider, demigods masquerade as humans or humans masquerade as demigods, only to end up with their own partners in what we might call a double-back-cross-play: as in a double-play, two people simultaneously play bedtricks on two other victims, but as in a double-back, they end up in bed together. The first variant, from a Jain Sanskrit text composed by a monk named Siddharshi in 906 C.E., is just a double-play: both the husband and the wife engineer bedtricks, but they do not end up together. For clarity, I will put the names of the celestials in capital letters:

"CLEVER" TRICKS "NAIVE"

A prince named Mugdha ["Naive" or "Infatuated"] was married to a princess named Akutila ["Not Crooked" or "Not Tricky"]. They were deeply in love. One day when they were picking flowers in different parts of their garden, a demigod [*gandharva*] named KALAJNA ["Knower of Timing," i.e., someone who knows what to do at the right moment] and his wife, a celestial courtesan [*apsaras*] named VICAKSHANA ["Clever"], flew over the garden. KALAJNA fell madly in love with Princess Akutila and VICAKSHANA with Prince Mugdha. KALAJNA thought he could trick Akutila; he descended from the sky to where she could see him but his wife, VICAKSHANA, could not; then he used his divine powers to turn himself into a magical duplicate of Mugdha, and he persuaded Princess Akutila to join him in a bed of flowers in a plantain bower. Meanwhile, VICAKSHANA used her powers to turn herself into Akutila's look-alike and persuaded Mugdha to go with her to a bower of creepers. But they went to the very same plantain bower where Akutila was with KALAJNA.

Both couples looked at each other in astonishment. They could not see a speck of difference between them. Prince Mugdha thought, "I have become two through the grace showered on me by the Blessed Goddesses of the Forest. My wife has also become doubled. This is a great cause for rejoicing." The king, too, Mugdha's father, regarded himself as lucky to have two sons instead of one and two daughters-in-law instead of one. And Akutila was delighted, as she thought, "I have become two."

But KALAJNA used his supernatural powers to find out who the second woman was; he realized, "Oh no, it can't be, it is my own wife VICAK-SHANA!" Then he got mad. He thought, "I'll kill that evil man. She is immortal, so I can't kill her. But I will make her so miserable that she will never go near another man again." When he had made up his mind to do this, his Fate ordained it to be otherwise. Fate made him think, "That was wrong of me. I must not torment VICAKSHANA. After all, I was no better. I did exactly the wrong deed that she did. . . ."

And VICAKSHANA thought, "My goodness! That's my husband KA-LAJNA, who now looks like this other one. How could it be anyone else?" She became ashamed of herself, thinking, "How can I be with another man when my husband is right here?" She also became jealous at the thought that her husband had another woman. They both stayed there like that.

One day a Jain monk came there and preached the Jain doctrine. When KALAJNA and VICAKSHANA heard the teaching, they were overcome by remorse at their wrongdoings. There emerged from both of their bodies a hideous woman whose body was made up of red and black atoms. Horrifying to behold, she stood far away from them all, her back to the group. KALAJNA and VICAKSHANA wept and fell at the feet of the monk and begged him to help them cleanse themselves of their sins, but he said, "Good people, do not despair. None of this was your fault. . . . It is the fault of that woman who has come out of your bodies. . . . She is called 'Thirst for Sensory Pleasures' [Bhogatrishna]." At that moment out of the bodies of all four of them emerged three children, one white and two black and hideous, representing Righteousness, Ignorance, and Sin. The Jain monk said, "When Ignorance is in their bodies, creatures cannot distinguish between a woman they may approach and one who is off-limits to them." The humans became ordained, and KALAJNA and VICAKSHANA thought, "See how fortunate these people are. Their lives are complete. . . . But we are gods and so are deprived of this opportunity, which is open only to human beings. . . ." That divine couple then returned home. Thirst for Sensory Pleasures went back into their bodies as they were leaving; only this time, because of the great power of their pure faith, she would cause them no harm.[56]

The mortals—who are defined, by their very names, as gullible—are delighted to find doubles. The immortals, whose names define them as clever, are angry to discover that they have *not* been doubled, because they realize that their genuine partners have been unfaithful. The male immortal does not, for once, invoke a double standard;† he holds himself to the same rules that he applies to his wife and forgives her her trespasses as he expects her to forgive his. The two mortals don't have to deal with this quandary: they're too naive to realize that they have been cuckolded. But both mortals and immortals are prey for the hideous woman named "Thirst for Sensory Pleasures," the very incarnation of dangerous female desire, who possesses their forms in a way far more sinister and destructive than the immortals' relatively innocent usurpation of the forms of the mortals.[57] In the Jain framework of this text, immortals are inferior to mortals‡ in their opportunities for Enlightenment.

A mid-sixteenth-century Hindu variation, in Telugu, on the theme of a mortal couple who get mixed up with an immortal couple reverses the flow of power; where in the Jain text both of the immortals desire mortals and masquerade to get them, in the Hindu text it is the mortals who desire the immortals and masquerade to get them. And where in the Sanskrit text the demigods figure it out first, in the Telugu text the humans figure it out first. In both cases, however, what they do or do not figure out is that they have been masquerading as the partners of their partners—which is to say, masquerading as themselves.† In the Telugu variant the double-play reaches its apogee (or nadir, depending upon your taste for this sort of thing) as a kind of double-back-cross-play: two double-backs and one double-play, arranged in a double-cross, two tricksters double-crossed into doubling-back. In what is probably a vain hope of keeping it all clear, I will again put the names of the celestials in capital letters:

THE DEFINITIVE LOINCLOTH

A celestial courtesan [*apsaras*] named RAMBHA was married to a demigod [*gandharva*] named NALAKUBARA. A human courtesan named Kalabhashini had fallen in love with NALAKUBARA, while a human poet named Manikandhara had fallen for KALABHASHINI when he saw the beauty of her feet.‡ The sage Narada told Manikandhara that Kalabhashini was more beautiful than a heavenly courtesan; and Narada said to RAMBHA, "Perhaps someday NALAKUBARA will meet a woman who looks like you."

Now, Manikandhara had generated dangerous amounts of inner ascetic heat, and Indra, king of the gods, sent RAMBHA to seduce him in order to dispel that heat. But as Manikandhara and RAMBHA were making love, she said, "NALAKUBARA, leave me, I'm tired," using the wrong name, the way men usually do. Then Manikandhara left her for a moment and used his ascetic power to take the shape of NALAKUBARA; in this new form, Manikandhara-as-NALAKUBARA returned to RAMBHA and continued to make love to her.

Meanwhile, Narada had given Kalabhashini the power to take any form, since he wanted to use her to humble RAMBHA. When RAMBHA had gone off to seduce Manikandhara, leaving NALAKUBARA alone, Kalabhashini used her magic power to take the form of RAMBHA. But Kalabhashini-as-RAMBHA came into the vicinity not of NALAKUBARA, who was still alone, but of RAMBHA and Manikandhara-as-NALAKUBARA. At that moment, RAMBHA was distracted by a deer and went away, leaving Manikandhara-as-NALAKUBARA alone. Kalabhashini-as-RAMBHA approached Manikandhara-as-NALAKUBARA, and they began to make love. But then RAMBHA returned and interrupted them.

There were now, in one place, one RAMBHA, one Kalabhashini-as-RAMBHA, and one Manikandhara-as-NALAKUBARA. Each of the two women claimed to be RAMBHA, and as a test each asked the other, "Tell me something about NALAKUBARA." Kalabhashini-as-RAMBHA knew some of the story and told what she knew, baffling Manikandhara-as-NALAKUBARA, who still could not tell which was RAMBHA.

Then RAMBHA said, "Come to the world of the gods and let us settle this before Indra." Kalabhashini-as-RAMBHA, however, who didn't have the power to go to the world of the gods, lamely argued that she did not wish to bother Indra with their trifling squabble. Manikandhara-as-NALAKUBARA then realized that Kalabhashini-as-RAMBHA was Kalabhashini, but RAMBHA still didn't know that he was not NALAKUBARA. Exposed, Kalabhashini-as-RAMBHA was humiliated and went away, and Manikandhara-as-NALAKUBARA said to RAMBHA, "Let's make love."

Meanwhile, the heavenly courtesans told NALAKUBARA that RAMBHA was making love with Manikandhara, and he went there. Now there were one NALAKUBARA, one Manikandhara-as-NALAKUBARA, and one RAMBHA, who was thoroughly confused. Manikandhara-as-NALAKUBARA said that NALAKUBARA was a demon. They began to fight and stripped off their clothes, down to their loincloths. Now, RAMBHA knew that NALAKUBARA wore a green loincloth, but Manikandhara-as-NALAKU-BARA was wearing an orange loincloth. RAMBHA stopped the fight, saying, "I know who is the real one," and she went home happily with NALA-KUBARA.

Manikandhara-as-NALAKUBARA took back his own form and encountered Kalabhashini. They told one another their stories and realized that by trying to take the shape of other people, they had made love with one another.[58]

This is a competition between courtesans on two levels, for the word *apsaras* signifies a celestial woman who is both closely connected with water (hence often translated as "nymph") and a dancer in the harem of the king of the gods. Rambha's husband, Nalakubara, is a *gandharva,* a demigod connected with horses,† magic illusion, music, and sexuality. His name, Nalakubara, may carry intended resonances with Nala, a man whose wife, Damayanti,‡ had to distinguish him from four gods who had taken his form;[59] this story may even be designed as a satire on that more famous one. One version of the Nala story even alludes to Nalakubara, when a swan tells Damayanti, "When Rambha heard about Nala from us, she was attracted to him, but when she failed to get him, she took Nalakubara, for the sake of the name of 'Nala.'"[60] But this Telugu text has more direct connections with another myth, the story of Nalakubara, Ravana, and Rambha. Ravana's rape of Rambha serves, in the Sanskrit epic, to explain why Ravana never rapes Sita:‡ Nalakubara cursed Ravana to die if he ever again took a woman against her will.[61] In the Telugu text, the cautionary tale of Ravana seems to serve, instead, to mock the elaborate masquerades of humans who desire immortals.

This is a farce that would make Feydeau turn green (or orange) with envy. If we are determined to sort out the actual sexual encounters in this vertiginous plot, it would look something like this:

1. RAMBHA makes love with NALAKUBARA.
2. RAMBHA makes love with Manikandhara.
3. RAMBHA makes love with Manikandhara-as-NALAKUBARA.
4. Kalabhashini-as-RAMBHA makes love with Manikandhara-as-NALA-KUBARA.
5. RAMBHA makes love with NALAKUBARA.

The first and last episodes are the same; the wheel has come full circle. The climax of all the masquerades is the penultimate episode, the fourth, when both of the bedtricksters meet and are mutually tricked; the human

man and woman later discover that they have gone to great pains only to end up in bed with one another. This is a rather one-sided solution to the asymmetry† with which the myth began, for Manikandhara desired Kalabhashini, but Kalabhashini did not desire Manikandhara. As in Shakespeare's *A Midsummer Night's Dream,* the night of magic illusion squares the human triangle, but it is not a perfect square, not even the intricate square-dance figure called a Grand Square.† The human male, Manikandhara, gets to make love to the human woman that he desires, as well as to the immortal woman (whom he does not particularly desire but, presumably, generically desires—and whom he decides to trick, even after he has had her *in propria persona,* just to get even with her for calling him by someone else's name in bed). The human female, however, Kalabhashini, never gets to make love with her fantasy man, Nalakubara, but only with the human man she does not desire, in the form of the fantasy man (and even then she is awakened before the dream is over, *somnus interruptus*). The text thus, like so many others, limits the eroticism of the human female, even a courtesan, and even in the maelstrom of the magic carnival. Rambha, of course, gets to make love with everyone, several times; that is, after all, the job description of a celestial courtesan.

The criteria for separating the men from the gods, and the women from the goddesses, function on two different planes, due to the usual asymmetry† of gender. The criterion for telling one female from another is knowledge:† Who knows the true story?† This fails, not because the women do not know the story, but because the man judging the case does not know the story: since he is not the real Nalakubara but simply Manikandhara-as-Nalakubara, he does not know what is supposed to be his own story. The myth is concerned with the type of knowledge required to choose the right story of one's life, or the right self—though in this case the criterion itself is undermined by the corruption of the judge.

The criterion for telling one male from another, by contrast, is green loincloth versus orange loincloth; Nalakubara's wife knows this and identifies her man. This is a ridiculously superficial (though submerged) criterion, which strips away the fantasy; if this is all that separates us from the gods, the theological masquerade is as thin as a G-string. Just as Kalabhashini-as-Rambha looks good but lacks the power to fly to the world of Indra, so Manikandhara-as-Nalakubara duplicates merely the outer garments, not the inner garments (let alone the inner soul), of the real Nalakubara. In *Double Impact* (1991), a film about twin brothers separated at birth, when one twin finds the other's girlfriend, she thrusts her hand down into his shorts—it's that sort of movie—and comments on his black silk underwear. The real boyfriend, who comes in on this scene, slams the girl across the room, shouting, "You of all people should know I don't wear black silk underwear."

But the loincloth test is actually no more superficial than the usual serious tests, which both mortals and immortals can manipulate. The silliness of the loincloth standard for the men provides a foil for the more serious criterion, which applies to the women, the criterion of knowledge. Yet, in this satire, knowledge fails, and the loincloth standard carries the day. The loincloth is the butt of other jokes in Hindu mythology, such as the story of the strip-poker game played by Shiva and Parvati, in which she analogizes the present loss of his loincloth to his previous castration in the Pine Forest.† Yet to the extent that the loincloth is, as in that story, a metonym for the genitals,† the loincloth test demonstrates that the one thing a woman knows her husband by is under his pants (even though, in this case, Rambha couldn't tell the men apart in bed). The contrast between green and orange loincloths is not a general way of telling a god from a mortal, like blinking or the lack of a shadow† in the story of Nala;[62] we are not led to believe that all gods wear green loincloths, and all humans orange. (Though we may note that green is the color of the goddess in South India, and orange the color worn by human renunciants; and that green, white, and orange are the colors of the Indian flag.) The loincloth standard is, rather, a specific way of telling someone who really knows you from someone who merely pretends to know you, a way of telling someone's individual identity within a known group.

Variants of the double-back-cross-play were also imagined in Europe. In John Marston's *The Insatiate Countess* (1610), two men who are enemies marry two women who are friends; each man plans to cuckold the other, but the wives exchange places in a double bedtrick and nobody has been cuckolded; both women become pregnant, however, and since both men are arrested later that same evening, each man believes the other has fathered his wife's child.[63] More complex, and more sinister, is a double-back-cross-play involving *five* people and two bedtricks, a revenge play concocted by Samuel Harding in 1640, in which the enemies come from two cities notorious for their pursuit of revenge,

SICILY AND NAPLES

Ferrando (1), king of Naples, wooed Felicia (2), daughter of Alberto, marquess of Durazzo, but then he switched his affection to Calantha

(3), daughter of the king of Sicily. Felicia thought that Ferrando had come to her in the night, constrained to secrecy by his engagement to Calantha, and had "filled her arms," seduced her and impregnated her, but in fact Ferrando's favorite, the evil Ursini (4), who was in love with Felicia, had perpetrated a bedtrick that Felicia never uncovered. When the king of Sicily broke off the match with Calantha, war broke out, in which Ferrando killed both Alberto and the king of Sicily; Calantha escaped, dressed as a soldier. Felicia came, masquerading as a page named Sylvio, to the court of Ferrando, and her brother, Frederico (5), also came to that court, masquerading as a Moor named Zisco, with a clubfoot; neither knew of the other sibling's survival. Calantha, too, came to the court of Naples, engaged, against her will, to marry Ferrando, though she was sick with grief for her father. All of this happened before the play begins.

Ursini realizes that Zisco is Frederico, but not that Sylvio is Felicia; he thinks Felicia is dead and soliloquizes: "I loved her once, Till I enjoyed her, but she's lost; so is her memory" (1.6). Ferrando insists on the wedding, but before he can consummate it, Felicia-as-Sylvio tells Calantha her story, still believing that Ferrando had impregnated her. "Our wrongs and sorrows," says Felicia, "have made us just so like one another, That each seems th' other's counterfeit." Each confesses to the other that Ferrando had killed her father, taken her dowry, and "mocked me with the title of a Queen," yet, each confesses, "I am lost in passion." Felicia offers to take Calantha's place on the wedding night, since Felicia has already lost her maidenhead (to Ferrano, she thinks), and Calantha still has hers. Calantha agrees to this.

Meanwhile, Frederico-as-Zisco, believing a rumor that Ferrando had had Felicia raped and murdered, offers to help Ursini in his plot against Ferrando; he tells Ursini, lying, that he himself was the Moor that Ferrando had hired to ravish and kill Felicia. At this, Ursini says, "And canst thou do't again?" Zisco: "Bravely." Ursini then tells him that he has arranged matters so that Frederico-as-Zisco can ravish and kill Calantha that very night. Frederico-as-Zisco agrees to do it, "An she were my mother." But Felicia takes Calantha's place, and it is she that Frederico-as-Zisco rapes and murders; he then stabs Ferrando. When Calantha comes to gloat over Ferrando as he dies, Frederico-as-Zisco discovers he has killed his own sister, Felicia. Ursini now confesses that it was he, not Ferrando, who had seduced Felicia; when Frederico-as-Zisco asks him why Felicia had not recognized him, Ursini says it was dark, and "I dissembled so the Prince in voice and feature." Frederico stabs himself, Calantha stabs Ursini, and, as he dies, Ursini stabs Calantha.

At the end, as William R. Bowden remarks, "Everyone is now dead, and it does not really matter whether the reader has been able to keep straight who has been a villain and who a victim."[64] Not so; Ferrando is guilty of murder and inconstancy, though not guilty of the seduction or murder of Felicia, for which he is blamed; and (rather like Berthold Brecht's "Sorabaya Johnny") he continues to inspire passion in the two women who blame him wrongly for the seduction of Felicia and rightly for the murder of their fathers. Zisco, who begins as the avenging hero, becomes a villain by pretending to be one; he ends up committing the very crime (the rape and murder of Felicia) that he lies about having committed and thinks he is avenging. Ursini is a villain through and through; his jealousy and hatred of Ferrando (for taking the love and, he thinks, the life of Felicia) drive him to set Zisco up to commit the crime, and his bedtrick impersonation of Ferrando triggers the retaliatory bedtrick that makes Felicia, rather than Calantha, the victim of the second bedtrick he engineers. The women are, as so often, the victims of both political† and sexual treachery, to which they can only respond with a bedtrick of their own.

The epicyclic doublings of the doublings, wheels within wheels, create a world in which nothing is sure, no trick achieves closure, no relationship (least of all a subversive one) is invulnerable to subversion. The escalating series of bedtricks within bedtricks deconstruct first marriage, then adultery, and then the pretense of adultery. The bedtricks whirl around and around into a *mise en abîme,* a sexual vortex in which no one ever knows who is tricked and who tricking—it's all a lie. The complex permutations dizzy the reader until the reader doesn't know, or care, who is who in bed—the very point the story aims to make.

THE DOUBLE-BIND

The double that stands for oneself (like the double of the victim in René Girard's sacrifice scenario)[65] is simultaneously the other "I" that achieves what I cannot otherwise achieve, the one who obtains the object of my sexual desire *for me,* and the other "I" that is my rival, that takes that same object away *from me.* This is the paradox of the double-bind: bedtricksters usually believe that they will be loved only if they cease being who they really are, a situation well captured in the original title of a film about a bedtrick: *Hollow Triumph* (1948, later known as *The Scar*†). Or, as the masquerading woman sings in *Bells Are Ringing* (1960): "He's in love with Millicent Scott, / A girl who doesn't exist. / He's in love with someone you're not; / So it was never you he kissed." Schnitzler's Casanova† was caught in this bind when, having tricked a woman into bed, he thought of "the so greatly desired and yet so intensely dreaded moment of revelation."[66]

Nietzsche imagined such a quandary even for the Superman in bed: "[He] asks himself whether the woman, when she gives up everything for him, does not possibly do this for a phantom of him. He wants to be known deep down, abysmally deep down, before he is capable of being loved at all; he dares to let himself be fathomed. He feels that his beloved is fully in his possession only when she no longer deceives herself about him."[67] Who is this phantom? It is the double in the double-bind, who haunts everyone who asks, "Am I loved for myself?" and who ensures that any victory achieved by a bedtrick will be truly hollow. This double-bind also applies to a woman who is possessed: she can say, "I am not myself,"‡ and assume the power of another voice,† but the trouble is, it is not her own voice; someone else speaks for her, or she for someone else.

In the renditions of the myth of Amphitryon‡ by Kleist and Molière, when Jupiter masquerades as Amphitryon he wants to be loved for himself, not for the sake of Amphitryon, that is, as Alcmena's lover as well as her husband. He wants Alcmena to say that the lovemaking on his night was better than ever, and she won't say it. In Giraudoux's retelling of the story, Jupiter-as-Amphitryon asks Alcmena, "Far and away our most delightful night together, wouldn't you say?" But she replies, "That remains to be seen. Don't you remember our wedding night, dear husband . . . ? That was our most beautiful night."[68] This is *not* what Jupiter wants to hear. ("All right, our most beautiful. But this was still the most *delightful*," he insists.)

When a bedtrickster pretends to be someone else who actually exists, it is usually someone of whom the trickster is already jealous from the start. But the bedtrickster who pretends to be someone nonexistent gradually becomes jealous of his or her own creation. This quandary crops up in a 1993 episode of *Star Trek*, "Second Chances," in which Commander William Riker of the *Enterprise* (in a red shirt) encounters a double of himself (Lieutenant Riker, in a yellow shirt) that had split off eight years ago (during a transporter malfunction, the usual source of doubles on *Star Trek*) and had been existing alone on an isolated planet ever since. The red and yellow shirts that distinguish the two Rikers are like the loincloths that distinguish the Telugu poet and the demigod. Deanna Troi and Commander Riker (red) had been in love eight years ago, but he had rejected her, hurtfully; now she and Lieutenant Riker (yellow) fall in love (again?), and Riker (red) tells her, "The look in your eyes—I recognize it. You used to have it for me." The nonhuman Worf tries to explain to Data, the robot, why the two Rikers hate each other: "Humans value their uniqueness, that sense that they are different from everyone else. The existence of a double would preclude that feeling." (Worf might have been paraphrasing Rosalind Krauss: "In being seen in conjunction with the original, the double destroys the pure singularity of the first.")[69] But Data—who has his own out-of-control brother, named Lore (science versus myth?), identical but dressed very differently—counters, "Perhaps it is more a matter of seeing something in your double, something you do not like in yourself."[70] Out of the mouths of robots.

The double-bind is brilliantly depicted in Edmond Rostand's *Cyrano de Bergerac*, composed in 1897, in which Cyrano, a great poet and soldier with an enormous nose, woos the beautiful Roxane, whom he loves secretly, on behalf of the handsome but rather slow-witted Christian de Neuvillette. When Christian dies, Cyrano keeps the secret of the trick for many years, until his own death approaches. Cyrano is grateful to his macho friend for allowing him to "have" Roxane in a way that would otherwise not be possible; but of course he also hates him for having what he, Cyrano, cannot really have. Both men lose, for each feels that Roxane truly loves the other. Each had hoped he would be himself *plus* the other and finds he has simply given away himself *to* the other and gotten nothing back in return. Where each had hoped to be the full part of the half-full glass, each now perceives himself as the empty part; where they had hoped to win her together, now each feels that he has lost her to the other as rival.

No bedtrick is consummated in the play, but the kiss,† as usual, stands for more, and both the implicit film version (*Love Letters*† [1945]) and the explicit film version (*Roxanne* [1987]) connect the dots and consummate the act. In the film *Roxanne,* when the Cyrano character (now named Charlie, or C. D.) succeeds in using his voice to persuade Roxanne to go to bed with Christian (now named Chris), he shouts out, "Oh god, I did it! Oh shit, I did it!" When later he claims to have been the one who won Roxanne, he argues, lamely, "It just wasn't the actual me that [he hesitates] did the honors." And when Roxanne, on discovering that she went to bed with Chris thinking that he was the author of the letters, insists, "I don't consider that I went to bed with him," C. D. replies, "It sure as hell wasn't me." This is the double-bind.

Roxane is wooed by a man compounded of two men, who explicitly regard themselves as a composite of wit (or soul) and beauty.† (In *Roxanne*, Chris tells C. D., "She wants somebody that looks like me and talks like you.") When, at the end, Roxane realizes the truth about the love letters, purportedly written by Christian but written by Cyrano and marked with his tears, she tells Cyrano, "They were your tears," and he replies, "The blood was his." Is Christian masquerading as Cyrano, or Cyrano as Christian? Cyrano assures Christian that Roxane loves him for himself, but he is wrong; she loves him only for his surface, as she herself later admits, and the self, or soul, that she loves is Cyrano's, as Christian comes to discover to his distress. When Cyrano "pretends" to love Roxane, and "pretends" to weep as he writes to her, he is masquerading as his true, concealed self.† But Christian, too, is caught up in this self-masquerade, as he realizes when he cries out, "She loves only my soul. That means you," and finally, "I am tired of being my own rival!" Christian and Cyrano become a tragicomic embodiment of the old folktale of the blind man who put the lame man on his shoulders so that, together, they could see and walk; together, Christian can be seen and Cyrano can be heard. Cyrano invokes and rejects a myth when he tells Roxane, "When Beauty said, 'I love you' to the Beast / that was a prince, his ugliness / changed and dissolved, like magic. . . . But you see / I am still the same." Cyrano, who has no faith in fairy tales like Beauty and the Beast,† mocks this choice when he remarks, correctly, that there is no value in Roxane's imagined "choice" of an ugly Christian, since he will not be magically transformed in that way when she bestows the magic kiss.†[71]

In the film *Roxanne,* which stumbles at the end into a version of Rudolph the Red-Nosed Reindeer, Chris ditches Roxanne for another woman, a friend tells Roxanne that C. D. wrote the letters, and they live happily ever after. In the play, Roxane figures it out herself, but not until Cyrano is dying. She has two chances to make the choice between the two men, both in darkness. The first time is during the balcony scene, when Cyrano stays below, in darkness, speaking words of love while Christian climbs to the balcony and claims the reward of a kiss. Roxane fails to recognize Cyrano's voice; she notices something wrong with it at first, but in the darkness the two men seem to her to be alike. At the end of the play, the darkness returns: Cyrano, dying, asks Roxane to let him read the letter that she thinks Christian had written to her when he was dying, a letter that she kept always in her breast. As night draws on, Cyrano continues to read the letter out loud, as Roxane remarks, "You read it so . . . in a voice . . . in such a voice . . . as I remember hearing . . . long ago." And then, "How can you read now? It is dark." Then she realizes, "It was you. And I might have known, every time that I heard you speak my name.† I understand everything now: The letters—that was you. . . . And the dear, foolish words—That was you. . . . And the voice in the dark—That was you. . . . And the Soul!—that was all you. . . . I never loved but one man in my life, and I have lost him—twice." (The film *The Truth about Cats and Dogs* [1996], a remake of *Cyrano* with the genders reversed, gives the male Roxane character an upbeat version of the same line: "I've never loved but one woman in my life, and I don't want to lose her twice.") It is in part the resemblance between the two darknesses that gives Roxane the clue (are all darknesses alike in the dark?): the fact that Cyrano is reading "Christian's letter" when *he cannot see* makes her able to *see him*.† But it is also the resemblance between the two dyings, the congruence of the moment when the letter was written (as Christian died) and read (as Cyrano died). Only in death† has Cyrano been able to become the man he pretended to be, his own rival.

The film *Love Letters* (1945) draws heavily upon *Cyrano de Bergerac*:†

LOVE LETTERS

During the war, a soldier named Allen and a young woman named Virginia who have never met fall in love through love letters that he writes to her on behalf of his friend Roger Morland. (Allen refers to her as "a kind of pinup girl of the spirit.") When Roger returns and marries her and she discovers what a bounder he is, there is a fight; he is killed and she goes mad, loses her memory, and calls herself Singleton. Allen is told that both Virginia and Roger died in a tragic accident, which no one will talk about. He meets Singleton and does not realize at first that she is Virginia Morland, though eventually a mutual friend tells him the truth and warns him never to speak to Singleton about her past: "If her memory ever came back, it should come back gradually, from within, of her own accord. If anyone told her of her past now, the shock would be so terrible that she'd probably lose her mind." Singleton is haunted by the memory of another man whom she had loved, who had written wonderful letters, and she fears that Allen, too, is still in love with someone else, someone she doesn't know, named Virginia Morland ("I'll help you find her," she says, cheerfully). They fall in love, but Singleton's guardian warns Allen that he is proposing to marry two women, Virginia and Singleton, and that only one, Singleton, can give her consent; how could Singleton give

Virginia's consent? And what if Singleton turned back into Virginia Morland? Still, they marry.

Singleton has forgotten how to write but now learns again, and one day she writes a verbatim quote from one of the letters she had written to Roger/Allen long ago. Then Allen quotes from one of his letters to her, and she realizes that he is the author she seeks. Now she remembers everything, but she does not, as he had feared, hate him for his deception. They live happily ever after.

If *Roxanne* imagines what might have happened if Roxane had slept with Christian and then found out that Cyrano had written the letters and chosen him instead of Christian, *Love Letters* imagines what might have happened if Cyrano had married Roxane after the death of Christian. Allen lies to Singleton as Cyrano lied to Roxane; people lied to one another most appallingly all the time in films of that era (remember *Dark Victory* [1939]?), but of course for noble reasons. Still, amnesia maintained in this way is a kind of false ignorance† on the part of the amnesiac's manipulative partner. Singleton sleeps with Allen only after the onset of her amnesia, so that there is no basis for comparison to jog the sexual memory. But, as in *Cyrano de Bergerac,* the words in the letters do the job of the magic awakening kiss†—the pleasures of the text† substituting for those of sex.

In many of these stories, amnesia makes a person into his or her own imaginary rival. A delightful inversion of this situation is provided by a genre of Indian texts in which stupidity prevents a husband from realizing that he really *does* have a rival, in which the mythology of the magical sexual double is invoked to sustain a straightforward case of adultery. This happens in a Sanskrit text dated to the fifteenth century:

The Husband in the Mango Tree

In a certain village there lived the wife of an honest man; she was beautiful and clever but in love with another man. One day she went to their place of assignation in the mango grove and there gave herself to her lover. But at that time her husband happened to come to the mango grove. When the wife's lover saw the husband approaching, he got up with a great flurry and stood modestly concealed. When the wife saw her husband, she cried out, "What I want is to eat a mango." "Then I will bring some for you," the husband replied. But she said to him, "My desire is to climb the tree myself and then to eat the mango." "Then do so," he replied.

When she ascended the tree she looked down at her husband and cried

out, "O my dear, how can you make love with another before my eyes!"
"How can you think this?" her husband replied. "There is no one else
with me here." "Could this be the peculiar nature of the tree?" asked the
wife. "You must come here and look at me standing on the ground."

Then she called her lover and had her pleasure with him in just the
manner that pleased her. Seeing this, the husband declared, "This tree
does indeed have a peculiar nature!" Thereupon the lover departed. So
that was how these two caused the tree to have a "peculiar" nature.[72]

This story satirizes the myth of the magical rival that makes a man
cuckold† himself. It has charmed people of many countries and times;
scholars have noted parallels with one of Chaucer's *Canterbury Tales* and
with tales from Boccaccio, the Bahari Danish, and the Turkish "Forty
Viziers,"[73] and it took on a new twist in one of the French fabliaux collected by R. Howard Bloch, "Du prestre qui abevete," in which a priest
bamboozles the peasant whose wife is the priest's mistress.[74] Folk traditions the world over laugh about adultery; it is the landed classes that
take it seriously.

A contemporary Kannada variant was collected by A. K. Ramanujan:

THE HUSBAND'S SHADOW

[A merchant had a pretty wife who was carrying on an affair with the
king. The husband became suspicious and said:] "Look here, woman. You
seem to be fornicating in my absence." . . . Being still suspicious, he appointed a man to guard over his wife, but the man was a nitwit. As soon
as her husband was safely out of sight, she sent for the king. He came to
her in a hurry and spent time with her. After he left, the nitwit asked her,
"Who is that man who came and went just now?" She said, "Oh, that is
my husband's shadow." "What is a shadow?" he asked. "A shadow is what
you see in a mirror. Look for yourself," she said. He looked into a mirror
and said, "Oh, that, I know that."

On another day, when the king and the merchant's wife were sleeping
together, the merchant returned home from his travels and banged on
the door. The king got up in a hurry, jumped the backyard fence, and
vanished. When she then opened the door for him, her husband was full
of suspicions. He called the nitwit and questioned him. "Did anyone come
here when I was gone?" "No, sir. Only your shadow came and slept with
the mistress. No one else." "My shadow? What do you mean by 'shadow'?"
"Come here, sir," said the nitwit, and took him to the mirror. He
showed his master his shadow and said, "Look there, that's the shadow
I mean." The merchant laughed. His doubts about his wife were cleared.

"Oh, that shadow? It's all right if that shadow comes to see my wife. You don't have to stop him," he said. Now his wife could sleep with her lover whenever the merchant was away. The nitwit didn't ever report it again.[75]

The "shadow"‡ is a reflection or image, the subject of an extended ancient Indian mythology of bedtricks. This text may also be seen as a satire on the famous Upanishadic passage in which the demons foolishly regard the image in a mirror as the entire self and lose their chance to attain true knowledge of the Self, the *atman*.[76] Here is self-cuckolding in a new key, subverting classical Indian philosophical ideas about the nature of the self as well as the literary trope of mirror images and shadows and deeply embedded cultural assumptions about female chastity.

Approach One

Philosophy, or Love/Sex = Mind/Body?

This essay summarizes, not what philosophers have said or might have said about bedtricks, but rather what the texts of the bedtrick tell us about human issues that have also intrigued philosophers: the relationship between the body and the mind and/or soul, and the different sorts of love. The bedtrick can be read as a parable of idealistic philosophy in bed. Its philosophical implications become apparent when we ask what is real and what is unreal in each of these stories. But reality differs from one variant to another, and something that is "unreal" in origin may come to have very real effects. There are a number of possible criteria for "reality," which we can explore by substituting different terms for "real" and by assuming different points of view. For example, we may ask which of two people competing for the same identity is more authentic from the standpoint of the author (outside the frame) or more desirable from the standpoint of the victim (inside the frame). Often one person is said to be "real" at the beginning, while the other is either a masquerade or a magical duplication. The copy is usually "worse" both in being a fake and in having evil motives for masquerading. But this paradigm is challenged by myths in which the bedtrickster is a god (Jupiter with Alcmena,‡ Indra with Ahalya‡) or a better lover than the original (ditto, plus Martin Guerre†) or nobler in spirit than the corrupt political† ruler who is noble only in blood (Sommersby,† the prisoner of Zenda†). Does this make them more authentic, more real, than the people they imitate?

In some myths (such as the tale of the Somnambulists†) and in some real-life cases of bedtricksters, we (and the victim) meet the masqueraders in medias res, in the false form, and only encounter the authentic form at the end. But in other myths (such as the stories of Shiva† and Casanova†), we begin with the authentic, move into the masquerade, and return to the authentic at the end. We encounter some masquerades at their moment of coding and others at their moment of decoding. We meet a different gaze, perhaps, and hear the story from the standpoint of the masquerader. Some myths (such as the tales of animal lovers† and Loathly Ladies†) regard the bedtrickster as Other, alien, caught in an inauthentic position; other myths (such as the tale of Rachel and Leah†) regard the Other as a valid form of the self, authentically constructed from the start. We may therefore encounter in some myths a greater nervousness about what the authentic is and, sometimes, a greater need to establish it from the start rather than let the reader/victim discover it gradually.[77]

BODY AND SOUL (AND MIND)

Although these stories seem to be about the boundary between mind and body in human sexual identity, they blur the boundary even when they assume it from the start. So, too, they are about the tension between sex and gender and between lust and love; but sex does not exactly correspond to body, nor gender to mind, and lust and love do not map easily onto these dichotomies. There are other metaphors for the problem of the real that fit many of our stories better than a simple dichotomy does, such as a hierarchy with "most real" at the top or a circle with "most real" at the center or a Möbius† strip twisting in upon itself or a Venn† diagram of family resemblances. All of these abstractions are ladders that we may use to climb up into these stories and then kick away. But I will focus on dichotomies here because they best approximate the strong tensions and choices that make for drama in narrative, particularly in myth.

Bedtricks present a challenge to our Cartesian understanding of the connection between the mind and the body. How does the masquerade of the body change the mind? And what about the soul, which is not at all the same thing as mind, especially in Indian texts, but seems to be interchangeable with it in some European texts? The legal† fights about adoptive versus birth parents are about body versus soul, as is, in the theory of parental imprinting,† the tension between mental and physical parenthood and the tension between fantasy† and the physical act. In Cartesian thinking, identity must fish or cut bait: it must make its home in the mind or in the body. Other cultures, however, are not so quick to jump to either conclusion, or even to take the question seriously in the first place. One Indian answer to the Western question "Mind or body?" is "Yes." But the question is debated in many stories about bedtricks. More spiritual myths argue that the mind—or the soul or speech or knowledge—supplies the touchstone of identity; but earthier myths assume that the body, particularly the sexual body, is the home of identity. These are matters of degree: for the myth expresses the paradox† as a tension between both of these points of view and challenges it by raising such questions as whether or not the bedtrick is a rape.† The argument that the sexual act is a source of knowledge is profoundly non-Cartesian.

Various cultures express the belief that what you *think* you are doing in bed is more important than what you actually *are* doing. The sexual act straddles the line between psychic and physical reality: sexual fancy† is bred both in the heart and in the head. The psychosomatic reality of the sexual act is also expressed in myths about dreams of sexual encounters, the reality of which is "proven" by semen or blood on the bed on the morning after.[78] The rabbis argued that Jesse,† the father of David, wasn't committing adultery if he *thought* he was in bed with his own wife. A similar idea is expressed in a Buddhist text that argues that a man who has intercourse with the wife of another man is not to be punished if he thought that he was with his own wife; and opinions differ as to whether a man who mistakes the wife of one man for the wife of another man should be punished; some say he should, since he both intended to enjoy another man's wife and enjoyed another man's wife (though not the same man); other say he should not, since, like a man who kills the wrong person by mistake, he did not enjoy the object of his desire.[79]

Which is the more "real" infidelity: when a woman has sex with her husband while she dreams of her lover, or when she is raped by a stranger while remaining true in her heart to her husband? While the villain in *The Queen of Corinth*† suggests that Merione, the woman he raped, might think she had dreamt it, her fiancé's friend says, "Imagine faire Merione had dream'd / She had been ravish'd, would she sit thus there / Excruciate?" Just as a woman who is raped might think of her husband in an attempt to remain undefiled, Kleist's Alcmena‡ keeps insisting that Jupiter is her husband, in an attempt to remain innocent. This paradox makes stories about bedtricks a paradigmatic expression of the problem of the mind and the body,† reality and illusion.

Mind and body jockey for position in the mind of a man who is tricked into committing adultery with his own wife. During the trick, the husband's head is not really sleeping with his wife, and his head takes charge of his body; it is because his fantasy is so powerful that he is fooled. But when the trick is revealed, he is forgiven, his adulterous mental intentions treated as peccadilloes: all that really counts in the end is the bald, literal fact that he has ended up bodily in bed with his own wife, whatever he may have been thinking and intending. The power of fantasy bound up with his intentions makes the deception possible, but his fantasies are not grounds for moral condemnation. How can male fantasy weigh so heavily in making the story work, and so lightly in the denouement?[80]

This paradox† drives the resolution of *Measure for Measure*† (5.1.450–60). Isabella argues that Angelo is innocent since he merely *intended* to kill her brother Claudio and debauch her but was bedtricked out of succeeding in either of these aims: "For Angelo, / His act did not o'ertake his bad intent, / And must be buried but as an intent / That perished by the way. / Thoughts are no subjects, / Intents but merely thoughts." If all is fantasy, no one should be punished (as is often argued in debates about pornography). When Angelo projects over Mariana his image of the body of Isabella, which is the object of his desire, he is sleeping with what Shakespeare calls an "imagined person" (5.1.213) and what Carol Thomas Neely characterizes as "part body, part fantasy."[81] But Janet Adelman reminds us: "We respond to Isabella not simply as an icon in a male fantasy about sexuality but also as a vividly and independently alive character with fantasies of her own. In fact the encounter of Angelo and Isabella is so explosive in part because the fantasies each embodies mesh so well."[82]

When the body takes on a new gender, the mind and soul may remain intact: the demons Jalandhara† and Adi† do not feel or think like Parvati or Shiva when they take on their forms; they just look like them but retain their own essence and mentality. These texts present a self with a mind that resists all masquerades; generally speaking, the characters (even in stories of magical transformations) wish not to *be* virtuous but to have what the virtuous have. Thus, Jeanine Basinger comments on the films in which the evil twin pretends to be the good twin: "When a bad woman pretends to be a good one, she always has a *bad* reason for it. It's never because she wants to be good for a while; it's because she wants something she shouldn't have, usually sex, her sister's man, or money."[83] So, too, Basinger continues, the good woman who pretends to be someone else does so in order to reify some evil that is already a true part of her repressed† identity; in films about a woman who splits into two‡ when she dreams or is hypnotized,† "The woman who goes to sleep and releases herself into a different form is uniformly a good woman whose inner self wishes to be sexier, naughtier, freer in some way. I don't know of any films in which a bad woman falls asleep and dreams that she's taking baskets to the poor."[84]

Sometimes tricksters are exposed when they do not behave like the originals. Indeed, we must distinguish between the masquerader who is not *who* he or she appears to be (one's husband, a human) and one who is not *how* he or she appears to be (unmarried, a king, faithful, and so forth). Behavior in bed, including but not limited to "sexual tricks,"† is paramount, but behavior out of bed is also a relevant factor. Shiva† is able to distinguish his wife Gauri/Kali from the impersonating demon because she is not *behaving*† like herself, and she can see through the impersonation of Shiva by the demon Jalandhara† when the demon does not do (in the sexual act) what Shiva does. The behavior of children often "proves" their identity and solves the riddle of the Family Romance:† Shakuntala's son[85] and Zeus's (and Amphitryon's‡) son catch their fathers' eyes by dealing fearlessly with wild animals. Many masqueraders are identified by their ability to cook† a particular dish; Nala‡ and Amphitryon are recognized by their horsemanship.† Often the trickster is exposed because he behaves *better* than the original, particularly in political† bedtricks; Martin Guerre's† wife, in the novelized account, accuses the impostor, "If you had been Martin Guerre you would perhaps have struck me just now."[86] This is the "Have you stopped beating your wife?" criterion of identity. And behavior is often the key to identity in films about bedtricks. In *The Dark Mirror*† (1946), the psychologist remarks, "Not even nature can duplicate character, even in twins." The reincarnate husbands in *The Reincarnation of Peter Proud*† (1974) and *Chances Are*† (1989) have personal ticks that convince their partners that they are who they claim to be; the same sorts of ticks, in *Prelude to a Kiss*† (1992), expose the impostor.

In *The Changelings,*† when the biologically female Chunagon masqueraded as a male, "four or five days each month he was unable to conceal the strange ailment about which he could do nothing. 'I am afflicted by evil spirits,' he would say, as he secretly went off to his wet nurse's village to hide. This worried people, who wondered what it was all about."[87] It should have more than "worried" them; it should have betrayed the truth about Chunagon, yet nothing came of it. On the other hand, only when a man named Saisho saw the biologically male Naishi no Kami (whom he knew as a heterosexual woman) in the form of "Chunagon" seducing a woman did it occur to him to ask himself, "Can this be someone else and not Chunagon?"[88] Saisho assumes that a woman does not seduce another woman (though Saisho himself had tried to seduce someone he thought was a man, Chunagon), but, even more important, Saisho believes that his true love, Chunagon, could not be promiscuous.

Behavior can also reveal the species of an animal bride,† as we learn from an ancient Roman story told by the Hellenized Roman author Babrius, in the second century C.E.:

A weasel fell in love with a handsome youth and by the grace of Aphrodite was transformed into a girl, so that she could marry him. But at the marriage feast a mouse ran past the bride's couch; she sprang up and began to chase it, thus revealing her true nature. That was the end of the wedding banquet.[89]

Behavior supplies the vital clue in some of the lawsuits involving sexual fraud,† such as the case of the woman who realized her bedmate was not her husband because he had just had a haircut and her husband hadn't, and he smelled of tobacco and her husband didn't smoke.[90] In all of these stories, the behavior of the bedtrickster remains unchanged when his or her superficial form changes. But behavior can be faked, too: the bedtricksters in "The Great Switcheroo"† teach one another how to behave in bed.

There are important exceptions to this rule of superficial transformations, stories in which the mask is not merely a superficial surface but something that encompasses the whole head, including the brain and the mind, of the person whose face appears on the mask. Sometimes the mask becomes real, and the soul as well as the body changes. Thus, when Vishnu mimics Jalandhara's† chest, height, and speech, he also mimics his "frame of mind," a factor that compounds his initial desire for Jalandhara's wife and makes him fall in love with her while pretending to love her. This also happens to the bedtrickster in the film *My Geisha*† (1962), who takes on the mentality of the character whom she creates to trick her husband, which is the mentality of a woman who would never trick her husband. Javier Marias's protagonist fears that his ex-wife, who may or may not be the prostitute he has just slept with, may have been transformed in this way: "If she was Celia, she would, by then, have spent some time working as a prostitute and would, therefore, be a prostitute. . . . *She wouldn't, in fact, be pretending.*"[91] Masks can convey qualities not merely to those who see them but to those who wear them; the masquerader may be entirely transformed into someone else. The masquerader may become his mask.[92]

The most dramatic changes of this sort occur in stories about transformed gender in which, unlike Adi masquerading as Parvati, the bedtrickster finds his mind transformed along with the body: this happens even to the gods Vishnu and Shiva.‡ The case of the real-life eighteenth-century French chevalier (or chevalière) d'Eon,† who pretended to be a woman pretending to be a man, also implies that a change of body, or

even a change of costume, may lead to a change of soul. In objecting to
being forced to give up his dragoon's uniform, d'Eon said, "My body is
like my mind. It cannot be content with being embroidered in lace."[93]
But when he "consented" to wear women's clothes, his body changed his
mind. As Gary Kates puts it, "His spiritual transformation was the result
and not the cause of his gender transformation."[94] After reinventing himself as Joan of Arc the transvestite, d'Eon took on, *volens nolens,* the rest
of the myth: Joan of Arc the Christian mystic. And d'Eon's idea that one
must become a woman in order to become virtuous finds a parallel in
those devotional Hindu movements in which male worshipers impersonate women in order to become self-surrendering and close to God, and
saints like Ramakrishna and Gandhi became women in their hearts and
(in the case of Ramakrishna) even crossed-dressed in order to conquer
their passion (like d'Eon attempting to "control . . . his virile behavior").
Not just virtue but villainy can be transmitted by a mask: Frederico, in
Sicily and Naples,† pretends to be a man who had raped and murdered
Frederico's sister and ends up raping and murdering her himself.

  The idea that the mind and soul change when the body masquerades
and changes is expressed in a story told of the demon Ravana‡ in response
to speculation on why, if Ravana could fool Sita by taking on the form
of a Brahmin sage, he could not seduce her by taking on the form of her
husband, Rama. A nineteenth-century Bengali text tells us:

> Someone said to Ravana, "You are taking various magic forms in order to
> get Sita. Why don't you take the form of Rama sometime and then ap-
> proach Sita?" Ravana said, "When I think of Rama and even the realm of
> Godhead seems a trifling thing, how could I think of such a trifling thing
> as another man's wife? And so how can I take the form of Rama?"[95]

Ravana is saying that when he thinks of becoming Rama, already he thinks
like Rama, and so he can't carry out a dirty trick like pretending to be
Rama. Ravana cannot switch into Rama's form, because he would get
Rama's mind along with his form. He would stop being Ravana—and,
presumably, paradoxically, stop wanting to change into Rama. Similarly,
a twelfth-century commentary on poems of devotion to Vishnu argues
that if Ravana would take the form of Rama, he would become virtuous,
since Rama is the very incarnation of virtue, *dharma;* even if he merely
pretended to be virtuous, he would be infected by *dharma.*[96] William Buck
expands upon this theme in his English translation of the *Ramayana.*
When one of the demons suggests to Ravana, "Take Rama's form by

magic, go to Sita, and she will willingly love you," Ravana replies, "No, I can't. The transformation would have to be complete; I'd have to take on all Rama's virtues as well to fool her, and then I could do no wrong, I couldn't lie to her and say I was someone I wasn't."[97]

Some modern texts in English imagine a situation in which the trickster keeps his own mind but *also* takes on the mind of the person he is pretending to be. In S. N. Behrman's retelling of the myth of Alcmena and Amphitryon,‡ Jupiter is explicitly said to give up his own mind while he takes on the form, and the mind, of Amphitryon. When Mercury asks, "What went on in your mind?" Jupiter replies, "Only that I was her husband. I had limited the compass of my mind to his."[98] But Jupiter neglects to take this precaution in another modern version, Garrison Keillor's satire, in which Zeus (as he is called here) enters the body of a Lutheran minister named Wes whose mind has been transposed into the body of a dog but who is also somehow still present in his own body (like both Steve Martin and Lily Tomlin in Martin's body in *All of Me*† [1984]):

> Diane undressed in the bathroom, and slid into bed sideways, and lay facing the wall. Zeus sat on the edge of her bed and lightly traced with his finger the neckline of her white negligee. She shrugged. The dog lay at her feet, listening. Zeus was confused, trying to steer his passion through the narrow, twisting mind of Wes. All he wanted was to make love enthusiastically for hours, but dismal Lutheran thoughts sprang up: Go to sleep. Stop making a fool of yourself. You're a grown man. Settle down. Don't be ridiculous. Who do you think you are?[99]

Who, indeed?

SEX AND LOVE

These stories play out the tension between love and sex or lust and desire or between different sorts of desire or between duty† and desire. The intimacy of sex is different from that of love and different again from the intimacy of marriage. All of these texts are about sex, and some are also about love. Falling in love is, of course, not at all the same thing as falling into bed; but the relationship between lust and love is complicated by the widespread belief (never, to my knowledge, tested scientifically) that sex is best when you're in love.

Andrew Lang, the Indo-Europeanist, disdained the bedtrickster heroine of *All's Well That Ends Well*† as "the thief, not of love, but of lust."[100] And in writing about Shakespeare's bedtricks, John Wain writes: "The mindless drive of lust, like the animal rush for survival, does not pause to recognize its object. . . . Love feeds on recognition and knowledge of the loved person; lust, by contrast, is blind; its patterns are laid down in advance and it feeds on whatever approximates to those patterns."[101] This is a true enough summary of the Romantic† view, which defines the difference between sex and love precisely on the grounds that love, unlike sex, can see the truth. But William R. Bowden adds a wise note of caution: "Wain's statement is not true of the bed trick in general. . . . sometimes blindness afflicts love rather than lust."[102] The evidence of our myths suggests that blindness afflicts both love and lust, and that the distinction between the two is not subtle enough to explain these stories: there are many kinds of love, and many kinds of lust, too, and some are more discerning than others.

Many cultures do seem to draw a distinction between emotions comparable to "love" and "lust" in English. But ideas about love vary greatly from one culture to another, and often we must rely on our rather shaky knowledge of what a particular author means by "love."[103] More to the point: since stories about sex often turn out to be stories about love, and the reverse, it is not always possible to draw and defend a line between the two. Indeed, these stories are generated by precisely that problem, by the ways in which love and sex masquerade as one another and thus both force and enable lovers to masquerade in bed; they are about the ways in which people mistake sex for love, about the tension between ways of knowing someone through the mind and heart (love) or through the body (sex). (Indeed, the Sanskrit word *manas* means both mind and heart, the organ with which one both falls in love and calculates the position of the planets.) Many stories seem to begin with the assumption that love/sex = mind/body or, perhaps, sex/body = love/mind. But this Cartesian assumption (which is not limited to cultures that know Descartes or always present in those that do) does not remain static; it is challenged, inverted, subverted, and, sometimes, reinstated after all. The myths negotiate the territory carved out by this paradox: we may assume that love is in the mind, sex in the body, but the myths often teach us that sex is in the mind, love in the body.

It is common to argue that you get to know people through love rather than through sex, but people in various cultures tend to mix up sex and love as ways of knowing. Thus some texts argue that you *do* know people through love and that you do *not* know people through sex (regarded as inferior to, and indeed opposed to, love); others, that you *do not* know people through love and that you *do* know people through sex (regarded as embedded in the body, which is closer to the essential self). Still others muddy the waters by regarding sex as caused by or causing love, or love as a form of desire, lust, or sex. Classical Indian texts, for instance, distinguish sex *(kama)* from love *(prema),* but different genres disagree as to which of these a woman experiences with her husband and which with her lover.

Bedtricks usually work quite well on the people who are *not* erotically attached, but are merely officially or physically attached, to the person who creates the surrogate; the one who cannot tell the difference is usually not the true lover but someone who does not care about and therefore does not really notice the other person; indifference† breeds contempt and conceals difference. Often a husband cannot recognize his wife when she plays the whore precisely because he cannot imagine her as an erotic partner. Ann Gold speaks of Rajasthani women whose songs, containing the lines "Bite, bite the whole body, / Don't bite the cheeks or husband will beat you," imply that "the husband would notice marks on the cheeks but fail to see those on the body—perhaps because in this context his vision is less lascivious than the lover's."[104] Indeed, the husband's vision is generally "less lascivious" and therefore less discerning than the lover's. The bedtrickster is, like the letter in Edgar Allan Poe's "The Purloined Letter," so obvious to the traditional partner as to fall beneath any notice at all.[105]

The husband's indifference, however, seems at odds with the point of many of these stories—namely, that it is precisely the man's powers of discrimination, the difference between his despised wife and his coveted mistress, that inspire the bedtrick. Presumably, if all women were as one to him, the one he happened to be married to would have sufficed, if only for reasons of convenience. Instead, his urgent consciousness of the difference between women, specifically between his wife and his mistress, has made him stray from the garden path of monogamy. The sexual surrogate may be created precisely because the person in love cannot tolerate the embrace of anyone other than the beloved—the one who knows the difference. All the effort that people take in setting up the masquerades that abound in these myths, the elaborate devices and ruses and tricks, is necessary because only *that* person's body, the body that one is not allowed to have, will do, rather than the body to which one has sexual

rights. Against this background, the ease with which the husband is ultimately deceived by the bedtrick becomes still more perplexing[106]—another paradox.†

Unlike the jaded husband, the true lover *notices* the woman and recognizes her; he can tell the difference. In *The Marriage of Figaro,*† the devoted Figaro recognizes Susanna's voice and is not fooled, but the promiscuous count does not recognize the voice of the countess and is fooled.
The gaze of true love was the subject of stories about women who wear
pelican skins,† stories told in Spanish villages where the women often
have goiters that resemble the pelican pouch: "Their metamorphosis
changes their problematic fleshly envelope, which has inspired such undesirable desire, until a chosen, more suitable, more lovable lover can appear
who will answer the riddle, undo the animal spell, disclose their identity
and their beauty and release them to speak again. . . . Only a true lover
will be able to see past the disfigurement to the real beauty of the person
beneath the outer, pelican skin."[107] This attitude more broadly characterizes the Romantic† belief in the beautiful† soul hidden beneath an ugly
body and the theological† belief that God's perfect love has the power to
make us all beautiful, lovable.

DESIRE, DUTY, AND DOMINATION

Our myths express different attitudes toward the uniqueness or interchangeability of a sexual partner. Hindu social theory recognizes three
goals that each individual (male) should satisfy in a lifetime: *kama,
dharma,* and *artha.*[108] These might be translated into English as "desire,"
"duty," and "domination." Our stories often express a conflict between
desire and either duty or domination, which gang up on desire by regarding marriage as a matter of property rather than sex. Traditional concepts of marriage or traditional marriage partners are keyed to concepts
of duty and domination (social, religious, and/or political) and do not
value individualism as an element of eroticism as do stories that privilege
desire; the official partner seeks not the personality but the persona of
the woman in bed. Stories about duty emphasize those basic human moments, indeed almost animal moments, that are the same for all bodies;
they are reinforced by biological† attitudes ("I must make sure my offspring survive"), which may be subdivided into male ("I need to put my
sperm in lots and lots of places") and female ("I need a male to stay and
protect my young"); or, again, male ("I have one person for children and

another for pleasure") and female ("I must marry the man my father chooses for me").

Desire, too, has many faces, some inclining toward lust, some toward love. Spiritual or Romantic† desire focuses on one person and applies equally well to both male and female ("One person is everything to me" and "I must choose the one person I fall in love with"). Stories keyed to spiritual desire emphasize the more cultural moments where not the body but the head does the remembering—the moments of personality, education, logic, and, above all, speech, when, like French structuralists, we identify ourselves with our heads. But the all-cats-are-gray variety of desire sides with duty in disregarding the individual; like the official partner, the husband in the grip of pure animal desire seeks not the personality but the body of the woman in bed. Moreover, "I am unique" argues against an assumed "You are all alike," and vice versa.

Desire for an individual is expressed in all the cultures I know—the Bible (Jacob for Rachel), ancient India (Nala for Damayanti‡), etc. But Romantic love, it has been well argued, is largely a construction of post-Enlightenment European culture. Enlightenment attitudes, like Romantic, may apply equally well to both male and female ("I must choose someone who shares my ideals"). The Enlightenment perspective, however, assumes that we carry around inside us, like true north in a compass, the knowledge of who we really are. Against this, many myths (and much of depth psychology†) assert the Romantic notion that we do *not* carry this sense around inside us but derive it from the mirror provided by those whom we love; we don't know who we are until someone else (and not just anyone else) recognizes us. Even those myths that do seem to value the individual argue that the *reason* it is essential to know the individual identity of the lover is that only by knowing the identity of the person we love, and by whom we are loved, do we know who we are; and this implies that our individuality lies, again, not in ourselves but in others, that it is socially constructed. Thus the whole emphasis on choosing the lover at all (even going by Enlightenment criteria) is, as a whole, anti-Enlightenment, in that it situates the identity of the self as dependent on the identity of the other: "Some day my prince will come" (even if he is a prince with a Ph.D. in computer science). This is one of the reasons rationalists (Hume, Kant, not to mention Plato) hate mythologists: mythology is seductive, and traditional mythology undercuts the primacy of the individual. So here is another paradox: certain myths assume both that we and our lovers are individuals and that it is essential to find ways to tell the true lover from the false one, but that we are not individuals, because our identity depends upon the identity of our lover.

Part of the fascination that the bedtrick has for us moderns stems from the sort of obsessive interest that people often have in the previous (or subsequent) spouses or lovers of their spouses or lovers. This obsession is a form of narcissism: "What of me is mirrored in him/her that she/ he should find us both attractive?" Since most European or American readers are victims of Romantic illusions that make them want to be unique to those they love, they find it deeply disquieting to encounter a double of this sort, to discover a chorus line of ex-lovers/spouses, who not only resemble one another unto twinship but often also share unusual behavioral traits. Such a discovery can be truly mortifying, for it implies that the entire group functions as nothing but a storehouse of inter-changeable parts. And this, in turn, arouses the suspicion that we, too, may be fungible to those we love. A form of vociferous individualism tends to assert itself here, for who does not take offense at being thought interchangeable?[109] To be replaced by a clone is to become a clone. We are held in the thrall of our desire to be unique to those whom we love, or even those whom we desire.

The Rape of the
False Mother

~~≈≈~~

T SEXUAL VIOLENCE IN ANCIENT INDIA
he myth of committing adultery with one's own wife may be a
married man's fantasy, but the wife may have fantasies of her own,[1]
and she may view this same plot either as one in which she seduces
him or as one in which he rapes her. These various points of view may
be expressed in a single myth,[2] and this complex pattern may be applied
to stories about goddesses, women with magical powers, and human
women, though the mechanisms by which the tricks take place and
the theological implications are certainly different in each instance.
Let us, as we did in chapter 1, begin with gods and then descend to the
human.

The myth we considered at the start of chapter 1, the seduction of
Shiva by a Parvati whom he mistakes for someone else, is the inversion
of a series of myths we are about to consider, the seduction of Shiva by
someone whom he mistakes for Parvati, often retold in the same texts
that tell the stories of Shiva and Parvati that we considered in chapter 1.
On some of the many occasions when Shiva and Parvati quarrel about a
game of dice,[3] Parvati does not transform herself into a seductive foreign
or tribal woman but, on the contrary, begins with a dark skin and goes
off to change it for a golden skin. In one variant of this story, Shiva,
tormented by unsatisfied desire, mistakes Savitri, the high-class wife of
the god Brahma, for Parvati (she "resembled Parvati in all her qualities,"
says the text) and begs her to make love with him. Savitri rebuffs him
("You fool, you should apologize to your wife instead of trying to take
another man's wife") and curses him so that he makes love to a human
woman, which results in yet another divine bedtrick (with Princess Tara-
vati†).[4] Another variant of this myth, in a late medieval Sanskrit text,
begins with the same premise—that Parvati goes off to obtain a golden

skin—but this time Shiva mistakes not a woman (high or low class) but a demon for Parvati:

THE RAPE OF THE FALSE PARVATI

One day the god Shiva teased his wife, the goddess Parvati, about her dark skin; he called her "Blackie" [Kali] and said that her dark body against his white body was like a black snake coiled around a pale sandalwood tree. When she responded angrily, they began to argue and to hurl insults at one another. Furious, she went away to generate inner heat in order to obtain a fair, golden skin. Her little son Viraka, stammering in his tears, begged to come with her, but she said to him, "This god is a woman-chaser when I am not here, and so you must constantly guard his door and peep through the keyhole so that no other woman gets to him."

While she was gone, a demon named Adi took advantage of her absence to attempt to kill Shiva in order to avenge Shiva's conquest of his father, the demon Andhaka. He took the form of a serpent to slip past the gaze of the guard and entered Shiva's bedroom through a chink. Then he sloughed the serpent form and took on the form of Parvati in order to make love with Shiva. The fool took an illusory form, more charming than can be imagined, perfect in all its limbs, complete with all the signs of recognition, and with various ornaments and clothes. But he placed a tooth as hard as a thunderbolt, with a sharp tip, inside the vagina of the form that he assumed, planning to kill Shiva by deluding his wits.

When Shiva saw Adi in the form of Parvati he was satisfied, and he embraced the great demon, thinking him to be Parvati because of the perfect detail of "her" limbs. Then he asked, "Is it truly you, and not some imitation, Parvati? Did you come here because you knew how empty my home was without you?" When the demon heard this he smiled a little, realizing that Shiva thought he knew him by means of the signs of recognition, and he said to the god: "I went to generate inner heat because you called me 'Blackie' [Kali], but there was no sexual pleasure for me there, and so I have come to you." When Shiva heard this, he smiled, but he began to have some doubts in his heart, thinking, "She was angry, and knew that I was angry, and it is her nature always to keep her vows. How could she have come back without getting what she wanted?" Then he searched for a sign of recognition, and he did not see the mark of a lotus made with a twist of hair on her left side. Realizing that this was the demon's magic power of illusion, he hid his feelings beneath his facial expression and, still smiling, placed upon his own penis a weapon with a sharp tooth. He killed the demon, who then resumed his true form.

When the goddess of the wind told Parvati that Shiva had been se-

duced by another woman, she became furious; in her tortured mind she
pictured her son and said, "Since you abandoned me, your mother who
loves you so, and gave women an opportunity to be alone with Shiva,
therefore you will be born among humans to a mother who is a heartless,
hard, numb, cold stone." Her anger came out of her body in the form of
a lion, with a huge tongue lolling out of a mouth full of sharp teeth. Then
the god Brahma came to her and granted her wish to have a golden body
and to become half of Shiva's body, in the form of the androgyne. She
sloughed off from her body a dark woman, named Kali, who went away
to live in the mountains, riding on the lion.

Parvati, now in her golden skin [Gauri, "The Fair" or "The Golden"],
went home, but her son Viraka, who did not recognize her, stopped her
at the door, saying, "Go away! A demon in the form of the goddess entered
here unseen in order to deceive the god, who killed him and scolded me.
So you cannot enter here. The only one who can enter here is my mother,
Parvati, who loves her son dearly." When the goddess heard this, she
thought to herself, "It wasn't a woman; it was a demon. I cursed my son
wrongly when I was angry." She lowered her head in shame and said to
her son, "Viraka, I am your mother; do not be confused or mistaken in
your mind. Do not doubt me, my son, or be misled by my skin or my
limbs; Brahma made me golden. I cursed you when I did not know what
had happened. I cannot turn back my curse, but I will say that you will
quickly emerge from your human life, with all your desires fulfilled." The
goddess then returned to Shiva, and they made love together for many
years.[5]

Parvati is a woman divided against herself or, rather, a woman forced
by her husband to divide herself into two polarized halves.‡ The creation
of a double is her solution to the problem of her husband's womanizing;
insulted and rejected, she walks out on her unfaithful, hypercritical husband, as she does in most of the stories about their quarrels. She does
not stay away for long: eventually she sends back a more acceptable form
of herself, her explicit double, the golden goddess. But before this happens, another double, the demonic false Parvati, replaces the true Parvati
in Shiva's bed in a double-cross† that is also half of a double-cross-dress.†
(The other half occurs in another myth, in which Shiva takes the form
of Parvati to foil the amorous demon Bhasmasura.†)

Ostensibly, this double is an agent entirely separate from Parvati, the
demon Adi; but we may also read it as an unconscious projection† of
Parvati herself, created, just as yet another double, the lion, is created,
out of her mingled anger and desire. That is, the bedtrick perpetrated by

the demon Adi in the form of Parvati, a double-cross, becomes a double-back if we allow a reading in which Parvati herself becomes the demon. The transformation of a wronged woman into an angry goddess is a paradigm that we will encounter again in the myth of "The Brahmin Woman and the Outcaste Man."† Here, the demonic false Parvati is created out of her resentment of Shiva's apparent revulsion for her dark skin† and her suspicion of his womanizing—a double problem that inspires many bedtricks—but also out of her frustrated desire for him. The energy of Shiva's mild abuse of Parvati (his philandering and cruel teasing) is escalated into a a sexual act that intentionally kills the partner—what some would call sexual violence and others, rape. And this sexual violence is then projected from Parvati onto the demon Adi, her sexual surrogate, whose intended rape of Shiva twists back upon himself in a grotesque switchback instance of the trickster tricked.†

The demon Adi and the goddess Parvati have more in common than may at first appear. Adi's father, the demon Andhaka, was born when Shiva's seed spurted into his own third eye at the touch of Parvati.[6] Through this connection, irregular though it may be, Andhaka is regarded as Shiva's son, whom Shiva impaled when Andhaka tried to seduce Parvati (regarded as his mother); this is why Andhaka's son, Adi, the grandson of Shiva and Parvati, attacks (and seduces) Shiva.[7] Like the goddess, Adi is androgynous; he is serially bisexual,‡ whereas she becomes vertically androgynous when she occupies the left side of Shiva's body—split once again. Both Adi and Parvati slough off their skins like snakes; Shiva likens her to a black snake when he teases her, and Adi becomes a snake to penetrate the otherwise "impregnably" guarded room of Shiva, utilizing a standard motif in Indian folklore (the deadly snake who gets into a room thought to be sealed off).[8] But Adi also transforms that general theme into a metaphor for sexual penetration by combining it with another standard motif, that of the amorous snake lover† who enters the house in his animal form to seduce the woman there in his anthropomorphic form. When Adi then transforms himself into a woman, his bedtrick is countered by an outright rape, the only trick of which consists in Shiva's pretense that he does not know† that he is being tricked—a common and effective countermeasure to a bedtrick. Yet another transformation occurs when Adi, in order to seduce the *man* there, takes not a male anthropomorphic form but a female (more precisely, theamorphic) form, the form of the man's wife, changing both his species and his sex. (Another version of the story makes this double shift explicit when it specifies

that Adi was granted a boon that he would die only when he had transformed himself *twice,* and that he remembered the prediction when he
transformed himself into a snake—and a woman.)[9]

In the tale of the mountain woman, Parvati appears to Shiva disguised
as a low-caste human with a dark skin;† here the dark-skinned Parvati
returns disguised in a light skin. The contrast between the demon's false,
beautiful external form and his true, devastating internal form, the two
sides of the Lovely Lady,† is the inverse of the contrast in the goddess
herself, who sheds her black outer sheath to reveal her golden inner form.
Yet we must assume that the demon's outer form is still black, since the
woman he imitates is the form of Parvati as Shiva last saw her, still with
her dark skin. At first the demon's bedtrick works, but ultimately the
impostor is exposed, first by his words, which the real Parvati would never
have spoken, and then by his lack of a certain twist of hair, a kind of
cowlick, which functions in many Indian stories like a unique fingerprint†
or birthmark.†

The disguises of the demon are mirrored by the disguises of the goddess, his alter ego. By setting her son as the guard, Parvati is utilizing
yet another standard motif (the guardian of the bedroom door‡)[10] and
transforming it, too: since the son has been (as she thinks) asleep, she
curses him to have (in a human rebirth) a mother who is asleep, an inanimate *(jada)* stone, a mother as heartless and cold in physical form as she
herself has just proved to be in spirit. (Being turned to stone is also a
punishment for an excessively sexual woman in Hindu mythology.‡) The
abandoning mother not only ignores her son's pitiful pleas as she goes
away but even throws his words back in his face when she curses him,
accusing him of abandoning *her* by failing to restrain his father's sexuality.
In another version of this myth, Viraka pleads with her as she leaves,
saying: "I will follow you; you are my mother, full of love for your child.
If you abandon me, I will not be able to bear Shiva's cruelty; a son is a
vessel to receive his father's cruelty in his mother's absence."[11] But it is
his mother, not his father, who proves to be the cruel one. The chopped-
off, negative Kali, the one who cursed her son, is banished to the liminal
area of the Vindhya Mountains (the southern region that composers of
the ancient Sanskrit texts in the northwest of India regarded as beyond
the Hindu pale, the place to dump things that you did not want in the
story anymore), together with the lion, whose toothy mouth recapitulates
the demon's *vagina dentata.*† (In one variant of the myth, Adi actually
places the tooth *in his mouth,*[12] not in his vagina,[13] presumably planning

to kill Shiva either with a kiss† or, perhaps, fellatio.)[14] The remaining golden form, the one who minimized her son's curse, becomes the female half of the androgyne.

Viraka fails to recognize his mother when she returns, mistaking her for a non-Parvati just as his father had mistaken the demon for Parvati; his failure to recognize her seems to be superficial—she has changed the color of her skin—but it has deeper, darker overtones, for he knows his mother loves him, and this woman has cursed him in a most unloving manner (though he does not yet know it). As David Shulman puts it: "The softer, inner part—a heated, reddish gold—eventually comes to the surface of Parvati's body, while inside she has become harsh and rigid; she curses her son (Viraka) to have a stony mother—that is, she curses herself to be frozen and unyielding. No wonder this son fails to recognize his mother when she finally returns, in her new golden exterior."[15] The failure of a son to recognize his mother often, though not here, leads to incest.†

Another goddess who splits herself into a dark and light form is Samjna,‡ who abandons her husband, the Sun, and her children, Yama and Manu, to avoid what we have now learned to call marital rape: she cannot bear her husband's embrace. She leaves in her place a surrogate, her mirror reflection or shadow (chaya)—a creature who at once resembles her and is her opposite in terms either of inversion (the reflection) or of color (the shadow).[16] Samjna's husband is fooled by the masquerading shadow, but Yama suspects the substitute, judging not by appearances (as his father does, and Shiva on occasion) but by behavior† (as Shiva does on other occasions). Parvati's curse of Viraka resonates with Samjna's shadow's unjust (and later modified) curse of Yama, her stepson. In one telling, Yama says, "I do not think she can be my mother, for a mother does not behave badly even toward badly behaved sons," and his father says to the shadow, "Surely you are not the mother of these [children]. You are some Samjna or other who has come here. For how could a mother curse even a bad child?"[17] In a closely related variant, it is also Yama, not the Sun, who notices the difference: "Daddy, no one has ever seen such an amazing thing, a mother who stops loving her son—like a cow that rejects her calf—and gives him a curse. This woman does not act like a mother to me as Manu told me she did [to him]; for a mother would not act badly even toward bad sons."[18] Or, in another text: "Sir, Mother got angry and cursed me for no reason. Well, in my childishness, I did raise my foot, just a little bit, once, but even though Manu tried to stop her, she cursed me. Surely, she who cursed me is not our mother."[19] In the contemporary comic book version of the myth of Samjna, the Sun remarks, "A son may change in his affections but a mother never ceases to care. . . . The children are right. She must be an impostor."[20] This was the very criterion that made Parvati's son Viraka believe, incorrectly, that the woman who seemed to be his mother could not be his mother: she did not love him.

The theme of the abandoning mother, the wife of the Sun, resurfaces in a transformation in a myth that is central to the great Sanskrit epic the *Mahabharata,* composed between 300 B.C.E. and 300 C.E.:

The Abandoning of Karna

When the princess Kunti was still a virgin, before she was married, she was given the boon of invoking a god whenever she wanted to have a child, and she tried out her boon on the Sun god, merely out of curiosity. The Sun god split himself into two, so that he came to her but still went on shining in the sky. As soon as Kunti saw him, she begged him to go back, pointing out that she was still a child, but he insisted on having her, threatening that if she did not give in to him, he would burn to death "your foolish father, who does not know of your misconduct." Kunti gave birth to a son, Karna, but to conceal her own misdeeds, she threw him into Horse River [*asvanadyam*], lamenting, "Fortunate is the woman from whose breast you will drink. What dream will she have?" Then she returned to the palace, sick with sorrow and with fear of awakening her father. Karna was retrieved from the river by a charioteer, whose wife, Radha, adopted him.[21] Many years passed, and Karna became an unrivaled warrior.

On the eve of the great battle, Karna bitterly berated his mother for abandoning him. Kunti, who wished to get Karna to fight on the side of her legitimate sons, insisted that he was her son, not Radha's, and a voice from the Sun in the sky affirmed, "Karna, Kunti is right; do what your mother says." But Karna insisted: "You have done me irreparable harm by casting me out. What enemy could have done me greater harm than you have? When you should have done something, you did not have the compassion you show me now. You have never acted in my interests like a mother."[22]

The Sun rapes Kunti; he forces himself upon her, in part by threatening to harm her father. But this time the rapist rather than his victim generates a double: the Sun splits himself in two in order to remain a celestial body even while he is raping Kunti, so that Karna in a sense has three fathers (the Sun in the sky, the Sun who raped Kunti, and the charioteer), as well as two mothers (Kunti and Radha). The psychological power of the Samjna myth colors the heartrending scene in which Karna accuses his mother of not acting like a mother. Manu and Yama might have said the very same thing.

IS A BEDTRICK A RAPE?

Goddesses (and, as we might assume by extension and will soon see in examples, women) play bedtricks to avoid sexual abuse or rape. This is a familiar mythological (and psychological) pattern: the victim of sexual violence splits into two or more personalities.‡ Myths on this theme often express or represent a woman's fantasy or a woman's personality dissociation in reaction to rape. But Parvati's surrogate, the demon Adi, is both the perpetrator and the victim of a rape. The bedtrick in this instance— made possible by the supernatural power of the sexual trickster not only to change his sex but to transform that sex into a lethal weapon—is a rape counteracted by the rape of the bedtrickster. What implications does this myth have for human women who do not have these powers?

Marliss C. Desens, considering primarily texts involving human women rather than goddesses, has asserted that to be the victim of a bedtrick is to be raped:

> The bed-trick explicitly requires that at least one partner not have informed consent to the sexual contact. The absence of physical violence in most bedtricks should not become a pretext for ignoring the physical and emotional violation that occurs whether the deceived person is female or male. . . . At least one partner is always physically and emotionally violated in a bedtrick; while that partner has chosen sexual involvement, he or she has not chosen it with the person unwittingly embraced in the dark. . . .
>
> The legal system . . . denies that a man could be sexually assaulted— particularly that he could be assaulted by a woman. Recent feminist and psychological theory has pointed out the limitations of these societal beliefs and their harmful effects on both women and men. I follow the lead of these theorists in defining rape as any sexual contact to which a person, either male or female, does not have informed consent. Whether that assault takes the form of physical violence or of manipulation and deceit is a difference only in means; for the victim, the violation is the same.[23]

The woman who plays the bedtrick is therefore, in this view, raping the man, in some cases the man who had intended to rape her, just as (with the genders reversed in two ways at once) Shiva rapes Adi when he realizes that Adi intends to rape him.

These arguments take on new meaning in the context of actual legal† cases about real women—legal disputes about marital rape, date rape, and sexual fraud. As Jane E. Larson argues, in a subsection of her essay entitled "Not as Bad as Rape": "By equating force and fraud in its working definition of coercion, the law demonstrates a nuanced grasp of how body and mind are fused in human personhood. If laws against force guard against threats to the will directed through the body, the rules against fraud protect against the 'shackled mind.' "[24] But Judge Richard A. Posner wants to keep the distinction between the rape of the mind and the rape of the body: "[I]f the woman is not averse to having sex with a particular man, the wrong if any is in the lies (and we usually do not think of lying in social settings as a crime) rather than in an invasion of her bodily integrity."[25] As Larson paraphrases this argument: "A woman suffers no additional harm in later discovering that she consented under false pretenses—'No harm, no foul.' Posner presumably means to distinguish fraudulently induced sex from forcible rape, which he believes should be regulated. This purported distinction, however, is one of degree rather than of kind. When sexual consent is coerced, whether by force or fraud, the result is nonconsensual sex, a moral *and* physical dispossession of one's sexual body."[26] Much of this argument turns upon each writer's assessment of the mental and emotional reactions of the victim of the bedtrick. Thus, Posner argues, "The act itself, were the true facts known to the woman, would be disgusting as well as humiliating, rather than merely humiliating as in the case of the common misrepresentations of dating and courtship."[27]

Posner distinguishes between the legal attitude to the sorts of lies† that people tell in bed and the sorts of lies that they tell in other circumstances:

[G]enerally it is not a crime to use false pretenses to entice a person into a sexual relationship. Seduction, even when honeycombed with lies that would convict the man of fraud if he were merely trying to obtain money, is not rape. . . . It is otherwise if the man is impersonating the woman's husband or claims to be administering medical treatment to the woman rather than to be inserting his penis in her.[28]

Apparently it is humiliating, but not a crime, to trick a woman into bed using lies that are criminal when used to trick her out of money. Posner assumes that it becomes disgusting as well as humiliating if the man pretends to be her husband (or a speculum), and disgusting a woman is, apparently, criminal. By this account, we must ask whether Martin Guerre's† wife was at the end disgusted (having been really fooled by the sexual lie) or "merely" humiliated (having been fooled at first by the small lies but then having seen through the big lie). The mind, at least the nonlegal mind, boggles.

This is a subject on which our fictional texts can shed some light. There are many reasons the big sexual lie† may be so destructive, and many of these stories sound a bitter note of tragedy that outweighs the high comedy† of sexual play. Even when the story actually ends with all wrongs righted, all wounds healed, the number of wrongs and wounds depicted on the long, long road to the happy ending leaves a bitter aftertaste of tragedy, and we doubt that "all's well that ends well."[29] The reactions of people who discover that they have been the victims of a bedtrick include disbelief, fury, sadness, embarrassment, loss of self-esteem, and sometimes madness. Most texts don't even describe the reactions to the bedtrick, assuming that they are obvious: the experience of loss, imperfection, and abandonment. Since we tend to believe that the sexual act reveals the most intimate truth about both our partners and ourselves,† our deepest sense of self may be challenged when this assumption is shattered by the violent deception of the bedtrick. The humiliating knowledge† lapse also applies in ordinary cases of sexual betrayal, but it is extreme in the case of a bedtrick. Nathalie (in E. T. A. Hoffmann's "The Doubles") one day sees that her lover is two people and she has been fooled: "A deep horror seized Nathalie when she saw the two youths, a double image of the beloved whom she carried in her heart."[30] O, in *Story of O,*† regards the bedtrick as worse than physical torture: "She was surprised that the whipping she had received had left her so untroubled, so calm, whereas the thought that she would probably never know which of the four men had twice taken her from behind, and whether it was the same man both times, and whether it had been her lover, quite distressed her."[31] In Ibsen's version of the myth of Siegfried and Brunhilde, the tricked woman later says to Sigurd (Siegfried): "You have poisoned my whole life! Remember it was you who played that shameful trick. It was you who remained with me in my room, making a mockery of love and laughing slyly to yourself."[32] When the heroine of the film *Roxanne*† discovers that she has been bedtricked, she socks the man she *thought* she was in bed with on the nose (it's a remake of Cyrano de Bergerac,† after all) and cries out, "You bastard! You were playing with me!" Even though the woman in Kobo

Abe's novel *The Face of Another* knows that her husband is playing a bedtrick on her, she is deeply wounded by it, as she later tells him: "My insides have almost burst with your ridicule. I shall never be able to get over it, never."[33]

Though it is less physically violent than a brutal physical rape, the bedtrick is a kind of delayed-reaction rape, a retroactive or retrospective rape, a rape with a time lag: first it fucks your body, and later it fucks your mind. Your body says yes, and then, later, your mind says no.† When you finally realize, ex post facto, that it was the wrong guy/gal, you reclassify the whole experience as rape. At the time of the act, the victim of rape experiences terror and the victim of the bedtrick experiences pleasure; later, the victim of rape experiences rage and shame, and when the truth of the act is revealed, the victim of the bedtrick experiences rage and a different kind of shame, tempered by mental remorse. There is a tension, in the mind/body world,† which is to say much of the Western world, between the view that if the mind is fooled, the body cannot be raped, and the view that it can; or, on the other hand, between the view that if the body remains pure, the mind can be raped, and the view that it cannot. But either form of the violation is profoundly disturbing; rarely does one get off scot-free by arguing that the glass is half empty—that since "only" the body was raped, or "only" the mind, the person has remained intact. Generally, both have to remain intact for the sense of self to survive in one piece (or even in several pieces). Desens explains this sense of a double betrayal: "The bed-trick thus depicts betrayal on the most intimate level. The deceived person is betrayed not only by the arranger of the bed-trick and by the substitute in the bed but by his or her own body, which responds sexually to the wrong person."[34] "You enjoyed it, didn't you?" is the ultimate humiliating taunt of the bed-trickster.

The great sexual trickster Casanova† recorded in his memoirs his revulsion when he realized he had fallen victim to a bedtrick in his country home at Soleure: "What increased my anguish, and made me loathe and despise myself still more, was that I could not help confessing that I had been perfectly happy [*parfaitement heureux*]. . . . I cursed love, my nature. . . . I resolved to die, after having torn to pieces with my own hands the monster who had made me so unhappy."[35] On the other hand, when Arthur Schnitzler's† fictionalized Casanova plays a bedtrick, he immediately feels a kind of remorse when he sees in his victim's face an expression of infinite sadness, "as if during the night that had just closed a nameless and inexpiable offence had been committed by cunning against trust, by lust against love, by age against youth."[36] The final two contrasts, in particular, are at stake in the bedtrick and account for a large part of its horror.

The greater the happiness at the time of delusion, the greater the unhappiness at the moment of enlightenment. Thus, the victim of the bedtrick in William Davenant's *Albovine*† undergoes "an emotional disintegration that ends with his descent into madness [caused by] his guilt at having acted on sexual feelings, and at having enjoyed them."[37] The guilt is triggered by his realization that he enjoyed his sexual feelings with the wrong woman. In this sense, at least, a woman can certainly rape a man; it is as if his own body raped him.

The horror and revulsion that the victim experiences are particularly strong in cases of transvestite masquerade; the reactions of victims of transsexual bedtricks reveal, in an exaggerated form, the factor that makes the bedtrick, in one sense at least, worse than a rape. In one of the many tales told of the Tibetan trickster Uncle Tompa,† a man is tricked into marrying Uncle Tompa; when Uncle Tompa subsequently brandishes his penis in public, "The groom was so shocked at what had happened that he hid himself in a very dark room for many days, ashamed to show his face to anyone."[38] In the film *The Crying Game* (1992), Fergus becomes physically ill and throws up when he realizes that he has been sexually tricked by a man whom he desired as a woman. In real life,† too, the victims of transvestite bedtricks express their sense of humiliation, anger, and disorientation: Teena Brandon's† successful masquerade as a man, with several women who found "him" an entirely satisfactory partner, ended when two men, enraged by her deception, first raped and then murdered her. Here the bedtrick was not explicitly caused by a rape or equated with one, but it was punished with one.

Most of the earlier, more classical versions of the bedtrick imply that the successful masquerader is a happy masquerader, that only the victim suffers. But there is no such thing as a permanently successful bedtrick *in a narrative:* as the trickster in *Bells Are Ringing*† (1960) goes on to point out, in the end, "It's time to wind up / the masquerade / Just make your mind up / The piper must be paid. . . . Now you must wake up / All dreams must end / Take off your make-up / The party's over, my friend."[39] Once the fantasy has been acted out, there is a price to pay; the masquerade is discovered, the trick does not work anymore, the dream lover vanishes.

Moreover, a bedtrick of any kind is tragic not just for the victim but also for the trickster, especially the trickster who realizes the tragedy of being caught in the double-bind.† The bedtrickster also suffers from the big lie, knowing that the victim is really responding to someone else; in some texts, the trickster, male or female, is shown to suffer an agony more exquisite than that of the victim. The male bedtrickster in Kobo Abe's novel *The Face of Another* says, later, "I felt intolerably sad. . . . Wasn't even rape more wholesome than this?"[40] And when his wife tells him that she knew† all along that he was her seducer, he feels even worse: "A swarm of shame, centipede-legged, streamed out, choosing the parts of me most subject to gooseflesh."[41] One victim, Boursicot,† after it was all over, said, "It's better to be cheated than to cheat. There is no dishonor to being cheated. I do not feel Shi [the bedtrickster] is a bastard. I am just sorry the story was not the one I was believing."[42]

In *All's Well That Ends Well* (4.4), the bedtrickster Helena says:

> But, O strange men!
> That can such sweet use make of what they hate,
> When saucy trusting of the cozen'd thoughts
> Defiles the pitchy night; so lust doth play
> With what it loathes for that which is away.

Janet Adelman asks the right question about this passage: "It's very hard to say just what is defiling what here."[43] Zvi Jagendorf glosses it very well:

> Such words come very close to imagining the reality in the conventional situation, here the disturbing mixture of passion, disgust, participation and observation that is the woman's burden as the knowing partner in the bedtrick. . . . Helena grapples with the lust that feasted on her body. She participated in it. She was used sweetly but she was also abused. She was aware of the hatred for her in the man coupled in intimacy with her. Helena is making us think here not of the saving fact of her impregnation, which is the point of the biblical episodes, but of the ordeal of consciousness that accompanied the moments of pleasure and of the defilement that her successful impersonation made her undergo.[44]

In this account, it is the trickster who is, in a sense, raped, for the mind can humiliate the body of the bedtrickster as well as that of the victim. The bedtrick induces in the trickster, too, a split between the mind (often full of hate) and the body (full of love or, more often, lust). Carol Thomas Neely, writing of the effect upon Mariana, the bedtrickster in Shakespeare's *Measure for Measure,* speaks of "the dark delusion and mechanical work-

ings of lust and the consequent fragmentation of identity."[45] Allan Bloom
reminds us that Isabella's reaction to Mariana's plight is to say that she
would be better off dead, and he suggests that her encounter with a man
who has never been sexually attracted to her (or anyone except Isabella),
and who is only doing it because he thinks she is someone else,

> is at the very least humiliating and argues for an ambiguity in her future
> sexual relations with the man she hopes will be her husband. Will he ever
> be aroused by her, or will he always have to imagine Isabella in order to
> perform the act? . . . Angelo will think he has had [Isabella] and, in a way,
> will think so for the rest of his life, even though he is to learn that it is
> untrue. . . . Angelo has had the experience of Isabella and will probably
> spend the rest of his life comparing Mariana with Isabella. . . . Perhaps the
> lesson is that these things are all the same in the dark, but Angelo will
> never believe that.[46]

Desens believes that women suffer from this particular humiliation as
tricksters more than men do as victims: "While the husband, at the most,
experiences some embarrassment at having been caught in his intended
unfaithfulness, the wife, through no fault of her own, experiences the pain
of having been rejected by her husband, and the humiliation of knowing
that in the dark her husband cannot distinguish one female body from
another."[47] But why, we might ask, is the husband not also humiliated
by the knowledge that he cannot tell the women apart? Perhaps because
of the macho assumption that the women are in fact alike.† But then why
is the man not equally humiliated when he succeeds in the trick and
proves that his wife cannot tell the difference between him and another
man? I think he is—sometimes. But when it comes to reactions to the
bedtrick, the gender of the trickster is not always as significant as the
gender of the victim; here, for once, the double standard† does not always
apply. Many male tricksters are after nothing but the body, not the mind
or the soul or the love,† of their victims and are perfectly happy to have
the trick work. But some are after more, and their victory is bittersweet,
at best; that is one reason there are relatively few triumphalist stories
about men who trick their wives in this double-backing† way, in comparison with the far more numerous stories in which wives trick their husbands into committing adultery with their disguised wives.

Natalie Zemon Davis, in *The Return of Martin Guerre*,† points out
how both trickster and victim suffer from the deception. She presents us
with a wonderfully detailed historical record of a sexual lie told by a man

called Pansette (Arnaud du Tilh was his full name), who claimed to be Martin Guerre and either fooled Martin Guerre's wife, Bertrande de Rols, or persuaded her to pretend that he had fooled her. Bertrande, the putative victim, "loved the new Martin, but he had tricked her once; might he after all not trick her again? And what if the other Martin Guerre came back?" Pansette, the putative trickster, "could never acknowledge his lie and never give them a chance to pardon him. In this way a deep uneasiness, uncertainty, and wariness would inevitably grow in village and family relations."[48] Davis's story of the real Martin Guerre poses problems that also arise in a number of the fictional tellings that we will encounter.

And while we are considering the painful aspects of the bedtrick, it is important to consider the feelings of the surrogate who saves the heroine from rape, often simply a magical construct with nothing but a visual presence, but sometimes a person (a sister, a maid) with feelings that relatively few of our texts take into consideration. For instance, in one telling of the story of the shadow Sita,‡ Sita introduces the shadow to Rama, saying, "She went with Ravana in my place and suffered unbearable hardships in Lanka. You must marry this woman who suffered so much on our behalf."[49] And the injured feelings of Brangane,† Isolde's maid, who substitutes for Isolde† on the wedding night with King Mark, are an important ingredient in the subsequent plot, as are the feelings of other women whose mistresses employ them in a double-cross.† For all of these people caught up in the big sexual lie, there is a price to pay.

Yet, for all of its humiliating qualities, in certain circumstances the bedtrick may prove to be a fate not at all worse than death and perhaps preferable to other alternatives such as straightforward clandestine adultery, let alone rape. In William Rider's *The Twins* (1635), a woman who falls in love with her husband's twin brother† and thinks she has committed adultery with him is overwhelmed by guilt; she is therefore delighted and relieved to learn that the twins had turned a bedtrick on her and that the man she slept with was actually her own husband.[50] The bedtrick was prescribed as therapy in John Fletcher's *The Two Noble Kinsmen* (1613), in which the Jailer's daughter, who had gone mad out of unrequited love for Palamon, was to be cured by another man who was her Wooer and would masquerade as her otiose lover. Dressed as Palamon, the Wooer kisses† her twice (the Doctor, when he hears of this, says, "Twenty times had been far better, / For there the cure lies mainly"), and then she says, "And then we'll sleep together." The Wooer hesitates, but the Doctor prompts, "Take her offer," and he says, "Yes, marry, will we." Her final words are, "But you shall not hurt me. If you do, love, I'll cry." It is not clear whether she is cured, or indeed whether she recognizes the deception (5.2).

A number of scholars have argued that the victim of the bedtrick may be, not only hurt, but also healed and restored in various ways;[51] at least, as we saw in chapter 1, many bedtricks replace an illicit partner with a legitimate one, "thereby 'making a marriage' instead of breaking one."[52] Neely has argued this case for *All's Well That Ends Well:* "The fact that Helen seems alone among the perpetrators of bedtricks in expressing her humiliation and defilement emphasizes the cost of her stratagem, not its success. But she also acknowledges the sweetness of her pleasure and the growth that will ensue."[53] Neely points out that, for someone like Helena's husband, Bertram, "bedtricks are employed to cure or transform male fantasy through its apparent enactment," and she argues that "the bedtrick is a sexual and psychological death and rebirth for both Bertram and Helen. . . . both fraudulent and fair, both corrupt and restorative."[54]

Is it worse to have your mind† raped or to have your body raped? Different people will make different choices. The situation is more complex than Desens and the lawyers make it. We need different words; both rape and the bedtrick are forms of illegitimate sexual access, one by force and the other by guile; but English is a rich language, and "rape" should not be applied to both situations. The two phenomena can neither be conflated in a term like "rape-trick"[55] nor be simply dichotomized. The anguish that a woman feels when, bound and gagged or at knife point, she is physically penetrated by someone she despises is different from the anguish that she feels when she realizes, after enjoying a night of passionate sex, that she had been with someone she did not love and could not distinguish from the one she did love—or, worse, that she half knew the difference and could not stop her body from responding. The shock with which most victims of the bedtrick react to it is not unlike the reaction to a conventional rape, but the bedtrick violates the trickster as well as the victim. Both the bedtrickster and the victim suffer a kind of debasement, each in his or her own way, whereas in physical rape the rapist does not usually share the sense of debasement that is felt by the victim. Neely wisely makes a distinction between the two great Shakespearean bedtricks: "Whereas *All's Well*'s bedtrick is a corrupt bargain that feels like prostitution, *Measure for Measure*'s is a coercive assault that feels like rape."[56]

The ambivalence of both bedtrickster and victim was vividly, even grotesquely, embodied in a woman, Chris Costner Sizemore, whose true life
story was told by her psychiatrists in 1957 (in *The Three Faces of Eve*,‡
quickly made into a film of the same name) and then retold in three
books by each of her three major personalities: Eve White, a rather dull,
meek woman; the flamboyant and sexy Eve Black; and the thoughtful,
intelligent Jane.[57] On one occasion, Eve Black seduced their husband,
Ralph, who was fully aware that it was not Eve White ("He immediately
recognized the changed timbre of the voice and groaned, 'Oh gawd, you
again!'").[58] Later, Eve Black speculated about his ambivalence:

> I don't pretend to know what went on in Ralph's mind as he watched Eve
> Black's deliberate semi-strip-tease. Perhaps he told himself that he had a
> legal right to that body no matter which personality was in control, so why
> not exercise it. Or perhaps Eve Black's occupancy of the body he knew so
> well lent an erotic piquancy to the situation which he found irresistibly
> titillating. Or it may be that he saw this as a golden opportunity to repay
> Eve White for the many blows she'd dealt his ego by her constant rejection
> of his advances. Whatever his motivation, he finally said, "O.K., it's a
> deal."[59]

But what of her motivation? As she later told it, Eve Black was frigid
and had to get drunk† to go to bed with Ralph; moreover, she often
insisted that she had never slept with Ralph: "Don't tell me I ever slept
with that jerk. . . . All right, sure this body bore the kid. But I wasn't
around when it happened."[60] And: "I wouldn't sleep with the son-of-a-
bitch. I've never slept with him."[61] When Eve White awoke to find herself
with Ralph in the hotel room, she was furious and sick. "Don't ever try
to see me again," she said, and left him for good. Later, she told her
psychiatrist, "I'm going to get a divorce. You may think I'm foolish but
I consider Ralph an adulterer, or worse."[62] Her psychiatrists described her
reaction at greater length:

> On learning that her husband had taken Eve Black to Jacksonville and spent
> the weekend with her, she knew that she would never go back to him,
> whether or not she eventually recovered from her illness. Her reactions
> indicated something even more complex than the hurt of a faithfully con-
> ventional wife who finds that her husband has spent the night with another
> woman who regarded him and the whole affair as a triviality. They reflected
> also deep horror in the awareness that her own person had, without her
> will or knowledge, been used in this peculiarly treacherous transaction.[63]

The "deep horror" that is here attributed to Eve White upon her realization that she herself was the *trickster* is precisely what E. T. A. Hoffmann's Nathalie felt on learning that she had been the *victim* of a bedtrick. Since Eve was both the original (White) and the surrogate (Black), she was humiliated both as victim and as trickster.

We might start with a triad, recognizing that "the same act of sex can be a source of pleasure (as in consensual sex) or a source of humiliation (as in the bed-trick) or criminality (as in the rape)."[64] But then we must acknowledge that pleasure, humiliation, and criminality are by no means mutually exclusive. The bedtrick is in some ways more painful than rape, in some ways less painful, but it is not "just" a form of rape or even "just" a defense against rape. It is a sexual fantasy,† rich in meanings that have shifted constantly over three millennia.

Whose fantasy is it? The bedtrick functions as a woman's fantasy that protects her from the trauma of rape,‡ but for every female fantasy there is a male fantasy, and this is no exception. Emily Detmer has pointed out that, just as bedtricks depend on men's inability to tell the difference in women's bodies, rape plots seem to assume that men can't tell the difference between consensual and nonconsensual sex. She sees support for a rape culture in the bedtrick's frequent dramatization of women lying about sex. Thus, where the rape mentality argues that when women say no, they mean yes (more precisely, as we will see, that when their mouths† say no, their eyes† say yes), the bedtrick argues that women say yes but, when the trick is revealed, say no. In keeping with the retroactive revision that is the source of the "deep horror" of the bedtrick, "the fantasy of the deceptive woman explains rape as deferred refusal rather than as withheld consent or forced intercourse." And men seem to find "both fearful and titillating" the idea that a change in a woman's mental state "can make a perfectly enjoyable act of sex into a criminal act."[65]

From the woman's point of view, a woman who resorts to a bedtrick to avoid a rape is replaced by another woman *before* the sexual act takes place, but from the male rapist's point of view, the woman who claims to have been raped is replaced by another woman *after* the act: the consenting woman the man says he went to bed with is replaced by a woman who does not (did not) consent. In other words, the shadow of the woman's fantasy of a bedtrick in reaction to the threat of being raped is the man's fantasy of a bedtrick in reaction to having raped. The long, tragic history of sexual violence, from the Hebrew Bible to contemporary police records, testifies to the deep roots and enduring power of the tension between the two aspects of this fantasy.

THE ABANDONING MOTHER AND LOVER

Stories in which women create doubles in response to (or in order to avoid) abuse by their sexual partners are bedtricks, at least from the standpoints of the man and woman involved. But from the children's point of view, the double masquerades as a mother as well as a wife, and the children suffer because their real mother has vanished and another woman, who pretends to be their mother, has taken her place. Different subsidiary episodes adhere to the basic bedtrick according to whether it does or does not involve, or emphasize, the birth of children. In general, myths emphasize children and the production of heirs, while later literary forms are concerned less about children and more about adult sexuality. But the two scenarios are inextricably linked: in myths as well as secular stories, the child may serve as the physical proof of the identity of the bedtrickster, treated merely as an object whose physical resemblance† to his father proves not his own identity but the fact that his mother is his father's wife. If we bear in mind the incidental damage done to the children of bedtricksters, we might do well to consider the children not as objects but as subjects and to analyze the myths from the standpoint of the child, the hapless mediator between the two divided (and subdivided) parents.

The mother who flees from her husband and abandons her child often inflicts damage on both her husband and her child. Parvati curses her son to have a stony mother, and the flight of Samjna‡ results in the mutilation of her husband and the quasi-fatal mutilation of her son. When the mother "splits" (as in the slang phrase for a hasty exit), her children may also be split—at worst mutilated or destroyed and at best deeply wounded. Although there is a significant difference between the harm inflicted by the mother who goes away and the mother who is a false copy or a shadow, they are often causally related: because one mother leaves, the other is a mere copy. When the mother vanishes, who or what is to be put in her place? What surrogates can the child find?

Myths such as the tale of the demon Adi speak to us out of a culture in which the frequency of maternal death, the routine remarriage of widowers, and a close-knit extended family with many available "aunties" made absent mothers and surrogate mothers far more common than they are in contemporary America. But depth psychology† tells us that every mother is, in a sense, an abandoning mother: we lose her when we realize that we are not a part of her, when we grow up, when she dies, when we realize that we cannot have her, that she is taboo, off-limits. And so Genesis tells us (2.24) that a man leaves his father and mother and cleaves to his wife, and they are one flesh. In this sense, the loss of the mother, any mother, is inevitable, and this loss, as Freud pointed out long ago,[66] sets us on the path for the search for a subsequent (nonincestuous) replacement, a substitute: a lover, a god, or a teddy bear. D. W. Winnicott† spoke of transitional objects that a child uses as substitutes both for himself as the totality of the world and for his mother—a breast, a thumb, a blanket, a teddy bear, and, perhaps most important, a story.†[67] A painting or statue‡ might also function as such an object. Marjorie Garber, rejecting the stark contrast between a "substitute" love and the "real thing," argues that "all loves function, in a sense, within a chain of substitutions."[68]

The desire to see one person as a double of another, to see one woman as like another, to see your mistress as a replacement for your mother, may be a desperate effort to achieve psychical conservation, a way of disavowing loss or denying aloneness. But what happens when we lose the puppy or the teddy (not to mention the lover or the god)? Or, perhaps worse, when the transitional object turns out to be a demon? For the man who "cleaves" to his wife may find that she cleaves† herself away from him, in the other sense of the word.[69] The sexual partner may abandon you just as your mother did or turn out not to be the person you think s/he is. The Sun, abandoned by his wife, Samjna,‡ relives the occasion when his mother, Aditi, abandoned him.[70] The loss of the abandoning mother makes us vulnerable to the destructive surrogate mother or the abandoning wife; two lovers make one, just as the child with the mother makes one, and when the lovers split apart they reenact that first, primal separation. The basic human problem of separation and identity that originates with the (abandoning) mother may be later reawakened, the old wound bled again, by a treacherous spouse or lover. Or, in a related scenario, the son who grows up and leaves home may perceive his loss of his mother as her loss of him, something to feel guilty about. Ruth Padel asks, "When a man leaves a woman he has loved, is he re-enacting the experience on which his adult self is built?"[71]

The compelling connection between betrayal by a mother and by a wife is inverted by Shakespeare in *Cymbeline* (2.5), where Posthumus, when he thinks his wife has betrayed him, imagines that his mother betrayed his father, too:

> We are all bastards,
> And that most venerable man which I
> Did call my father was I know not where
> When I was stamped. Some coiner with his tools
> Made me a counterfeit; yet my mother seemed
> The Dian of that time. So doth my wife
> The nonpareil of this. O vengeance, vengeance!
> Me of my lawful pleasure she restrained
> And prayed me oft forbearance.

Posthumus has been taken in by falsified evidence of his wife's infidelity, but there is absolutely no evidence of his mother's infidelity. He leaps to this conclusion perhaps because she died just as he was born (hence his name, Posthumus), a loss that, coupled with his wife's apparent sexual coldness to him, produces the scenario of the abandoning mother doubled by the abandoning wife and the transformation of rejection into sexual betrayal, by both women at once.

The chain of substitutions appears in the mythology of the bedtrick as a cluster of masquerades (a disappearing mother/lover/self) that the victim simultaneously longs to uncover and fears to uncover, a series of paradoxes† that are expressed differently according to the point of view of the character in the drama. We can express this cluster of substitutions in the form of a three-point syllogism:†

1. "My mother is not my mother." This may be a happy discovery (or fantasy): my real mother is someone better than this one, who is really just a stepmother; my real mother would not treat me as badly as this mother does. This fantasy of other, better parents is what Freud called the Family Romance†[72]—the myth of the child who is taken from his parents at birth and raised by strangers who pretend to be his parents. Thus, Freud would add, the child reasons that since this apparent mother is not in fact related to him, he can acknowledge his sexual feelings for her. But the realization that "my mother is not my mother" is also an unhappy discovery (or fantasy): my real mother has abandoned me and therefore clearly does not love me.

In the film *The Three Faces of Eve* (1957), Eve White says, thinking of her daughter (Bonnie) and Eve Black: "How do you explain to a little girl that her real mamma's never comin' back, but a woman that just looks like her?" In the book by the psychiatrists, Eve White remarks of Bonnie: "What hurts me is for her to climb on my knee, touch my face with her tiny hands and ask, 'Are you my Mommy or is it one of the others?'" And when the psychiatrist asks Eve Black, "Don't you *love* your daughter?" she replies, "Bonnie's *her* child. I got nothing to do with her."[73] Or, in the words used in a book by Eve Black herself, "The brat's hers."[74] In *Invasion of the Body Snatchers*† (1956), the first person we meet who detects the clones is a little boy who is dragged into the doctor's office, screaming, "She's not my mother!"

2. **"My wife/husband/lover is not my wife/husband/lover."** This scenario, too, which is the bedtrick, may be a happy discovery (or fantasy): the person in my bed is not my familiar, boring partner but an exciting stranger. However, it may also be unhappy: my lover has gone away and betrayed me, and I am in bed with a potentially dangerous stranger.

3. **"Therefore, I am not who I am."** The happy aspect of this discovery (or fantasy) is: I am of higher birth than I appear to be (the Family Romance). On the other hand, depth psychologists'† studies of mirroring† suggest an unhappier fantasy: I construct myself through the eyes of those I love, my mother or my lover or my god, and now that I realize that I have been looking into a false mirror, I no longer know who I am. This applies even in ordinary cases of sexual betrayal, when the victim retroactively realizes that, since the lover was not what s/he appeared to be, the victim, too, must have been someone else, not someone loved but someone fooled. Sometimes the child tries to take the place of the lost loved object (as the French diplomat, for instance, becomes his fantasized lover, Butterfly, at the end of *M. Butterfly*†). This may be the most basic of all masquerades: to become the person that you long to have with you to tell you who you are. The loss of this most intimate substitute is the final link in the tragic chain of betrayals that tears away the identity of both the bedtrickster and the victim of the bedtrick. Thus, the mother and the lover as the betraying others make us doubt that we know who we are.

Approach Two

Psychology

The Case of the Missing Identity

Bedtricks are about that great Lost and Found department known as human identity; they tackle the case of mistaken identity at its most intimate level, in bed. What Hegel called the human need "to be recognized, to be desired and valued by other human beings,"[75] varies from one culture to another, and people in different cultures do not react in the same way to the shock of discovering that their lovers, and hence their selves, are not who they thought they were. Some cultures do not construct identity sexually, though surprisingly many do.

Bedtrick myths weave fantasies on the theme of individuality; they are about the fragility, indeed the fictive nature, of identity. All three of the key players in a bedtrick—the trickster, the victim, and the impersonated partner—may feel the ground of their identity shifting beneath them. The person whom the bedtrickster imitates or replaces becomes disoriented when he learns that he has an impostor. Amphitryon‡ loses his sense of who he is when Alcmena does not know him: "If she can recognize her husband in him, / I will inquire no further who I *am*, / But I will hail him as Amphitryon."[76] So, too, the real Martin Guerre† might have asked himself, "Who am I . . . if another man has lived out the life I left behind and is in the process of being declared the heir of my father Sanxi, the husband of my wife, and the father of my son?"[77] This prompted him to return to a wife and a village that he had happily abandoned (though he may also have returned because his hated father had died): "The original Martin Guerre may have come back to repossess his identity, his persona, before it was too late."[78] And we have noted, throughout this chapter, the damage that the bedtrick does to the trickster's sense of self.

The threat to individuality is posed not only by our own double but by the double of the one we love, who challenges the assumption that the person we love is different from everyone else—and that we ourselves are, therefore, different from everyone else. Bedtricks force us to confront the issue of the sexual object:† do we define ourselves, including our sexuality, in terms of who we *are* or in terms of who we are *with*? Those who view the sexual act as an extension of the self, a form of self-knowledge, define their sexuality with reference to the sexual self, the subject of desire. The authors of texts that express this point of view seem to ask, "Who are you regardless of who you are in bed with?" This attitude limits the destructive capacity of a partner's sexual betrayal: even if the partner is other than you thought, you may still be who you thought you were.

For those who define themselves by their partner, however, the knowledge that the lover is other than what they had thought is particularly devastating because it means that they themselves are other than they had thought. The intimate partner is a kind of finger painting of one's own identity, a place to hang up one's emotional hat. The mutual exchange of intense physical pleasure and responsiveness is a powerful medium for the merging of identities. Bedtrick myths express a longing not just for the real him or the real her but for the real me, indeed, the real *mes*, and the real *us*.

People in love tend to become more and more like the people they love, or to believe that they are already more like their lovers than like anyone else. The romantic ideal that drives this mythology insists that both men and women (though particularly women‡) define themselves by, and take their self-images from, the mirrors† of the eyes of those whom they love and/or who love them.

The bridegroom in Basile's "The Old Woman Discovered"† is in the thrall of this paradigm when he reflects, on finding his beautiful young bride apparently changed into a hideous old woman:† "Am I myself, or not myself?"[79] When Kleist's Alcmena‡ cannot tell if the man she has slept with is her husband (Amphitryon) or Zeus in Amphitryon's form, her entire self-perception is deconstructed:

> I'd sooner be mistaken in
> Myself! I'd sooner take this firm conviction
> That I drank in while at my mother's breast
> And which assures me that I am Alcmena,
> And say I was a Parthian or Persian.
> Is this hand mine? And is this bosom mine?
> Is my reflection in the mirror mine?
> Would he be stranger to me than myself?
> Remove my eyes and I will hear him still;
> My ears, I'll feel him still; my touch, I'll breathe him;
> Take eyes and ears and touch and sense of smell
> And all my senses, and but leave my heart,
> And you will leave me with the bell I need
> To find him in this wide world.[80]

The identity that she found at her mother's breast, when she was mirrored in her mother, she has now lost in her false husband's arms.

When Joseph Roth's shah of Persia discovers that he fell for a bedtrick, he doubts his infallibility for the first time:

> [The eunuch]: "Sire, it wasn't the same woman, it was a similar one!" "Are you telling me I'm blind?" "We are all of us blind," said the Chief Eunuch. The Shah felt uncomfortable. He pushed the dishes with honey, butter and fruit to one side. He thought or rather he gave the appearance of thinking, but his head remained as empty as a hollow pumpkin. "Well, I see, I see!" he said. And then: "But she made me happy!" "Indeed, indeed!" affirmed the Chief Eunuch. "Just tell me," the Shah began again, "be candid: do you think I made mistakes, mistakes in other, more important matters as well?" "Sire, candidly, yes! You err because you are human."[81]

In a similar vein, when the victim in the film *Dream Lover* (1994) starts to figure it out, he asks his wife, the bedtrickster, "If the things you tell me aren't true, what is true?" She replies, "That I'm your wife," and asks him, "Isn't the real question, Who are you?" This is not merely a Western construct; when the wife in the Japanese novel *The Changelings*† finds herself in bed with the substitute and finds him strange, she says, in verse: "The one I knew, / He whom I was wont to see, / You seem not to be he. / Is it I who am different? / Or is it you who have changed?"

Marjorie Garber asks: "When we say that we want to be loved 'for ourselves,' what 'selves' do we have in mind?"[82] The stories of bedtricks pose this riddle of sexual identity in two forms: How can two people become one? And, the greater riddle, how can one person ever be one?[83] Given the multiplicity of each of us, the problem is to explain not doubling but unity. How is it that we are perceived as one when we are so many? Indeed, we should expect much more multiplicity; since each of us is several persons, often one of us gets us into a situation that another one of us has to get us out of.

The wish to be multivalent may take either (or both) of two forms. In the Romantic† model, or the paradigm of desire, some people, or perhaps some parts of each of us, want to have all the parts known at once, to be and to appear to be integrated; we desire to find a single person who loves *all* parts of us, who fulfills our sexual needs, family needs, intellectual needs, and so forth. But, in the traditional† model, or the paradigm of duty, some people, or some parts of ourselves, seem to want to play one part at a time and to keep the separate selves separate, validated by different people. This involves us in another paradox:† though we may want to find a single person to perceive all of us at once, rather than being seen in fragments, one part at a time, yet we reserve the right to be as many separate people as we are. A part of each of us rejoices to find a different self, and a part is terrified by this. This paradox is compounded by another factor that often intersects with it: we expect others to show us always the same face, and we may feel betrayed when we see different sides of them, just as we may feel shortchanged when they see only one side of us.

In these stories, intolerable conflict moves the characters simultaneously in two apparently opposite directions, toward splitting (one person creating a second, different person, real or imagined—the double) and integration (one person pretending to be the same as another person, real or imagined—the masquerade). In the myths of rape, for instance, the woman does *not* want the man and produces a substitute in order to avoid him. But in the stories of the man who commits adultery with his own wife,† the woman *wants* the man and pretends to be two women (herself and the woman he desires) in order to get him. We may see this as a tension between patterns of avoidance (through the double) and seeking (through the masquerade) or as a single act interpreted from two different points of view: to the person who produces the double, the story is about doubling, splitting, avoidance; to the double who takes the place of the original, it is about masquerading, integrating, seeking. To the question "Which is real, the split form or the integrated one?" the answer is "Yes."

The integrating masquerade extends the personality by allowing the original to do more than he or she can do within the original persona; the splitting double limits the personality by doing the things that the original does *not* do, or does not acknowledge doing. One set of stories regards splitting as the solution: the self is unable to accept the identity of some aspect of the personality (the woman cannot believe that she has been raped; Dr. Jekyll will not accept that it is he who has done what Mr. Hyde‡ has done) and so splits it off into another personality. Another set of stories regards splitting as the problem: the self does not wish to be regarded as only partial but wishes to play more roles than those that the partner would allow (the wife wishes to be both the mother and the mistress†) and so slips into the role of another personality ("I am both this person and that person"). Splitting the double away from ourselves begins by denying the otherness within us, saying, "I am not that person."

Masquerading as someone else begins by denying the otherness of the other, saying, "This other person is not different from me."

Other myths of splitting and masquerading, and other readings of the same myths, go on to deconstruct the initial dichotomy, reading the mythological glass as half full rather than half empty, so that the myth of the splitting double acknowledges the other within us, accepts that all the forms of us are in fact us, and the myth of masquerade acknowledges the otherness of the other, allows us to understand that even though the other is us, it is a different us. Many of our stories express both points of view simultaneously.[84] And some masquerades have a developmental aspect: people change, learn, become embroiled in new problems out of the solutions of the old. Masquerading is not something weird that only deranged people do, or even something that we ourselves do only once in a while when we are in extremis. It is natural and unavoidable, since we are all multifaceted (if not necessarily two-faced). There are, from one culture to another, different ways of distinguishing "healthy multiplicity" from "pathological schizophrenia." The idea that people who "see double" are mad has a long literary history in the West, from Plautus's *Amphitryon‡* through Shakespeare's *The Comedy of Errors†* to Craig Lucas's *Prelude to a Kiss* (1992).†

But who is crazy, the bedtrickster (for engineering it) or the victim (for falling for it)? Given our vacillating standards, the best we can probably do, in real life, is to judge whether or not a fantasy is nourishing and sustaining or interferes with (as Freud would say) work and love. We do not declare a person legally insane, Ralph Slovenko points out, when "[a]lcohol or drugs may turn a soft-spoken individual into a ranting madman. We say, 'I don't know what got into me,' or, 'I was beside myself.' "[85] In this case, the cliché† is just a cliché. But if you take it literally, and start introducing people to your double, they lock you up.

FREUDIAN BEDTRICKS

Psychological observations of a general nature inform all of my readings of the myths, and I have concentrated on the psychological aspects of identity that the bedtrick threatens (though the bedtrick is also about a lot of other psychological concepts). The psychology of identity has been best excavated by depth psychologists, the literary branch of the psychiatric family, who have also illuminated the aspects of identity that the bedtrick myths explore: the literary, rather than "scientific," aspects. Let us therefore consider what depth psychology has to teach us about the ways in which a person's psychic integrity may be shattered (or, rarely, mended) by various forms of bedtricks. We will be concerned primarily with psychological theories that illuminate puzzling aspects of our texts and only secondarily with the evidence that our myths offer in support of those theories. And we will concentrate on three seminal thinkers in this field: Sigmund Freud, Otto Rank, and Jacques Lacan.

I have already used many of Freud's concepts and terms in my discussions of texts about bedtricks throughout this book: splitting,‡[86] the Family Romance,† repression,† projection,† multiple personalities,† the Freudian error or slip† (an unconscious slip that reveals a deeper truth), and upward displacement† (the belief that parts of the body often stand in, as it were, for other parts; in particular, that the genitals are often displaced upward to the head, mouth, nose, or eyes). Other, less familiar, Freudian assumptions, also relevant to the bedtrick, deserve to be glossed at greater length now.

In "The Uncanny," Freud sees a paradigmatic example of uncanniness in the motif of the double, that is, in the relation between "persons who are considered identical by reason of looking alike," which represents the return of something once "familiar" but eventually "repressed."[87] Hysterical symptoms, too, force us to acknowledge that the body sometimes remembers† what the mind has repressed, a hypothesis supported by many aspects of bedtrick mythology. A famous insight of Freud's—that all women are imperfect substitutes for the one woman, a man's mother[88]— illuminates important aspects of the bedtrick. First, according to Freud, the original love object, the parent, is taboo and must be replaced by a permitted surrogate; then people in love overvalue this surrogate, which leads to disillusionment and eventually to the replacement of the love object,[89] who becomes interchangeable with other love objects, part of a long series, all alike in the dark. "Her disposal is revenge. And now comes lying."[90] Thus, the abandoning mother produces compulsive Don Juans.

Freud also established a highly influential paradigm for interpreting one of the central forms of the bedtrickster, the split woman.‡ He saw the tension between the mother and the whore as a universal factor in the psychic life of men.[91] From the husband's standpoint, the mother (of his children) is the permitted woman, sometimes in contrast with the erotic woman, the whore. From the wife's standpoint, she is simultaneously maternal (to her children) and erotic (to her husband). But from the standpoint of the (male) child, the combined image of mother and erotic woman may be threatening and intolerable, forcing the child to split her apart and to fantasize that he has two sets of parents, or to split himself apart and to fantasize that there are two of him. Freud argued that in myths of the Oedipal type, the man projects double parents or splits himself (and/or his mother) in order to avoid or deny his erotic attachment to her. That is, he splits her into one woman who is maternal and another who is erotic, and then splits himself so that there is one of him for each of his emotions.

In her variant of the mother/whore hypothesis, Melanie Klein attempts to explain the split image of the good and bad mother through her concept of projective identification. Her theory of the good and bad breast,[92] which might have a stronger claim for universality than Freud's male-oriented Oedipal syndrome, tells us that it is natural and inevitable for very young children of both sexes to distinguish two female figures, the breast that gives milk and the breast that feeds itself, the loving mother and the devouring mother, and that this dichotomy is the basis of all subsequent moral judgments. Anna Freud applied the term "splitting" to defense mechanisms in which "a person experiences, in mixed form, two attributes that she would rather keep separate, and so assigns them, in fantasy, to two different persons or entities."[93] Thus, the split within the self can, again, be traced back to the original split between the mother and her shadow.‡

In his analysis of Schreber,‡ Freud also dealt with what he saw as the deceptions and self-deceptions that homosexuals generate: "It is a remarkable fact that the familiar principal forms of paranoia can all be represented as contradictions of the single proposition: '*I* (a man) *love him* (a man),' and indeed that they exhaust all the possible ways in which such contradictions could be formulated."[94] Eve Sedgwick notes that these "eroto-grammatical transformations, . . . unspeakable under a homophobic regime of utterance," form a kind of syllogism:† (1) "I do not *love* him; I *hate* him." (2) "I do not love *him;* I love *her.*" (3) "*I* do not love him; *she* loves him." And finally, (4) "I do not love him; I do not love anyone."[95]

The first and second transformations are what Garber glossed as "delusions of persecution" (I hate him because he hates me) and erotomania,[96] which, together, result in the cuckolding† scenario: "Because I hate him, I love her." The third is what Garber called the formula for delusional jealousy,[97] which also motivates myths of cuckolding but rebounds, as well, into a variation of the splitting† scenario, when the denied love is painful or violent: "It is some man (or woman) other than me who loves her (or him)." The fourth transformation often shades off into, "I love only myself," leading to megalomania, the sexual overestimation of the ego.[98] This transformation is not often represented in our texts, for it means that there will be no erotic story at all—except, perhaps, for someone like Narcissus,‡[99] who fell in love with his own reflection, or like the Prince Who Married His Left Side.‡ Indeed, Freud investigated this scenario in his reading of Ovid's tale of Narcissus.[100] But it shades off into a fifth transformation, which, Sedgwick argues, "underlies Freud's project so intimately that it does not occur to Freud to make it explicit. . . . I do not *love* him, I *am* him."[101] This appears in our narratives with relation not to the love object but to the rival, the other, the double, in the integration scenario: Cyrano† becomes his rival; the wife (Parvati†, Tamar†) becomes the mistress.

A similar taxonomy underlies an instance in the so-called Capgras syndrome, named after a multiple-personality case published by Jean Marie Joseph Capgras in 1923 but which Capgras himself named after the character of Sosia‡ in the myth of Amphitryon.‡[102] In a 1976 update of this scenario, Edwin J. Mikkelsen and Thomas G. Gutheil related the Capgras syndrome to "Family Romance" and fictional works involving doubling, such as *The Picture of Dorian Gray*,‡ "William Wilson,"‡ and various doppelgänger‡ legends.[103] The patient in this case ("Mrs. M.") experienced various delusions of doubles, forming another syllogism:†

1. Her true mother was just "the woman who raised her," while she regarded a neighbor as her "real mother."

2. Her husband was not really her husband, "not the man he said he was." This is said to have "contained a cogent element of existential truth: he was not the man he had 'said' he would become. . . . At issue here is the basic notion of a 'kernel of disguised truth' that axiomatically forms the core of all paranoid delusions."[104]

3. Her youngest son was not really hers; "a switch was made at the hospital" and her own child had been taken elsewhere. She gave six reasons in support of this intuition, including the fact that the delivery was under general anesthesia,† so she did not see the baby immediately afterward, and that "a court had placed her children in foster homes (because of Mrs. M.'s neglect), which implied to her that the children could not have been truly hers."

4. She was not the real Mrs. M. She insisted that "she herself was a good loving mother while the real Mrs. M. was a 'no good bitch.'" Here the authors remark that "the self as impostor" is "the psychotic expression of an ambivalence about mothering that is consciously intolerable": "She was partially correct when she said, 'There are two other Mrs. M.'s running around out there.' The 'other Mrs. M.' who is *most* important in her life, however, is her husband's mother, whom she despises. . . . The ambiguity about which of the two Mrs. M.'s—patient or mother-in-law—is being called a bitch cannot, we feel, be entirely coincidental."[105] And, finally, inevitably:

5. Her therapist was not the real doctor. When her outpatient therapist visited her at home, the patient said, "You're not the real Dr. Mikkelsen; he wouldn't do this."[106] We may take this as the therapeutic surrogate for the theological† hypothesis "my god is not God."

After Freud's analysis of the bedtrick in E. T. A. Hoffmann's "The Sandman,"[107] his successors applied psychological theory to other literary bedtricks.[108] Fredric Jameson includes among "the classic themes of all psychoanalytic literary criticism since Freud" many that are prominent in bedtrick myths, such as "the Oedipus complex, the double, splitting, the phallus, the lost object."[109] Other, more general aspects of Freud's work are also applicable. We might, for instance, analyze the story in terms of a wish component (the wish to be in bed with a certain person) and a defense mechanism (the wish not to be in bed with another person or, indeed, with that same person). Or we might see it in terms of Freud's belief that the ego is capable of splitting itself, thus causing a subject/object relationship within the self that passes judgment on itself, the ego in conflict with the superego, the self in self-reflection.[110] Freud's basic argument that you pretend you don't know what you do, especially but not only with regard to incest, is a broader example of the more particular argument that the bedtrick depends on this sort of self-delusion.† Thus, when the *Zohar* suggests that Jacob† was lying to himself about Leah, we may see an early source of Freud's well-known rabbinic thinking.

OTTO RANK ON THE DOUBLE

Of all the studies of bedtricks that Freud inspired, Otto Rank's *The Double* remains the classic text. Like Freud, Rank focused his analysis on a story by E. T. A. Hoffmann, but where Freud chose "The Sandman"† (as Rank notes at the end of his study), Rank chose "The Story of the Lost Reflection." (In opera,† which has a good instinct for myths, Offenbach chose these two stories plus one more for his *Tales of Hoffmann*.) Oddly enough, neither Freud nor Rank paid much attention to Hoffmann's most explicit tale of a bedtrick, actually called "The Doubles"† ("Die Doppelgänger,"

1821). Though Rank's insights apply primarily to nineteenth-century Gothic doubles (more specifically to German ones, though also to British— Jekyll/Hyde‡ and Dracula‡) and are not limited to bedtricks, he also makes several suggestions that, on the one hand, generally illuminate our more circumscribed theme and, on the other, focus specifically upon sexual aspects of the double (as when he associates the loss of the shadow with castration‡ and impotence).[111] Rank summarizes these themes as they are employed in the literature of the nineteenth-century Romantics such as Hoffmann: "We always find a likeness which resembles the main character down to the smallest particulars, such as name, voice, and clothing—a likeness which, as though 'stolen from the mirror' (Hoffmann), primarily appears to the main character as a reflection. Always, too, this double works at cross-purposes with its prototype; and, as a rule, the catastrophe occurs in the relationship with a woman, predominantly ending in suicide by way of the death intended for the irksome persecutor."[112] Not merely the image in the mirror† but name† and voice† are stolen by the double.

Rank saw narcissism (Freud's fourth reformulation: "I do not love him; I do not love anyone") as the key to the myth of the double.[113] The narcissistic aspect of the double expresses an excess of self-love, which prevents one from loving anyone else; the schizophrenic aspect of the double expresses an excess of self-hate, which makes it impossible for one to take responsibility for what one has done (or, more often, for what one wishes to do and fantasizes about doing). In its social form, this tension would explain doubling and splitting in terms of the conflicting claims of distancing and intimacy.

Rank connects the fear of death and aging with "the threat to narcissism by sexual love," which may take either

> the form of pathological self-love as in the Greek legend . . . or . . . the defensive form of the pathological fear of one's self, often leading to paranoid insanity and appearing personified in the pursuing shadow, mirror-image, or double. On the other hand, in the same phenomena of defense the threat also recurs, against which the individual wants to protect and assert himself. So it happens that the double, who personifies narcissistic self-love, becomes an unequivocal rival in sexual love; or else, originally created as a wish-defense against a dreaded eternal destruction, he reappears in superstition as the messenger of death.[114]

In Rank's view, narcissism denies "the idea of death, which is extremely painful to our self-esteem. . . . the most general example of the repression of an unendurable certainty."[115] He sees this in the myth of Narcissus itself (particularly in the Pausanias variant, in which the reflection is mistaken for Narcissus's twin sister)[116] and in Oscar Wilde's Dorian Gray:‡ "The intimate friendships with young men . . . are attempts to realize the erotic infatuation with his own youthful image. . . . Dorian shares this defective capacity for love with almost all double-heroes."[117] The fear of death and "dreaded eternal destruction" is also expressed in stories in which the passage of time† produces an inadvertent bedtrick staged by the aging† self in competition with the young self. Thus, the sexual double is a manifestation of both sexual megalomania and sexual inadequacy, both longing for sex and fear of sex; this makes good, human sense and constitutes another cluster of paradoxes.†

LACAN ON THE MIRROR STAGE

I have argued that many of the myths of the bedtrick, or indeed of common or garden-variety sexual betrayal, assume that such a masquerade or betrayal is so devastating because we derive much of our sense of our own identity from the mirror embodied in those who love us and whom we love—our mother† or our lover.† The idea that this mirroring lover is the mirror of the mirroring mother was encapsulated by Winnicott: "The precursor of the mirror is the mother's face."[118] Rank illustrated the "defensive attitude toward the mirrored self" by citing an actual legal case in which a young lord had locked up his beautiful, unfaithful sweetheart for eight days in a room whose walls were mirrors; there is also a variant of Snow White in which the wicked stepmother is punished for her vanity by being locked up in a room of mirrors.[119] Henry Abramovitch cites the actual case history of a man who moved from woman to woman, job to job, "without an inner center. . . . Only by physically seeing himself reflected in the mirror could he regain a sense of his own identity." Abramovitch likens this man to the bedtricksters Jacob† and David† in the Hebrew Bible.[120] Mirror images often function as masqueraders, but here we see that masquerade, too, can be a mirror.

Some Hollywood films satirize the magic mirror. In the classic Marx Brothers film *Duck Soup* (1933), both Harpo and Chico dress just as Groucho is dressed at that moment (moustache, glasses, nightshirt, and nightcap), and posing on different sides of the frame of a giant mirror that has just been shattered, each mimics the other's gestures to persuade him, for several zany minutes, that he is looking at himself in a mirror— until Groucho breaks it up. Woody Allen pays transsexual tribute to this scene in his film *Sleeper* (1973), in which our hero (Woody), transported to the futuristic future, shaves in an electronic mirror in which another actor (also Woody) mimics his every move, until he pushes a button and a woman appears, eventually shaving to match him (a scene that in turn inspired the transsexual mirror scene in *All of Me*† [1984]). The Marx Brothers scene is also visually quoted in *Big Business* (1988), in which a woman meets her unknown identical twin, wearing the same suit, in a powder room in which a series of mirrors is separated by a series of open spaces, and the two of them play the mirror scene until they realize that they are twins. This is the Family Romance as comedy.†

The mirror is a stage both in the sense of an arena in which we present an image of ourselves, on which we act out our various selves (like the often revolving mirrors of glass or water on which Busby Berkeley staged the dances of hundreds of identical women), and in the sense of a stage of our development as individuals. In this latter sense the mirror is a central theme in the writings of Jacques Lacan, though, as Marina Warner has wisely remarked, "The play between self-knowledge and self-image gives the mirror a role in identity long before Lacan named the Mirror Stage."[121] Lacan distinguishes three dimensions in the human mind.[122] The Mirror stage is the Imaginary, in which the dyadic relation of an infant (*infans*, not-speaking) to his mirror image (in a mirror or in his mother's face) makes him believe that he has a stable social identity, equated with his image. The Imaginary is the dialectic between the lost object and the totalized, complete ego; the pull between them is what inevitably splits the subject. In terms of our mythological actors upon the Mirror stage, the original narcissist, still fixated in the Imaginary, incestuously engaged with his mother or himself, judges only by the visual, by the mirror. Like Harpo and Chico in *Duck Soup*, he thinks there is no one there but himself, when actually there is someone else; the supposed mirror image is another person. Here he is trapped within an infinite *mise en abîme*, locked into a conflict with infinitely proliferating doubles of the self. As Margaret Trawick put it: "The self imagines itself to be an image of an image (the baby sees the mother and himself in her). This vision is static and closed, an eternal, mutual reflection between two images. It is a mirage." In this stage, the mother is the other, who generates the illusion that she makes us real, "the illusion that there is something on the other side of what we perceive that will complete us."[123] Where Winnicott sees the mirror as a positive source of identity, a "loving gaze," Lacan sees it as a distortion. The mirroring gaze is thus the site of both aspects of desire, distortion and true recognition; and as the child in either case loses this mirror in growing away from the parent, it is also the site of the loss of a stable sense of self.

The Symbolic stage is the world of language and hierarchy, which is reached by mastering the codes of culture represented by the father and by the phallus. The Lacanian paradox is that one becomes trapped between the terror of losing one's mirror image and the desire for language, which requires the loss of that image.[124] This is the equivalent of what the myths depict as the tension between the eye and the mouth.† Here the father is the other, who breaks in—like Groucho breaking up the scene in *Duck Soup,* Groucho with his cigar, which may or may not be just a cigar—to generate the Oedipal conflict. "The Symbolic order (or language itself)," writes Fredric Jameson, "restructures the Imaginary by introducing a third term into the hitherto infinite regression of the duality of the latter's mirror images."[125] With the intrusion of a third person, the father, language breaks the spell of the magic mirror, and we develop into that mythological beast, the speaking animal. But this gain is also a loss, as Toril Moi argues: at this stage, "[t]he speaking subject that says 'I am' is in fact saying 'I am he (she) who has lost something'—and the loss suffered is the loss of the imaginary identity with the mother and with the world. The sentence 'I am' could therefore best be translated as 'I am that which I am not,' according to Lacan."[126] This is a self-referential version of Freud's syllogism† on homosexuality, an outgrowth of the fifth gloss, the one that Freud did *not* make. To be what one is not, as in this syllogism, is to be a masquerader, more precisely someone who masquerades as himself or herself.† But, as Sedgwick pointed out for Freud, I would suggest that our myths admit of yet another possibility: the intrusion of a double of the mother or a false lover as the other who breaks the cycle of self-reflection; the mother who makes us real is later replaced by the beloved who makes us real. Finally, the Real stage is generated by the tension of the dialectic between the Imaginary and the Symbolic. The masquerade dissolves this tension, too.

Lacan, glossing Freud's "Wo Es war, soll Ich werden" ("Where It was, there shall I be," sometimes translated "Where Id was, there shall Ego be"), wrote: "Who, then, is the other to whom I am more attached than to myself, since, at the heart of my assent to my own identity, it is still he who agitates me? His presence can be understood only at a second degree of otherness, which already places him in the position of mediating between me and the double of myself, as if it were with my counterpart."[127] Many bedtricksters live in the world glimpsed through the Lacan-glass. Lacan is talking about what we are talking about, and like many of the bedtricks in our myths, it's all done with mirrors.

The three-point syllogism that begins "My mother is not my mother" and ends "I am not who I am" is often theologically† squared: "My god is not God." This fourth mirror may show us true or false images. Hindus and Buddhists represent the guru's face as a mirror in which the devotee's face is truly and compassionately reflected, undistorted by fear or self-hate. The fifteenth-century poet Kabir spoke of the guru that resides in one's own heart:

> Within the heart a mirror
> but no face shows.
> You'll see the face when the heart's
> Doubleness goes.[128]

The mirror of the guru's heart, like the lover's face, may reflect the duplicitous self, but unlike the lover, it reflects it truly.

THREE

Waking Up in Bed with an Animal

ANIMAL LOVERS: BEAUTY AND THE BEAST

Many bedtricksters are animals whose trick consists in a transformation: the demon Adi becomes a snake, Parvati, a lion. Waking up in the morning to discover that you have been in bed all night with an animal (or a deity or a human in the form of an animal) is the fantasy that underlies both the folktales and the literary retellings of those tales about figures that folklorists sometimes call "animal lovers." (Unfortunately, this term is often spelled with a hyphen, which produces a potential confusion with animal-lovers, people who are fond of stray cats and dogs. The hyphen distinguishes our animal brides or grooms—the latter term meaning here, not people who curry horses, but people who marry brides—from those who dote on their pets, although the *partner* of an animal lover is in a most literal sense, even a bestial sense, an animal-lover.)

The Family Romance† often involves animals, for the changeling child may be raised by or among animals who serve as maternal surrogates, like wet nurses, impersonating a mother; or the child may be sent out to be killed, whereupon the compassionate killer relents and kills an animal instead, taking back its heart (or tongue†) as proof of the murder, so that the animal is a sacrificial surrogate, impersonating the sacrificial victim. The Family Romance presents two complementary animal paradigms. Lowly animals may be assimilated to the lower-class† people who adopt a royal child; as animals are below humans, so lower classes are regarded as naturally below higher classes. On the other hand, animals may be assimilated to gods and regarded as the higher parents of children who appear to be lower—merely mortal. Animals are similarly high and low on the continuum that Edmund Leach has articulated between the animals we eat and those we don't eat, paralleled by the continuum of the women we marry and those we don't marry.[1] Some are tabooed because they are too near, some because too far; in between they are safe to eat or marry, respectively, but there is uneasiness at the edges of the categories, and the considerable overlap between the two systems (such as words for edible/inedible animals applied to available/unavailable women) inspires many of the myths of animal lovers.

Not all animal lover stories involve masquerades, for often the humans encounter the animal forms first and know perfectly well that their partners are humans bewitched to become animals. But sometimes the animal lover is first encountered in human form, and the transformation then functions as a bedtrick; and when the animal not only pretends to be a human but takes the place of an actual human, the story follows the pattern of a bedtrick of substitution.

A paradigm of the male aspect of this genre is Beauty and the Beast, in which a monstrous groom of unspecified zoological nature is equated with ugliness, in contrast with the defining beauty† of his bride. This story, which Marina Warner regards as "a founding myth of sexual difference,"[2] occurs in many, many variants[3] but is itself a variant of an even more basic story, best known from Apuleius's second-century C.E. romance of Cupid (or Amor or Eros) and Psyche, which is actually embedded within the tale of the transformation of a Greek man into an ass.[4] As Warner points out, "The first Beast of the West was Eros, the god of love himself."[5] In this story, Cupid, the son of Venus, makes love in the dark to a mortal Beauty—Psyche—whom he forbids to look at him. When she can resist no longer, she breaks the prohibition, lighting a lamp to look at her lover while he sleeps; seeing how beautiful he is, she becomes transfixed and allows several drops of tallow to fall upon him from her lamp. He awakes, sees her looking at him, and vanishes. That Psyche sees Cupid's true form in his postcoital sleep† is a manifestation of one of the sexual tests† of identity. The inability to identify the lover without the light of a lamp or, later, a candle,† underlies the sexist metaphor of the sameness of all women, but in the case of Cupid and Psyche it cannot be sexist in any feminist sense, for it is the male partner whose beauty (or, as the case may be, animal or human nature) is in question.

The tale of Beauty and the Beast calls into question the difference between the human and the animal and, in myths that assume that the beast is ugly, between beauty and ugliness. Moreover, since, like Cupid, the beast has divine or at least superhuman powers (he may be a magician and/or a powerful lord), these myths are also about the tension between the human and the superhuman‡ and between the two species that bracket the human: the animal and the divine. The real beast in most versions of the story is the heroine's father, who sells her to the prince who merely appears to be a beast. As Salman Rushdie wisely comments, "It was once explained to me by one of the world's Greatest Living Poets . . . that the classic fable *Beauty and the Beast* is simply the story of an arranged marriage."[6]

The female counterpart of the animal groom is the animal bride, a woman from another world who marries a mortal man, stays for a while, and then abandons both him and their child(ren) when the man displeases her. Often she is an animal who sheds her skin† and is captured by a man who hides that skin. (The skin plays an essential role in tales about animal grooms, too: the serpent lover may leave his wounded skin behind; the turtle lover, his shell.) As A. T. Hatto remarks of the animal bride: "At the human level the story has to do with the pitiable lot of a girl from another tribe and territory who has been trapped into an unsuitable union through the guile and strength of a man."[7] Thus, whether the animal is the bride (who is captured and forced to stay with a man she doesn't want to stay with) or the groom (to whom the woman is given, usually by her father, again usually against her will), the tale tells of the oppression of a woman, an interesting asymmetry.† Beauty begins by hating the Beast and ends up by loving him, while the Swan† Maiden begins by loving her husband and ends up by hating him. But in both genres, no matter whether she or he is the beast, the woman is captured, forced, raped†—until she escapes.

Let us set aside the tension between the human and the divine and postpone until chapter 4 the discussion of beauty, concentrating here on the beast.

HORSES AND SWANS

Horses are closely associated with bedtricksters and visual deception. When the goddess Samjna‡ runs away from her husband, the Sun, and transforms herself into a mare, he takes the form of a stallion and tries to cover her; not recognizing him, she turns her hindquarters away from him but he impregnates her through her mouth. She gives birth to the twins called the Ashvins, who are half horse and half anthropomorphic god, the Hindu form of the Greek Dioscuri or the Roman Gemini.‡ The theme of the equine mother survives in the story of Karna† only in the form of "Horse River," which receives the child, a body of water that is not mentioned elsewhere in the epic, to my knowledge. The ambivalent sexual availability of Samjna makes her into a mare, both too wild and too tame; the sexual violence of her husband against her anthropomorphic form is muted and projected onto her equine form, where it bursts forth brutally and grotesquely. When a mare presents her hindquarters to a stallion, that act is itself ambiguous: she presents herself as sexually ready but she also presents her hind-legs, which are her most dangerous weapon. But Samjna "turned to face him, determined to protect her hindquarters,"[8] because, unlike him, she was (in this case, wrongly) suspicious of the identity of her sexual partner in his equine transformation; she did not trust her eyes. (The mare's action inverts the human situation in which a prostitute, for instance, will sometimes allow intercourse but not a kiss,† which is regarded as more intimate.) The Sun raped† her, as the texts make clear: "He coupled with her by joining with her in her mouth, for she was struggling against him in her fear that it might be another male." "Tormented by lust, the Sun took the form of a horse and mated with her right in her mouth; Samjna was terrified and her mind was agitated, and from the cavities of her nose she vomited that semen."[9] The recurrent statement that the Ashvins were conceived from the nose (*na-sat*) may also have been inspired by a desire to account for their Vedic epithet of Nasatyas, which has traditionally been interpreted in India as "Nose-beings"[10] or "not false" (*na-a-satya,* literally, "not-not-true" or "not-not-real")[11]—the latter an interesting assertion in light of the fact that the Ashvins are the "true" sons of Samjna, in contrast with their "not-real" brother Yama (cursed to live among the dead) and their "not-true" half-brother Manu (son of the unreal surrogate mother).

Some texts are troubled by the implication of bestiality in this episode. One Sanskrit text, from the tenth century, eliminates the equine element entirely by saying that the Sun had a third wife, *named* "Mare" (Vadava),[12] not a horse, but just a woman named Mare. The same euhemeristic tendency inspired a twentieth-century commentary that insists that the horses are not horses: "'In the form of a mare' . . . implies that she ran at a great speed. . . . 'In the form of a horse' . . . implies that the Sun being overpowered with passion ran with the speed of a horse to enjoy himself in the company of Samjna."[13] Euhemerism and bowdlerization lead this commentator also† to omit the reference to the Sun's fellatio with his equiform wife; the Sun is simply said to have "enjoyed himself in the company of Samjna," which makes it difficult to understand how "she consequently ejected the semen virile through her nostrils."

The commentary that denies Samjna's equine nature tells us in greater detail why she "could not recognize her Lord at the first sight": "She met the Sun after a long time, and quite *unexpectedly,* and then there was a great difference in his features, as his power was moderated by [Samjna's father, the artisan Tvashtri]. The Sun, of course, recognized Samjna, and mixed with her in the usual way. Samjna, being overpowered, became helpless, but was very much agitated in mind."[14] This is an unusually realistic approach to the excuse for many *human* bedtricks: over time,† people change. Other readings, which include the equine transformation, assume quite reasonably, if flat-footedly, that when people change themselves into horses, they become unrecognizable. But, if this were so, how could the Sun recognize Samjna when she is a mare?

The comic book version (which calls her Sanjna) is simultaneously so sexually squeamish and so literally naturalistic that it paints itself into a corner where it cannot cope with the bestiality issue and entirely omits the rape. The Sun searches for his wife, remarking, "I have divined that she turned herself into a mare." When he goes to find her, he asks a passerby, "Have you seen a mare go by?" "Yes! A quaint one . . . by the river." The Sun: "Why do you call it a quaint one?" Passerby: "I speak the truth, sir. This mare talks!" To which the Sun makes the wonderful reply, "It must be Sanjna."

Now, "mare" in ancient Indian and medieval European mythology has many of the connotations of "bitch" in English. Leach notes that, for most Indo-Europeans, the bitch is the "wrong" animal among canines, the inverse of the relationship among felines (good dog/bad bitch = good cat/bad tom),[15] and I have argued for the same relationship among horses and cattle (good stallion/bad mare = good cow/bad bull).[16] This is one of the reasons why Samjna is a mare, and why the hypersexual Helen of Troy, sister of the equine twins the Dioscuri, is also associated with a deceptive mare (the Trojan horse).[17] Tales of masquerading mares persist in the European mythology of witchcraft, in which the witch resumes her true equine form at night and is often identified by the horseshoes that are put on her feet when she is a mare and that remain on her hands and feet when, by daylight, she resumes her human masquerade.[18] In the Ozarks, the tale acquires a class† element: the equine witch, caught and shod, proves to be a rich merchant's missing daughter, found naked in a barn, shod with horseshoes; "they just hushed the whole thing up and sent the girl off to a big hospital somewhere."[19] Here Modern Science lands at the eleventh hour, like the Marines, to extricate the myth from its tragic ending. The foot, particularly the mutilated foot,‡ is often a clue

to the animal nature of a bedtrickster; the folklorist Stith Thompson†
even lists it as a motif: K 1911.3.3.1, "False bride's mutilated feet."

Myths about stallions follow a very different path from myths of
mares; this is a highly gendered, which is to say asymmetrical,† mythology. The father of all centaurs was born from a double of Hera that Zeus
created to protect her from being raped by Ixion.‡²⁰ Greek stallions are
also associated with incestuous bedtricks. Aristotle, of all people, tells a
story about a horse who covered his own mother by mistake and threw
himself over a cliff as though horrified at what he had done, "because
some animals even have a natural respect for those that have begotten
them."²¹ In the ancient Indian horse sacrifice, the chief queen panto-
mimed copulation with the slaughtered stallion, who was said to "be"
both the sacrificing king (to whom he transferred his powers) and the
god Prajapati. In Hindu mythology, Indra, the king of the gods, is one
of several gods designated as the recipients of the horse sacrifice, but he
is unique in that he is himself famed for having performed more horse
sacrifices than anyone else and is jealous of this preeminence.²² He thus
(unlike the usual human worshiper) normally combines the roles of sacrificer and recipient. In one text, the *Harivamsha* (the appendix to the Sanskrit epic the *Mahabharata,* composed a few centuries after the final re-
cension of the *Mahabharata,* perhaps in the sixth century), he adds to
these roles that of the victim:

INDRA AND THE QUEEN

Janamejaya was consecrated for the sacrifice, and his queen, Vapushtama, approached the designated stallion and lay down beside him, according to the rules of the ritual. But Indra saw the woman, whose limbs
were flawless, and desired her. He himself entered the designated stallion
and mingled with the queen. And when this transformation had taken
place, Indra said to the priest in charge of the sacrifice, "This is not the
horse you designated. Scram."

The priest, who understood the matter, told the king what Indra had
done, and the king cursed Indra, saying, "From today, kings will no longer
offer the horse sacrifice to this king of the gods, who is fickle and cannot
control his senses." And he fired the priests and banished Vapushtama. But then Vishvavasu, the king of the demigods [*gandharvas*],
calmed him down by explaining that Indra had wanted to obstruct the
sacrifice because he was afraid that the king would surpass him with the
merits obtained from it. To this end, Indra had seized upon an opportunity when he saw the designated horse and had entered the horse. And

the woman with whom he had made love in that way was actually Rambha, a celestial courtesan. Indra had used his special magic to make the king think that it was his wife, Vapushtama. The king of the demigods persuaded the king that this was what had happened.[23]

Janamejaya was already familiar with shadow sacrifices, nightmare sacrifices. It was he who had performed the surreal sacrifice of snakes instead of horses (to avenge the death of his father, from snakebite) at the beginning of the *Mahabharata*.[24] Here, at the very end of the epic, his sacrifice goes wrong in yet another way: he defies the god implicitly simply by doing the extravagant sacrifice at all, which makes him the object of the god's envy,[25] and then at the end he defies him explicitly, by excluding Indra from the sacrifice because the god has spoiled it by taking the form of the animal. Vedic texts tell us, cryptically, that Indra on one occasion became the *wife* of a man named Vrishanashva[26] (whose name means the "stallion bursting with seed," or "bull-stallion"), which is why one should sacrifice a castrated‡ animal for Indra.[27] In the story of the queen and the sacrificial stallion, Indra becomes the lover of the sacrificer's wife— or does he? Is the demigod telling the truth? His story makes Indra's bedtrick into a double-cross:† while Indra engaged in his bedtrick (substituting for the stallion), a celestial courtesan engaged in another (substituting for the queen). In Norse folklore, the anthropomorphic trickster god Loki masquerades, like Indra and Samjna's husband, as a horse in order to seduce a horse, and like Indra elsewhere, Loki changes gender as well as species: he becomes a mare to distract the stallion Sleipnir, whose master will win Freyia as his wife if he finishes a certain task within the time specified in the contract.[28] (On another occasion, Loki keeps Freyia from leaving the gods by getting Thor to take on the female form of Freyia herself.)[29]

Horses are closely related to birds in many mythologies, which depict both horses and birds as solar and winged animals. The mare maiden is often a Swan Maiden:[30] Urvashi, the Vedic Swan Maiden, is compared to a horse biting in its loveplay.[31] When Zeus becomes a swan to rape Leda, she gives birth not to swans (as one might expect) but to the *equine* twins Castor and Pollux, as well as to Helen, the double woman. This becomes less puzzling in the light of the Sanskrit parallel of the birth of the equine Ashvins to the equine Sun amd Samjna; this equine element from the mother remains, atavistically, even when the father is not a stallion but a swan.

Female swans, too, are bedtricksters, and the Swan Maiden is often regarded as the paradigmatic animal bride.[32] The earliest version of the Swan Maiden myth that I know is the story of Pururavas and Urvashi.‡ Like many Swan Maidens, Urvashi (who is an *apsaras*, a celestial water nymph and courtesan) leaves her human husband when he violates his promise to her, but she does not, strictly speaking, masquerade; Pururavas always knows that she is a bird woman.[33] Yet on one occasion she does masquerade—as a male charioteer.[34]

The story of Urvashi survives in transformation in a story that is very much a bedtrick, the ballet *Swan Lake,* first performed by the Imperial Ballet at the Bolshoi Theatre in Moscow in 1877.[35] This Swan Maiden is not really a swan at all but a princess bewitched into the false form of a swan. The ballet adds a bedtrick, a second masquerade, through the folk motif of the black and white substitute bride:† the white swan, Odette, is impersonated by a black† swan, Odile, who fools the prince, thus condemning Odette to remain forever under the swan spell.[36] The dark side of the hero is revealed at the start by the motif of the fatal error† (in this case a near-fatal error): the prince mistakes the princess for a swan and is about to shoot her when she changes her form. But the ballet whitewashes the hero by transferring from him to the character of Rothbart, the evil magician, the treachery that dooms the swan princess. The treachery of the bedtrick gives the prince an excuse: it was not the prince's fault that he was fooled by the second swan; the evil magician cast a spell so that he could not tell the difference.

In an attempt to eliminate the racism that modern consciousness came to see in the black† swan, a 1986 production by the New York City Ballet (designed by Alain Vaes) dressed all the swans, except for Odette, in black, while a 1989 production directed by Mikhail Baryshnikov dressed all the swans, including Odile, in white.[37] Erik Bruhn's 1967 production for the National Ballet of Canada changed the evil magician into a Black Queen, the alter ego of the Prince's mother.[38] Reversing the genders in a different way, Matthew Bourne's 1995 production for Sadler's Wells made all the swans *male,* arguing, against a long tradition, that swans are intrinsically male, "big, aggressive birds" whose wingspan "is better suggested by male musculature than female" (not to mention the long neck . . .). He also hoped to make sense of the original scenario, which he found "pretty weird—a man falling in love with a bird, then not being able to spot the difference between a white swan and a black one. . . . I just wanted to explain how the story could happen, in a plausible context, without magic spells."[39] It is hard to see how the shift in gender contributes to this euhemeristic† enterprise, nor how it covers the ground of the black/white bedtrick (unless, of course, the male swan were to appear as a female in the second act, in drag or in the closet, as it were . . .). The Ballet Trockadère de Monte Carlo actually put on a hilarious Swan Lake, in drag: casting men but dressing them as female swans.

There already are, of course, male versions of the Swan Maiden myth. We have briefly noted that Zeus/Jupiter took the form of a swan in order to rape Leda, resulting in the birth of Helen.‡[40] The story remains one of the great themes of European art, and like all great themes it continues to take on new meanings. When S. N. Behrman's Alcmena suggests that Leda‡ should substitute for her in Jupiter's bed, she speaks of this role as that of a black swan, assimilating Leda to *Swan Lake*. As with *Swan Lake*, bisexual tricks could be played with this bedtrick: at a "come-as-the-person-you-most-admire" costume party in Hollywood in 1935, the notoriously bisexual Marlene Dietrich went dressed as Leda *and* the Swan.[41]

A famous descendant of Zeus the Swan is the medieval German knight Lohengrin, whose story, told in Wolfram von Eschenbach's *Parzival* and in the later thirteenth-century anonymous German epic called *Lohengrin*, is best known to us in its Wagnerian incarnation. The knight Lohengrin, in disguise, rescues Elsa von Brabant and remains with her as long as she keeps her promise never to ask him his name. She breaks the promise and he departs—riding on his faithful swan (to whom he addresses an aria more passionate than anything he sings to Elsa: "Mein lieber Schwann"). This is a theme we know not only from the Swan Maiden Urvashi but from Mélusine‡ and Cupid and Psyche‡ and from the river Ganges' contract with King Shantanu in the *Mahabharata*, which results in the birth of Bhishma:† "Do not ask to know who I am; do not look at me naked; do not shine a light at me; do not, in short, discover that I am Other."[42] As Bram Dijkstra summarizes the story of Lohengrin: "Wagner ultimately dumped Elsa on the trash heap of perfidious wives simply because she dared to ask her husband the simple and perfectly reasonable question, 'Who are you? Where are you from?' That mild sign of insubordination was enough to send Lohengrin packing in disgust over the inability of women to keep their mouths shut."[43] Why are we not surprised to note that the man who violates his contract with the animal bride is usually treated far more sympathetically?

SNAKES AND MERMAIDS

When the (male) demon Adi takes the transitional form of a snake to sneak into Shiva's bedroom and then takes the (female) form of Parvati, who has just been compared to a snake herself, he evokes two complementary myths: the male serpent lover and the female serpent lover. Let us consider them one by one.

The tale of the animal groom usually involves the transformation of one actor into another; it becomes a bedtrick when the snake imitates the victim's spouse. More specifically, this story overlaps with the pattern of bedtricks by gods who take the form of husbands, like Indra with Ahalya.‡ The mother of the emperor Octavian claimed that Apollo had taken the form of a snake and impregnated her (with Octavian) in her sleep; similarly, the priest Nektanebos‡ took the form of Apollo to impregnate Alexander's mother, and then, when her husband, Philip† of Macedon, accused her of adultery, Nektanebos took the form of a snake who rested his head in her hand, coiled down to her knees, put out his forked tongue, and kissed her to demonstrate his love for the benefit of the onlookers.[44]

Indian folklore abounds in male serpents who play bedtricks; the story is often told by women in the course of rituals to honor snakes. A very early version of the story, called "The Girl Who Married a Snake," appears in the Sanskrit *Pancatantra*, a collection of fables recorded in about the sixth century, from much earlier sources:[45] a girl marries a snake, who turns into a human husband. In the following contemporary Kannada retelling by a woman, the snake masquerades not as *a* husband but as *the* husband, so that there are two of them:

THE SERPENT LOVER

There was a newly wedded woman named Kamakshi whose husband never slept with her; he spent every night with his mistress, a courtesan, and returned to his wife only to eat, in silence, the food that she prepared for him. She made a magic potion to win his love but then threw it away in fear that it might kill him; a snake in the garden drank it and fell in love with her. He entered the house. When she peeped at him through the chink in the bedroom door, the man outside looked like her husband. When she talked to him, he talked exactly like her husband. She took him in without asking too many questions and he made her very happy that night. He came to her night after night, and in a few days she was pregnant.

When the snake came to know of it, he wanted to tell her the truth. He said, "Kamakshi, who do you think I am? Your husband? No, I'm the king of snakes. I fell in love with you and came to you in the shape of your husband." Then he shed her husband's form and became a five-headed cobra. She was terrified and shut her eyes. He changed back into her husband's form again and said, "You know now I'm the king of snakes." When her husband discovered her pregnancy, he accused her of adultery, since he knew that he himself had not slept with her. But the cobra helped her to prove her chastity through an act of truth: handling a deadly cobra. She put out her hand and took the cobra, who was no other than her lover, the king of snakes. He hung around her neck like a garland, opened all his five hoods, and swayed gently. She was exonerated.

After several months, she gave birth to a son. Her husband began to be attentive to her and to make love to her; the mistress was spurned by the husband; and the wife, with the help of the serpent lover, tricked the mistress into becoming her servant (carrying water for her). Her husband gave up the concubine's company, favored his wife in all things, and was supremely happy with her.

In the happiness of regaining her husband, Kamakshi forgot the king of snakes. She was wholly absorbed in her husband and son now. One night, the king of snakes came to see how Kamakshi was doing. He saw her lying next to her husband and child, fast asleep, contentment written on her face. He couldn't bear this change: he twisted himself into Kamakshi's loose hair, which hung down from the edge of the cot, and hanged himself by it.

She said to her husband, "This is no ordinary snake. I had made offerings to him to get my husband back. It's because of him you're with me now. He's like a father to my son. A snake is like a Brahmin, twice-born. Therefore, we should have proper funeral rites done for this good snake and our son should do it." The husband agreed, and the son performed all the proper funeral rites, as a son should for a father. Kamakshi felt she had repaid a debt and lived happily with her husband and son.[46]

The story begins with the purely human problem that we considered in chapter 1: the man has two women, one to be his official woman and to nourish him, the other to be his sexual partner. The wife wishes to be both to him; indeed, she cannot fulfill even her most important official role, to give him a son, unless she can find a way to make him engage her in the other role of sexual partner.[47] When she takes measures to achieve this reintegration of herself, however, to double herself as a mistress as well as a wife, she fails and succeeds instead only in doubling *him*—or, rather, in splitting him: one half of him is the phallic snake, a purely erotic partner and nothing else to her. (The snake lover is a kissing cousin of the frog prince of European folklore, who, in return for some service—usually fetching something precious that the princess has lost under water—demands that the princess let him eat beside her and sleep beside her and, finally, that she kiss him, whereupon he turns into a handsome prince. The frog prince may, like the snake lover, function like a phallus: it begins small and shriveled, little and ugly, and then, when the princess kisses† it, VA-VOOOM! Prince Penis!)[48]

The myth raises questions in our mind that the author does not address directly. Does the wife know the difference? Is she faking? She does not seem to see through the illusion—or perhaps she does see but pretends not to, indulging in false ignorance:† "She took him in without asking too many questions and he made her very happy that night." This text short-circuits this question, which occupies so much space in so many other variants, and moves quickly on. She certainly knows the difference when he *tells* her who he is; and after that she does not sleep with him anymore. In Girish Karnad's play based on this story, *Naga-Mandala: Play with a Cobra,* the snake in his cobra manifestation during the day is attacked by a mongoose; when he comes to her that night in his human form, he is covered with scars,† inescapable proof that he is not in fact her husband. From then on, the woman sees that "her husband" has no scars by day but has scars by night. Still she persists in convincing herself that she is not committing adultery.

We may also ask what the husband thinks after the ordeal "proves" that his wife had not committed adultery (in images strikingly similar to the ordeal that exonerates the mother of Alexander). That she is a goddess? That he himself slept with her without knowing it? The folktale does not care to tell us about that, but it tells us other things about his feelings: he starts to love his wife because she has given him a son, who is her source of power over him. But the existence of this son also shatters the magical fantasy episode, for the son must be the son of her husband, not the son of her lover. In order that this may be so, the fantasy lover must vanish; first he ceases to be her lover, and then he dies. (Here we may note in passing yet another double standard:† the story begins by assuming that the husband may have a mistress and the wife may not have a lover; yet in the end both of them give up their paramours.)

At midpoint, it would seem that the woman is once again reduced to one half of the possibly integrated woman: all maternal and not at all erotic. But the story finds its way to a happy ending within the realm of the purely realistic. The *real* mistress vanishes, not magically, like the snake lover, but in the degradation of class;† and both the wife and the husband are integrated at last. A. K. Ramanujan points out that the wife gets everything she wants—a husband, a passionate fantasy lover, a child: "Even her conscience is clear because her lover is a double, a lookalike of her lawfully wedded husband, and conveniently kills himself in the end."[49] Indeed, the happy ending is made possible only through the continuous intervention of a magical helper for whom the story ends in tragedy. The sloughing of the skin is here compared to the transformation of a Brahmin, who becomes "twice-born" at his initiation, when he sloughs the skin of his former self and is reborn as an adult male. But though the snake's regenerative powers are explicitly mentioned in the woman's pun on the sloughed skin, he dies, bequeathing children and the rebirth of her marriage to the woman.

The word for cobra, *naga,* also designates a mythical creature who is a cobra from the waist down and anthropomorphic from the waist up. The female of the species, the Nagini, brings sexual pleasure, hidden treasure, valiant sons, and, occasionally, death to her human male paramours.[50] A close parallel to the Nagini in French folklore, the paradigmatic French animal bride, is the snake maiden named Mélusine,‡ who appears to be a beautiful maiden but demands to be left alone on Saturdays; one day her husband discovers her in her bath, "her lower extremities changed into the tail of a monstrous fish or serpent." She kisses him and embraces him for the last time, then disappears, leaving behind her the impression of her foot on the stone and a ghostly form that returns at night to nurse at her breast the two babies she had left behind, the usual twins.[51] Her present absence is also captured in her footprint,‡ a particularly poignant symbol of a snake woman who, like the closely related mermaid,‡ has no feet until she marries the mortal who will betray her. When Mélusine is seen naked, she is also seen for the first time as an animal, and the revelation and/or mockery of her animal nature is what triggers the catastrophic end to the relationship.[52]

Another European cousin of the female snake lover is the mermaid, an aquatic creature who also has much in common with snakes, including the tendency to be joined to the human at the hip. In form, therefore, the mermaid is like a Nagini; but in function she is more like another aquatic Indian female, the *apsaras,* the seductive celestial water nymph and courtesan, such as Rambha,† Urvashi,† and Varuthini.† (Stella Kramrisch even calls an *apsaras* a "celestial mermaid.")[53] The mermaid's story is best known in our day from Hans Christian Andersen's story "The Little Mermaid,"‡ about a mermaid who sacrifices her voice† and suffers excruciating pain in order to exchange her tail for the sexual fork of two legs, all for the love of a man whose life she has saved and who rejects her for another woman.[54] This is masquerade not *in* sex (where the trick takes place in bed) but *of* sex (where the trick lies in the mermaid's pretense that she is sexually open, cloven‡). It also attracts to itself another bedtrick: the prince, who does not know that the mermaid has saved his life, marries another woman, whom he mistakes for his savior and who looks like the mermaid.

Walt Disney's 1989 film version adds another bedtrick. The prince loves the mermaid expressly for her voice, which she, as usual, sacrifices to get legs for his sake, a Catch-22 bargain reminiscent of O. Henry's "The Gift of the Magi." The witch who gives her the legs uses the voice herself, recycling it, as it were, instead of, presumably, throwing it away like Andersen's wasteful witch. Disney's witch may be the mermaid's mother; she is explicitly the rejected ex-partner of the mermaid's father, and in Disney, what else could that be? If she is, this version of the story is a variant of the tale of the mother who masquerades as her daughter.†

The Disney plot places new emphasis upon the element of recognition. Unlike the villain of Andersen's text, this prince *does* recognize the mermaid, when she gets her voice back, so that he does not betray her but, *au contraire*, is able to kill the witch and achieve the happy ending. (He is also the bearer of the magic kiss,† borrowed perhaps from Snow White's prince; even in the light, all Disney princes do tend to look alike.) Disney also introduces a new character, the mermaid's father, who finally gives the mermaid her legs. If only she had asked him in the beginning, none of this would have happened. How foolish of Andersen not to have thought of that.

THE FATAL ERROR

Animals of various species appear in the mythologies of nonhumanness and otherness. One of Stith Thompson's† motifs is K 1223.1, "Bride leaves goat as substitute in bed (Type 1685)." In Thomas Deloney's *Jack of Newbury* (1597), a would-be bedtrickster is double-crossed† when he finds himself in bed with a drugged sow placed there by the husband of the woman he intended to seduce. In *My Little Chickadee* (1940), Mae West† puts a goat, horns and all, into the bed in her place while W. C. Fields is engaging in his precoital toilette. She turns down the light and tells him she's going to surprise him. He gets into the bed and exclaims with surprise that she is still wearing her fur coat and indeed suggests that it has been a while since she's had it cleaned. Finally, he pulls off the covers and discovers the truth.

Just as there are generic ways of telling a god from a human,‡ so there are traditional ways of recognizing a demonic or magical animal in human form. The Japanese fox-masquerader is not hard to spot:

> A fox took the shape of the consort of the Lord of Shikoku, and the latter found to his unbounded astonishment two women sitting in his house, who were exactly alike and who both pretended to be his real wife. A physician believed that it was the so-called "soul-separating" illness, which causes one woman to become two. . . . As [the husband] saw that one of them ate quite different food from the ordinary, he examined that one by torture, whereupon she became a fox.[55]

The "soul-separating" illness is the Japanese explanation of a phenomenon of splitting‡ that is explained quite differently in the European and Indian parallels. It is detected here by a combination of the usual fictional clues of food† and behavior† and the more realistic and political† method of torture.

The story of the animal lover will be told differently depending upon whether the bedtrickster is an animal pretending to be human or a human bewitched into an animal form and depending upon whether the bedtrickster is happy or unhappy about being translated to a different world. For these stories present two sides of the single truth that a human being is really an animal; when the story ends, and the masquerade is over, either there is a human or there is an animal. It does matter.

When the seal folk, or silkies, for instance, are conceived of as originally humans, they are usually unhappy as seals: the woman in the sealskin coat may be a deviant mortal whose longing for the sea is a betrayal of her human husband; a mortal "whose longing for the sea speaks to an aberration that must be remedied"; a human transformed into a seal by falling under a spell, so that "the pleasures of the supernatural realm do not compensate for the loss of her soul";[56] or a human undergoing punishment for having committed a sin.[57] When the silkies are conceived of as originally animals, on the other hand, they are usually unhappy as humans: the seal maiden's stay on earth may involve infidelity to her seal lover, and her human existence may deprive her of what she needs to be happy. Her human husband violates her essential being by forcing her to stay in his world.[58] But sometimes, like Mélusine and other demonic aquatic women, the seals are happy to masquerade as humans: they may be seductive demons capable of assuming human shape to tempt a mortal being into their realm‡ or otherworldly beings who seek "some infusion of the real world into what would otherwise be a sterile existence."[59]

These myths argue that we often mistake animals for people, and the reverse, in sexual (or quasi-sexual) situations. They also imply that people become animals, and therefore in a sense unrecognizable, in their sexuality, in the sexual act that Shakespeare's Iago† imagined as a "beast with two backs" (*Othello* 1.1) The ultimate result of this conflation is that human hunters often mistake other humans for animals, particularly when they are mating—a mistake that has fatal consequences not only for the animals but for the unlucky hunter. In the *Mahabharata*,† Pandu, the father of the Pandavas, is cursed to die in the embrace of his own wife because he mistook a sage for a stag when the sage was mating with his wife (they had taken the form of a stag and a doe to do this) and killed him.[60] This pattern extends to other related Hindu stories: the warrior Karna† kills a young calf by mistake (presumably mistaking it for a wild animal) and is cursed to fail in a crucial battle;[61] a hunter kills mating curlews and inspires a grief-stricken observer to invent a poetic meter;[62] Rama's father mistakes a boy for an elephant and is cursed to lose his own son.[63] These stories form a corpus that links a chain of themes: succumbing to the lust for hunting, mistaking a human for an animal and killing the "animal," interrupting the sexual act (by killing one or both of the partners), and creating a poetic language.

Another telling tale in the *Ramayana* ties together the themes of separation from a spouse, the deadly nature of erotic love, and the language of birds:

> The father of Kaikeyi, Rama's evil stepmother, had been given the boon of understanding the cries of all creatures, but he was warned that he must not tell anyone about it. Once when he was in bed with his wife, he heard a bird[64] say something funny and he laughed. She thought he was laughing at her, and she wanted to know why, but he said he would die if he told her. When she insisted that he tell her nevertheless, he sent her away and lived happily without her for the rest of his life.[65]

As an indirect result of his unusual ability to comprehend the language of birds, Kaikeyi's father was forced to become separated from his wife, who would have killed him, just as Dasharatha was cursed to become separated from his son Rama, Rama was cursed to become separated from his wife Sita, and Pandu was cursed to die if he made love to his wife. Kaikeyi herself, however, is the paradigmatic evil co-wife, who uses sexual politics to force Dasharatha to disinherit Rama, an act that is regarded as directly responsible for Dasharatha's death. She resembles the unfaithful women in folktales who are exposed by parrots who tell the truth about them. In a broader sense, all hypersexualized women are represented as talking animals.

There are logical links between, on the one hand, killing a human (who has human speech) whom you mistake for an animal (which lacks human speech) or who has become an animal (to express the bestial sexual impulse) and, on the other hand, becoming a human who has a uniquely poetic language; between, on the one hand, sexual substitution (the animal acting as the surrogate for the human, particularly in the sexual act, regarded as an animal act) and, on the other hand, the creation of speech, which distinguishes humans from animals. Ovid, writing at the turn of the common era in Rome, tells a story that elaborates on these themes:

CEPHALUS, PROCRIS, AND AURA

Procris would have preferred her husband, Cephalus, to Jove, and he would not have been tempted by Venus. Just two months after Procris and Cephalus had married, Aurora, the dawn, fell in love with Cephalus as he was out hunting. She carried him away with her, but when he kept protesting that he loved Procris, the furious goddess let him go, warning him that he would live to regret his loyalty to his wife.

As Cephalus went home, Aurora's warning made him begin to fear that Procris had been unfaithful to him, especially since he himself had stayed with a notorious goddess. Aurora egged him on and changed his face; unrecognized, he tried to seduce Procris to test her. At first she resisted, but his offers of wealth made her begin to waver; then he revealed himself, insisting that he himself was not a real adulterer, but that he had seen, with his own eyes, her faithlessness. Ashamed, Procris left him, but when he begged for pardon and acknowledged that he was the one who had sinned, she came back to him.

One day, Procris began to suspect Cephalus of infidelity, for she followed him when he went out hunting again, and when he called out to the breeze, "Aura," she thought he was calling a woman. He heard a sound that he thought had been made by the movement of an animal, threw his javelin, and hit Procris, who clutched her wounded breast and cried out. Cephalus recognized the voice of his own faithful wife. As she died she said, "I beg you: do not let Aura take my place as your wife in our wedding bed."[66]

The trouble begins when Cephalus attempts to get his wife to commit adultery with him,† to test her—always a dubious proposition. Procris, who mistakes her husband for another man on this occasion, later mistakes the word for breeze *(aura)* for a nymph, mistakes a name† for a thing; or perhaps she mistakes Aura for the goddess Aurora, who really did try to seduce Procris and whose curse upon him is fulfilled in this episode. In the culmination of all of these sins and curses, Procris herself is mistaken for an animal, a beast that has no words; too late, her husband recognizes her by her voice.† The two errors fatally intersect, and her faithful husband, who had previously doubted her fidelity, now (accidentally) kills her for her lack of faith in his fidelity.

ANIMAL HUSBANDRY AND ANIMAL BRIDES

It is useful to distinguish stories about animal brides from those about animal grooms, for men and women have different sorts of animal lovers and become different sorts of animal lovers. The confusion between them was reflected in a *Newsweek* article that quoted Senator Al D'Amato announcing his engagement to Claudia Cohen: "I feel like the frog who has been kissed by the princess. Claudia is my Cinderella." *Newsweek* remarked, "You know it's love when a politician can't keep his fairy tales straight."[67] In fact he had, like many storytellers, straightened them out to his liking, producing a conflated story of an animal groom (frog) joined by a magic kiss† to an animal bride (Cinderella in her catskin or donkeyskin).

Some of these stories seem to imply that the woman tends to be an animal and must be forced, by her husband and family, to be a human. As Barbara Fass Leavy puts it: "The woman may prefer the beast to the prince, prefer, that is, debased nature as she resists the restraints of civilization: it is then *she* who is the animal, her beast paramour virtually an extension or projection of herself." "Women will almost invariably kiss frog princes, whereas a noteworthy number of men cannot kiss the frog princess."[68] Marina Warner sees the animal metamorphosis as a source of liberty and empowerment for women: "The animal disguise of the heroine equips her to enter a new territory of choice and speech; the apparent degradation works for her, not against her. Being a beast . . . can be preferable as a temporary measure to the constrictions of a woman's shape."[69] (Cross-dressing† in men's clothing often achieves the same ends.)

But the animal skin that the woman wears also symbolizes the very sexuality that she is fleeing, for this is a two-way stretch of the imagination: "The wronged and runaway daughters wear the pelts of beasts, coats of rushes, and other 'natural' disguises because they have been violated, by their father's assault or by another's, and it has contaminated them, exiled them. Although they have suffered wrong in all innocence in the fairy tales, they accept the taint and enact it on their own persons."[70] The paradox that emerges from this corpus is: the woman in the animal skin is simultaneously more sexual and less sexual than the man who pursues her. Samjna becomes a mare to flee either her husband's excessive sexuality or her own.

A vivid Jewish tale of a woman whose sexuality took the form of a beast was recorded in Egypt in this century. It tells of a prediction that a certain young man would be devoured by a beast on his wedding night. His parents, with misgivings, allowed him to marry and tried to protect him by having the marriage take place on a small island, uninhabited by man or beast. Then he saw his bride:

> She was astonishingly beautiful, with raven hair that reached to her waist . . . fine, slender fingers and long nails. He smiled shyly at her, but she seemed afraid to lift her eyes from the floor. When at last she did, the young man was astonished to see a look of wild desire in them unlike anything he had ever seen. When he stepped forward to embrace her, he heard a low growl. The young man looked around in confusion, wondering where it could have come from. He turned back just in time to see the fangs of the beast as it leaped at him from the very place his bride had been.[71]

Nothing of the animal's form is actually described; what astonishes and confuses the young man is the "look of desire" that he defines as wild.

A single story about an animal bride or groom may carry different messages for men and for women. From the woman's point of view, as Germaine Greer noted, tales of the Swan Maiden may be fantasies of escape from the dreariness of earthly married life,[72] but they may also reflect a man's memory of his painful separation from his mother and his fear that his wife, too, will leave him.† The frog prince also carries different messages for men and for women (and for different male scholars). Bruno Bettelheim regarded the frog prince genre as an expression of repressed† *female* sexuality and argued that the animal groom stories tell us "that it is mainly the female who needs to change her attitude about sex."[73] But since the heroine often prefers the beast in his *un*transformed form, the story seems to argue less that the woman must overcome her sexual repression† than that, on the contrary, she likes sex and her animal mate too much. Moreover, Stuart Blackburn challenges Bettelheim and argues that the Indian turtle tales express not female but *male* anxieties about adulthood and married life.[74]

Bettelheim also argued that the alternation of human by day, animal by night,† expresses female sexual fears, while tales in which the animal form appears during the day are a projection† of the woman's inability to face reality on the morning after (the very essence of the fantasy of the bedtrick†): "What seemed lovely by night," he writes, "looks different by day."[75] And he accounts for the male perspective when he hypothesizes that the animal husband's nocturnal bestial form represents a man's wish to keep his sex life separate from everyday life.[76] But Blackburn has argued for the need to interpret the other arrangement—"animal by day, husband by night"—from the man's point of view, too:

> It remains curious that the non-sexual identity is the animal form. (Is the man, too, overcome by morning-after guilt and denial?) A separation between sexual and ordinary experience exists in our tales, too, but it is maintained neither by a masculine need to isolate sex nor by a female fear of sex. Rather, I believe, the "turtle by day, prince by night" pattern of our tales reflects a male fear of sexuality, at home, and a male wish fulfillment, outside the home. The distinction to be made, then, is not day/night, but internal/external, the domestic versus the public.[77]

This is in harmony with Ramanujan's interpretation of the snake lover story as a tale of two realms, private and public.[78]

The animal skin taken on as punishment becomes the skin of the scapegoat, the beast who bears away, and at the same time bears, human sin. But the sloughing or burning of the Swan Maiden's feathers or the turtle groom's shell represents the moment when the animal trickster loses the original self, perhaps the true self, and becomes the mask; it is the moment when the masquerader is caught in the masquerade and can't go back again. This happens to human tricksters, too, not just to animals.

Night and Day

These stories often turn upon the contrast between day and night. The myth of Samjna‡ is about sunlight and shadow; a caste that still worships

Samjna, under the name of Randhal-ma, explains her double form by saying that there is one of her for the night and one for the day.[79] Max Müller, who was obsessed with solar myths, not surprisingly saw Psyche as "the Dawn with its sweet breath" and Cupid as "the Sun, who leaves her and plunges beneath the sea. Through the weary hours of the night she seeks him, to be reunited with him at last."[80] In Apuleius's tale, Psyche cannot bear the anonymity of making love in pitch darkness and brings a lamp to make night into day; when at last she has won him back, she has joined together the pleasures of the night and the pleasures of the day.

"My night is your day," says the Beast in Jean Cocteau's film *Beauty and the Beast* (1946). The Hindu queen Cudala,‡ gifted with magic yogic powers, was transformed into a woman by night and a man by day; the serpent lover allows the woman to experience her husband as an intimate lover by night and a distant partner by day. In a Turkish narrative, a horse's masquerade links the bride's delights to a rich fantasy life in which she has the best of both worlds: in the daytime, she has a horse for a husband and a stable for a dwelling; by night the stable is transformed into a rose garden and the horse into a handsome youth.[81]

Often the forms are distributed as in Stith Thompson's† motif B 640.1: "Marriage to beast by day, man by night." This is the pattern of Beauty and the Beast, Cupid and Psyche, the snake lover in India, and the fox woman in Japan: by day a beast, by night a handsome prince or desirable woman. The reverse also occurs, however, where the lover appears as a human by day, an animal at night, as in Shakespeare's *Midsummer Night's Dream,* when the magic of the dream and the night and the moonlight gives Bottom the Weaver the head of an ass and bewitches Titania into believing that he is a handsome suitor; in the light of day, Bottom becomes a weaver again, and both he and Titania have only a dim memory of his animal form. When the play employs double casting, with the same actress playing Titania and Hippolyta, the final scene can allude to a quadruple bedtrick: by daylight, Hippolyta sees through her own night-form as Titania and through the fictional character of Pyramus as played by Bottom to recognize her night-companion, the Ass.

Vampires, night creatures, are like Bottom in this, as Nina Auerbach has remarked: "The vampire comes to life under the same moon that gives Bottom an animal's head so that he can have intercourse with a fairy; it unites disparate orders of being."[82] And werewolves assume their original animal form by night, while by day the wolf climbs into bed and pretends to be Red Riding Hood's granny. (The bed, by the way, alerts us to a submerged bedtrick; in some of the older tellings, Red Riding Hood eats her grandmother and climbs into bed with the wolf.)[83]

Sometimes the victim of the animal masquerade can choose which form s/he wants by day and which by night. In a French tale, the snake† reassures the woman that he can become a man when he chooses and asks when she prefers him to do so, by day or by night; his wife replies that she prefers him to be a man at night, for she would be less afraid to have a beast near her by day than by night.[84] In American folklore, the bride of Whitebear Whittington, a human under a spell to become a bear, responds similarly to his proposition:

> "Now I got a spell on me and I can't be a man but part of the time. From now on I can be a man of a night and stay with you here and be a bear of a day, or I can be a bear of a night and sleep under your bed and be a man of a day. Which had you rather I'd be?"
>
> So she thought about it and she didn't like the idea of a bear layin' under her bed of a night so she told him she'd rather he'd be a man of a night. So that was the way it was. He was a bear in the daytime and he'd lie around outside while she kept house, and when dark came he'd be a man.[85]

Here the nightly form is the original form, as well as the chosen form, the private form.

The alternation between night and day cannot be simply mapped onto other alternations in this corpus, such as the tension between the original and the masquerading form or the male and female forms. In many myths, the original form is the one that appears at night—an assertion of the authenticity of what is hidden, the time of dreaming, over what is apparent, the time of the workaday world. Night is when most people make love, and this variant of the myth asserts its view of sex as truth.† In this genre, the original, nightly form may be human (when a man or woman has been bewitched into becoming a beast, like Cupid or Mélusine) or animal (as in the case of the witchwomen who reveal their true nature as horses at night). The pattern of diurnal women and nocturnal animals (as well as the contrast between culture and nature) is expressed in an Oriya proverb about women: "Beautiful as a picture by day; a cobra-woman by night."[86] But sometimes the daytime form may be the original form, hence perhaps the authentic form, as is the case with the original animal forms of the snake lover in India and the fox woman in Japan.

And, as we have seen, men and women are differently represented in the contrasts between animal/human, day/night, and original/false.

The Kannada story of the snake lover may reflect an imaginative version of the actual situation that prevails in traditional Hindu marriages: custom prevents the husband from expressing any affection for his wife in public, so that he may well be one man to her by day (cold and indifferent) and another by night (warm and loving). "At night, in the privacy of the bedroom, or at least in the dark, the husband may change into an amorous and passionate lover."[87] For the wives of other animal lovers, however, the story may express the experience of a woman married to a man who is a pillar of the community by day but gets drunk (or sexually lit) every night and turns into an abusive beast who beats her up, or to a rich old man who buys her presents in the day but condemns her to the horrors of his bed at night. Thus, the tales of animal lovers raise complex issues of intimacy, sexuality, and authority.

The images of female animal by day and male animal by night are conflated in *Ladyhawke* (1985), said (by the filmmakers) to be "based on a 13th-century European legend," in which a wicked bishop, spurned by a beautiful lady, makes a pact with the devil and curses her and her lover so that she becomes a hawk every day and he a wolf every night. "Only the anguish of a split second at sunrise and sunset when they can almost touch, but not. Always together, eternally apart. As long as the sun rises and sets; as long as there is day and night. And for as long as they both shall live." They are able to break the curse by appearing together in their human forms "when there is a day without night, a night without day"— a solar eclipse. When they ride off into the sunset, the cliché† Hollywood finale takes on new meaning: at last the hero and heroine are able to bear the dangerous, liminal moment that separates the human from the animal.

The meanings, the angles of vision, can change in the chiaroscuro of these extreme day/night, animal/human juxtapositions. The central questions remain: What is animal? What is human? Where (if anywhere) is the line between them? Is sex most deeply human or most deeply animal? Where on the continuum between human and animal do we locate our longings and fears? How do different cultures, classes, genres, periods, valorize some possibilities and constrain others?[88]

There is an hour of twilight that the French call *entre chien et loup*, "between dog and wolf." This is the charged moment in which these transformations take place, for the transitional, marginal, liminal animal transgresses the boundary between nature and culture: the wild wolf turns into the domesticated dog, not at every dawn but through the long day of human history. Stepping outside the text for a moment, we may see that day and night may also serve as analogies for the worlds of life and fiction,† as Elaine Showalter has argued: "The double life of the day and the night is also the double life of the writer, the split between reality and the imagination."[89] Or, as I would put it, the twilight of the animal lover is the twilight of the myth.

Approach Three

Zoology

The Cuckoo's Nest: Sexually Deceptive Animals

Our myths and rituals represent as masquerades our relationships with animals: in rituals, humans often literally wear the masks of animals, and animals stand in symbolically for human victims, while in myths we imagine that animals masquerade as humans and humans as animals. Since ancient mythmakers often lived closely with animals and could see how they behaved, they used animals consciously as natural metaphors to express their ideas about human and divine sexuality and masquerade ("All cats are gray"†), and by looking at the animals in myths we can learn something about those ideas.

The depiction of relationships of masquerading bestiality (as in Beauty and the Beast†) may be seen as a dream of intimacy with animals, like the widespread mythologies of talking animals, or as a nightmare of incest, with the animal masking a desire for parent or sibling.[90] Some animals symbolize a particular form of sexual deception. The word "cuckold"† comes from "cuckoo," by the obvious analogy (the cuckoo lays her eggs in the nests of other birds), though with an interesting switch of gender: the (female) cuckoo's eggs and the (male) cuckolder's sperm masquerade as those of another (female) bird or (male) human. Thus, in the *Nibelungenlied,* when Hagen hears Siegfried accused of sleeping (through a bedtrick) with Gunther's wife, Brunhilde, he says, "Are we to rear cuckoos?"[91] which seems to imply that Siegfried has laid his eggs in Gunther's nest.[92] In comparison with human males, who are obsessed with their offspring's resemblance† to them, the female birds who foster cuckoos do not seem to recognize their young or distinguish them from other birds: all that they recognize is the nest (a bourgeois habit) and the generic gaping maws of the small intruders.

In addition to seeing animals through the mythmakers' metaphors, we can also look at animals ourselves, noting aspects of their behavior that the mythmakers may have been unaware of; and we can make our own, different mythological judgments about our own animal natures. Moreover, myths may express the animal parts of ourselves, the parts that our bodies† remember and that our minds—our superegos, formalized by society—may suppress in open discourse and express in myths only in a censored transformation. This realization, along with a knowledge of animal mating habits, especially camouflaging and masquerading mating habits, may help us to understand some of the unconscious levels of symbolism in the myths.

Sexual deceptions by animals begin on the microbiological level. The immunological work of Roald Hoffmann, a Nobel Prize–winning chemist, takes the sexual masquerade to the level of DNA itself. (Significantly, another of Hoffmann's books is called *The Same and Not the Same*.) Working with Shira Leibowitz, Hoffmann first likens the strategy of drug design to the Trojan horse (a classic image of the fatally seductive mare†) and then goes on to describe how a drug fools the disease into thinking that it, the drug, is actually the body on which the disease wishes to feed: "It turns traitor and it effectively stops further DNA synthesis."[93] Hoffmann and Leibowitz then turn to the metaphor of two bedtrickster sisters, Rachel† and Leah, suggesting that the NK (natural killer) cells might be renamed NL (natural lover) cells.[94] "How much more appealing to deal with L cells (after Leah) which mimic R cells (Rachel cells), snuggling up to the unsuspecting bacteria. Immunological terror can be turned into erotic trysts, and battles into orgies. As Laban set up his daughter for his duplicity, so drug designers craft molecules that deceive. . . . Could it be that the appropriate metaphor for the drug designer is not that of a general, but a playwright? Or a matchmaker, in a game of elective affinities?"[95] If Goethe's *Elective Affinities* (in which each of the two original partners fantasizes about a different person) is to provide the model for the matchmaker, rather than Rachel and Leah, it is a matter of substituting a fantasy lover for a real lover—indeed, two fantasy lovers†—precisely what the drug in question must do.

As for animals that we can see without microscopes, our anthropocentrism drives us to use as the key to our own ability to tell animals apart the animals' ability to tell one another apart in the defining situation of reality,† sex: if two animals will not mate, we say they are of different species.[96] Midas Dekkers expresses a toad's options in the form of a syllogism:† "If a male [toad] sees something moving, there are three possibilities: if it is larger than I am, I run away from it, if it is smaller, I eat it, and if it is the same size, I mate with it. If the creature with which it is mating does not protest, then it is probably the right species and the right sex."[97] We all know men like that toad, and not every frog turns into a prince when you kiss him.

How *do* toads (or cats†) tell one another apart in the dark? And do we care? It is particularly important for animals to recognize one another's mating signals, for sex is the one breach in the nigh impenetrable wall of their xenophobia, the one moment when they allow a strange animal to get close to them. Only in sexual matters, then, do they have to tell the difference: "In nature, red in tooth and claw, every other animal is a potential danger. Even creatures that live in herds, swarms or packs usually keep some distance from each other. At mating time, however, that distance can be reduced to zero. For this there are all kinds of rituals, which in the case of human beings have resulted in the discotheque and in the case of animals in display, sniffing, spawning and chorusing."[98] Here we may recall the elaborate rituals that Nala and Damayanti and Odysseus and Penelope impose upon one another before they are willing to recognize one another as true mates.‡ Among animals, these are often referred to as "sexual strategies."[99] Given the quantity of stories in which bedtricks lead to death, not to mention the wider corpus of lethal love, fatal instincts, fatal errors, poison damsels, *Liebestods,* and other sex-linked murders, our human protagonists are just as vulnerable as other animals, though apparently not nearly as careful.

For an animal, a bedtrick is a very serious matter indeed, as Dekkers notes: "In order to prevent the male's semen entering the wrong female or the female having semen foisted on her which will be rejected by the eggs inside her, each partner closely monitors the other's identity. From the trills in their song, from that specific smell of urine, from that wonderful look which occurs in no other courting repertoire, the owner of the semen and the owner of the eggs conclude that their semen and their eggs will shortly be compatible and grow into new male and female owners. Everything else is capriciously rejected."[100] Animals can tell the difference in the dark: while visual clues may play an important role in the initial courtship, smell† and a baroque complex of other clues are essential to an animal's decision to lower its defenses in order to mate.

Despite these clues, however, the criterion of instinctual sexual response is far from watertight as a mechanism for mating only with animals of one's own species, for animals often trick one another in the course of the mating game. It is sobering to realize that even insects can undergo face-lifts (grasshoppers impersonating branches, moths with false eyes† on their wings, and so forth) and that they are quite successful in cross-species masquerading: "Females of [a] species [*Photuris pennsylvanica*] of firefly accurately imitate the light code of the smaller *Photinus scintillans;* exactly one second after two short flashes they give a flash of exactly the correct strength and duration. Eager to mate, the males head for the light source, whereupon they are seized and devoured by the despicable Lore-lei."[101] Even mammals occasionally sink to such low tricks, though in a more playful key: "a dolphin was put in the same tank as a sea-lion. Both were males. At a certain moment the dolphin began playfully imitating the sea-lion, until the latter became so confused that it tried to mate with the dolphin. The dolphin did not welcome the advances, and a few bites returned the sea-lion to the real world."[102]

Sometimes the problem consists in distinguishing, not between two females of two different species, but between a male and a female of the same species (the *M. Butterfly*† scenario). Where the cuckoo fakes its species, other animals fake their gender. One of the great piscine gender-benders is the fish known as the "sneaker":

THE BLUEGILL AND THE SNEAKER

It is noteworthy that in certain conventional male-and-female species, members of one sex may turn such coordination to their advantage by imitating members of the opposite sex. Such activity may be thought of as another nongenetic form of sexual differentiation.

The bluegill sunfish engages in an intriguing form of such gender bend-ing. . . . Male bluegill sunfish exist in three different forms. Large, colorful males court females and defend their territories. A second kind of male—often known as a "sneaker"—becomes sexually mature at a much younger age and smaller size. These small males live on the periphery of a big-ger male's territory and clandestinely mate with females while the domi-nant male is otherwise occupied. Sneaker males mature into a third kind of male, one that assumes the behavior and drab coloration of a female sunfish. These female mimics intervene between a territorial male and the female he is courting. The female mimic, rather than the courting male, usually ends up fertilizing the eggs.[103]

Apparently the male victim wastes his sperm on the "sneaker" male (the female mimic), who can then fertilize the female with his own sperm.

The bluegill is not unique; nature abounds in such transsexual trick-sters, like the male red-sided garter snakes in the grass:

THE MATING BALL

At times of peak sexual activity, males congregate around females, forming a so-called mating ball. . . . In 16 percent of the balls, the snake being courted by the males was in fact a disguised male, what we call a she-male. She-males have testes that produce normal sperm, and they court and mate with females. But in addition to exhibiting male-typical behav-iors, she-males produce the same attractiveness pheromone as do adult females. In the mating ball, this second source of the pheromone confuses the more prevalent conventional males, giving the she-male a decided mating advantage.[104]

Is the mating ball like the great balls held in Europe where young women came to find their suitors? Where Cinderella met her prince? Do red-sided garter snakes lie about, like Alice in Wonderland, waiting for a frog-footman to bring them "an invitation to the mating ball"? The mind boggles.

Thus, animals are capable of both perpetrating and detecting bedtricks, and they provide both basic metaphors and basic data that can inspire our own bedtricks. We are, moreover, capable of perpetrating bedtricks upon animals. Animals are usually not so concerned to recognize our faces as they are to recogize the faces of their own species, but sometimes they mistake humans (of either sex) for their mates, often through the process of imprinting† made famous by Konrad Lorenz and his duck-lings.[105] Imprinting works like the magic drug that Oberon in *A Midsummer Night's Dream* (2.1) has Puck procure and use on Titania: "The juice of it on sleeping eyelids laid / Will make or man or woman madly dote / Upon the next live creature that it sees." In the case of animals, "the next live creature that it sees" upon emerging from the womb or egg strikes it as a kind of mirror† (like the "mirror" that the mother provides for the identity of a human child in the psychoanalytic,† particularly the La-canian,† paradigm); it thinks it must be like that and, upon sexual maturity, falls prey to narcissism and tries to mate with it. Thus, animals in captivity often try to mate with their keepers: "Sometimes such animals are simply deranged, but mostly it is a case of false imprinting."[106] (Significantly, "parental imprinting"† or "false imprinting" is the term also used to describe the effect upon the embryo of the fantasies† of a woman who imagines a man other than her actual partner at the moment of impregnation: she imprints the embryo with the features of her dream lover.)[107]

Humans have sometimes capitalized upon this false perception in animals. A crane in the Rotterdam Zoo, "completely imprinted on human beings, tried to mate with its vet, but the latter used this exceptional opportunity in order to take sperm from the creature, thus providing the zoo with a large number of young."[108] But usually it happens just by accident: "Occasionally people unintentionally seduce animals with inanimate objects. . . . Local male sword crabs regarded everything in the water, from old boots and bricks to anchors and boats, as females on heat. . . . The old joke about a tortoise falling in love with a German helmet is based on fact."[109] The *Key West Citizen,* December 31, 1995, announced: "Chi Chi the Pig is arrested by Monroe County Animal Control after allegedly sexually assaulting a Harley Davidson motorcycle. The amorous pig caused $100 in damage during the tryst." Animals, too, have their sexual illusions, and for some of them, if they are excited enough, in the dark not only all cats but all objects are gray.

THE (TEASER) MARE'S NEST: "NOT AS GOOD AS STALLIONS"

Konrad Lorenz, one of the great animal-lovers and animal-knowers of this century, once apologized to a woman at a cocktail party for failing to recall her face or her name; but, he added, it was a funny thing: he could remember the faces and names of all of his 458 greylag geese.[110] So, too, Barbara Smuts, who lives and works with gorillas in the wild, can recognize over 450 gorilla faces, far more than the people she knows. And of course the gorillas themselves recognize one another; they know one another as individuals, with idiosyncratic histories.[111] To a gorilla, all gorillas do not look alike in the dark. People notice distinctions between individual instances of what they care about.

The animal matings we care most about are those that involve species in which we ourselves have an investment, such as horses, who are valuable not merely as companions, pets, and partners in film and sport but because breeding and racing are major industries. Horses provide useful metaphors for sexual discrimination (and play a pivotal role in the identity crises of the great horsemen Nala‡ and Amphitryon‡). Carlo Ginzburg suggests that the tracking of footprints† was one of the earliest ways of determining the identity, as well as the health and other characteristics, of an animal being tracked, and he draws an analogy between this process and falling in love (in terms of Freud's† notions of overvaluation and delusion in sexual love):[112] "It was once said that falling in love meant over-valuing the tiny ways in which one woman, or one man, differed from others. This could of course be extended to a work of art or to horses."[113] But this sort of overvaluation could be good, from the Romantic point of view: "The ability to tell an unhealthy horse from the state of its hooves . . . would certainly not be learnt from treatises on the care of horses. . . . [but was] born of experience, of the concrete and individual. . . . One need only think of the gulf separating the rigid and schematic treatises of physiognomy (judging character or mood from the appearance) from its perceptive and flexible practice by a lover or a horse-dealer or a card-player."[114] Horse owners in both ancient India (according to the *Ashvashastra*) and present-day England identify their individual horses by "skin colours and markings and where exactly on the body the hairs of the coat grew in whorls"[115]—like the missing "twist of hair" that enabled Shiva to distinguish the demon Adi† from Parvati.

Husbands are often unable to describe their runaway wives,[116] but they could probably describe their horses; people who care about animals see them as individuals, often at the cost of blindness to the individuality of people. In Joseph Roth's† novel about a Viennese bedtrick, both the victim, the shah of Persia, and the man who orchestrates the bedtrick, Captain Taittinger, find women interchangeable but horses unique. The captain loves only his horse, Pylades, and will ride no other after he is forced to sell Pylades. So, too, the shah falls in love with the supreme Lippizaner stallion: "He kept two thousand eight hundred horses in his stables in Tehran. They were finer and considerably more valuable than the women in his harem. [Then he saw the Lippizaner dance.] In the great harem of the Shah of Persia—so far as he could remember—not one of the women had displayed as much loveliness, dignity, grace, and beauty as that gray Lippizaner. . . . The Shah thought only of the gray."[117] The shah's failure to purchase the gray (owned by the Austrian emperor, whom no one dares to approach on the shah's behalf) precipitates his attempt to purchase Countess W. (ditto Count W.), for whom Captain Taittinger substitutes his own mistress, the prostitute Mizzi. Thus, Mizzi is, in a sense, ultimately a surrogate for the Lippizaner.

Our finely honed ability to discriminate among horses has led, paradoxically, to an equine breeding policy that depends upon our ability to subvert the horses' own ability to discriminate among themselves. Sexual deception is the essence of the surrogate mare used to lure the stallion to the AI (artificial insemination) tube. Before bringing the stallion to the tube, the breeder often teases the stallion with a real mare in heat (often a mare for whom the stallion is known to have a particular affection) and then leads him to the dummy to collect his sperm. (He thought it was Rachel† and it turned out to be Leah. Does he mind? Can he tell the difference?) This procedure has a low-tech precedent: mule breeders used to put a big jack donkey to a mare, but the jack wouldn't respond unless teased with a jenny, a female of his own species. Further complications are introduced by the use of a surrogate on the other side of the fence.

"Teaser" stallions of no particular breeding value are sent to the mare to detect the moment when she comes into heat (her estrous period), at which point she is whisked away from the teaser and shipped over to the designated stallion, the prizewinner who commands the high stud fees. The teaser is thus a kind of stand-in or stunt-stud (a species well known, appropriately, from films about cowboys and horses), of so little value that no one minds if he is damaged by being kicked by a mare who is not in the mood. (She thought it was another man, but it turns out to be her husband.) A related procedure, for milking rather than mating, is so common among breeders of camels as well as horses that the Arabs have a word for a "stuffed camel-hide for deceiving a she-camel when milked."[118]

A kind of double-cross† occurs when a mare, called a "teaser mare," is used as a surrogate for the stallion (the "teaser") who is used as a surrogate for the real stallion. Cows are natural teasers of this sort, through a kind of inversion: when a cow comes into heat, she "bulls," that is, acts like a bull, mounting other cows, which the observant breeder immediately recognizes as a sign that that cow really wants, not to mount, but to be mounted by a bull. But the inversion of the teaser mare is of a different order, as we learn from a relevant article, entitled "Teaser Mares: Not as Good as Stallions," from the newsletter of the Cornell University College of Veterinary Medicine: "Using a mare (one 'androgenized' or given some male characteristics by drug therapy) as a teaser [is a] good idea but, alas, one that doesn't seem to work very well. . . . Androgenized mares are nowhere near as good as real stallions in detecting estrous periods. . . . It is known that the individual characteristics of stallions make some better as teasers than others."[119] Among horses, individual differences matter and can be detected.

But if some of the mares are *too* good at their job, they end up fooling not only the other mares but themselves. For there is yet another twist, the case of "the teaser mare who wound up, in effect, teasing herself": "This androgenized mare actually experienced two estrous periods of normal length—in spite of the hormones given to keep her androgenized. The mare was even observed responding to her own urination and defecation with male-type sexual behavior, including sniffing, flehmen, and the elimination and covering responses." This mare was a surrogate for the stallion (the "teaser") used as a surrogate for the real stallion. (This is the house that the Jack-donkey built.) The mare who became androgynous and fell in love with her own urine is a cousin of Narcissus,† who fell in love with his own reflection. She is the victim of a sexual fantasy—not her own, but her owner's.

The sex lives of mares are now intimately connected with those of women. Premarin, a hormone-replacement drug widely taken by post-menopausal women, is made from the urine of pregnant mares and contains more than twenty horse estrogens, none of which is native to the human body. This prompted Molly Haskell to quip, "How can you tell if you've overdosed on Premarin? Answer: You start craving oats, hay and wide-open spaces and start looking for a stud." She suggested that some women who had "bonded with horses" in their adolescence may have developed horse hormones that would later react with the Premarin to make them "move toward the finish line like some weird female centaur, half beast, half human, galloping into the sunset, another of the modern world's hermaphrodites of nature and technology."[120] The sunset,† indeed: *entre chien et loup,* the right place for a liminal creature like a centaur or a postmenopausal woman.

Is Zoology Destiny?

Zoology therefore teaches us that the ability to deceive sexually and to be deceived sexually is built into the very structures of reproduction, as is the sexual asymmetry† that makes so many of the human masquerades necessary. The biological paradox, embodied in many of our myths, argues that it is biologically advantageous for men to be polygamous (the drive to scatter their genes everywhere, promiscuously) and for women to be monogamous (the drive to concentrate on raising one set of children). Among the many human paradoxes† that the bedtrick addresses is the tension between the male claim that promiscuity is necessary to keep desire fresh and the female claim that a stable relationship is needed to ensure progeny and child rearing. (This asymmetry is often justified in humans by the so-called Coolidge effect, named after the president's well-known banter with his wife: when she called to his attention the frequency with which the rooster mounted the hens, he reminded her that it was a different hen each time.)

Besides the biological differences in the opportunities for women and men to dissemble about such things as pregnancy and erections,† a biological bias underlying the double standard may also contribute to the fact that, in life as well as in our texts, the consequences for men's adultery are so much milder than the consequences for women's adultery. For although many of these stories are about desire, they are also about fertility, which is biological, and inheritance, which is not. Marjorie Garber, after pointing out the cognate meanings of "p/matriarchy," "p/maternal," "p/matricide," and "p/matronymics," calls our attention to the *lack* of literal correspondence between the terms "matrimony" (meaning marriage, "with the implication of impending motherhood") and "patrimony" (meaning inheritance). And she remarks, drily, "It would be naive to ask how these two words, so apparently similar in structure and etymology, came to diverge in meaning."[121] ("Alimony," alas, is not derived from the Latin *alius,* "other," meaning, therefore, "money paid as reparations for sleeping with someone *other* than your spouse"; it is derived from *alere,* "to nourish.") Biology works insidiously within the patterns of the bedtrick mythology. In order to bear children who will have all the advantages of legitimate children, as opposed to the children of the mistress, a wife merely has to bed her husband *periodically* (sometimes only once), until she becomes pregnant. She might prefer not to have her husband gallivanting about impregnating other women, but she can achieve her biological ends, at least, through her husband's intermittent fidelity. On the other hand, for the man to fulfill his wish for legitimate offspring, he must be *perpetually* sure of his wife's fidelity; in some hardheaded sociobiological way, the man cares about his wife's fidelity, virginity, and so forth because he has no other way of guaranteeing that her child is "genuinely" his. As Lorraine Daston has put it, "The men want all or nothing from their wives; the women can afford to be satisfied with something."[122] This gnawing paternal insecurity† is, in part, what impels some husbands to test their wives with bedtricks. Why, then, does she care about his fidelity? She knows damned well that the child is hers. His infidelity, however, jeopardizes not the public identity of the child but the private identity of the mother, to the extent that she defines herself through her husband's fidelity to her.

Biology is not everything; we are animals, but we are not *just* animals. (The fact that many animals eat their young is not usually taken as a paradigm for human behavior.) Biology, moreover, is not a constant. Our ability to regulate pregnancy and childbirth (through the labyrinths of abortion and adoption, and now in vitro fertilization) moves forward constantly, and the mythology of mating shifts in its wake. The revolutionary changes in women's rights to dispose of their children and their property that have taken place in this century will surely effect corresponding (but unpredictable) changes in the mythology of the next millennium. Yet the double standard of biology spreads to the sociology, as well as the psychology, of men and women in our texts. Jealousy,† for instance, transcends biology when culture constrains it, and although jealousy is asymmetrical for the two genders in some ways, it is symmetrical in others. Nervous husbands are tormented, just like their wives, by the sexual jealousy that stems from desire and the need for a sexual mirror of identity. Some tomcats kill their own kittens in order to have sexual access to the mother cat, who will not mate while she is nursing her young; at such moments, even for an animal, desire outranks biological survival. Both men and women care about sexual fidelity for reasons of both biological lineage ("if I do not know who my sexual partner is, I do not know who my child is") and cultural identity† ("if I do not know who my sexual partner is, I do not know who I am"). But both biology and culture are structured in such a way that most men care about lineage more than women do, while culture is structured in such a way that most women link their identity to their sexual partner more than men do. The bedtrick is about that, too. The zoological data tell us what we share with other animals, and the myths reveal how deeply embedded in us are our ideas about ourselves as animals. These are givens. But we can challenge both our zoology and our myths, to strive for a sexual humanity that is not given.

The Lovely/Loathly Lady

The Lovely Lady

We have seen Kali, the dark side of Parvati, sloughed away from the fair side, Gauri, and the serpentine Adi masquerading as Parvati. Implicitly in this myth, and explicitly in Beauty and the Beast, the masquerade of a god or animal as a human is superimposed upon the masquerade of ugliness as beauty and enacted in the twilight zone between the dark and the light, night and day. These contrasts also hedge the myth of the Lovely/Loathly Lady, a doubled double, for she appears in two forms, each a double (which can be still further doubled in its male variant): the Lovely Lady is ugliness masquerading as beauty (like the demon Adi as Parvati), and the Loathly Lady is beauty masquerading as ugliness (like Parvati before she sheds her black outer sheath [Kali] to reveal the fair beauty beneath [Gauri]). The two polarized forms of the myth alternate according to where the author believes reality lies. The bedtricks of the Lovely Lady or Substitute Bride take place when an ugly (old) woman takes on the (false) appearance of a beautiful (young) woman, usually because she desires a man, while the Loathly Lady only appears to be ugly, through a curse, until *his* desire for *her* (or his kiss) restores her true loveliness. When she succeeds in fooling her victim in bed, the Lovely/Loathly Lady becomes a bedtrickster; until then, she is a bedtrickster *in potentia,* a bedtrick waiting to happen.

The connection between Beauty and the Beast and the Lovely/Loathly Lady was noted by Salman Rushdie in a question his hero wanted to ask a wise man of his acquaintance:

> Whatif, whatif a Beastji somehow lurked *inside* Beauty Bibi? Whatif the beauty were herself the beast? But I think he might have said I was confusing matters: "As Mr Stevenson has shown in his *Dr Jekyll and Mr Hyde,* such saint-and-monster conjunctions are conceivable in the case of men; alas! such is our nature. But the whole essence of Woman denies such a possibility."[1]

The wise man was wrong: Bibi in this story turns out to be, as the hero fears, not the traditional Beast (beauty masquerading as ugliness, the Loathly Lady), but the reverse, a Lovely Lady (ugliness masquerading as beauty, Hyde masquerading as Jekyll).

If Pandora is the paradigmatic Greek Lovely Lady *(in potentia)*, Shurpanakha‡ is her Hindu counterpart. This is how Shurpanakha's story is told in the poet Kamban's Tamil version of the *Ramayana,* composed in South India in the seventh century:

SHURPANAKHA

The demoness Shurpanakha, the sister of Ravana, well aware of her ugliness, fell in love with Rama; he rejected her but offered her to his brother Lakshmana, who mutilated her by cutting off her nose, ears, and breasts. She then transformed herself into the image of the divine form of Sita. When the real Sita appeared, Shurpanakha told Rama that the other woman (the real Sita) was a deceitful, man-eating demoness who was skilled in the arts of illusion and had adopted a false form. Rama knew who was who, but continued to tease Shurpanakha. But when Sita ran to Rama and embraced him, Rama rejected Shurpanakha.[2]

The poet makes explicit the demoness's motive. She reasons, "He will never look at me while she who has no equal is near him. / Best for me to run there fast, take her and hide her away somewhere quickly / and then I will assume that form that he loves and I will live with him."[3] But she does not, in fact, hide Sita away; the two Sitas, the original and the double, stand there, side by side.

In other tellings of the *Ramayana,* Shurpanakha is neither ugly nor beautiful; as an ogress *(rakshasi),* she is capable of assuming diverse forms at will.[4] This is a basic characteristic of all demons and demonesses; they are called *kamarupa,* literally, "desire-form": their imagination is their shape. Kathleen Erndl asks the right questions about Shurpanakha: How did she actually appear in Rama's eyes, beautiful or ugly? If she could take on any form she pleased, why did she appear ugly? Was the poet describing her "true" form rather than her "apparent" form? When Rama commented on her beauty, was his comment serious or sarcastic?[5] Why, indeed, are demonesses generally described as ugly? (In the Sanskrit version of the story, the monkey Hanuman describes the demon women as deformed, sallow-skinned, misshapen, with huge heads and monstrous bodies.)[6] Perhaps they assume such forms because they see the world upside down from us and regard as ugly what we think beautiful—and also because their default position, as it were, is ugly. Shurpanakha, therefore, changes her appearance, not because she wants to be "beautiful," but because she wants to be what Rama wants. At one point, Shurpanakha tells Rama that Sita is ugly, "deformed, without beauty, unsightly, grim-visaged, with a lean abdomen."[7] But she tells Ravana that Sita is beautiful when she encourages him to seduce her,[8] and she recognizes Rama as beautiful and wants him for that very beauty. Which is the lie? Is beauty itself ugly? This passage creates an ambiguity not only about demonesses but about women and about beauty itself: each of them looks like one thing but is another.

That the ogress changes her voice as well as her visual appearance (she makes her speech as soft as that of the Indian cuckoo)[9] makes this one of the more subtle transformations. But when she persists in propositioning Rama, his brother Lakshmana mutilates her, cutting off her nose, ears, and (in the Tamil version) breasts—precisely the mutilation prescribed in Hindu law and folklore for a promiscuous (beautiful) woman. Since Shurpanakha's beauty is false, the punishment restores her to her true ugliness. But Shurpanakha accuses Lakshmana of having mutilated her nose to keep her for himself: "So that no stranger might ever look at me, you cut it, / didn't you?"[10] This reasoning is predicated on the assumption that a woman cannot be both beautiful and faithful, a belief that the other demons share. When they see Shurpanakha with her nose cut off, they speculate, "It must have been Khara, / her protector, thinking she was unchaste and had soiled / the honor of the family, who took away her beauty."[11] Another version of the story insists that the motive for mutilation is not only punishment but deterrence (destroying her beauty): "It was really a matter of his duty to punish the wicked. He disfigured S[h]urpanakha in order to keep her away from sin."[12]

In the Tamil telling, when Rama sees Shurpanakha again after the mutilation, he doesn't recognize her.[13] At this point, Shurpanakha claims that superficial beauty means nothing: "So what if you made me lose my nose, now that it's gone, if you can't bear it, / instantly I will create it again! I will be beautiful again! Am I / any less a woman if in this way I gain the fortune of your grace? / Isn't a long nose rising on a woman's face only a frill?"[14] The text regards this as a ridiculous argument, but the idea that a nose is just a frill, and even that a woman is better off without her beauty, indeed without her sexuality altogether, is developed quite seriously in other Hindu and Buddhist texts.

The mythology of Indian Buddhism plays upon the discourse on the impermanence of the body and the superficiality of beauty, inspiring a revulsion against beauty itself. A famous instance of this argument occurs in a text composed by Ashvaghosha in the first century C.E. The future Buddha, the prince Gautama Shakyamuni, escapes from the palace by night and passes through the harem, where he sees the women asleep in unflattering, revealing, and disgusting postures: "Another lay as if sprawling in intoxication, with her mouth gaping open and saliva flowing out, and with her limbs spread out so as to show what should be concealed. Her beauty was gone, her form distorted."[15] Thus, sleep (often specified as postcoital sleep†) reveals the hideous truth underneath the seductive surface of women just as it forces demons to assume their true form. The Lovely Lady in the Buddhist parable is not a masquerader: she is Everywoman.

A bedtrick on this theme appears in several variants of the canonical episode of the temptation of the Buddha by Mara (the archenemy of the Buddha, who represents the forces of sex and death)[16] and his beautiful daughters (variously translated as Desire, Discontent, and Passion, or Greed, Hate, and Delusion, or Lust, Thirst, and Delight). Usually they tempt him with their beauty, but in Ashvaghosha's telling, after they have tried and failed to seduce him by assuming the forms of beautiful young women, they try another tack:

MARA'S DAUGHTERS AND THE BUDDHA

When the three daughters of Mara saw that their father had failed to defeat the Buddha, they went to the Buddha and tried to seduce him through infatuation, flattery, and threats, but he remained absorbed in meditation. Then all three took on the appearance of young women and asked him to receive them as renunciants; still he kept his eyes closed. Then they took on the appearance of older women and approached him in order to delude him; they said, "We come to you after wandering as slaves, and we have grown old; teach us the true Buddhist teaching. We are older women; pity us. We are bewildered by our fear of death; fix us firmly in the Release that will stop all rebirths." When he heard the words of those magicians, he did not get angry; but he fixed them firmly in old age through his own magic power. When they realized that he was immovable as a mountain, they turned away their faces, but they could not get back their beauty. Dragging their feet with their worn-out limbs, they asked their father, "Lord of the Realm of Desire, Daddy, fix us firmly again in our own shapes." But, though he loved his daughters, their father had no power to change what the Buddha had done, and he told them,

"Seek refuge with the Buddha." They begged the Buddha, "Forgive us, for our minds were intoxicated with youth." Silently, he forgave them and restored them; and they went home rejoicing.[17]

This is a trick, not quite a bedtrick, that gets the trickster (the Buddha) out of, rather than into, the bed of the victim(s) (the daughters of Mara). The women's own magic accelerates their age, but his magic "fixes them firmly" in it even as he is firmly fixed in his own freedom from aging† and as no mortals can ever be firmly fixed in youth and beauty.† Then he makes them young again, but presumably no longer "intoxicated with youth." As Elizabeth Wilson remarks: "The Buddha . . . pulled a . . . real rabbit out of his psychic hat when he froze Mara's daughters into the decrepit forms of old women. . . . Such transformations need not be magically induced. As the backfired seduction by Mara's daughters would suggest, the minions of Mara will often reveal their true nature when left to their own devices. Sooner or later, all of Mara's daughters will decay and die."[18] Indeed, the transformation from youth to old age is hardly magical; it happens every day. Thus, when the lovely sirens pretend to be old women, they are, in a sense, masquerading as themselves.† Their old age is designed to excite not his lust but his pity. In another version of this myth, the daughters of Mara reason, "Men's tastes are various" (literally, "high and low"),[19] and they offer the Buddha, in vain, a hundred maidens, a hundred women who had given birth once, a hundred mature women, and finally a hundred old women.[20]

This sequence—from virgin to primipara to old woman—is one that the Buddha in other texts projects onto his sister, called Abhirupa Nanda or Rupa Nanda ("Delighting in Fine Form"). One Buddhist text composed in Pali develops this motif with the same sort of inversion of a conventional bedtrick that we saw in the story of Mara's daughters: the transformation takes place in the body of the victim (the sister) rather than the trickster (the Buddha):

THE BUDDHA'S SISTER

[The Buddha], concluding that her disintoxication from intoxication with form would be best achieved by form itself, just as one draws out one thorn using another, conjured up a beautiful woman by his psychic power at the moment Rupa Nanda entered the monastery. She was the very definition of sweet sixteen. . . . He caused the body to age in appearance, so that Rupa Nanda suddenly saw a twenty-year-old woman. His sister noticed the difference instantly, and "her mind was a little displeased."

The Buddha then caused the spectral woman to age in a time-lapse sequence. First, he gave her the appearance of a woman who has given birth once, then the appearance of a middle-aged woman, and then the appearance of "an old woman broken with decay." Rupa Nanda, aware of the changes wrought by each stage of the phantom's aging process, became disgusted upon seeing the last stage: a grey-headed, toothless, hunchbacked, palsied old woman leaning on a walking stick. On the verge of achieving his goal, the Teacher moved in for the kill: "Then the Teacher mastered her with disease. Screaming loudly, she . . . fell to the ground, and rolled back and forth, wallowing in her own urine and feces. Seeing her, Rupa Nanda was extremely disgusted. The Teacher then caused her to see the death of this woman. Her body immediately assumed a bloated condition; putrid lumps and maggots oozed out through the nine gaping wounds. Crows and the like fell on her and tore into her flesh. Rupa Nanda, observing this, thought, 'This woman has fallen prey to old age, to disease, to death right here in front of me: my body will also experience old age, disease, and death.' "[21]

The three images that Rupa sees—of old age, disease, and death—recapitulate the three images that the future Buddha himself, Gautama, saw and that prompted his Enlightenment, the Four Signs (the fourth being a renouncer) that reminded him of his own mortality and the path to Freedom.[22] Here they are transposed onto the female body, where they contrast not with political power (which Gautama rejected at the time of his Enlightenment) but with sexual power (which he rejected then and rejects again now).

THE LOATHLY LADY

The "loathly lady/bride" (or "loathsome lady/bride"), the beautiful young woman masquerading as an old hag, is a female counterpart to the male Beast (with Beauty) or the invisible, presumably ugly Cupid (with Psyche). The story is represented in several of Stith Thompson's† motifs, such as D 732 (Loathly Lady) and T 327.6 (Princess assumes loathsome disguise to avoid demon lover). The Loathly Lady in European folklore involves the hero in a rather specific plot. First, she solves a riddle† that saves his life and then she sets him not so much a riddle as a puzzle, which consists in the choice between her ugliness and her beauty. He is quite willing to disenchant her, but he balks, at first, at her real desire, that he should marry her—which he seems to regard as a fate worse than death. She insists, he submits, and she becomes Lovely.

Four of the theme's most famous expressions in early English literature are John Gower's *Tale of Florent* (the first recorded version, c. 1386),[23] the incomplete *Marriage of Sir Gawaine*,[24] *The Weddynge of Sir Gawen and Dame Ragnell* (mid–fifteenth century),[25] and Geoffrey Chaucer's "Tale of the Wife of Bath" (1397–1400).[26] These stories ask, "What do women want?" which became the essential question for Freud and for some feminists, together with its equally interesting partner, "What do men want?" The Loathly Lady's answer to the question about women is "power over men" (a rather different thing from the modern feminist's "empowerment"), more precisely, sovereignty over husbands. But Chaucer's Wife of Bath puts a twist on this answer. She demands that women have the same power over their husbands that they have over their lovers, assuming that (1) a woman has a lover (as she has); (2) a woman has sovereignty over her lover; (3) a woman has no sovereignty over her husband— though his mistress does (see assumption 2); and (4) a woman wants to have sovereignty over her husband (i.e., to control him as she controls her lover, to keep him in her erotic thrall). The assumed contrast between the erotic woman (young, not married, Freud's whore, the mistress of the man who commits adultery with his own wife†) and the wife (aging,† no longer erotic, Freud's madonna, the wife who tricks the husband into mistaking her for his mistress†) is here subverted: the wife is to continue to use her (erotic) sovereignty over her husband.

But this is not the last surprise that the Wife of Bath has in store for us. The other three authors pose the puzzle in the same way: is it more important to be beautiful by day or by night? But they do not answer it in quite the same way. John Gower's protagonist takes the old woman to bed, turns his back, and, at her remonstrance, turns over and sees a beautiful, eighteen-year-old woman. As he tries to take her, she bids him choose whether he will have her in that condition by day or by night. This question was foreshadowed by the knight's plan to hide the old woman away on an island, avoiding the public encounter of the day, and his hope that she would soon die, avoiding the private encounter of the night. It is a wonderful statement of the quandary of public beauty and private sex, of the tension between the inner, private soul and the outer, public body. Now he asks her to make the choice, and she promises that she will never lose her present beauty, day or night, until she dies.

Unlike Gower's hero, Gawaine in *The Marriage of Sir Gawaine* at first makes the choice himself. He prefers to have her foul in the day, rather than in the night, when he would play with her. But the hag then complains that she must then hide herself when he is with his drinking companions. When he then asks her to make the choice for him, she replies (presumably after becoming beautiful) that he will have her henceforth just as she is now. As Barbara Fass Leavy has remarked, "What his loathly wife told Gawain is that women want sovereignty; what the story actually reveals is that what she most desired was Sir Gawain."[27] In *The Weddynge of Sir Gawen and Dame Ragnell,* Gawen is, unlike Gower's knight, willing to take on the old hag, Dame Ragnell, just as she is, before she is transformed, and his courage (or gallantry or both) is what transforms her, not his answer to the puzzle. In bed, she begs him at least to kiss her, to which Sir Gawen replies, "I will do more than kiss, and God before!" And when he turns around to her, he sees the fairest creature that ever he had seen; they make love with great pleasure. Only afterward does she tell him the problem: "My beauty will not hold." And so she asks him the $64,000 question: will he have her fair at night or by day? The rest goes at first as in Gower, and they live together for five years and have a son, and Gawen never loved any woman as he loves her. But even after she is transformed back into the beautiful woman, Dame Ragnell still has the problem of all women: her beauty will not last. In this case, the statement that she will remain beautiful as long as she lives is proven true simply by having her vanish or die within five years, another unmagical solution. How easy some things are in fairy tales.

The genius of Chaucer's version, a stunning innovation upon the other texts, is that he keeps the basic pole of old and ugly versus young and beautiful but replaces the night/day distinction of the other variants with the contrast between cuckolding and faithfulness: the knight can have the woman old and ugly and faithful, or young and beautiful and unfaithful (a line of reasoning that we recognize from the justification for the mutilation of Shurpanakha). The Wife of Bath presents her husband with an unmagical choice reminiscent of the old misogynist equation of women with translations (sex and language†): they cannot be both beautiful and faithful. It is echoed in Oscar Wilde's *The Picture of Dorian Gray*‡ when Lord Henry remarks, "Young men want to be faithful, and are not; old men want to be faithless and cannot: that is all one can say."[28]

Yet this is, in its way, an argument in favor of making love to older women, not unlike Benjamin Franklin's‡ notorious satire.[29] Moreover, since "beautiful" is as usual equated with "young," the Wife of Bath speaks in praise of old women when she speaks in praise of ugly women. The assumption that old women are faithful, quite an irony in the mouth of this lecherous old hellcat, is subtly twisted when, after she promises that she will be "both" to him and specifies that she means "both" beautiful and faithful, the transformation takes place and he sees that she is "both" beautiful and *young;* he cannot of course see whether she will be faithful. The choice that she offers him is merely a way of characterizing two sorts of real women, ugly faithful ones versus beautiful promiscuous ones. Yet she will apparently stay young "to the end of her life," like the other Loathly Ladies and unlike real women; either she is lying or joking or she doesn't expect to live long or there is magic at work here after all. The true miracle, however, the Wife of Bath implies, is that she will remain faithful.

In chapter 3 we encountered people forced to choose between human and animal, night and day. In other stories, they must choose the desirable, though apparently inferior, even ugly, mortal instead of the glamorous (beautiful) but metaphysically incorrect god.‡ Leavy connects these scenarios with the tale of the Loathly Lady: "Choice as a theme in folklore can be found in animal groom tales whenever the Psyche character is asked whether she would prefer her husband an animal by day or by night. . . . Chaucer's tale has been held to be a rationalization of the animal bride type story."[30] To the question, "Do you want the animal form or the human, the ugly or the beautiful?" the answer is "Yes."

But the stories of masquerading animals and gods also raised another question: Which was the original, the animal (or divine) or the human form? Indeed, which was the authentic one? Whatever the original form may have been, the form that the human partner chose (often by burning the animal skin,† if the human was the chosen form) became the authentic form forever after. This question—Which is real?—is also relevant to the issue of beauty versus ugliness (now equated not with human versus animal but with youth versus age) in the tale of the Lovely/Loathly Lady. Thus, the story poses another double-headed question: (1) Which is better and (2) which is real, the beautiful woman or the ugly woman? The two are explicitly combined when the Loathly Lady asks the knight to choose which of her forms is to remain.

In James Shirley's *The Lady of Pleasure* (1635), the myth of the Loathly Lady is assumed and makes possible another unmagical bedtrick, but one attributed to magic:

THE LADY OF PLEASURE

A beautiful young married woman who desires a young gigolo gets an old bawd to bring him to the bawd's house, blindfolded. She offers him

gold and jewelry if he will sleep with her, but he fears she is a succubus,†
"so cold, an incubus would not heat her"; he asks her if she wasn't a cat
in former days. But she assures him: "Yet thou wilt find by light of thy
own sense, for other light is banish'd my chamber, when our arms tie
lovers' knots, and kisses seal the welcome of our lips, I shall not there
affright thee, nor seem old . . . ; my skin is smooth and soft as ermines,
with a spirit to meet thine." And so he goes to bed with her, for the gold
and because he fears she will curse him if he does not. When he next
meets the married woman, he gives her the gold and jewelry as a gift and
tells her he had gotten it from "an old witch, a strange ill-favored hag . . .
a she-devil, too, a most insatiate abominable devil with a tail this long."
When she asks him if he saw her, and if he is sure "it was the devil you
enjoyed," he admits it was all in the dark but insists, "I did the best to
please her, but as sure as you live, 'twas a Hellcat." When he leaves, his
unrecognized mistress muses, " 'Tis a false glass, sure I am more deformed. What have I done?"[31]

Either he is telling what he believes to be the truth and has projected
his sexual fantasy† upon the actual woman in his bed, enhancing the
power of her disguise; or he is pretending that he did not recognize his
mistress, to tease her. His mistress believes that he is telling the truth,
which sobers her up so that she breaks off the affair; he has in a sense
turned her into a witch. Yet the old bawd told him to expect a beautiful
woman in his bed, transformed by his magic kiss; did he not believe her?

The character of Papagena in Mozart's opera *The Magic Flute* appears
at first to be a hideous old woman and, at the end, a beautiful young girl.
Jacques Chailley has remarked: "Certain lines in the libretto . . . invite us
. . . to ask ourselves if, in the minds of the authors, the ugliness of the
old woman is not, fundamentally, the image of her true nature as a
woman, the pretty appearance that she reveals at last an illusion of the
man inflamed by wine and desire."[32] This is the point of all Lovely Ladies,
but it is also a plausible reading of the more cynical (or realistic) among
the Loathly Ladies: all flesh will wither, all passion die, and beauty is the
most ephemeral quality of matter. The love of visible beauty is a delusion,
and beauty, more than anything else in human life, is subject to what the
Buddhists call *anicca*, impermanence.

THE MAGIC KISS

Like the true nature of the animal bride or the animal groom, the true
beauty of the apparently foul Loathly Lady is not so much transformed

by the magic kiss† (Stith Thompson's† motif D 735, "Disenchantment by kiss") as revealed by this standard diagnostic test for bedtricks. The kiss is part of the masquerade in those variants in which the hero believes that the woman is hideous and is happily surprised to find her, post-kiss, beautiful. The knight transfers his choice to the Loathly Lady in two ways, by word and by deed. The words amount to saying, "You may choose when to be beautiful," the second form of the puzzle of women's wish for power over men and over their own beauty. But the deed is to kiss her (or make love to her) before she is transformed into or revealed as a beautiful woman, which amounts to saying, "Beauty does not matter to me." The kiss is thus the physical analogue to the puzzle; sex and words replace one another, through the mental (puzzle) and physical (kiss) aspects of the mouth. In some variants, the hero knows that the hideous form is unreal—but he also knows that it may kill him before he can disenchant it. Thus, the hero of Wagner's opera *Siegfried* awakens the terrifying Brunhilde with a kiss, one of many tests of his valor and of his worthiness to win her.[33] This "awakening kiss" similarly transforms Snow White and Sleeping Beauty into beautiful (live) women, not from beasts or ogres, but from apparently dead beautiful women.

What I would call the brave kiss or the magic kiss is often called the *fier baiser,* the "proud" or "noble" kiss. It is a test of courage: if the knight refuses the kiss, "if, indeed, as in some cases he even shudders or shows his repugnance,"[34] the window of opportunity for disenchantment closes. (Ananda Coomaraswamy refers to the stories where the knight fails to kiss the monstrous female as "the Fier Baiser *manqué.*")[35] Repugnance against ugliness may cause the faint of heart to close their eyes‡ in the clinch—often with tragic consequences.

The courage required to bestow the brave kiss is emphasized by texts that go into gruesome detail regarding the loathsomeness of the Loathly Lady, particularly of her mouth.† The kiss may function as a euphemism for a more intimate sexual encounter, and some variants actually stipulate a full sexual act. Several levels of intimacy are set forth in a Norse tale in which an enchanted woman is transformed into a hideous troll: "She might be restored to her own form if some man would consent to three things: to accept life at her hands, to kiss her, and to share her bed."[36] "To accept life at her hands" seems to be the equivalent of the sovereignty demanded by the Loathly Lady. The kiss and the bed are separate here, as they often are in the tale of the frog prince,† who wants to drink from the princess's cup and sleep in her bed (which is not, in this case, a euphemism for sex) and then, finally, to be kissed. The Loathly Lady demurely asks to be "married," but on the wedding night she makes it clear that she expects the marriage to be consummated. This is what makes her deception a bedtrick.

OLD WOMEN MASQUERADING AS YOUNG WOMEN

It is noteworthy that Mara's beautiful young daughters think that some men (perhaps religious fanatics?) might be aroused by old women, for there is another essential factor in these myths besides the tension between beauty and ugliness: the contrast between youth and age. The Lovely Lady is not just ugliness masquerading as beauty, but an old woman masquerading as a young woman in bed. One such story was told by Giambattista Basile (1575–1632), who called it

THE OLD WOMAN DISCOVERED

[An old woman hid under the trees near one of the windows of the king. The king, hearing her talk, thought she must be beautiful and proposed that she come to his bed. She accepted his invitation but insisted, "Let me] be received in thy bed at night without a candle, because I could not bear to be seen naked." The king [agreed, and when the night grew dark, the old woman] came in the gloom, covered from head to foot with a thick veil looped up behind. And reaching the king's bedchamber, she unrobed at once, and went into bed. The king, who had waited like a match near a powder-cask, when he . . . heard her get into bed, perfuming his person with sweet scented musk and civet, and anointing his beard with perfumed ointment, jumped into bed. And it was well for the old woman that he was thus anointed and perfumed, so that he could not smell the stink of her mouth, and the vinegar of her arm-pits, and the mustiness of that ugly thing. But as soon as he felt her limbs, he perceived the deception; he felt her bottom and found it fleshless, the limbs thin and withered, and the breasts as empty bladders; and he marvelled with exceeding marvel, but kept silence, so as to be better assured of the case; and forced himself to do that for which he had no more desire. . . . But when sleep overtook the old woman, the king drew out . . . a small lanthorn which he lit, and made a perquisition under the bed-linen, and beheld a harpy instead of a nymph, a fury instead of a grace, Medusa instead of Venus. [He shouted,] "This, and worse, deserveth he who buyeth the cat inside the bag." [He threw her out the window, but then some fairies made her young, beautiful, and rich; when the king saw her, he said,] "Am I sleeping, or awaking? Am I in my right senses, or am I mad?" [He begged her to marry him, and she agreed.][37]

The woman at first is old: she has disheveled hair, wrinkled brows, crooked, stiff eyebrows, eyes red and watery, yellow skin full of wrinkles, large and crooked mouth, hairy breasts, and shriveled arms; she is hunchbacked, lame, and cloven† footed.† But then she undergoes a triple transformation: first she is apparently transformed from ugly/old to beautiful/young (when the king hears her but cannot see her), then from young to old (when the king, in bed, sees through the trick), and, finally, from old to young (by the magic of the fairies). The Lovely Lady (ugly inside, beautiful outside) becomes a Loathly Lady who is, in turn, transformed from ugly to beautiful—in part by the willingness of the king to embrace her even when she is ugly. He is fooled at first by his own good smell,† but the sense of touch serves him in the dark. At the end, he is fooled again—for when he sees the bride as beautiful as he had originally perceived her, he assumes not that there was a substitution or transformation between then and now but, rather, that she has been beautiful all along, and that there is something the matter with him,† not with her.

Carlos Fuentes's novella *Aura* is about an old woman who seduces a young man through the magical projection† of a double of herself as a young woman named Aura. Aura seems to be merely a silent reflection of the old woman, and only at the end does the young man realize that Aura is not *like* a mirror image of the old woman but actually *is* the old woman, in her youth; and at that moment he realizes that he too has "come back," that he is the reincarnation of the old woman's dead husband. Perhaps Fuentes named his heroine Aura to echo the Aura who was the mirror rival of Procris (the wife of Ovid's Cephalus†), the double who was not there at all.

A soft-porn flick called *Double Threat* (1992) used the device of the "body double"† as the pivot of its plot:

DOUBLE THREAT

An aging star, Monica Martel, making her comeback, insists on having a young girl, Lisa Shane, replace her in the sexual scenes. Eric, who plays her lover on camera and off, also becomes the off-screen lover of the "body double." When Monica finds out, she is surprisingly cool and forgiving, but she and Lisa plot together and murder Eric. Before she shoots him, Monica says to him, "You were once attracted to me; it makes sense that you would be attracted to my daughter." The policeman who figures it out doesn't prosecute her because, he explains, Eric had murdered his (the policeman's) sister.

The rather obvious plot suddenly veers, at the end, into a Family Romance,† indeed a double family romance: the Loathly Lady is replaced by her lovely daughter, and even the avenging spirit at the end turns out to be a blood relative of the parallel victim. What appeared at first to be a case of older woman versus younger woman turns out in the end to be a case of the girls against the boys, while the incestuous implications of the double-cross† hover salaciously in the air.

THE SUBSTITUTE BRIDE. 1: MOTHERS

Ugly old women do not have to be the natural mothers of the beautiful young women whom they counterfeit, but they often are. The paradigmatic mother in many myths is exactly like her daughter in every way but one: she is old,† and the daughter is young. Thus, many Cinderella† stories begin with the incestuous premise that the widower father determines to marry only a woman who looks exactly like his dead wife—a category of one, his daughter. The woman who impersonates her daughter is not becoming someone else; that would happen if she impersonated someone else's daughter. By impersonating her own daughter, she is becoming herself, young again.

Many bedtricks, particularly but not only incestuous† bedtricks, turn upon the failure of brothers and sisters (or parents and children) to recognize one another through their mutual resemblance or the failure of other people to tell them apart. Family resemblance could occasionally be used to unmask an impostor (Natalie Zemon Davis suggests comparison with other members of the family as a way to test a claim of identity in the premodern age),[38] but far more often it enables the bedtrick to take place, when one family member masquerades as another whom s/he resembles.

Sometimes the mother colludes with the daughter against the man, as in the Roald Dahl story "The Visitor,"† about the beautiful mother and daughter and the leprous daughter.[39] More often, however, the mother acts *against* her daughter by remaining in her sexual world and competing with her. A series of cosmogonic myths recorded throughout the Pacific Rim and in Southeast Asia tells of an old woman who sloughs her skin† in order to masquerade as a young woman.[40] James George Frazer cites several myths of this type about the origin of death,‡ including one fetchingly entitled "The Composite Story of the Perverted Message and the Cast Skin."[41] Several other versions, from Tanna Island in New Hebrides (Vanuatu) and from the Admiralty Islands, depict a son who rejects his mother when she sheds her skin; he says, "I don't know you. . . . You are not my mother."[42] Geza Roheim glosses these stories for us: "A child or grandchild refuses to recognize the rejuvenated grandmother or mother in the young woman. In the last version quoted above and belonging to this group the difficulty lies in the Oedipus complex. If mothers were to cast their skins and hence mankind were to live forever, sons would want their mothers for their wives—hence we must die."[43] Often the unnatural suspension of aging leads to incestuous† bedtricks.

The story becomes a bedtrick when the old woman thus transformed gets into bed with a young man. An ingenious sexual twist occurs in a story recorded in East Greenland, in which, when a man goes away to fish, his mother provides her daughter-in-law with the meat of seals she hunts, and in return the daughter-in-law acts as her wife—which includes making love to her with a dildo made of seal bone. When the son/husband returns and spies on them, he kills his mother, and his wife weeps and cries out, "You've killed my dear husband."[44] Here the daughter herself serves as the surrogate husband, and the son, not the mother, intrudes between "husband" and wife—mother and daughter.

In an Inuit myth about the hero Kiviok,‡ an old woman usurps the skin from the younger woman's whole head and body.[45] Annie Dillard retells a version of this myth:

The Woman Who Stole Her Daughter's Skin

A young man in a strange land falls in love with a young woman and takes her to wife in her mother's tent. By day the women chew skins and boil meat while the young man hunts. But the old crone is jealous; she wants the boy. Calling her daughter to her one day, she offers to braid her hair; the girl sits pleased, proud, and soon is strangled by her own hair. One thing Eskimos know is skinning. The mother takes her curved hand knife shaped like a dancing skirt, skins her daughter's beautiful face, and presses that empty flap smooth on her own skull. When the boy returns that night he lies with her, in the tent on top of the world. But he is wet from hunting; the skin mask shrinks and slides, uncovering the shriveled face of the old mother, and the boy flees in horror, forever.[46]

This variant is particularly noteworthy for the implication that the motion of the sexual act itself dislodges the skin and allows Kiviok to see through the masquerade. Dillard tells her story in answer to the question that she poses: "Is beauty itself an intricately fashioned lure, the cruelest hoax of all?" This question lies at the very heart of the myth of the Lovely/Loathly Lady.

A man's mother may also compete with his wife for his love. In addition to the problem of rivalry with her daughter-in-law, she often poses incestuous† problems for her son. Some masquerading mothers-in-law play the role of what is known in folklore as the Substitute Bride.[47] Ibrahim Muhawi and Sharif Kanaana tell a Palestinian story about a mother who steals her daughter-in-law's eyes† and succeeds, for a while, in sleeping with her own son.†[48] Lila Abu-Lughod records a more complex, contemporary Bedouin version:

THE WOMAN WHO STOLE HER DAUGHTER-IN-LAW'S EYES

Once there was a barren woman who asked a traveling holyman for some medicine to make her fertile. He gave her something that looked like eggs and instructed her to cook them but not to eat them until the next morning. She cooked them, then left to fetch water. While she was gone, her husband returned, peeked in the pot, found the "eggs," and ate them.

When she came home and saw the empty pot, she was alarmed. "Oh no!" she said, "now you'll get pregnant." Her husband didn't believe her but later realized that he was pregnant. Time passed. Then one day he felt labor pains. He came to his wife and asked her what to do. She replied, "Go out and squat behind that bush and deliver the baby. If it's a boy, bring it home. If it's a girl, just leave her there." He went and pushed and pushed, hanging onto the bush until he gave birth. He took off as fast as he could.

A bird came along and carried away the baby girl. He put her in a nest high up in a tree and brought her food every day. She grew up to be the most beautiful girl imaginable. No one surpassed her in beauty.

Now, under this tree was a spring. Muhammad buh Sultan, living in a castle not far from there, had a beautiful horse [later referred to as "she," apparently a mare] which he sent with a slave to be watered under there. But when they approached the spring, the horse reared and refused to drink. Muhammad buh Sultan was furious when they returned, shouting, "What do you mean she wouldn't drink?" So he beheaded the slave. The next day, he sent another slave to water the horse. The same thing happened. So the third day, he decided to go himself. When they approached the spring, again the horse reared, but as it did, he caught a glimpse of the girl's reflection in the pool and immediately fell in love with her. . . .

Now Muhammad buh Sultan had hidden himself nearby, and when the girl stooped over he jumped out and grabbed her, put her on his horse, and took off. She cried and screamed all the way. . . . She did not stop screaming until they got to the castle. Then he talked to the girl. He said, "Please live with me. If you want me as a father, I'll be that. If you want me as a brother, I'll be that. If you want me as a husband, I'll be that." She married him. (She knew what was in her best interest!)

The only other person in the castle was his mother, an old woman. Now, Muhammad buh Sultan decided to make the holy pilgrimage to Mecca. Before he left, he gave his mother and wife a ram, saying, "If one of you dies, the other will slaughter this ram over her. If my mother dies, bury her in the courtyard." Then he went to his wife and told her, "For my sake, do anything my mother asks of you, even if she asks you to take out your own eyes." (She had gorgeous eyes.) Then he set off.

Immediately the mother-in-law started picking on the girl. She asked her to take out her eyes and the girl agreed. The old lady, with these beautiful new eyes, threw the girl out of the castle. Now blind, the girl left. She rescued a *magass* [a scissors or walkingstick] from a large snake. In return, the *magass* gave her what she asked: a castle twice as big as her old one, a new pair of eyes, and an orchard full of every conceivable fruit tree. He granted her these wishes, and they lived together in the castle.

When Muhammad buh Sultan returned from the pilgrimage, the woman he found started weeping. "We slaughtered the ram over your poor old mother," she said. Indeed, he found a grave in the courtyard. But he found his wife quite changed. "Why is your skin so tough? Why has your body aged so?" he asked. She replied, "You've been gone a long time." So they lived for a while as man and wife (Muhammad and his mother).

Then one day, the woman announced that she was pregnant. (A lie, she was too old to conceive.) She said she had a pregnancy craving for some grapes. So Muhammad sent a slave to the castle that had sprung up in his absence to ask for some grapes. The slave went off to the castle and said to the mistress who greeted him, "The wife of Muhammad buh Sultan has a craving for some grapes, won't you give us some?" The woman answered, "That's a lie! That's not his wife; that's his mother!" She told the *magass* to cut out the slave's tongue so he wouldn't talk. The slave came back empty-handed with his tongue cut out. Muhammad was furious. The next day he sent another slave, who also returned with his tongue cut.

Finally, he decided to go himself. When he got there he said, "Don't you have any grapes for the wife of Muhammad buh Sultan? She has a pregnancy craving." He heard the woman respond, "What a lie, that's not his wife; that's his mother." He was shocked and asked, "What do you mean?" Just as the *magass* was about to cut out his tongue the woman recognized her husband and stopped him. She related what had happened in his absence: how his mother had taken her eyes, thrown her out, and buried the ram whole in the courtyard.

Muhammad returned to his castle and demanded that his "wife" dig up his mother's grave. She tried to dissuade him, pleading, "No, no. Why do you want to see her?" He insisted, and when they dug it up he found the ram. Furious, he threw his mother into the fire. [The listeners, mostly young girls, were shocked. The woman telling the story commented, "That's what she deserved!"] Then he brought his true wife back to live with him.

They said that it is because of what his mother did that women's veils are black.[49]

This is, among other things, a tale of incest:† the husband "mistakes" his mother for his wife. Indeed, he is suspicious at first ("Why is your skin† so tough? Why has your body aged so?" he asks), but he settles for a lying version of the truth: "You've been gone a long time,"† his mother replies, expanding the relatively brief period of her son's absence into the significantly long period of her life. He is too easily fooled, perhaps because he is from the start incestuously inclined; when he first proposes to his wife, he gives her the extraordinary option of being, if not his wife, his daughter or sister. But his wife is able to recognize him at the crucial moment and saves him from having his tongue cut out (in vivid contrast with his implication in cutting out her eyes).

The heroine has only a father, no mother (a situation that often leads to incest,† as in the Cinderella† story). As Abu-Lughod glosses this, "The good woman is the most male woman, symbolized by the father giving birth to her. . . . She is chaste, claiming not to want a man and protesting violently when forcefully abducted." But she chooses the sexual, rather than the nonsexual, relationships offered to her, as the storyteller herself wryly notes. The heroine's father is falsely pregnant (because men can't be pregnant), and then her mother-in-law is falsely pregnant (because old women can't be pregnant). (As Abu-Lughod remarks, "Stories of older women who get pregnant meet with mild signs of disapproval despite the admiration for fecundity.")[50] The father eats the wrong thing (objects that look like eggs but aren't, and are in any case meant for his wife), and the mother-in-law desires to eat the wrong thing (the grapes meant for a genuinely pregnant woman). The theme of the bird† that rescues the newborn daughter assimilates the story to tales of abandoned children (often children of double mothers) adopted by animals. But there are other animals, too, who are or have doubles: the horse† is doubled by its reflection, and the ram doubles the mother (by being buried in her place).

Eyes† are obscured in various ways in this myth. The girl puts out her eyes, and the story as a whole explains why women are veiled. Two slaves are beheaded, and two others have their tongues cut out. How are these mutilations related? Beheading‡ is the extreme form of blinding; the tongue† and the eyes, vision and speech, are two senses that are in opposition throughout the myths of masquerade; and veiling is a practice that is the inverse of putting out a woman's eyes: it obscures the sight of everyone but her. This is a brilliant variant on the theme of blinding: the villainess does not just put out the heroine's eyes but steals them, in order to become her double, as Disney's witch steals the mermaid's† voice. The eyes thus function here not just as the subjective instrument of identification (the organ in your own head that lets you recognize someone else) but as the objective thing identified (the organ in someone else's head that lets you recognize them): if the other woman has the eyes, the husband is fooled. Veiling has a lot to do with hiding, too, and with seeing and not being seen. But it has other meanings in this particular culture: it identifies, and protects, women between childhood and menopause, the years in which they are sexually active.[51]

Blinding and veiling are not the only things that obscure true vision in this story. The king falls in love with an upside-down reflection that prefigures the whole series of reversals to come. He is stupid but not malicious. He is the one who first suggests, metaphorically one presumes, that she give her eyes to his mother—apparently little suspecting that she will literalize the metaphor,† as so often happens in myth. (We should, however, bear in mind that in many nonsexual myths the protagonist plucks out his eyes, or her eyes, the most precious thing in the world, to give to the deity.)[52] The husband is not the villain of the piece, nor is the father, who bungles the pregnancy.[53] It is the heroine's mother who, sharing the culture's evaluation, tells her pregnant husband to abandon the child if it's a girl. Already the women are against the women: the mother is against her unborn daughter. I read this as a story of old women against young women: the heroine's mother abandons her, and her mother-in-law blinds her; both are her enemies. And here, as so often, we encounter different points of view: the storyteller enjoys taking revenge on the mother, while the listeners apparently do not.

The advent of modern science allows females (human and animal) to have other females' babies through the use of in vitro transplants and foster wombs, not to mention frozen sperm, artificial insemination, and all the rest. Such techniques are prefigured by the actions of the devil in the *Malleus Maleficarum,* who takes the form of a female succubus‡ to get a man's semen and then the form of a male incubus to use it to impregnate a woman.[54] Science, as so often, plays the role of the devil in an article in the *Ladies' Home Journal* in 1992 about Arlette Schweitzer, who became the first American woman to give birth legally to her own grandchildren through the in vitro offspring of her daughter, Christa, who was unable to carry them because she was born without a uterus. Told partly in Arlette's own words, the article was entitled "My Children, My Grandchildren," but I would call it

THE MOTHER WHO STOLE HER DAUGHTER'S EGGS

I said [to Christa's doctor], half jokingly, that I wished he could transplant my uterus into Christa's body. "After all," I said, "I'm not planning to use it anymore." Dr. Ory looked at me and said, "How old are you?" I said, "Thirty-seven." He paused for a moment and said, "I don't think a uterus transplant is possible, but . . ." He didn't have to say another word. It was as if a light had gone on. Now it all seems so simple. Why couldn't I carry a baby for Christa? . . . What bothered me most were the quotes from an ethicist who said that the pregnancy was a bad idea because Christa's children could be confused about who their mother really is. Another expert said that my pregnancy might create tensions in the family. I told the reporter that our case goes beyond ethical questions. I am simply a mother who is trying to help her daughter fulfil her dreams. What mother could do less?[55]

Muhammad buh Sultan's mother or Naomi† (in the Book of Ruth) is the answer that comes immediately to mind. Yet, clearly, the surface agenda here is entirely benevolent, and the child (and the husband) ended up belonging to the daughter, not to the mother. The mother did not steal the eggs, she was given them. (Christa's body, however, reacted violently, as Arlette admits: "I don't think any of us anticipated that it would be as agonizing as it was for Christa. They gave her morphine to dull the pain, but it couldn't blot out everything. . . . I told her to remember this day, in case anyone ever tells her that she didn't endure the pain of childbirth. I really feel this was Christa's labor.") But it certainly wasn't as "simple" as Arlette blithely assumes, and I'm with that ethicist, perhaps because of the heavy mythological overtones of the story, so reminiscent of the confusion of the generations of women in the tales of Tamar† and

of Ruth.† The mythology extends even to the twins—a boy and a girl—
who were born to Arlette and Christa.

THE SUBSTITUTE BRIDE. 2: SISTERS

When the bedtrickster is not the mother but the sister of the woman that
she replaces, the myth often combines the themes of the Lovely and
Loathly Ladies: the older/uglier sister pretends to be young and beautiful
(a Lovely Lady), while she forces the younger/prettier sister to hide her
beauty (like a Loathly Lady). These stories manage simultaneously to
maintain two unexamined assumptions that, if examined, would prove
mutually contradictory, paradoxical:† the sisters in these stories are assumed to look alike, but one is more beautiful than the other. Their resemblance is assumed from their parentage even when they are, as is usually the case, only half sisters; and when they are raised together, nurture
as well as nature conspires in the bedtrick. Kirin Narayan's informant,
Urmilaji, notes in her down-to-earth way that since both of the sisters in
her story about a bedtrick were healthy young girls, they probably looked
very much alike.[56] So, too, Thomas Mann's Jacob,† trusting all the senses
other than sight, including touch and smell, and ignoring the fact that
"Rachel's" voice† sounds like Leah's and her shoulders feel like Leah's,
reasons that, after all, sisters are very much alike.[57] The physical resemblance between Viola and Sebastian in *Twelfth Night*,† despite the differences in both their sexes and their genders, is easily transformed into an
explanation for the physical resemblance between "Cesario" and Sebastian, who are of the same gender, though still of different sexes: that is,
both appear to be male, but one is biologically female, the other, male.
In *Rosenkavalier*,† Baron Ochs is struck by the resemblance between
Oktavian and his masquerade as "Mariandel" ("The likeness! The very
image!"), but the Marschallin allows him to think that Mariandel is an
illegitimate half sister of Oktavian. The discovery of a hidden, shared illegitimate father (or grandfather) explains the resemblance in *The Prisoner
of Zenda*.† When the man masquerading as Mrs. Doubtfire in the film
of the same name (1993) meets a woman who knew him as a man, Mrs.
Doubtfire identifies her male persona as her brother, inspiring the other
to remark, "You have his eyes."

Yet the contrast between the ugly and beautiful sisters is at the heart
of one of the most famous examples of this theme in Europe, the episode
in the Cinderella story in which ugly sisters or stepsisters substitute for
the beautiful heroine. The contrast between two sisters who look alike is

even more emphatic in another variant, as important and widespread as the Cinderella theme, the tale type (403) called "The Black and White Bride." The basic text, as collected by the Brothers Grimm in the nineteenth century, could be summarized as follows:

THE BLACK AND WHITE BRIDE

The Lord asked two stepsisters the way to the village. One refused to help, and the Lord cursed her to be black as night and ugly as sin. The other was helpful, and the Lord granted her wish to be as beautiful and fair as the sun. The king saw the fair girl's picture, fell in love, and asked her to marry him. But as the bride was traveling to the castle, the stepmother used her magic to make the coachman (the fair girl's brother) half-blind and the fair maiden herself half-deaf, and the black girl put on the clothing of the fair girl and pushed her from a bridge. A white duck emerged from the water. The black girl married the king, whose sight had been clouded by the stepmother's magic. The white duck revealed herself to the king, who cut off her head with his sword, and she changed back to the white bride, just like her picture. Now knowing what had happened, the king had the witch and her black daughter put to death, and he married the white bride.[58]

The white duck may be an atavism of our old friend the white swan† maiden (with the black double) or simply an example of the more general European tendency to depict beauty with a white skin† ("fair" in both senses of the word). "Magic" is all that is needed to explain why the king cannot tell the difference between his white beloved and a black copy of her in bed.

A paradigmatic tale of a substitute bride occurs in the Hebrew Bible story of Jacob, Rachel, and Leah. Jacob wishes to marry Rachel, but her father, Laban, substitutes Rachel's older sister, Leah, in the bed, and Jacob cannot tell the difference until the morning, when, "Behold, it was Leah" (Genesis 28.15–24). This story is a fine example of the minimalist plots† of the Hebrew Bible: the barest outline is given, in true mythic fashion, leaving the later tradition free to invent *midrashim* (commentaries) either to flesh out what the commentators think is there or to use the text as a springboard for later theories (or both: the two agendas are seldom separate). What, for instance, is Rachel thinking? She must know what Laban is plotting, since she herself does not go to Jacob's bed that night, and so she is a party to the deception. We might then assume that Rachel both does and does not want her sister to sleep with Jacob, or that she does not want it but is forced to obey her father. This, then, may be not merely the story of a man caught between two women (Jacob between Rachel and Leah) but also the story of a woman caught, in a different way, between two men (Rachel caught between her love for Jacob and her obedience to Laban—though that obedience wears rather thin later, when she defies him by running away with his idols and lying to him about them). Or, to put it differently, we may see it as the story of a woman caught between duty† (her duty to let her sister marry first) and desire† (her desire for Jacob).

In terms of the patterns of folklore, we might identify Leah as a Lovely Lady (the older, plainer sister pretending to be the younger, prettier sister), but Rachel is actually the Lovely Lady, for her superficial beauty hides what the Hebrew Bible regards as a female flaw far worse than ugliness: infertility. And by this logic, Leah is the Loathly Lady: she appears to be ugly but is in fact beautiful—that is, fertile. Indeed, even Rachel's youth, traditionally a Good Thing, is, in the Hebrew context, a negative factor in the plot: Jacob is supposed to marry the older sister first, not the younger. But the Hebrew Bible, reversing the superficial value of the folk structure, expands upon its more complex underlying agenda, the tension between beauty and fertility, desire and duty. And, as usual in the discourse on beauty, the clever hero in the end has his cake and eats it: he gets the beautiful girl *and* the fertile girl.

The text implies that Jacob and Leah's lovemaking took place in silence and perhaps in darkness. The commentaries generally insist on the darkness and also on a veil (which is not mentioned in the biblical text). Jacob's wits may also have been dulled by the "feasting" that took place at the wedding—that is, by drunkenness.† More elaborately, some commentaries suggest a kind of double-back† by Rachel: in one text, Rachel colludes first with Jacob against Leah but then with Leah against Jacob; Jacob and Rachel agree on "certain signs by which they could recognize one another at all times, and when Rachel saw that they were about to bring Leah to him for the marriage ceremony she thought, 'My sister will now be embarrassed or shamed,' and she therefore readily transmitted these signs to her."[59]

Rachel actually hides under the bed during the wedding night according to a *midrash* composed in the fifth and sixth centuries C.E. that imagines what Rachel said to God when the First Temple had been destroyed and many Jews had been killed and exiled, presumably in punishment for their sin in worshiping idols such as the Golden Calf. She says:

RACHEL'S BEDTRICK

"Jacob loved me very much [best], and served my father for seven years, for *me*. When the time came for him to marry me, my father insisted that my sister be married instead of me. This was very difficult for me. I told my husband [i.e., Jacob, her husband-to-be], and I made a secret sign between him and me, so that he could distinguish the two of us, in order to thwart my father's plan.

"But then I changed my mind, and I mastered my passion. And I felt pity for my sister, lest she be disgraced. In the night, they substituted my sister for me. All the secret signs that I had made with my husband, I told my sister, so that he would think she was me. Not only this: I went under the bed where he was making love with my sister. Whenever he spoke to her, she was silent, and I would answer, so that he would not recognize her voice. I did this out of my compassion and kindness to her. And I wasn't jealous of her. I would not allow her to be disgraced. And if I, who am only flesh and blood, dust and ashes, was not jealous of my co-wife [Jacob subsequently married Rachel as well] and did not permit her to be shamed and humiliated, then You, O Living King, why are You jealous of idols, though they are nothing, as You Yourself know? You exiled my children, and they were slain and ill-used by strangers."

Then God was moved; his mercy rolled around, and he said, "For *your* sake I will bring the Jews back. As it is said, 'Rachel weeps for her children and will not be comforted.' 'Stop your voice from lamenting, and your eyes from weeping, for there is a reward for your action.' Stop weeping; your children will come home."[60]

This is a very literal sort of bedtrick, which this *midrash* introduces in order to deal realistically with the problem of deceiving a man who has known a woman well for seven years, who knows her voice† as well as the external form of her body. Significantly, Rachel's voice gets into bed with Jacob seven years before she does. Why does she help her sister like this? The *midrash* implies that Rachel's jealousy is overcome by her realization that the other woman is a true human form of herself, related not only by family blood but also by a broader humanity, by common goals, by being part of the same people; that the other woman really *is* her double, not merely her surrogate. The sexual jealousy that is overcome in this way is then theologically† analogized, in a brilliant original stroke of this text, to the divine jealousy that God feels toward *his* surrogates— toward the images of him that substitute for him in heathen temples even as false lovers substitute for one another in lustful beds. But we might speculate on other, lower motives: maybe she does it to spoil things for her sister, whose pleasure will surely be cramped by her awareness of her sister's presence under the bed. And who is fooled by all this? Perhaps, on some deep level, Jacob really knows it is Leah and merely pretends that he doesn't; maybe all three of them know and are just fooling Laban. Maybe Rachel actually got into bed and just *said* that it was Leah. . .

Some of these speculations are far from the spirit of the *midrash,* let alone the Hebrew Bible, but one—that Jacob subconsciously knew the truth—may be implicit in a later Jewish gloss on this story. In the *Zohar,* a man who makes love to his wife while he is thinking about another woman is said to "sow false seed" (through parental imprinting†), and the child is considered a kind of changeling.[61] (In the film version— though not in the written text—of Isaac Bashevis Singer's story about Yentl,† the girl who became a yeshiva boy, the disguised Yentl, trying to stay out of bed with the woman she has married, cites the Talmud: "It is written: A woman must not give herself to one man when she's thinking of another.") Although Jewish law regards adultery in thought† as legally distinct from the corporeal act of adultery,[62] the law considers it morally reproachable: "If a man defiles himself by evil thoughts when he comes to have intercourse with his wife, and sets his thoughts and desires upon another woman, and emits semen with these evil thoughts, then his thought effects changes in the world below [fn.: an exchange of women in one's thoughts]. . . . The body of the child that he begets is called 'a changeling' [fn.: because the body was created while the father 'changed' his thoughts during procreation]."[63]

The *Zohar* uses Jacob's mistaken belief that he is with the woman he loves to explain the statement in 1 Chronicles 5.1–2 that the birthright went from Reuben, Leah's son (and the firstborn), to the sons of Joseph, Rachel's child. The *Zohar,* which apparently assumes that Reuben was conceived on the wedding night, when Leah was substituted for Rachel and Jacob still did not know, insists that Reuben was *not* a "changeling," because Jacob was thinking about the woman he should have been in bed with and thought he was in bed with; this is why he had "truthful thoughts." Had he known he was in bed with Leah and still thought of Rachel, the child would have been a changeling.

Perhaps to counteract the explanation given in Chronicles (that Reuben "polluted his father's bed" by seducing his father's concubine), the *Zohar* constructs a rather different sexual triangle: not Jacob, Reuben, and the concubine, but Jacob, Rachel, and Leah. This text argues that the seed that left Jacob's body was still controlled by his *thought* of Rachel:

"On the night when he had intercourse with Leah he was thinking of Rachel. He lay with Leah but thought of Rachel, and his semen followed his thought, but it was not intentional, for he did not know. . . . And because the Holy One, blessed be He, knew that it was not intentional and that Jacob had truthful thoughts during his desire, [Reuben] was not disqualified from being counted among the holy tribes. Otherwise he would have been disqualified."[64] The implication is that God considers Rachel to be Reuben's mother, since Rachel was the object of Jacob's thought and desire, and therefore Reuben is legitimate. "Thus the Zohar, having to accept the fact of the trick, defeats it by making Rachel pregnant with a thought."[65] "His semen followed his thought" is a statement that explains the power of mind over matter in most bedtricks.

Yehuda Liebes glosses the *Zohar* passage in the context of the Jewish mysticism that arose during the era when that text was composed. He argues that, subconsciously, Jacob really wanted Leah all along and that Leah was the hidden deity (the feminine Shekinah) above him, symbolically his mother. Because he could not accept the idea that he wanted his mother, he *thought* (consciously) that he wanted Rachel, his wife. That is, he repressed† his incestuous† desire for his mother, Leah, and only acknowledged his desire for his wife, Rachel; and, through a kind of double-back,† he got the woman that he (secretly) wanted.[66] This reading brings out something that is latent in the Hebrew text: the distinction between the act (for Jacob is apparently quite happy in bed with Leah) and the perception of the act (for afterward, he is appalled that he has slept with Leah). The element of quasi incest suggested by this reading is balanced by another sort of quasi incest: according to Leviticus (18.18), "Neither shalt thou take a wife to her sister, to vex her, to uncover her nakedness, beside the other in her lifetime." The breach of this rule leads to predictable human problems. The bedtrick in the dark allows Jacob to overcome the incest taboo, either with a maternal figure (as, in Liebes's view, the *Zohar* argues) or with a sister (as Leviticus would dictate).

Jacob is the trickster tricked.† Before Leah tricks him, he deceives his blind† father in bed (a different sort of bedtrick), masquerading as the hairy Esau when his father feels him (and is fooled, even though he rightly recognizes Jacob's *voice*, a point that we have noted in the *midrash* on the story of Rachel and Leah). Touch is the equivalent of vision for the blind Isaac and, as usual, it outranks the other senses—hearing, in this case—and, as usual, it lies. Later, too, Leah gets Rachel to sell her her right to Jacob's bed for a mandrake, and Leah goes out to meet Jacob as he comes in exhausted from the fields, just as Jacob tricked Esau into selling his birthright for a mess of potage, going out to meet Esau as he came in exhausted from the hunt.

Another *midrash*, on Genesis 29.18, makes this parallelism explicit: "In the morning, however, Behold, it was Leah. He said to her, 'You are a deceiver and the daughter of a deceiver.' She answered, 'What teacher is there who does not have pupils? Your father called you "Esau" and you answered him. So you called me and I answered you.' "[67] Leah regards her trick as an appropriate revenge on Jacob for his treatment of Esau. The *midrash* on Genesis 29.17 ("Leah had weak [*rakkoth*] eyes") reads this correlation with Jacob and Esau back into the very nature of the two women from the start: "Rabbi Johanan said, 'They had grown weak through weeping, for people used to say, "This was the arrangement: the elder daughter (Leah) is for the elder son (Esau), and the younger daughter (Rachel) for the younger son (Jacob)." And she used to weep and pray, "Let it be Thy will that I do not fall into the hands of that wicked man.' " Rabbi Huna said, 'Prayer is great, for it cancelled the rule and she even [married] before her sister.' " Leah weeps in fear of her proposed husband, and so her eyes are weak. Rachel, by contrast, is famous for weeping for her children, and so she is beautiful. This text also says that Leah "wept over her fate until her eyelashes dropped from their lids." But another folk tradition says that Rachel, not Leah, feared that her father would marry her to Jacob's brother Esau instead of to Jacob, and that Esau was a notorious adulterer.[68] Even the *midrash* of Rachel under the bed may imply that although the voice is Rachel's (and Israel's), the hands of Leah are like the hands of Esau (the impersonated one).[69]

A final twist is provided by a bedtrick, also in a *midrash* (composed between the seventh and eleventh centuries C.E.), in which Jewish law is at first apparently evaded but then finally validated by a good woman who replaces her evil sister *after* the adultery:

THE POISONED KISS

A tale is told of two sisters who resembled one another. One of them committed adultery. The thing came to the attention of her husband, and he decided to take her to the priest to have her drink the bitter waters of the adultery ordeal [see Numbers 5:11–31]. What did she do? She went to her sister, and said to her, "My husband suspects me, and I know that he intends to make me drink the bitter waters. Now, we look a lot alike, and you are my bone and flesh. Be a loving sister, and cover my shame and disgrace, for you also will bear it otherwise. So, make ready and go with my husband and drink the bitter waters—for you are innocent, and there is no impurity in you!" And her sister replied, "I'll do as you ask." That night, the two of them spent the night together, and the next day, the look-alike rose early to go off with her sister's husband to the priest. There, the priest gave her the poisonous brew to drink, and it had no effect on her, for she was innocent. When she returned, she encountered her sister, and the latter came up and threw her arms around her and kissed her, for she felt great love for her and great happiness, and she said to herself, "From now on, I'll have many lovers!" But it was the Lord's wish that the following should happen. At that moment, just as she kissed her sister, she smelled the aroma of the bitter waters, and immediately her face went green, her belly swelled up, and she fell to her knees and keeled over dead.[70]

The "shame and disgrace" that the evil sister begs to be protected from, and threatens her sister with, is precisely what Rachel decided to save Leah from. Here the intimacy of the sisters is extreme: they sleep together and kiss on the lips. Indeed, the good sister inadvertently kills the evil sister by a traditional folk weapon generally used by women upon their male lovers: the so-called poison kiss.† Yet here, as usual, the evil sister initiates the fatal embrace, though the poison is on the lips of the good sister. A muted sexual death (sororal, incestuous) exacts payment for a blatant sexual sin (adulterous) in a bedtrick displaced onto an ordeal.†

TWIN SISTERS

In some variants of the Substitute Bride, the substitute is not only the natural sister of the heroine but her identical twin, a plot device that supplies a more realistic explanation for the success of the bedtrick. For example, in Yasunari Kawabata's *The Old Capital*, a Japanese girl gets her long-lost twin to substitute for her in a marriage to a man she does not love. Lawrence Wright, in a study of real-life identical twins separated at birth, saw different aspects of the problem of identity posed by this variant of the Family Romance, including what I have termed the paradox of the double-bind,† the hope for and fear of the double:

Babies actually do get lost or separated, and, however rare such an event may be, when a person finds his twin it feeds the common fantasy that any one of us might have a clone, a doppelgänger; someone who is not only a human mirror but also an ideal companion; someone who understands me perfectly, almost perfectly, because he is me, almost me. It is not just the sense of identity that excites us but the difference; the fantasy of an identical twin is a projection of ourselves living another life, finding other opportunities, choosing other careers, sleeping with other spouses. . . .

But there is a darker and more threatening side to the story, and this may be the real secret of its grip on our imagination. We think we know who we are. . . . Suppose, then, we meet an Other who is in every outward respect ourself. . . . If we discover that we are fundamentally alike despite our various experiences, isn't there a sense of loss? A loss not only of identity but of purpose? We are left wondering not only *who* we are but *why* we are who we are.[71]

There is something typically American about this approach to the problem; the hope that the double will *understand* us is not a desideratum, at least not an explicit one, in most of our texts, though it does raise the underlying question of the asymmetry of knowledge† in a bedtrick. Wright notes, however glancingly, a theological† implications of twins: "Twins have been confounding humanity from the earliest times, almost as if they were a divine prank designed to undermine our sense of individuality and specialness in the world."[72] This prank is indeed often engineered by gods, but also by humans.

Angela Carter's great mythological novel *Wise Children*† is about identical twin girls, vaudeville actresses, Dora and Nora Chance. Their father was Melchior Hazard, a Shakespearean actor, who falsely denied them, while his fraternal twin brother, Peregrine (Perry) Hazard, falsely acknowledged them. One episode of the self-consciously Shakespearean plot begins when Dora (the shy one) falls for one of Nora's many men and begs her sister, "Give me your fella for a birthday present."[73] Dora, the narrator, tells the story:

NORA AND DORA

I'll only do it once, I said. He's really stuck on you, Nora, he's crazy about you and he's never given me a second look. But won't he be able to tell the difference? I don't know, we won't know until we try; but why should he notice any difference? Same eyes, same mouth, same hair. If it was only the once and if I keep my mouth shut. . . . Why should he guess? . . . She put on my Mitsouko and I put on her Shalimar. . . . I nearly fainted when we kissed, I was scared witless, I thought he'd recognise the ruse at once and suddenly I didn't want to go through with it. . . . But he was just my own age, just seventeen, a child, too; nothing to be afraid of. And for the purpose of the act, I wasn't Dora anymore, was I? Now I was Nora, who was afraid of nothing provided it was a man. So I kissed him back and we slipped off. . . . He never said: "Nora, there's something different about you, something more enchanting, tonight." I never wanted him to, either. I'd have been ashamed. I'll never know if he could tell the difference. If he did, he was too much of a gent to say. . . . Afterwards, I pretended to be asleep, I didn't dare talk. . . . I breathed in the smells of him and me that were really the smells of him and Nora and I kept a little sentimental tryst with silence and the night and the full moon over Croydon and he never would have done it if he'd known I wasn't Nora. He was the faithful type. Did we betray the innocence of the boy with our deception? Of course we did. Does it matter? Let the one without sin cast the first stone. He really thought I was the one he loved so he was not deceived. And I got the birthday present that I wanted and then I gave him back to Nora.[74]

That was the first bedtrick, in which the women switched the smells,† liquor† dulled the perception, silence† kept the secret of identity, and the will to self-delusion†—or male gallantry—carried the day. Some time later, at a big party, Dora recognized the man she had borrowed from Nora on her birthday, who again mistook her for Nora. They went upstairs to a bedroom, and Dora started to take off her makeup, thinking, "Tonight, this night of all nights, I wanted to look like myself, whoever that was." But after they had made love, all he said was, "Nora, you've changed your perfume." And she did not correct him.[75]

DOUBLE TAKES: THE TWIN SISTERS ON FILM

Hollywood borrows the identikit of myth and supplements it with its own clichés for mythic themes like "the good and evil twins," who seldom engage in a consummated bedtrick on screen (largely because the censors would not allow it) but enjoy all the fringe benefits of the bedtrick plot. Tricky camera work allows one actor to play two parts simultaneously in those melodramatic tours de force in which the great women and men of the silver screen play their own twins. In the same year—1944—when Betty Hutton sang duets with herself in *Here Come the Waves,* Gene Kelly danced with his alter ego in *Cover Girl.* Danny Kaye practically cornered the market on male twins: *Wonder Man* (1945), *On the Riviera* (1951), and *On the Double* (1961). In *The Divorce of Lady X* (1938), a rather stuffy lawyer falls in love with Lady Mere, who presents herself to him as both the simple, chaste (mere?) girl she really is and the wicked, much-divorced woman for whom he mistakes her (and whom she fears he may prefer to her). Both of them appear at his flat one day when he is out, and when he asks his servant what Lady Mere was she like, he replies, "She was two, sir."

In *Two-Faced Woman,* Greta Garbo's last film, made in 1941 when she was thirty-six, she plays a healthy, athletic ski instructor married to a sophisticated New Yorker (Melvyn Douglas). When he begins to stray, she invents a twin sister who is a scandalous demimondaine. He is uncertain when he first meets the twin but knows the truth when he kisses† her; he then pretends to fall for the siren song of the "twin" until in the end he accuses her of being a female Jekyll and Hyde† and confesses that he loves them both. In the very same year, 1941, the other reigning European goddess of the American cinema, Marlene Dietrich, made a film *(The Flame of New Orleans)* in which she plays a promiscuous nightclub singer masquerading as a demure countess. When the rich man she hoped to marry overhears her speaking in her own voice,† and when another man identifies her as a promiscuous woman he had known, she attributes these phenomena to a nightclub singer who is her "cousin." That is, through a double-back,† she creates a fictional character who is her true persona. We can extend the frames of masquerade even farther by taking into account the fact that the promiscuous nightclub singer was the persona that Marlene Dietrich had created for herself in what "real" life she had.

Other Hollywood actresses won their spurs by acting the parts of the good and evil twins. In *The File on Thelma Jordan* (1949), Barbara Stanwyck plays a murderess who fools the district attorney with a false identity. As she lies dying, with him beside her, she confesses everything and ends: "In a way, I'm glad it's over, the struggle, the good and evil. Willis [her lawyer] said I was two people; he was right. You don't suppose they could let just half of me die?" (a request that had been granted to the Greek twins Castor and Pollux‡). In the film *In This Our Life* (1942), Bette Davis and Olivia de Havilland starred together, not as twins, but as sisters: Davis, the bad sister, stole the man who belonged to de Havilland, the good sister. In subsequent films, Davis and de Havilland split apart; each played both the good twin with the guy and the evil twin who took him away.

In 1946, Olivia de Havilland made *The Dark Mirror,* which ends with the psychiatrist saying, only half jokingly, to the remaining, good identical twin, "Why are you so much more beautiful than your sister?" (In the 1986 remake, the line is given to the evil twin, who says to the good twin, "You're so much more beautiful than me." To which the good twin replies, "You know that's hardly possible.") In that same year, Bette Davis made *A Stolen Life*, in which, as usual, the evil Davis (Pat) steals the fiancé of the good Davis (Katie); when Pat dies in a boating accident, and no one knows which is which, Katie pretends to be Pat. The twist comes when the masquerading Katie-as-Pat learns that the envied original (Pat) was not in fact loved but hated (a cinematic surprise already known from the film of Daphne du Maurier's *Rebecca* [1940]), so that she has gained nothing by the masquerade. This is an inversion of the double-bind† that plagues all bedtricks, and it explains the success of the trick: since Bill has stopped sleeping with Pat, he never sleeps with Katie-as-Pat and so has no chance to compare the two women in bed. In fact, he so dislikes Pat that he doesn't even allow himself to look closely at Katie-as-Pat, and so he is fooled out of bed as well. (The twins' elderly guardian, by contrast, realizes from the start of the masquerade that Katie-as-Pat is not Pat.)

Davis starred in the double of this film, *Dead Ringer* (1964), almost twenty years later, but this time the plot involves murder rather than accidental death; the good (albeit murderous) twin (Edie) kills the evil twin (Maggie). The irony of the trickster tricked† works here, as in *A Stolen Life:* the bad (i.e., murderous) trickster ends up impersonating someone who turns out to be even worse (i.e., more murderous) than she is herself. She escapes unjustly from a crime she did commit (the murder of Maggie) only to pay, unjustly, for a crime she did not commit (Maggie's murder of Maggie's rich husband). *Killer in the Mirror* (1986), made twenty years after *Dead Ringer,* appears, at first, to be a shameless rip-off of the (second) Bette Davis film, a mirror-image double, even using some of the same names and following the old plot (Karen, taken for Samantha, is charged with the murder of Samantha's husband and insists that she is Karen) with most of the old details (the right hand burnt to avoid being asked to produce an identifying signature, and so forth). But then we begin to realize that, despite their superficial resemblance, the twin films are as different as the twin sisters. The first change is stolen from the *first* Bette Davis twin film, *A Stolen Life:* the evil sister, Samantha, is not murdered but apparently dies in a boating accident. But then, some time after the switch, Karen-as-Samantha discovers that Samantha is not dead at all but has been living Karen's old life ever since the switch, that Samantha had planned it all and faked the accident in order to take over Karen's life when she realized that she was about to be indicted for the murder of her husband. Both sisters claim to be Karen, and Karen-as-Samantha is sentenced to death. Only an accidental tape recording of Samantha's confession—the disembodied voice†—saves Karen.

In all of these films that share what Jeanine Basinger calls the "My God! There's two of her!"‡ theme (from the poster for *The Dark Mirror*), "there will be a discussion about which of the two women is more beautiful than the other, and a moment in the plot will arise in which one of the two will decide to pretend she's the other one. Both of these things are inherently ludicrous, since an actress can't be more beautiful than herself, and since she is already the other one in the first place."[76] But the paradoxical assumption that identical twins cannot be told apart, even though one is more beautiful than the other, is, after all, one of the basic clichés† of the bedtrick, deeply embedded in the folk traditions we have seen and explicitly noted in both takes of *The Dark Mirror*. And it is manipulated by the male directors of all of these films in ways that are not so ludicrous; makeup easily renders one twin more beautiful than the other (what else is Hollywood about?), and the actress's skill makes her into two very different people. All that the two women share is their basic physical appearance. By accepting these assumptions, ludicrous or not, the audience allows these "films to become stories about 'what makes a woman beautiful' and 'why she should behave one way and not the other.' "[77] Thus, bad girls are aggressive, sexy, career women, and so forth, while good girls are passive, modest, and so forth. While the two women may be physically identical, their behavior,† particularly their *sexual* behavior, distinguishes them (just as it distinguishes the real Lucy, in Bram Stoker's *Dracula*, from the otherwise identical Lucy the Vampire‡). And so, in *A Stolen Life*, "Although Pat and Katie are easily told apart by everyone who knows them throughout the film, no one except the Airedale can tell that Katie is not really Pat when she undertakes the impersonation. We are seriously asked to believe that Pat and Katie are totally defined by their wardrobes and sexual attitudes, so that if Katie wears Pat's clothes and is willing to undertake her sex life, there should be no problems."[78] But this is more than a mere film convention; in other genres, too, the bedtrickster knows that most of what determines one's apparent identity is superficial and can be easily faked.

In Hollywood films about double women made in later decades, as in some of the original films noirs, murder often upstages sex. Sometimes the women are not twins or even sisters but unrelated women, one of whom turns herself into an apparent twin of the other and commits a murder for which the other is suspected. This is the case with a number of films ranging from Alfred Hitchcock's classic *Vertigo* (1958), in which Kim Novak masquerades as a woman she has in fact helped to kill,[79] to *Basic Instinct*† (1991), in which Jeanne Tripplehorn masquerades as Sharon Stone when she commits a murder. *Single White Female* (1992) was made from a novel by John Lutz whose excellent title, *Single White Female Seeks Same,* expresses the longing for sameness that characterizes both urban and sexual paranoia.

Some contemporary films about twin sisters are about politics rather than murder. In a Hungarian film, *My Twentieth Century* (1990), one twin sister (Dora) is sexy and given to luxurious tastes like diamond necklaces and champagne, while the other (Lili) is poor and dowdy and revolutionary, given to throwing bombs. Do they perhaps represent the cold war capitalist West and communist East? A mirror of *My Twentieth Century* is the Polish/French film *The Double Life of Véronique* (1991), about the parallel lives of two women, Véronique and Weronika, born at precisely the same time, one in France and one in Poland. Here, as in the Hungarian film, the "twins" are separated not by a magic mirror but by an Iron Curtain, yet here, too, they invade one another's sex lives.

Finally, and predictably, the story of the good and evil twins generated at least one pornographic double, *Mirror Images* (1991), in which Delia Sheppard plays twin sisters, one promiscuous and the other sexually repressed† (an exaggeration of the usual contrast), who replace one another in various beds belonging to men who do not really seem to care who they are in bed with. The surviving sister sums it up with a classic sexist remark in the last line of the film: "Does it really make any difference?"

CATS AND CANDLES IN THE DARK

Throughout this mythology, mothers and daughters, sisters, and unrelated women slip in and out of one another's beds unnoticed. One factor that enables one woman to be mistaken for another is the misogynist assumption that all women are alike. As Janet Adelman puts it, commenting on the "pitchy night" in Shakespeare's *All's Well That Ends Well*† (4.4), the bedtrick "becomes the epitome not only of the dark waywardness of desire but also of its depersonalization, the interchangeability of the bodies with which lust plays."[80] After all, the essence of prejudice has been defined as the assumption that an unknown individual has all the characteristics of the group to which he or she belongs. The comments "people like you" or "they're all alike" (frequently said of women) are always offensive.[81] Myths, as I have argued, often enact and embody metaphors† and clichés;† in this case, they enact the metaphor of the cats and candles in the dark.

The old women who put their daughters' skins over their own faces are in a sense putting bags over their own heads in order to fool men. But the phrase "put a bag over her head"‡ generally carries a very different meaning: it is a macho locker-room joke, implying that even an ugly woman can be sexually useful in the dark. Benjamin Franklin‡ explicitly connects the sexist advice "put a bag over her head" and the sexist claim "in the night, all cats are gray" in the course of his satirical praise of older women;† together the two phrases express men's belief that all women not only look the same but actually are the same, that women are fungible, like certain kinds of money. The cats and the bags also appear together in the adage, cited by Basile in "The Old Woman Discovered,"† that a man who buys a cat in a bag (= a [male chauvinist] pig in a poke) may get an ugly woman. The sameness is also implicit in the use of "gray" rather than "black" for the invisible animal, indicating something neither black nor white, neither the white bride nor the black bride,† something that lacks all color, all character.

But is it true everywhere, or only in France, that "de nuit tous les chats sont gris"? The saying is best known in French, perhaps because of the felicitous French rhyme—which requires the change from the more general "dark" to "night" *(nuit,* to rhyme with *gris).* In some early texts, the cats in the proverb are male. In *Alphonsus, Emperor of Germany* (1594, attributed to George Chapman), Alphonsus, persuading Alexander to rape another man's bride on the wedding night with a bedtrick, argues, "By night all Cats are gray, and in the dark, / She will imbrace thee for the Prince of Wales, / Thinking that he had found her Chamber out, / Fall to thy business and make few words."[82] The cat remains male in Beaumarchais's play *The Barber of Seville* (1775), when the aged Bartholo, intending to force young Rosina to marry him, sings, "In the night, in the shadow, I'm well worth my pay; and when it is dark, handsome cats all are grey."[83] Here the implication is that age may have destroyed his good looks, but not his sexual prowess; he is still a tomcat.

Casanova,† in the eighteenth century, applied the metaphor to men in his reply to the bedtrickster (an ugly old widow) who taunted him for having mistaken her for the pretty young married woman with whom he was infatuated at Soleure. She wrote: "I have avenged myself because you can no longer pretend to think her a marvel of beauty, as having mistaken me for her, the difference between us must needs be slight. . . . But I have done you a service, too, as the thought of what has happened should cure you of your passion. You will no longer adore her before all other women who are just as good as she."[84] The belief that women are all alike in the dark was thus a comfort to this ugly old woman. To confute her, Casanova argued that she was the one who had been fooled (as in fact she had not): "It is easy to see that you took my servant for myself, for in the night, you know, all cats are grey, . . . and I congratulate you on obtaining an enjoyment you certainly would not have had from me, as I should most surely have recognized you directly from your breath and your aged charms, and I can tell you it would have gone hard with you."[85] Thus, he argues simultaneously that no woman can tell one man from another in bed (using, for men, the metaphor that later came to be applied primarily to women) and then that he can always tell one woman from another—particularly an old woman from a young woman. In fact, the situation was just the opposite: the woman knew perfectly well who she was in bed with, and Casanova did not. To save face, he pretended to have engineered a double-cross.†

In later texts the cats are almost always female, often with an implicit play upon the obscene meaning of *chat*. Robert Darnton notes, "*Le chat, la chatte, le minet* mean the same thing in French slang as 'pussy' does in English, and they have served as obscenities for centuries." He gives several examples: "As he loves his cat, he loves his wife," and, nastier, "He has other cats to whip." The proverb was explicitly glossed in an eighteenth-century collection: "That is to say that all women are beautiful enough at night."[86] Darnton snaps back, "Enough for what?" There is also, perhaps, an unintended irony in invoking for this metaphor an animal, the cat, whom we believe to be able to see in the dark and whose eyes we can see gleaming in the dark. To say therefore that you can't see cats in the dark is to deny and confuse what cats (and women) see subjectively with the way that men see them as (sexual) objects—a very old sexist move.

Freud made what can only be called a Freudian slip† in using the metaphor of the cat in his discussion of Dora when he proclaimed his determination not to use euphemisms in discussing sex or the genitals: "I call bodily organs and processes by their technical names, and I tell these to the patient if they—the names, I mean—happen to be unknown to her. *J'appelle un chat un chat.*"[87] Jane Gallop calls him on this one: "At the very moment he defines nonprurient language as direct and non-euphemistic, he takes a French detour into a figurative expression. By his terms, this French sentence would seem to be titillating, coy, flirtatious. And to make matters more juicy (less 'dry'), *chat* or *chatte* can be used as a vulgar (vulva) slang for the female genitalia. So in this gynecological context, where he founds his innocence upon the direct use of technical terms, he takes a French detour and calls a pussy a pussy."[88] By arguing that he was simply playing doctor, being scientific, and so forth, Freud was implying that a woman was just a body to him, not an occasion for erotic countertransference. And the French metaphor of the cat does just that: all gynecological objects are alike in the dark. (The dark was also the key to one of Freud's notorious categorizations of woman as object: "the dark† continent.")[89]

The metaphor of cats alternates with the metaphor of candles. John Heywood's *Proverbs,* in 1549, invokes both the cats and the candles: "When all candles be out, all cats be grey."[90] Erasmus, in 1500, had linked the two by citing the French proverb about cats ("De nuici tous chats son gris") and a story by Plutarch in his gloss on the Latin adage "When the light is out there is nothing different between women" (sublata lucerna nihil interest inter mulieres).[91] The story from Plutarch (writing in the first century, in Greek) may be one of the oldest sources of the metaphor of the candles (here lamps, as candles had not yet been invented):

> One day a woman said to Philip [of Macedon], who was trying to make her come to him against her will: "Let me go. Every woman is the same when the lamp is out." This is a good thing to say to adulterous and lustful men, but a married woman should be, *especially* when the light is out, not the same as random women. On the contrary, when her body cannot be seen, her wisdom, her constancy, her affection, and her belonging person- ally to her husband alone should be apparent.[92]

Thus, the Greek urtext of the metaphor for ignoring difference when sight is obscured enters recorded European literature as a remark not about cats at all but about women (and lamps). Plutarch's proverb of the lamp has a double edge: if a rapist thinks all women are alike, he might be dissuaded from raping any particular one; but if a husband knows that all women are not alike, he will appreciate his wife's good qualities— including the quality that he prizes most in her, which is her belief that *he* is unique. It also has a certain irony in the light of the tradition that Philip's† son Alexander‡ was begotten through a bedtrick.[93]

The lamps may have entered the story from another Latin source, the story of Cupid and Psyche,† in which a woman who feels that all men are *not* the same in the dark insists on shining a lamp on her lover, thereby awakening him and putting an end to the bedtrick. In later European literature, the lamps become candles and develop a paradigm of their own. Kleist's Amphitryon‡ protests, "In rooms where candlelight was shining fair / No one who had five healthy senses has / Mistaken friends until today."[94] Shakespeare uses the candle metaphor to suggest homeliness masquerading as beauty in *As You Like It*† (3.5) when Rosalind, masquerading as a man, mocks Phoebe: "What though you have no beauty,—As by my faith, I see no more in you / Than without candle may go dark to bed." And he twists the metaphor in another direction in *Measure for Measure*† (5.1) when Lucio suggests that a judge should go "darkly to work" with a woman because "women are light at midnight."

Casanova, whom we have just seen invoking (tom-)cats, also cites the Latin proverb of the lamps (sublata lucerna nullum discrimen inter feminas [When the light is out, all women are the same]) and remarks: "A true saying insofar as it regards material pleasures, but false and very false concerning the affairs of love."[95] The image is often used to make a point about class.† Robert Herrick, in 1648, substitutes class for beauty and the phrase "in the dark" for "without candle" in a poem actually entitled "No Difference i' th' Dark," which includes the lines "Night makes no difference 'twixt the Priest and Clerk; / Joan as my Lady is as good i' the Dark."[96]

Class is also at the heart of the poet William Butler Yeats's use of the candles in his poem, published in 1938, about a woman who sends her maid† to substitute for her in the dark with her lover—for fear of losing his love:

THE THREE BUSHES

> Said lady once to lover,
> "None can rely upon
> A love that lacks its proper food;
> And if your love were gone
> How could you sing those songs of love?
> I should be blamed, young man."
> O my dear, O my dear.
>
> . . . .
>
> "I love a man in secret,
> Dear chambermaid," said she.
> "I know that I must drop down dead
> If he stop loving me,
> Yet what could I but drop down dead
> If I lost my chastity?"
> O my dear, O my dear.

"So you must lie beside him
And let him think me there.
And maybe we are all the same
Where no candles are,
And maybe we are all the same
That strip the body bare."
O my dear, O my dear.

.   .   .   .

When the lover dies, the lady dies of grief. The chambermaid cares for their graves, on which two rosebushes grow together. And when she dies, the priest, to whom she has confessed all, plants a third rosebush, whose roots grow together with the other two.[97] When Yeats writes, "And maybe we are all the same / Where no candles are," he is explicitly speaking of one person masquerading as another (and perhaps quoting the cliché about candles in the dark), putting into the mouth of the woman the assumption that is enforced when she sends her female servant in her place. Yet the poem gives a measure of power back to the servant, for by burying her, too, beside the lover, the wise priest suggests that she, who knew his body, has a claim to him as great as that of the lady who loved his soul—indeed, that she knew him in a way that the lady did not.

The metaphor of cats and/or candles in the dark comes to function primarily as a sexual metaphor, with only secondary philosophical or po-litical overtones. Women are implicated in this metaphor not merely when they are analogized to cats but as soon as the phrase "in the dark" or "without candles" is taken to imply "in bed" or "for sex" (and, of course, a male subject). Indeed, the phrase implies not that men have regarded women as indistinguishable *even* in the dark (in bed, in situa-tions of intimacy where we might most expect a difference) but that men have regarded them so *especially* in the dark, since it was precisely wom-en's sexuality that was taken as their essence and that was regarded as essentially the same in all women in the dark, just as their beauty was essentialized and universalized in the light. Milan Kundera's womanizing Tomas thinks that all women are alike in 999,999 parts of all significant respects: "Tomas was obsessed by the desire to discover and appropriate that one-millionth part; . . . he was obsessed with what in each of them is unimaginable, obsessed, in other words, with the one-millionth part that makes a woman dissimilar to others of her sex." And, discounting things like gait and cooking,† "he sought that dissimilarity in sex and nowhere else."[98] Thus, he argued, women are different *only* in the dark.

In Sir Philip Sidney's *The Countess of Pembroke's Arcadia* (1593), a man who has spent the night with a woman he mistook for another exclaims in the morning, "O, who would have thought there could have been such difference between women!"[99] Like the victim of the bedtrick in Julian Barnes's "Experiment,"† he sees a difference between women where there is none.

Women can also treat men that way, can fail to tell the male tomcats apart, and some male authors argue that (all) women think that all men are alike in the dark—an argument advanced by men in those relatively rare texts in which the men themselves play the bedtricks and the even rarer texts in which they take the time to wonder how the women feel about that. But are all tomcats gray? I think not. Women seem to have better night vision than men. The stories, at least, seem to say that more men find women all alike than women find men all alike; in most texts in which men substitute for other men against the will of the women, women insist that the men are different in the dark. Some male authors argue that women are not so easily fooled‡ as men, an argument used to accuse women, on the one hand, of promiscuity and hypocrisy when they are seduced and, on the other hand, of the cunning to avoid seduction and the power to fool those tomcat Casanovas. Other texts attribute higher powers of discrimination, and higher motives, to the female victims of bedtricks and to female bedtricksters.

Thus, when men try to inflict the levirate or the droit du seigneur† on women, the women move heaven and earth to get out of it, because they do *not* want to let *that* guy touch them; the bedtricks that women turn are necessary precisely because they find men different. When Dick Francis's hero, in *Straight*, sleeps with the mistress of his dead brother Greville (in what he wryly refers to as a "memorial service" for his brother, a horsey pun,† since stallions† are said to "serve" or "service" mares), he remarks: "Women said men were not all the same in the dark, and I knew both where I'd surprised her and failed her, known what I'd done like Greville and not like Greville from the instinctive releases and tensions of her reactions. . . . [She said,] 'What I had with Greville was unforgettable and unrepeatable.'"[100]

Are women smarter? Or more alike? Or do they simply value the parts of people that are not alike, while the men value the parts that are alike? In any case, women are often able to subvert the powers of men precisely because men regard women as indistinguishable or not worthy of distinction. The man's sexism (or his traditional, duty†-driven attitude to the woman as a thing rather than a person) may make him regard the woman as a mere object, so that he does not take the trouble to find out who she really is. Because men think women are alike, they do not notice them, and that invisibility can be used as a weapon of the weak† when women need to masquerade. Husbands of runaway wives "prove surprisingly obtuse when asked by detectives to describe the runaway, revealing how long it had been since they had truly looked at their wives as persons, 'really seen' them."[101] But since the wife cares about who her husband really is, she takes pains to get away from him.

ARE ALL BEAUTIFUL WOMEN ALIKE IN THE LIGHT?

The ideal of beauty imprisons women in many ways, one of which is by assuming that all beautiful women look alike—indeed, that all beautiful people look alike. Why do beautiful male-female twins, who in real life can look very different (consider the gorgeous Cary Grant as a stupefyingly ugly woman in the film *I Was a Male War Bride*† [1949]), look alike in stories such as *Twelfth Night*† and the Japanese novel *The Change-lings*†? A particular culture at a particular time tends to regard beauty as a single ideal, a universal norm ("36-24-36, blond hair and blue eyes . . ."), and to see all beauties as looking alike even in the light, in contrast with ugly people, each of whom is ugly in a different way, like Tolstoy's† unhappy families. Beauty blinds in much the same way that otherness blinds, for beauty itself is often construed as other, as nonhuman ("angelic," "divine"). All women look alike not only to men who *don't* care about them but to those who care too much, whose lust drives them to project† the desired face, the perfect face of Helen of Troy,‡ onto all the faceless others. At the start of *The Stepford Wives* (1974), the husbands *can* tell the difference between their wives, and that is precisely what makes them replace their wives with computerized robots who love to clean house and praise their husbands' sexual performances, and who lose their desire to do anything that makes them individuals. That is, the doubles are created precisely for their sexuality, and to do this all of them must be precisely the same. Two actresses, one cool, the other sexy, played the heroine in Luis Buñuel's last film, *Cet obscur objet de désir* (1977). Salman Rushdie makes a telling comment on the reception of this film: "The two women looked utterly dissimilar, yet it was not uncommon for people to watch the entire movie without noticing the device. Their need to believe in the homogeneity of personality was so deeply rooted as to make them discount the evidence of their own eyes."[102]

"Vive la différence," the punch line of several old jokes, celebrates the difference *between* the two sexes. But within each sex, more particularly within the female sex, and more particularly within the female gender (defining "gender" as a system that establishes and valorizes the particular social meanings attached to biological, sexual difference), it is sameness, not difference, that misogynists celebrate. R. Howard Bloch defines "misogyny as a speech act in which woman is the subject of the sentence and the predicate a more general term. . . . Even the sentence, 'All women are different' is included in such a definition, since there are among women as among men, points of resemblance that reduce such a statement to a violating generalization."[103] Significantly, Bloch's defense of an individual's difference includes the right to resemble another individual.

The idea that all women are alike (both in the light and in the dark), the refrain of rapists and seducers, became a staple of misogynist quips. In the film *The Truth about Cats and Dogs*† (1996), when the protagonist encounters two women who pretend to be a single woman, he complains to a friend, "She seems entirely different from one day to another"; to which the friend replies, "Women are like that." That is, one of the ways in which all women are alike is that all women differ from themselves from one day to the next. But all misogynists are not alike, even in the darkness of their misogyny. A commentary on the *Kamasutra* puts a peculiar twist on the sexist logic:

> Formerly there was adultery [*paradarabhigamanam*] in the world, as it is said:
>> Women are all alike, just like cooked rice, Your Majesty; therefore, one should not get mad at them or get attached to them or take pleasure in them [*rameta*].
> But [the sage and author] Audalaki forbade this state of affairs, and so people said:
>> [The lawgiver] Manu forbids Brahmins to drink wine, and Audalaki forbids common people to take other people's wives.[104]

Thus, in the good old days, adultery didn't matter, since women didn't matter; if all women are like rice, there is no reason to make a fuss if someone dips his spoon in your bowl, as it were. But Audalaki changed all that and distinguished between women that one can and cannot have sex with. Romantic love or desire does not always regard all women as so much "cooked rice." This "oriental" metaphor of the cooked rice was satirized in the musical *The King and I* (1956) when Anna, pleading with the king to set free one of the many slave girls in his harem, said, "To you one woman is like another, as one bowl of rice is just like another bowl of rice"; to which he replied with another metaphor: the bee goes from flower to flower, but the flower must not go from bee to bee. The rice metaphor, which, as so often, equates sex and eating,† remained current in India. At the end of the nineteenth century, a variant resurfaced in a Bengali text:

> A guru said to his disciple, a certain king, "Everything is the same." In the night the king went into [his] room and said to his wife, "This woman is [the same] to me as you. Tonight I will sleep with her." The wife said, "Whatever happens tomorrow will happen." The next day the queen went to the guru and told him everything. The guru said, "Today at mealtime give him a cup of shit with [his] vegetables." The queen did this. The king, seeing the cup of shit near the rice, got angry and began to scold the queen. The queen said, "You have attained the realization that everything is the same—so why do you get angry whether it's fish soup or shit?" The king then regained his composure. He realized that he did not understand the teaching about the realization of the same.[105]

The metaphysical idea of monism (which Hegel, contra Schelling, characterized as "a night in which all cows are black")[106] is translated first into sexual promiscuity and then into omnivorousness. In the implicit exchange of sexual favors for food, the wife invokes the values of distinctiveness in the kitchen to remind her husband of the values of distinctiveness in the bedroom.

The connection between adultery and the sameness of women is constructed in a different way in another Hindu myth of the origin of adultery, the myth of Indra and Ahalya.‡ According to one of the earliest tellings, in the *Ramayana,* all women were created identical, but then the Creator made one, Ahalya, with unique beauty. Ahalya, however, was forced to share her beauty with everyone else as punishment for having committed adultery.[107] Thus, it is implied, if all women are the same, adultery will not take place—or, perhaps, not quite so often.

In the late nineteenth century in Europe, a sustained argument was made for the indistinguishability of women. Otto Weininger used this argument to prop up the double standard,† as Bram Dijkstra notes:

> Since each man was an individual, this argument went, a woman who decided to sleep with several men showed her inability to recognize the glorious contours of her chosen mate's unique masculine individuality. In her

unwillingness to cleave to one man, she thereby offended the special dignity of every other man's personal identity as well. But the male who roamed from woman to woman was seen as a poet in search of the ideal. Among the unvariegated shadows of a single undifferentiated form, he made a ceaseless, heroic search for the perfect embodiment of his sense of beauty.[108]

So a woman who thought all men alike was stupid, unable to recognize her man's individuality and cleave† properly, but a man who thought all women were alike and searched for the ideal—the true Helen‡—was smart.

Women in the twentieth century still feel that they must defend their individualism. An advertisement for a vaginal cream states, sympathetically: "Who says we're all the same? You thought all yeast medications were the same. But Gyne-Lotrimin® knows that every woman is different with different needs at different times. . . . Now, who says we're all the same?"[109] Precisely the part of the female anatomy that is the locus of sameness in the sexist paradigm is positioned here as highly individual.

Female sameness is asserted, then subverted, and then desubverted in a passage in a short story by Italo Calvino:

A girl begins to come to the room. I could say it was always the same girl, because at first there's no difference between one girl and the next; they're all strangers, and you communicate with them according to a prescribed ritual. You have to spend some time and do a lot of things with this girl in order to understand the whys and wherefores; and then begins the enormous-discoveries phase—the real (perhaps the only) exciting season of love. After that—spending still more time and doing still more things with this girl—you realize that the other girls were like this, too, that you, too, are like this, that we all are, and that everything she does is boring, as if repeated in a thousand mirrors. Bye, girlfriend.[110]

The transition from same to different to same is the double-back† logic characteristic of bedtricksters, as is the multiplication of one stereotype in many mirrors.†

A particularly low blow was dealt by those misogynists who argued not only that all women were alike but that they were all trying in vain to be like men. "The female is as it were a deformed male," Aristotle suggested.[111] Thomas Laqueur argues that in what he calls the one-sex model of pre-Enlightenment anatomy, woman is merely a flawed double of man, and there is no *difference* not only between women but between women and men.[112] The one-sex model of language† is mocked in Muriel

Rukeyser's humorous and feminist version of the myth of Oedipus† in her poem "Myth":

> Long afterward, Oedipus, old and blinded, walked the roads. He smelled a familiar smell. It was the Sphinx. Oedipus said, "I want to ask one question. Why didn't I recognize my mother?" "You gave the wrong answer," said the Sphinx. "But that was what made everything possible," said Oedipus. "No," she said. "When I asked, What walks on four legs in the morning, two at noon, and three in the evening, you answered, Man. You didn't say anything about woman." "When you say Man," said Oedipus, "you include women too. Everyone knows that." She said, "That's what you think."[113]

Sexist language blinded Oedipus; he didn't recognize his mother because he didn't distinguish women from men.[114]

A Hindu meditation on the identity of all beautiful women, parallel in many ways to the Buddha's† deconstruction of his sister's beauty, was recorded by Ann Grodzins Gold in Rajasthan in the 1980s. This is my summary of her long, detailed text:

SEVEN HUNDRED AND FIFTY QUEEN PINGALAS

King Bhartrhari goes hunting, taking pains to kill only male animals, but after he kills a magnificent talking stag, the seven hundred talking does who are the stag's wives commit suicide [*sati*] by impaling themselves on the stag's horns, cursing the king to suffer as they have suffered. But he thinks, "These sluts are just barking; they are animals," and ignores their curse. Then he decides to test his wife, Queen Pingala, to see if she too would commit *sati* for him. He soaks his handkerchief in the does' blood and sends it with a message to say that he has been killed while hunting. Meanwhile, the great yogi and trickster Gorakh Nath arrives and chastises the king for killing an innocent animal and making seven hundred widows, and Gorakh Nath revives the stag.

When Pingala sees the bloody handkerchief and hears the message, she commits *sati*, even though the god Shiva himself tells her that the king is alive and she herself knows this through her own magic powers; she realizes that it is a test and decides, stubbornly, to use her powers to fulfill it. When the king returns and finds her dead, he begs Shiva to revive her, and the god summons Gorakh Nath and tells him to "put an end to King Bhartrhari's stubbornness." As Gorakh Nath hears the king moaning, "Alas, Pingala!" he drops his jug, which shatters into many pieces, and he begins to moan, "Alas, my jug!" Gorakh Nath promises to bring back seven hundred and fifty Pingalas "just like yours" if the king will have his potters make seven hundred and fifty jugs "just like this one." The potters make the jugs, but Gorakh Nath points out that they are the wrong color. The king, who does not want to wait for another batch of jugs to be made, agrees to accept Pingalas "good or bad, black or fair, . . . black or yellow."

Gorakh Nath worships Shiva, and there appear seven hundred and fifty Pingalas, all looking alike, exactly like Pingala, with her face, her exact face, her eyes, her bangles and clothes. "Not one of them was missing something. Or else the king might not have recognized her." Gorakh Nath tells the king to grab his Pingala by the hand, threatening to flay him alive if he grabs any but the one that is his. Blindfolded, the king grabs one and the others disappear. Gorakh Nath says, "Here is your Pingala."[115]

The tale begins with a fatal error,† the slaughter of a talking animal separated from its mates; the does' vivid sexual death, impaled on the stag's horns (which here signify not cuckolding,† as in Europe, but destructive male sexuality), inspires the king (or curses him, as the story puts it) to be similarly separated from his own mate; in effect, he kills his own wife, as Gorakh Nakh reminds him repeatedly. The king tests Pingala just as the hunter Cephalus† tests, and kills, Procris in the course of his fatal error.

The metaphysical lesson teaches the king first not to discriminate between black† and fair women, and then that there is more difference among jugs than among women. In fact, jugs and pots often stand in for women as parthenogenic wombs, sometimes giving birth to sages with the matronymic of "pot" (such as Drona in the *Mahabharata* and Kumbha, the fictional male form of Cudala,‡ in the *Yogavasishtha*). Then Gorakh Nath defies the king to find the Pingala that is his, just as Damayanti‡ had to choose her own Nala from among five look-alikes. But in fact he cannot tell the difference between the queens, and the threat of punishment for failure—a flayed skin—is appropriate both to a hunter, who strips animals of their skins,† and to someone who cannot see beneath the surface. Only when he is blindfolded† does the king touch and get to keep his own Pingala. But is she real or just one of the many fakes? The king thinks she is real, and Gorakh Nath tells him she is his own, but is he telling the truth? The storyteller later told Ann Gold that "the 'real' Pingala was no more real than the magic replications of her form.

Bodies are not real. Name and form are not real."[116] This conclusion begins with the same assumption that animates sexist texts—that all women are alike—but it ends in a very different metaphysical place, a place where, not merely beautiful women or even all women or even all human beings, but indeed all living creatures are alike in their lack of metaphysical essence; their very existence is the ultimate illusion.[117]

Approach Four

Feminism, or Women Are Good to Think With

The tales of the bedtrick address many issues that I would classify in a general way as feminist, issues about the ways in which men have injured and controlled women in real life and have produced texts that present a distorted view of women, and the ways in which women have resisted and subverted those controls and those views.[118] You don't have to be a radical feminist to realize that men do an awful lot of really lousy things to women in these stories. Many, if not most, of the sexual unions in this book would be described as rape† by our present standards, and a few are explicitly designated as rapes even within the texts. Still more of these stories tell of miscellaneous acts of forced marriage or of what we would call marital rape; many of the animal brides† are taken against their will, and the women on the receiving end of levirate† marriages and the droit du seigneur† are bought and sold like pieces of meat. But the stories of rape are also about women who use the bedtrick to avoid rape; the stories of the droit du seigneur are, almost without exception, about the *subversion,* rather than the passive experience, of that custom.

Women are implicitly denigrated in texts from every culture treated in this book. In texts written by men (which is to say most texts), the woman is almost always the other, and the other is frequently incomprehensible and irrational. Yet, time and again, the text undercuts the patriarchal assumptions with which the story seems to begin, and here I would detect a woman's point of view, if not necessarily a woman's voice. Even patently misogynist texts may be read to reveal female revenge and/or tricksterism when edited (if not actually rewritten) by a woman writer for a female audience. The story damns women, but who is telling the story? Women may be using the tales—and the lessons within the tales—toward their own ends. Just as, within the stories themselves, characters want to know if women's voices are being heard (when their faces are not seen), so, too, as readers we want to know if women's voices are being heard outside the text, in the frame of the storytelling. We may try to sort out the different views of the men and women inside the stories, but it is far more difficult to know whose voice is speaking to us through the outer frame of the narrator, the voice of a woman or a man (or, in some cases, an androgyne).[119] Many of these texts hold misogyny and feminism in tension together like asceticism and eroticism or truth and falsehood—another paradox.† Perhaps it is best to speak of voices *on behalf of* women rather than *from* women. Let us confine ourselves here to the voices within the story, but bear in mind the parallel outer frame, so that we may, for instance, read stories about cutting out women's tongues as stories about suppressing the voices of the women telling the story.

THE SILENT WOMAN

We have noted that one of the many things that tales like Beauty and the Beast† or the Swan Maiden† are about is the common practice of exogamy, which forces women at marriage to leave their native home and move away to live with their husbands, who may be so foreign as to appear like beasts. This foreignness may also bring the bride to a place where a different dialect is spoken, so that she literally loses her voice, her native language, her *mother* tongue (which A. K. Ramanujan taught us to contrast with the more public *father* tongue).[120] Rarely, a man in our stories is rendered voiceless (Secundus† undertakes a vow of eternal silence when he seduces his mother and she kills herself), but women are often silenced. In many variants, the Loathly Lady† "has been bound by a spell and cannot speak the truth of her state."[121] Hindu women are expected to remain silent when they are subjected to impregnation by surrogate husbands in the levirate.†[122] Some bedtrickster women give up their voices expressly in order to win the love of a man. Disney's version of the story of the mermaid† puts the case most cynically, through the voice of the evil sea witch, Ursula: "You'll have your looks, your pretty face, and don't forget the importance of body language." Yet the prince recognizes the mermaid primarily by her voice, not by her face; he rejects her when she loses her voice, and he accepts the surrogate (the sea witch herself), who has the voice. More often, however, the female victim of the bedtrick is silenced against her will. The Greek nymph Echo, in love with Narcissus,† is forbidden to speak and may use her voice only to repeat what someone else says (like E. T. A. Hoffmann's Olympia in "The Sandman"†). Silencing a woman obscures not only her own identity (which the bedtrickster may actively wish to conceal) but the identity of the man who rapes her (which the rape victim may wish to reveal). In our stories, women are often silenced by being beheaded,‡ like the woman on the English inn sign "The Silent Woman," which depicts a headless female body, "a Draconian way to shut women up."[123] Yet in South Asia, and other places, "talk" is a euphemism for sex; this makes the silence of the bedtrick a paradox: how can you have sex without "talking"? Perhaps the answer is that some cultures allow women *only* this kind of talking.

Male bedtricksters sometimes willingly disguise their voices, for the voice can reveal or conceal; a person's speech patterns, nuances, rhythm, and accent are all identifiable marks, but they can be hidden or changed as part of an effective disguise. The timbre of the sound and the content of speech together often unmask a bedtrickster, particularly when vision is obscured; speech and, sometimes, silence identify the true person, overcoming the false evidence of vision. Stith Thompson isolates a motif (H 38.2.3) that he calls "Recognition of maidservant substitute by her habitual conversation." Not surprisingly, bedtricksters in operas† are often revealed by their voices—Mozart's Don Giovanni,† Susanna in *The Marriage of Figaro*† (Figaro insists, "I recognized the voice I adore"); and so is Cyrano.†

For both men and women, the successful imitation of the voice often makes a bedtrick succeed; the snake† lover talks like his victim's husband. In one *midrash,* Jacob is fooled by Rachel's† voice, and in Thomas Mann's version he recognizes Leah's voice but explains it away. In *The Changelings,*† it is said: "How could their voices differ when not only were they similar to begin with, but Naishi no Kami had long been imitating a woman, while Chunagon had grown accustomed to acting like a man?" But, later, "Worried lest the Emperor suspect that this was the voice of Chunagon that he had been accustomed to hearing, Naishi no Kami spoke unevenly and quietly."[124] In the film *True Lies*† (1994), the bedtrickster husband sits in the dark and plays a tape recording of the voice of a French colleague, for he knows his wife would recognize his voice. So, too, in Roald Dahl's "The Great Switcheroo,"† one of the men planning the bedtrick says, "No talking, I presume," and the other replies, "Not a word." The voice functions in these myths as a kind of prescientific voiceprint, an auditory fingerprint.† As Ralph Harper put it: "Through all the changes in the bodies of a man and woman, the voice alone usually survives unchanged."[125]

But women are silenced both as bedtricksters and as women, *tout court.* Angela Carter's† masquerading sister is careful to keep her mouth shut. Men sometimes cut out women's tongues, to silence a sexually aggressive woman or to silence a woman who is the victim of male sexual aggression. The huntsman cuts out the tongue of a deer in place of Brangane's† tongue, which counterbalances the use of Brangane's maidenhead in place of Isolde's† maidenhead. In a Roman myth, Tereus rapes Philomela and cuts out her tongue, but Philomela uses her hands to weave the story into a piece of cloth. In revenge, Philomela's sister, married to

Tereus, remarks to their son Itys, "How very much you look like your father," then stifles her maternal feelings, kills him, and feeds him to Tereus.[126] In Shakespeare's *Titus Andronicus,* the rapists cut out Lavinia's tongue, and the mute girl uses the stumps of her arms to point to them—for her hands, as well as her tongue, were cut off expressly so that she would not be able, like Philomela, to write the story out. (She points, in fact, to a book that tells the story† of Philomela.) Appropriately, Titus, Lavinia's father, gags the rapists when he tortures them in revenge. Rape is marked by silence just as incest† is marked by riddling speech; both are "unspeakable acts," protected by the further unspeakable act of cutting out the woman's tongue. But the silence about a rape rebounds because it, too, is a statement, a speaking silence. In *The Queen of Corinth,*† when Merione is asked to identify the man who had raped her ("His tongue, / Did you not heare his tongue, no voice?"), she replies, "None, none Sir: / All I know of him was his violence." Here the man's silence, rather than the woman's, testifies to his sexual violence.

The female tongue may serve as a weapon that can kill a sexual enemy more literally than can a mere poison pen(-is) or barbed words. The tongue and the vagina together function like the *vagina dentata,* the vagina with teeth; this is the weapon of the (male) demon Adi,† trumped by the razor-sharp penis of Shiva. Shiva inherits this mythological trope from the god Indra,†[127] whose deadly penis(es) and phallic thunderbolt often come in handy in his combats with women who have excessive and aggressive genitalia and tongues.‡ Such women pose a threat for which there is only one solution: castration, or an (upwardly) displaced† clitoridectomy.[128] The mouth must first be castrated (the tongue cut out) and then penetrated. But the stories also tell us that the mouth is not the same as the genitals at all, because it has the power of a particular sort of speech that the genitals, articulate though they may be, lack: ambiguity.

NIGHT BLINDNESS

Eyes, like tongues, are sexual weapons. The truism of the cats in the dark can be presented from either a nonsexist or a sexist point of view: (1) People may look different but in all other aspects they are alike; hence, when you can't see them, they become alike. (2) Women may look different but, unlike men, in all other aspects, particularly in their sexuality, they are alike; hence, when you can't see them, they become alike. Let us begin with the more general visual aspect of sexual sameness, which applies to both men and women in bed, and then consider its sexist aspect.

The war between the senses—between vision and other senses such as hearing, or the broader power of mind—looms large here. We call it the deed of darkness, but so much of human sexuality is really visual, often deceptively visual; and the person who is tricked is blind even in the light. Which of the senses do we trust when they compete? As human beings (in contrast with, say, dogs), we tend to privilege our eyes, in many ways our most highly developed contact with the outside world. Since, for humans, vision is the king of the senses, it is vision that must be stymied when a human is to be sexually flummoxed. If love is blind, lust is stone blind. More precisely, in most European texts Cupid is blind (though according to Apuleius he is invisible and will make love to Psyche† only in the dark), but his Hindu equivalent, Kama, is invisible,[129] so that *we* are blind to *him*—a more appropriate location of the blurred vision of lust.

Desire influences vision in another way, as well: it causes us to project† upon the face we really see the image of the face we would like to see. After someone we love dies or goes away, or even when our children leave home, we keep thinking we see them when we are looking at people who resemble them in even the most general way—the same height or baseball cap or color of hair or way of walking. At the end of the film *Multiplicity*† (1996), the protagonist's wife happens to see all three of his clones driving away in an open convertible car; she blinks and says to the children, "You know how you can tell if you really love someone? When everyone you see reminds you of him."

People in myths often use their eyes to make sexual discriminations, but some myths seem to imply that they should not. In a way, the emphasis on the physical identity of doubles is an argument *against* the visual: it demonstrates that we are wrong to judge by appearances. When two people look alike, we are forced to distinguish between them by searching for more subtle, more profound, signs of identity. In traditional,† impersonal contexts, the visual element of sexual love predominates, and all that binds the doubles together is their appearance, while other, more intimate factors such as actions, words, smell, feelings, and personality don't count. If the impostor *looks* like the other person, the trick works. By contrast, the voice† and other senses play a central role in some stories that take a more spiritual or Romantic approach to the uniqueness of the individual. These are more than two variants on the theme of recognition; they are two very different approaches to the problem of human identity.

Night blindness is often evoked, metaphorically, to explain why someone "accidentally" gets into bed with the wrong partner. Sleeping customs in many cultures are such that a husband and wife may never ever see each other naked. Joint family arrangements also make nocturnal masquerades both more likely and more possible than in cultures where married couples sleep alone. Salman Rushdie imagines precisely such a situation in a Pakistani house in which all the women sleep in one room,[130] and Donald Keene argues that very similar conditions limited the vision of a lover in Japan in the Heian era.[131] The dormitory atmosphere prevails in Gabriel García Márquez's *One Hundred Years of Solitude*† when an adolescent boy finds himself in a darkened room with his mother and several other women, one of whom (his mother?) he makes love to.[132]

But are we not all night blind when it comes to sex? What deep human instinct, linked to fantasy and self-deception, makes us close our eyes,‡ sometimes literally, often figuratively, when we kiss or make love?[133] Varuthini† is made to close her eyes during a bedtrick, and Isak Dinesen's Joseph begs Mary† to close her eyes and imagine that he is the Holy Ghost.[134] The eroticism of not being really seen is an element of all of these myths: when the lights are out, the victim is blind, and beauty does not matter. The fantasy of having a blind lover, dramatized in a bedtrick in the film *Sirens*† (1994), may be a fantasy of being loved for one's true self, for one's soul, forever, for qualities that will not decay. When the woman's face is invisible, veiled, for instance, the man has to judge her by her body—or her soul. The tenuous link that connects the fantasy of making love in the dark with the elements of jealousy,† hatred,† and paranoia† that drive many of these stories may be seen in a story that Chaucer tells ("The Merchant's Tale"), in which the wife of a blind man makes love to her lover in his presence, epitomizing the "blindness" of the cuckold.†

In tracing the role of the eye in narratives of bedtricks we may speak, on the one hand, about the gaze, about what we see through our eyes (vision as part of the judging subject), and, on the other hand, about the eyes that we see (the eyes as objects to be judged). The eye is both a mirror—often called the mirror of the soul—and a window, the point through which the soul moves out of the body. As a mirror, it reflects the world; as a window, it is what we look through and into to see who a person is. These ideas are conflated in the belief that we see ourselves mirrored† in the eyes of those who love us and whom we love. Shakespeare used this concept in a brilliant, protostructuralist joke about infidelity in *Merchant of Venice* (5.1), when Bassanio, swearing his love to Portia, says, "I swear to thee, even by thine own fair eyes, / Wherein I see myself,—" and she breaks in, "Mark you but that! / In both my eyes he doubly sees himself; / In each eye, one: swear by your double self, / And there's an oath of credit." And in *Troilus and Cressida* (5.2), Cressida says: "Troilus, farewell! one eye yet looks on thee, But with my heart the other eye doth see. / Ah, poor our sex! this fault in us I find, / The error of our eye directs our mind." The doubleness of eyes makes inevitable the duplicity of sexual love.

Eyes recur throughout our texts as things to look not through but at, as objects rather than instruments of identification. The evil Bedouin† mother-in-law steals her daughter-in-law's eyes in order to replace the young woman in her son's bed. In the film *My Geisha*† (1962), it is only when the color of the actress's eyes, reversed from blue to brown by contact lenses, are re-reversed (doubled back†) on a negative film that her husband can see who she is. But it is hard to keep the subjective and objective aspects of the eye separated. In the film *The Scar*† (1948), when a woman puts her hands over a man's eyes, *she* doesn't see *him,* doesn't notice that he is masquerading as the man she thinks she loves. Urvashi† demands that she not be forced to look upon her human husband when he is naked and Mélusine† demands that *he* not look at *her* naked.

An Oxford anecdote is told, variously, about Maurice Bowra, David Daube, Isaiah Berlin, and other local characters. There has long been a bathing spot on the River Charwell known as Parsons' Pleasure, where men can swim naked. (More recently, there has been another, for women, known as Dames' Delight.) One day when Bowra (or Daube or X) was bathing there with a group of friends, a punt carrying a group of women strayed into the forbidden pool. Panic-stricken, all the men scrambled to find towels to put around their loins. But Bowra (or Daube . . .) simply picked up a handkerchief and put it over his head, remarking, "I don't know about you, gentleman, but in Oxford I, at least, am known by my face."[135] Here, as in the quandary of the transvestite in the wo/mens' room,† there is a conflict between two aspects of the gaze. In this instance, it is a conflict between the generic (Victorian, Oxonian) belief that a woman should not see *any* male genitals and the sense of personal embarrassment underlying the belief that a woman should not see *one's own* genitals. It is also a conflict between the face and the genitals as the locus of personal identity—upward displacement† again. The tale of Parsons' Pleasure may be rather flimsy and highly apocryphal, but it rides on the crest of a very serious myth indeed, the myth of sexual blinding.

A similar point was made in the film *Body Heat* (1981, a remake of *Double Indemnity,* 1944) when the adulterous (and murderous) lover, who is caught in the act by a little girl, dreads that she will identify him— until he discovers that she was so mesmerized by the sight of his naked, erect penis that she never looked at his face at all. In a neat twist on the theme of "sexuality as revelation," the preemptive force of sexuality gives it the power not to reveal but to conceal. (It also reflects the bedtrickster's own inability to distinguish one sexual object from another; in *Body Heat,* on one tryst he approaches his mistress from the back and calls out, "Hey, lady, you wanna fuck?" only to discover, to his great embarrassment, that it is another woman with the same sort of blond hair.) The metaphorical blindness of the male toward the inner nature of the "official" woman, often coupled with the temporary blindness of the woman, who closes her eyes in her resistance to the "official" man, may be expressed as the literal blindness of the child who results from such a union, like the child begotten by Vyasa.† The blindness of the child may also express the fact that, without the visual element, the sexual act of the parents was some- how incomplete, and so the child is incomplete.

If one person cannot see another, it may be because the viewer is blind or because the object of vision is invisible. These two conditions have the same result—the viewer cannot see the truth—but they are not symmet- rical inversions of one another. In darkness, both the bedtrickster and the victim are literally blinded, but the bedtrickster "sees" (i.e., knows) both the body and the soul, while the victim sees neither. Both instances are degrading for both partners, through the loss of their individuality and identity and through the incompleteness that the blindness of each inflicts upon the other.

THE MOUTH SAYS NO BUT THE EYES SAY YES

These unisex aspects of sexual blindness form the basis of the more partic- ular sexist form of the adage about cats in the dark, meaning female cats. In bedtrick stories, women's eyes and mouths are often functionally op- posed, like the literally transposed mouth and eye of the Loathly Lady in *The Marriage of Sir Gawaine.*† In *Twelfth Night* (2.2), Viola in drag com- plains that Olivia "made good view of me, indeed so much, / That sure methought her eyes had lost her tongue." The trickster masks both eye and tongue; in *Measure for Measure* (3.1), the wily duke advises Isabella to carry out her bedtrick with a combination of "shadow and silence"—eliminating any sensual contact at all but the sexual, since darkness stymies vision, and silence stymies hearing. Just as the woman's mouth is threatening and must be blinded, so, too, her gaze must be silenced.

His gaze—what feminists have taught us to recognize as the male gaze, an organ of penetration—appears in direct opposition to the female mouth. The female impersonator in *M. Butterfly*† speaks eloquently of the rape mentality, the macho argument that "her eyes say yes when her tongue says no," with its embedded pun on "eye" and "aye (yes)." The rape mentality splits the woman into a welcoming eye and a rejecting mouth; it ignores speech and relies only upon vision, while the raped woman claims, by contrast, that the man falsely saw a vision of sexual seduction when she was sending verbal messages of sexual resistance or revulsion that he failed to hear. Vision is what the rapist fixates on, the message of the eyes, communication on the animal level; speech is what the rapist denies, the message of the tongue, the message on the cultural level of the individual. All cats may be gray in the night, but cats can't speak; women can, and hence are not alike.

When Casanova† was confounded by the person who was either a castrato or a woman, he later recalled: "It was at this moment that I saw he was a man, and believed that I saw it against his will. . . . I could not look into his eyes and not burn with love. I told him that since his eyes were a woman's and not a man's, I needed to convince myself by touch that what I had seen when he had run away was not a monstrous clitoris. . . . 'All that I ask of you is to let me touch an object which cannot but fill me with disgust!' "[136] The eyes say yes, as usual, though in this case it is the crotch, rather than the mouth, that says no. Downward displacement††?

The Double Standard:
Asymmetrical Gender Patterns

If we isolate contrasting patterns in the behavior of men and women in comparable situations, we find that the same stories are told about men and about women, but the plot takes a different turn when a woman is the subject; the same acts have different consequences when men or women engage in them.‡ Sex is never an equal opportunity employment. In tales of transvestism, for instance, men usually masquerade to kill† or to have sexual access to other men,† while women usually masquerade to avoid rape† or to have the social freedom of a man, not to have sexual access to other women but, on the contrary, to have nonsexual—or, occasionally, sexual—access to men. As Carol Thomas Neely points out, "The pervasive analogy in *Measure for Measure* implies that sexuality, like death, is corrupting—fatal. The analogy means that men and women are in different relation to the play's substitutions. . . . The men are threatened with death and the women with sex."[137]

There are good reasons why the bedtrick is more to the advantage of women than of men, and why there are asymmetrical patterns of gender in stories about animal lovers.† On one level, the threat to identity posed by the bedtrick is the same for both genders. Some men invest their identity in their women, partly through their desire for paternal security† but partly because a man, too, may confirm his sense of self by seeing his reflection in the mirror† of the eyes of the woman who replaces his mother.† This is evident from the terror of infidelity and the shock of betrayal expressed by men in stories even when children are not at stake. But this loss of a sense of self does not occur in the same way for the women in our texts, whose identity is often defined, as a man's is not, by their marital fidelity.

Moreover, the asymmetries of biological aging,† compounded by the asymmetries of social and political power and the pressure of paternal insecurity,† result in two distinct genders of the mythology of the bedtrick. The different biological consequences for his and her adulteries account for the far milder recriminations for men tricked into committing adultery with their own wives, in comparison with women tricked by their own husbands.† Even on those relatively rare occasions when a woman does turn a bedtrick in order to sleep with a man who does not want to sleep with her, that man is her own husband,† who has been sleeping with another woman, his mistress. Lorraine Daston has noted another asymmetry in stories in which husbands and wives test one another with apparent adulteries:

> Whereas the man has gone astray on his own, and his long-suffering wife reacts to this provocation, the wife/fiancée had every intention of remaining faithful until actively tested by her disguised husband or his friend. That is, in both male and female variants of the story, it is the man who propels the action, who initiates the adulterous situation. Presumably both husband and wife have grounds to fear recidivism: a husband who has once chased a mistress is likely to do so again; a woman once seduced by a lover is an easy mark for the next gallant. Yet only the husbands who

have played the bedtrick on their wives seem to feel the full force of this here-we-go-again threat.[138]

Indeed, the stories begin by assuming that he *has* already lapsed, and will continue to do so, but that she has not, and must not. They end, however, on a very different note; even as she wins according to his rules, the woman deconstructs those rules and wins, if not his heart, the heart of the audience.

DECONSTRUCTING AND RECONSTRUCTING BEAUTY

Annie Dillard asks, of the story of the woman who skinned† her daughter, "Is beauty itself an intricately fashioned lure, the cruelest hoax of all?" Let us see how our texts wrestle with this question.

Plato equated beauty with goodness, love, happiness, wisdom, truth, and knowledge, ugliness with old age, evil, ignorance, lies, hate, unhappiness, waste, and destruction. Following Plato, in "Ode to a Grecian Urn" Keats equates the beautiful not only with the true (in contrast with the false, the surrogate) but with the good. As Max Lüthi has perceptively remarked, "Beauty stands for visible perfection and represents the divine in many popular European fairy tales." Thus, the fairy tale seldom tells us anything about particular parts of the body, like eye color or stature or type of build; instead, there is a "beauty of the extreme."[139] Naomi Wolf's *The Beauty Myth* and Nancy L. Etcoff's *Survival of the Prettiest* attempt to demolish this paradigm, but the myths themselves have been demolishing it for centuries. David Tracy has cast light on this tension in the dialogues of Plato: "In the greatest dialogues there is a world where the beauty of particular persons and particular art objects is both affirmed as emblem of the Good and suspected as a distraction from the pure search for the Good."[140]

Many myths seem to devalue youth and beauty in this way; we have noted Buddhist and Hindu stories that expose the hideous underside of apparently gorgeous women. In a Japanese story, a beautiful girl hides under a skin that transforms her into an ugly old woman;[141] the magic skin is a shield to protect her from her own beauty—and, presumably, also from her intelligence, since the young master who spies on her seems to be even more astonished that she can read than that she is beautiful. This story of the young woman who puts an old woman's skin over her head is an inversion of the Kiviok† stories in which an old woman puts a young woman's skin over her head. (It is also a gendered inversion of the story of the frog† prince, for one variant ends, "The old woman who gave the skin to the girl was a disguised old toad.")[142]

Beauty is depicted as evil in our myths above all because it is illusory and deluding, especially when contrasted with true inner beauty. In Balzac's *Sarrasine*,† a man named Sarrasine falls in love with a castrato† named La Zambinella, thinking that she is a woman. Roland Barthes points out the self-destructive syllogism† that allows Sarrasine to persuade himself that a (beautiful) man is a (beautiful) woman: "Beauty obliges me to love, but also what I love is inevitably beautiful. By declaring La Zambinella adorable, Sarrasine establishes one of the three proofs (narcissistic, psychological, aesthetic) he will continually use in order to deceive himself about the castrato's sex: I am justified in loving her because she is beautiful, and if I love her (I who cannot be mistaken), it is because she is a woman."[143] But the woman whom the narrator is trying to seduce also remarks that La Zambinella is too beautiful to be a man.[144] Beauty, which is always misleading, here disguises the essential sexual truth.

The choice of (apparently ugly) truth over false beauty is enshrined in Shakespeare's *Merchant of Venice* (and in Freud's essay on the three caskets in that play)[145] and in the myth of the Judgment of Paris (who wrongly chooses Aphrodite, beauty, over Athene, wisdom, thereby precipitating the disaster of Helen‡ and the Trojan War). The truth of beauty is certainly subverted by the myths of Beauty and the Beast and the Lovely Lady.

Here is another of the basic paradoxes† that inform these texts: the surface of the myth and the fairy tale argues that beauty is truth, that the beautiful woman is the symbol of all else that is good. But just as the hero must penetrate the surface of the Lovely/Loathly Lady, the reader must penetrate the seductive surface of the old archetype. And beneath that surface a Christian or Buddhist fifth column may undermine the blithe equation of the beautiful and the good and argue that what is real is not the surface but the interior, and that the interior may be the true beauty of an apparently ugly woman, or the true ugliness of all that appears beautiful.

Our myths hold the two opposed paradigms in suspension as a paradox: (1) ugly women are evil; (2) ugly women are good. But they subvert the basic equation of beauty with truth in various ways:

1. Beauty (with its correlates) is good, but it is hard to be sure that it is real. This is the message of the Lovely Lady.
2. Beauty is bad. This is the message of the Wife of Bath and of the Buddhist Lovely Lady.

3. Beauty is bad, but if you are smart enough to make the right choice, to reject beauty, you are rewarded by being given a beautiful partner—because beauty is good. This is the paradoxical message of the Loathly Lady.

Sometimes the story may begin with subversion (the heroine is independent and smart) but end by capitulating to the traditional paradigm (she dances, displaying her lovely body, and gets the prince to help her overcome the villain). In the end, youth and beauty win the day. The paradox of evil beauty goes on to become part of its own inversion in yet another paradox, for many stories end by deconstructing their own premises. After Jacob† and Rachel† have come to accept that Rachel's beauty is not as valuable as Leah's fertility, Rachel is made fertile after all; beauty wins. So, too, the Loathly Lady saves the knight's life, an act that establishes her goodness as well as her quite reasonable expectation that, in return, he will be good to her; he is, and she ceases to be Loathly. In the end, the heroine or hero who has rejected beauty is rewarded by having the beast made handsome, or the wife beautiful, after all, which means that superficial beauty is a good thing after all; like reconstructive surgery,† reconstructive narrative is retrograde. Thus, we have a third, paradoxical term in the paradigm: (3) One should value ugly women— so that one will be rewarded with beautiful women. The story sells out in the end; the subversive paradigm subverts itself in a double-back.†

WHY IS OLD UGLY?

Not only is beauty good; beauty is young. Rachel is younger than Leah, as well as more beautiful. Here again we encounter a paradox: (1) old women are wise and kind; (2) old women are horrid witches. The switchback works here, too: though it is better to be a wise, kind, old woman than to be a witch, it is better, this mythology argues, to be young and beautiful than to be old and ugly.[146]

Our texts assume that the reader assumes that old women, jealous of young girls, are not only ugly but the personification of evil. Why is it that old is always ugly? Who is it that thinks this? Men? Young women? Old women? Claude Lévi-Strauss presumes that this is a human universal when he writes: "The Nambikwara have only one word for 'pretty' and 'young,' and another for 'ugly' and 'old.' Their aesthetic judgments are thus based essentially on human, and especially sexual, values."[147] The misogynist author of the medieval *Lamentations of Matheolus* said it all when he said this of his wife: "I complain, for by vision was my knowledge deceived. . . . Alas! now my heart is really sad, for she is now so mangy, stooped, humpbacked and pot-bellied, disfigured and undone that she seems to be a deformed person. Rachel has become Leah, all gray, white-haired, rough, senile, and deaf."[148] Age has bedtricked him just as Leah (and Rachel) tricked Jacob.

For both sexes, both genders, aging produces obstacles to the recognition of a stable self. Terence Cave comments, "Sameness always gives way to difference, and no doubt the man Penelope‡ went to bed with, even if he was Odysseus, was still a stranger."[149] The loss of youth and beauty, for a woman, or of virility and power, for a man, is felt as a loss even without the threatening presence of some other woman or man who has not lost them—yet. As Adam Phillips puts it, speaking of Anna Freud: "She must have known very early the agony of sexual jealousy: that it is not a question of rivalry—competitions, after all, can be won—but of something far worse. It confronts us with the impossibility of being some-one else."[150] And the impossibility of being someone else (someone who, unlike oneself, has not already started to age and die)—or of avoiding being someone (oneself, who is aging and dying)—is the challenge that inspires the bedtrick. Flagging desire and sexual performance may be more painful for men than flagging interest and/or response are for women; at least, male desire is harder to fake than female response.

But our stories bypass this factor by their emphasis on the male gaze, the requirement that women, not men, must be beautiful. Old women are ugly, in these stories, in ways that old men are not. Some of their perceived ugliness is natural, not cultural; biologically,† men and women do age differently in some ways, though not in others. Women by and large outlive men, but they do not remain fertile as long. Less significant than fertility, though often more prominent in mythology, is the fact that the softness of women's tissue makes more dramatic changes in their bodies as they age (their breasts, for instance, soften more obviously than do the chests of men). And physical aging reverses the genders in different directions, forming a double set: mature women are like young boys, mature men like old women. Mature women are smaller than mature men, more like children (i.e., young men), and mature men are thicker and rougher than mature women, more like older women (who do become more masculine, with more male hormones, mustaches, etc.). As Marjorie Garber points out: "The authors of *Information for the Female-to-Male Crossdresser and Transsexual* cite Molloy [John T. Molloy, *The Woman's Dress for Success Book*] specifically and by name when they address the problem of 'How to Look 30 When You Are 30.' 'The biggest problem when going female-to-male is that a 30-year-old female, when cross-dressed as a man, can end up looking like a 14-year-old boy. What can the female-to-male crossdresser do to look older?' "[151] When women dress as men, they look younger; and when men dress as women, they look older.

The different ways in which men and women age make it possible for young men to play the parts of older women and young women to play the parts of young boys. A thirty-year-old woman can play the part of a fourteen-year-old boy (both have a short stature and high voice), and a thirty-year-old man can play a fifty-year-old woman (both have a thick waist and low voice). There are practical benefits in using the opposite sex in the theater to portray characters at the ends of the age spectrum where actors are unreliable (if children are too young to behave or to master the part, a woman can play a boy; and if old people are too infirm to project their voices, a man can play an old woman). Beaumarchais's program notes for the part of Cherubino† make this clear: "The part can only be played, as it was in fact, by a young and very pretty woman: we have no very young men in our theatre who are at the same time sufficiently mature to appreciate the fine points of the part."[152] And in the traditional British Christmas pantomime, a young girl plays the boy hero and a man plays the ugly old woman. In the theater, as well as in opera,† the genre may also dictate the direction of the asymmetry† between voice† and appearance, as Slavoj Žižek notes: the "caricature image of a transvestite" male parodying a female, the drag queen, has a "heightened feminine voice," abnormally high; but the realistic, sinister, and convincing masquerade of Norman as his mother, Mrs. Bates, in Hitchcock's *Psycho,*† "the monstrous apparition of an apathetically cold woman using a man's voice," has a voice *lower* than a woman's voice.[153] Garber remarks, "Why is Peter Pan played by a woman? Because a woman will never grow up to be a man."[154]

These biological changes are exacerbated by cultural factors that differ dramatically between men and women and that reinforce the biological paradigm that makes older women sexually less attractive than older men. Ugliness can be perceived as a male problem: the paradigmatic contrast is then between beauty (the female, essentialized as beauty) and the beast (the ugly male). Cyrano† de Bergerac suffers from his youthful ugliness the same tragic loss that is usually suffered by ugly and/or aging women. Nevertheless, men usually fear the loss of strength, power, and virility more than the loss of beauty, while the problem of aging in women is usually inextricably connected with the loss of beauty. Our society does not set the same premium on physical beauty in men as in women, or even construct "beauty" for older men as it does for older women (compare, for instance, the aging Gary Cooper, Clint Eastwood, Paul Newman, and Robert Redford with the aging Bette Davis, Lauren Bacall, even Elizabeth Taylor, let alone Gloria Swanson). Biological decay (wrinkled skin and sagging flesh) is compounded by social construction (a preference for one sort of flesh and skin over another) and a double standard (wrinkles that are acceptable on a man's face but not on a woman's). Moreover, although for both genders, old age often brings power,[155] such power is socially constructed as a positive, erotic factor in men but as dangerous and antisexual (masculine, castrating, etc.) in women. And ugly old men can use power to get young women into their beds; they therefore do not resort to bedtricks as often as old women do.

The myths never argue that old is beautiful, but they subvert the paradigm of youth and beauty at least to the extent of arguing that old is good (wise, kind, and so forth), and that ugliness, too, may be good. Benjamin Franklin's‡ notorious preference for old women over young women as sexual partners was cynical and almost certainly tongue-in-cheek.[156] More recently, the inevitable links between old age, ugliness, and women have been disputed by feminists of various persuasions. Betty Friedan's *Fountain of Age,* for instance, attempts to demolish the mythology of old women much as Naomi Wolf's *The Beauty Myth* and Nancy L. Etcoff's *Survival of the Prettiest* attempt to demolish the mythology of beautiful women. But they are attacking a powerful and firmly entrenched power: the mythology of female youth and beauty.

FACE-LIFTS

The process of aging and changing presents us with new versions of ourselves, both the same and different, like new tellings of the same story. Some people totally reject the selves of the past, the former lives, the former wives or husbands, and become each new person, each new mask. Some acknowledge the truth and value of all the masks at the same time and strive to recognize themselves in all of them. But others totally reject the present self and strive to put on the masks of youth, through the magic of the Nautilus machine, the younger and younger lovers, the haunting of high school reunions.

And the face-lift. The primary obstacle to the recognition of a stable self transformed by aging is the retransformation of the face; the mythology of the bedtrick imagines people who attempt to swim upstream against the current of time by changing their faces back in the other direction. Face-lifts embody the belief that to remain yourself you must stay the same, and to stay the same you must change your skin into the skin that belonged to what you were—though with the face-lift you actually change into someone else, away from who you really are *now* (a person with a soul and a face that are formed and scarred by experience). Charles Siebert describes watching a face-lift operation: "With each snip, I imagined the ghosts of the myriad worries that furled this woman's forehead flying free: there, the times she troubled over school exams; there, the long waits for loved ones who were late; and there, the years of confusion and doubt."[157] And he records the misgivings of a woman hesitating to have the surgery: " 'But then,' she said, a nicely furrowed frown indicating a still-intact corrugator muscle, 'I looked at my nose in the mirror and thought, That's my father there, and that's my mother right there in the upper eyes.' "[158] The myth of family resemblance† here serves to anchor personal identity in the surface of the face that changes with age, not with surgery.

A Clairol advertisement for a dye to make gray hair black or blond or red again proclaims: "Grey Hair Lies." That is, time lies, age lies, death lies. The outer surface of the old woman lies, by concealing the young soul beneath, and the dye restores the truth of youth. Marjorie Garber questions the meaning of such face-lifts in the context of the sexual soul: "Why does a 'nose job' or 'breast job' or 'eye job' pass as mere self-improvement, . . . while a sex change (could we imagine it called a 'penis job'?) represents the dislocation of everything we conventionally 'know' or believe about gender identities and gender roles, 'male' and 'female' subjectivities?"[159] The face-lift offers a quick fix to stave off the inevitable flood of a deeper change. Saul Bellow's Armenian cynic spoke of that other change: "On any certain day, when you're happy, you know it can't last, but the weather will change, the health will be sickness, the year will end, and also life will end. In another place another day there'll be a different lover. The face you're kissing will change to some other face, and so will your face be replaced. . . . You make your peace with change."[160] "Your face will be replaced" has so many meanings here: your own present face will be replaced by your aging face or by the face of another person with whom your lover will replace you or, as a result of the first and in order to prevent the second, by a face-lift. The anguish with which the victims of bedtricks react to their betrayal indicates that they, at least, have not made their peace with change—or, at least, with the betrayal that claims change as its excuse.

What is the relationship between our sexuality and our faces, our skins? Our texts both express and challenge the mythology of the face-lift. Parvati and Kiviok's† mother-in-law sloughed their skin in what we might regard as proto-face-lifts; Kleist's Sosia‡ expresses to his look-alike (Mercury) the impossibility of doing what Kiviok's mother-in-law did: "I can't annihilate / Myself, transform myself, slough off my skin / And hang my skin around your shoulders."[161] The characters in the films *Shattered*† (1991) and *Face/Off*‡ (1997) undergo face-lifts that enable them to masquerade as other people. The plastic surgeon functions as a kind of a deus ex machina in many bedtricks, such as Kobo Abe's *Face of Another;*† in *A Face to Die For* (1996), the plastic surgeon gives his patient the face of his dead wife, an inadvertent masquerade that she only discovers later; but she masquerades on purpose in order to murder her unfaithful lover.

Angela Carter's Dora describes a woman whose ex-husband is in love with Dora, and who, like many wives of straying husbands, has undergone a face-lift; but this face-lift, like the bedtricks turned by such wives, makes her look like the woman her husband fancies (Dora):

> A hand-made, custom-built replica, a wonder of the plastic surgeon's art. The trouble she'd gone to! She'd had her nose bobbed, her tits pruned, her bum elevated, she'd starved and grieved away her middle-age spread. She'd had her back molars out, giving the illusion of cheekbones. Her face was lifted up so far her ears had ended up on top of her head but, happily, the wig hid them. And after all that she looked very lifelike, I must say, if not, when I looked more closely, not *all* that much like me, more like a blurred photocopy or an artist's impression, and, poor cow, you could still see the bruises under the Max Factor Pan Stik, however thickly she applied it, and the scars round where the ears should be. Oooh, it must have hurt! . . . [She] loved her man so much she was prepared to turn herself into a rough copy of his beloved for his sake. . . . [He] and the imitation Dora lived happily ever after, once he'd got over the shock, and if you believe that, you'll believe anything.[162]

The pain that the rejected wife endures for her man is not unlike the pain that the mermaid† experiences when she slices apart her tail to make legs for her lover's pleasure. It didn't work for the mermaid, and we are led to believe that it will not work for this woman either. It never really works.

F I V E

The Cuckolds
of the Heart

❧

Cuckolding to Kill

The demon Adi† played a bedtrick not because he desired Parvati but because he wanted to kill Shiva. Hatred of the alien rival, and paranoid† fear of him, are central to many bedtricks in which desire is outranked by hate, or at least by a spirit of revenge or rivalry. Often the antagonism between the men takes the form of violence, which may rebound upon the woman, as well. Sometimes the wife's seduction is simply the by-product of another plan aimed primarily at her husband. Men may force their bedtricks upon their female victims in collusion with other men,† and they may also masquerade as their male enemies against the enemies' will. Some of the men in these stories attempt to destroy an opponent by sleeping with his wife, as the wife's chastity functions as a shield for her man. Yet men tell stories of cuckolding not only against one another but also against women, who are depicted as too easily seduced or fooled and who also retaliate strongly against the efforts of men to erase their individuality. In all of these stories, though hate, rivalry, and revenge are said to be the primary motives, desire constantly reasserts itself and often causes the aggression to miscarry. The film *Excalibur* (1981) cuts back and forth between the scene in which the duke of Tintagel is breathing hard and moaning because he is dying and the scene in which Uther, magically transformed into the form of the duke (played by the same actor), is breathing hard and moaning because he is approaching his sexual climax with Igraine, the duke's wife. The merging of the two movements emphasizes not only the lethal aspect of cuckolding but the lethal aspect of sex itself, *la morte douce*: as the husband dies, the child is engendered. (Death and sex also overlap, according to Jain and Buddhist theory, when the soul escapes from a dying body—released as the seed is released—and immediately engages with a copulating couple.)[1]

The *Kamasutra* condemns a man who commits adultery out of love or lust for the woman in question but condones the act when its purpose is to harm her husband. The adulterer reasons: "If I become intimate with this woman and kill her husband, I will get for myself his great wealth and power, which ought to be mine." Or "This woman's husband has defiled the women of my harem; I will therefore defile *his* wives in return."[2] This total disregard for the woman taken in adultery characterizes the many bedtricks in which the primary target is not the seduction of the wife but the destruction of the man. The droit du seigneur† was often a way to assert power over a male subject rather than (or in addition to) a way to have access to young women. We must not forget, however, the self-deception implicit in the "progress narrative":† sexual tricks usually have, even if only at an unconscious level, sexual motives (though they may also have hidden power motives).

The title of this chapter is taken from a slip of the pen in the review of a play that was, the text said, "a delightful blend of wit and drama that is sure to warm the cuckolds of the heart."[3] The cuckolds of the heart are often the victims of bedtricks. A Hindu story of a cuckolding bedtrick, much retold in texts of the late medieval period, is the tale of the demon Jalandhara, who, like the demon Andhaka,† was born of Shiva alone and tried to seduce his father's wife, Parvati (regarded as his mother). At Jalandhara's birth, Brahma predicted that he could not be killed by anyone but Shiva and that his wife would be faithful and beautiful,[4] unlike Chaucer's Loathly Lady.† But it did not work out quite that way when Jalandhara grew up:

JALANDHARA IMPERSONATES SHIVA

Jalandhara reigned with justice, but he usurped the prerogatives of the gods. They asked the sage Narada to help them, and he went to Jalandhara and inspired in him the desire to abduct Parvati. Jalandhara sent an emissary to Shiva asking him to give up Parvati; instead, a great battle ensued, in the course of which Jalandhara created the magic illusion of celestial courtesans. While Shiva was fascinated by the courtesans, Jalandhara, driven by lust, went to the palace where Parvati lived. With his power of illusion he assumed the form of Shiva, with ten arms, five faces, three eyes, and matted hair, seated on the great bull—in every way the image of Shiva. When Parvati saw Shiva approaching, she was full of love for her beloved; she came forward to meet him. But as soon as the beautiful Parvati came into the demon's range of vision, he released his seed and became impotent in all his limbs. Realizing that he was a demon, Parvati disappeared immediately, and Jalandhara returned to the battle.[5]

Jalandhara begins by lusting for power and is then sidetracked into lust tout court. There is a double meaning here, for Parvati recognizes the demon not only because he takes on his own form after he releases his seed but because she knows that her husband, Shiva, has, by virtue of his yogic powers, the ability to make love for thousands of years without releasing his seed at all.[6] Jalandhara is thus exposed not just by a generic sign (for gods as well as demons resume their true shapes when they release their seed†) but by a universal sign (truth resulting from sexuality) as well as a specific sign of an individual (since one particular person, Shiva, never sheds his seed prematurely). The fact that Parvati is Jalandhara's stepmother adds yet another significant layer of incestuous† non-recognition to the myth, like that of Oedipus† (or, culturally closer, Kutsa†): Parvati at first mistakes her (step-) son for her husband.

Another, roughly contemporary version of the myth elaborates upon the sign—virility—that distinguishes Shiva from Jalandhara:

Jaya Impersonates Parvati

Vrinda, the wife of Jalandhara, said to Jalandhara, as he was arming, "Do not fight, my lord, with that despicable yogi. Forget about Parvati. Why do you desire her? Is Parvati better than me? She wants a son, but she is barren and has only artificial, adopted sons. Leave her alone and enjoy me." But Jalandhara replied, "Vrinda, look after the country and the treasury; remember me always, if Shiva kills me." And then he went to fight with Shiva.

Shiva said to Parvati, "I am going to the battle. Stay here, even though you will be alone and full of longing." When Jalandhara realized how difficult it would be to conquer Shiva in battle, he thought to himself, "I have not seen Parvati, whom Narada told me about. I will go to see her today, and afterward I will fight with Shiva." He said to the demon Shumbha, "Take a form just like mine and fight the battle, while I go to see Parvati, who has captured my heart." And he took off the ornaments from his own body and gave them to Shumbha. Then he took the form of Shiva, and another demon took a form just like that of Nandin, Shiva's ally. The two demons, disguised as Shiva and Nandin, approached Parvati.

When Parvati saw Jalandhara-as-Shiva approaching, wounded by arrows, leaning on Nandin's shoulder, his garments smeared with blood, she was amazed. Her friends, Jaya and the others, went to him and said, "What happened?" And when Parvati saw that he was carrying the severed heads of her sons Ganesha and Skanda, she cried out, "O Skanda, O Ganesha, O Shiva!" Jalandhara-as-Shiva sighed and said, "Your two

sons were killed some time ago. Why are you grieving in vain? You
should protect me now by uniting your body with mine." But when she
heard these words, which were unbalanced and inappropriate for the moment, she replied, "What you are saying is wrong. Wise men forbid sexual
intercourse at the time of grief, danger, meditation, fever, traveling, a
funeral, or in the presence of teachers or old people. How can you ask
me to make love with you when I am suffering from grief, oppressed
by sorrow for my sons, weak, flooded with tears, and thoroughly upset?" But Jalandhara-as-Shiva, who was deluded by the form of Parvati, pressed his suit to get what he wanted: "Women who refuse to
make love with a man who is suffering will undoubtedly fall into a terrible hell." Then she heaved a long sigh, for though she was paralyzed
by grief, the goddess who deludes this whole universe had been deluded
by Jalandhara.

Yet Parvati had been disturbed when Jalandhara-as-Shiva had asked
her to make love with him, and she began to worry and brood. She went
outside, bathed in the Ganges, and said to her friend Jaya, "Take my
form and go to him, my friend, and find out truly if he is Shiva or
someone else. If he embraces you and kisses you and so forth, then
you will know that he is a demon who has come here with his power of
illusion. But if he asks you how I am, well or ill, then surely it will
be Shiva; come and tell me." When Jalandhara-as-Shiva saw Jaya-as-
Parvati coming, he was overwhelmed by lust and embraced her, thinking that it was the form of Parvati. But he immediately released his seed,
for he had small virility; and so she said to him, "You are a demon, not
Shiva; you have small virility and very low habits. And I am not Parvati,
but her friend." She took back her own form and went back and said to
Parvati, "This is Jalandhara, not your husband, Shiva." Then Parvati
hid in a lotus bud.[7]

Parvati's suspicions are based not on the demon's appearance (which
thoroughly deludes her) but on his behavior:† he is asking her to do
something that her own husband wouldn't ask; he has "low habits," as
Jaya puts it. It is the fact that he asks her to make love with him at all
under these circumstances, rather than the manner in which he does it
or the fact that he loses control during it, that betrays him.

When Jalandhara takes Shiva's form, he gets someone else to take his
own form and a third player to take the form of Shiva's attendant; the
construction of a social world supports the central illusion. But the demon
overdoes it, and so the illusion of the dead sons is counterproductive,
inspiring maternal grief rather than erotic longing. Vrinda invokes her

own fertility against the erotic barrenness of Parvati, who, like most goddesses after Samjna,‡ has no natural children: Ganesha was born of the
rubbings from Parvati's body, and Skanda, like Jalandhara and Andhaka,
was born from Shiva's seed, without Parvati's help.[8] Perhaps it is because
he recalls his wife's mocking words about Parvati's artificial motherhood
that Jalandhara underestimates the depth of her maternal grief. But that
grief is part of what sobers Parvati up, as grief for lost children often
sobers up people who have forgotten who they are.[9] Capital punishment
here focuses the mind wonderfully.

And once she becomes suspicious, Parvati takes action. Shiva has expressly forbidden her to change her own form, perhaps because he suspects she might do so to play erotic games of her own, for he acknowledges
that, with him away at war, she might be prone to longing, and she does
change forms to play bedtricks on other occasions.† But Shiva did not
forbid her to let someone else take her form. Jalandhara ultimately reveals
himself sexually: he fails because he has "small virility" (*alpendriya*), a
complex pun implying a lack of virile staying power, a small penis, or a
penis that quickly becomes small by losing its erection. But he does not
reveal himself to Parvati, for unlike the first text we considered, in which
the demon sheds his seed at the mere sight of Parvati, this text assumes
that Jalandhara will shed his seed—and therefore lose his powers—only
if he actually consummates the sexual act. To avoid polluting Parvati in
this way, the myth introduces a substitute for her, as Tulsi Das did to
protect Sita,‡ not a magic double this time but just the standard surrogate
to stymie a rape or droit du seigneur:† the maid† or friend. This results
in a double-back-cross,† in which the trickster meets another trickster.
(Shiva himself takes the form of Parvati to stymie another demon who
lusts after her, Bhasmasura, whom Shiva kills while merely dancing with
him, before any sexual act is consummated.[10] In this he is the counterpart
of the demon Adi, who takes the form of Parvati in an attempt to kill
Shiva; the difference lies in the fact that Parvati is Shiva's wife, not Adi's.)

There are still further twists in the plot, for this text adds another
bedtrick after the exposure of Jalandhara, a retaliatory seduction of Vrinda
by Vishnu, who is said to be motivated not by demonic lust but by the
divine knowledge that only by destroying the fidelity of the demon's wife
can the god destroy the demon. Several texts insist upon the tit-for-tat
nature of the counterseduction; in one, as soon as Parvati has penetrated
Jalandhara's disguise she summons Vishnu, tells him what has happened,
and demands, "He himself has shown the path: destroy the *dharma* of

fidelity of *his* wife. There is no other way for the great demon to be killed, for there is no *dharma* on the face of the earth equal to the fidelity of a wife."[11] Sometimes it is Vishnu himself who says this.[12]

But Vishnu's altruistic motives in undertaking this deception are undermined in another telling elsewhere in the same text, which begins with the statement that, after Jalandhara married Vrinda (with the *gandharva* rite of mutual desire), "She gave up her fickleness, and so did he; he did not desire the wife of another man."[13] To conquer Shiva, however, Jalandhara attempted to seduce Parvati, and Jaya took Parvati's place, as above. Then:

VISHNU IMPERSONATES JALANDHARA

The Garuda bird said to Vishnu, "You should go there and engage in a war of illusion against Jalandhara, whose wife I have seen: she is a hundred times more beautiful than Parvati, Rambha, or Urvashi. So, abduct her. Do a favor for Shiva and give yourself pleasure." Deceiving his wife, Lakshmi, Vishnu used his yogic power of illusion to assume another form, for he was deluded by passion for Vrinda. He gave Vrinda nightmares, portending her own widowhood: she saw the severed head of Jalandhara, its eyes plucked out by a vulture. She awoke and entered a terrible forest; suddenly she realized that the female mules pulling her chariot had stopped neighing, and that the wheels made no sound, nor the bells. Then a horrible demon devoured the mules, seized Vrinda, and said, "Shiva has killed your husband in the battle, or so I have heard. Take me for your husband and drink sweet wine and eat the meat of large animals." When she heard that, the life went out of her.

Vishnu then appeared in the form of an ascetic, wearing bark garments, and reduced the demon to ashes. Vrinda, fooled by Vishnu's illusory power, threw her arms around Vishnu's neck, a touch which gave him much pleasure, and he said to her, "By your embrace, the head of your husband will come back again, and all his limbs, even better than before." She lay down on the divine bed and picked up the head of her husband and drank kisses from his lower lip and closed her eyes in waves of pleasure. Then Jalandhara seemed to appear, for Vishnu had taken on a handsome form just like his, with his chest, his height, his speech, his frame of mind. Seeing the full form of her beloved, Vrinda cried out, "I will do whatever pleases you, my master. Tell me about the battle." Vishnu-as-Jalandhara said, "My darling, Shiva cut off my head, but just then by your power of yoga, the severed head was brought here and revived by the touch of your body." Then Vrinda, lusting for sexual pleasure, embraced him closely and kissed him. Vishnu thought that the plea-

sure that came from deluding Vrinda was greater than the delicious
pleasure of the love of his wife Lakshmi, and that this sexual release was
greater than the pleasure of metaphysical Release. He enjoyed Vrinda's
body for a number of days, and then he thought about what he was supposed to do for Shiva.

One day, at the end of their lovemaking, Vrinda saw Vishnu in his
own form, with his two arms around her neck. She loosened the noose
of his arms from her neck and said, "How is it that you came to delude
me in the form of an ascetic?" And he said, to calm her down, "I am the
beloved of Lakshmi. Your husband went to seduce Parvati in order to
conquer Shiva, and I am Shiva, and he is me. Jalandhara has been killed
in the battle. Make love with me now." Furious, she cursed him, and then
she said to her friend, "The sight of my beloved was just an object of the
senses made of my own longings." And she killed herself and went to
heaven.[14]

When Vrinda finally sees Vishnu as Vishnu, she asks him only why
he took the form of the ascetic, not why he took the form of her husband.
It appears that she goes to her death believing that it was she herself, not
Vishnu, who conjured up the image of her husband in bed, out of her
own longing, as she herself admits, tacitly acknowledging the projective†
power of sexual fantasy.

Vishnu works much harder at his successful seduction of Vrinda than
Jalandhara does at his unsuccessful seduction of Parvati (though one can
hardly call it work). Where Jalandhara's bedtrick fails, Vishnu's bedtrick
succeeds—or, rather, succeeds long enough for him to seduce the woman
he desires. What success he achieves is due in part to his greater skill as
a magician: he mimics not only Jalandhara's chest, height, and speech
(and, presumably, his multiple arms, which distinguish him from the anthropomorphic, two-armed form of Vishnu) but his "frame of mind,"†
a factor seldom taken into account in these myths. Moreover, the textual
convention demands that Vishnu succeed at least long enough to let Shiva
win the fight: demons must fail, gods must win. In one text, Jalandhara's
own demons tactlessly point out the contrast and parallel when Jalandhara
has failed to seduce Parvati: "Shiva has destroyed your army, and you
will not get Parvati. How can a jackal get the lion's queen?[15] And Vishnu
has taken away *your* queen. As you do to others, so they do to you. You
came to abduct Parvati, and Vishnu abducted your wife."[16]

Where Jalandhara's trick with death (the mirage of Parvati's dead sons)
was anti-erotic, Vishnu's trick with death (the mirage of Jalandhara's

corpse and the rejoining of the severed head‡) is erotic: Vrinda is so happy to see him alive again that she doesn't look too closely. The illusion of the dead man plays upon a necrophiliac streak in Vrinda, who kisses, and revives, the dead head of her husband, as Richard Strauss's Salome kisses the head, indeed the mouth, of John the Baptist and as a number of heroes bravely kiss† enchanted (and, occasionally, dead) women in order to disenchant them. Vishnu's trick may have been inspired by several episodes in the Valmiki *Ramayana*.‡ Ravana's son produces an illusion of Sita being killed in order to dishearten Rama in the battle,[17] just as Jalandhara produces an illusion of celestial courtesans *(apsarases)*[18] and of Parvati[19] to distract Shiva. Ravana attempts, in vain, to bed Sita by producing the illusion of the severed head of her husband; Sita falls for it but grieves without seeking comfort from Ravana, and the illusory head vanishes when Ravana leaves.[20] So, too, Jalandhara produces the severed heads of Parvati's sons in his vain attempt to seduce her, and Vishnu produces an illusion of Jalandhara's corpse in his successful attempt to seduce Vrinda.[21] In these instances, unlike the episode with the heads of Parvati's sons, capital punishment unfocuses the mind.

But Vishnu, too, is ultimately exposed, after lovemaking, through the revelatory power of sex,† perhaps because his motives turn out not to be so pure after all, for he falls in love with Vrinda just as Jalandhara falls for Parvati; that is, Vishnu actually *becomes* the person whose mask he assumes: a person who is in love with Vrinda. These myths generally assume that the demon can take on the body of someone else in a masquerade without taking on the soul contained in that body. Jalandhara does not feel or think or remember like Shiva; he just looks like him. But Vishnu with Vrinda poses an exception to this rule. He does not take on Jalandhara's memory or sense of self; he knows that he is Vishnu pretending to be Jalandhara in love with Vrinda. Gradually, however, he forgets that it is just a game. He then justifies the transformation (Vishnu = Jalandhara) by translating it into a theological equation (Vishnu = Shiva); if the gods are one, what does it matter if a woman sleeps with her husband or one god or another? Thus, polytheism (more precisely, what Max Müller called henotheism† and I would call serial monotheism) justifies polygamy.

From the start, Vishnu admits that he prefers Vrinda to his own wife, whom he deceives, and even after he is exposed, he tries to persuade Vrinda to go on making love with him. Several texts address a problem that remains after the fight between Shiva and Jalandhara (or Parvati and

Vrinda) has come to an end: Vishnu remains in love with Vrinda, who becomes reincarnate as the Tulsi plant (a kind of basil), regarded as a wife of Vishnu and worshiped in conjunction with Vishnu.[22]

In other variants, in which the demon is named not Jalandhara but Shankhacuda, Vishnu *fails* because of his greater skill as a lover: "Then he lay down on the bed with her, and she made love joyously with him. The wise woman guessed everything, because of the excess of the attraction that gave rise to her joy [or because of her enjoyment and pleasure],[23] and she said, 'Who are you? You have had me by means of illusion, and since you have ruined my fidelity, I will curse you.'"[24] She can tell the difference between him and her husband by something different that he does at the very end of the act of intercourse, something therefore perhaps related to the orgasm, as was the unmasking sign of Jalandhara. There was more, or at least different, pleasure for her when the god seduced her than she was accustomed to from her demonic husband. (Ahalya‡ and Alcmena‡ sometimes notice a similar superiority in the sexual techniques of the divine impersonators of their husbands, in addition to suspecting them because they want to make love at all, as Parvati suspected Jalandhara).

Vishnu is cursed by Jalandhara's wife because, in contrast with the noted fidelity of Jalandhara (who must be tricked into seducing Parvati), Vishnu is overcome by gratuitous lust for Vrinda. And he is cursed all the more by Shankhacuda's wife because, unlike Jalandhara, Shankhacuda has not even touched Parvati, so it is impossible to justify Vishnu's actions in the name of revenge.[25] The weakness of Shiva's own moral position is betrayed by his decision in both myths to get Vishnu to do the job for him and to receive the punishment as well, splitting the evil part of himself away and projecting it onto someone else.‡

The textual history comes full circle when Vrinda curses Vishnu, saying that someone else disguised as an ascetic will abduct his own wife— that is, that Ravana, disguised as an ascetic, will abduct Sita when Vishnu becomes incarnate as Rama in the *Ramayana*.‡ I have noted the ways in which the Jalandhara story is, itself, modeled on the illusions in the *Ramayana*. Indeed, Jalandhara becomes reincarnated as Ravana to take away Sita in Tulsi Das's sixteenth-century Hindi version of the *Ramayana*, the *Ramacaritamanasa,* when Vrinda curses Vishnu (here called Hari or the Lord): "By a stratagem the Lord broke her marriage vow and thus accomplished the purpose of the gods. When the lady discovered the deception, she cursed him in her wrath. Hari, the Blessed Lord, sportive and gracious, accepted her curse. It was this Jalandhara who was reborn as Ravana."[26] What was "the stratagem"? One translator, W. D. P. Hill, explains in a helpful footnote: "Vishnu took the form of Jalandhara and approached Vrinda, who at once ceased to pray, with the result that Jalandhara fell down dead."[27] Ceased to *pray?* This English scholar takes us a long way from the Sanskrit and Hindi texts. The folk tradition also bowdlerizes the sex, but not the necrophilia, of the Sanskrit tradition. In a variant recorded in Kangra in 1995, Vishnu takes the form of Jalandhara and is brought to Jalandhara's wife (here already called Tulsi) as a wounded body; when she lifts the body to tend it, she has touched a man other than her husband, and the protection she was giving Jalandhara vanishes.[28] And in a variant recorded in Central India in 1975,[29] Vrinda doesn't even touch the body; she just has to *say* that it is her husband, and that suffices to seal Jalandhara's doom.

Thus, despite the initial premise of the myth of Jalandhara—that it is the reality of the sexual encounter† that exposes the true nature of the bedtrickster—the escalating levels of illusion finally prove the opposite, the illusoriness of sexuality. For none of the sexual partners turns out to be what he or she appears to be. First we encounter Jalandhara-as-Shiva, then Jaya-as-Parvati, and then a whole series of false Jalandharas: Shumbha, Vishnu, the corpse of Jalandhara, an anonymous corpse, and finally just a gleam in Vishnu's eye. This is a far cry from the immediacy of the texts in which Jalandhara's premature ejaculation is described in such blunt and realistic detail.

SLEEPING WITH THE ENEMY

We have seen that desire often enters the ostensibly political scenario of cuckolding—desire for the wife. Sometimes desire for the husband enters the scenario, too, and when two men collude together to trick a woman into cuckolding one of them, the element of male homoeroticism can become quite blatant.

The cuckolders in these myths may be sleeping with the enemy in the sense of making love with the purported enemy, for the man who is ostensibly in competition for the woman may, on some deeper level, desire her man. Occasionally, women can play this game, too: in *Single White Female†* (1992), the passion of Ellie (also called Hedra) is really directed, not toward Sam, Allie's boyfriend, but toward Allie, whose place she takes in Sam's bed and in a sense cuckolds: she seduces Sam, not because she lusts for him, but to prove to Allie (whom she loves) that Sam is unfaithful, so that Allie will no longer love Sam and will, presumably, love Ellie. As Marjorie Garber nicely sums up such a situation: "We always fall in love with a fantasy, and it is sometimes as easy to fantasize about the rival, who is so desirable that he or she might take away the beloved, as it is about the more familiar and 'known' beloved. . . . If we desire what the rival desires, we also sometimes desire the rival because of his or her desire."[30]

The Freudian† view of cuckolding emphasizes the repressed† desire that the cuckolder has for his victim. The uneasy relationship between the two men is somewhat differently characterized by Javier Marias† in his story of the man who is not sure if the prostitute he has sex with is his ex-wife, Celia. Recalling that his friend Ruiberriz has told him that he has seen Celia working as a prostitute, he thinks, "If it was Celia and Ruiberriz had hired her and had spent the night with her, then there would have been established between the two men—between him and me, between us—a relationship that our languages no longer reflect, but that certain dead languages do."[31] And he wonders if there might perhaps be an Anglo-Saxon noun that would mean "co-bridegroom" or "co-fornication," or refer to men who are "co-fornicators" or "co-fuckers."[32] This fictional kinship system is a grotesque satire on the charts and family trees known from anthropologists and genealogists; this tree has nothing but bars sinister. When Javier Marias's protagonist (the authorial voice, even called Javier) himself has had sex with the woman, calling himself Victor, he wonders "if she suspected that I suspected her of avenging herself on me by imposing on me all those non-blood relationships, and without my consent or my knowledge. But how can there be consent? Perhaps she was going to make me become related to myself, Javier and Victor, and then there would be consent."[33] And finally he considers the implications of this "Anglo-Saxon relationship": "Both men and women are often ignorant of that relationship or link, and its most tangible, visible manifestation is disease. . . . Perhaps the verb described what was principally a bond of hatred, . . . a connection based on rivalry and unease and jealousy and drops of blood."[34] The connection with disease makes explicit the parallel with syphilis, transmitted from one lover to another, and the reference to "drops of blood" evokes the blood transfusions that Bram Stoker's Lucy, as well as Dracula, employed to forge links between her lovers.‡ Both of these images in our day of course evoke AIDS, and Javier's pyramid is like the AIDS pyramid constructed to teach people the necessity for safe sex: the person who thinks s/he is connected with only one partner discovers that s/he is in fact related to thousands of others through sometimes fewer than six degrees of separation: it's a small, small world.

The mythological enactment of sexual male bonding through cuckolding occurs in magical stories in which a man takes the form of a certain woman and engages in a heterosexual act with her man. We have seen this happen when the demon Adi† becomes a woman (Parvati) in order to seduce and destroy Shiva, the one he really wants in one sense or another. Indeed, in one variant of that myth, Shiva discovers, inside the demonic fabrication of his wife, a golden *linga* (phallus) with a trident in the middle—a replica of his own fatal male organ. Even though this made him "a little worried," the text remarks, "Shiva was so tortured with desire that he continued to make love to her."[35] Despite the unmistakable sign of the demon's male sexuality, Shiva continues to experience desire— a powerful expression of same-sex desire in cuckolding. Shiva's lust delays his recognition and makes it possible for the demon to approach him; then it drives him to continue making love to Adi, despite his suspicions; and, in the end, it gives him the weapon with which to kill the demon, his enemy and sexual partner.

Another sort of masked same-sex eroticism may link some of the men who impersonate one another in bed not, as in standard cuckolding stories, in secret and through mutual aggression but, as in the levirate† scenario, in collusion and through mutual, perhaps erotic, affection. These stories are the male counterpart to stories of female collusion, such as the tale of Rachel and Leah.† The underlying tension between love (lust) for the male friend's girl and love (ostensibly affection, perhaps also lust) for the male friend pervades this corpus. It is the key to the story of the twin gynecologists in the film *Dead Ringers*† (1988) and to an ancient story recorded in the *Gesta Romanorum* (tale 171)[36] and retold by Boccaccio:†

TITUS AND GISIPPUS

Titus fell in love with a young girl betrothed to his best friend, Gisippus; he told Gisippus of his love. Gisippus celebrated the wedding banquet at home, where Titus's chamber adjoined that of Gisippus and one might go from the one room into the other. Titus went to her in the dark, and the girl fell for the trick; she wept bitterly later when she was told.[37]

This is a very fishy story; the fact that Titus and Gisippus have communicating bedrooms is surely not insignificant. The men care for one another far more than either cares for the girl; when Titus does for a moment take into consideration the girl's feelings, he says, "If it appear to her that she has been deceived, it is not I who am to blame therefore, but she, who did not ask me who I was." This is precisely what judges have ruled in cases of date rape† very much like this story, one man replacing another in the dark: that it was a woman's own fault if she was fooled. And there is surely irony in Boccaccio's voice when he remarks that the wise woman "readily transferred to Titus the affection she bore Gisippus." This twisted sexist argument implies that since, to a woman, all men are alike in the dark,† women do not deserve sexual choice as men do.

A vivid example (myth or reality?—it is hard to tell) of the same sort of ostensibly nonsexual male bonding evinced in a bedtrick is told in a captivity narrative, published in 1778, about the Revolutionary War period in America, involving British soldiers and Native Americans ("Indians"):

BRADDOCK'S SOLDIER AND THE INNOCENT SQUAH

An officer under General Braddock having contracted with a pretty Indian girl an engagement, which she at least considered to be matrimonial, and having promised her favours to an intimate, after he had often tried ineffectual persuasion, and once narrowly escaped being killed by her in abetting violence; was at last driven to this stratagem, in order to cuckold himself;—he placed his friend under the bed in which he was with his perverse spouse, and pretending to fall out by accident, changed places with him; and thus ingeniously triumphed over the virtue of the innocent Squah [sic].[38]

The sexist disregard for the woman in this story is blatantly tainted with racism:† the "Indian" girl is mocked both for her promiscuity and for her chastity (which is, perversely, regarded as perverse); and she foolishly believes him when he promises to marry her. The men conspire together to deceive and corrupt her, hiding under the bed like Rachel† when she conspires with Leah to deceive Jacob. The men are virtually in bed together.

In *Story of O*,† Pauline Réage's Sadeian novel, published in 1954, heterosexuality is visible on the surface, while homoerotic bedtricks take place in the realm of fantasy, often in darkness:

STORY OF O

[René seduced O, blindfolded her, and made her submit, in his presence, to other men—multiple, anonymous, undifferentiated sex partners.] All of a sudden they removed her blindfold. . . . Two of the men were standing and smoking. Another was seated, a riding crop on his knees, and the one leaning over her fondling her breasts was her lover. All four of them had taken her, and she had not been able to distinguish him from the others.[39]

Here, as in films about amnesiac† women, the trick is meant to conceal from the woman the identities not of the men who are her partners but of the woman herself. Even conventional bedtricks tend to cause a loss of the sense of self,† and René intends to do this, to destroy O's ego so that she will become the ideal pornographic woman: her name is a cipher, and her treatment is designed to empty her of all individual identity. But unlike conventional bedtricks, which also tend to weaken the victim's attachment to the partner, these humiliations are also intended to strengthen O's dependence upon René, to make her his slave. To René's surprise, this does not happen; instead, the result is the same as that of the conventional bedtrick on both counts: O loses her sense both of herself and of him.

The normal psychology of cuckolding is turned on its head when René willingly gives O to other men, reifying his fantasy† by physically substituting other men for himself instead of making love to O while imagining another woman (or her husband) in her place. O cannot distinguish René from the other men who take her, even though she suspects that he might be among them; and, on the other hand, as her humiliation deprives O of her own identity in her own eyes, she loses her uniqueness in René's eyes, too. When René gives O to Sir Stephen, Sir Stephen in a sense becomes René's double, so that René mates with O through Sir Stephen. But in another sense, the two men mate with one another through her, so that O, not Sir Stephen, is René's double; O is the surrogate through whom René expresses his repressed† desire for Sir Stephen. As the author remarks, "Everything would probably have been much simpler if Sir Stephen had liked boys, and O did not doubt that René, who was not so inclined, still would have readily granted to Sir Stephen both the slightest and most demanding of his requests."[40] But when did a bedtrickster ever want to make things simpler?

In *Story of O*, the bedtrickster loses his woman; in other stories that begin with male collusion, the bedtrickster loses his male friend. This happens in an English Renaissance drama called *The True Trojans*, in which Hiraldus arranges a bedtrick so that his friend Eulinus may sleep with Landora, who has rejected Eulinus's love and pursues Hiraldus. Afterward, however, Hiraldus teases Eulinus: "Landora loves not you, but me in you." Eulinus: "But I in you enjoy Landora's love." Hiraldus: "But she enjoys not your love, 'cause unknown." Eulinus: "No matter, I in you, or you in me, / So that I still possess my dearest dear." Later, Eulinus kills Hiraldus in a fit of rage during what was to be a mock sword fight at a funeral masque. Eulinus grieves for the loss of his friend, but even more for the loss of his access to Landora, since he can no longer masquerade as Hiraldus: "Yet how / Borrow can I his shape, or use my own?"[41] That this is a transaction strictly "between men," to borrow Eve Sedgwick's† phrase, is revealed by the simple fact that no female character ever appears onstage at all.[42] In contrast with the story of Titus and Gisippus, however, the friendship between these two men crumbles under the tension of the bedtrick; the mock fight that becomes real doubles the mock sexual encounter that becomes real for Eulinus. The "accidental" killing of Hiraldus by Eulinus is clearly motivated by the jealousy that Eulinus experiences as the unreal double, in the familiar double-bind,† despite his insistence that he is satisfied to possess Landora physically, even under another man's identity. Hiraldus's tactless reminder that Eulinus, like all bedtricksters, is not loved for himself, seals his own doom.

The repressed† antipathy between the two men who collude in a bedtrick may amount to no more than sexual rivalry, a grown man's version of little boys competing to see who can pee farthest. This is the point of the most realistic successful bedtrick that I know, contrived by Roald Dahl in 1965, in which two men, Vic (married to Mary) and Jerry (his next-door neighbor, married to Samantha), plot to replace one another in bed without their wives' knowledge, in what we might call a double-play:† two bedtricks simultaneously perpetrated by two tricksters. Vic, the narrator, tells Jerry his idea, but then:

THE GREAT SWITCHEROO

[Jerry objected,] "Everybody knows that a wife and a husband who have been married for some years develop a kind of routine. It's inevitable. My God, a new operator would be spotted instantly. . . ." "A routine can be duplicated," I said. "Just so long as every detail of that routine is described beforehand." . . . The only thing one had to watch out for was not to get carried away and start improvising. One had to follow the stage directions very carefully and stick to them.

[They began to compare notes on their lovemaking techniques.] At the end of it all, it turned out that the only real difference between Jerry's routine and my own was one of tempo. But what a difference it was! He took things (if what he said was to be believed) in such a leisurely fashion and he prolonged the moments to such an extravagant degree that I wondered privately to myself whether his partner did not sometimes go to sleep in the middle of it all. . . . Jerry was not so discreet. . . . "My God, you go through it like an express train whizzing through a country station!"[43]

This is the joke: each thinks that the other is a terrible lover, and despite all the preparations, each reverts to his own usual technique at the moment of truth. Like Jupiter as Amphitryon,‡ each husband hopes that the woman has enjoyed him, the bedtrickster, more than she enjoys her own husband. The second part of the joke then consists in the dashing of this hope, the reactions of the women. On the morning after, the wife of Vic (the bedtrickster, the perfunctory lover) sends the kids out of the kitchen and tells him:

> I've never really liked [sex]. If you really want to know, I've hated it. . . . It's never given me even the slightest little bit of pleasure. . . . I wasn't ever going to tell you. And I never would have if it hadn't been for last night. Last night, I suddenly found out what the whole crazy thing is about. Oh, darling! . . . Thank you so much for last night! You were marvellous! And I was marvellous! We were both marvellous! Don't look so embarrassed, my darling! You ought to be proud of yourself! You were fantastic! I love you! I do! I do!

At this moment, it seems unlikely that the trickster regarded the bedtrick as successful in every sense of the word. He got away with it, and he was not literally tricked. But the woman *did* notice the difference; and like the wives of so many political† rulers replaced by impostors, she preferred the impostor. The trickster was, therefore, unmasked in other, more troubling ways, as was his dissembling wife ("I wasn't ever going to tell you"). As usual, the mask reveals the truth.

PATERNAL INSECURITY, FAMILY RESEMBLANCE, AND MALE JEALOUSY

Cuckolding is a problem not primarily, or not only, because it mocks a man's virility but because it casts doubt upon the (male) progeny who are going to inherit his property. Cuckolding myths also reflect another deeply embedded human concern: the search for the identity of a child or a parent through the identity of a sexual partner. For people who define themselves in terms of someone else, lover or child, cuckolding renders the identity of that other person more elusive than ever.

Many people in the ancient world probably did not know who their parents were: fathers died, mothers died, and the tribe or society helped out and farmed out the abandoned children. "Pater semper incertus," as the old Latin saying goes; the father is always uncertain (with the double meaning† of that word). The Hindus say, "(Only) god knows the 'Song of God,' (only) the mother knows the father" (krishna jane gita, mata jane pita), and Salman Rushdie suggests that the god Shiva beheaded his son Ganesha because he suspected his paternity, as mysterious as that of Jesus Christ.⁴⁴ The problem of being certain of your father is pointed out in the *Odyssey* (1.215–16) when Telemachos, asked if Odysseus is his father, replies, "My mother says that I certainly am his, but I myself do not know. For no one himself knows his own father." A rejected suitor in Fumiko Enchi's *Masks†* expresses the man's fear:

> A man may try as hard as he likes, but he'll never know what schemes a woman may be slowly and quietly carrying out behind his back. Children— think what endless trouble men have gone to over the ages to persuade themselves that the children their women bore belonged to them! Making adultery a crime, inventing chastity belts. . . . but in the end they were unable to penetrate even one of women's secrets. Even the sadistic misogyny of Buddha and Christ was nothing but an attempt to gain the better of a vastly superior opponent.⁴⁵

This is a brilliant statement of the power of male paternity paranoia and of the even greater subversive power of women.

The uncertainty persists in present-day Euro-American culture, too. Apparently there was (in 1998) a paternity case pending for one of every 100 children in the United States, about 750,000 cases. DNA testing has become commercially popular, advertised on billboards (1-800-DNA-type), taking the mystery out of this once mysterious matter even as it testifies to its enduring human appeal. "An incredible number are just doing it for their own peace of mind," said Caroline Caskey, president of the Identigene lab that answers the call to 1-800-DNA-type. But Dr. Amanda Sozer, director of another lab, remarked, "It gives people the chance of getting an answer they may not want to get."⁴⁶ Nowadays, the scientific permutations of surrogate motherhood, egg donors, and other reproductive technologies exacerbate parental instability—and extend it into new legal† tangles—far more than DNA testing assuages it.

The uncertainty of biological† paternity skews the symmetry† of the bedtrick: it is a truism (and was an article of faith for both Jews and Nazis) that you are more likely to know who your mother is than who your father is, presumably because (unlike your father) your mother must have been present at your birth. Uno Harva remarked of the asymmetry in myths about animal spouses: "An expectant mother can dream that she has been visited by such-and-such an animal, and nobody can contradict her, since there comes the child for all to see: whereas a man can dream that he mated with a Swan and have nothing to show for it."[47]

But in fact you do not always know who your mother is, as myths like the tale of Parvati and the demon Adi remind us. Mothers are harder to lose than fathers, but as Oscar Wilde pointed out in his satire on the Family Romance,† people are careless ("To have lost one parent might be considered a misfortune, but to have lost two seems like carelessness").[48] Salman Rushdie has imagined a situation in which one of three sisters, who live together in a pregnable castle, has a child: "But who was pregnant? . . . Nobody ever discovered, not even the child that was born. . . . The sisters, by virtue of dressing identically and through the incomprehensible effects of their unusual, chosen life, began to resemble each other so closely that even the servants made mistakes."[49] And the child never learns who his true mother is.

If the mother bears a child in concealment and hands it over to someone else, she knows, though the father may not, who the mother is; but she, too, may be fooled by the people to whom she entrusts the child. This point is well argued by Angela Carter's† Perry (in *Wise Children*), who, after he has gone to bed with Dora, reassures her that he is not her father, and adds: "But . . . has it ever occurred to you that your mother might not be your mother?" He suggests that the woman Dora calls Grandma and regards as her guardian might have been seduced by her father. Dora objects: "Come off it, Perry. 'Father' is a hypothesis but 'mother' is a fact." "Mother is as mother does," said Perry. "She loved you just as much as if—."[50] The belief that "a mother is always a mother, since a mother is a biological fact, whilst a father is a movable feast," as Dora continues to reason, underlies the pervasive problem of paternal insecurity;† but the belief that "mother is as mother does" underlies the darker side of the mythology of both stepmothers (or abandoning mothers) and unfaithful wives.

We can understand how a son might not know his mother (he was not thinking clearly when he first cast eyes on her, fresh from her womb), but how could a wise mother not know her own child? Tapati,† the daughter of the shadow Samjna,‡ is rendered unconscious immediately after the birth of her child and forgets his existence.[51] When she meets her son, she cries out, "Child, my love recognizes you, but not I."[52] Similarly, a Tamil princess who does not know she has a living son—because she was drugged when she was impregnated, blindfolded as she went into labor, told that she had given birth to "a blunt coconut-scraper [smeared] with dark used lamp-oil," and made to believe this incredible lie through "powerful magic"—this gullible woman almost commits incest with her son when she meets him later.[53]

Resemblance was the ancient weapon most often used to slice the Gordian knot of paternal insecurity. We have seen that the resemblance (or falsely stated resemblance) of bedtricksters to their siblings usually conceals the truth, but the resemblance of children to their parents usually reveals the truth. Many bedtricks about women's adultery pit the father's ability to recognize his child through its resemblance to him against his wife's apparent inability to distinguish the father from another man who resembles him. Such myths express the father's fear that his child is not his child or, rather, that he can never be sure that his child is his child—unless, of course, he trusts his wife.

Herodotus told of a place where all the women were promiscuous, and a child could know his father only by looking for the one who most resembled him.[54] If the child does not resemble the parent, the assumption is that the mother has been unfaithful. Both the positive and the negative aspects of this assumption are presented in Fletcher's *The Queen of Corinth*† (1616–17): Crates, wondering at his brother's superiority, invokes the Amphitryon‡ myth when he remarks (at 4.4), "Jove surely did descend / When thou were gotten in some heavenly shape / And greet my Mother, as the Poets tell / Of other women." On the other hand, when the queen argues that the wretched Theanor cannot be her son, and he insists that he is, she says (5.2), "Thou lyest, lyest falsly, / My whole life never knew but one chaste bed, / Nor e'er desir'd warmth but from lawfull fires, / Can I be then the Mother to a Goat?" The link between family resemblance and female chastity was expressed in a line in Thomas Middleton's *The Family of Love* (1602), in which a woman who had been the victim of a bedtrick played by her husband† argued that she really recognized him from the start:† "As if I knew you not then as well as the child knows his own father!"[55] As Marliss C. Desens notes, "This proverb had become a satirical reference to female infidelity, and its uses in the drama raise a secondary issue about cuckoldry."[56] If the wife recognizes her husband, the child recognizes his father, and the father his child; if she does not, however, neither do they. The proverb supplied both the title and a part of the essential philosophy of Carter's *Wise Children:*†

> "Our father denied us," is how Dora remembered it. "It's a wise child that knows its own father," hissed Peregrine, . . . "but wiser yet the father who knows his own child." [Later, Dora said,] "Biology is biology. You can't fool a sperm. . . . We were not flesh of his flesh. But then, again, a person *isn't* flesh of its father's flesh, is it? One little sperm out of millions swims up the cervix and it is so very, very easy to forget how it has happened."[57]

Or to worry that the wrong sperm might have made the trip—a shot in the dark.

The belief that a child can instinctively recognize a parent she or he has never seen before, or a parent a child, is so widespread that Stith Thompson† identifies it as a motif: H 481, "Infant picks out his unknown father." The ancient Indian king who does not recognize his wife, Shakuntala, instinctively responds to his son, born by her: "How is it that I feel love for this little boy as if he were the son born of my own loins? If my limbs thrill so to his touch, what bliss must he give to the man from whose body he grew?"[58] And in the *Arabian Nights,*† when a father sees a boy who is, though neither of them knows it, his son, "his stomach began to flutter, and he felt happy, as the blood hearkened to the blood, driven by instinctive sympathy and the divine mystery—Glory be to Him who controls everything."[59] In an Italian story told by Basile,† when a woman gives birth to twins out of wedlock, her father, the king, refrains from killing them only so that, when they grow older, he will "be able by their favour to recognise their father." When they are seven, the ministers decide to give a great banquet "and seek with our own eyes him to whom the children incline most by the inclination of nature: for that one without fail will be the father, and we will at once get hold of him like goat's excrement." The father "had hardly entered the place of feasting when the two pretty children ran to him and embraced him."[60] In the film *Duplicates*† (1991), the brainwashed father of a boy named Joey shouts, "I know my son when I see him and nobody is going to tell me that I don't, not you, not the guy who just walked out of here, not Joey himself!" The idea of instinctual recognition is satirized, along with the whole concept of the Family Romance,† in Beaumarchais's *The Marriage of Figaro,*† when Marceline, having tried to seduce Figaro, now realizes that she is Figaro's mother and says, "My heart was drawn to him. Only in my motive was I mistaken. It was blood calling to blood." To this Figaro replies, "In my case my own good sense served me for instinct when I refused you."[61] Thus, family feeling may be invoked as a proof, akin to sexual feeling.†

But the fear that the child and the father, however wise, might not recognize one another underlies a great deal of the suppression of women by men who wish to ensure that only their children will be born from their women. On the one hand, we view our children as our doubles ("He has his father's eyes," "Spitting image of her mother," we lie to please the parents) and therefore as a rebuttal to death: we are perpetuated in our children, and we love them for that. This need to be doubled in his children may drive a man to place a premium on the chastity of his wife; for if some other man should replace him in the marriage bed, the cuckolding would destroy not merely the husband's virile pride in this life but his only means of survival after death. On the other hand, by creating a child one creates one's rival and, sometimes, one's killer.† Men are jealous of their sons and envious of them for replacing them; this is one of the bases of the conflict between father and son, as well as between mother and daughter. And it is a two-way road. As Karl Miller has put it, "While the notion of the double life has testified to marital ambivalence, the notion of the double has testified to the mixed feelings of the adolescent who wants both to supplant and to emulate the father he resembles."[62] The desire simultaneously to create and to destroy one's sexual double is also one of the bases of the ambivalence inherent in the levirate marriage.†

Parental Imprinting

According to many texts in many cultures, the resemblance of a child to its parent may be destroyed not merely by physical adultery but by mental adulteration. A surprisingly large number of people have believed that a woman who imagines or sees someone other than her sexual partner at the moment of conception may imprint that image upon her child, thus predetermining either its appearance or aspects of its character or both. This belief in mind over matter—what you think about is what you get— is documented in ancient India, Greece, the Hebrew Bible, medieval Europe, and modern Europe.[63] It is variously referred to as maternal imagination, impression, or imprinting, although since there are less common but equally relevant instances of paternal imprinting, and since maternal imprinting itself only became problematic as it threatened the assumed paternal imprinting, it might be better to call it parental imprinting.

Aside from the implausibility of the imprinting mechanism, the value of this theory is fatally undercut by the consideration that if every woman

who thought of another man in bed changed the form of the child conceived on that occasion, very few children would resemble their biological
fathers. As if this were not bad enough, the theory was turned on its head
to show that resemblance, too, could dissemble. Thus, Nicolas Venette,
in 1687, agrees with the wise lawyers and doctors who "claim that a
woman who thinks strongly about her husband in the midst of illicit
pleasures can produce, through the force of her imagination, a child that
perfectly resembles him who is not the father. . . . Resemblance is not
proof of filiation."[64] Now, it is easy enough to imagine that a woman
might dream of her lover while in the embrace of her husband, but why,
one might ask, would she think of her husband while in the embrace of
her lover? (Oktavian, in Richard Strauss and Hugo von Hofmannsthal's
Rosenkavalier,† is appalled to hear the Marschallin say, after their night
of passionate lovemaking, "Last night I dreamt of my husband." "Last
night? *Last night!?*" Oktavian asks, in disbelief and wounded amour
propre.) One answer is that if she, too, subscribes to the theory of parental
imprinting, she will think about her husband when she is with her lover
on purpose, to conceal her adultery. This is a mental variety of the double-
back.† Thus, the mother is no longer regarded as a victim of her own
passion or desire but is in control of her own imagination to such a degree
that she can produce, through that imagination, "not a monster but its
exact opposite: a child who actually resembles the legitimate spouse who
did not father it."[65]

The backlash from this switchback was very serious. For where the
theory of parental imprinting doubtless saved the necks of a number of
adulteresses whose children did not resemble their fathers (for they could
argue that they were not sleeping with other men, merely thinking about
them), the corollary theory that an adulteress could imprint her lover's
child with her husband's features cast suspicion upon *all* women, indeed
particularly upon faithful women whose children *did* resemble their legitimate fathers (for their husbands could argue that the women *were* sleeping with other men but took care to think of their husbands).[66] Women as
a whole were cast as body snatchers† who could at will replace a seemingly
normal child with a monster conceived in the pods of adulterous beds.
This was truly a no-win situation; women were damned if they did, and
damned if they didn't, produce children who resembled their husbands.
And the cognitive dissonance† that resulted from this uncertainty drove
men both to attempt to control women's sexuality and to project† their
images upon their sons. Thus, M. Boursicot, the French diplomat in the

real-life affair that inspired David Henry Hwang's *M. Butterfly*,† explained why he thought his (male) Chinese lover was a woman and that she had borne him a son; speaking of that son, he said, "He looked like me."[67]

In *Sicily and Naples*,† a similar error is made by Felicia, who is the victim of a bedtrick that makes her believe, wrongly, that King Ferrando has impregnated her. Felicia imagines how she will show the child to its father: "Can he not love himself? Here, here I bear him, / Himself in a less model. This I'll show him. / If he mistrusts 'tis none of his, let him / But rip me up. There he shall see each limb / As like to his as his one hand, one eye, / One cheek, is like another." The violence of the image—that, to prove her faithfulness to him, she will let Ferrando rip out the unborn child and examine it—collapses the interval between the pregnancy (the occasion for accusations of infidelity) and the birth of the child (that validates the mother). The irony is that she is wrong; if the child resembles anyone, it is the villain who bedtricked her, and who will ultimately cause the death of Felicia, Ferrando, and the unborn child. Projection† here hath made its masterpiece.

Theology, or When God Has Lipstick on His Collar

The Sexual Masques of God

In most mythologies, to forgive is human, to err, divine. The more or less rigorous strictures that traditional societies place upon human sexuality have as their shadows myths in which deities violate all of those strictures. The divine escapades thus shed light upon the human dilemma of sexual misbehavior; but beyond that, the human situation helps us to understand what it means to worship a goddess who sends a demonic surrogate in her place, or a god who cheats on his worshipers.

Ralph Harper sees in several passages from Proust, ostensibly about human love affairs, a sense of grace, of the presence of god. Then he remarks: "Perhaps underneath some of the casual talk about sex these days is a secret hope that in sex we may still be able to experience the intimacy of real presence. But for most people it is probably a simulacrum at best. The mystics of the past at least understood the fullness of presence, its demands as well as its satisfactions, and, paradoxically, they made use of the language of sexual love. Too often human beings speak of one kind of experience in terms of another that they know only by hearsay."[68] The idea that the sexual act is the locus of ultimate truth† need not always have religious overtones, but it often does. These overtones are manifest throughout the mythology in which sexual desires drive the gods to masquerade in human forms, as Zeus became incarnate as Amphitryon‡ to seduce Alcmena and the Hindu god Indra became incarnate as the sage Gautama to seduce Ahalya.‡ Incarnation is the supreme masquerade, often achieved through a bedtrick that makes it possible for a god or goddess to have children with a mortal by masquerading as a human, becoming human and at the same time not becoming human, to produce the man-god (such as Heracles as the son of Zeus and Alcmena).

Bedtricks pervade the canons of Judaism and Christianity. In addition to the Hebrew lineage that comes to Jesus† from a long line of sexual tricksters and masquerading mothers, and the Greek male lineage of bedtricks that comes to Jesus from Amphitryon, the early Gnostic tradition maintained that Eve used her reflection (rather than her shadow, as the Hindu goddess Samjna‡ does) to protect herself from rape.[69] The evil powers fall for the reflection—not merely the image but the echo, not merely the shadowy reflection but the voice†—and defile it. Eve herself escapes by becoming a tree (as Daphne changes into a laurel tree to avoid Apollo, and Samjna not only produces a double but changes into a mare), and so the rape is ultimately meaningless: "The 'spiritual Eve' remains untouched by the lust of the powers, who can only defile/impregnate her shadow."[70] Thus, as Roberto Calasso said of the phantom Helen:‡ "Helen was a reflection on water. How can you kill a reflection without killing the water? And how can you kill water?"[71] Elaine Pagels has called this "a case of mistaken maternity,"[72] not a bad name for the story of Parvati and the demon Adi,† too.

In other Gnostic texts, it is Adam who loses his celestial nature as a result of falling in love with his own image glimpsed in the mirror of water.[73] In Milton's *Paradise Lost* (455–75), Eve falls in love with her reflection, until God's voice tells her that it is her self and bids her follow him to "where no shadow stays / Thy coming, and thy soft imbraces, he / Whose image thou art, him thou shalt enjoy"—that is, instead of loving her own image, she is to let Adam love *his* own image, her. The deceptions proliferate, as such deceptions tend to do: the evil powers of darkness rape the reflected image of Sophia in the water, engendering certain classes of beings.[74] Sophia—whose name means "knowledge" and whose domain, *gnosis,* is cognate with the name of Sam*jna*—is the key to a Gnostic mythology in which carnal knowledge† is deconstructed in favor of spiritual† knowledge. The bedtricks in early Gnosticism may be viewed as an offshoot of the basic Gnostic contention that god herself is a double, and that we are all the children of a lesser god(ess) than god.

In India, Samjna's bedtrick creates the ancestor of the human race; it is the source of the illusory nature of all of human existence. This basic masquerade is perpetrated by *maya,* illusion: the one godhead is shattered into multiple images in the phenomenal world, and we must look to find the single image behind all the false forms.[75] Hinduism is highly accessible to the idea of having more than one body per soul, and the multivalence of certain Hindu gods leads to an image of a multivalent whole, which functions not merely on the level of sexual metaphors, polygamous gods, and polytheism (what Max Müller† called henotheism or kathenotheism, and we might call serial monotheism: worshiping one god as supreme and then another and then another) but also on the level of the personality. All of the Hindu myths of illusion, not merely the myths of sexual illusion, catapult us into a new reality that forces us to recognize not merely our multiplicity but, sometimes, our illusory existence, and this transition is particularly vivid in the mythology of Shiva and Parvati.

DIVINE BETRAYAL

Theology and psychology intersect at the point of abandonment. The human experience of the terror of being abandoned by human agents, first the mother and then the spouse (sexual jealousy but also, at a deeper level, the fear of rejection and sexual inadequacy), and the theological hypothesis of being abandoned by god reinforce one another. The loss of the lover and the loss of the mother foreshadow the loss of the deity who abandons humankind. Thus, to the syllogism developed in chapter 2 we must add a fourth assertion:

4. **"My god is not God."** This is an entirely unhappy discovery, which does not even leave us the dignity that Existentialism, for example, found in the absence of god, the challenge to create our own fate. For the myth does not say that there is no god at all; on the contrary, it says that there are several, and the human race was created by a second-rate one who does not care for us. The abandoning mother behaves like god in the deist argument, who made the world and then left it here for us, without him (or her) to run it, a watch with no watchmaker—and, the myth adds, leaving us to the mercies of the substitute. The god or goddess in these myths is otiose, hidden, vanished, a layabout: like a policeman, she's never there when you need her. Or she is *absconditus,* like a criminal with the loot: when you need her, she is feasting with the Ethiopians, like Poseidon in the *Odyssey* (1.22, 5.282), or temporarily indisposed, like Baal (off answering a call of nature)[76] in the contest with Elijah (1 Kings 18.27). In Woody Allen's film *Mighty Aphrodite* (1996), when the Greek chorus call out to Zeus, they hear the sound of an answering machine with the voice of Zeus inviting them to leave a message after the tone. The Hebrew Bible tells us how Moses and the Jews lost the original tablets of the Ten Commandments, written by the very hand of God, and had to settle instead for the surrogate, written by the hand of Moses (Exodus 31.18, 32.15–19, 34.1–5, 27–28). Once again, the myth tells us that all that we have is the double.

We must, however, distinguish between the mother who abandons her child and the woman who betrays her husband. In the human narrative, this may be the same woman, viewed by the child or by the husband. In the theological narrative, it is manifest in two aspects of the divine betrayal: god goes away, or god turns out to be a fake (the real god having gone away). Male gods can also be absentee fathers, dud dads, or, more often, abandoning lovers. In Hinduism, the otiosity of god is also expressed through the erotic metaphor of *viraha:* the longing for a lover (often an adulterous lover) from whom one is separated—the longing of Shiva and Parvati for one another. God is not with us, the poem says, because he is making love to some other woman instead; god (Krishna,‡ for instance) doubles himself for his various women and comes to us with some other woman's lipstick on his collar (or the Hindu equivalent: the scars of her nails on his back). In the Neoplatonic reading of the paradigmatic tale of Cupid and Psyche,† Psyche's search for true knowledge of her hidden lover was analogized to the soul's search for the concealed godhead.[77]

Avishai Margalit and Moshe Halbertal have demonstrated the use of human adultery as a metaphor for the betrayal of god—betrayal in both the objective and subjective senses, the worshiper's betrayal of god and god's betrayal of the worshiper.[78] God's abandonment of his worshiper and human adultery often become mutual metaphors for one another: Tamil and Telugu love poems are enlisted in the service of poems for the love of god, but then those devotional poems are recast as poems sung by courtesans about their customers—or, perhaps, about god.[79] Sex may begin as what is signified (with its symbols that signify it), but then it is religion that is signified (by sex and its symbols, as well as by the symbols of religion), and finally, in a kind of second naiveté or double-back,† sex is signified by religion and its symbols, which is in turn signified by sex and its symbols, as well as by the symbols of religion . . . until it is impossible to distinguish between signified and signifier. Sex masquerades as religion masquerading as sex; the love poem masquerades as itself.† We are left asking: "What is sex? What is religion?" Though other religions also mix religion and sex, Hinduism is notorious for it; a character in a David Lodge novel suggests helpfully to a friend who is groaning under the yoke of Christian repression: "But if you must have religion, why not Hinduism? Then you can have sex as well."[80] Hindus themselves, as we have seen, find this conjunction far more complex than Lodge's Orientalist Catholics think they do.

Sexual and theological arguments can be made simultaneously so as to inform one another. For example, one response to the argument that god has abandoned us is the theological assertion that god is indeed here and that we are the ones who create the disjunction because we cannot see god, not because s/he has vanished and left nothing but a shadow,‡ but because what is familiar becomes invisible to us, as a woman becomes invisible to her husband.† This is what happens in a sixteenth-century Telugu poem about the god and his wife, but also about the god and us:

HE'S STANDING RIGHT NEXT TO HER

Tell her he's standing right next to her,
and he's amazed she doesn't see him.
She's thinking so much and missing him
that when he comes to her door and calls her
she doesn't hear.
Right from the beginning,
this separation has worn her down.
Now, if anyone tells her the truth,
she doesn't believe it.

. . . .

[W]hen he comes for real,
she says it's a lie.

. . . .

He lies down beside her
and she doesn't see him.
Then he looks up and makes love to her
and she says she's had the strangest dream.
He's standing right next to her.[81]

This philosophy argues that when we mistake the reality for a dream, we ourselves make the real lover/god into a fantasy lover, a god who has failed us; or, mistaking the dream for a reality,[82] we do not recognize the real lover/god when s/he comes to us. But when the god makes love to his wife (or to the worshiper), she wakes up; sex is not just reality,† it's Enlightenment.

How are we to unpack these sexual/theological metaphors? What does it mean to say that you have been raped by god (like Alcmena and Ahalya), or that god herself (like Parvati) has been raped? What sort of a theodicy is implied by such a violation? What sort of a theodicy is implied by divine adultery, such as the infidelities of both Shiva and Parvati? The lesson that the adulterous and/or sexually violent god teaches the worshiper is manifold: god cannot belong to any one person; love (whether of god or of a human lover) respects no boundaries, particularly possessive boundaries; and love is painful and unequal. The worshiper may be "possessed" by god in a trance, but god is never possessed.

Both religious and Romantic† philosophies distrust visual† recognition. St. Theresa, who had a most erotic relationship with her god, said:

> If I say that I do not see Him with the eyes of the body or the eyes of the soul, because this is no imaginary vision, how then can I know and affirm that he is beside me with greater certainty than if I saw Him? If one says that one is like a person in the dark who cannot see someone though he is beside him, or that one is like somebody who is blind, it is not right. There is some similarity here, but not much, because a person in the dark can perceive with the other senses, or hear his neighbor speak or move, or can touch him. Here this is not so, nor is there any feeling of darkness. On the contrary, He appears to the soul by a knowledge brighter than the sun.[83]

The argument here is that human partners *should* be able to recognize one another in the dark, by the senses other than vision, which should tell us that someone is "standing right next to her" (in the Telugu) or "beside me" (St. Theresa). But since there is "not much similarity" between partners in bed and worshipers in the presence of god, this is not how one knows god—or how god sees us.

Can we trick the gods in bed the way that they trick us? There is a Herodotean text, from the fifth century B.C.E. in Greece, that argues this question rather obliquely. It is literally a bed trick, though it is not, strictly, a bedtrick:

XERXES' BEDTRICK

[Xerxes had a dream urging him to attack Greece, against Artabanus's advice. He summoned Artabanus and said,] "If it is a god that sends it, and it is entirely his pleasure that this expedition against Greece should take place, then this same dream will hover about you too and will lay the same charge on you as on me. And I think this would be most likely to happen if you would take all this raiment of mine and put it on and sit upon my throne and then go to sleep in my bed." [Artabanus replied,] "Let the vision appear to me with the same orders. But there is no necessity that it should rather appear to me because I am wearing your clothes rather than my own or sleep in your bed rather than my own—that is, if it is minded to appear at all. The vision that appears to you in your sleep, whatever it is, has hardly attained such a degree of simplicity that it will think me to be you when it sees me, drawing its evidence solely from your clothes. If it shall disdain me altogether and shall not choose to appear, whether I wear your clothes or my own—that is what we now have to find out. . . ." So spoke Artabanus, and, hoping to prove that

> Xerxes had been deluded, he did as the King bade him. He put on
> Xerxes' raiment and sat upon the royal throne and afterwards went to
> bed, and in his sleep the dream vision came to him as it had to Xerxes,
> and standing above Artabanus it said, "You are the man who turns Xerxes
> from making war upon Greece. . . ."[84]

Xerxes was right in thinking that the dream would come to the person
in the bed, the person in the official position of the king. But Artabanus
was also right in thinking that the dream would know who was in the
bed; it addressed him, not Xerxes. Even when we appear to trick the gods,
therefore, they see through us; as in the myth of Prometheus,‡ the human
trickster is, in the end, outtricked by the divine trickster. To the gods,
apparently, humans are not all alike in the dark.

HUMAN BLINDNESS AND DIVINE INVISIBILITY

Is there any point in distinguishing the "mythical" variants of the theme
from the "realistic" ones? Does the divine lover vanish because of human
blindness or because of divine invisibility? When these stories appear as
myths, they involve deities in magical situations, and when they appear
as tales that function on a more banal and human level, servants or siblings often assume the role played by magical doubles in the myths. The
myth of the woman who creates a magical double of herself in order to
avoid an unwanted liaison also appears as the tale of the woman who
sends her servant girl in her place, and the man who transforms himself
into a woman in order to sleep with another man also becomes the man
who simply puts on women's clothing to get a job. Pausanias rationalized
the story of Narcissus‡ by arguing that Narcissus loved not his own reflection but an identical twin sister.[85] When Herodotus (1.8) told the story
of King Candaules,† he had him urge Gyges to hide behind the bedroom
door to see the queen naked; but when Plato told the story in the *Republic*
(2.359D–360D), he substituted for the bedroom door a magic ring of invisibility.

   Often, we may read the same myth on the level of realism or on the
level of fantasy. But in a sense, *all* of the tales of bedtricks, even the realistic
ones, are mythological in one sense of the term: they imagine what cannot
ever be in real life. More precisely, they imagine what might be most
natural to *real* real life devoid of the constraints of human culture (a
situation that can never exist for us). The supernatural and the realistic
stories are alike in some ways, different in others. They are alike in that

they deal with the same sets of human problems, but they express those problems differently according to the idioms of each genre, and they imply different ultimate meanings.

Many stories about gods turn out to be largely about human problems, and many stories about human beings raise theological questions. The psychological and theological concerns of the myth stand as metaphors for one another, like the Escher drawing of the hand drawing the hand drawing the hand. Myths about the relationship between the body and the soul,† however psychological or political their concerns, are religious myths. It is not the case that one can ask psychological and/or political questions only of "realistic" myths and theological questions only of "fantastic" myths. As Ernest Gellner has remarked: "[Hum]ankind in general is seldom if ever conceptually kosher. The transcendent is *not* neatly and conscientiously separated off from the empirical. Most traditions are appallingly unfastidious about their conceptual crockery."[86]

Franz Rosenzweig once remarked that theological problems seek to be translated into human ones, and human problems to be projected into theological ones.[87] If we view the human concerns as the logical and psychological base from which the theological versions were derived, we are following in the footsteps of the ancient school of interpretation called euhemerism, which argued that all myths evolved in this way: from a "rational" core of legend about human heroes there developed an "irrational" overlay about gods. And by attempting to unravel this unfortunate process, the euhemerists rationalized the myths: that is, they took stories ostensibly about the gods and made them (back, as they saw it) into stories about humans. Freud† may be regarded as a latter-day euhemerist when he argues that stories that appear to be about god are really about your father.† The interpretive process of rationalization (regarding the supernatural as derived from the natural) argues that the myth itself has *irrationalized*, turning what is rational (observable human behavior) into what is irrational (unobservable divine behavior). Thus, the *midrash* on Lamentations takes the (human) story of Rachel† and Leah and turns it into a story about the jealousy of god; it makes one sort of theology (mixed with psychology and history) into another.

We can also see the opposite process at work in our stories, the derivation of human meaning from theological texts. That is, theological questions are posed, and to answer these questions, human images, human concerns, are projected into myths about the divine world. The meanings of these myths, however, must be sought not merely in superficial

anthropomorphic forms and quasi-human events but in the darker theological questions that are posed. Thus, both rationalization and irrationalization may occur in the making of myths as well as in their interpretation. Irrationalization occurs when ideas about men and women are
transformed into myths about gods and goddesses, when stories about
human women and men, entangled in the toils of human sexual tragedy,
take flight in the illusion provided by myth. But the opposite process,
rationalization, is equally common and important, when ideas about gods
and goddesses are translated into myths about men and women, when
insoluble theological problems take on flesh and seek their solutions, always in vain, on the human stage. The banal and the magical are by no
means mutually exclusive, for the myth is a bridge between the actual
human sexual experience and the fantasy that grows out of that experience
and in turn transfigures it. But it is also a bridge between the terrifying
abyss of cosmological ignorance and our comfortable familiarity with our
recurrent, if tormenting, human problems. Some variants narrow the gap
by rendering the fantasy in almost realistic terms; but the gap, however
small, remains nevertheless. The tension gives rise to the myth.

S I X

Designated Hitters

ᕦᐟ✦⎯

LEGAL MALE SURROGATES

In many stories a man substitutes for another man in bed—not secretly but officially, using instead of magic or family resemblance family connections (in the case of the levirate†) or political power (in the case of the droit du seigneur†). Such a man may act as a sexual pinch hitter or designated hitter not only to achieve his own projects but, sometimes, to help out a friend. If the man who is replaced is not being tricked, if the arrangement is entirely official, this is hardly a masquerade, though we may still speak of doubling or surrogation. On the other hand, though the men may agree to it, the woman may not be told, or be bedtricked into it. Even when it is official and she knows about it, the woman may find unofficial ways to subvert it, through a double-crossing bedtrick of her own. Instead of remaining the passive field in which the man sows his seed, instead of closing her eyes and thinking of England (or Bengal), the woman becomes active and refuses to follow the script. Indeed, the levirate and droit du seigneur are dramatized in narrative primarily in their subversion through bedtricks.

The levirate is a legal way for a man to produce an heir for his dead brother by impregnating his brother's widow. The term is derived from the late Latin *leviratus,* "son-in-law," although the levirate marriage is sometimes (apparently wrongly) said to be so called because of its occurrence in the Hebrew Bible, where Levi's brother begets a son on his behalf (and where a descendant of Levi, Onan,† husband of Tamar, resorts to the sin of onanism in order *not* to function as a levirate husband). Raphael Patai lists the conditions that "had to be present in the social mores of the society in order to make levirate both possible and necessary": the society had to be polygynous ("Only in a society where a man was allowed to have several wives could he be expected to marry his childless brother's widow irrespective of his own marital status"), patrilocal (with brothers living together with their father, to ensure the "availability of a brother to fulfil the law of levirate"), patrilineal, and patriarchal (only then "could the law function without having to countenance objection or even refusal on the part of the widow").[1] (The widows often do object and refuse.) These conditions apparently prevailed in ancient India and in biblical times and still prevail in some parts of the world to this day.

The competition between fathers† and sons may lead them to masquerade as one another, but it is the need to produce those sons in the first place that forces many fathers to resort to other types of masquerades. The need for the substitute usually arises when the intended father of a child has proved impotent or died before begetting a child. One rather extreme solution to this problem is to invoke the dead man himself, whose corpse may miraculously return to impregnate his widow.[2] In our day, science produces the same miracle, as we learn from an article in the *New York Times* (March 27, 1999, A1) entitled "A Birth Spurs Debate on Using Sperm after Death":

> In the first known birth of its kind in the United States, a California woman has given birth to a girl using sperm retrieved from her dead husband, raising ethical questions over whether a man must give his consent to be a father. The sperm was retrieved 30 hours after the man's death and then frozen for 15 months before use. His wife, Gaby Vernoff, became pregnant in July 1998 and delivered the girl on March 17 in a Los Angeles hospital. . . . "Is it appropriate to consciously bring a child into this world with a dead father?" said Alexander M. Capron, professor of law and medicine.

It may or may not be appropriate, but it happens all the time in mythology—and now in California, much the same thing.

But the usual male sexual substitute was the dead man's brother, whose right (indeed, whose duty) to beget a child upon his brother's widow was legitimized and institutionalized in the custom of the levirate marriage. Claude Lévi-Strauss suggests that, in at least some instances, this practice may have arisen to compensate for the lack of women as a result of the chief's privilege of taking more than his share (the practice of droit du seigneur,† often closely related to the levirate): "A . . . factor which compensated for the unfair allocation of the women was the levirate—the inheriting of widows by their dead husbands' brothers. . . . 'He lends [his wife] to his brother,' because 'brother is not jealous of brother.' "[3] Ah, but brother *is* jealous of brother, and there's the rub in the levirate.

For the myths of levirate marriage are about yet another series of paradoxes.† The first is a metaphysical mystery: How can a dead man beget a child? Answer: Through his brother. This riddle resurfaces at the end of a bedtrick in *All's Well That Ends Well*† (5.3), referring to a woman instead of a man: "One that's dead is quick" ("quick" meaning both "alive" and "pregnant"). Then come the psychological paradoxes. On the one hand, a man must never have sex with his brother's wife; on the other hand, he must have sex with his brother's wife—if the brother is dead. On the one hand, the person you most want to have sex with your wife, when you are dead, is your brother, because he has your genes; on the other hand, the last person you want to have sex with your wife, even when you are dead, is your brother, because of sibling rivalry. On the one hand, the child that results is your child, because the law says he is; on the other hand, he isn't your child, because he does not spring from your loins. On the one hand, your widow wants to have sex with your brother, because she wants to bear a child; on the other hand, she may very well not want to have sex with your brother, because he is not the man she chose to marry. (This paradox interacts with and further complicates the one in which you fear that your wife *does* want to sleep with your brother.) Fraternal sibling rivalry yields to the necessity for the levirate marriage, expanding the sexual boundaries of women at least in principle, but then this necessity rebounds into the need for ultimate control of women so that *they* do not encourage illicit surrogations. Whether the brother is doing his dead brother a favor or an injury is the source of considerable tension within the mythology. This is a variant of the double-bind:† when one man officially invites another to substitute for him, the resulting bedtrick still humiliates him, not by fooling him but by forcing him officially to acknowledge that the other man can do what he cannot.

Brothers

The mythology of the levirate is best understood in the context of the more general corpus of stories about brothers who substitute for one another in bed. Like sisters,† brothers often use their innate resemblance to work with or against their siblings in bedtricks—a theme so common that Stith Thompson† lists it as a motif: K 1311.1, "Husband's twin brother mistaken by woman for her husband." A Buddhist text (dating from sometime before the fifth century) tells of a king who is a previous incarnation of the Buddha himself; it employs motifs that European folklore usually associates with women: the Substitute Bride† (here, groom), the ugly† bride (here, groom), and the contrast between the wise-and-ugly† sister and the foolish-and-beautiful sister (here, brothers):

KING KUSA AND HIS HANDSOME BROTHER

Queen Silvati had a wise but ugly son, named Kusa, and a son who was foolish but handsome, named Jayampati. She found a very beautiful bride for Kusa, named Pabhavati, and arranged the marriage, but then she began to worry, "This maiden is very lovely and my son is ugly. If she sees him, she won't stay for a single day but will run away." So she said to the girl's father, the Madda king, "In our family a wife is not allowed to see her husband by daylight until she has conceived." The girl agreed to this, but when Kusa wanted to see his bride by daylight, the queen arranged to have him disguised as an elephant keeper when Pabhavati came to see the elephants (he pelted her with a piece of elephant shit), and as a groom in the horse stable when she came to see the horses (he pelted her with a piece of horse shit). Then Pabhavati expressed a desire to see her husband, and the queen arranged for her to see Prince Jayampati instead.

But after a while Kusa, as the elephant keeper, made gestures toward her with his hands, and she began to suspect that he was King Kusa. She returned to her father's city, but Kusa came to her in disguise as a cook, underwent many trials, and eventually won her.[4]

In another variant of this story, Kusa himself does not know that he is ugly, "for he had never been allowed to see a mirror; and he had always been prevented from bathing, for fear that the water might serve as a looking-glass and let him know what manner of man he was."[5] (This might have been yet another reason why his wife shunned him.) Making the victim close his eyes† and showing one woman and giving another are tricks usually played on a man, as Laban played them on Jacob.† The second half of the story, too, follows a pattern far more typical of women's stories, and more particularly of Cupid and Psyche: after the wedding, the bride (here groom) loses the groom (here bride) by indulging her (his) forbidden curiosity and must undergo trials to win him (her) back. But both Kusa and Cupid are invisible to their brides, and the fact that Kusa's only flaw is that he is ugly links this tale with a related pattern of stories about male bedtricksters: Beauty and the Beast.†

Brothers frequently jump in and out of beds in real life (and in legal cases,† by no means the same thing). I cannot resist citing a little-known episode from the life of the real Abraham Lincoln. It seems that in 1829 the Lincoln family was excluded from the list of guests invited to the double wedding of their neighbors, the Grigsby boys, Charles and Reuben, and Lincoln felt mortified by this slight, the more so since an enemy of his named Josiah Crawford, a man with a "long, huge, blue nose," had been invited. This is what happened, in the words of James C. Richardson, from an interview recorded in September 1865:

Abraham Lincoln and the Mistaken Partners

After the infair was ended the two women were put to bed. The candles were blown out upstairs—the gentlemen—the two husbands—were invited and shown to bed. Chas. Grigsby went into bed with, *by an accident* as it were, with Reuben Grigsby's wife and Reuben got into bed with Charles's wife, by accident as it were. Lincoln, I say, was mortified and declared that he would have revenge. Lincoln was by nature witty and here was his chance. So he got up a witty *poem*—called the Book of Chronicles, in which the infair—the mistake in partners—Crawford and his blue nose, came in each for its share—and this poem is remembered here in Indiana in scraps better than the Bible—better than Watts's Hymns. This was in 1829—and the first production that I know of made us feel that Abe was truly and really *some.* This called the attention of the People to Abe intellectually. Abe dropped the Poem in the road carelessly—lost as it were—it was found by one of Grigsby's boys satirised who had the good manly sense to read it—keep it—preserve it for years—if it is *not in existence now.*[6]

Elizabeth Crawford recited "The Chronicles" from memory on January 4, 1866, and her son transcribed it; is is truly terrible doggerel (a sample: "So Billy and Natty agreed very well; / And mama's well pleased at the match. / The egg it is laid, but Natty's afraid, / The shell is so soft that it never will hatch").[7] This is the literary work that first put Abe Lincoln on the map, a poem that people in Indiana found even funnier than the Bible (which has many similar stories in it) or Watts's hymns (which, to the best of my knowledge, do not). Richardson's version of the incident that inspired the poem suggests that someone led the brothers to the wrong beds on purpose (the use of "by an accident as it were" is rendered sarcastic by its repetition and by the use of the phrase "as it were" when Lincoln "loses" the poem on purpose). Another version of the story, more cryptic, gives Lincoln the role not merely of archivist of the plot but its author: "young Abraham became the moving spirit in a plot that resulted in maneuvering the brides into the wrong bedchambers on their wedding night. The mistake was rectified before too late, but not without considerable chagrin to those involved, a state of mind not assuaged when Lincoln publicized the incident throughout the country-side by writing an account of it in Biblical language, titled, 'The Chronicles of Reuben.' "[8] Whatever actually happened, the story found its proper resting place in mythological fiction.

TWIN BEDS

As with twin sisters,† the problem of mistaken fraternal identity is exaggerated in the case of twins. Claude Lévi-Strauss, in his analysis of the story of Splitting Hares,† defined twins as "two individuals which are exactly similar or identical because they are both a part of a whole."[9] But what is that whole? Otto Rank argued that twins are to be understood as one being—a single soul contained in two vessels—and that the special status of such a soul indicates immortality.[10] More often, I think, the male twin is associated with death, particularly the death triggered by the rejection and masquerade perpetrated by a false parent or lover. Samjna's‡ son Yama,† whose name actually means "twin," is the king of the dead; one of the two Gemini,‡ Castor and Pollux, gives half his life to the other.

But the twin mistaken for his brother in bed has also been one of the great comic themes from the time of the Romans. In Plautus's *Menaechmi* (or *The Two Menaechmuses*), Menaechmus of Syracuse unwittingly masquerades in Epidamnus as his brother from Epidamnus and enjoys both his brother's dinner and his courtesan, Erotium, who believes that Manaechmus the Syracusan is the same Menaechmus she saw moments before and whom she has entertained in the past. (The local twin puts on a dress and compares himself to Ganymede, Zeus's boy lover.) *A Comedy of Errors,* Shakespeare's great slapstick treatment of the theme of twin brothers, written between 1589 and 1593 and well adapted in the 1938 musical comedy *The Boys from Syracuse,*[11] is itself an adaptation of both *Menaechmi* (in which, though there are two brothers, there is only *one* servant) and another play by Plautus, *Amphitryon*† (in which two gods impersonate a man and his servant). But *A Comedy of Errors* doubles the doubles in a tale of twin brothers and their twin servants. The theme is a perennial favorite, the innocence and comedy inhering in the fact that, like the brothers in *Menaechmi* rather than the gods in *Amphitryon,* the double *does not intend* to take over his twin brother's life—or wife. On the contrary, the joke is that he does *not* desire her as she hopes he will. Although no sexual act is explicitly consummated (perhaps because the courtesan in Plautus, whom the unconscious impostor explicitly says he has bedded [*scortum accubui,* "I lay with the whore"], becomes a wife in

Shakespeare), the mistaken "dinner" with the woman (the courtesan in Plautus, the wife in Shakespeare) takes its place. Shakespeare is usually quite explicit about sex, but there may be more implied here than a mere *souper intîme*. In David Bell's 1998 production for the Shakespeare Repertory Theatre in Chicago, the unwitting double staggers out after the "dinner" half naked, pulling on his pants, and more than a shared meal is expressed by the horror in the wife's face when, learning that her husband has an identical twin, she asks, "Which of you two did dine with me today?" (5.1). This is the plot:

THE COMEDY OF ERRORS

Identical twin brothers were separated in youth as the result of a shipwreck, and each was called Antipholus. One (Ephesan Antipholus, henceforth E.) lived in Ephesus, the other (Syracusan Antipholus, henceforth S.) in Syracuse, and each had a servant named Dromio (E. Dromio and S. Dromio). E. was married to Adriana, and E. Dromio was engaged to Luce, Adriana's maid, but neither S. nor S. Dromio was attached. One day, S. came by chance to Ephesus with S. Dromio.

The sexual "errors" turn upon sexual jealousy and rejection. The wife wonders why her husband (as she thinks, but actually her husband's twin brother) does not love her, and indeed, her worries are not unfounded: for her husband is suspiciously friendly with a courtesan, as he himself admits. Thus, where a wife (rightly or wrongly) often suspects what we have come to call "the other woman," this wife begins to believe that her husband actually is "another man"—which he, or rather his twin brother, is. By contrast, the unattached S. Dromio is puzzled to discover that E. Dromio's comically fat girlfriend, who of course seems to S. Dromio to be a total stranger, regards him as her boyfriend.

The Comedy of Errors is about asymmetry† in sexual love: one partner expects intimacy, while the other regards him or her as a stranger. This distancing is wonderfully expressed by Adriana to S., whom she mistakenly regards as her (straying) husband:

Ay, ay, Antipholus, look strange, and frown:
Some other mistress hath thy sweet aspects,
I am not Adriana, nor thy wife. . . .

. . . .

How comes it now, my husband, O! how comes it,
That thou art thus estranged from thyself?
Thyself I call it, being strange to me,

That, undividable, incorporate,
Am better than thy dear self's better part.

. . . .

For if we two be one, and thou play false,
I do digest the poison of thy flesh,
Being strumpeted by thy contagion. (2.2)

"I am not Adriana," she says to him, because if she defines† herself by him, and he is false, she is false. "I know you not," he replies, and means it literally (in both senses of "know"†), while she thinks he is merely speaking metaphorically, as she was. The behavior of S. supports the misgivings Adriana already has about her relationship with her husband; she says that for weeks E. "hath been heavy, sour, sad, / And much, much different from the man he was" (5.1). And now he is really really different. The unusual accident of double twins (with the even more unusual accident of masters having the same names and having servants with the same names and ending up in the same town) triggers the not-so-unusual accident of marital infidelity and estrangement: the feeling that one simply does not recognize one's official partner is expressed in the dream (or nightmare) that that partner is actually a total stranger. In David Lodge's *Small World*, the titles of Shakespearean plays are translated into Japanese paraphrases and then retranslated back into English; *The Comedy of Errors* is called "The Flower in the Mirror and the Moon on the Water,"[12] a pair of "oriental" metaphors for twin illusions that could stand for many of the stories in this corpus.

The theme of twin brothers who share one woman is inverted in stories in which one man pretends to be his twin in order to sleep with two women. The lighter side of this theme was developed by A. R. Gurney in a two-act comedy entitled *The Perfect Party*, in which a man invents a twin who limps‡ and has a mustache (put on with black shoe polish), an Italian accent, and, he claims, "a considerably larger penis."† This paper-thin disguise is sufficient to fool the woman he seduces but not his wife, who catches him in the act and mocks him: "You cultivated a grotesque limp and a ludicrous accent. You didn't even bother to change your costume." When the husband invokes the double-back,† asking, "How do you know I'm not my twin brother pretending to be me?" his wife counter-invokes other, better authors: "That is a question only Pirandello could answer. . . . By inventing this brother, you went against everyone's advice and imitated Oscar Wilde.†"[13]

This theme underwent several successful reincarnations in the cinema.

In *Two Much* (1996), a man (Antonio Banderas) assumes two identities in order to seduce two sisters ("Mr. Banderas, mugging desperately, changes identity mostly by adjusting the rubber band in his hair").[14] Here the theme of good-and-evil sisters† (in this case, stupid and intelligent, or promiscuous and choosy) is combined with the theme of the man who pretends to have a twin brother; in one Feydeau-like scene, he is in bed with both sisters, racing back and forth between their rooms through a shared bathroom and pool room, changing hairdos (or rubber bands) and bathrobes en route. The person he pretends to be, an artist, is the person he once was (before he sold out), the real person, and the one he remains in the end.

The mythology of twin brothers who replace one another in bed is balanced by a mythology of twin brothers who do *not* replace one another in bed, despite all temptations to do so. The Brothers Grimm recorded a paradigmatic form of this story in which one brother lays his sword in the bed between himself and his brother's wife (who has mistaken him for her husband) to protect them both.[15] The knife that separates the brothers was given a bizarre twist in the film *The Corsican Brothers* (1941), in which conjoined twins,† Lucien and Mario, are separated shortly after birth; years later they become bitter rivals when Lucien falls in love with the woman who loves Mario. Attacking Mario, Lucien says, "The doctor's knife couldn't separate us; but my knife will do it now." The irony is that Lucien always experiences whatever pain is inflicted on Mario; if he were to cut him, he would wound himself (as in Théophile Gautier's story *Avatar*‡)—an extreme case of the double-bind.†

The twin who tries not to sleep with his brother's wife fails hilariously, several times, in a modern variant of this story, the 1996 film

MULTIPLICITY

Doug wants more time to meet his increasing workload as an engineer and more "quality time" with his kids and his wife, Laura, who wants to go back to her job in real estate. He lets a geneticist create two clones of himself (Doug 2 and Doug 3), and Doug 2 on his own produces a clone of himself, Doug 4, who is, like the blurry Xerox of a Xerox, flawed—an idiot. Doug warns the clones away from his wife (Rule Number One: "No clone nookie; original nookie only"), which he has anticipated by joking, "It wouldn't work if Laura rolls over in bed in the morning and finds two Dougs." Laura notices the discrepancies, memory lapses, and so forth— "I feel like I don't know you anymore," she says. But one night when Doug is away, though Doug 3 loyally puts a pillow between them in the

bed, Laura aggressively and irresistibly seduces first him and then the
other two clones. Each time she notices the difference: "That was so unusual. I've never seen you cry like that before, Doug" (with 3); "That was
so athletic of you, Doug" (with 2); and "You really have surprised me
tonight, Doug" (with 4). But she never figures it out.

"I feel like I don't know you anymore," says Laura, like the wife of the
twin in *The Comedy of Errors,* and she wonders aloud about bipolar dis-
orders† and multiple personalities†—but she still thinks there is just one
of him. When she threatens to leave Doug in fury at something one of
the clones did, he protests, "It wasn't me," like the raped women in the
myths, invoking the old split-level alibi.‡

At one point, the clones suggest that they "clone Laura," but in fact
it is because Laura is already about to do the opposite of cloning, because
she is about to split (into mother and real-estate agent), that her husband
in desperation doubles himself (and then, to outdo her, trebles and qua-
druples himself into the mythological lineup). He defends himself by accusing her: "It's happened to you, too. You want to be a mom but you also
want to work." As in Marjorie Garber's progress narrative,† the original
masquerade was not intended for sexual purposes, but it still ends up, as
usual, in bed. In justifying the infringement of Rule Number One, the
clones say that Laura was "unstoppable," "a very powerful woman" (an
idea confirmed by our own witnessing of the three seduction scenes).
Believing that they must resist her, one of the magical doubles invokes
the mythological technique of the sword (here a pillow) laid between him
and Laura in the bed, but to no avail.

Doug is both the trickster and the victim: he creates the doubles but
never intends to have them replace him in bed. Nor is Laura simply the
victim; she never finds out that she has been victimized, and she is defi-
nitely portrayed as the sexual aggressor; in a very real sense it is she who
cuckolds Doug. Doug has to get rid of the clones because he finds himself
in the usual double-bind† of the man who both does and does not want
his double to sleep with his wife: he is jealous of the clones and feels that
he has not doubled himself, as he hoped, but, rather, halved (or quartered)
himself. When he finds out that Rule Number One has been broken and
reacts with shocked fury, the clones reassure him: "She thought I was
you"; "She thought *I* was you too." And then: "We're not perfect." This
last statement ostensibly means just "We were susceptible to her," but in
this context it also means "We are not perfect copies; you alone are you."
Now Doug asks them, as Jupiter asked Amphitryon's wife Alcmena,‡ "Do

you think she liked you more than she likes me?" "Of course not," Doug 2 says. "You *are* me; I *am* you." But Doug himself admits, "I wasn't really *there* for her. Even when I was there, I wasn't *there.*" The psychobabble cliché is here cunningly applied to a liminal situation in which "there" means simultaneously "existentially real," "sexually intimate," and "orgasmically on the G-spot." The sensitive Doug 3 reassures Doug: "Trust me; it's all quality time." But the question of time†—which is, ultimately, the question of death—is what justified the cloning in the first place.

Real twins don't always behave like the ones in the stories; the fantasy and the experience of having a twin are quite different. A study of fifteen hundred pairs of twins (a project statistically flawed but still anecdotally interesting)[16] was carried out in Minneapolis (the twin city in more ways than one). The results suggest that "although twins competing for the same mate is a staple of television talk shows"—and, I would add, of myths—identical twins in real life very rarely replace one another in bed. They tend not to be attracted sexually to the same sorts of partners: "The extraordinary difference between identical twins lies in whom they choose to marry."[17] This evidence comes from left field (sociobiology) to confirm the mythological assumption that sex is the touchstone of difference in identity.† The researchers found that "when the twins were asked to evaluate their twin's spouse, about as many disliked the spouse as not. The spouses, for their part, returned the favour, although one would expect that the spouses would be at least somewhat attracted to the identical twin." They note what they call "a curious and disquieting conclusion" and I would call a paradox: "Although we do tend to choose from among people like ourselves, another person who is remarkably like ourselves (our MZ [identical] twin) is not likely to be drawn to the same choice we make."[18] Although some of us do tend to marry women just like our mothers or men just like our fathers—and the Minneapolis study revealed one set of gay twins, separated at birth, who met as adults and became lovers[19]—many of us desire an Other who is different from us, and though there is only one way in which our double can resemble us exactly, there are infinite ways in which our Other can be other.

This emerges as the moral of the true story of one set of identical twin brothers who were "as physically alike as identical twins can be, both of them dark-eyed, long-lashed, full-lipped Latin-lover types," yet as the girl who married one of them explained, "Who knows what one sees in another person—physically, emotionally, or intellectually—that makes him different from everybody else." One twin brother met her first, but the other fell in love with her and immediately called his brother to ask if he had any "romantic intentions" toward her, for as he later remarked, "Most twins know that this area is a big, fat hot potato. . . . It would be very difficult going through life wanting the same spouse."[20] Although the actors knew the way the story could go ("I don't want you to say ten years from now that I stole a girl you were interested in," one said to the other), they didn't pick up their mythological clues. The woman could tell them apart immediately; one brother called the other to ask permission; and, most important, *they didn't both want her,* or, in the words of the storyteller, they didn't both have "romantic intentions" toward her. They demythologized the story.

Yet Lawrence Wright, the author of this study of studies of twins, speaks of the fantasy of an identical twin as "a projection of ourselves . . . sleeping with other spouses,"[21] and the bedtrick is the pivot of his understanding of this fantasy. Perhaps the mythology of twins is polluted by the mythology of the magic clone, who is not a real twin at all, of course, and whose very raison d'être is often to seduce another person's lover. Or perhaps the myth expresses many twins' fantasy of sleeping with their twins' sexual partners—a fantasy that they repress† in real life, a sublimation that adds fuel to keep the myth alive.

And some twins do live out the fantasy. We have noted some cases of non-twin brothers who replace one another in bed (including some acquaintances of Abraham Lincoln†). From time to time, instances are reported in contemporary mythological texts like the *Weekly World News* (February 13, 1990): "Evil twin masquerades as his brother! Stole his money & Porsche. Took over his big buck job! Moved in with his sexy wife!" The true-life story of Cyril and Stewart Marcus[22] inspired the film *Dead Ringers* (1988), in which the twin gynecologists collude together in a bedtrick. In the film, a woman who was the victim of their bedtrick says to the twin she had chosen, "Were you afraid that, when it came right down to it, I really couldn't tell the difference?"

THE LEVIRATE, HINDU STYLE

Let us turn now from stories in which brothers unofficially replace one another in bed to stories in which they do it legally, through varieties of the levirate.

In ancient India, the *Rig Veda*, composed in Northwest India in about 1000 B.C.E., speaks of the wife of a dead man sleeping with his brother ("Who invites you, as a widow takes her husband's brother to her bed, as a young woman takes a young man to a room?"), but the text says nothing about legal progeny resulting from this union.[23] Later, the Hindu levirate, or *niyoga,* became both paradigmatic and stigmatized in myth and social law *(dharmashastra);* sometimes it was secretly longed for but publicly disavowed, and in other times or situations, it was publicly approved but secretly avoided.

The conflicting Hindu attitudes to the levirate are systematized in the great compendium of laws attributed to Manu, who both justifies the practice of the levirate and expresses, in no uncertain terms, his revulsion toward it and his complex reasons for disapproving of it: "The appointed man, silent and smeared with clarified butter, should beget one son upon the widow in the night, but never a second."[24] There are two different duties at stake here: the brother has a duty to give an heir to his dead brother, but he also has a duty to allow the woman, his brother's wife, to fulfill her own duty to produce a child. This second duty is less important than the first, but it, too, counts. Thus, Hindus speak of the law that a man must unite with his wife during her fertile season (the *ritugamana*); in many myths, a woman attempts to seduce a man who is not her husband by arguing that if he refuses her, her fertile period will be fruitless.[25] The levirate served a similar purpose in ancient Israel, as Mieke Bal stresses: "This law has two sides to it, as well: it protects the widows and, probably in the first place, insures posterity for the dead."[26]

Levirate marriages fell into desuetude and disrepute in later Hinduism (perhaps because of abuses such as we are about to see, at least in literary texts, and in tandem with the development of a law against the remarriage of widows) and were sometimes replaced by the widespread and ancient custom of inviting an unrelated Brahmin to impregnate or deflower a woman whose husband was unable or unwilling to do this.[27] Until quite recent times, in Kerala, high-caste Nayar ladies were deflowered by Brahmins.[28] This tradition grows out of the ancient Indian belief that the bride poses a danger to the groom, a theme well known in world folklore as the murderous bride.[29] In the *Rig Veda* hymn recited to this day at Hindu weddings, the priest defuses the black magic of the blood of defloration on the bride's gown.[30] According to this hymn, on the wedding night a double of the bridegroom, a demigod *(gandharva),* deflowers the bride, and a double born of the incarnation of the bride's bloodstained gown threatens the husband (until the priest neutralizes it): "It becomes a magic spirit walking on feet, and like the wife it draws near the husband." Significantly, the bride in this hymn is Suryā, the daughter of the Sun and, presumably, of Samjna,‡ who made a likeness of herself to "draw near her husband."

The belief that a priest should defuse the danger of deflowering a bride survives primarily in the wedding hymn. More often, Brahmins were called upon to impregnate women whose husbands were unable to give them male children, although this was usually accomplished, not through intercourse, but by blessing a pot of water or a kind of rice pudding.[31] This custom is mythologized in the tales of Dirghatamas and Vyasa in the *Mahabharata*. It begins with

THE SONS OF DIRGHATAMAS

Dirghatamas fathered many sons, but they threw him in the Ganges on a raft, not wishing to support him since he was blind and old. He came downstream to King Balin, who recognized him and said, "Please father sons on my wives, to continue my line." The virile seer agreed, and the king sent him his wife Sudeshna. Seeing that he was blind and old, the queen did not go but sent the old man her nurse, on whom he fathered Kakshivat and ten other sons. When Balin saw them, he said, "They are mine," but the great sage said, "No, they are mine, fathered on a slave woman, since your queen rejected me and foolishly gave me her nurse." Balin pacified the seer and sent Sudeshna to him again. This time, Dirghatamas felt all her limbs and said, "You will have a great son." And so the sage Anga ["Limb"] was born from Sudeshna.[32]

The first time, Dirghatamas is foiled by the double-cross:† while he is substituting for her husband, the queen sends a substitute for herself. The second time, Dirghatamas feels her limbs, presumably to determine that he is in bed with the real queen this time, since, being blind, he must rely on touch rather than on sight. (A similar tactile test is carried out by Isaac on Esau† and by the prince in Basile's "The Old Woman Discovered."†) This test is then reflected in the child's name, Anga, "Limb." The argument as to whether the children really belong to their biological father (Dirghatamas) or their official father (Balin) is an early instance of a paternity suit. It is also one of the eternal paradoxes of the levirate and of the other forms of legal male surrogation that came to supplant it in Hindu mythology.

The story of Dirghatamas and King Balin is told in the *Mahabharata* when Bhishma‡ wishes to convince his stepmother to support the proposed levirate of Vyasa on behalf of his dead half brother, King Vicitravirya (for whose sake Bhishma himself has endured complex woman

problems). Persuaded, she summons Vyasa and sends him to Vicitravirya's two widows, Ambika and Ambalika. The essence of what happens
is this:

The Sons of Vyasa

Since Ambika closed her eyes when she conceived her son, Dhritarashtra,
he was born blind. Ambalika turned pale and conceived Pandu the Pale.
When Vyasa was sent to Ambika a second time, she sent in her place a
slave girl, who conceived Vidura, a servant.[33]

The narrative of the bedtrick used against Dirghatamas, which seems to
go directly against the purposes of the apparent narrator (Bhishma),
serves well the purposes of the actual narrator (Vyasa himself, the ultimate
author of the entire epic): it tells us that the levirate of Vyasa will also
be subverted and prove disastrous. And indeed, that is precisely what
happens; the story of Dirghatamas is the template for the disastrous levirate of Vyasa. Ambika‡ closes her eyes† (and, presumably, thinks of
Kurukshetra), and her child, Dhritarashtra, is blind,† by attraction to both
his mother and his blind ancestor Dirghatamas. Ambalika turns pale and
gives birth to a pale (and functionally impotent) son. When Ambika sends
a slave girl in her place, staging a bedtrick that duplicates the one used
against Dirghatamas, her son becomes a servant. Vyasa appears in the
epic as a kind of walking semen bank; the widows of Vicitravirya reject
him because he is old and ugly and smells fishy, a characteristic that he
inherited from his grandmother (another long and interesting, but not
entirely relevant, story).[34] Moreover, he is said to be the wrong color†
(too dark? too light?), and this, plus the mother's temporary pallor, results
in the birth of a child who is the wrong color, Pandu. (Is this an echo
of the theme of skin color† that haunts the tales of Parvati† and Sam-
jna‡?) So, too, the blindness of Dirghatamas is passed on, through the
narrative, to Dhritarashtra.

Another tragedy is also part of the indirect fallout from this disastrous
levirate. There is an awkward imbalance here between the number of
wives (two) and the number of sons (three), doubly and hence counteref-
fectively patched by the double statement that the third son was born to
a servant girl and that the first wife (Ambika) was supposed to sleep with
Vyasa twice. In fact, the arrangement was originally more symmetrical,
for there had been a third woman, Amba,‡ clearly the basic name, of
which Ambika and Ambalika are variants. (These are the names of the
three queens that Vedic texts describe as pantomiming copulation with

the dead stallion† who pinch-hits for the king in the horse sacrifice, a grotesque distortion of the droit du seigneur.†)³⁵ Amba dies in a complex transsexual act of revenge against Bhishma, bringing about his death. Amba is driven by hate, but the two other women's hatred of their surrogate lover, though much milder than Amba's, results not in their deaths but in a confusion over the throne, which leads to a more general death: war, and the destruction of all the sons of Pandu and the sons of Dhritarashtra.

The epic goes on to tell us how the pale and impotent Pandu allowed his wife, Kunti, to invoke gods to father "his" sons, the Pandavas;³⁶ she calls on five divine husbands, Indra† and the other gods whom Damayanti‡ rejected. The five Pandavas, in their turn, marry a single woman, Draupadi.† The text thus depicts, in three successive generations, three women (Ambalika, Kunti, and Draupadi) who have several husbands, the first two through the levirate, the third through a polyandry that troubles the epic on several crucial occasions. Vyasa, the "author" of the text, is the "author" (the grandfather) of the five heroes, but he is a problematic substitute for the true parent, producing unsatisfactory offspring (one pale, one blind, one a servant). Vyasa partially redeems the guilt incurred in his flawed begetting of their fathers by telling the story† of the sons of Pandu, the Pandavas.³⁷ Bhishma, too, the other grandfather (and narrator), is a problematic father, to put it mildly. Beneath these impotent fathers lie angry women, and the midpoint solution to the steadily escalating hierarchy of male surrogates is the invocation of the gods—traditional fathers of so many special sons of virgin mothers. On this highest, mythical level the substitute is relatively satisfactory to the woman, freeing her at least from having to supply her own female surrogates to accommodate the unsatisfactory male surrogates provided for her bed. But even on this level the surrogation is highly problematic, as it was in Kunti's disastrous connection with the Sun† god, resulting in the birth of Karna.†³⁸

For all its flaws, the levirate of the gods was later used as a positive paradigm. Walter Gill tells a story about Hindus in the colonial diaspora in the nineteenth century in which an Englishman connives with two old women to allow the wife of a man who will not admit his sterility, and who threatens to destroy his wife for her presumed sterility, to become "secretly" impregnated by another man, claiming that it was the work of a god. While they are plotting the "god-assisted pregnancy," the Englishman asks: "'Suppose they were characters in a story, what would be the end according to the story-teller?' They liked the idea. Mahalatchmi went first. 'Because of the girl's unhappiness, a god would sleep with her and get her with child.' Sannicheri cackled. It is the sort of mind she had. 'If it was Ganesh, I would like to talk with her afterwards,' she said. Ganesh was the elephant god . . ." The plot succeeds (though the woman gets a girl, not the desired son), and when she is pregnant and the husband is delighted, the Englishman, who tells the story, remarks: "Before he went, he reminded me that the Gods must also be credited with the pregnancy. After he had gone I thought what a queer foursome we would be; our elderly Priapus [the man they got to impregnate her], the two old girls, and me in the halls of the Hindu Pantheon."[39]

So the Englishman plays god and narrator (lamely; Ganesha is not an elephant god, with all that that seems to imply here, but a chaste, plump human figure with an elephant's head); he does not, we assume, play the levirate role himself (as Vyasa does). The fiction of the divine levirate proves useful to everyone, including him. But the unofficial levirate father need not be divine; Ann Gold has noted nontheological fictions of this sort in villages in Rajasthan, where husbands who are able to admit to themselves the possibility of their own sterility tolerate the adultery of their wives in order to get the sons they so desperately desire.[40]

THE LEVIRATE, JEWISH STYLE

Like the Hindu stories we have seen, the two great tales of the levirate in the Bible—the stories of Tamar and Ruth (which record oral traditions that may date back to the eighth and seventh centuries B.C.E.)—tell of *failed* levirates, levirates called into question. The double standard† operates here because the law tells us what the man can do if he does not want the levirate but not what the woman can do if she does not want it. The stories address only the former situation, but in two permutations: the problem of the man who refuses the levirate and the problem of the woman who has to deal with such a man.

The law of the levirate (*yibum* or *meyabbem*) and the conditions under which it could be abrogated (*halitsa*)—the fabric of the law and its unweaving—are proclaimed together (as they are in the Hindu texts) in Deuteronomy 25.5–10: "If brothers live together, and one of them dies and has no child, . . . [the widow's] husband's brother shall go in unto her and take her to him to wife. . . . And if the man like not to take his brother's wife, . . . then shall his brother's wife come unto him in the presence of the elders, and loose his shoe from off his foot, and spit in his face, . . . and his name shall be called in Israel, The house of him that hath his shoe loosed." The woman is doubly controlled and humiliated here: required to sleep with a man not of her choice and then publicly rejected by him, though she does get to spit in his face. This law appears to conflict with, or be an exception to, the prohibition against marriage with a sister-in-law in Leviticus (18.16). But the levirate may have been regarded as not a real marriage but an ad hoc measure, as Ephraim Neufeld suggests, citing the parallel with the Hindu *niyoga,* in which "a brother-in-law's duty was fulfilled by a mere temporary union (not marriage)."[41]

Indeed, the parallels between the Hindu and Hebrew levirates were noted in the other direction as well, by a Tamil Christian named A. N. Sattampillai, who wrote tracts in favor of widow remarriage in which he cited the levirate of Ruth in the Hebrew Bible as a parallel to the *niyoga.* He published a pamphlet entitled *Ruttammavai,* a retelling of the story of Ruth set to the meter of a popular style of Tamil folk song, drawing on citations from both Hebrew texts and Brahmanical texts of religious law *(dharmashastras).*[42] He justifies this eclecticism by arguing that both the ancient Hebrews and the Aryans are direct descendants of Noah, whose ark was stranded "in the region of the Himalayas" when the waters of the great biblical flood subsided. I would prefer to argue that the resemblances between the Hindu and Hebrew levirates are analogical rather than homological—that is, that they are the result of parallel independent origination rather than diffusion.[43]

The culminating and by far the most explicit example of both the levirate and the bedtrick in the book of Genesis is played upon Judah, Jacob's son not by Rachel† but by the bedtrickster Leah; like the curse in a Greek tragedy, the character of the bedtrickster does seem to be transmitted through the genes. Like Jacob, Judah is both the perpetrator and the victim of bedtricks involving double women and double brothers. In the first part of the story, Tamar marries Er, Judah's firstborn son, but when Er dies Judah instructs Er's brother, Onan, "Lie with your brother's wife and fulfill your duty as a brother-in-law, providing seed for your brother." But Onan, knowing the child born of his seed would not be his, lets the seed go to waste on the ground whenever he lies with his brother's wife. This displeases God, who takes Onan's life, too. When Judah keeps postponing Tamar's marriage to his third son, Shelah, Tamar takes matters into her own hands:

TAMAR AND JUDAH

A long time afterward, Judah's wife, the daughter of Shuah, died; after being consoled, he went up toward Timnah to his sheepshearers, together with his friend Hirah the Adullamite. And Tamar was told, "Your father-in-law is coming up to Timnah for the sheep-shearing." Then she took off her widow's garments, covered her face with a veil, wrapped herself up, and sat down at the entrance to Eynaim on the road to Timnah, for she saw that Shelah was grown up and she had not been given to him as a wife. Judah saw her and took her for a harlot [zona] because she had covered her face. So he turned aside to her by the road and said, "Look here, let me lie with you," for he did not realize that she was his daughter-in-law. She answered, "What will you pay me for lying with me?" He replied, "I'll send you a kid from my flock." She said, "Only if you leave a pledge until you send it." And he said, "What pledge should I leave you?" She replied, "Your seal and cord, and the staff that you carry." He gave them to her and he lay with her and she conceived by him. Then she got up, went away, took off her veil, and put on her widow's garments. Judah sent the kid by his friend the Adullamite to redeem the pledge from the woman, but he could not find her. He inquired of the men of the place, "Where is the cult prostitute [qedesa], the one at Eynaim by the road?" and they answered, "There has been no cult prostitute [qedesa] here." So he went back to Judah and told him, "I couldn't find her, and the men of the place said, 'There has been no cult prostitute [qedesa] here.'" Judah said, "Let her keep the things, or we shall become a laughingstock. I did, after all, send her this kid, but you could not find her."

   About three months later, Judah was told, "Tamar your daughter-in-law has played the harlot [zona] and what is more she is with child by harlotry [zenunim]." And Judah said, "Take her out and let her be burned." As she was being taken out, she sent word to her father-in-law, "By the man to whom these belong, by him am I with child." And she added, "Please recognize, to whom do these belong, this seal and cord and staff?" Judah recognized [them] and said, "She is more in the right than I for I did not give her to my son Shelah." And he had no carnal knowledge of her again. (Genesis 38)[44]

Judah makes a double error: he mistakes Tamar not only for a woman who is not his daughter-in-law but for a woman who is a whore rather than a cult prostitute. We are explicitly told that he reads her veiled presence by the wayside as characteristic of a harlot (zona), and he does not correct those who, later, accuse her of being a zona; but his friend asks about a cult prostitute (qedesa), a related but significantly distinct persona. The term may be derived from an Akkadian word for a type of priestess *(qadistu);* the Jerusalem Bible identifies the *qedesa* as a Canaanite prostitute, that is, as belonging to a tradition of sacred prostitution originating in Canaan. Judah's wife was a Canaanite, and Tamar may have been one, too. More significantly, the *qedesa* was not merely a prostitute; she might also be a midwife.[45] As Mieke Bal sums up Tamar's shifting status, "She starts as a virgin, becomes, but ambiguously, a wife, only to be widowed immediately; she then acts as a ritual 'prostitute' and is considered a whore—a significant error—and ends up as a mother without a husband. Her sexuality is clearly rendered problematic by the men in her life."[46] Judah's friend refers to the woman by the road, in conversation both with Judah and with others, only as a *qedesa,* never as a *zona;* it may well be that Judah told him to ask for a *qedesa* instead of a *zona* in order to appear to be looking for a more respectable woman. Tamar "plays the harlot" not in the sense that Judah agrees to (meaning simple promiscuity) but in the sense of playacting the harlot; and he does not "know" her (i.e., recognize who she is) when he "knows" her (i.e., has carnal knowledge of her). To him, ultimately, all women-of-the-night look alike.

Having married two of Judah's sons, Tamar bears him a replacing set of twin sons, who battle in the womb, the hand of the one coming out first and being marked with a red thread, even as Jacob and Esau had battled in Rebecca's womb, the hand of one coming out on the heel of the one marked by red hair. And just as, in the *midrash,* Leah explicitly connects her deception of Jacob by masquerading as Rachel with Jacob's deception of his father by masquerading as Esau,† so, too, the trick played against Judah is blamed upon a related deception which immediately precedes the story of Tamar: Judah's deception of his father (Jacob) by bloodying the coat of his brother Joseph.[47] The *midrash* spells out the connection: "The Holy One, praised be He, said to Judah: 'You said to your father, *haqer-na* [recognize]. By your life, Tamar will say to you, *haqer-na* [recognize].' "[48] It is also worth noting that the Hebrew text that Robert Alter (and most others) translated "Judah recognized them [the seal, cord, and staff] and said . . ." actually says merely "Judah recognized and said" (vayaqer jehudah v omer). It may well be that it is only at this moment that he recognizes *her* as the woman he slept with.

As always in the Hebrew Bible, the key to the story of women lies in the men, for the question of male lineage is the pole around which the Hebrew Bible winds the motif of the bedtrick. One *midrash* euphemistically refers to Onan's method of contraception as "plowing on roofs."[49] In Hindu mythology, a man who sheds his seed on the ground is a saint,[50] but in the Bible such a man is a sinner. This is because the Hindu mythological tradition regards the unilateral shedding of semen by a sage to be the procreative technique of choice (especially for a celibate sage, who deposits his seed in a bird or fish or river, where it produces a child), while the realistic Hebrew tradition emphatically does not.

Tamar is doing something similar to what Lot's daughters did when they aggressively and incestuously played a bedtrick upon their drunken father (Genesis 19.31–36). Tamar's seduction of Judah is a far less grievous sin, since Judah is her father-in-law, not her natural father, but Leviticus (18.15, 20.12) prohibits a father from uncovering his daughter-in-law's nakedness and adds: "If any man lies with his daughter-in-law, both of them shall certainly be put to death. They have done an abominable thing. Their blood is upon them." In this respect, the Hebrew Bible story of Tamar is liminal. Middle Assyrian law specifically gives the father-in-law the right to beget children by his sons' widows,[51] but Hammurabi's Code forbids a man to sleep with his daughter-in-law,[52] and a later text, Jubilees (second century B.C.E.), explicitly points the finger of guilt: "And Judah knew that the deed which he did was evil because he lay with his daughter-in-law. And he condemned himself in his own sight" (2.41.30). In Genesis, Judah does not take the Assyrian option by choice, but he admits that Tamar was more righteous than he in tricking him into taking it in fact. Thus, Judah's act is poised liminally between incest (with a natural daughter, a serious crime) and a quasi levirate (with his son's, rather than his brother's, widow, a crime by Jewish but not by Assyrian law); it is and isn't a crime.

The confrontation between Judah and the woman he mistakes for a prostitute takes place right after the death of Judah's wife, the daughter of Shuah, a troublesome woman who is said, in Jubilees (2.41.130), to be indirectly responsible for the final debacle, because she prevented Shelah from marrying Tamar. After Judah's wife's death, and after the period of mourning, as Robert Alter points out, "Tamar can plausibly infer that Judah is in a state of sexual neediness."[53] Despite the way that the story presents itself, as a story about Judah's sons, we might read it as a story about Judah himself, about the indirect way in which he is forced to replace his ·wife in order to produce a lineage by skipping over his sons, a grandfather producing his own unmediated grandsons.[54]

In this, Judah resembles Oedipus.† But Bal argues that "Judah's goal

was an impossible one: to have offspring and to keep his sons in safety.
. . . Judah finds a way out of this dilemma: he replaces the son. . . . Judah
protects his son, but he does so by making him powerless, as powerless
as his dead brothers."[55] Judah thus inverts the Oedipal pattern and replaces his son in the bed of his daughter-in-law—but in a way that his
tradition regards as, if not strictly kosher, still somehow necessary. Judah
needs Tamar as much as she needs him, for she heals his barrenness by
giving him the sons/grandsons that he otherwise could not have. As Judah
Goldin remarks: "An attractive symmetry has been achieved. Judah, who
had lost two sons, Er and Onan, now begets twins—a sign certainly that
Judah has been forgiven."[56] And, presumably, Tamar.

In fact, no levirate ever takes place in this story; no brother substitutes
for Er. Nor do we ever find out what happened to Shelah, who drops out
of the story that turns out to be Judah's story. Why didn't Tamar masquerade as a prostitute for *him?* And afterward, why didn't she marry
him? This actually happens in the Testament of Judah, in which Shelah,
rather than Judah, is said to be the father of the surviving twins, whose
birth is never actually described.[57] Thus, the Hebrew Bible assimilates the
theme of sexual doubling to a theme that it regards as more essential—
the doubling of sons. And it uses this theme to move from the depiction of
conscious and consensual incest, in the early chapters of Genesis (between
Adam and Eve), to a combination of conscious and consensual incest (on
the part of Lot's daughters) and unconscious and unconsensual incest
(on the part of Lot), to quasi incest and trickery, in the later chapters of
Genesis. Like Lot, Judah may have been drunk;† he is drunk explicitly in
The Testament of Judah [12.3–10] and perhaps implicitly in the biblical
text, for sheep-shearing was generally accompanied by riotous drinking,
a proto-stag-party (or ram-party).

The other great levirate marriage in the Hebrew Bible occurs in the
tale of Ruth and Boaz, told in the Book of Ruth:

RUTH AND BOAZ AND NAOMI

[Naomi's husband died, and her two sons married Ruth, the Moabitess,
and Orpah. When the two sons died, Naomi decided to return to her
home, Bethlehem. Orpah remained behind, but Ruth protested her love
for Naomi ("Whither thou goest . . ."). In Bethlehem, Ruth went to work
in the fields of Naomi's kinsman, Boaz. Boaz noticed Ruth; he spoke to
her and liked her. Naomi told Ruth to bathe, adorn herself, and go to
Boaz, to make herself known to him only after he had feasted and drunk
well, and to uncover his feet and lie with him and do whatever he asked.]

Ruth went down to the threshing-floor and did just as her mother-in-law had charged. Boaz ate, drank, and felt free of care. He then proceeded to lie down at the edge of the grain pile. Approaching quietly, Ruth bared his "legs," and lay down. Around midnight, the man was shaken by fright; he twisted away—there was a woman lying close to him! "Who are you?" he exclaimed. "I am Ruth your handmaid," she replied. ". . . Spend the night here," said Boaz, ". . . Lie down until morning." Ruth stayed by him until daybreak, but rose before a person's features could be recognized, for Boaz had thought it best that her arrival to the threshing-floor remain unnoticed.

[When Ruth came to her mother-in-law, she told her all that they had done. Boaz purchased from the nearer kinsman the right to marry Ruth; to confirm the transaction, he drew off his shoe. Boaz married Ruth, and the elders said:] "May the Lord make the woman, who is coming into your house, like Rachel and Leah, who together built up the house of Israel. May you prosper in Ephrathah and be renowned in Bethlehem; and may your house be like the house of Perez, whom Tamar bore to Judah, because of the children that the Lord will give you by this young woman." And Boaz took Ruth as his wife, and cohabited with her, and she bore him a son. And the women said, "A son has been born to Naomi." They called him Obed. He is the father of Jesse, the father of David.[58]

The text of the story of Ruth, and its explicit parallelism with the stories of Leah and Tamar, present us with a series of riddles.† There are two fathers and two mothers, for Obed is supposed to be the son of Ruth's dead husband (Mahlon) but is said to be born to Boaz, and although he is born to Ruth he is called Naomi's baby. Two tricky women (Leah and Tamar) are invoked as role models. The law of the levirate is mentioned several times, in a negative form, but the child is not regarded as the descendant of the dead husband. And there is, at midpoint, a surprising surprise: Is Boaz just surprised to find any woman in his bed? Or is he particularly surprised because the woman is Ruth? If so, whom did he expect?

Why does the Book of Ruth cite the stories of Leah and Tamar as parallels to itself in the elders' final blessing? Bal argues that all three (Ruth, Leah, and Tamar) are women who collude with other women against men in levirate or pseudolevirate marriages.[59] I would add that each of the three women pretends to be another woman in bed. But who, then, is the other woman for whom Ruth substitutes, even though it is Ruth whom Boaz desires? Who is the woman whom Boaz expected, so that he was frightened and drew back when he saw Ruth there? I think

Boaz is surprised to see Ruth and asks who she is because he expects Naomi—but hopes for Ruth.

The problematic points would be cleared up if Ruth were, like Leah and Tamar, a bedtrickster—but the text does not say she is. They would be cleared up if Boaz thought (and hoped) that he was getting Ruth but got Naomi through a bedtrick in the night—but he does not. They would be cleared up if Naomi wanted Boaz to marry her (despite his obvious interest in the younger Ruth), persuaded Ruth to make an assignation with Boaz, and, when he was drunk, got into bed with him herself, instead of Ruth—but none of this happens. Instead, Boaz both does and does not know that it is Ruth; the semidarkness provides a permeable veil, an alibi: he wants Ruth and gets Ruth, though he should have Naomi. I certainly do not wish to argue that any of the scenarios I have just reconstructed constitutes the true or original form of the text. I simply wish to suggest that the parallels with the stories of Leah and Tamar hovered over the story of Ruth and seeped into it from time to time, coloring it with images and words and incongruous details suggesting a different sort of story, sometimes producing minor inconsistencies or conundrums, until they were explicitly invoked at the end. The story of the bedtrick is present as a kind of ghost—an invisible shadow double—of the story of Ruth. The elements of the explicitly invoked parallel plots of Leah and Tamar lead us to expect Naomi to replace Ruth, just as Schnitzler's† references to the bedtrick that the old woman played upon Casanova† at Soleure lay a false trail that the reader follows in the false expectation that the aged Amalia will play the same sort of bedtrick on Casanova† now. The trick, in both cases, is that there is no trick.

Boaz is of Naomi's generation, not Ruth's; he is Naomi's brother-in-law, the brother of her husband, Elimelech (4.3). If Naomi is the sister-in-law whom Boaz *should* marry, then when Naomi sends Ruth to Boaz, she is substituting the desirable younger generation for the appropriate older generation, in a *reversal* of Rachel/Leah and Shelah/Judah, where the appropriate (or, in the case of Judah, necessary) older generation was substituted for the desirable younger generation. I would suggest that Obed is "Naomi's baby" because he should have been born (physically) to Naomi or (officially) to Naomi's dead son. A later Jewish *midrash* glosses over the Bible's statement that Boaz begat Obed, interpreting the statement that Obed was born to Naomi as meaning, "A son is born to Naomi—to Naomi, not to Boaz," because Boaz died on his wedding night, after (or in the very act of) begetting a son.[60]

Naomi herself considers and rejects the possibility of a real marriage for herself that might produce new husbands for her two widowed daughters-in-law to marry, in turn, through their own levirates. At the very start of the story, Naomi says to them, "Turn back, my daughters, go your way, for I am too old to have a husband. If I should say I have hope, even if I should have a husband this night and should bear sons, would you therefore wait til they were grown?" (1.12). This is exactly what Judah had asked Tamar to do after Onan died, and the same verb, "he was grown," is used to indicate when Tamar had a right to expect to be married to Shelah, although Judah failed to arrange the marriage. Naomi, then, might have acted like Judah and produced another son for Ruth to marry.

But Naomi is too old—not necessarily too old to bear children, as she herself points out (when no one had asked her); the ambiguous Hebrew allows us to believe either that Naomi can bear children or that she cannot. After all, these women are the descendants of the laughing Sarah, who became pregnant when she was much older than Naomi—for with God, all things are possible (Genesis 18.12–15). But Naomi is too old, as the Hebrew literally puts it, to "be with a man" or "for or of a man"— that is, to attract a husband. Indeed, Naomi may well have urged her daughters-in-law to abandon her not, as is usually argued, out of a selfless concern for their welfare ("I'll just sit here in the dark") but to get rid of younger women who would (as in fact Ruth does) attract men away from Naomi herself. There is an interesting variation in the ancient written version of the text (Mona Fishbane calls it "Naomi's slip† of the tongue") when Naomi uses the first person instead of the second in instructing Ruth: "Bathe, anoint yourself, and *I* will put on your dress, and *I* will go down to the threshing floor . . . and uncover his feet, and *I* will lie down." This slip may represent, in Fishbane's opinion, "the conflation of identities in Naomi's mind"[61] or, in my opinion, the relict of a bedtrick, Naomi in Ruth's clothing. The implied division of motherhood between the two women is very like the one that is falsely deduced from the bedtrick in *All's Well That Ends Well*,† in Janet Adelman's gloss: "[Helena's] pregnancy is thus presented as the result of Bertram's copulation with Diana, as though the child were Helena's by a magical transference through which Diana gets the taint and Helena gets the child."[62] Caught up in the vestiges, the traces, of the story of a bedtrick, the child is Naomi's by a narrative transference through which Ruth gets the child and Naomi gets the credit.

Both the widow Naomi and the widower Judah are surviving parents who have lost two sons and are left with the wife of one of those sons. Both are of the generation above the woman who actually works the bedtrick. Both confront the ostensible problem of finding a young husband for the young widow, yet the obvious candidate (the "nearer kinsman" for Ruth, Shelah for Tamar) is rejected, and someone of an inappropriate, older generation is taken instead (Boaz or Judah). (Boaz has an imaginary double, the "young man who will molest Ruth," who is constantly feared, though he never appears.) Like Judah, Naomi uses Ruth to skip a generation and beget her own grandchildren. In yet another connection with Tamar, the Kabbalists said that Mahlon and Chilion (the two sons of Naomi) were reincarnations of Er and Onan (the two sons of Judah).[63] For the true problem that both texts address is that of finding a spouse for the surviving parent (Judah or Naomi). And in both stories, though a great fuss is made about the problematic levirate, the lineage is *not* traced through the line of the dead husband and official father but through the line of the older surrogate male and natural father (Judah or Boaz).

The story jumps the track of the levirate through a bedtrick that leaves clues in the form of certain narrative clichés. Boaz gets drunk† enough to pass out in the barn instead of staggering home to his own bed, which allows us to speculate that Ruth may have used any of several hackneyed bedtrick devices involving drunkenness: Did Ruth find Boaz too drunk to be of any sexual use and then, when he woke up and she realized that he was also too drunk to remember what had happened, encourage him to *think* that he had made love with her? *Was* Ruth molested by one of those nameless young men and made pregnant, so that Naomi engineered the whole thing to get Boaz to believe that he was the one who had impregnated Ruth and would have to marry her? Did Ruth want people to *think* she had slept with Boaz, in order to get out of another relationship she didn't want?

Darkness is used, as usual, to explain the masquerade (at 3.14): "So she lay at his feet until the morning, but arose before one could recognize another." This explicitly means that Boaz, who has been told that she is Ruth, doesn't want anyone to see Ruth leaving his bed. But it has overtones of another meaning from the alternative plot line of the bedtrick: that the episode took place before Boaz could recognize the woman who had shared his bed. And what actually happened on the threshing-room floor? The text says that Ruth uncovered Boaz's feet (Alter says legs). Feet‡ may serve as a metaphor for genitals in the Hebrew Bible (as in the old

adage that the size of a man's feet† indicates the size of his genitals†),
thus implying that Boaz and Ruth made love.

Feet and shoes also play a role in the ceremony by which Boaz makes
Ruth legally his, the ritual enacted with the man otherwise entitled to her.
This ceremony, which involves "drawing off the shoe," seems to resemble
the *halitsa*, the abrogation of the levirate, mentioned in the original Deu-
teronomic text that we considered in connection with Tamar. Thus,
when Ruth uncovers Boaz's feet—which might well involve taking off his
shoes—she seems to be drawing off the shoe of the levirate, releasing
Boaz from a levirate with her. Boaz *claims* to be engaging in a levirate—
he insists that he is marrying Ruth "the wife of Mahlon, to raise up the
name of the dead upon his inheritance" (4.5, 10)—but the levirate in the
Book of Ruth is not really a levirate. So, too, this apparent *halitsa* is not
a *halitsa*: the "nearer kinsman" whose shoe Boaz draws off is not obliged
to perform the levirate and so is not shirking any duty. On the contrary,
Boaz volunteers to do it, thus *taking on* the levirate that is normally canceled by the *halitsa*. And, as we have noted, Boaz is not Ruth's brother-
in-law, her designated Jewish levirate hitter, but Naomi's. In fact the story
represents a different ritual, a kind of shadow of the *halitsa*, a ritual not
about sex but about real estate. The competition between Boaz and the
"nearer kinsman" is between two potential redeemers *(goel)* of Naomi's
land. When Boaz is first introduced, he is called a *goel*, a redeeming kinsman to Elimelech; Ruth reminds him of this when she comes to him in
the night, and he speaks of being a *goel* when he buys off the nearer
kinsman (4.4–9). The Book of Ruth therefore turns out to be a bedtrick masquerading as a *goel* masquerading as a *halitsa* masquerading as
a levirate.

BEDTRICKSTERS IN THE LINEAGE OF JESUS

The line of masquerading women from Leah to Tamar to Ruth leads in
the New Testament to the birth of Jesus, the child of double fathers.[64]
Matthew's lineage of Jesus, from Abraham and Isaac through Boaz, Jesse,
and David, to Joseph, includes only four women: "Judah the father of
Perez and Zerah *by Tamar,* . . . Salmon the father of Boaz *by Rahab,* and
Boaz the father of Obed *by Ruth,* . . . and David the father of Solomon
by [Bath-Sheba,] the woman who had been Uriah's wife" (Matthew 1.2–
6). Matthew has to mention all the fathers—that is the whole point of
the male lineage—but gratuitously he adds the names of four of the mothers. Why those four? Edmund Leach has sought the underlying structures

by virtue of which Tamar, Rahab, Ruth, and Bath-Sheba "have something in common which makes them specially significant as ancestresses of Solomon"—and, by extension, Jesus.[65] I believe that what they have in common is that they are all bedtricksters, women who fool their husbands in sexual situations—culminating in Mary, with whom Matthew's genealogy concludes: "Joseph the husband *of Mary,* of whom Jesus was born" (Matthew 1.16).

Tamar and Ruth we have just considered. Let us turn now, briefly, to the other two women in Matthew's list, Rahab and Bath-Sheba.

Rahab, the mother of Boaz, according to Matthew, is usually identified as the harlot named Rahab who (in Joshua 2, 6) hides Joshua's messengers and is alone saved, of all her people, when Joshua's army captures Jericho; she is mentioned elsewhere in the New Testament (James 2.25, Hebrews 11.31). Whether or not Matthew identified the Rahab of his genealogy with the one mentioned in Joshua, early Christian commentators on the New Testament took the identification for granted. Rahab is a trickster, liar, and whore (*zona*) but is on the side of righteousness and, according to rabbinic tradition, one of the four most beautiful women in the world,[66] even as she is one of the four memorable female ancestors of Jesus. Rahab is, like the other women in the group, a marginalized, foreign woman who saves the center.

About Bath-Sheba a lot more is known, beginning with the story told in 2 Samuel 11: During a time when he was at war, David saw Bath-Sheba, the wife of Uriah, wanted her, sent for her, lay with her, and made her pregnant. He told Uriah, who was with the army, to go home, but Uriah refused to go home and lie with his wife while all his people were camped in tents. Then David made him drunk, but still he did not go home. Finally, David wrote a letter and sent it by Uriah's hand, instructing Joab to put Uriah in the front ranks and then withdraw support from him, so that he would be killed; and he was. David married Bath-Sheba, and she bore him a son, who died; then Bath-Sheba bore David another son, Solomon. Thus, David killed Uriah in battle (more precisely, used what has come to be known as a "Uriah's letter" to make him an unconscious accomplice in his own death) and then produced a child in his wife.

Leach emphasizes the qualities of Bath-Sheba that make her worthy of inclusion in Matthew's select group: "The son that dies was genetically David's but legally Uriah's. David's marriage to the widow ignores the levirate principle which has been emphasized in the Tamar and Ruth stories."[67] But, as we have seen, Tamar and Ruth do not so much "emphasize" the levirate as subvert it; nor is David Uriah's brother (far from it; Uriah is a Hittite). Thus, Bath-Sheba joins Tamar and Ruth both in ignoring the levirate and in having two fathers for her son. She is also of a tribe (Hittite) foreign† to that of the man she sleeps with; similarly, Tamar is often said to be a Canaanite, and Ruth, the Moabitess "amid the alien corn,"[68] is descended from Moab, the offspring of Lot's daughters and their father (Genesis 19.31–36). Moab is himself the father of daughters who sleep with the sons of Israel (in what Mieke Bal calls "illegal cleaving"†).[69] But more important qualities link three of the four women (excluding Rahab) with Mary: they are, like Mary, impregnated by males other than their husbands and, as a result, faced with "the crucial question of the true paternity of their sons."[70]

David himself is conceived through a bedtrick according to a Jewish tradition about Nazbat, the wife of Jesse (the father of David and son of Obed the son of Ruth and Naomi). A late rabbinic tradition states that David was a bastard, engendered not in Jesse's wife but in his servant woman, a belief probably based on David's statement in verse 5 of Psalm 51 ("Behold, I was shapen in iniquity, and in sin did my mother conceive me")[71] and perhaps bolstered by David's own irregular biblical sexual track record.[72] This troublesome interpretation of David's birth was later undercut by arguing that Jesse only *thought* he had committed adultery with a servant woman whom he had attempted to trap and seduce (despite her resistance to his harassments), but had unknowingly impregnated his wife. The *Yalqut Makhiri*, a medieval anthology of commentaries, tells this story:

JESSE'S WIFE AND THE SERVANT GIRL

For three years, Jesse did not sleep with his wife; then he acquired a beautiful handmaid and lusted for her. The handmaid went and told everything to her mistress, who said, "My daughter, what can I do, seeing that he has not touched me for three years?" The handmaid replied, "Prepare yourself, as will I, and at night when he tells you to close the door, you will come in and I will go out." So she did. At night the handmaid got up and blew out the light and went to close the door, and her mistress entered when she left. She made love with him all night and got pregnant with David. And because of [Jesse's] love for the handmaid, David was redder than his brothers. After nine months had passed, her sons wished to kill her and her son David when they saw that he was red. Jesse said to them, "Leave them alone and let him be our slave and tend the flocks." And the matter remained a secret for twenty-eight years.[73]

The redness of the child presumably reflects the parental impression† of Jesse's belief that he was in bed with a red-headed servant girl; redness is also associated with the bedtricks of Esau† and Tamar.† This commentary assumes that Jesse was not sleeping with his wife and that he noticed her pregnancy. Neither of these assumptions is preserved in Louis Ginzberg's retelling of the tale, which transfers the agency from the handmaid to Nazbat:

> In spite of his piety, Jesse was not always proof against temptation. One of his slaves caught his fancy, and he would have entered into illicit relations with her, had his wife, Nazbat, the daughter of Adiel, not frustrated the plan. She disguised herself as the slave, and Jesse, deceived by the ruse, met his own wife. The child born by Nazbat was given out as the son of the freed slave, so that the father might not discover the deception practiced upon him. This child was David.[74]

Pierre Bayle, in a controversial article on David in his 1697 Dictionary, sticks closer to the Hebrew text but still gives the agency to the wife:

> David's father was in love with his servant girl, and after having cajoled her several times, he told her finally that she must sleep with him that night. She, having no less virtue than beauty, complained to her mistress that Jesse gave her no respite from his solicitations. "Promise to content him tonight," her mistress told her, "and I will take your place." The affair took place for two or three consecutive nights. When Jesse realized that his wife, with whom he had no longer slept for a long time, was nevertheless pregnant, he accused her of adultery, and absolutely refused to have faith in the story that she had made an agreement with the servant girl. Neither he nor their sons wished to see the infant that she brought forth, for they regarded him as a bastard. He treated her with the greatest contempt, and had the baby raised in the country among shepherds.[75]

Lacking the foresight of other clever wives, Nazbat fails to take the precaution of stealing Jesse's ring or any other physical evidence,[76] and so she is rejected not only at the start, like the others, but even after she brings forth the child. The child is therefore "raised in the country among shepherds," like other heroes of the Family Romance.†

Another commentary cited by Bayle argues that if Jesse had thought he was in bed with his servant girl when he was really in bed with his wife, he had committed adultery; but if, believing in good faith that he was making love to his wife, he had actually impregnated his servant

woman, he would not have committed adultery at all.[77] This argument
of mind over matter,† much debated in Jewish tradition, prevailed in a
story in the Babylonian Talmud about Rabbi Hiya Bar Ashi, in which the
heroine, as usual, had to masquerade as another woman to get her husband into bed.[78]

Read in this light, Matthew's lineage of Jesus would serve, not to situate
Joseph (who is, after all, not Jesus' father) in the male line, though this
is explicitly stated to be the purpose of the litany of names, but rather to
situate Mary in the line of the Hebrew women who became pregnant even
though their legal husbands did not, or thought they did not, sleep with
them (Tamar) and/or who had, or seemed to have had, two husbands
(Tamar, Ruth, and Bath-Sheba). The lineage simultaneously establishes
Joseph as the official father, descended, physically, from famous Jewish
patriarchs who were themselves official fathers, and Mary as the real
mother, descended, spiritually (or narratively, which may amount to the
same thing), from famous Jewish women who had children by men other
than the official fathers.

Isak Dinesen played with the human implications of the relationship
between the two fathers of Jesus: "In Egypt, in the great triangular shadow
of the great pyramid, while the ass was grazing, St. Joseph said to the
Virgin: 'Oh, my sweet young dear, could you not just for a moment shut
your eyes and make believe that I am the holy ghost?' "[79] Shut your eyes
indeed, and let the masquerade take place. According to one Jewish tradition (recorded sometime after the tenth century C.E.), Joseph actually
played a bedtrick on Mary:

JOSEPH'S BEDTRICK

The beginning of the birth of Jesus. His mother was Mary (a daughter)
of Israel. And she had a betrothed of kingly seed, of the house of David;
and his name was John. And he was learned in the law, and feared heaven
greatly. Now, over against the door of her house (there dwelt a man) of
fair appearance (a warrior), Joseph the son of Pandera: he cast his eyes
upon her. It was Saturday night and a man entered the door of her house.
She thought in her heart that he was John her betrothed and she hid her
face and was embarrassed. He hugged and kissed her. And she said, "Don't
touch me. I have separated myself from others because of my menstrual
impurity." But he did not pay any attention to what she had said, nor
did he worry about her impurity. He lay with her and she became pregnant
by him. Then he left.

In the middle of the night her betrothed, R. John came to her. She

said to him, "What is this! You have never before behaved like this—
from the day of our betrothal—coming to me twice in one night!" Her
betrothed answered her, saying, "One time only have I come to you tonight, right now!" She said to him, "You came to me and I said to you
that I had separated myself from others because of my menstrual impurity
but you didn't care and you did what you wanted with me and then you
left." When he had heard these things he immediately recognized that
Joseph ben Pandera had set his eyes upon her and had done these things.
He left her.[80]

Instead of God taking the place of Joseph, Joseph takes the place of John;
and Jesus, like David, is wrongly said to be a bastard. Mary's failure consists either in not enforcing the rule against intercourse for a menstrual†
woman or in not recognizing that a man who was willing to ignore that
rule could not have been the man she was going to marry or both. Solomon's wife was wiser than Mary in this regard: according to the Babylonian Talmud,[81] when the demon Ashmedai took the form of Solomon,
Solomon's wife noticed the difference because he transgressed the taboo
against making love to her when she was menstruating (and also called
for his mother, Bath-Sheba†).

The text about Joseph goes on to relate how Mary was accused of
adultery, as in the Christian Gospel, but in this version of the story her
betrothed husband does not forgive her or take her back. It happens thirty
years later, when Jesus begins to attract the displeasure of the rabbis.
When the story of the deception is told, they accuse Mary again and pardon her; "there is no judgement of death upon her, for she did it not
willingly." They spare Mary precisely because she did not recognize the
bedtrickster, but they call Jesus a bastard and the son of a woman in her
separation and worthy of death; and "after the saying concerning Jesus
was spread abroad, he went forth and fled to Jerusalem."[82] In this Jewish
satire, the persecution of Jesus is fueled by his father's bedtrick and his
mother's failure to see through the trick.

To return to our Gospel text, we might argue that Matthew needed
the bedtrickster women to justify Mary's irregular sexuality. Could the
lineage of Jesus that the Evangelists read in (or into) predictions in Isaiah
and elsewhere among the Prophets have inspired them to tell the story
of his birth the way they did, with a virgin mother and two fathers? One
Jewish bedtrickster woman who does *not* appear in Matthew's list—
Leah—played an essential *negative* role in the Christian appropriation of
the Hebrew Bible. Mary Douglas has noted how, in Numbers, the arrange-

ment of the tribes around the Tabernacle stations the sons of Rachel opposite those of Leah, and those of Rachel's maid opposite those of Leah's maid, thus continuing the story of fraternal inheritance in terms of surrogate mothers.[83] This influenced the subsequent history of anti-Semitism, when Christians applied to religious history the stories of the second wife supplanting the first in the affections of her husband and identified the Christian Church with the second bride, Rachel, more beautiful, more beloved, more virtuous than the first, the Hebrew bride, Leah.[84] Christians, from the time of Patristic literature, identify themselves with Rachel, and they identify the Jews with Leah. In medieval Jewish texts, the Jews identify themselves with Jacob, the Christians with Esau. The claim that one or the other of the two sisters is "more real"—older, wiser, younger, or more beautiful—has therefore had serious historical consequences.

Certain medieval European Christian texts explicitly connect the irregularities of the birth of Jesus to Mary with another sort of problematic maternity—maternal imprinting,† which they regard as "a blasphemous parody of the cult of the Virgin Mary. In erasing all traces of the progeny's legitimate father, the monstrous mother replicates, and derides, the Immaculate Conception. She also demonstrates that such births are not miracles."[85] David Tracy has described Christianity as consisting largely of Greek ideas about Hebrew stories,[86] and the idea of parental imprinting or mis-conception is shared by Hebrew and Greek traditions. But the mythology of Mary also combines the Hebrew lineage of bedtrickster mothers such as Tamar and Ruth (a tradition that is not so well represented in ancient Greece) with the Greek lineage of bedtrickster fathers, gods masquerading as mortals, such as Amphitryon‡ (a tradition that is not so well represented in ancient Judaism). Mary resembles not only Tamar but Alcmena and Leda,† who were impregnated by Zeus in the form of a husband and a swan, respectively. The Evangelist may have had both the Hebrew stories and the Greek ideas in mind when he chose the women to include in the lineage of Jesus in his Gospel.

Transformations of the Levirate

We have seen that, though the levirate is ostensibly an act of collusion between two men, there is often uneasiness on the part of one or both of the men (in the Jewish variants) or distaste on the part of the woman (in the Hindu variants), and bedtricks frequently occur as a means by which women circumvent the plans of men. In the Hindu stories of Dirghatamas and Vyasa, the women object to the levirate and avoid it with a double-cross:† while the sage is substituting for her husband, the queen sends a substitute for herself. In the Jewish story of Tamar, by contrast, the man objects to the levirate, and the woman has to trick him into it. What is the meaning of this contrast? Why do the ancient texts about the bedtrick (which may or may not represent more general cultural trends) depict Jewish women and Hindu men as the perpetrators—or, if you prefer, Hindu women and Jewish men as the victims—of these enforced matings? Complex and deep cultural differences, beyond the scope of this study, would be relevant to the answer to these questions, but our narrative texts alone suggest an indirect answer to a related question. For the Hindu and Jewish texts agree that the women are the bedtricksters—either to perpetrate or to avoid the levirate. In this, at least, gender trumps culture.‡

Bedtricks are turned to subvert the levirate in cultures far beyond Israel and India. The emotional complexities of African levirate arrangements are hilariously depicted by Laura Bohanan (a.k.a. Elizabeth Smith Bowen) in her novelized account of her anthropological fieldwork in Africa.[87] In another part of Africa, among South African Xhosa and other Bantu speakers, the ultimate criticism of the levirate husband reduces him to nothing but a disembodied penis,† like the one that appeared to impregnate the mother of Romulus and Remus.† The trouble begins with a boy's preparation for initiation:

> The boy is told, "You used to call this your penis, but from now on you must call it X" (the clan name). And when he marries, the wife calls the penis X. If the man dies and the wife marries his brother, she calls the brother X. So people think, "When you die, your brother becomes your penis." Therefore, a brother does not like to take on his brother's wife, even if he gets her house and so forth, because he becomes nothing but his brother's penis.[88]

This is a particularly vivid, and particularly Xhosa, expression of the problem. But some of the emotions it describes are both African and more than African.

And there is something more than Indian about the emotions described in parallel incidents in India, and more than Japanese about the bedtrick in a modern Japanese novel, Fumiko Enchi's *Masks* (1958):

MASKS

Mieko was married to a man whose mistress caused her to miscarry their child. Mieko then took a lover and by him conceived twins, a girl,

Harume, and a boy, Akio. Harume, who was brain-damaged by her brother's feet during the birth, was hidden away immediately; Akio married a
woman named Yasuko but died in an accident only a year later, leaving
her childless. Harume then came back to live with Mieko, and Mieko
contrived with Yasuko to have Yasuko's lover, Ibuki, spend a night with
Yasuko, during which Ibuki was drugged and Harume was substituted
for Yasuko. When Ibuki realized that he had been tricked, he could
not imagine "what strange configuration in Yasuko's heart might have
prompted her to bring another woman into the bedroom and to switch
places with her so adroitly." Harume conceived a boy, gave birth to him,
and died, and Yasuko raised the boy as her own, saying to Mieko, "I'm
as excited as you by the prospect of a baby with Akio's blood in its veins."
When the baby was born, Yasuko said, "He looks so much like Akio I
could almost believe he is mine."[89]

The foot‡ of the brother that bruises his twin sister's head at birth is
reminiscent of the contest between the hand and the foot of the twins
Jacob† and Esau in the womb (Genesis 25.21–26) and between the hands
of Tamar's twin sons in the womb (Genesis 38.27–30). As so often, the
competition between twins in the womb prefigures or reflects the competition between two women in bed. Mieko arranges the bedtrick in order
to get Ibuki to father a child in Harume, so that she, Mieko, might continue the line of her own blood and that of her lover, but also, indirectly,
the blood of her son, Akio. The configuration of this levirate is complex:
when Akio dies without an heir, his mother enlists not his brother (he
has none) but his wife's lover and, in place of his wife, his sister, to supply
the genes that the nonexistent brother would have provided.

Differences among these stories are intriguing, and we must grant that
the emotions that they express are always modified by culture, certainly
by the time they are encased in narrative and arguably even when they
are experienced by each person in the culture. Yet the parallels between
these stories of subverted levirates are stunning and must give us pause.

THE DROIT DU SEIGNEUR

The levirate overlaps with two other sorts of male surrogation: in one,
the king has (or takes) the right (or duty) to deflower a virgin, and in
the other, a priest has the duty to deflower the bride in order to protect the bridegroom from the danger of the blood of defloration. We have
seen how the role of the priest was transformed into a more conventional
levirate in the story of Vyasa; now let us consider how the role of the
king undergoes permutations in Europe.

Just as the levirate offered a legal way for a man to sleep with another man's wife, so the droit du seigneur offered a means (somewhat less legal) to a related end—the right of the king or feudal lord to substitute for any of his vassals on the wedding night—though in this case the husband was still alive and not the protagonist's brother. In India, well into the twentieth century, the temple dancers *(devadasis)* of Orissa were traditionally deflowered by the king.[90] But, in contrast with the magical defloration by the priest that takes place presumably at the wish of the groom (though perhaps against the wish of the bride), the royal droit du seigneur (right of the lord) or *ius primae noctis* (law of the first night) was asserted despite (perhaps against) the wishes of both the bride and the groom, as the king's duty to deflower turned into his right to the pleasure of defloration. The duty and pleasure are conflated in texts that construct defloration as something that a man would rather have someone else (a priest or a king) do on his behalf; even the king needs to have this service performed for him. In some variants of the Norse and Germanic myths of Brunhilde, King Gunther secretly asks Siegfried to deflower his bride, the murderous Brunhilde; thus, he uses his royal prerogatives in order *not* to deflower her.[91] Indeed, Gunther points out that Siegfried can do this for him since they have sworn blood brotherhood, making this an episode in which all three surrogate pinch hitters are present at once: brother (or quasi brother, in a quasi levirate), priest (as magic deflowerer), and king (who exercises his droit du seigneur not on his wife but on the man he gets to deflower her).

We must here acknowledge the problem of distinguishing between evidence that this really happened and the idea that it could happen. The *Encyclopaedia Britannica* asserts that the custom of the droit du seigneur "is paralleled in various primitive societies, but the evidence of its existence in Europe is almost all indirect, involving records of the redemption dues paid by the vassal to avoid enforcement, not of actual enforcement. Many intellectual investigations have been devoted to the problem, but, although it seems possible that such a custom may have existed for a short time at a very early date in parts of France and Italy, it certainly never existed elsewhere."[92] Alain Boureau, in *The Lord's First Night,* has demonstrated that this right was more myth than reality. The historical records show primarily resistance, which might mean either that there was nothing but resistance or that only the resisted instances were recorded. We should also take into consideration the possibility that, just as a woman might have *wanted* to sleep with her husband's younger brother, so too she may have preferred the king to her husband (just as women in myths often preferred gods to their husbands‡), for reasons of sex or power or both.

But surely the use of political power to secure sexual favors is ancient and widespread. The droit du seigneur in the broadest sense—political pressure for sexual favors, what we now call sexual harassment—must have been invoked informally all the time but was formalized in the myths as if it were a kind of unofficial law or right, one that was, from the start, intolerable. It may never, or seldom, have been technically legal, but it was not "just a myth." We may even see it at work in the abuse of divine† power: in Jean Giraudoux's *Amphitryon,*‡ Jupiter threatens to destroy Thebes, Alcmena, and Alcmena's unborn child if she does not sleep with him; if she does, he will keep alive the children that death would have taken during that very week, including her own daughter Charissa. At this, Alcmena cries out, "This is blackmail."[93] In a satirical piece about the Clinton impeachment, Christopher Buckley imagined a headline: "Signalling New Aggressiveness, Kendall Asserts Presidential 'Droit du Seigneur' in Widow Case."[94] Indeed, part of the animus against Clinton was resentment against a king who thought he could have all the women—still trying, in the 1990s, to get away with the droit du seigneur.

We might regard the myth (or reality) of the droit du seigneur, in which the king controls the sexuality of his female subjects, as merely the extreme political form of the much more common practice of arranged marriages, in which the father controls the sexuality of his daughter. The myths dramatize the tension between duty,† in which women had little or no choice, and desire,† in which they had some choice. Stories like "Beauty and the Beast"† make explicit the connection between the father's familial power over the girl and the Beast's royal power over the father. As Marina Warner comments, "In a cluster of stories—hagiography and fairy tale—there recurs a figure of a wronged daughter, a young woman in flight from the unwelcome desire of a man, who is her own father or otherwise a man in power, an emperor, a prefect, a tyrant."[95] In this light, the droit du seigneur is no fantasy but, alas, a commonplace of women's sexual existence. And even if we consign the story of the droit du seigneur to the ranks of all the other fantasies† in this corpus, we must ask not whether, or why, it happened but why people went on talking about it, *especially* if it never happened.

EUROPEAN SUBVERSIONS OF THE DROIT DU SEIGNEUR

Even more than the levirate, the droit du seigneur is dramatized in narrative primarily in its subversion. A man betrays his wife with another man, as it were, when he inflicts a designated hitter on her; and when she sends a covert substitute, substituting a maid for the princess, her bedtrick response is a kind of double-cross.† The levirate and droit du seigneur are social fictions, which lead in turn to the antisocial fiction of the double-cross.

Some subversions fail. In William Kemp's drama *A Knack to Know a Knave* (1594), a man who does not trust his new wife and rightly fears that the king has designs upon her insists that the kitchen maid put on his wife's clothes and go to the assignation in her place; but "the disparity between the two women is so great that the king perceives the deception immediately."[96] Most subversions in stories succeed, however, as they do in Shakespeare's *Measure for Measure*,† in which Angelo threatens to kill Isabella's brother unless she submits to him. Shakespeare is never untimely. At a production of this play in 1992, at the height of the Clarence Thomas/Anita Hill debates, when Angelo sneered, "Who will believe thee, Isabella?" the audience gasped as perhaps no audience for this play has ever gasped before. It is not hard to imagine Judge Clarence Thomas saying to Anita Hill, in response to her threats to expose him, an updated version of what Angelo said to Isabella: "My unsoiled name, th' austereness of my life, / My vouch against you, and my place i' the state, / Will so your accusation overweigh, / That you shall stifle in your own report, / And smell of calumny. . . . As for you, / Say what you can; my false o'erweighs your true" (2.4). Isabella escapes the droit du seigneur by double-backing† the villain into sleeping with his rejected fiancée, Mariana. Yet Isabella may be the victim of yet another droit du seigneur. She is silenced,† literally dumbstruck, at the end of the play by the duke's offer of marriage, which confronts her, like the other offenders onstage, with a forced marriage as punishment for the offense of slandering a prince. Indeed, the duke, not Isabella, is the one who orchestrates her bedtrick—to get her away from Angelo, perhaps the better to turn his own powers on her. Here, as in so much else, the duke and Angelo are twins.

The servant girl here plays an ambiguous role: usually she takes the place of a noble lady (such as Isolde) to get her *out* of an unwanted situation, but occasionally, as in the story of Jesse's wife Nazbat, the noble lady may save her maid from harassment by a man whose bed the lady wants to get *into*—her husband. The device of putting the harasser's wife in place of the harassed woman is also used in Mozart's *Marriage of Figaro*,† both in Beaumarchais's play and in Da Ponte's libretto. The opera opens with Figaro and his bride, Susanna, planning their wedding; then she tells him that Count Almaviva regrets having abolished his feudal privilege of droit du seigneur and wishes to revive it for her. Figaro and Susanna approach Almaviva together with a group of villagers to thank him for abolishing the droit du seigneur, "a privilege so painful to lovers." They ask him to crown the bride, "whom this gift of yours has preserved spotless, with this white veil, symbol of virtue." Almaviva, furious, replies, "That privilege exists no more. . . . It was an unjust privilege, and by abolishing it in my domain I have restored to nature and duty their rights." In Beaumarchais's version, the count is quite brutal in the use of his powers; he tells Susanna, "If you go back on your word, let us be clear, my dear: no rendezvous no dowry—no dowry no marriage." To which she cleverly replies, "But no marriage also means no *Droit de Seigneur,* My Lord!"[97] Beaumarchais's Figaro adds a twist to the dagger: "If His Lordship hadn't abolished the infamous privilege when he got married himself I would never have married you within his domains." And later Almaviva insists, "The abolition of a shameful custom is no more than an acknowledgement of what is due to common decency." But the official abolition of this privilege proves to be the problem, not the solution, because it makes Almaviva rely on his personal sex appeal rather than the aphrodisiac power of his office; this drives him from the official to the unofficial arena of combat, where he is potentially even more dangerous. In response to the unwanted sexual double presented by the *seigneur,* Susanna helps the count's wife, the Countess Rosina, to double-back† and substitute herself for Susanna.

THE *DIRITTO DELLA SIGNORA*

There is a chain of subjugation in many of these stories, as the exercise of power travels down the line: when the king inflicts his will upon a lady who loves another man, oppressing both the man and the woman by exercising the droit du seigneur, she inflicts her own power on an inferior. Many a lady of quality, like the woman in Yeats's "The Three Bushes,"† sends her maid in her place, using her power over the maid as the king or husband uses his power over her. A Russian noblewoman uses her power over her maid almost as blatantly as a man, though indirectly, in

Grushenka, a quasi-pornographic novel attributed to "J. D." The woman who does this is oppressing another woman to avoid her own oppression, for any bedtrick inflicts sexual damage on both the bedtrickster and the victim,† but the bedtrickster in a double-cross† is doubly humiliated, simultaneously as victim (of the first quasi bedtrick, the levirate or droit du seigneur) and trickster (of the second bedtrick, the subversion).

Janet Adelman argues that in *Measure for Measure* Mariana "is introduced into the plot only when the bed trick needs her; she never becomes a fully realized figure."[98] But Shakespeare shows concern for the fate of the surrogate, Mariana: not only does Isabella escape Angelo, but Mariana marries him, as is her inexplicable wish. Usually the feelings of the lower-class surrogate woman are disregarded, but occasionally, as in *Measure for Measure,* her own rights and desires may also be satisfied by the bedtrick. In a few later tellings of the story of the false Sita,‡ too, some concern is expressed for the feelings and the fate of the surrogate.

The women who trick their unwilling husbands into sleeping with them in a double-back† are, in a sense, satisfying a narrative need that remains unfulfilled in most subversions of the levirate or the droit du seigneur, the need for the sexual surrogate, too, to be justified, if not satisfied. Thus, Isabella's need to have Mariana take her place in the bed of the despised Angelo is justified by the subplot that makes Angelo not only Mariana's object of desire but her fiancé, the subplot of a double-back. In myths of escape from unwanted sexual encounters, the double-back tells the bedtrick from the standpoint of the surrogate, who has an agenda of her own.

Another solution to this dilemma was imagined in Angela Carter's† version of Beauty and the Beast,† "The Tiger's Bride," in which the heroine's father loses her to Milord (the tiger beast) in a game of cards, thus simultaneously exercising a kind of droit du seigneur (his absolute ownership of his daughter) while himself succumbing to that of the tiger (who is richer, more powerful, and a better gambler). When her father expects her to return, the girl, who has fallen in love with the tiger, looks at her maid (a robot who looks just like her) and decides: "I will dress her up in my own clothes, wind her up, send her back to perform the part of my father's daughter."[99] This fantasized bedtrick would allow the heroine both to escape the lower droit du seigneur (the power of the father) and to embrace the higher (the power of Milord).

When a servant woman is substituted for the heroine of an epic recorded in Norwegian, German, and French sources from the thirteenth century c.e., the injuries to her become an important factor in the subsequent plot:

(Tristan and) Isolde and Brangane

> When King Mark sent Tristan to woo Isolde on Mark's behalf, Tristan himself fell in love with Isolde on the voyage home to Mark (they drank a love potion prepared by Brangane, Isolde's maid); and so, when Mark expected Isolde to be a virgin on the wedding night, Brangane took her place in the dark. Only the three of them (Mark and the two women) were present in the king's bedroom; Brangane wore the queen's robes, they put out the lights, and Brangane "suffered her ordeal" in silence. Worried that Brangane might say something to betray her, Isolde remained "as close as possible to them during the night to ascertain what they said."[100] After the consummation, Brangane slipped out of the room and Isolde slipped in; the lights were turned on, wine was drunk, and, to Isolde's distress, Mark resumed his lovemaking. He noticed nothing: "To him, one woman was as another; so he found Isolde, too, to be of good deportment. There was nothing to choose between them—he found gold and brass in either. Moreover, they both paid him their dues, one way and another, so that he noticed nothing amiss."[101]

Thus, the servant Brangane substitutes (unofficially) for Isolde to atone for her sin in serving the love potion that made the servant Tristan substitute (unofficially) for the king. They might have assumed that since it is the first time Mark will have slept with Isolde, he has no basis for comparison; but even when he *does* have such a basis, he cannot tell the difference. Isolde hovers over the bedtrick as Rachel† hovers over Leah (in the *midrash*), but she needn't have worried: Mark notices neither the switch nor the switch back (to Isolde), because it is dark,† he is drunk† from the wedding feast, nobody says a word, and it's in everyone's best interest† to allow the deceit to succeed.

But there is more. When Isolde turns against Brangane, another double appears. For when Isolde commands a servant to take Brangane to the forest and kill her, the servant, as usual, balks at the last minute and kills a deer instead, taking back its tongue† as proof of the murder. The animal that is killed instead of Brangane is thus a sacrificial substitute, and the physical proof provided by Brangane's tongue is a double of the physical proof of the dragon's tongue that Tristan used earlier to prove that he, and not the false Steward, killed the dragon and had the right to Isolde. But Brangane's tongue lies (it is not, in fact, Brangane's tongue at all, and Brangane is not dead), while the dragon's tongue tells the truth: Tristan is, in fact, the rightful dragon-slayer.

Sometimes the trick with the maid backfires, as in this French tale attributed to Pierre de Villiers and published c. 1462:

THE OLD MISTRESS AND THE YOUNG MAID

[A knight was the lover of a woman who, during his absence, married an elderly knight, who seldom made love to her more than once a month. The lover returned and came to stay with the elderly knight and his lady and schemed to get into bed with his former mistress. She summoned the maid and explained the problem: "My husband is in the habit, as you well know, of turning toward me in the night, to feel around for me a bit, and then to leave me alone, once again dropping off to sleep." So the maid got into bed with the old knight; the lady, with her lover.] As was his custom, the lord awoke about an hour before daybreak, and turned towards his chambermaid, assuming that it was his wife. In groping around, his hand happened to strike her breast, which was very firm and pointed to the touch. He immediately knew that it was not his wife's, which was nowhere so firm. "Aha!" he exclaimed to himself. "I see very well what is going on. They've played a trick on me, and I'll play one on them in return." He turned towards this lovely girl, and despite some misfortune, he broke only one lance, but she let him do it without saying a single word, or even half a word. [Then he called out to his guest, saying,] "I'll make the same exchange as last night with you anytime you so wish it. . . . I'll trade an old woman whose youth is passed, and who is dishonest and disloyal, to boot, for a beautiful, good, fresh young thing. This is what you have done for me by your visit here." [The knight left and never returned.][102]

Like Casanova,† the old knight saves face by claiming false knowledge,† but here the situation is reversed, and a double-cross† (or even the pretense of a double-cross) is not called for. For where Casanova was tricked into mistaking an old woman for a young one, this old knight was "tricked" into mistaking a young one for an old one—but did indeed notice the difference. The mistress promises the maid, apparently in good faith, that she will not have to submit to an actual sexual act; the old knight, however, responds to the younger woman with unaccustomed vigor, and the maid must suffer in silence.† Perhaps the exposure of her mistress is some compensation for her; perhaps not.

Some women wield not merely the power of any rich and/or noble woman over her servants but special royal (or divine) power over men.

This is a female droit du seigneur of a different sort, what we might call, because of its notorious use by several Italian women, the *diritto della signora* (a woman's direct use of political power to demand sexual favors). *The Marriage of Figaro* suggests a *diritto della signora* in another subplot: Marcellina tries to force Figaro to marry her against his will, through legal coercion, and is foiled only when it is revealed that she is his mother, in a comic variant of, simultaneously, the droit du seigneur, the *diritto della signora,* and the Family Romance.† In such cases, a woman may use her power not to force her maid to get her out of a sexual situation but to force a lower-class man into one. Potiphar's wife (Genesis 39), the seductive goddesses/queens (Aphrodite,‡ Astarte), and even, perhaps, Iocasta (who doesn't exactly force Oedipus† to sleep with her but perhaps buys him or seduces him with the power of the throne) may be included in this category, to say nothing of all the older women who keep gigolos (though here it's hard to say who's using whom). But the female variant of the droit du seigneur, though common enough in the first sense (her power over female servants), is relatively rare in the second sense (her power over lower-class men).

A Lombard queen combined a bedtrick with a protofeminist use of the *diritto della signora* against a man who was the servant of her husband the king, in this eighth-century Latin text:

King Alboim's Wife

[King Alboim killed the father of his wife, Rosemund, and made her drink from a cup he had made from her father's skull. To take revenge] she put herself at night in the bed of her dressing-maid with whom Peredeo was accustomed to have intercourse, and then Peredeo, coming in ignorance, lay with the queen. And when the wicked act was already accomplished and she asked him whom he thought her to be, and he named the name of his mistress that he thought she was, the queen added: "It is in no way as you think, but I am Rosemund," she says, "and surely now you have perpetrated such a deed, Peredeo, that either you must kill Alboim or he will slay you with his sword." [Peredeo helped her to kill the king.][103]

This story owes much to the story of King Candaules,† who, having made the mistake of falling in love with his own wife, urged Gyges to hide behind the bedroom door (according to Herodotus 1.8) or to wear a ring of invisibility (according to Plato, *Republic,* 2.359D–360D) to see for himself how beautiful she was. When the queen learned that Gyges had looked upon her naked, she exercised her *diritto della signora,*

insisting that he sleep with her and kill her husband. But the female variant is not a symmetrical† inversion of the male practice. Although King
Alboim's wife has the power to command the murder of the king, she
must use this power with double indirection, being a woman. First, she
must play the bedtrick in the dark, and then she must arrange elaborate
traps to get someone else (male) to murder the king. Were she a man,
as king she could simply have seduced a woman in the retinue in her
own persona—or, indeed, murdered the king, as he had murdered her
father.

The story of King Alboim was dramatized, greatly expanded, and
somewhat modified in William Davenant's *Albovine* (1628), in which
Rhodalinda (= Rosemund), the queen, seduces Paradine (= Peredeo) by
substituting herself not for her own maid but for Peredeo's newly wed
wife. This changes the ending, too. Since Paradine, unlike Peredeo, did
not intend to be unfaithful to his wife, he is deeply upset by the bedtrick,
and this has the perverse effect of leading him into a continuing affair
with the queen, who persuades him that his wife has been unfaithful. He
kills the king, but then his confused sexuality becomes violent, and he
pretends to kiss† the queen, bites her on the lips, and then stabs her to
death.[104] Clearly, the female variant of the theme was regarded as deadlier
than the male, and troubled the Italian male; the *diritto della signora* is
inverted, rather than subverted, in Boccaccio's story of the Lombard (now
Longobard) queen, Rhodalinda (now Theodolinda), who is seduced by
a low-born stableman.[105]

Hindu Subversions of the Droit du Seigneur

Some of the victims of the droit du seigneur circumvent it with double-
cross bedtricks that involve transvestism† (double-cross-dressing†): in
South India, they celebrate the death of a local warrior lord and landowner
who forced every virgin to sleep with him the night before her wedding—
until the goddess Gangamma,‡ in trousers, tricked him and murdered
him.[106] But Brahmins as well as kings used their power, in this case their
power to curse, to force women to submit to their sexual demands, exercising a kind of ecclesiastical droit du seigneur. When the sage Kapota
demanded that the princess Taravati† "save him with the boat of her
thighs from the ocean of desire in which he was drowning," she sent her
younger sister† in her place, explaining, "He would burn us up with his
curse if I sent anyone else; but you resemble me in all qualities, and overwhelmed by desire, in his delusion the sage will not know." The sage was

fooled and only realized the trick later, when he saw the two women together; then he cursed Taravati to be raped by someone else in disguise (the god Shiva,† as it transpires).[107]

In a story told in a Sanskrit text of c. 900 B.C.E., a woman uses a bedtrick to escape from a Brahmin:

YAVAKRI AND THE BRAHMIN'S WIFE

Yavakri had the brilliance and glamor of a Brahmin. If he called a woman to him and said, "Hey!" to her, she had sex with him and she died; even if she did not have sex with him, she died. He called the wife of a certain Brahmin to him and said "Hey!" to her. She reflected, "If I have sex with him, or if I do not, I will surely die in any case. Hell, let me have sex with him; if I am to die, let me at least die giving pleasure to a Brahmin." [Or, in an alternative reading, "A woman who does something displeasing to a Brahmin will die."] She said to him, "Stay there, and I will come to you."

As she was preparing herself, weeping, her husband came to her. He said to her, "Why are you adorning yourself, and why are you weeping?" She said, "I am full of self-pity when I realize that I am going to die. For Yavakri called me to him and said 'Hey!' to me." Her husband made an oblation and said, "Fire, bring to me the beloved of Fire, prepared and adorned for Yavakri, and she will save me today." With this he created a celestial nymph of the same form [as his wife], saying to her, "There is Yavakri. Go to him." Then he made a second oblation and said, "Bring me a fierce demigod, lusty, rock-hurling, blindingly bright, to be the killer of Yavakri." And with this he created a jealous demigod with an iron club in his hand, saying to him, "Your wife has just gone to Yavakri. Go to him."

As the nymph came to Yavakri, Yavakri spread out the bed, and she smiled at him. He said to her, "Little woman, you're smiling, but you don't have anything to smile about." "Why so?" "Because you are going to die," he said. She stretched out her foot and said, "Man, you have surely never 'cooked' a woman with feet like this." For the bottoms of her feet were covered with hair. The two of them went together, and when they finally pulled apart, just at that moment the demigod with the iron club in his hand came to them. Yavakri said to him, "Honor to you. How can I avoid paying for this?" "Maybe there is a way for you to make up for it, and maybe there is not," said the demigod. "If you cut off the head of everything that your father possesses, before sunrise, that might make up for it—or maybe it won't."

Yavakri began to cut off the heads in that way. People said, "Yavakri has gone crazy. Let's tie him up." "No," said his father; "my son acts as if he is driven by the gods. He is the one who knows what is best to do in this matter." Now, there was a woodcutter in the village who was deaf, and so he had not heard the prohibition (against stopping Yavakri). Yavakri came to him and began cutting off his [animals' heads]. The woodcutter said, "What person is this [who is] ruining us?" and he killed Yavakri—this is what some people say. But others say that the sun rose and shone upon Yavakri as he was still slaughtering the cattle, and as the sun rose, the demigod killed him. In any case, he died; that is what did happen. But doubtless it was the demigod who killed him.[108]

The Brahmin's wife (who has no other name) remains chaste and is split apart from the nonhuman woman, who is, apparently, the wife of the god of fire. Her supernatural nature is betrayed, as she herself hints, by the hair on the soles of her feet‡—a hint that Yavakri fails to take, at the cost of his life. The Brahmin's wife is powerless, but her husband allows the sadistic Brahmin to seduce the wife's magic alter ego so that the wife may be protected and the seducer may be killed. The husband also produces a male double to do his dirty work, the demonic double's jealous husband, the alter ego of the wife's presumably jealous husband. Sexual jealousy,† one of the most common motivations for sexual masquerading, is here transformed into an instrument of revenge: by creating a jealous ogre, the husband destroys the would-be cuckolder, Yavakri. And since, in this text, it is not the woman herself but her husband who uses magical powers to produce the surrogate, this is a war between two men, indeed two Brahmins, the husband and Yavakri. As is often the case, the story that begins with sexual violence against a woman (one Indologist regards Yavakri's act as a "forced rape")[109] concludes with fatal violence against a man.

JEWISH SUBVERSIONS OF THE DROIT DU SEIGNEUR

Jewish tradition, which calls the levirate into question, also suggests ways of escaping the droit du seigneur. Esther, in the Book of Esther in the Hebrew Bible, is an orphan adopted by Mordecai, her cousin. Pretending not to be Jewish (already a masquerade!), she marries King Ahasuerus. But according to a Jewish tradition recorded in various sources between 100 B.C.E. and 500 C.E., Esther was married to Mordecai, and that tradition, troubled by her relationship with Ahasuerus, took a route that the reader by now should almost be able to predict:

The Shadow Esther

When Esther had grown to maidenhood, Mordecai had espoused her. Naturally, Esther would have been ready to defend her conjugal honor with
her life. She would gladly have suffered death at the hands of the king's
bailiffs rather than yield herself to a man not her husband. Luckily, there
was no need for this sacrifice, for her marriage with Ahasuerus was but
a feigned union. God had sent down a female spirit in the guise of Esther
to take her place with the king. Esther herself never lived with Ahasuerus
as his wife. The old sources do not know of this docetism, and maintain that the last Darius was the offspring of Ahasuerus' marriage with
Esther.[110]

"The old sources" may not know of this particular Docetism, but they
know the bedtrick very, very well, and they know that it can be used not
only to protect a woman from an unwanted sexual liaison but sometimes,
even more usefully, to allow her to *say* that it has protected her from such
a liaison, claiming false knowledge.† Moreover, where the other stories
we have considered seem to express a woman's response to rape or an
unwanted sexual liaison, the revisionist story of Esther more obviously
reveals the concern of its (male) author to remove any possible stigma
from one of the heroines of Jewish tradition.

Stories about the subversion of designated hitters may be so numerous
simply because acquiescence doesn't make much of a story, but they may
also be evidence that subversion was a popular fantasy, or perhaps even
a popular stratagem. The male surrogates in different cultures come from
different directions and are subverted in different ways. The levirates of
brothers (Hindu and Jewish), drawing upon a broader cross-cultural mythology of brothers who replace one another in bed, are subverted in
ways that refract upon early Christian mythology and undergo different
transformations in African and Japanese cultures. The droit du seigneur,
an early European variant of male surrogation, is resisted in many ways
in texts such as *The Marriage of Figaro* and *Tristan and Isolde,* as is its
female counterpart, the *diritto della signora*. Its Hindu and Jewish variants
also intersect with the mythologies of Brahmins and tyrants who oppress
not merely individual women but an entire religion and ethnic group. It
is also the focus for a more general kind of political sexual harassment,
still operative in contemporary European and American culture, which
we will consider in chapter 7.

Approach Six
Law, or Loopholes in the Penal Code

Rape and Sexual Fraud

Twentieth-century variants of the bedtrick deal with scientific issues—cloning and the creation of life—which, in our litigious society, find their way into the law courts in the form of fights about abortion, adoption, artificial insemination, and rape. I have already noted, in different contexts, some of the legal† repercussions of new technologies of in vitro implantation,† as well as the implications that medical techniques of surrogation† have for bedtrick concepts such as the *diritto della signora.*† The fallout from what have been called "Sperm Wars," the techniques of artificial insemination and frozen sperm, constantly touches the media. An adopted child created by donor insemination wrote a *Newsweek* essay in which she complained: "The process is centered around deception. . . . Some doctors encourage the couple to lie, to say that the husband's infertility has been treated successfully. Then friends and family will assume the child is the natural offspring of the husband and wife."[111] These legal issues remain highly mythologized; the courts are haunted by the real counterparts of our mythological evil stepmothers, multiple mothers, multiple fathers, and custody fights. The shadow mother casts her shadow on the raging controversy and surreal legislation that have been generated by the complexities of surrogate motherhood, such as the case of Baby M (where the birth mother fought the surrogate mother for possession of the child) and the custody case in Florida in which a healthy child was switched for an unhealthy child in the maternity ward in which they were born. The Family Romance† has been subjected to heavy litigation in the past half-century in America, but the ancient mythology of the levirate should warn us that these problems are not likely to be settled in any court of law. In contemporary legal debates about sexual fraud,† as Judge Richard Posner points out, "the problems of proof of seduction by false pretenses . . . are exquisitely difficult."[112]

One doctor who lied about artificial insemination became involved in a bedtrick. Our source is a 1992 article in the *New York Times,* entitled

Fertility Doctor Gets Five Years

Dr. Cecil B. Jacobson was sentenced today to five years in prison for using his own sperm to inseminate female patients who sought help for their infertility and for tricking other women into believing they were pregnant. Dr. Jacobson, convicted on 52 counts of fraud and perjury, caused his patients "extreme psychological injury," ranging from depression and guilt to a fear of doctors, said Federal District Judge James C. Cacheris. . . . Dr. Jacobson, who is married and has eight children by his wife, was allowed to remain free during appeal. "I was totally unaware of the anguish, the anger and the hate that I have caused," he told the judge. "I am deeply sorry." Dr. Jacobson was convicted on March 4 after former patients testified under anonymity they never would have let him inseminate them if they had known he was using his own sperm, rather than that of anonymous donors supposedly matched to characteristics of their husbands. . . . On the witness stand Dr. Jacobson acknowledged occasionally using his own sperm when other donors were not available. He said he did not know how many children he had fathered, and his lawyer, James Tate, argued that in any case it was not illegal.[113]

The "fear of doctors" that Dr. Jacobson induced in the women to whom he gave children ("physicophobia"?) hardly seems evidence of "psychological injury"; it strikes me as a pretty smart idea. Yet the fact that Dr. Jacobson's method was not only legal but, mythologically speaking, legally sanctioned might have gotten his sentence commuted—if he had done it openly. Instead, he masqueraded as anonymous donors "supposedly matched to characteristics" of his patients' husbands—the age-old lust for paternal resemblance.†

The ancient myths also cast light on modern legal and psychological aspects of rape,† including date rape, marital rape, and what we have now designated, in contrast, by the strange phrase "stranger rape" (stranger than what?). In legal terms, a bedtrick is one subdivision of sexual fraud, which includes not only other sorts of lies (such as saying that you are using contraception when you are not, or that you do not have AIDS when you do) but two senses of "impersonating a spouse," one of which is our bedtrick while the other simply involves the banal pretense that you have married your victim when you have not. These legal cases turn upon deception about the nature of the act or the personal identity of one of the participants. The Model Penal Code paragraph 213.1(2)(c) contains a provision criminalizing the seduction of a woman by impersonating her husband. About forty states had similar laws in 1995, and prosecutors have won rape-by-fraud cases across the country.[114]

Such cases usually come down to a matter of consent or choice. In a California case decided in 1981, a friend of the victim's boyfriend undressed, climbed into bed with the sleeping victim, and undertook "prolonged erotic touching and caressing" before the victim realized who it was and protested.[115] In another case, the woman woke up at the moment of truth: "The evidence reveals that on the 1st day of May, 1955, some minutes after 3:00 o'clock P.M. [?] the petitioner made forcible entry into the home of the victim and criminally assaulted her as both she and her husband lay, in a normal slumber, in bed. She was awakened by the act of the petitioner and aroused her husband who pursued the petitioner from the house with a knife."[116] Perhaps if she had aroused him sooner, this would not have happened; the last line in the case is: "Penetration was established by competent testimony."

Some of these multiple men fool multiple women, as did a man from Nashville, Tennessee, in a 1995 episode that one newspaper called

ODD SEX SAGA OF "FANTASY MAN": BLINDFOLDED PARTNERS THOUGHT HE WAS SOMEBODY ELSE

Nashville, Tenn. The phone rings late at night. In a sexy whisper, a man persuades a woman to unlock her door, undress, put on a blindfold and wait for him in bed. At least three women did so, thinking he was their boyfriend, and had sex with the so-called Fantasy Man. One woman had sex with him twice a week for two months. Now they want police to charge Raymond Mitchell III with rape. The 45-year-old businessman says he was just fulfilling the women's fantasies and the sex was consensual. Police are not sure what to do. Investigators are looking at whether Mitchell claimed to be someone else, which could constitute rape by fraud. . . . But Connie Vaupel, who got Mitchell, a co-worker, charged with attempted rape in 1989, defended the alleged victims. "These are not stupid women," she said. "They were convinced of something that was not true. He had enough information beforehand to convince them. Believe me, this guy is slick." . . . The Tennessee Sentencing Commission . . . in 1989 updated an 1870 criminal statute on "fictitious husband rape" and came up with Tennessee's current rape-by-fraud statute.

More information is given in the "box":

Raymond Mitchell's accusers are: A 26-year-old woman who realized that Fantasy Man was not her boyfriend as soon as he touched her. She feared that he would hurt her if she resisted. A woman in her mid-30s who thought Fantasy Man was a man from Texas she had met a week before. She had sex with Fantasy Man twice before calling the Texan and realizing the truth. A woman in her early 20s who said she had sex with Fantasy Man twice a week for two months because she believed he was her boyfriend. She realized the truth when her blindfold slipped.[117]

Thus, one woman *did* see through the trick but was virtually raped. The others, however, saw and heard just what they hoped to see and hear,† just like the people in myths.

A legal case involving identical male twins† in Nassau County, New York, appeared in a 1994 law journal, headlined

SEXUAL MISCONDUCT COUNT DISMISSED IN DECEPTION OF TWIN'S GIRLFRIEND

A twin accused of deceiving his brother's girlfriend into having sexual intercourse won dismissal of a sexual misconduct charge this week after a Nassau County judge decided there was not statutory basis for prosecution. The judge ruled that what amounted to loopholes in the Penal Law mandated dismissal tied to facts in a case he described as "truly novel." The key elements missing in the statutory framework, District Court Judge John Michael Gallaso explained in People v. Lamont Hough, was the Legislature's exclusion of *fraud, deception or impersonation* in defining sexual misconduct where there was lack of consent. . . . The charge against Lamont Hough alleged he made an early morning visit to the home of the girlfriend of his twin brother, Lenny. The woman, in her complaint, said she consented to intercourse in her darkened apartment believing the man was her boyfriend. Only afterwards, when the man asked, "Are you going to tell Lenny?" did she realize the deception. . . . The judge wrote . . . "The lack of consent results from the complainant's mistaken belief, resulting from defendant's alleged fraud, that *the body she made love with* was that of her boyfriend."[118]

The "loopholes in the Penal Law" reflect the blind reasoning that is the driving force behind the folklore on this theme; if the judge had read those stories he would not have found this case "truly novel." The belief that the woman made love with a body, rather than a person (or a mind†), is a masterpiece of the legal mind at work.

The court transcript notes several inconsistencies:

It is interesting to note that complainant states that she left the door unlocked for her boyfriend, yet she stated that she had just given him a key. . . . Complainant got out of bed and, curiously enough, turned off the light located near the door rather than turn it on. . . . Complainant began talking to the male as if it were her boyfriend Lenny but was looking away from him while they were in the bed.[119]

(Another man, in a similar case almost a hundred years ago in Texas, was convicted in part because his testimony, rather than that of the woman he raped, contained a crucial inconsistency: "Appellant says he recognized her by the light of the moon. The record shows that there was no moon on that night.")[120] Both by insisting on darkness ("curiously enough") and by looking away, the victim stymies sight.† But are there no other ways of telling who you are in bed with?

The other bases of the woman's nonrecognition of the man in her bed are quite traditional:

> Complainant believed the male was her boyfriend because it sounded like him. . . . Complainant opened the door and thought it was Lenny who entered the apartment, as it was dark and she couldn't see. The male, who smelt of alcohol, got into bed next to the complainant. . . . The male began to touch the complainant's breasts and complainant responded "Oh boy, your [sic] drunk and horney." He then asked her to have sex with him and she told him to make it quick because she had to work in the morning. . . . Complainant wasn't looking at the male's face.

Darkness,† inattention,† time ("make it quick"),† drunkenness,† and self-deception,† as well as the voice†—they're all there. Equally traditional is the reason given for the trickster's self-revelation: male pride,† sibling jealousy,† and the double-bind† ("When the act was over, the male said, 'Was that the best sex you ever had?'"—as Jupiter said to Alcmena‡). Case dismissed.

In yet another case of this type, in Arizona, a woman was at first fooled by the man's silence† but then came to realize the deception, not by his behavior in bed, but by other, more trivial factors. The defendant testified: "When I got in bed with her, she thought I was her husband and kept calling me 'Charlie.' I didn't want to talk, because she would know I wasn't her husband and I took her pajama bottoms off. She didn't know that I wasn't her husband until we had had intercourse." Again the clue of the voice is deflected. But then, how did she know? She told the judge: "Well, at that time something came to my mind that it couldn't be my husband because the defendant had his, just recent, a haircut, I could feel it, and my husband hadn't had a haircut, and the smell of tobacco on his breath. My husband doesn't smoke."[121] That's how.

Judge Posner discusses another sort of sex by fraud: a medical practitioner who inserts his penis into a patient's body under the guise of administering "medical treatment."[122] Similarly, a gynecologist who repeatedly had intercourse with a young and, apparently, very inexperienced patient under the pretext of treating her menstrual cramps was convicted of rape.[123] In other cases, too,[124] the woman apparently believed that the "instrument" used to perform the examination was a speculum or other medical instrument, when in fact it was the physician's penis.†[125] One physician used his penis in place of a medical instrument during an examination to discover the source of a patient's problem with her *vision*.[126] Unless we resort to Freudian ideas of upward displacement† or take into consideration the linguistic ambiguity of a "speculum," used to examine not eyes (as its name suggests) but vaginas, it is difficult to imagine how this misunderstanding came about.

RAPE AND MULTIPLE PERSONALITIES

Multiple personalities have always given the courts a headache, and when sex is involved, it reaches the proportions of a migraine. Eve White,‡ it may be recalled, wanted to sue her husband for divorce when he slept with her alter ego. A judge found "mind-boggling" (but rendered a verdict of not guilty by reason of insanity) the 1977 case of William Stanley Milligan, a twenty-three-year-old Ohio man accused of nine rapes, who argued that "the rapist was not Milligan, but Adelena, a 19-year-old lesbian, one of his personalities."[127] In a 1990 lawsuit in Oshkosh, Wisconsin, a woman who had been diagnosed as having a multiple personality disorder (she had forty-five personalities) claimed that the personality who was flirtatious and promiscuous had accepted a date with a man who had pressed his sexual claims upon another of her personalities, who was shy and chaste. The whore invited him into bed and the nun kicked him out:

THE UFO OF PSYCHIATRY

Jurors heard psychiatrists disagree over the 27-year-old woman's contention that she was unaware one of her personalities—described as a fun-loving 20-year-old woman—was having sex. She said she learned of it from another personality, a girl the age of 6. . . . Darold Treffert, a psychiatrist who testified for the defense, said he feels she comprehended her conduct. Treffert said the woman's various characters were encouraged by her therapists who believe in multiple personality disorder, which he called "the UFO of psychiatry."[128]

Six of the woman's personalities testified in the trial. The little child who blew the whistle was Emily, "a personality who is approximately 6 years old and sometimes eats crayons that the other personalities are then obliged to spit out."[129] The ruling sustained the law on the books, that it was a crime to have sex with someone known to have a multiple personality disorder.

The woman in this case resembles in certain respects not only the three Eves‡ but the conjoined twins† Millie and Christine, whom Mark Twain called "A Wonderful Two-headed Girl": "She has a lover, and this lover is in a quandary, because at one and the same moment she accepted him with one mouth and rejected him with the other. . . . He wishes to sue for breach of promise, but this is a hopeless experiment, because only half of the girl has been guilty of the breach."[130] Apparently, in those halcyon days, the suitor did not sue—nor did the other twin sue *him* for date rape.

But in a case in St. Paul, Minnesota (the twin† city), in 1995, a woman named Jeanne Chacon, who had previously accused her fiancé, Paul Erlinder, of domestic abuse, later made another claim:

CHACON À SON GOÛT

In a flashback to childhood abuse, she reverted to being "Little Jeanne." As "Little Jeanne," she says, she attacked Erlinder, who restrained her. Now that she's back to being "Big Jeanne," Chacon wants the case dropped. But prosecutors won't comply. So Chacon wants to defend Erlinder herself (as "Big Jeanne") and turn in "Little Jeanne" to police.[131]

We might see the Wisconsin and Minnesota cases (what is it about those cold midwestern states?) as exaggerations of the more usual claims in date rape, that the man misunderstood the woman's intentions or even that he disregarded her explicit protests. This is the "rape" mentality, which argues that "her mouth says no, but her eyes say yes."†

The myths support both of these views, the man's and the woman's. Some of these myths argue, like the woman who is the victim of rape, that the man does not see both sides of the woman he is with. Other myths, or other parts of the same myth, argue, like the man who is accused of rape, that the woman herself is more than one woman, that the woman who wants the man is replaced by another woman who does not want him (or the reverse, depending on your point of view). This latter view, however, the view that a woman has several doubles, may also express another fantasy that the raped woman herself creates to deal with her memory of the rape.‡

When both the rapist and his victim have multiple personalities, the bed gets very crowded† indeed. A double-cross† of this sort in real life (or at least in the newspapers, which is not quite the same thing) took place in 1944:

Accused, Victim, Both Claim to Have Multiple
Personalities

They met, he says, in group therapy last spring, and as they became better friends so did their multiple personalities, who fell in love and talked of marriage. Now Edward B. Kelly, 44, of Falls Church, Va., has been charged with breaking into the woman's Prince William County home, binding her hands with wire and raping her. Mr. Kelly says he didn't do it. He says that the incident was one of consensual sex between "Spirit"—one of 30 personalities that inhabit his body—and "Laura"— one of the woman's many selves.

The disorder has been used as a defense in rape cases in other courts, including an Arizona case in which eight of the defendant's 11 personalities took the stand and a Wisconsin case in which the defendant claimed that one of the victim's personalities gave consent. But this case is unusual in that both parties say they suffer from the disorder.[132]

We have noted the Wisconsin (Oshkosh) case; the difference here, the paper says, is that both of the partners multiplied. But when we look a bit closer we see that only one of them claimed that it happened that way: the woman says she was raped by Edward, while he says that "Spirit" and "Laura" had consensual sex. He was arguing that it was a double-cross; † apparently she, or at least one of her, maintained that it was plain rape. As in so many enduring myths, an insoluble paradox† is embedded in a tale of desire, sexual violence, and masquerade.

Color, Class, and Clout

Color-Blind and Outcaste

In the tale of the rape of the false Parvati (the demon Adi†), Shiva is white (covered with the white ashes of corpses and illuminated by the crescent moon in his head) and Parvati is dark ("with skin like the petal of a blue lotus at night"). When he teases her about the contrast in their skin colors, she sloughs off her dark shadow, Kali,† and creates, instead, a bright shadow of herself, Gauri. In one version of the story, Shiva gives the issue of skin color a strange twist: "People like us, whose dark bodies are smeared with white ashes, have one sort of thought in the heart, but our words express the opposite thought."[1] Is Shiva referring to what we call "passing"? Can we call his remarks racist?

One single Rig Vedic hymn refers to the Dasyus (slaves), the enemies of the Aryans [*sic*], as coming from "dark wombs,"[2] which may indeed be a slur on the ethnic stock of India at the time when the authors of the *Rig Veda* arrived. But since later classical Sanskrit texts (composed at a time when the Aryans and Dasyus had intermarried for centuries) have no clear expression of a concept of race, let alone a correlation between race and skin color, we would do better to identify this negative attitude to dark skin in terms of class and otherness: in India during most of recorded history, people with dark skins were generally regarded as social inferiors (or, in the case of Krishna and Kali, whose very names mean "black" or "dark," as gods). Since most bedtricks are about the deceptive surface, the skin, it is not surprising to find many variants that deal with the most dramatic aspect of skin, its color. Skin color and caste intersect in several stories, such as those about Parvati's disguise as a dark-skinned Outcaste,† Pandu's† pathologically pale skin, and King Bhartrhari,† who so longs for his dead wife that he is willing to accept her "black or fair."

In teasing Parvati, Shiva also says that her dark skin against his white body looks "like a dark night touched by the light of the moon."[3] The imagery of night and moon evokes the myth of Samjna,† whose husband, the Sun, is regarded as both too bright and too dark for her. I have dealt elsewhere with the problem of his (and her) excessive brightness;‡ here let us return to an abbreviated form of that text (the *Harivamsha*, c. 700 C.E.) to consider the problem of the Sun's darkness:

THE DARK SUN

The Sun married Samjna, the daughter of Tvashtri, the artisan of the gods. She was not satisfied by the form of her husband, for she was filled with her own bright ascetic heat, and the form of the Sun, burnt by his own fiery brilliance in all his limbs, was not very attractive—excessive, it constantly overheated the three worlds. When Samjna saw that the form of the Sun had a dark color, she was unable to bear it. Transforming her own shadow into a similar, earthly female, Samjna went to her father's house. When the Sun discovered the deception, he went in fury to Tvashtri, who mollified the Sun's anger and trimmed him on his lathe, removing his excessive fiery brilliance. Then the Sun was much better to look at; he showed Samjna his handsome form, and when she saw her husband, she was satisfied.[4]

This idea, common in premodern and modern Europe, that the skin of dark-skinned peoples got that way by being burnt by the sun was formulated as a reductive, quasi-scientific astronomical parable in this myth in which the sun itself is burnt black by the sun, for this text implies that the Sun gave himself a suntan—"He was burnt by his own fiery brilliance in all his limbs." His meteorological brilliance makes him, anthropomorphically, dark. Samjna rejects him because of his blackness and creates an appropriately black mate for him (*chaya* here perhaps indicating the dark shadow rather than the bright reflection)—someone who, being dark like him, is at least in that sense similar to him (*sa-varna*, literally "of the same color"). Through her shadow, Samjna passes for black. The counterintuitive idea that the sun is both black and golden may be an expression of the black spots we see when we gaze directly at the sun‡ or of the sun's black color during its underworld journey, when it is night on earth.[5]

Later variants of this myth explicitly connect the color of the skin with class. The word for "color" (*varna*) also means "class" in Sanskrit and thus has social, as well as aesthetic, overtones, which overlap in the idea that the lower castes have darker skins than the upper castes. These concepts color, as it were, Indian attitudes not only to the Sun but to his children. One British scholar in 1840, noting that Samjna's son Manu was called "of-the-same-kind" *(sa-varna)*, glossed this as meaning that he was "of the same caste as his elder brother" Yama.[6] In some Sanskrit texts, Yama is described as a black man (with red eyes). In the comic book version, he is depicted as dark brown with thick red lips. This color may have come from his father or from his own dark role as the god of the dead or may simply be this genre's racist way of depicting ugliness: the comic book version of King Kusa† has the same dark skin and red lips as Yama. A contemporary South Indian version of the story says that the Ganges River, the symbol of purity, was given in marriage to the Sun but substituted her shadow, Chaya, for herself; she cursed Yama to become a Candala, an outcaste.[7]

These associations between skin color and class are deeply embedded in the literature of the bedtrick in other cultures, too. Casanova,† expressing his disbelief that he could have been fooled by a bedtrick, remarks, without any conscious reference to skin color, "It was an unpardonable mistake, as the two women differed as much as white does from black."[8] Eve White and Eve Black, the alter egos of the protagonist of *The Three Faces of Eve*,‡ were apparently so named by the therapists who collected the semantic data; critics of the book drily remark, "We suppose that the 'White' and 'Black' have some connotative significance."[9] This seems a pretty good supposition to me. But precisely what is the "connotative significance" of black and white in these stories? Barbara Fass Leavy notes that the heroine of animal groom tales is often imprisoned by a black man instead of the traditional beast and remarks, "The racist implications of the equation of blackness with loathliness or evil are obvious."[10] But the assumption in these stories that black is not beautiful is not merely racist. The primary experience, long anterior to the social fact of racism, might well be the experience of night and day or, with Melanie Klein,† the milk and the nonmilk of the two breasts, also a black/white experience if you wish. Without reference to skin color, black may also be associated with goodness (cool shade, creative chaos) or evil (darkness, dirt, death, or danger). People who hunt at night, who live where it is too hot to do much during the day, or who like to go out to buy cigarettes at 3 A.M. prefer the night; other people are happier in the light. In the ancient world, not everyone cared about skin color as a factor in identity, and those who did didn't usually connect it with a race or ethnic group. The kind of color-coded prejudice that we would call racism might be regarded as preracist, perhaps.

But even if these oppositions were originally metaphysical or personal, as soon as people with racial ideas tell these stories, race gets into it and rides piggyback on, indeed "appropriates," other sorts of symbolism that might be keyed to skin color. As Leavy points out, "Although folktales may not be intentionally racist, they often perpetuate damaging stereotypes."[11] Marina Warner's meditations on the blonde are very much to the point: "The adjective's double resonance—in French, Italian, German, Spanish—of beauty and light colouring corresponds to the English usage of 'fair' since the middle ages: the Old English meaning of beautiful, or pleasing, developed by the thirteenth century into 'free from imperfections or blemish' and by the sixteenth carried explicit connotations of 'a light hue; clear in colour.'"[12] The Nazis, of course, took up the theme of light and dark (a.k.a. blond and swarthy) from their own version of Indo-European mythology and racialized it in a different way, to use primarily (though not only) against the Jews.

The Hindu preference for brides with light skin color, already attested in the ancient period, was of course exacerbated by the colonial experience. And when stories about light and dark women, such as the "Black and White Bride,"† were recorded in the European tradition, they almost always took on racist overtones. White animals abound in the stories of animal lovers (Whitebear Whittington,† the white witch mare,† and so forth), but black women are even more significant: "The blackness of the substitute bride . . . is clearly symbolic. Where she is not specifically black, she is often ugly and swarthy, such as the Arab girl in a Turkish variant and the impostor in a Norwegian version, where one would not expect to find a dark-skinned woman. . . . In many Hispanic examples, the stories . . . focus . . . on the conflict between a wife and a wicked Negress who tries to impersonate her."[13] The symbolism of the black and white brides was used to make Odile, the alter ego of Odette in *Swan Lake*,† a black swan—a move that inspired some subsequent, race-sensitive productions to make all the swans white or black.

Distinctions of skin color are endemic to this mythology. The lower-class woman in the Chinese novel *The Carnal Prayer Mat* accomplished her bedtrick in the dark because, "although her skin was as dark as could be, it was not really coarse."[14] As in India, dark skin identifies some of these people as lower class, and others as foreign. "Moors" appear in bedtricks in a number of English Renaissance dramas, including Samuel Harding's *Sicily and Naples* (1640),† John Marston's *Sophonisba* (1605), William Rowley's *All's Lost by Lust* (1619), and Philip Massinger's *The*

Parliament of Love (1624) and *Novella* (1632?), playing roles that, as Marliss C. Desens puts it, encourage the audience "to focus on this symbolic humiliation of class and race rather than on the actual sexual humiliation."[15] And racial and sexual violences may compound, rather than deflect, one another. In John Fletcher's *Monsieur Thomas* (1615), the hero reacts with horror when he sees the Moor (whom he takes for a devil) instead of his beloved; and when he realizes that the women have arranged a double-cross† bedtrick, "his fear turns to anger, and he converts his intended sexual violence into physical violence by beating the maidservant before he leaves."[16] So common is this theme that William R. Bowden suggested, "A psychologist might be curious as to why a surprisingly large number of bedtricks involve Moors, real or pretended."[17] So might a cultural critic.

Moors play a key role in a story called "Starlight," attributed to the early-eighteenth-century French writer Countess Henriette-Julie de Murat, a tale in which the fair heroine is not replaced by a dark surrogate but actually becomes, herself, that surrogate.[18] Starlight is disguised twice over: first as a lowly slave (in a Family Romance†) and then as an Ethiopian/Moor (to avoid the exercise of a droit du seigneur†). The pseudo-Arabian Orientalism† of the tale hints at its indebtedness to one of the *Arabian Nights*,† but the Arabians in this story are not the Others; that role is saved for the Ethiopians,† leaving the Arabians to mediate between us French and those Ethiopians. The story is racist to the extent that the princess's dark skin is regarded as a total negation of her identity: after she has been transformed, the prince doesn't recognize her. But it does not negate her beauty; perhaps because he senses, on some level, that she is really white, or perhaps because his racism, too, is only skin deep, the prince finds the Ethiopian "fascinating and lovely" despite her skin color.

PASSING

Hindu bedtricks often engage the theme of double-casteing—Outcastes (in this case shoemakers, who are polluted by handling leather that is the skin of the cow) masquerading as Brahmins:

THE BRAHMIN WOMAN AND THE OUTCASTE MAN

A Brahmin girl began to menstruate† before she was married; in keeping with the custom, her father blindfolded her eyes and left her in a jungle. A man who pitied the girl took her home and raised her as his own daughter. An Outcaste fell in love with her, dressed himself in Brahmin-style clothes, and married her. She bore him two sons, but one day they spied on their father at work and saw him measuring people's feet and sewing sandals for them. Then they went home, gathered big leaves, and cut out the outlines of their feet, telling their mother, when she questioned them, "We are doing exactly what Daddy does." When she realized what caste of man she had married, her anger rose, and she grew bigger and bigger and became a terrifying goddess. She put out her tongue and went in search of her husband. Her children, terrified, hid themselves in two goats, but she broke off the goats' heads and drank her children's blood. The Outcaste man entered a he-buffalo, but she slit him open and drank his blood.

She met a religious mendicant and told him to walk in front of her, not looking back; but he looked back, and she lashed out with her tongue at him, killed him, and drank his blood. She went on killing people, drinking their blood, until she came to rest.[19]

This story, from contemporary Kannada-speakers in South India, connects the bedtrick with blinding and the telltale foot.‡ The visual masquerade is entirely superficial (it is a matter of mere clothing), in contrast with a narrative of caste-passing in a Buddhist Jataka story[20] in which the low-caste masquerader is betrayed by his speech.† The visual masquerade is supported by the motif of blindfolding, the bag over the head:‡ the Brahmin girl is blindfolded ostensibly so that she will not find her way home from the jungle, but really in order to blind her to what is being done to her. The prohibition "Do not turn around and look at me" is a motif that we know not only from Lot's wife but also from Mélusine,† Lohengrin,† and Cupid and Psyche.† Thus, the goddess is visually betrayed by three different men: her father, who blindfolds her; her husband, who masquerades for her; and the luckless mendicant, who looks at her when she tells him not to (a violation that brings into play the male gaze†). The blindfolding of the girl is a weak form of a myth told over large parts of South India about Yellamma under the name of Yellamma-Renuka,[21] in which her Brahmin husband has her beheaded in punishment for a minor act of mental infidelity and she gets the head of an Outcaste woman;‡ this set of variants structures the motifs of concealed sexuality, blinding, an abusive husband, and Outcaste status in different ways.

In response to the curtailment of her powers of sight, the goddess lets loose the powers of her destructive tongue.† Her children are among the first whom she destroys; this is the fate of the offspring of the betrayed mother.† The animals, here explicitly said to explain "why goats, sheep, and a buffalo are sacrificed to her when she is angry,"[22] are also inherited building blocks from the corpus of women and goddesses (like Parvati and Samjna) who take the forms of animals to flee from sexual violence; here, men and children attempt, in vain, to take the forms of animals to escape from violence at the hands of the goddess herself.

The terrible goddess is created through the parallel, and implicitly analogized, forces of men abusing women and lower castes polluting Brahmins. In Sanskrit texts narrated by Brahmins, and even in many vernacular texts, such as this one, that reflect a male and Brahmin ideology, these stories are told from the standpoint of the Brahmins (high in status in comparison with Outcastes) but they also sympathize with the women (low in status in comparison with men). Generally speaking, however, the Indian folk tradition tolerates passing, just as it tolerates adultery,† more than the Sanskrit tradition does. Kirin Narayan recorded in Kangra a story about a Brahmin who thinks he has married his daughter to a Brahmin but later discovers that the groom is a Sweeper, a member of a very low caste. The Brahmin dies of shame, but he does not tell anyone else what he has discovered. The daughter stays married, and the storyteller, a woman, was not particularly bothered by this fact: as long as no one knows, the marriage is valid.[23]

Sexual and ethnic masquerades overlap in many texts in which people of one ethnic group pass as people of another group—and, occasionally, another gender. Much of the psychology of sexual masquerades applies equally well to ethnic masquerades, though there are some considerations that are unique to each problem. Narratives of passing dramatize in an extreme manner the problems of knowledge, identity, and concealment, the epistemological impotence of vision, and the consequences of recognition and misrecognition. The folklore of "telltale signs" that we know from sexual reality-testing† is utilized, and sometimes satirized, in these stories of passing.

The Ethiopians we encountered in "Starlight" play a role in this mythology from a very early period. The *Aithiopika* of Heliodorus, who lived in Syria in the third or fourth century, may be the earliest "passing" novel. In it, Persinna, queen of the Ethiopians, abandons her daughter because the child is, unlike her mother, white, and the queen fears accusations of adultery, though in fact the child's color is the result of parental imprinting:† during the act of conception, Persinna gazed on a picture of

Andromeda.[24] Andromeda was the daughter of the king of Ethiopia, but Greek artistic convention generally represented her with white skin.[25] Ethnically black, conventionally represented as white, she is the ideal liminal creature to lure Persinna across the color barrier. Jerome, one of the Church Fathers, writing between 386 and 390, cites a lawsuit of Quintilian's that gave a similar explanation for a white woman who gave birth to an Ethiopian child.[26] This would seem to be a more meaningful problem for a white author, which is to say for the authors of all of the extant relevant documents. Yet, though some later texts (Jewish and Christian) do regard blackness, rather than whiteness, as problematic (in the children of white parents), it was Heliodorus's version, the black woman giving birth to a white child, not Quintilian's, that was more often cited in later Jewish and Greek literature. This is puzzling, unless we assume that the whole story, which is after all *about* a reactive back-formation ("What could have produced a child of the wrong color? Perhaps it was the sight of someone of the wrong color . . ."), is itself first expressed in a reactive back-formation ("Imagine if a black queen were as concerned about a white baby as we white people [like Quintilian] are concerned about a black baby. . . .").[27] These stories are not racist or even preracist; on the contrary, the idea of parental imprinting is a force against racism (and hereditarianism in general); the Lamarckian or Lysenkan idea of the inheritance of acquired characteristics argues against the idea that one's racial stock determines who one is.

In Mark Twain's 1894 novel about passing and racism (and by this period we can certainly call it racism), *Pudd'nhead Wilson,* a white baby and a black baby are exchanged, and the black child, who looks white, is raised as white. The racial masquerade is shadowed by a sexual masquerade, for, like so many of Twain's characters, both the black mother and the passing son cross-dress. The ease with which the son escapes from the house where he has committed a murder, simply by jettisoning his female disguise, raises questions about the superficiality of both sexual and racial identity, as Susan Gillman argues: "If 'male' and 'female' are as readily interchanged as 'black' and 'white,' then gender difference may prove to be as culturally constituted, as much 'a fiction of law and custom,' as racial difference."[28] The ongoing racial masquerade works because no one really notices slaves; and the temporary gender masquerade works because the black man who passes as white also passes as a woman on the day of the murder—and no one really notices women. That he escapes by putting on (and taking off) his *mother*'s clothing makes him at last, symbolically, entirely assimilated to her and to her race, which he has so viciously denied throughout his childhood and early manhood. But when, after that, his mother masquerades as a man to escape from slavery (slavery into which her son has sold her), she has completed the circle, rejecting the maternal persona that drove her to sacrifice herself for her undeserving son. Racial and sexual "passing" overlap similarly in Harding's *Sicily and Naples*† when Alberto's daughter masquerades as a boy, and his son masquerades as a Moor.

Racial and sexual issues conflict in a different way in Nella Larsen's 1929 novel *Passing,* which focuses upon the trauma of recognition, particularly the fear of a "throwback," when a woman passing for white gives birth to a child with blatantly black characteristics. Where the concept of parental imprinting† argues that the child's appearance reveals the mother's hidden thoughts, the mythology of passing argues that it reveals her past; the "throwback" is an extreme test of sexual deception. Thus, in *Passing,* a woman who "passes" and is pregnant by her white husband, who knows she is black, worries: "They don't know like we do, how it might go way back, and turn out dark no matter what colour the father and mother are. . . . It's awful the way it skips generations and then pops out. Why, he actually said he didn't care what colour it turned out, if only I would stop worrying about it. But, of course, nobody wants a dark child."[29]

Another black woman, Clare, is married to a man who does not know she is black. Her lie of passing is equated, in the eyes of her (black) friend Irene, with Clare's lie of pretending she isn't sleeping with Irene's husband—or, in the eyes of the author, with Irene's lie of pretending that she doesn't know about the presumed adultery (or, in the eyes of some critics,[30] with Irene's lie that she herself does not desire Clare). In one scene, Clare masquerades as herself in a double-back,† pretending to be a white woman pretending to be a black woman. On another occasion, Clare's husband calls her "Nig" and explains why: "When we were first married, she was as white as—as—well as white as a lily. But I declare she's gettin' darker and darker. I tell her if she don't look out, she'll wake up one of these days and find she's turned into a nigger." And he laughs, and Clare laughs with him.

The double-back takes a different form in films about passing. Mary Ann Doane notes that relatively few films have been made about the quandary of "passing" because of the visual dilemma that it poses: What does the actress look like when she is supposed to look like a black person who looks like a white person? The simple answer is, a white person.[31] The irony of racism inheres in the fact that people who do not *look* black at all are defined as black by nonvisual criteria, invisible genealogical criteria, though the convention still assumes that they may be identified by skin color. Thus, where Larsen depicted black as white as black, casting a white woman as a passing black woman results in white as black as white. The viewer experiences "a curious distanciation. . . . There is one body too much."[32] A third extra body produces a triple-back when the film puts a frame around the original double-back of the novel, as in the two films based on Fannie Hurst's novel *Imitation of Life* (1934, and then the imitation in 1959). On one occasion, a black woman passing as white is asked by friends to serve at table; she carries the tray of food on her head and announces, "I learned it from my mammy and she learned it from her massuh befo' she belonged to you." As Doane comments on this scene, "The representational convolutions involved in this scene are mind-boggling. The spectator is faced with a white (Susan Kohner the actress) pretending to be a black pretending to be a white pretending to be a black (as incarnated in all the exaggerated attributes of southern blackness). Ontology is out of reach."[33] But it was well within the reach of Rosalind in *As You Like It*:† a male actor pretending to be a woman (Rosalind) pretending to be a man (Ganymede), who in one scene pretends to be a woman (Rosalind). Given the parallels between transvestite passing and racial passing, it is not surprising that the double- (and even the triple-) back applies to racial as well as sexual masquerades. Just as the girl serving the tray pretends to be black, which she is, her mother on one occasion pretends to be her mother, which she is—a trick she might have learned from Moses'† mother, in a very similar situation. (In both *Passing* and *Imitation of Life*, the women who "pass" are usually also neglectful mothers and/or oversexual women.)

Skin color (often compounded by eye color) is regarded as a dramatic sign of paternity. Hence, these myths may simply be using racist criteria in the service of another agenda, broader than racism: the agenda of paternal insecurity.† In vitro† impregnation replaced the theory of parental imprinting† (and the test tube replaced the male bedtrickster) in a modern variant of the myth of Ethiopian parents and children, a 1995 legal suit:

Black and White Twins

[A Dutch couple who had failed to produce a child on their own had twin boys by means of in vitro fertilization. One was blond, the other dark;

blood tests confirmed that the dark one was the child of a man from the Caribbean island of Antigua, whose sperm had accidentally been given to the woman along with that of her husband. The couple made public their distress:] "There's always the suggestion that Wilma has been to bed with someone else," [said Wilma's husband, Willem]. [The biological father, however, asked the right question:] "Do they love the child?"[34]

Apparently they did; in any case, they kept them both. Although the phenomenon of two fathers for twins is rare in humans (it happens only when a woman has sexual relations with several men in close succession at a time when she has more than one egg susceptible to fertilization), it is quite common among animals†—and in mythology. Alcmena gives birth to twins when she sleeps first with her husband and then with Zeus (in the form of her husband); one twin is like her husband, the other like Zeus.

It happened again in March 1999. Two women, one black, one white, who were being treated for infertility by the same doctor in the same midtown Manhattan fertility clinic had appointments to be implanted with fertilized eggs on the same spring day. A month later, the white woman was pregnant with twins, and the black woman was not. But a mistake was made: some of the eggs that impregnated the white woman were her own and had been fertilized by her husband, but DNA tests showed that some came from the black woman. And indeed, the white woman gave birth to twin boys, one white, one black. The black couple sued for custody of the black child, and the white mother gave him up. According to her lawyer, "She is doing this because she loves her boys, and she is a victim here, not the culprit. She doesn't look at them as white and black. She looks at them as her sons. She is torn apart by this. She holds the babies, she feeds the babies, she cares for them. But at the same time, she doesn't want to deprive her son of being with his biological mother."[35] Barbara Katz Rothman, a City University sociologist, compared this incident with the "similar case [that] occurred recently in Holland" and noted that in that case the woman is now raising both children. "Such cases, she said, raise murky philosophical questions."[36] Indeed they do, and have done for centuries.

IN THE LIGHT, ALL BLACK CATS ARE BLACK

The children of the "wrong" color in the mythology of parental imprinting are soon found out. But in myths like "The Black and White

Bride,"† magic allows a dark person to pass as a fair one; and in more realistic literature, a fair person defined, racially, as "black" may pass for white. A different sort of passing takes place when one person defined as "black" substitutes for another. Color prejudice produces a scorn for the other, for the person of a lower class or darker color, who is not worth looking at carefully. In *The Great White Hope* (1970), the prizefighter Jefferson jumps bail by getting another man to double for him while the FBI is watching his house. When his friends and family remark that the other man doesn't look like him, Jefferson points out that he is big, black, and wearing the same bright pink shirt and adds, "Don't you know that people say all Niggers look alike?" In *Watermelon Man* (1970), a white bigot wakes up one morning to discover that he is black. Previously, while still white, he had said to a black man under suspicion of committing a crime, "It would be hard for the police to identify you. All you cats look alike." The phrase took on a new twist in *Men in Black* (1997) when the black FBI agent said to the extraterrestrial—a gigantic, hideous bug— "You guys all look alike." (The producers of the film, speaking of the limited number of ways in which aliens are portrayed in Hollywood, confirmed this opinion: "They all look similar.")[37] Ralph Ellison's novel, *Invisible Man,* depicts the invisibility of black people in America as a source of both humiliation and freedom.

Both sexism and racism (as well as classism) cloud the judgment so that the other is beneath contempt, or at least beneath recognition; they dehumanize, deindividualize, the sexually and racially other. Racism and sexism are often conflated not merely through people's shared belief in the sameness of the sexual or racial other but in their *equation* of the sexual and racial other. The sexist "In the dark, all cats are gray" is usually applied to women; but it is also applied to black men (and, rarely, to black women) as a racist slur, implying not only that black cats are all alike in the light (that, in a sense, they are their own darkness) but that they are like women. Another metaphor of darkness links them, too: the depiction of the woman herself as dark, through the usual conflation of the sexual other—the woman—with the racial other. Freud's use of the term "dark continent" (in English) to describe female sexuality[38] has racial implications, as Sander Gilman points out: "In using this phrase in English, Freud ties the image of female sexuality to the image of the colonial black and to the perceived relationship between the female's ascribed sexuality and the Other's exoticism and pathology. It is Freud's intent to explore this hidden 'dark continent' and reveal the hidden truths about female sexuality, just as the anthropologist-explorers (such as Lombroso) were revealing the hidden truths about the nature of the black."[39]

But racism and sexism do not look alike in the dark. Henry Louis Gates, Jr., has argued: "Race is the ultimate trope of difference because it is so very arbitrary in its application. The biological criteria used to determine 'difference' in sex simply do not hold when applied to 'race.'"[40] But Doane has pointed out the problems in this approach: "Even for a theorist so acutely aware of the social construction of difference, there is a certain obviousness about the biology of sexual difference—as though the body were immediately readable in this respect and this respect alone."[41] For it is just as hard—or, for that matter, just as easy—to distinguish sexual others as racial others.

Just as transsexuals and transvestites† are often unmasked at death, people who "pass" often flunk the autopsy. The overlapping masquerades of race and gender end in the morgue in Richard Wright's 1953 radio play, which sidesteps the problems of representation of "passing" encountered in films by omitting visual representation altogether:

MAN OF ALL WORK

A black man named Carl dresses as a woman named Lucy in order to get a job taking care of a child, Lily Fairchild. At the start, Carl teases his own wife, "How will anybody know? Lift up my dress?" But then, in the house where Carl-as-Lucy works, Lily asks him about Red Riding Hood and then asks why the voice of Carl-as-Lucy is "heavy, like a man's." The husband makes a pass at Carl-as-Lucy, and the wife in a panic shoots Carl-as-Lucy dead. The doctor who makes the preliminary postmortem examination asks, "Did you, for some reason, *make him wear that dress?*" Mr. Fairchild immediately changes his story and insists that he (not his wife) shot the man—who must have been a rapist: "That's our answer! I was protecting white womanhood from a nigger rapist impersonating a woman! A rapist who wears a dress is the worst sort!"[42]

"Passing" leads to becoming the object of a "pass"; one stereotype replaces another. As Marjorie Garber points out, "'Passing' here itself passes from the category of race or color to the category of gender; a black man sees that he can pass as a woman because he is, in white eyes, always already a woman: 'We all look alike to white people.'"[43] The logic here seems to be: since all women look alike, and all black people look alike, black men look like women.

A muted bedtrick in a very old, one-minute silent film, made by

Thomas Edison in 1903, satirizes both racism and sexism: "*What Happened in the Tunnel* takes place on the set of a moving train. A young man retrieves a handkerchief dropped by a young girl seated with her [black] maid. As the man returns the kerchief to its owner, he attempts to kiss her. At that moment the train enters a darkened tunnel, and the screen blacks out. When the train emerges from the tunnel, the man is horrified to discover that he is embracing the maid, who is black."[44] As Judith Mayne remarks: "This film could be read . . . with a racist twist. The man looks and wants to possess what he sees, but he kisses the 'wrong' woman, the inappropriate object of spectacle. However, if the two women in this film are objects of the male look, they turn the tables by laughing at the man."[45] The initial premise is indeed racist, but the twist comes in allowing the collusion of the two women against the male to override the collusion of the two whites against the black. The innocent kiss is magnified by what must be one of the earliest recorded instances of the recurrent film convention of the train entering the tunnel as a metaphor for the man entering the woman (as in *The Lady Eve, North by Northwest*, etc.). The tunnel is the dark place—the womb—where light and dark women look alike.

WHY ORIENTALS MAKE GOOD (MASQUERADING) WIVES

The patterns of race take on different permutations in fiction about colonialism: colonizer is to colonized as penetrator is to penetrated as male is to female. Colonialism, of course, deals not only with "blackness" but with "yellowness" and "brownness" and views these hues through what Edward Said has taught us to call "Orientalism"—the Western tendency to present "the Orient" (and, in particular, "the Oriental") as exotic, erotic, feminine, and even worse. Orientals, like black people, are invisible. In Paul Scott's novel about the British in India, *The Jewel in the Crown*, the Indian, Kumar, who has been educated in England is not recognized by his British school buddy Linsey when they meet in India. "I am invisible, Kumar said, not only to white people because they are white and I am black but invisible to my white friend because he can no longer distinguish me in a crowd. He thinks—yes, this is what Linsey thinks: 'They all look alike.' "[46] A quasi bedtrick takes place when the British accuse Kumar of being one of a group of men who raped Kumar's English girlfriend. The police imply that she could not tell him from the others in the dark, though of course she knew the difference—knew that he was not one of her attackers—but remained tragically silent, as did he.

The silence of the woman and of the "Oriental" are conflated in "The Case of Lady Sannox,"† written by Sir Arthur Conan Doyle in 1894, during the reign of British Orientalism:

THE CASE OF LADY SANNOX

[A surgeon, Douglas Stone, was carrying on an adulterous affair with a married and notorious ex-actress, Lady Sannox. One evening when Stone was about to go out to meet Lady Sannox, a rich Turk came to his house and said that his wife had cut her lower lip on a poisoned dagger and would die from the swift-acting poison unless her lip were cut off, which he offered the surgeon a hundred pounds to do. The surgeon, who wanted the money, went with the Turk to a house where there was] a couch in the corner, on which lay a woman dressed in the Turkish fashion, with yashmak and veil. . . . But the surgeon was not thinking about the yashmak. This was no longer a woman to him. It was a case. [He could see only her lower lip and her eyes, which showed that she was, as the Turk said, drugged with opium. Stone hesitated to perform the operation.] "The defiguration will be frightful." "I can understand that the mouth will not be a pretty one to kiss." Douglas Stone turned fiercely on the man. The speech was a brutal one. But the Turk has his own fashion of talk and of thought. [The Turk persuaded Stone to do it for the money. Stone cut a V-shaped piece out of the woman's lip; she jumped up and screamed.] Her covering was torn from her face. In spite of that protruding upper lip and that slobber of blood, it was a face that he knew. [She put her hand over "the bloody gap."] He was conscious that the Turk's hair and beard lay upon the table, and that Lord Sannox was leaning against the wall with his hand to his side, laughing silently.[47]

The mutilation of the lip takes away the woman's voice,† for, as Elaine Showalter comments: "Excision of the lip is an act against speech as well as against sexuality . . . with the 'under lip' a metaphor for the female genitals."[48] Destroying a promiscuous woman's beauty by mutilation† is a standard ancient punishment for adulterous "Oriental"† women (like Shurpanakha† in the *Ramayana*). But getting the woman's lover to do the mutilation in place of her husband (or the legal powers) is an unusual use of the double-cross:† the lover mistakes his mistress for another man's wife (which she is) and mistakes her husband, too, for another man. He remarks that "the Turk has his own fashion of talk and of thought," an Orientalist assumption that tricks him into behaving as brutally as he assumes the Turk—and his wife—would act. The woman does not willingly perpetrate the bedtrick, but she is drugged† into silence even before her mouth is cut; she cannot speak, cannot demonstrate that she does *not* have a brutal "fashion of talk and of thought"—until the two men render her incapable of any sound but a scream. She is, as it were, raped in her drugged sleep,† in a nightmare in which she is paralyzed, unable to defend herself.

The surgeon, too, is in the end paralyzed with terror and literally turned to Stone.⁴⁹ Here we may recall all the people (beginning with Ahalya) who are turned to stone‡ in Hindu myths as punishment—an alternative to mutilation—for their sexuality. As Showalter remarks upon this story, Stone is persuaded "because he has stopped seeing the person in the veil as a human being: 'This was no longer a woman to him. It was a case.' She has become the Other, the veiled woman who is a possession to be displayed and revealed by the Turk."⁵⁰ And so she is desexed, fleeing to the convent that is a common European solution for sexual aporias.

Lord Sannox, too, is silent at the end, but his silence is a silence of power, cynical and sadistic. His brutal revenge is made bearable (and, perhaps, believable) for the British audience by being not bowdlerized but Orientalized. The mutilation that Sannox engineers and the surgeon performs they would not inflict upon a White Woman, let alone a Woman of Title; but it is suitable for an adulterous "Oriental" woman, who is veiled both by the cloth on her face and by her status as an (invisible) alien.

"All Japanese look alike," another Orientalist variant of the "cats" cliché, had its heyday in World War II but did not vanish in 1945. An Orientalist and sexist fusion surfaces in *Our Man in Havana* (1959) when someone looking for a stripper in a strip joint asks the actor (Alec Guinness) passing as a vacuum cleaner salesman passing as a spy passing as a vacuum cleaner salesman, "Which one is Teresa?" to which he replies, "They all look the same without [hands mimicking a brassiere] . . . like Japanese." (That is, women below the neck are like Japanese above the neck.) And in 1996, I heard Senator Robert F. Bennett (Utah) argue in public in Washington, D.C., that since Japan has a single ethnic base, in contrast with multicultural America, "All the Japanese look alike. . . . They're all related to one another."⁵¹ The war film *Destination Tokyo* (1943) inverts the usual conflation of anti-Japanese jingoism and sexism when the captain tells his men how he met and fell in love with his American wife on a blind† date when it was so dark that he couldn't see her: "I liked her voice, and I liked what she said. I liked everything about her. I still do." He goes on to say that the Japanese have no real feeling for their women, that they treat them like slaves. Thus, the usual sexist/Orientalist argument (Japanese should be our slaves, just as our women are our slaves) is given a twist and comes out: Japanese should be our slaves, just as their women are their slaves—so that we can set their women free.

Orientals, like black people, are equated with women. The feminization of racial others provided colonial rulers in India with a symbolic solution to the problem posed by the confusion of several different models of polarized racist sex roles: the Black Man as Stud, the Black Woman as Whore, and the Black Man as Slave. The "solution" was the Black Man as Impotent Man, emasculated whore (*kliba*‡). His counterpart, as feminists have pointed out, is the non-European woman, or "subaltern feminine," construed as doubly shadowed, black on black.[52]

Orientalism plays a crucial role in the film *My Geisha* (1962):

MY GEISHA

A famous movie director married to a more famous actress named Lucy Day decides to make a film of *Madama Butterfly* in Japan. His wife wants to play the part of Madama Butterfly, but he wants to prove his own talents, without her help, by casting a real Japanese geisha in the part. When he flies to Tokyo to cast the film, his wife follows him, masquerades as a geisha named Yoko (she wears a black wig over her red hair, dark contact lenses over her blue eyes, and white paint over her pink skin), and fools him (though he does remark that the geisha reminds him an awful lot of his wife). She gets the part and continues to fool everyone, in part through pseudo-Japanese modesty: she keeps her head lowered in the Japanese manner and always dims the lights when she is close to her husband. When her geisha pal assures her that she couldn't tell that Lucy was not Japanese, Lucy replies, "My husband knows me a lot better than you do." But when he is waiting for her in a public place, he does mistake another Japanese woman for her at first. When she kisses the leading man, whom she has often kissed before as Lucy, she so bowls him over with her sexual proficiency (geisha style) that his head swims and he doesn't recognize her. But Lucy remarks to a friend at one point that she is so possessive of her handsome husband that "I am even jealous of Yoko." She begins to worry that she has done a bad thing, an idea that is confirmed when a real geisha gives her a fan with a motto: "No one before you, my husband, not even I."

The director chances to see a negative of the film, in which Yoko has red hair and blue eyes, like Lucy, and then he realizes that Yoko is Lucy. Furious and depressed, he takes revenge on her by making love to Yoko, pretending that he still does not know that she is Lucy. When he kisses her, she rejects him, devastated by his infidelity. He decides to leave her right after the premiere. On that night, as she prepares to go onstage and reveal that she was the actress so as to take all the credit (the producer has suggested that she might even get an Oscar for the part), she thinks about the geisha's message and hesitates, looking in the mirror as she has one contact lens still in (brown) and one eye nakedly blue. At the last minute, she comes out (as Lucy) and says that Yoko has retired to a convent and will never be seen again, and that she is very proud of her husband for making such a wonderful picture. As they take their bows (she bowing only in her capacity as his wife), he whispers to her the words that Yoko had said to him during the seduction. "You knew!" she says, in relief. "I knew," he confesses smugly, implying that he had known all along.

The assumption is that white women can play Japanese women better (or at least can fool white men better with their clichés of Oriental women's behavior) than Japanese women can, an Orientalist transformation of the sexist argument that only men know what women should be like. The Orientalism is emphasized by the moments of recognition that depend upon the racist criterion of the color of the eyes; but it is then somewhat modified by the sexist codicil that Japanese women are properly submissive to their husbands, a lesson that this uppity American actress must learn from the Japanese. Only when she decides *not* to reveal to the public that she was masquerading as the geisha (i.e., that she is a fine actress, compounding the felony by fooling her own husband so that he did not recognize her, the ultimate betrayal) does her husband decide to withdraw his counterattack and tell her that he knew she was masquerading as the geisha. He lies when he says he knew "all along," but all she cares about is that he knew who she was when he made love to Yoko, and that is true. She sacrifices her artistic persona for her sexual persona, finally taking on in life the attitude and mentality† of the double she has invented in her art, the character that she assumed to trick her husband, which is the mentality of a woman who would never trick her husband. Indeed, she also takes on the mentality of the heroine of the Puccini opera, in which the hero is named, significantly, Benjamin Franklin ("In the dark all cats are grey"†) Pinkerton.

Orientalism made possible the seduction of the Frenchman in David Henry Hwang's 1989 play

M. BUTTERFLY

A French diplomat named René Gallimard went to China and met a famous male opera singer named Song, who played female roles. Gallimard
took Song to be a woman, fell in love with her/him, and lived with him
for a number of years in China and, later, in Paris. Eventually it transpired
that Song was working for the Chinese Communists and had used Gallimard to gain access to secret documents. Gallimard was tried for treason,
and only in the course of the trial did he learn that Song was a man. He
committed suicide.

The Orientalism inheres, first of all, in the fact that the Frenchman
doesn't bother to find out that the Chinese always have men play the
roles of women in operas (a factor that Hwang may have borrowed from
Balzac's Frenchman, Sarrasine,† who didn't know about the roles of
castrati in Italian opera). Moreover, the confusion in Gallimard's mind
between the Japanese heroine of the Puccini opera (which Gallimard
keeps talking about) and the Chinese heroine of the play is yet another
instance of Orientalism: all Japanese not only look alike but look like all
Chinese.

Bernard Boursicot,† the real-life Gallimard, accounted for his mistress's refusal to strip as a manifestation of Oriental modesty, but Hwang,
a Chinese American, later remarked, "I am aware that this is *not* a Chinese
custom, that Asian women were no more shy with their lovers than are
women of the West. . . . I inferred that, to the extent that the Chinese
spy encouraged these misperceptions, he must have played up to and
exploited this image of the Oriental woman as demure and submissive."[53]
Hwang explains the bedtrick through the Orientalist equation of "Orientals" with women, which makes it easy for "Oriental" men to be mistaken
for women. As Hwang remarks, "Given the degree of misunderstanding
between men and women and also between East and West, it seemed
inevitable that a mistake of this magnitude would one day take place."[54]
Song argues that the masquerade worked primarily through the masquerader's ability to understand, circumvent, and manipulate the confluence
of sexism and Orientalism in the victim of the masquerade (who was the
political oppressor of the masquerader). Song says:

> The West has sort of an international rape mentality towards the East. . . .
> "Her mouth says no, but her eyes say yes." The West thinks of itself as
> masculine—big guns, big industry, big money—so the East is feminine—
> weak, delicate, poor . . . but good at art, and full of inscrutable wisdom—

the feminine mystique. Her mouth says no, but her eyes say yes. The West believes the East, deep down, *wants* to be dominated—because a woman can't think for herself. You expect Oriental countries to submit to your guns, and you expect Oriental women to be submissive to your men. That's why you say they make the best wives. . . . Being an Oriental, I could never be completely a Man.

The contrast between mouth and eye† is a sexist construct that has nothing to do with Orientalism; but it is conflated with a racism that feminizes the Other.

Indeed, the racism then turns back to reinfect sexual relations even between Asians themselves, in the absence of Westerners. The image of the "Rice Queen"—a gay Caucasian man who is attracted to Asians—became, as Hwang points out, "so codified that, until recently, it was considered unnatural for gay Asians to date one another. Such men would be taunted with a phrase which implied they were lesbians."[55] In other words, Western men had persuaded Asian men that they would become not feminine men (the Western racist view of Asian men) but masculine women (the false consciousness of themselves imposed by Western men on Asian men) if they attempted to assume the roles assigned to gay Western men.

Close Your Eyes and Think of England

The sun never sets on English xenophobia; it is not limited to the "Orient" but also colors bedtricks in Renaissance plays that depend upon the foreignness of the foreigner.[56] In William Haughton's 1598 play *Englishmen for My Money,* a foreign merchant who has married an Englishwoman and settled in London wants his three thoroughly Anglicized daughters to marry foreign merchants, but they want to marry Englishmen. The father sets up a bedtrick for the foreigners to replace the Englishmen, but "the suitors' accents give them away as each arrives for the night."[57] The Anglophile foreigners are fooled, however, through a double-back-cross† in another drama of this period, Thomas Heywood's *The Fair Maid of the West* (1631). Being royals, these foreigners can invoke their droit du seigneur,† but, as usual, that does not protect them from bedtricksters:

The Fair Maid of the West

Mullisheg, a Moor king, despised his wife Tota and wanted to sleep with Bess, an Englishwoman; Tota vowed to revenge herself by sleeping with Bess's English husband, Spencer. Spencer set up a bedtrick so that the Moor king and queen slept together, ecstatically, and Bess and her husband escaped. The next morning, Tota praised the "sweet and loving bedfellows" of "this great nation," and Mullisheg raved: "Venetian ladies, nor the Persian girls, / The French, the Spanish, nor the Turkish dames, / Ethiope, nor Greece can kiss with half the art / These English can, nor entertain their friends / Wi' th' tenth part of that ample willingness / Within these arms."[58]

The English playwright tells us that foreigners *believe* that the English are superb bedmates, although in this case, they never have a chance to validate that hypothesis.

The assumption that the English are recognizably different, if not necessarily better, in bed is challenged in Julian Barnes's 1995 short story

EXPERIMENT

[Uncle Freddy told his nephew—the narrator—about his meeting in Paris in 1928 with the Surrealists, who questioned him about his sexual practices. He had told the Surrealists that he used to dream of twin sisters on his street who were in all visible respects identical.] If you were having sexual relations with one, how could you tell it was she and not the other? . . . And this in turn provoked a further question. What if there were two people—women who in their . . . sexual movements were exactly the same, and yet in all other respects were completely different. . . . erotic doppelgängers yet social disparates . . . so that if you closed your eyes you couldn't tell the difference. . . . In sex we note distinctiveness, not similarity . . . we don't as a rule think, Oh, being in bed with her was much like being in bed with So-and-So a couple of years ago. In fact, if I were to close my eyes. . . . We don't, on the whole, think that way. Courtesy, in part, I expect; a desire to maintain the individuality of others. And perhaps a fear that if you do that to them, they might start thinking the same back about you.

[The Surrealists then challenged Freddy to tell the difference between an Englishwoman and a Frenchwoman in bed, blindfolded; on two successive days, they sent him two women who used the same perfume. He said he could tell the difference, though he wouldn't tell his nephew how. Without reporting back to the Surrealists, he sailed back to England; on the boat train he met a woman named Kate, whom he married within three months; he never told her about this adventure because she was, he said, "as pure as driven snow." Many years later, Aunt Kate and Uncle Freddy died, and the nephew learned that the Surrealists had often used, in their experiments, an Englishwoman referred to simply as "K."]

Both uncle and nephew insist, against the force of most of our myths, that people behave† differently in bed (even if they are twin sisters,† even if they smell† alike, even if you close your eyes†). And they admit that you want your partner to think that *you* are different in bed. But all of these apparent challenges to the old cliché are then subverted at the end, in two stages. First comes the hint that one of the women, presumably the Englishwoman, was "K.," the "secretive" Aunt Kate, who is therefore not "as pure as driven snow," so that Freddy unknowingly slept with the woman who was to become his own wife.† Then the narrator meets a well-known Master of Wine, a woman, who tells him that if you decant a magnum into two different bottles, "It's extremely rare for even wily drinkers to guess that the wine in those two particular bottles is in fact the same one. People expect all the wines to be different, and their palates therefore insist that they are." (The womanizer in Roald Dahl's "The Visitor" uses the same metaphor for telling women apart in the dark— "A connoisseur, a supreme connoisseur, should always be able to guess the vintage without seeing the label on the bottle"—and is, like Freddy, fooled.) This testimony (significantly, from a woman) that people who hope for difference will find it even in sameness makes us realize that "K." must have been *both* of the women. This means that Freddy is not only incapable of telling a Frenchwoman from an Englishwoman† but incapable of telling his own "pure" wife from a Parisian whore. Barnes is telling us that women are one big sexual magnum (the Magnum Mater?), decanted into containers that only appear to be different—old wine in new (young?) bottles, as we say.

Some bedtricksters pretend to be foreign, and sometimes real foreigners masquerade, their foreignness affording them an incidental advantage. In a broad sense, women† are often foreigners, linguistically and culturally, to the men who marry them and whom they trick. This is true of several bedtricksters in the Hebrew Bible: Ruth, Judah's wife, and Tamar,† as well as Laban,† an Aramean (one commentary makes a pun on that name to make him an Arami, a trickster—with the implication that all foreigners are tricksters).[59] How could Jacob not have known, after seven years, that the older sister had to be married first? This is an example of the political ignorance of the Other that makes foreign sexual masquerades possible, for in several commentaries, Laban's people and Jacob certainly regard one another as foreigners, and the trick takes place "in another country," like fornication in Marlowe's *The Jew of Malta* ("and besides, the wench is dead").

In George Bernard Shaw's *Pygmalion,* the cockney girl masquerading as a noblewoman escapes exposure because the expert mistakes her for a Hungarian—and, therefore, a princess. This trick is reused in *Victor/ Victoria*† (1982), in which the woman pretends to be not just male but a Polish aristocrat who speaks very little English; her gay friend assures her that his/her Polishness will create the necessary "plausible diversion." A similar diversion is employed by the masquerading suitors in Mozart's *Così fan tutte,*† who pretend to be "Albanians." Foreign settings often facilitate bedtricks. Bertram goes to Florence to betray Helena in *All's Well That Ends Well,*† and Celia in *As You Like It,* when she makes her face dirty (to keep from being robbed or raped), calls herself Aliena, literally, "the [female] alien." When the South Indian goddess Gangamma‡ cross-dresses, she also assumes the guise of a foreign ruler, a "prince from an-other place."[60] The gullibility of the squaw† who is tricked by the British soldiers is explained by her foreignness, and much is made, in Richard Strauss's *Arabella,*† of the foreignness of the man who is taken in by the bedtrick.

DOUBLE PENETRATION AGENTS

Thus far we have considered the ways in which political ideologies such as racism, sexism, casteism, Orientalism, and xenophobia—all versions of stereotyping others as groups and denying their individualism—are played out in bedtricks to the advantage of the bedtricksters who are the victims of these political prejudices. Let us now consider the ways in which people in positions of political dominance—spies and dictators—are dis-armed through bedtricks.

The bedtrick is often set in the context of some other (often related) concern that a particular culture may regard as even more basic than sex, such as fraternal succession or political rivalry (an important motive for cuckolding†). Many of the men who replace one another in bed are not sexual enemies but political enemies, and they hide in bed primarily to escape from other dangers (like the two cross-dressing musicians in the film *Some Like It Hot,*† who are running away from gangsters—if we accept this progress narrative). The men who exercise the droit du seigneur† are using political power for sexual ends, but on the other hand, political power (which means, in many traditional cultures, royal power) is often at stake in a bedtrick: many Substitute Brides† care more for ruling than for romance.

Political masqueraders, such as spies, have to be careful because they know that people will be suspicious, will try to find out who they really are; but sexual masqueraders know that their victims will do everything possible to ignore the glaring inconsistencies in their disguises.† On the other hand, spies, knowing that they do not exactly resemble the people they are impersonating, get away with it by keeping other people at a distance, while bedtricksters are subject to a much closer scrutiny. We therefore often expect sex to unmask political masqueraders.

One political form of masquerading is censorship, which our texts use as a metaphor on several levels. Freud used censorship as the metaphor for the mechanism that the superego uses to control the id, for political oppression is closely related to mental repression;† where there is no repression, there is no symbolism. On the level of unconscious symbolism, the superego censors the wish to commit incest,† for instance, with the result that people dream of incest in symbolic forms, often by masquerading in the form of animals;† many of the tales of bedtricks are masked tales of incest.† On the political level, the law censors freedom of speech, resulting in political repression but also in secret plans for revolution. And on the level of language, people use riddles† and myths to express what cannot be said directly for one reason or another. Oppressed people know how to make words have two meanings; they use language simultaneously to satisfy and to defy their oppressors.

The double-backs in "Spy versus Spy" in the old *Mad Comics* grow out of the same Möbius strip logic that pervades the more complex bedtricks: the double-back,† the double-cross,† and the double-play.† The very term for a certain type of spy—"double agent" or, even better, "double penetration agent"—speaks volumes. As Ron Rosenbaum remarked of a "mole" like the great double (or, perhaps, triple) agent Kim Philby: "His entire being, every smile, every word he exchanges, is an intimate violation (an almost sexual penetration) of all those around him. All his friendships, his relationships, his marriages become elaborate lies requiring unceasing vigilance to maintain, lies in a play-within-a-play only he can follow."[61] In this instance, the sexual relationships ("marriages" in the plural, perhaps significantly) are overshadowed by the political deception ("an almost sexual penetration") and the art form (the play-within-a-play†); but the lies can originate in the sexual realm, too, and spill over into the political.

There is a special parallel between the lies of international spying and the lies of transsexual masquerading; the lover of *Victor/Victoria*† (1982), who deals with gangsters and pretends to be operating legally, confesses to the transvestite, "We're both pretenders." In the real-life drama that inspired *M. Butterfly*,† the need for secrecy under the more and more oppressive government of China made it impossible for the French diplomat to spend much time with his Chinese lover, and this made it easier for the lover to deceive him. In those days, too, to be gay posed a particular danger for a public figure like a diplomat, who could be blackmailed; this might have led the Frenchman to channel his same-sex eroticism into his love for a woman who was like a man. Politics conspires with self-delusion and closet sexuality to make the trick work.

A great political/sexual masquerader, allegedly inspired by the life of Vanessa Redgrave, was created by that master of spy fiction John Le Carré in his novel *The Little Drummer Girl*. A British actress named Charlie, a sympathizer with the Zionist cause, fell in love with an Israeli spy named Joseph, who constructed a fictional character for her in order for her to infiltrate a Palestinian terrorist organization: that she was a sympathizer with the Palestinian cause and was in love with an Arab spy named Michel (to be played by Joseph). The doubles began to be unable to distinguish themselves from the originals. Joseph's penetration of the mind and heart of the fictitious Michel was so profound that when Charlie fell in love with Michel, she did not always know whom she was in love with, or which political side she was on. At one point, referring to the characters that they were playing, she asked him, "Do *we* exist as well? Or is it just the other two?" And he replied, "Of course we exist. Why not? We are Berkeleyans, you see. If we do not exist, how can they?" The moment of truth came when Charlie and Joseph finally got into bed together as their original selves: "Suddenly it was clear to her that their whole shared fiction was nothing but foreplay for this night of fact. . . . If she had been blind, she would have known it by his touch; if she had been dying, by his sad victorious smile that conquered terror and unbelief by being there ahead of her; by his instinctive power to know her, and to make her own knowledge more."[62] Charlie's name makes her a kind of sexual double, an androgyne, from the start, as does her old profession (an actress) and her new profession (a spy). The undoubling comes only in bed, with the truth in blindness and touch, the transcending of death through merging with the double, and carnal knowledge† as true knowledge.

"True lies" is a phrase that well expresses the theme of people who masquerade as themselves,† and the film by that name (1994) produces clever, if by now predictable, variations:

TRUE LIES

A spy whose wife thinks he is merely a businessman neglects her. When she becomes bored and depressed, she totters on the brink of an affair with a used-car salesman who pretends to be a spy and claims credit for certain acts, reported in the press, that were actually committed by the husband. To keep his wife happy, the husband trumps up a spy scenario for her to play in and summons her to the hotel room of a mysterious stranger. When she comes to the hotel room, he sits in the dark and plays a tape recording of the voice of a French colleague (knowing that she would recognize his own voice). As he watches her strip, he sees her with fresh lust in his eyes, and then he makes her close her eyes while he kisses her. At this moment, the real spies who are his enemies break in on them, and the seduction does not proceed.

Later, the husband becomes suspicious of his wife's fidelity and has her interrogated as if she were under suspicion for spying; in the course of the interrogation he keeps asking her if she has had an affair with another man and if she loves her husband. In the same way, when the enemy has injected him with truth serum, she takes that opportunity to ask him if he has had an affair with another woman. Together, they kill all the bad guys and live happily ever after.

The husband is a political masquerader from the very start, and when he takes on the sexual masquerade he is impersonating himself, producing a fantasy figure who may be his secret self but is also his wife's fantasy lover. In the hotel room, the play-within-a-play† is recast by "real" spies, political spies (though none of it is very real; when she finally discovers his true profession, she asks him, "Have you ever killed anyone?" to which he replies, with deadpan self-satire, "Yes. But they were all bad."). The lies of spying are used to force sexual truths when husband and wife politically "interrogate" one another about sex. Her shock in finding out that he has been a spy all these years when she didn't know it, that he has not been as intimate with her as she thought, is balanced by his shock in finding out (as he thinks) that she has been unfaithful to him when he didn't know it, that she has not been as intimate with him as he thought. But her shock is grounded in reality—he has indeed lied to her. His is not—she has told the truth. This is an asymmetry† that is all too familiar.

Spying and sex converge when the "bag over her head" is used on captives in war to make them helpless (and, perhaps, feminized): unlike a blindfold, a bag over the head† simultaneously blinds them, constrains their arms, and silences their mouths.[63] A bag is placed over the head of

Bertram's alter ego in Shakespeare's *All's Well That Ends Well*† when Parolles, blindfolded and thinking himself captured by the enemy, betrays his own friends, who are, unknown to him, present (who are, in fact, his captors) and who babble in a hilarious nonsense language. There is a clear parallel between Parolles and Bertram, who, thinking himself captured in Florence by a foreign woman to whom he falsely believes he cannot speak, betrays his own wife, who is, unknown to him, present in the bed, and who does indeed speak his language. Parolles, with a bag over his head, is a grotesque metaphor for blind lust. (I have seen productions in which, to emphasize the parallelism, Diana blindfolds Bertram before Helena appears to take her place.)

Another variant of this trope occurs in Shakespeare's other play about a bedtrick, *Measure for Measure*,† in which, while Angelo is in bed with Mariana, whom he mistakes for someone else (Isabella), the duke, disguised by a hood over his head, allows Lucio to slander the duke to the hooded man, whom Lucio mistakes for someone else (a nonexistent friar). In both plays, as so often, the speech† act and the sexual act are conflated, and a political† betrayal is assimilated to a sexual betrayal. In *Measure for Measure*, moreover, the substitution of Mariana for Isabella is echoed not only in the official substitution of Angelo for the absent duke but in the triple-play substitution of Ragozine's head for Barnadine's head for Claudio's head. When, at the end, the duke proposes to cut off Angelo's head to pay for Angelo's beheading of Claudio (who has not, in fact, been beheaded) and makes him marry Mariana for having raped her (when he thought he was raping Isabella), the surrogations seem to cancel one another out: Angelo's head for Claudio's, Mariana's maidenhead for Isabella's; but also, chiasmically crossing over, Angelo's head for Isabella's maidenhead, a sexual surrogation for a political surrogation.

This same conflation of sexual and political dehumanization in the metaphor of bagging the head occurs in the film *The Crying Game*† (1992). In an early scene, the prisoner, Jody, has a bag over his head, ostensibly so that he will not be able to recognize his kidnappers and later identify them (or the place where they kept him) if they should decide to set him free. But the bag serves another function: it prevents his captors from seeing him as an individual human being, a sight that might make it more difficult for them to murder him. It keeps *them* from seeing *his* face, the face of the Other—as Emmanuel Levinas puts it, the face that says, "Do not kill me."[64] Later, this mutual blindness is mirrored, as in *All's Well*, in a bedtrick: Jody's captor, Fergus, eventually discovers that

Jody's girl, Dill, is in fact a boy. Jody is blindfolded, but Fergus is the one who is blind: he cannot recognize Dill, cannot see Dill's true sexuality, even when he finds him in a gay bar surrounded by obvious transvestites, and even when the bartender says, "There's something you should know about her . . ." When Fergus realizes that he was wrong about Dill's sexuality, he realizes only in retrospect that he was wrong about Jody's sexuality and, perhaps more important, wrong about himself, both politically and sexually: he is not a straight IRA man. The film ends with the blurring of all categories, good and evil, black and white, Irish and English, and male and female. Thus, the bag over Jody's head serves both the same manifest purpose as the bag on Parolles (to blind a political prisoner) and the same latent purpose (to mimic a bedtrick). In both cases, a bedtrick is accompanied by a political trick in which the political victim has a bag put over his head to dehumanize him like the dehumanized woman in the dark.

The bag over the head appears with a twist in the film *Mission: Impossible* (1996), in which the trickster places over his own head a bag *which is actually the mask of his enemy*. He uses this bag to trick the enemy's wife, who has been sleeping with both of them, into revealing an essential secret to the man she thinks is her husband: his plan to kill the hero— the man she is actually talking to. (A similar trick, doubled, was used in the film *Face/Off*‡ [1997].) Once again, sexual and political betrayal wear the same mask.

Pretenders

Like spies, political stand-ins must fool the wife and/or mistress of the original. Films often conflate the "body double" or the stand-in,† who substitutes for a valuable and vulnerable actor in dangerous or strenuous scenes in films, with the stand-in who substitutes, in real life, for equally valuable and vulnerable political dictators; and actors who play dictators in films can use their own cinematic stand-ins, doubles to the third degree.[65] A classic of this genre is *The Prisoner of Zenda*, which began as a novel by Sir Anthony Hope (in 1894) and was filmed several times, first, and best, when Ronald Colman buckled on his swash in the 1937 film directed by John Cromwell, which followed the book quite closely. The plot concerns an English nobleman, Rudolph Rasendel, who is a dead ringer for the rather dissipated king of Ruritania and takes the king's place during an assassination plot. Rasendel also falls in love with Flavia, the future queen of Ruritania, who notices the difference between the two personae but does not realize that they are two different men. In the end, the pretender reveals himself to her and goes back to England.

This is a period piece of British romanticism, in which honor among men easily outweighs love for women—or, to put it differently, politics outweighs sex. When she learns who he really is, Flavia assures Rasendel, "It was always you, never the king . . . I would love you if you were not the king, if you were a humble beggar," and he rejoices when she says she never loved the king until the coronation (when the switch took place). Yet, in the end, she goes for the real king, and her choice is foreshadowed by her belief in the positively transformative effects of a coronation; before she realizes that there are two of them, she explains the difference between the king before and after the Rasendel replacement by saying that he was like Prince Hal in Shakespeare's *Henry IV, Part 1,* who was transformed from an apparent lightweight to a heavy when he became king. She admits, "It might be the crown—I loved you from the coronation." As usual, the impostor is a better man than the original, who learns in the end to imitate his imitator.

Stewart Granger proved only a pale shadow of Colman in 1952, but Peter Sellers created an ingenious comic mirror image in 1979. The happy ending is made possible in this version by two factors not available in the original: the true king's desire not to be king, and his love for a woman other than Flavia. This time the king's double (named Fruen) is not a nobleman but a cockney cabdriver, whose actress mother had been seduced by the king's womanizing father years earlier; the present king, too, is a womanizer (as well as a drunk). At the end, the king is not reconstructed, as in the Colman variant, but returns happily to his old wicked ways in London, and Fruen, now king, drives his cabhorse off into the sunset with Flavia.

Flavia can tell the difference between Fruen and the king, but the king's French mistress can't, because unlike Flavia, she loves the king only for his power, his position. In fact, the mistress's *husband* can't tell the difference, either; he mistakes Fruen not only for the king but for his own wife, when Fruen stumbles into the bed of the Frenchwoman and her husband thinks the form under the covers is his wife. The issue of class is radicalized here: where in the original it was the bond of nobility between the men that made them transcend the desire for the same woman, and the flawed king was regarded as a blot on his class ("letting the side down"), while Rasendel (of the Coldstream Guards) was a credit to it, now the joke is that the impostor is of a far lower class (though he and the king are even more closely related than in the book, sharing not just a distant ancestor but a father) but of far higher morals.

The ultimate degradation of the myth (to use the Eliadean term) came in a 1996 cable TV film entitled *The Prisoner of Zenda, Inc.,* which grafted the plot onto another Hollywood stereotype: the teenage twins (ultimately descended from Hayley Mills in *The Parent Trap* or, behind that, the two young boys in *The Prince and the Pauper*). The resulting bricolage makes the kingdom of Zenda into a billion-dollar computer company (Zenda, Inc.), Ruritania into Berkeley, the king a teenage nerd† (named Rudi) whose father has just died and left him the company, and the look-alike a jock, a champion baseball player (named Ollie) whose father is out of work. When, after the trick has been revealed, Fiona (i.e., Flavia) asks Ollie, "When you said you wanted to get to know me better, were you talking as Rudi or Ollie?" he makes no reply, and she indicates to her girlfriend that she likes them both. No sex here (even in the older genera- tion: Ollie and Rudi are unrelated, just chance ringers) and no conflict (Ollie and Rudi become friends, promising to teach one another about computers and baseball and, presumably, to share Fiona, as friends). The final line is "This could be the beginning of a really cool friendship." I wonder if anyone young enough to sit through this movie (for pleasure rather than research) would recognize the variant of the final line from *Casablanca* (1942).

The Zenda formula, without the name, was used again in 1988 in *Moon over Parador,* in which a look-alike actor impersonates a South American dictator after his sudden death. The dictator's mistress recognizes him immediately as an impostor—and proceeds to teach him the "expressions and gestures" of the real man, whom, she points out, she knew better than anyone else. When the press asks her if she approves of the ways in which he has changed (he suddenly "lost" twenty pounds and made politi- cal reforms), she replies with the usual ambiguous line: "He's certainly not the same man I first met." As in the original Zenda scenario, the impostor decides to return to his old life; but now the mistress becomes the new—and benevolent—dictator, and the impostor (better than the original) improves the system (by instituting a number of reforms) before he leaves it. This is after all the people's dream: get Nixon out and put in his place a guy who looks just like Nixon but is actually Abraham Lincoln† (or Lenin or St. Francis, depending upon your taste).

Class and power here supply yet another reason for the political or sexual masquerade to succeed: when those with power masquerade, the weak, who are doubly victimized (by the system and by the trickster), are forced to pretend to be fooled. The servants immediately notice that the dictator has been replaced by a surrogate; in the servants' hall they say, "It's not him. The walk is different. The eyes, too innocent. The hands of a peasant." But then one of them declares, "I don't care who I serve. When they say he's a dictator and he acts like a dictator, what's the difference?" Fearing that they will be killed if they tell the truth, they keep their mouths shut. The perpetrators of the masquerade are counting on this, too, for when the actor forced to play the dictator worries, "Somebody's gonna know," they tell him, "Knowing and saying are two different things."

The same plot was used yet again in *Dave* (1993), in which a look-alike replaces the womanizing president of the United States when he is permanently incapacitated by a stroke. David Ansen remarked that "Screenwriter Gary ('Big') Ross may have borrowed his look-alike premise from 'The Prince and the Pauper' and 'The Prisoner of Zenda,' but *Dave* is delightful proof that old fables can be wittily recycled."[66] Terrence Rafferty spelled out the new variations on the old formula: "When the First Lady finds herself attracted to Dave, what she's falling for is an airbrushed version of her husband—the man she once loved, but new and improved, with all the flaws and scars of their disillusioning years together magically eliminated. 'Dave' encourages us to dream about turning back the clock on corrupted government (by means of a rededication to old-fashioned American idealism and common sense) and on soured love (by means of something that amounts to moral cosmetic surgery)."[67] It also encourages us to "turn back the clock" to the notorious adulteries of Jack Kennedy (or, as the case may be, to turn it forward to those of Bill Clinton). The romantic fantasy of the First Lady is not that her husband is another man but that he is the man he used to be (restored by the spiritual face-lift,† "moral cosmetic surgery"), and that he sees her as the woman she used to be. Like the impostor in the film *Sommersby*,† the good-guy impostor is held responsible for crimes that the real president committed; the solution here is to bring back the real president (in a coma) and let him die for his own crimes.

The Zenda theme continued to be recycled. Between the Colman (1937) and Granger (1952) takes of Zenda came World War II, which inspired a subcorpus of political/sexual masquerades linked to the invasion of Normandy. In *The Man Who Never Was* (1955), the Allies use a double to fool the Nazis about the invasion. In *The Eagle Has Landed*

(1977), a Nazi attempt to kidnap Churchill almost succeeds—except that the Nazis capture only Churchill's double, who is in Ireland while the real Churchill is in Teheran; many lives are lost, all for a phantom Churchill. Danny Kaye doubled himself both in *Wonder Man* (1945) and in *On the Riviera* (1951), in which the wife of a French aviator (Kaye) for whom a cabaret artist (Kaye) doubles wakes up happy one morning but then has a moment of panic when she thinks (wrongly) that she slept with the double. In 1961, Kaye took a shot at the Normandy/Zenda formula, impersonating a general in *On the Double;* like the pretenders in *Dave* and the Sellers version of *Zenda,* the double loves the wife of the original, while the original (a notorious womanizer) does not. The wife immediately knows he isn't her husband and calls for the military police, who are in on the masquerade. When the impostor confesses his failure to them, saying, "I guess I didn't fool her at all," one soldier replies, "Don't worry, sir. The general never does either." As in the post-Zenda variants, the original conveniently disappears (the general gets killed) and the double gets the girl. In Olivia Goldsmith's *Switcheroo,* the sexual implications of the political masquerade in this genre were taken for granted by the wife who plotted to masquerade as her husband's mistress, inspired by "those World War II films her dad always watched where someone like Gregory Peck would have to go behind enemy lines and impersonate the Nazi general because of a coincidental resemblance; then you'd see army intelligence tutoring Peck in German, giving him a dueling scar, and briefing him on all the general's personal habits."[68]

There are also historical instances of political pretenders to various thrones who had to pass sexual muster with the wife of the true heir. In 1591, Dimitri, the third son of Ivan the Terrible, was murdered, presumably by Boris Godunov. Dimitri had married a Polish noblewoman named Marina Mnishek only a few days before his death, and Marina and her father were not allowed to return to Poland after his death. But in 1607 a pretender arose saying he was Tsar Dimitri, who had never been slain. He wrote affectionate letters to Marina as to his wife, and her father made her pretend that this man was her husband. Some sources say he did such a good imitation of Dimitri that Marina welcomed him to her bed and stayed with him until he was murdered on December 10, 1610.[69] If we assume, with most historians, that the Dimitri who appeared in 1607 was a pretender, then it seems that his wife knowingly allowed herself to be fooled,† presumably feeling "that any live husband was going to do more for her than a dead one."[70]

The false tsar resurfaced in this century in Lenin, Hitler, and Stalin, who were believed to have had doubles, both to divert assassins[71] and to extend the range of public appearances, to stand in when the original had two appointments in the same place or was ill. The idea of the doubles for each of the three dictators inspired satires. Salman Rushdie conjured up a Jewish Marxist who imported to the Jewish settlement in Cochin not one but seven Lenins, like the seven dwarves: the too tall Lenin, the too short, too fat, too skinny, too lame, too bald, and toothless Lenins.[72] A satirist in *Punch* (February 7, 1940) suggested that Hitler had used a stand-in since his rise to power to take his place at ceremonies and polite functions "that not even dictators can wholly avoid." Stalin apparently eventually purged his doubles, but an inspired satire fantasizes about the Stalin doubles, more precisely about the "first annual meeting of the Stalin's Doubles (ret.) Association . . . in the autumn of 1953" and its subsequent meetings until 1956.[73] According to this spoof, the imperson-ation of Stalin by people who did not really resemble him, even by a woman ("she would scarcely have been recognized as a former look-alike at all, now that she had ungummed her mustache and gone in for a blond perm, were it not for a certain squareness about the jaw and coldness in the eyes"), was made possible by the fact that no one ever really looked at Stalin himself ("After all, His image was known only through idealized portraits and touched-up photographs, plus the occasional blurry news film, so no one expected a Stalin in person to resemble the iconic version too exactly"). This inverts the more common sexual masquerade, where the original is a woman or foreigner too low to be noticed; here we are reminded of the widespread taboos against looking at a king or a god, or the argument about the multiple Helens,‡ who were so high, so ideal-ized, that they resembled all women. But the essential irony in this text is in the suggestion that all, or most, of Stalin's evil acts were committed by his doubles: "Looking back, we realized we had been given quite a free hand in the construction of the role, and possibly we had exaggerated the bloodthirstiness. In fact, on reflection, we doubles had been responsible for a number of the more tragic aspects of that sorry era. It might have been that Stalin Himself was reasonably gentle."[74] This is a cynical inver-sion of the already cynical general rule that political doubles are better than the originals that they replace. In *Face/Off,*‡ the political double is better than the original, in *both* directions: when the evil terrorist imper-sonates the virtuous FBI man, he is nicer to his staff (gay and playful where the original was somber and obsessed) and to his wife (sexier and,

again, more playful); while the virtuous FBI man is better than the terrorist when he plays the terrorist: he sometimes lets people go (especially
FBI agents whom he knows) instead of shooting them.

Pretending to Be an American in Hollywood

The flawless copies that are achieved by magic in myths are achieved by
science in science fiction films: artificial intelligence and machines that
masquerade as people (robots and clones). The perfect replication of the
robots or clones forces people to rely upon super- (or, more often, in-
fra-) scientific senses, such as the heart and other instinctive, somatic†
forms of knowing, to detect modern masqueraders. Fritz Lang's *Metropolis* (1926) makes use of the sexual double (a robot clone of the heroine)
who fools everyone except the man who loves her, a role later played by
the robot in *Blade Runner* (1982) and the Borg in *Star Trek*. Later films
depict elaborate computer techniques used to program memory banks
to steal the victims' minds,† including their memories† and identifying
knowledge,† and give them to the tricksters. The great classic of this genre
is the 1956 film

Invasion of the Body Snatchers

Seed pods from outer space land in a small town and begin to replace its
inhabitants one by one. One of the few people who realize what is going
on complains of a familiar character who has been replaced, "He looks,
sounds, acts, and remembers" like the original. When Miles proposes that
they test an alleged clone's memory by having his suspicious friend ask
him about "certain things that only you and he remember," the suspect
performs perfectly. "No one could impersonate him without you knowing.
There are a thousand little things you'd notice," insists Miles; but the
thousand little things, such as scars and fingerprints, are in place or can
be accounted for. Only the actual discovery of the clones being formed
in the pods persuades the doubters.

At the start of the film, Miles says, jokingly, to Becky Driscoll, "I'd
hate to wake up one morning and find that you weren't you" (a presumptuous remark, since they have not yet been intimate and there is no reason
for him to expect to "wake up" with her at all). "How can you tell?" she
asks, flirtatiously. "You really want to know?" he asks, and thereupon
kisses her thoroughly, smiles, and says, "Mmmmm. You're Becky Driscoll." They become lovers, though they do not marry. At the end of the
film, Becky falls asleep and a clone takes over her body. Miles does not
notice her change at first, but then she falls, and he falls on top of her

and kisses her, and a look of shock and horror passes over his face. He is speechless, but his eyes tell her (and us) that he knows. She shouts to the other clones, betraying him, and he runs away. When he tells his story later, he says, "I've been afraid a lot of times in my life, but I didn't know the real meaning of fear until I'd kissed Becky."

The film carefully constructs and then deconstructs all of the evidence and finally throws it all away for a kiss. The protagonist is a doctor, portrayed with all the fifties' confidence in a man of science (though the clone psychiatrist debunks his suspicions by saying, "Doctors can hallucinate, too."). But the doctor is outscienced by the science of the invading aliens.

The clones' lack of emotion is a clue to the film's function as a thinly veiled anti-Communist tract. The possessed hand over their minds to Mars; that is, they become mesmerized by a message from Moscow; the anti–Communist Party line traditionally depicted Communists as emotionless (recall the deadpan Garbo in *Ninotchka* [1939]). One woman knows that her uncle is not her uncle, despite overwhelming evidence that he is, because "there used to be a special look in his eyes," and that look is now gone. Another insists that "the feeling is different," though this is neutralized by a (clone) psychiatrist who discredits the evidence for clones by saying, "Don't try to rationalize everything" and "The trouble is inside you." The flaw is thrown back at the questioner when someone who begins to be concerned about the clones is told, instead, to "worry about what's going on in the world." (The cliché lives on in the Animorph books, by K. A. Applegate, in which sluglike evil aliens "crawl into the ears of other beings and take over their minds. There is no outward sign that a person is possessed by a slug, except for an occasional cold emotional falseness.")[75]

That the psychiatrist is one of the villains makes this another skirmish in the ongoing duel between Karl ("The trouble is in society") Marx and Sigmund ("The trouble is inside you") Freud; that the psychiatrist is Jewish adds to the American scenario of Jewish/intellectual/Communist aliens, a scenario in which (Jewish) Marxists and Freudians, one another's enemies on one level, are depicted together as the enemies of the Right on another. ("Brainwashing" is, after all, just a stone's throw, and I do mean a stone's throw, from "headshrinking.") The Nazis whom *we* invaded by doubling, in the Normandy-invasion genre of pretender films, here give way to the far more subtle, and more threatening, invasion of *us* by *them*, the Reds. The body snatchers, the Blob, the Thing, became, in the 1950s, a common metaphor for the (Russian) controllers of Communist zombies. The aliens/Jews are foreigners, marginal figures who invade planet Earth just as they invade our minds. (That *Invasion of the Body Snatchers* was also read, by liberals, as a tract against the spread of McCarthyism, with the clones as McCarthyites, Red-baiters, is a testimony to the chameleon powers of myth.)[76] What "paranoid gothic"[77] was for those in the sexual closet, paranoid bourgeois was for anti-Communist witch-hunters.

The fear seems to be that aliens are out to strip Americans of the emotional life that makes us who we are. One of the born-again clones argues the body snatchers' case: "You're reborn into an untroubled world—there's no need for love, no emotions. You've been in love before; it didn't last; it never does." True enough; but the hero's girl, Becky—before she is corrupted—defends the world of love and grief and, above all, difference: for all the clones are the same. The political assumption that the clones have no feelings supports the mythological belief that the hero's sexual feeling about his girl is the only true test of her identity. The fact that Becky sleeps with Miles before she gets the ring on her finger is a vital clue, for in 1950s films, girls who "do it" before marriage are bad girls, and alien invasions ultimately function, like Old Testament plagues, to bury Sodomy and Orgy in fire and brimstone. Therefore, we should not be surprised when Becky falls asleep† and is possessed by the aliens. The one absolutely reliable standard of knowledge, as applied even to Communists/clones, is the kiss,† which in this case turns out to be the "brave kiss,"† the knight's test of courage; Miles's immortal comment "I didn't know the real meaning of fear until I'd kissed Becky" echoes the line spoken by the masquerading Siegfried† after he has awakened Brunhilde with a kiss: "You alone have taught me what fear is."[78]

An update of *Invasion of the Body Snatchers* was made in 1978, with Kevin McCarthy in a different role. And a film by a different title, *They Live*, made in 1988, is a remake with an inverted political agenda: the aliens are Reaganite entrepreneurs and yuppies who quote lines from Reagan's 1984 reelection "Morning in America" speech verbatim, and the resistors say, "They're saying we're a bunch of Commmies." A brainwashing, mind-bending television station sends out rays that keep people from seeing the truth (seeing who is and is not an alien) unless they wear magic sunglasses and contact lenses. The hero's girl is not an alien but she defects to their side, and the sexual act is, again, where the final unmasking takes place. In the final scene, we see another man and woman in bed making love, with the woman on top. Suddenly the brainwashing television station is destroyed, and she looks down and sees him as he really is, an alien. When she stops pumping, he looks up and says, "What's wrong, baby?" End of film.

Let us conclude this brief foray into Hollywood films about Communist and other political masquerades by jumping out of the frame to consider the masquerades necessitated in Hollywood itself, during the McCarthy era, by the blacklisting (my mother used to call it redlisting) of writers and actors accused of being Communist Party members or sympathizers. Several writers and actors who had been blacklisted made a self-referential film in 1976, *The Front,* in which a semiliterate and politically ignorant man making a bare living as a cashier and bookie agrees to pretend to be the author of television scripts written by a friend of his who has been blacklisted; later he also fronts for other writers. He falls in love with a left-wing woman who edits the television show that buys "his" scripts, and she with him, but they begin to fight when he does not express the political sentiments she expects from the scripts. Eventually he begins to live the part, stands up to the House Un-American Activities Committee, and is jailed for contempt of court.

The front's quandary is the double-bind† of Christian, the soldier who speaks Cyrano's† lines: he can't get the girl by being himself, for she admires artists and first loves him for his scripts (in defense of his deception, he points out to her that she wouldn't be caught dead in bed with a cashier). But he knows she loves someone else even while believing she loves him; she says she loves the writer but not the man. (There is a hidden inversion here: where, in Cyrano, the writer was ugly and the soldier handsome, here the writer is played by Michael Murphy, the usual handsome straight man in Woody Allen films, and the front is Woody Allen, who usually plays the nerdy intellectual who gets the gorgeous women.) The solution is for him to become, at least partly, the person he pretends to be (a left-wing writer): though he cannot become a writer (like Christian, he is occasionally trapped in awkward situations where he cannot produce the lines expected of him), he can at least become left-wing. Thus, the fragmentation of the original (the separation of politics from aesthetics) allows the surrogate to remain simultaneously himself (semiliterate) and the man she loves (left-wing).

Approach Seven

Weapons of the Weak

Certain issues central to the discipline known as "critical studies," particularly to its postcolonial branch, pervade this corpus. Class raises its ugly head throughout the texts of bedtricks: the Family Romance,† after all, is predicated on the child's fantasy that his true parents are of more noble birth, a higher class, than his apparent parents. The more specific use of class power in the droit du seigneur† inspires many bedtricks: Figaro,† subverting both the droit du seigneur and the paradigm of the servant who perpetrates the bedtrick on his master's behalf, plots to bedtrick his master. And the secret of the caste takes the place of the secret of the name† in one Indian variant of the story of the snake lover:† a snake has two wives, one of whom, choosing to lose her husband rather than share him, incites the other to ask the tabooed question that drives him away forever: what is his caste?[79]

Class influences the form that sexual fantasies take in these stories. A man may fantasize, hypergamously (i.e., in a marriage system in which the husband is of a higher class than the wife), that he is in bed with a whore (like Judah with Tamar†); or a woman may fantasize that her husband is in bed with a whore, as in the story that a woman told of the snake lover† in which an "upper-class† woman's fear of the rivalry of a supposedly more vigorous lower-class woman is also evident. . . . Her rival ends up as her servant, hauling water to her door."[80] Or a man may fantasize, hypogamously (in a system with the husband lower than the wife), that he will win a princess. The woman, too, may fantasize about the lower classes (the Oliver Mellors scenario, seducing the gatekeeper or the stableboy, the *diritto della signora*†) or dream that someday her prince will come. Class is a factor for both in both directions.

Class can trump gender in a transsexual bedtrick. In *Some Like It Hot*† (1959), the men who masquerade as women try to act so upper class, so grotesquely la-dee-da (they pose as graduates of a ladies' conservatory), that the down-to-earth types in the band attribute much of the masqueraders' inconsistent behavior and weird appearance to their class affectations. "They're real ladies," says the male manager of the band, in answer to the female manager's comment "There's something funny about those new girls." Just as age† can mask gender (a woman pretending to be a man can explain the inconsistencies of voice and height by pretending to be a young boy), so class can mask gender: the refinements of upper-class men (or any Englishmen, for Americans) may be coded as "feminine" for the lower classes, and so a woman pretending to be a man can explain her femininity as a quality of class. Contrariwise, the woman in boots and jodhpurs, carrying a whip, is regarded as sexy if she is upper class, but masculine, butch, or into S & M if she is middle or lower class. A woman usually rises in status when she cross-dresses within her own class, gaining freedom and a voice; but she may explicitly masquerade as a man of a lower class, as when *Queen Christina* (1933) goes slumming as a man. Men more often cross-dress as upper-class women (*Some Like It Hot*, Dame Edna, *Tootsie* [1982]).

Different stories express different attitudes to the dominant power, subverting or upholding either pole of any of the many oppositions at play in the bedtrick. Both the dominant ideal and the subversive ideal may be expressed in the same story. Sometimes the story may begin with subversion but end by capitulating to the traditional paradigm; sometimes the reverse.[81] And considerations of class offer an answer to questions that may occur to anyone who reads or hears these stories: Why is it permissible for the hero (or, more often, the heroine) to lie? Why does a culture that endorses the telling of truth (as most cultures do) tell these stories? Why do certain cultures set forth masquerade and deception as a good thing? The answer lies, I think, in our sympathies: we are on the side of the survivor, and the survivor, who is often an underdog, weak in status if not necessarily weak in physical power, must survive through the power of her wits, the power of language, the power, in short, to tell a good story. The stories,† made of words, appreciate people who make words work for them. It might also be noted that a tradition often repudiates the trickery that was necessary *in illo tempore*, distancing itself from the emergency of the founding when the ends justified the means; thus, the rabbis point out that the tricks played by and against Jacob† took place before the Jews were given the Torah.

Isaac Bashevis Singer discusses the theme of Jewish masquerades in *Enemies, A Love Story*:

> The Jew had always managed to smuggle his way in through crime and madness. He had stolen into Canaan and into Egypt. Abraham had pretended that Sarah was his sister. The whole two thousand years of exile, beginning with Alexandria, Babylon, and Rome and ending in the ghettos of Warsaw, Lodz, and Vilna, had been one great act of smuggling. The Bible, the Talmud, and the Commentaries instruct the Jew in one strategy:

flee from evil, hide from danger, avoid showdowns, give the angry powers of the universe as wide a berth as possible.[82]

It has been said that tyrants make liars. Singer seems to be saying that Gentile tyrants made Jewish masqueraders.

We can take Singer's insights into Jewish masqueraders and weave them back into our more general fabric of bedtricks throughout the world. Not merely women and children, but also Outcastes and servants and, above all, foreigners, Others, are depicted as tricksters. The weak have to lie and trick because they lack the power to win in a direct confrontation. This is particularly true of women. In fact (and here we may note yet another asymmetry†), while men are more often depicted as tricksters of a general nature,[83] women are more often depicted as sexual tricksters.‡

Thus, the dishonesty of the trickster is justified, in the texts, by the need to subvert oppression. As Susan Gillman notes of the mother in Mark Twain's *Pudd'nhead Wilson,*† "Assuming false roles, then, as both she and her son repeatedly do, is a learned response in this slave society, perhaps most of all for those who have historically been the victims, not the perpetrators, of the 'fiction of law and custom' that defines racial identity."[84] Twain gives us the key in the motto at the very start of the book: "Tell the truth or trump—but get the trick."

The mental rigidity of the oppressor becomes a means of resistance by the oppressed, who are able to use ruse, a weapon of the weak (to use James Scott's term),[85] against naked force, to "pass" because their survival depends on their powers of observation and role-playing. The masquerade succeeds because the victim of the masquerade, the oppressor of the masquerader, believes that "they are all alike," an attitude that gives the underdog the tool with which to subvert: if you think we all look alike, we can fool you. The weak use their wits, as storytellers use their traditional texts, like judo techniques to make the big bullies throw themselves. Before fingerprinting,† lower-class people were often able, by virtue of their illiteracy, to duck under the radar of police identification.[86] (Though the rich and powerful resemble one another, too: commenting on a news item about a man who wore a mask that was "a likeness of Ronald Reagan or Richard Nixon, but investigators weren't sure which," the *New Yorker* commented: "Republicans all look alike to us, too.")[87]

The weak wield their weakness as a weapon in *Revenge of the Nerds* (1984), in which our heroes the nerds† (intellectuals, Jews, and blacks, who are grotesquely victimized by the fascist jock fraternity boys) use their brains to overcome the brawn of their enemies, thus reaping not only political but sexual revenge:

REVENGE OF THE NERDS

At the college homecoming celebration, the nerds, led by Lewis, and the jocks, led by Stan, set up competing kissing stands. When Lewis approaches Stan's girlfriend, Betty, who is selling kisses for the jocks, she scorns him, saying, "I'm not kissing a nerd," and Stan produces a surrogate in her place: a very fat girl. When Lewis sees Betty wander off into the House of Mirrors, he puts on the cloak and mask that Stan has been wearing and follows Betty into the House of Mirrors. As they begin to make love, she says, "Take off your mask," but he shakes his head in refusal, to which she simply remarks, "Oh Stan, you're so kinky." Later, aglow with happiness, she says, "Oh Stan, that was wonderful. You did things to me you've never done before." At that, Lewis takes off his mask and she screams, "You're that nerd!" "Yeah." "God, you were wonderful. Are all nerds as good as you?" "I guess." "Why?" "All jocks think about is sports; all we think about is sex." She gives Stan's frat pin back to him, saying, "I'm in love with a nerd!" and runs off after Lewis.

Like Woody Allen in *The Front*,† the nerd takes the place of the hunk and gets the girl. There is the vestige of a double-cross† here: Lewis's substitution of himself for Stan with Betty pays Stan back for substituting a fat girl—one of several stereotyped scapegoats—for Betty with Lewis. Stan's emasculation, the inversion of his sexual power, is underscored by the fact that, at the moment when Betty ditches him for the second and final time, he is in drag: for the stage performance at the end of the homecoming celebration, the jocks have dressed as pompom girls and the girls as football players. But there is a subversion of political power as well: the nerd who steals the jock's girl simultaneously seizes his office. He does this with the help of the physically powerful branch of the nerds' fraternity, who are black, a racial stereotype employed in the interest of the intellectual stereotype of the nerd; this sort of bigotry, too, travels down the line. There is mythology here: the inversion takes place on the Moon Walk in the House of Mirrors† (Betty asks the masked Lewis, "You wanna do it on the moon?"), with Lewis wearing the mythologically charged mask and cloak of Darth Vader (the evil father from *Star Wars*). Lewis's heavy breathing inside the mask simultaneously conveys Darth Vader's telltale personal noise (like the ticking of the clock inside the crocodile in Peter Pan) and Lewis's sexual excitement, like the double meaning of the heavy breathing of the two men dying and climaxing in *Excalibur*† (1981). And there is the less magical mythology of all bedtricks: the jocks and their girlfriends always look right through the nerd without noticing him. At first, when Betty tells Stan, "One of those nerds asked me out," and he asks, "Which one?" she replies, "I don't know; they all look alike to me." (Even the father of one of the nerds says to him, "You college guys are all alike; all you care about is getting laid.") But Lewis reverses the stereotype when, in his moment of triumph, he maintains that *all* nerds are good in bed, in the dark. By the time he is unmasked, Betty is already in his sexual thrall, having learned that beauty† may or may not be truth, but it isn't sex.

It is impossible to write about sex in the post-Foucault era without an awareness of the ways in which sex and power masquerade as one another.[88] Henry Kissinger's famous aphorism, that power is a great aphrodisiac, is just one-half of a greater truth, for sex is also a powerful political tool. Politics may make strange bedfellows, but bedfellows make even stranger politicians. Paula Jones's alleged identification of the exact configuration of the presidential genitals† *when erect* posed a political, more than a sexual, problem for the president. Oscar Wilde's† famous line about sexual surrogation and transposition ("To have lost one parent might be considered a misfortune, but to have lost two seems like carelessness"†) is transposed into the political realm in Tom Stoppard's *Travesties* when Lenin says, "To lose one revolution might be considered unfortunate; to lose two looks like carelessness."[89]

The mythology of the bedtrick plays upon the complex tension between the power inherent in knowledge† (which is the weapon of the trickster) and political power (which may or may not be the weapon of the victim). Knowledge often results from power, for those in power can force others to reveal themselves; and power often results from knowledge, when knowledge is used to manipulate, to blackmail, and so forth. But often the dominator does not need to know anything about the objects of domination in order to dominate; power and ignorance may coexist. And ignorance (false or real) may occasionally serve the interests of power, as Eve Sedgwick points out:

> Knowledge, after all, is not itself power, although it is the magnetic field of power. Ignorance and opacity collude or compete with knowledge in mobilizing the flows of energy, desire, goods, meanings, persons. . . . The epistemological asymmetry of the laws that govern rape, for instance,

privileges at the same time men and ignorance, inasmuch as it matters not
at all what the raped woman perceives or wants just so long as the man
raping her can claim not to have noticed (ignorance in which male sexuality
receives careful education).[90]

The myths, however, also argue that knowledge is the weapon of the
weak against the strong. Ignorance on the part of the dominators may
deprive them of the power to dominate; their ignorance of the other may
render the powerful weak. The bedtrickster—Tamar,† Song in *M. Butterfly*†—wins by having knowledge that the victim lacks. And it is essential
for the weak not only to understand the powerful, to know their enemies,
but to *tell them apart*, as Sedgwick acknowledges: "It was the long, painful
realization, *not* that all oppressions are congruent, but that they are *differently* structured and so must intersect in complex embodiments that was
the first great heuristic breakthrough of socialist-feminist thought and of
the thought of women of color."[91] In myth, as in life, knowledge, not
ignorance, is power, and knowledge of *difference* is the key to both sex
and politics.

EIGHT

Cross-Cultural
Cross-Dressing

Some myths ask, How do you tell a human from a god or an animal in bed? Others ask, How do you tell one human from another in bed? Now let us consider myths that ask, How do you tell a man from a woman in bed? Many bedtricks involve transformations into someone of the other biological sex, with different physical sexual organs, and I would call these transsexual bedtricks. The story of Parvati and the demon Adi† is such a story, as is the transsexual masquerade that takes place when Vishnu takes the form of a woman, Mohini, in order to seduce, and kill, certain demons; Shiva is also overcome with lust for Vishnu/Mohini and, in some texts, rapes her.‡[1] David Shulman sees the androgyny of both Shiva and the goddess as interdependent: "The goddess always has the male inside her, while she is somewhere inside of him. . . . If one gender is thus effectively wrapped inside the other, largely deriving from the other, we would perhaps do better to think of gender generally as an infinite concentric regress, male within female within male within female. . . ."[2] This regress leads us to what I will call the double-back-cross-dress, the double-back-cross-dress-play, and the double-cross-dress-back-play.†

Such stories of transsexual transformation‡ are, like so many myths, exaggerations of or fantasies on a more realistic theme, in this case the theme of transvestite bedtricks, which may be said to take place when someone of one sex and/or gender is perceived by a sexual partner as being of a different sex and/or gender. It is this aspect of the bedtrick, involving transformations of gender rather than of sex, the bedtrick made possible merely by a change of clothing and makeup—in a word, cross-dressing—that will be my concern in this chapter.

CROSS-DRESSING TO KILL

In the *Mahabharata,* men who masquerade as women generally do so to get close to men, not to women, for martial, rather than sexual, reasons, and are therefore almost always depicted as lethal. The final, fatal masquerade in the epic takes place when the adolescent boy Samba, son of Krishna,† dresses in women's clothes and pretends to be pregnant in order to tease a group of elderly (male) sages. As a result of this prank, he is cursed to give birth magically to a big iron club, surely phallic, through which the entire race of the heroes of the *Mahabharata* is massacred.[3]

But before that happens, a transvestite bedtrick in the fourth book of the *Mahabharata* reveals the grim sadism of a veiled same-sex attack. This is yet another story of a bedtrick invented to avoid the exercise of the droit du seigneur.† The rapist in this story misses the same double entendre that Yavakri† missed: "I bet you've never 'cooked'/touched a woman like this before." But where Yavakri wielded the power of a Brahmin, this story is about the power of a general. It takes place at the court of Virata, where the hero Arjuna‡ is disguised as a transvestite dancing master, his brother Bhima as the cook, and their joint wife, the princess Draupadi,† as the queen's personal maid:

KICAKA IN BED WITH BHIMA

The evil general Kicaka harassed Draupadi until he forced her to agree to an assignation. But she told her strong and headstrong husband Bhima, who went to the palace in the night ahead of Kicaka, lay down on the bed, and covered himself up, awaiting him like a lion awaiting a deer. Kicaka, dressed up in his finest to meet Draupadi, entered the dark room; deluded by lust, mad with joy, smiling, he approached Bhima, who said, "I bet you've never before known a touch like this, which you will appreciate because you are a man of the world, clever in the ways of lovemaking."

Then Bhima jumped up and laughed and grabbed Kicaka by his perfumed hair and beat him to death; long after Kicaka had ceased to move Bhima beat him, until all his bones were broken and he was a shapeless mass of flesh. Then he called Draupadi and showed her what was left of Kicaka, and she rejoiced and called the people and said, "Here lies Kicaka, who was deluded by his lust for other men's wives and has been slain by my husband." People came by the thousands and saw Kicaka lying there, covered with blood, and they said, "Where is his neck? His arms? His hands? His head?"[4]

The rapist becomes the victim of the bedtrick and experiences a double shock, which sweetens the bedtrickster's revenge, adding insult to injury: first the shock of sexual betrayal and rejection and then the shock of the terror of death. Not only is he not going to get laid, he is going to get killed. And the trickster who inflicts this double punishment is doubly disguised: first as a cook and then as Draupadi. The ultimate revenge on the promiscuous womanizer who cannot tell the difference between one woman and another is to mutilate him so that no one can recognize him as a human being, let alone a particular individual. He becomes a symbol of the chaos that is threatened by the erasure of sexual boundaries. (The same sort of ball of flesh is produced when two queens mate after the death of their husband the king[5]—here the product of female, rather than male, same-sex union.) This episode became a kind of sexual parable in Hinduism. The otherwise quite permissive *Kamasutra* invokes Kicaka with Draupadi as an example of a man destroyed by desire, comparing him to Indra with Ahalya‡ and Ravana with Sita;‡ elsewhere it cites him as the paradigmatic victim of a sexual trick carried out by someone in someone else's form and compares his deception by Bhima with Rama's deception by Shurpanakha.†[6]

The transvestite masquerade has a different, but still ostensibly non-sexual, motive in a story told in several Sanskrit, Tibetan, and Bengali variants. The following version is from a twentieth-century Bengali Buddhist text:

THE REVENGE OF KABIKUMAR

King Satyarata of Kampila had two wives who bore him two sons, named Alolamantra and Kabikumar. Since it was predicted that Kabikumar would kill Alolamantra, the king ordered his minister to get rid of Kabikumar. The minister put a girl in Kabikumar's place before the execution and entrusted Kabikumar to a fisherman. Kabikumar grew up incognito until he heard that Alolamantra was now the king. To win back the kingdom and take revenge on his enemies he traveled to the city of Kampila, where he assumed the form of a dancer so beautiful that she captivated all the people of the city with her performance. The king heard of her skill in dance and music and traveled with his ministers to see her; when he saw Kabikumar's beguiling dance, he thought he was like Vishnu in the form of Mohini, who stole back the nectar for the gods. The dots of perspiration on her body watered his tree of lust. That evening the king gave the dancer a prize of fine gems and brought her back to his home like a man in his dying hour who craves what will harm him.

In seclusion, the dancer became the very essence of Death as the lover of the impatient, undisciplined king. And so, when the king climbed into bed for a long sleep, Kabikumar shed the form of the dancer and said, "Your greed made you keep the fruits of kingship for yourself. I want revenge." Then Kabikumar imprisoned the king and gained the kingdom. But he soon began to fear his own defeat and stoned the king to death without mercy. Kabikumar enjoyed the fortunes of sovereignty but proceeded to hell when he died, because he was smeared with the blood of fratricide.[7]

This is the Family Romance,† complete with competing co-wives† and uncomfortable incestuous overtones. There is, however, a twist: a girl is sacrificed in her brother's place (as a girl was killed in place of the infant Krishna),[8] a surrogation that feminizes Kabikumar from the start. When he becomes a deadly dancing girl he is unraveling the image of the girl who died for him. The motif of the Lovely Lady, too, is given a new turn and explicitly assimilated to the myth of Mohini,‡ the transsexual enchantress (Vishnu in a female form): when the king likens the dancer to Mohini, he is saying more than he knows, for, like Mohini, she is a male disguised in order to kill.

The murderous transvestite is a Hollywood mytheme, too, epitomized in Alfred Hitchcock's *Psycho* (1960), in which a man masquerades as his mother (a double inversion of the story of the mother who masquerades as her daughter†) and murders a beautiful woman in a shower. *Psycho* has had many imitators, such as Brian de Palma's *Dressed to Kill* (1980), which begins with a woman in a shower, though the murder, by a man in drag, takes place later in an elevator. In Roman Polanski's *Bitter Moon* (1992), a woman on a ship lures a man to her room in the dark, where he finds the husband in the bed instead.

Like male-to-female (MTF) cross-dressers, FTM transvestites can be both lethal and comic, sometimes at the same time. The Chinese tale of Shang Sanguan is a kind of mirror image of the Indian story of Kabikumar, for the story seems to combine and invert two premises: that the woman must become a man to kill a man in revenge in battle (as when Amba becomes Shikhandin‡); and that a man must become a woman to kill a man in revenge in bed (as Kabikumar becomes a dancing girl). This early-eighteenth-century Chinese text, however, assumes that to have access to the murderer the girl must become a boy:

THE REVENGE OF SHANG SANGUAN

A man was murdered by a powerful local bully. His two sons did nothing. His sixteen-year-old daughter, Shang Sanguan, was engaged to be married, but because of her father's death, the marriage did not take place. She dressed as a male actor named Li Yü and was hired to perform on the murderer's birthday; this "actor" had great beauty, like that of a lovely young woman, and took pains to keep filling all the cups with wine, especially that of the host, the murderer. As the host's desire mounted, he dismissed his servants and kept only Li Yü with him. After some time, the servants discovered them: the host's head had been severed from his torso, and Yü had committed suicide by hanging herself. Then it was discovered that she was a female.[9]

This text assumes that filial piety to the father can justify female cross-dressing. By masquerading as a male (aided, as usual, by drink†), the daughter becomes the death of her father's murderer, and she herself is unmasked only by her own death. Significantly, the men who carry the putatively male actor's corpse into the courtyard are surprised to find it so light in weight; then they discover, inside his shoes, "a pair of white silk slippers as tiny as hooks, for this was in fact a girl." As Judith Zeitlin remarks, "The revelation of female identity has been displaced† from the genitals to the feet.†"[10]

CROSS-DRESSING FOR LOVE

Sometimes cross-dressing is playful and erotic, in vivid contrast with the more sinister register of the ancient Indian and Chinese stories just presented. The masquerades of Arjuna‡ and Cudala‡ demonstrate the comic side of ancient Indian transvestism. An inadvertent, complex, and farcical English transvestite bedtrick occurs in Henry Fielding's novel *Joseph Andrews* (1742):

PARSON ADAMS'S MULTIPLE MISTAKES

Beau Didapper went one night to what he took to be Fanny's bedroom but was actually the room of Slipslop, Lady Booby's servant woman, who mistook him for Joseph Andrews. Eventually both discovered their error, she immediately, he a bit later. She shouted rape, and Parson Adams rushed naked into the room in the dark and mistook Didapper for the victim and Slipslop for the rapist. Didapper escaped, and Lady Booby, now entering the room, thought that Parson Adams was raping Slipslop. Adams left the room but accidentally went into Fanny's room instead of his own and got into bed beside her, neither knowing that the other was there. At dawn, Joseph Andrews, who had an assignation with Fanny, entered her room and found Adams there . . .[11]

The first double-play† is soon compounded by a series of errors too frivolous to chart. This is good dirty fun.

A famous example of a FTM cross-dresser who becomes embroiled in comic situations, though the tale as a whole is sad, if not tragic, is Isaac Bashevis Singer's "Yentl the Yeshiva Boy."[12] Comedy doubles as tragedy, and cross-dressing as both convention and reality, in George Frideric Handel's tragicomic opera *Alcina* (1735, based on Ludovico Ariosto's *Orlando Furioso*, 1516). Here two women are dressed as men, but one is an alto cast as a man, outside the frame, in a conventional trouser role† (a part originally played by a *castrato†*), while the other is a contralto cast, within the frame, in the role of a woman cross-dressing as a man. When they kiss, two women are kissing, two men appear to be kissing, and the plot tells us that a man is kissing a woman.

Richard Strauss's Oktavian† in *Der Rosenkavalier* (1911), is in double drag: a woman, in a trouser-role in the outside frame, plays a man who cross-dresses, within the frame. In Strauss's *Arabella* (1933). Hugo von Hofmannsthal's libretto depicts, within the frame, a woman who dresses as a man:

ARABELLA AND ZDENKA/O

Count Waldner and his wife, Adelaide, in reduced circumstances because of his gambling losses, hope to marry their older daughter, Arabella, to a rich man. Adelaide explains why their younger daughter, Zdenka, is dressed as a boy (called Zdenko): "She is a girl, but because she was always wild like a boy we let her go about as a boy from that time. We aren't rich enough to bring up two daughters properly in this city." Mandryka comes to Vienna to meet Arabella; Waldner had sent a photograph of her to Mandryka's wealthy, elderly father, but the old man had died and his heir fell in love with the photo. At the Shrove Tuesday ball, Arabella accepts Mandryka's proposal of marriage but asks him to let her "bid farewell to her maidenhood" by dancing at the ball, where she will also bid a final farewell to all her rejected suitors, and he happily agrees. But one of those suitors, the penniless Matteo, becomes so unhappy that Zdenko gives him a key and tells him: "Go back to the house; the key is to the room next to hers. Arabella will come to you in a quarter of an hour and, without making a sound, will do everything to make you happy tonight."

Mandryka overhears this speech and becomes suspicious, though he muses to himself, "There may be many girls named Arabella here." But his suspicions are confirmed when Arabella disappears from the ball and sends him a note saying, "For today I bid you goodnight; I am going home. From tomorrow on I am yours." Bitterly, Mandryka departs to take Adelaide home. As Arabella enters the house, singing to herself of going home to the forest with Mandryka, Matteo emerges from an upstairs bedroom. Each is surprised to see the other. He begs her for "just one look, to tell me that you are still the same deep inside." "The same?" asks Arabella. "The same as you were a quarter of an hour ago," he replies. "But," she answers, innocently, "a quarter of an hour ago I was somewhere else." "Yes! Upstairs!" "I don't know what you mean," she says, and he replies, "We were in the dark; I didn't see your eyes. Now give me one look, to seal everything for the last time, and you are free forever."

At that moment, Mandryka enters and confronts them, saying, "I would have to be blind but unfortunately I have sharp eyes. I would have to be deaf, but unfortunately I have good ears. I would have to be weak in the head—then perhaps I would not be able to recognize individuals or understand what games people play here in the night." Though Arabella continues to protest her innocence, Mandryka is about to duel with Matteo when Zdenka emerges from the room, in a negligee and with her hair down.

"Haven't I seen that face already somewhere today?" Mandryka says to himself. Zdenka starts to explain everything to Arabella, saying, "He is innocent. He knew nothing. He believed that it was you. I did it out of fear for him. He still doesn't know that it was me." Matteo asks, "What sweet voice calls to me?" and Zdenka replies, "The voice of the woman who tricked you, Matteo. Your best friend, your Zdenko [*sic*] stands before you. I am a girl—indeed I was never anything else." Then Matteo says, "The room was too dark, and I didn't hear your voice. And yet it seems to me as if I suspected it right from the beginning, sweet little Zdenko [*sic*]."

Deeply ashamed of his mistrust, Mandryka apologizes to Arabella and insists that Waldner allow Matteo to marry Zdenka. Then, "Will you stay as you are?" asks Mandryka. To which Arabella replies, "I cannot be otherwise. Take me, as I am."

It all takes place on Shrove Tuesday, Mardi Gras, the time of masquerades and crossed boundaries but also the last day before Lent, the Carnival when everyone must say goodbye to meat *(carne-vale)*, Arabella must officially (and Zdenka unofficially) say goodbye to maidenhood, and Zdenka must say goodbye to her trousers.

Matteo, the victim of the bedtrick, is buffeted back and forth between what he sees as the double nature of Arabella. He wants to be reassured that she is "the same deep inside" *(im Innersten)*, the same in public as she was in the privacy of the bed (the quandary of the knight of the Loathly Lady†). But of course this is impossible; Arabella protests that she was "somewhere else"—the traditional escape of women who get other women to substitute for them in bed.‡ Matteo is caught in the crosscurrent of a double trick, the cross-dress of gender combined with the bedtrick of individualism: he mistakes Zdenka for both Zdenko and Arabella. He blames the voiceless† darkness for his stupidity, but then he claims that he suspected everything from the start—though clearly he did not (the claim of false knowledge†), and his last words still refer to Zdenka as Zdenko.

To Mandryka, however, the apparent duplicity of Arabella can be explained by the dichotomy between the wicked ways of the city and the gullibility of a country bumpkin like him, what the Marschallin in *Rosenkavalier* calls "Viennese masquerades." Unconsciously he senses that Arabella is doubled, rather than duplicitous, when he wonders how many girls could be named† Arabella (the argument of coincidence†), but then his jealousy† cuts in and erases his half-insight. Mandryka, too, is doubling, replacing the old man whom Arabella's father (like the father of Beauty with her Beast†) had intended as her husband in order to pay his gambling debts.

Since Zdenka's cross-dressing is part of the narrative, instead of conventional† (and hence invisible), it can be discussed. The deeper reason for it is never stated outright but merely hinted at in the statement that Zdenka was always wild and wanted to run around like a boy. When she protests that she doesn't want to be a girl, she adds only as an afterthought that she doesn't want to be a girl like Arabella: "I'll remain a boy to the end of my life. I don't want to be a woman—a woman like you, proud and coquettish and cold." The theme of sisters† in conflict and collusion takes on new meaning here because one of the sisters is a loving brother.

The opera questions the ways in which we use our senses to recognize the people we love. Matteo's excuse for being fooled is that he wasn't able to *see her eyes* or hear her voice in the dark, and he keeps begging her for just one look; but when he hears Zdenka speak, he asks whose sweet voice it is, and she has to tell him that it is the voice of the woman who was in his bed. And no one—including Matteo—ever recognizes that Zdenko is a girl; the only masquerade that is discussed is her masquerade as Arabella. Mandryka at first distrusts his senses, and with good reason, for they lie; only when Zdenka confesses does he truly understand the "games people play in the night"—the double game of cross-dressing and impersonation. The opera ends on a most ambiguous note, for Mandryka asks Arabella to promise what we know (from the Loathly Lady:† "My beauty cannot hold") that no woman can promise: to stay as she is. Her reply, "I cannot be otherwise," implies that the doubling, at least, is at an end. But of course she will be otherwise, both inside and outside, and so will he.

GENDER-BENDING IN HOLLYWOOD

Women wear trousers and men wear skirts in a genre of films sometimes known as "gender-benders," films that "cross . . . the wires of the specta-tor's libido."[13] We have stumbled onto several scenes of this genre in films that belong primarily to other contexts, but now let us focus on them.

In the more magical variants of the theme, as in several myths about transposed heads,‡ the mind of a man is put into the body of a woman, or the reverse. A transsexual variant of the reincarnation motif (which we know from nontranssexual films like *Heaven Can Wait* [1978] and *Chances Are*† [1989]) results in a kind of mythological transsexual equiva-lent of the realistic transvestite double-cross-dress.† In *Dead Again* (1991), a man and his wife die and become reincarnated—he as a woman, she as a man—and fall in love again. At one moment, he looks into a mirror and sees the image of the earlier incarnation of the woman, as if he were just thinking about her. But as we later understand, this is a clue that he really is her, or perhaps his own former self as well as hers: he is looking at his soul, through the common convention of a mirror.† The implication is that they were so deeply in love that they became one flesh, an androgyne, which then burst apart again in a sexual reversal.

Magical transsexuals have appeared from time to time. George Axel-rod's play *Goodbye, Charlie* (made into a film by Vincente Minnelli in 1964) depicted a womanizer reincarnated as a woman. This theme was taken up again in Blake Edwards's *Switch* (1991), about a male chauvinist reincarnated in the body of a beautiful woman but still retaining the soul of a man—that is, a soul with the memory† traces of a male body. S/he (meaning, in this case, not the nonsexist "she *or* he" but the androgynous "she *and* he") attempted to make love with a gay woman but was so homophobic that s/he could not bear to be with gays of either sex: his mind† would reject one, and her body the other. Finally, a man raped her in her sleep† (when her male mind was out of commission—just as King Budha impregnated the transsexual Ila/Ilā‡ when she was suffering from amnesia) and got her pregnant.

Jokes about death combine with banal criteria of identity proliferated to the nth degree in a story about transsexual reincarnation—Craig Lucas's film (1992, based on his play)

PRELUDE TO A KISS

A young man named Peter and a rich young woman named Rita fall in love. When Peter tells her he loves her, she says, "What about when I'm a hundred years old and have yellow teeth and a moustache? And when I never want to make love, and I can't remember anything?" "I'll still love you. And you can't remember anything now." They get married, and as Peter nervously prepares to walk down the aisle his best man tries to relax him by joking, "There's nothing to it. It's just like sliding down a banister—that turns into a razor blade." During the wedding ceremony, a poor, old, ugly, dying man named Julius Becker kisses Rita, and at that moment their souls enter one another's bodies.

On the honeymoon, Peter begins to feel that Rita is somehow not herself; as he later recalls, "Our first full day of being married, and she seemed like a different person. I said, well, it's the excitement." On his return, he asks his best man, "Have you ever been having sex with someone, and everything is all right, more or less, but they've stopped doing certain things they used to do . . . ?" "You mean, like oral sex?" his friend asks, but Peter means something more subtle. He says that she does only conventional things, not innovative and personal things, when they make love. Eventually he becomes certain that Becker-as-Rita is not Rita; and when he meets Rita-as-Becker, he recognizes her. They live together, but Peter says to Rita-as-Becker, "I'm sorry, I'm not attracted to you," to which Rita-as-Becker replies, "What, are you nuts? That's not the issue here." When Rita-as-Becker finally confronts Becker-as-Rita, together they remember the moment of the switch—He: "I wished to god I were that bridegroom, or the bride, for that matter." She: "I wanted to be you. To just be and not be afraid." He: "My whole life would be ahead of me." She: "My whole life would be behind me." Both together: *"Nothing to lose."* At that moment, they willingly switch back again.

This is a variant of the fairy tale motif of the Substitute Bride,† with the substitution taking place at the wedding. At the end, both Rita and Becker realize that the initial transfer took place because each wanted to be in the other's place on the continuum of time, to have what the other had, including the change of sex. The old man wanted to be a woman, who could make babies, "To see life from the other side of the bed," the Teiresias‡ experience, while the young woman, when she saw him, wanted to be "a father." But more important than gender was age, the fact that each was afraid of the future: the young woman of having children, and the old man of dying.

During the ceremony, the one line that Rita can't remember and has to have repeated is "for better or for worse, in sickness or in health." This is the clue to the problem of aging† and identity: are you still yourself when you're sick and old? Becker describes the terrors of his natural aging, "You can't recognize yourself in the mirror,"† just as Rita reveals her fear of aging in what becomes a running joke about yellow teeth.† The film then gives her the years and the yellow teeth, and he does still love her—but he also wants her young body back. In a variant of the quandary of the Loathly Lady's† lover, Peter must choose between the soul and mind† of the woman in the loathsome body of the old man and the body of the young woman with the alien mind and soul of the old man. The lover is not satisfied with the woman's body when he realizes that the soul is different, but still he misses her body very much, and he misses sex with it.

The film sketches a spectrum of ways to determine whether a person is the original or a double, some of them used to prove that the person in Rita's body is *not* Rita, some to prove that the person in Becker's body *is* Rita, some for both. The criteria range from the intimate (a kiss,† things that you do in bed†) to the superficial and banal (favorite brands of Scotch and beer, the yuppy insignia). The sensitivities of the people making the judgment determine their position on the spectrum: the lover, who has only known Rita for a few weeks (and so, one might think, does not know her), senses immediately that something is wrong; her father, though he has known her all her life, does not know her at all; and, in the middle, the mother senses that something is amiss and that her daughter is "not herself"—but does not have the metaphysical range to guess what has happened. The film juxtaposes the sorts of coincidences† and shared tastes that strike people as significant when they are falling in love and the importance that these same idiosyncrasies have, and do not have, in helping one person to recognize another.

We never see them in bed after the switch, but we see that he is unhappy. There is bitter irony in the best man's joke about the razor's edge and in other jokes about clichés† (the girl you woo is not the girl you marry, people are different in bed and out of bed, and so on) that Peter uses to rationalize away his own suspicions, to delude himself.†

Newsweek's David Ansen saw something else in the film: "This is a contemporary fairy tale that takes the old magical rules, in which princes can be transformed into frogs or beasts, and transports them into the anxious modern world, where AIDS and other horrors have given the link between love and death a new urgency. . . . Though the movie is not about AIDS, . . . it's hard not to think that this deceptively slight romantic comedy was conceived in response to that disease, which, like a witch's curse, can transform a young beauty into a physical beast."[14] The mélange of fairy tales—frog prince† and Beauty and the Beast†—includes several more that Ansen does not mention: Little Red Riding Hood and the Loathly Lady, Snow White and Sleeping Beauty, princesses bewitched by an *old* woman and awakened by a young prince's kiss.† The film is indeed about death, but even in our disenchanted state, we do not need AIDS to teach us that youthful beauty will be transformed into diseased old age.†

There are even more complex twists in another variant of the reincarnation genre, *All of Me* (1984), in which one body contains two minds, his and hers:

ALL OF ME

When a crusty old woman named Edwina dies, her soul enters the body of a young man named Roger, which continues also to contain the soul of Roger. Roger's androgyny becomes a problem when he attempts to go to bed with a woman named Terry and the soul of Edwina inside him revolts against this. She persists in thinking of very old nuns or dead kittens, which makes him unable to perform with Terry. He goes into the bathroom to look into the mirror so that he can talk to Edwina, and he persuades her (she is a virgin) that sex is something she should try, in his body. But her fantasies about Clark Gable taking off his undershirt are even more detumescent for him. Determined to get Edwina out of his body, he consults a Tibetan guru, who masterminds a soul-transfer. When Edwina's soul is projected into the body of Terry, the soul of Terry is, by her own choice, projected into a white horse that she has always loved.

The mirror† (the age-old dwelling place of the inner soul) here becomes the essential cinematic device to depict one actor inside another. Caught between two women with androgynous names (Terry and Edwina), he is also caught between a woman whose mind he comes to love despite her surliness (Edwina) and a rather horrid woman whom he loves only for her body (Terry). The perfect solution is to have Edwina's mind not in his body (where, as an androgyne, he cannot make love to her) but in Terry's body (where he can, incidentally also getting rid of Terry's mind). A happier solution was devised, in the less homophobic climate of 1999, by *Being John Malkovich*, in which the woman who enters the man's body is bisexual and hence does not resist but, on the contrary, engineers his/her seduction of another woman, so that both the heterosexual man and the bisexual woman inside him desire the woman in his bed.

Far more common than these films about magic transsexuality are more realistic films dealing with (mere) transvestism. In one series of films a double-back-cross-dress† (or, as the *New York Times* said in 1995 of *Victor/Victoria*, the musical,[15] "Julie Andrews in Drag, in Drag") enables a woman to masquerade as a woman. *First a Girl* (1935, directed by Victor Saville) is about a woman who surreptitiously stands in for her husband, a dance hall female impersonator, during his illness; thus, she pretends to be a man pretending to be a woman—even offstage.[16] This story was made into Blake Edwards's 1982 film *Victor/Victoria*, about a woman who pretends to be a male impersonator. Transvestism here really does not seem to be about sex at all; it's about showmanship (which is also about sex), and this is why the final scene, the best scene, is a show. When Victoria decides to give up the stage, her friend, an old drag queen, takes her place: a man pretending to be a woman pretending to be a man pretending to be a woman. (If we want to stretch it as far as it can go, we could say that an actor [Robert Preston] is masquerading as a drag queen [Toddy] masquerading as a drag queen [Victoria] masquerading as a Spanish woman.) Since Toddy is an *old* queen (as he points out from the start), he is funny, whereas Victoria, a *young* queen, poses a real sexual threat to the macho hero who falls in love with her.

Though Peter Marks complains that "Ms. Andrews, of course, was not believable as a man,"[17] I have never found Julie Andrews's imitation of a *woman* particularly convincing, and her even less convincing imitation of a man consists entirely of taking off her wig (revealing a most becoming short haircut), wiping the characteristic sunny smile off her face, and assuming the stern, noble look of a pointer scenting a pheasant. These problems were reversed when the unmistakably female Raquel Welch replaced Julie Andrews in the musical version on Broadway, of which Peter Marks commented, "With its new leading lady, the show could be retitled, 'Victoria/Victoria.'" Here was a woman *who looks like a woman* playing a woman playing a man playing a woman, an inverted drag queen to match Toddy: a hilariously womanly man, instead of a hilariously manly woman. The critics panned it, but I wish I had seen it. (Or, better yet, I wish they had done it decades earlier with Elizabeth Taylor, whose greatest role was, after all, as a transvestite—*National Velvet,* made in 1945, when Ms. Taylor was twelve years old.)

As for MTF masquerades, a great classic is *I Was a Male War Bride* (1949), based upon the true story of a French officer named Henri Rochard.[18] Rochard marries an American WAC and finds that the only way to cut the army's red tape to get to America with her is to apply under the quota for spouses of army personnel—assumed, however, to be female spouses of male personnel. One of the forms he must fill out asks, "Any female trouble?" to which he writes, "Nothing but." He can't sleep in the room for the American women because he's a man, and he can't sleep in the room for the American men because he's French (hence the British title of the film: *You Can't Sleep Here*). Finally he dresses in drag to sneak onto the boat that is taking troops to America. As usual, the transvestism has ostensibly political, nonsexual motivations but sexual repercussions. The men in the army don't notice that Rochard is a man rather than a woman for several reasons: he doesn't speak† ("Can you talk like a woman?" the WAC asks him and, when she hears his falsetto, advises, "Keep your mouth closed, not a word, leave everything to me. And keep your head down."), and he pretends to be the wife of an admiral (class† distancing). Most important, he turns out to be a very ugly woman, so that people just glance at him and turn away in disgust. He knows he's ugly ("I don't think I'll be called upon to defend my honor," he remarks), made uglier still by a wig made out of a horse's tail. The film is one big structuralist† joke, played, appropriately, on the French. Rochard is a category error: since, in the U.S. Army's mytheme, male = American and female = French, Rochard occupies an empty category of French male. (A similar quandary faced many men of other races,† symbolically and politically defined as female.) The only way out is for him to masquerade as one of the existing categories: a French woman, a.k.a. a war bride. The film counterbalances him with another category error, his wife, who literally wears trousers† and drives a motorcycle with him as the passenger.

Cary Grant was broadly connected with this genre both in his reputation for being bisexual in his private life[19] and in his association with cross-dressing in films. He played against the cross-dressed Katharine Hepburn in *Sylvia Scarlett* (1935) and wore a woman's negligee, again

with Katharine Hepburn, in *Bringing Up Baby* (1938). He was also implicated in the greatest of all Hollywood films about transvestism, Billy
Wilder's 1959 classic *Some Like It Hot,* through Tony Curtis's burlesque
of him. Indeed, Jack Lemmon at one point mimics Curtis mimicking
Grant—thus masquerading as a male jazz musician (Lemmon as the bass
fiddler) masquerading as a female jazz musician (Daphne) masquerading
as a male jazz musician (Curtis as the tenor saxophonist) masquerading
as a female jazz musician (Josephine) masquerading as an upper-class twit
(Curtis as the yacht owner) masquerading as Cary Grant:

SOME LIKE IT HOT

Two jazz musicians who inadvertently witness the Saint Valentine's Day
massacre escape from the mob by posing as women musicians (Josephine
and Daphne) in Sweet Sue's girls' band. There they meet Sugar (Marilyn
Monroe, in full sexual spate), who confesses to the saxophone player, Josephine (Curtis), her fatal weakness for (male) saxophone players and her
desire to break this habit and marry a millionaire. The sax player then
pursues her by masquerading as a millionaire. First the bass fiddler (Lemmon), still in drag as Daphne, and then the sax player, as the millionaire,
who says he's impotent, pretend not to become aroused when Sugar innocently (to Daphne) and purposefully (to the millionaire) exposes her extraordinary charms. Meanwhile, a genuine millionaire (Joe E. Brown) gets
a crush on Daphne, proposes to her, and is accepted. Eventually the gangsters catch up with them, and they escape. Josephine, still in drag, says
goodbye to Sugar by kissing her passionately, whereupon she realizes who
he is and runs after him. Daphne, still in drag, on the way to the millionaire's yacht finally tells him that he can't marry him because he is a boy,
to which the millionaire replies, "Nobody's perfect."[20]

Though Daphne argues to Josephine, reasonably enough, that they
won't be able to get away with it ("I tell you, it's a whole different sex"),
they do, for several reasons: (1) Chutzpah: They are so exaggeratedly,
hilariously female that a careful investigation is out of the question. (2)
Self-deception:† Sue doesn't follow up her suspicions because she desperately needs two women to play in her band. (3) The beauty syllogism†
(one of the "proofs" or syllogisms† that Roland Barthes applied to Sarrasine:† if it is beautiful, it is a woman),[21] here inverted, as it was in *I Was
a Male War Bride:* Ugliness is female, insofar as no one pays close attention to the men in drag because they are so ugly. Thus, when Daphne
objects, "I feel naked. . . . I feel like everybody's staring at me," Josephine
replies, "With those legs? Are you kidding?" and "They don't care, just

so long as you're wearing a skirt" (another cliché, a variant of "They're all alike in the dark"). The only one who sees through the masquerade in the end is the pursuing gangster (George Raft playing George Raft), who wants them to be men so that he can kill them. When his cronies refer to them as "dames," he says, "Maybe those dames ain't dames—same faces, same instruments," and goes after them.

Although no bedtrick is actually consummated in this film, the kiss† constitutes a euphemistic equivalent, calculated to pass muster with the censoring Hayes office that reigned in Hollywood from the 1930s to the 1960s. The first kiss comes when the virile saxophone player (pretending to be a girl saxophone player) pretending to be an impotent millionaire gets Sugar to kiss him, and his leg (his *leg*†?) rises slowly up from the couch where he is lying. At the end of the film, when the sax player (in drag as Josephine, though with very little makeup) sees Sugar singing a torch song about being brokenhearted (over him, as the millionaire), s/he rushes in and kisses Sugar passionately on the mouth. Sugar cries out in astonishment, "Josephine!" whereupon Josephine says to her in his own (Tony Curtis's) voice† (a Bronx accent that she has never heard undisguised), "None of that, Sugar. No guy is worth it." At that moment Sue, evidently viewing the kiss as a lesbian attack, shouts for help, and one of the gangsters, evidently viewing the kiss as a heterosexual embrace, shouts out, "That's no dame!" and starts after Josephine. Then Sugar's big eyes grow bigger yet; she looks down at the diamond bracelet that the millionaire has given her and smiles. The three images coalesce for her and she recognizes, through the female saxophonist and the male millionaire, her true type and destiny: a male saxophonist.

At midpoint, Daphne finds himself in an upper berth on a train, first alone with Sugar and then covered with other gorgeous half-naked women. This is a variant of the old motif of the prince who smuggles himself into the harem by dressing as a woman. But where the prince is in heaven, Daphne is in hell, because he cannot change back into a man (like the prince) but must remain in drag, chanting his magic detumescing mantra: "I'm a girl, I'm a girl." The crowded upper berth is a Hollywood mytheme that Wilder took from the Marx brothers in *A Night at the Opera* (1935) and from his own use of upper and lower train berths in *The Major and the Minor*† (1942). That film, like *Some Like It Hot*, drew its humor from the tension between the official surface message of the film ("Of course no man could possibly be sexually attracted to a man/young girl") and its darker, unofficial subtext, of which the sophisticated audience was undoubtedly aware ("Of course men are sexually attracted to men/very young girls"). Alfred Hitchcock also used the upper berth (and the train in the tunnel† as a sexual metaphor) in *North by Northwest* in the very same year (1959), with—who else but Cary Grant?

THE DOUBLE-CROSS-DRESS

When two people of opposite genders cross-dress and then exchange places, you get what could be called a double-cross-dress. In the mythology of the bedtrick, this happens most often to brothers and sisters, who often masquerade in bed as one another, sometimes accidentally, sometimes on purpose. Roland Barthes writes of the moment when Sarrasine,† finally admitting that the person he has regarded as a woman, La Zambinella, is a castrato, asks La Zambinella, "Have you any sisters who resemble you?" This device, which seems to me to be eminently Shakespearean (and is also a standard pick-up line), is viewed quite differently by Barthes: "The hoped-for sisters permit imagining a rectified, re-sexualized, cured castrato who would slough off his mutilation like some hideous envelope, retaining only his correct femininity."[22] The essence of such a person is more than mere family resemblance;† it transcends gender.

A double-cross-dress of siblings occurs in a story by Barnabe Riche (1540–1617):

PHYLOTUS AND EMELIA

A rich old Roman named Phylotus fell in love with a young virgin named Emelia, whose equally old father, Alberto, forced her to submit to the marriage. A young man named Flanius fell in love with Emelia; she said she would marry him if he could find a way to help her escape from her father's house. He brought her a suit of men's clothing, and she escaped. A servant told Alberto what she had done but did not know where she had gone. Now, it happened that Emelia had a brother, Phylerno, who had been raised from birth at Naples and came now to Rome to seek his father for the first time. As Alberto and Phylotus pursued Emelia, they "happened to meet with Phylerno in the streets, who was so like his sister Emelia" that they assumed he was Emelia (in the expected drag). Phylerno did not know who they were but went along with the joke. Phylotus brought Phylerno-as-Emelia to his house, sent for Emelia's clothes, and kept Phylerno-as-Emelia, for safekeeping until the marriage, with his (Phylotus's) beautiful daughter, Brisilla. Phylerno-as-Emelia told Brisilla that Phylotus was going to force Brisilla to marry Alberto, just as Alberto was forcing Emelia to marry Phylotus;

s/he wished aloud that their elderly fathers would find brides their own ages, concluding, "I would to God, my Brisilla, that I were a man for your only sake." S/he assured Brisilla that such things were not impossible, citing as precedent the story of Iphis, who was born a girl but whose mother raised her as a boy (to escape death at the hands of her father, who would kill any daughter), and whom Isis finally transformed into a boy. Phylerno-as-Emelia then prayed to Venus for the same boon and told Brisilla that the goddess had granted her request. As Phylerno embraced Brisilla in his arms, Brisilla perceived indeed that Emelia was metamorphosed, which contented her very well; they made love happily together in secret.

Phylerno-as-Emelia married Phylotus in church, but when they were alone in the bridal chamber, s/he grabbed Phylotus by his gray beard and "so bepommels him about the face that he was like to have been strangled with his own blood which gushed out of his nose and mouth." S/he then told Phylotus that she would come to his bed once a month, beginning tonight; s/he left the room and sent back a whore.

Meanwhile, Flanius had happened to see Phylerno-as-Emelia in church with Alberto; hastening home, and finding another Emelia awaiting him there, he cast her out as a fiend sent to him by witchcraft. She went to her father, who asked her how she liked her bedfellow, meaning Phylotus; she, meaning Flanius, complained that he had turned her out for no cause that she knew. Matters continued at cross-purposes until Emelia told her father about Flanius, who was summoned to the house of Phylotus. On hearing Flanius's tale, Phylotus insisted that *he* was the one who had married the satanic impostor. Then Phylerno, still in drag as Emilia, returned and there were two Emelias—until the tales were told, and the two young couples married: Emelia and Flanius, and Phylerno and Brisilla.[23]

Both age and gender are called into question here. The bridegroom is of the wrong age, and the bride (when played by the brother) is of the wrong gender—but both problems are resolved when the brother weds Phylotus's daughter. Phylerno, undisguised, is taken at first for Emelia in her male guise and, in female drag, for Emelia undisguised. But he masquerades with Brisilla and Phylotus in very different keys. His masquerade with the girl is all in the name of gender-bending fun, but his treatment of the man is ugly, reminiscent of the punishment of Kicaka and of Kabikumar's brother. Riche waxes deadly serious, at some length, about the wickedness of marrying young girls to old men, and his bitterness breaks through in the brutal beating of Phylotus.

Love Tricks (1625), a play by James Shirley (author of *A Lady of Pleasure†*), further complicates the plot of *Phylotus and Emelia*. Shirley changes the characters' names, but to demonstrate both his indebtedness and his innovations I will keep Riche's names and put Shirley's changes in italics:[24]

LOVE TRICKS

A rich old man named Phylotus *was passionately loved by* a young virgin named Emelia, whose father, Alberto, *tried in vain to dissuade her from* the marriage. A young man named Flanius fell in love with Emelia. *On the eve of her wedding to Phylotus, Emelia decided she loved Flanius after all.* In a suit of *shepherd's* clothing, she escaped *to the forest, where she met her sister Felice, who had run away some time before to escape a marriage to Gasparo.* Emelia's brother, Phylerno, *pretending to search for her,* dressed in Emelia's clothes, and Phylerno-as-Emelia married Phylotus in church. (Phylerno commented, "Either I am infinitely like my sister, or they are all mad with credulity. But our good fathers are blinded with their passions, and that helps me much.") When they were alone in the bridal chamber, Phylerno-as-Emelia threw Phylotus down and made him promise *never* to come to "her" bed and *to keep, instead,* a whore in "her" place. Phylotus, crying out, "Oh, I have married a Devil," but concerned to keep up appearances, *asked Phylerno-as-Emelia to sleep in the bedchamber of* his beautiful daughter Brisilla, whom Phylerno *already loved* but whom Phylotus was going to force to marry *a fool named Bubuculus.*

Gasparo found Felice and Emelia in the woods, and eventually their father and the others discovered them and learned the truth. Phylerno's servant Gorgon, in drag as a woman named Mopsa, got Bubuculus to admit having fathered several bastards on "her"; humiliated at the revelation of "Mopsa's" identity, Bubuculus retreated. So, *too,* on seeing Phylerno as a boy, Phylotus cried out, "Ha, how's this, my wife become a man? I confess she plaid the man with me." The *three* couples married: *Felice and Gasparo,* Emelia *and* Flanius, *and* Phylerno and Brisilla.

The changes here erase the crucial moment in Riche's story when Phylerno, undisguised, is thought to be in male drag; instead, he goes directly into female drag, and his sister Emelia remains in male drag for much longer. Emelia at first desires the June-September marriage, but she sees the light soon enough, and although her resistance is displaced onto a sister who was apparently created for this express purpose (and who quickly capitulates when she meets her rejected lover in the forest), there is no sermonizing on forced marriages. The end ties up more threads than Riche did (three marriages instead of two), but there is also an extra loose end, another undesirable elderly suitor: Bubuculus, who, like Phylotus, is punished for his attempt to marry a woman who wanted someone else. Even more than *Phylotus and Emelia,* the cross-dressings in *Love Tricks* serve to subvert the paternal variant of the droit du seigneur.†

THE DOUBLE-BACK-CROSS-DRESS AND DOUBLE-BACK-CROSS-DRESS-PLAY

When two people of the same gender cross-dress and end up together, you get a situation whose sexual point escapes me but that is catalogued by Jonas Balys and Stith Thompson as K 1321.3.2: "Two men fooled in love affair; both men, disguised as women, are locked in the same room; each starts making love to the other." The story that they cite concerns a bedtrick even less consummated than they imply. It is a South Indian folktale about the notorious trickster Tennali-rama, jester to King Krishnadeva Raya (1464–1530), who tricks the king (the Rayar) and his minister (the preceptor) into dressing as women and coming to his house at night, assuring each that he will there meet a beautiful woman. The king, in drag, gets in bed with the minister, also in drag, and the jester locks them in: "And inside when the men met with amorous intentions each taking the other to be a woman, the Rayar came to know his preceptor, and the preceptor the Rayar." Ashamed and humiliated, they agree to the jester's terms before he will let them out.[25] I suppose we could call this a double-cross-dress; it doubles the relatively straightforward cross-dress in such a way that it maintains the same-sex encounter, though in this case not merely the victim but both men expect a cross-sex encounter. We have seen that cross-sex desire produces many switchbacks, uncertainties, ambiguities; so does same-sex desire. And when the two agendas interlace, the bedtricks are very tricky indeed.

Many of the complications of this genre move through an apparent same-sex union to end up back with cross-sex encounters after all. What do you get when you cross a double-back (the man who commits adultery with his own wife) and a cross-dress? You get a man who commits adultery with his husband, a double-back-cross-dress. One of the finest examples of this theme is the Indian tale of Cudala,‡ who transforms herself first into a man, then into a man transformed into a woman, in order to win her husband both as a sexual partner and as an intellectual partner.

A much darker exploration of this theme appears in the *Arabian Nights* "The Story of Qamar al-Zaman and His Two Sons,"[26] in which a beautiful princess named Budur, who looks just like her (unrelated) beautiful husband, Qamar, becomes separated from him, puts on his clothes, marries a princess of another kingdom, becomes a king, and threatens (as a man) to rape her husband, who does not recognize her. This theme also appears in the Kashmiri tale of the woman who cross-dressed as a merchant and forced two kisses† on her unrecognizing husband, who "thought that there was no harm in that, if nobody saw it."[27]

In the double-cross-dress *(Phylotus and Emelia)*, the pairs of cross-dressers replace one another but do not sleep with one another. And in the double-back-play ("'Clever' Tricks 'Naive'"), a husband and a wife disguise themselves (without cross-dressing), only to end up in bed with one another. If we cross the double-cross-dress and the double-back-play, we get a story in which a husband and wife cross-dress and end up in bed with one another, in the same cross-sex embrace that they would have been in had they dressed according to their biological sexes (though here no other partners are involved, as there would be in a classic double-cross). We might call this a double-back-cross-dress-play, which is usually playful rather than destructive, producing no mayhem and a great deal of pleasure (as well as comedy).

Sir Philip Sidney's *The Countess of Pembroke's Arcadia* (1593) is a double-back-cross-dress-play,[28] as is the tale of the marquis-marquise de Banneville, attributed sometimes to the Abbé de Choisy, a notorious cross-dresser, and sometimes to Charles Perrault, the creator of the French fairy tale.[29] In Virginia Woolf's *Orlando*,‡ the hero/ine switches back and forth between male and female genders. When she is still a man, she tries to escape from a man dressed as a woman, and when she becomes a woman, and that man sheds his drag and still pursues her, she falls in love with another man who suspects that she is a man, while she suspects that he is a woman.[30] The most elaborate of Mark Twain's many transsexual spoofs, "1,002nd Arabian Night," a parody that he wrote in 1883, is a double-back-cross-dress-play: a person with the sex of a girl but the gender of a boy, forced to dress like a girl but hating it, goes in drag as a boy and eventually marries his/her opposite number (who has the sex of a boy and the gender of a girl). Eventually, the gendered girl tells her father, the ailing sultan, "The miracle of miracles has come to pass, and thy daughter and thy dynasty are redeemed: for lo, *not I but my husband is the child's mother!*" And the people say, "To think that the father, and not the mother, should be the mother of the babes! Now of a truth are all things possible with God."[31]

Switchbacks of this sort also occur in real life. Marjorie Garber tells of "a man who considers himself to be a lesbian and who dates a woman who cross-dresses as a man."[32] And then there is the *News of the Weird:* "After two years of marriage, a couple confessed to each other in 1979 that they wanted to be transsexuals. Although they had two children, the couple decided to seek sex-change operations. Harry, the 6-foot-8 husband, became the wife, Sheila Marie. Jean, the 5-foot-4 wife, became the husband, Thomas Eugene."[33] The tensions that are so painfully encoded in transsexuals‡ find a moment of release, sometimes comic relief, in the fantasies expressed in these stories.

THE DOUBLE-CROSS-DRESS-BACK-PLAY

A brother and sister (actually half siblings) of remarkably similar appearance, despite being of both different sexes and different genders (though not the same sexes as their genders), change places in the classical Japanese novel *The Changelings*. This text is of unknown date and authorship and may well have been written by a woman,[34] but almost certainly it was written no later than 1202[35] and probably between 1115 and 1170. It tells of siblings who do not sleep with one another but cross-dress to *become* one another. Because of a natural disaffinity between their gendered characteristics and their biological sex, both enter the social world as people whose gender proclaims them to be of a sex opposite to their biological sex. (The terms "homosexual" and "heterosexual" are inappropriate here for a number of reasons, the most practical of which is that we need to distinguish between same-sex and same-gender desire and union, and so I will use those terms.) Eventually, as a result of romantic entanglements, the siblings revert to roles that agree with their biological sex, each assuming the individual identity previously occupied by the other. In the process, an array of erotic relationships, each same-gendered from at least one perspective, resolve themselves in cross-sex unions.

I have tried, in the following outline, to simplify the labyrinth of the plot by rearranging some of the episodes so that the reader can follow the fate of each of the main characters. The novel (which I will quote from time to time) tells the story from the point of view of appearances, using male pronouns and a male name (Chunagon, which literally means something like "Counselor") for the person whom everyone thinks is a male but is physically female, and then, in the second half of the book, using the *same* male pronouns and the same male name (Chunagon) for the one whom everyone thinks is still that same person but whom we know now to be someone else—Naishi no Kami, who is physically male but has a woman's name (it means "Lady-in-Waiting"). Are you still with me?

Gregory Pflugfelder, in his analysis of the book, finds it "less confusing to designate the siblings according to their unchanging biological sex rather than their mutable social or gender identity."[36] But in the perhaps vain hope of achieving greater clarity while respecting the spirit of the book (and the translation), I will use the names (which are already encoded as masquerades, indicating one sex and a different gender) and the pronouns "he" and "she" according to the characters' apparent genders, but I will signal each sibling's sex (in uppercase) and gender (in lowercase after a slash), and I will also indicate when one character is appearing as another after they have switched places in the second half of the book. Thus, the reader will be able to distinguish between two different people who may appear to be the same person but whose actual gender and sexuality and name are closeted in the parentheses. Thus, Chunagon (the biological female, gendered male) will be "Chunagon [F/m]" when dressed as a male; "Chunagon [F/f]" when dressed as a female; and when dressed as his putative sister (the biological male, Naishi no Kami), "(Chunagon [F/m] as) Naishi no Kami [M/f]." Naishi no Kami (the biological male, gendered female) will be called "Naishi no Kami [M/f]" when dressed as a female; "Naishi no Kami [M/m]" when dressed as a male; and when dressed as her putative brother (the biologically female Chunagon), "(Naishi no Kami [M/f] as) Chunagon [F/m]" (are you *still* with me?). Here goes:

THE CHANGELINGS

Part I: The Masquerade Phase. Chunagon [F/m] behaved and dressed like a boy, and Naishi no Kami [M/f], Chunagon [F/m]'s half brother, behaved and dressed like a girl. Chunagon [F/m] married a woman named Yon no Kimi, whom their male friend Saisho seduced and impregnated; Yon no Kimi bore Saisho a girl, who was regarded as the daughter of Chunagon [F/m]. Saisho tried in vain to seduce Naishi no Kami [M/f] and succeeded in raping and impregnating Chunagon [F/m]. Naishi no Kami [M/f] seduced and impregnated the imperial princess.

Part II. The Transitional Phase. Chunagon [F/f], now dressed as a woman, went into seclusion at Uji and bore Saisho a son. Naisho no Kami [M/m], dressed as a man (she said she was the brother of Chunagon

[F/m]), met Chunagon [F/f]. Chunagon [F/f] left her son and Saisho and changed places with Naisho no Kami [M/m].

Part III. The Switched Phase. (Naishi no Kami [M/f] as) Chunagon [F/m] seduced Yon no Kimi (who had been married to Chunagon [F/m]) and impregnated her; she bore him a son. Saisho tried in vain to renew his intimacy with Chunagon [F/m], not realizing that he was now (Naishi no Kami [M/f] as) Chunagon [F/m]. The imperial princess, whom Naishi no Kami [M/f] had impregnated, now bore a son to (Naishi no Kami [M/f] as) Chunagon [F/m]. Saisho married the younger Yoshino princess and gave her his son (born to Chunagon [F/f]) to raise. The emperor seduced (Chunagon [F/m] as) Naishi no Kami [M/f], impregnated her, and married her. She bore him the crown prince.

This is a gender-bender so confusing that we truly cannot tell the players even *with* a score card. Indeed, it may be designed, as I think "The Definitive Loincloth"† may have been designed, to force the reader or hearer to admit that one cannot keep track of the players and that, therefore, such distinctions do not really matter. As one scholar suggests, "At one point the two grow quite confused as to who is she and who he, and there are points when the reader is equally at sea—which is obviously part of the fun and theme."[37] The storyteller is like a Zen master inspiring a pupil to question his assumptions, as is the apparent intention of another convoluted Buddhist tale about two women who are reborn over and over again, always as enemies; as Ranjini Obeyesekere, who retold the story, points out: "By the time we reach the middle of the story we have lost track of who is good, who bad, who originally guilty, and who the wronged one. The text deliberately blurs the distinctions."[38] Where that story is a lesson in moral dualism, the story of the changelings is an object lesson in bisexuality and androgyny, teaching us that if we cannot keep track of sex and gender, we might as well ignore them. This point, too, is explicitly argued in other Buddhist texts, such as *The Holy Teachings of Vimalakirti*:‡ "Women . . . are not women in reality, they appear in the form of women. With this in mind, the Buddha said, 'In all things, there is neither male nor female.'"[39] Indeed, the story of the changelings has an explicit Buddhist subtext, with various characters becoming nuns and monks in their flight from excessive and convoluted sexual aporias. As Pflugfelder remarks, critics of the novel shortly after its composition found the story "neither immoral nor implausible, but instead perfectly comprehensible within a Buddhist framework."[40]

Let us now see how the novel puts flesh on the bare bones of some of the main episodes. There is only one bedtrick, which take place after the switch, when Naishi no Kami [M/f] masquerades as Chunagon [F/m] in the bed of Chunagon [F/m]'s wife, Yon no Kimi. (Naishi no Kami [M/f] as) Chunagon [F/m] also goes back to the bed of the imperial princess, but now the imperial princess is *told* of the former masquerade and *knows* she is in bed with the same person in a different form, the biological male who formerly appeared to be a woman and now appears to be a man. Since the two most important male sexual partners of the changelings, Saisho and the emperor, sleep with only one version of each person, Saisho in part I and the emperor in part II, neither is the victim of an actual bedtrick. And Chunagon never engages in a bedtrick as Naishi no Kami.

But there are a number of quasi bedtricks of two sorts. In part I, people have sex with people whom they assume to be of one sex and soon discover to be of another sex (Saisho with Chunagon [F/m] and the imperial princess with Naishi no Kami [M/f]). In part III, people who do not have sex with them mistake (Naishi no Kami [M/f] as) Chunagon [F/m] for Chunagon [F/m] and (Chunagon [F/m] as) Naishi no Kami [M/f] for Naishi no Kami [M/f]; this group includes Saisho, the emperor, and the imperial princess, as well as, on other occasions, the bedtrick victim Yon no Kimi and, during the transitional period, the changeling tricksters themselves.

Let us first consider the genuine bedtrick in part III. Yon no Kimi may have realized that (Naishi no Kami [M/f] as) Chunagon [F/m] was not her original husband and was just relieved to have a real man living in the house at last. The big test comes when (Naishi no Kami [M/f] as) Chunagon [F/m] gets into bed with Yon no Kimi, who thinks he is still Chunagon [F/m]:

> Yon no Kimi and Chunagon had been used to being very close and simply passing the time by speaking tenderly with each other. Since Chunagon seemed the same, Yon no Kimi assumed things would go on the same as before. But Chunagon showed an amazing change of heart in his sexual treatment of her now, and she was even more embarrassed than when Saisho had first lain with her. She was still more upset that she could not protest. Her reaction was obvious, and Chunagon mused sadly that she must find him truly odd.
>
> Finally, she wondered whether this man was not indeed different. Again and again she considered her situation strange and incomprehensible; it was unbearable for her.

She sighed:

> The one I knew
> He whom I was wont to see,
> You seem not to be he.
> Is it I who am different?
> Or is it you who have changed?

Chunagon thought it amusing and natural that there should be aspects about him at which she would wonder.

> Your heart's confusion,
> A heart that has been given
> Not to one alone;
> Therein may lie the reason
> You think me not who I was.

He spoke these lines, imitating the former Chunagon's manner, and Yon no Kimi was apparently unable to tell the difference. (172–73)

Why is she "even more embarrassed than when Saisho had first lain with her"? One might think that because, on the previous occasion, she had never had sex before and was committing adultery (more precisely, was the victim of an adulterous rape), this consummation with her husband would be *less* embarrassing. Is it because she now realizes, in retrospect, what was wrong with the earlier relationship? Or because she now realizes that her husband must have known how she got pregnant before? In her confusion, she wonders whether she or he is the one who is different, changed, and with amusement he assures her that she is the one, that she thinks he is "not who I was" because *her* heart is confused by having been given to more than one man.

"An amazing change of heart" is an extraordinarily delicate way to describe the behavior of a man who replaces a woman in bed and for the first time consummates a sexual act. But talk about chutzpah! His poem lies: it is a false riddle,† accusing his wife of not recognizing him because she has slept with Saisho, even though he knows perfectly well that she has a perfect right not to recognize him, since "he" has never slept with her himself (for "he"—that is, the man she thought to be her husband—was Chunagon [F/m], someone else, someone biologically female). And she falls for it! Attack is the best defense.

Now let us consider the quasi bedtricks. The author tells us how it is that the two siblings can get away with each of the two masquerades in part I (man as woman, woman as man) and then, in part III, with the exchange in which each substitutes for the previous occupant of a bed, so that the man enacts the man, the woman the woman, each impersonating himself or herself. In all cases, family resemblance† makes the two half siblings look very much alike: when Naisho no Kami [M/m] replaced Chunagon [F/m], "she looked exactly like the missing Chunagon. Even when the two had been conversely male and female their faces had been mirror images" (129). The personalities are very different, but in the end the physical resemblance carries the day, aided somewhat by the way in which the siblings train one another to behave† as one another.

The people who go to bed with the changelings in part I, when there is a disparity between sex and gender (Saisho, Yon no Kimi, and the imperial princess), do not notice the disparity for any or all of several reasons: (1) They themselves respond to cross-sex but same-gender eroticism, and so they respond to a same-sex surface but a cross-sex body. (2) They love a particular person in any form or gender, androgynously. (3) They are so promiscuous that they will make love to anyone of any gender (Saisho alone). (4) They are bisexual, attracted to both men and women. (5) They are attracted to cross-dressing people of the opposite sex. But each victim faces a different quandary. Moreover, as Pflugfelder puts it, in "a situation in which one partner is accurately apprised of his or her partner's sex, and the other is not, . . . the same relationship might be experienced by one individual as cross-sex and cross-gender, and by the other as cross-gender but same-sex."[41]

Naishi no Kami [M/f] takes an active role in seducing the imperial princess in a cross-sex embrace that the princess regards at first as a same-gender embrace. The princess is appalled by the overtures of Naishi no Kami [M/f] but presumably is pleased to discover that she is a man. This is a same-gender but not a same-sex act:

> For some time she [Naishi no Kami] went to the princess only at night when she would not be clearly observed, and they lay together behind the same screen. . . . Though terribly shy and withdrawn, Naishi no Kami could not withstand the charm of the princess's innocence and frankness, and in attending her night after night she must have become much too bold. The princess was amazed at this unforeseen development. But there was nothing the least bit loathsome to her about Naishi no Kami's appearance and manner—indeed, the girl seemed surpassingly lovely and grace-

ful. The princess, thinking that there must be some reason for this behavior and finding the girl an earnest and good companion, clung to her and loved her as no other. (34)

"This behavior" may mean either the fact that Naishi no Kami [M/f], a man, pretended to be a woman or the fact that this apparent woman made sexual overtures to the princess—probably the latter. From this euphemistic passage, I think we must assume that Naishi no Kami [M/f] makes love to the princess not as a man but as a woman, for the princess continues to regard her behavior, rather than her appearance, as puzzling. In her acceptance of what she regards as a same-gender affair, the princess differs from the more sophisticated Saisho, who knew what Chunagon [F/m] was once he had stripped her, but even the princess must have figured it out by the time she became pregnant. Apparently the princess either swings both ways or simply loves Naishi no Kami [M/f], androgynously, no matter whether s/he is gendered male or female; she sleeps with no one else.

How does Saisho rape Chunagon [F/m], whom he regards as a man? Again this is a same-gender but not a same-sex act. At first, Saisho, who is after Naishi no Kami [M/f], is attracted to Chunagon [F/m] on the rebound, as it were; when he sees Chunagon [F/m], he notes that his features are identical to those of Naishi no Kami [M/f] (just as Narcissus,‡ in Pausanias's telling, loved his own reflection because it reminded him of his twin sister).[42] Then:

> "How beautiful he is! Should there be a woman like this I would languish for love of her," thought Saisho, his passions aroused as he gazed at Chunagon, and he lay down beside him. "It's too hot," said Chunagon, annoyed, but Saisho paid no attention. . . . When Saisho embraced Chunagon and declared his love for him, Chunagon said, in annoyance, "I can believe that. It's because you think of me in connection with both of the ladies you love." . . . Chunagon arose. What could Saisho have been thinking of? Upset, he could not stand to be separated from Chunagon now. In the grip of his passion he seized Chunagon. "What are you doing? Have you lost your mind?" snapped Chunagon in disgust, but Saisho paid no heed. . . . He could do nothing when Saisho seized him, and his heart grew weak. "What is happening?" he wondered. He wept tears of shame. Saisho was amazed at what he had discovered. (83–84)

"Too hot" may express an absence of desire (like "I have a headache") or just a feeling that there's too much passion in the air, while "Should there be a woman like this . . ." reveals a denied desire, like Freud's syllogism† of the man who denies his homosexual urge: "I do not love him, I love her." The words say no but the actions say yes. "What is happening?" suggests the first awakening of passion, first desire. Chunagon [F/m] is apparently disgusted by what he knows to be a cross-sex embrace, while Saisho shows enthusiasm for what he thinks to be a same-sex embrace and is actually a same-gender embrace. Or, to put it differently: Chunagon [F/m] is apparently disgusted by what he thinks his partner believes to be a same-sex embrace, while Saisho shows enthusiasm for a same-gender embrace that turns out to be a cross-sex embrace. For Saisho intends to make love to Chunagon [F/m] as a man but is happily surprised and content to switch to raping him as a woman. After they have become lovers, Chunagon [F/m] says, "My appearance is unusual [i.e., I cross-dress], but since our hearts have found one another [i.e., we are sexual partners], if you behave in such a way as not to embarrass me in public [i.e., you keep the secret of my genitality] I shall know you truly love me [and will go on sleeping with you]." This tension between public and private appearances† inspires many bedtricks.

Once Saisho realizes Chunagon [F/m]'s sex, he forces her to switch her gender identification. But Saisho's attentions to Yon no Kimi make Chunagon [F/f] jealous:† "I have been made to seclude myself like a woman; I even have a rival. I surely should not have to go on waiting anxiously like this for Saisho to come to me. . . . At times Yon no Kimi looked reproachful. Is this my retribution for those days—that I am to experience, in her place, the misery of being forsaken by a man?" (143). This is an interesting twist on the theme of the man who commits adultery with his own wife.† Here a man is in sexual competition with his own wife and in effect abandons himself, is otiose to himself, betrays himself to himself; and he is simultaneously cuckolded and pregnant. When Chunagon [F/f] finds that her own wife is her rival for Saisho's love, she muses, "How wretched it is to have become the woman I now am" (143). But Chunagon [F/f] does not get jealous when Saisho cuckolds him, enacting the Freudian† cuckolding scenario by sleeping with both the husband and the wife. Apparently only biological males mind cuckolding; biologically female, gendered males mind male promiscuity.

The situations of Yon no Kimi and the imperial princess in part III differ in several ways. Yon no Kimi goes to bed with two different people—Chunagon [F/m] and (Naishi no Kami [M/f] as) Chunagon [F/m]—but she thinks she has bedded the same person. The imperial princess goes to bed with the same person twice—Naishi no Kami [M/f] and (Naishi no Kami [M/f] as) Chunagon [F/m]. But although at first the imperial princess thinks they are two different people, she is told the truth before the second sexual act is consummated. She begins to figure it out by herself: "There's nothing different about her, yet all the same she does not look like the one with whom I was intimate. . . . What has happened to the one with whom I have exchanged vows? Might he be called Chunagon now? . . . In that case, though, who is this one? I had not heard he had many brothers and sisters" (181). Why does the princess figure it out--and reject the "family resemblance" excuse—when Yon no Kimi does not? Perhaps because the princess has been faced with the opposite proposition from that of Yon no Kimi: a move from sexual intimacy to sexual aloofness, from cross-sex union to same-sex rejection, a sobering experience.

Saisho desires Chunagon [F/m] as the princess loves Naishi no Kami [M/f], androgynously, gendered female or male, but the great libertine is fooled by both siblings; presumably, to him all women (and some men) are alike in the dark.† Happy to have sex with anybody beautiful, male or female, he does not look too closely, and his indiscriminate sexuality makes him vulnerable to bedtricksters. Even when he sees the truth, he remains blinded by lust. Despite his realization that (Naishi no Kami [M/f] as) Chunagon [F/m] must be a man, his desire persists, and if (Naishi no Kami [M/f] as) Chunagon [F/m] cannot be the same person as his old mistress Chunagon [F/m], maybe he is her brother; family resemblance, as usual, comes to the rescue, falsely branding Naishi no Kami [M/f] as his own sister. Since no same-sex acts are consummated in this book (though same-sex eroticism is more prevalent than same-gender eroticism), Saisho fails to seduce Naishi no Kami [M/f] and apparently never thinks of trying again when she is a biological woman, (Chunagon [F/m] as) Naishi no Kami [M/f] (the one cross-sex opportunity he misses).

We might assume that (Chunagon [F/m] as) Naishi no Kami [M/f] would have no problem when she is seduced by the emperor, who has never slept with either of them before and hence has no basis for comparison. But since the emperor has known her as Chunagon [F/m] for many years, and (Naishi no Kami [M/f] as) Chunagon [F/m] is still present at court, the emperor notices not the difference but, in this case, the opposite problem, the similarity: "The Emperor looked closely at Chunagon. . . . Suddenly he recalled Naishi no Kami's face so like Chunagon's in every respect" (189). And, finally, the emperor does, rightly, suspect that (Chunagon [F/m] as) Naishi no Kami [M/f] has had a child by another man, though he never suspects that she had that child when she was supposedly a man herself (Chunagon [F/m]). Thus, people are fooled but not fooled; they are swept up in the superficial construction of forms, while true sexual passions undergo their astonishing transformations under the surface.

There are a number of significant asymmetries† here. Chunagon [F/m] has two sexual partners before the switch, his wife and Saisho, while Naishi no Kami [M/f] has only one (the imperial princess). But after the switch, (Naishi no Kami [M/f] as) Chunagon [F/m] has *three* (Yon no Kimi, the imperial princess—again!—and the elder Yoshino princess), while (Chunagon [F/m] as) Naishi no Kami [M/f] has only one—though this one is the emperor. Significantly, Chunagon never engages in a bedtrick as Naishi no Kami. These asymmetries reveal the novel's bias: of the four changelings (two in part I and two in part III), those who are gendered male have more sexual partners than those who are gendered female (4 to 1 [unless you count the imperial princess twice, in which case it is 5 to 1]), and those of male sex have more sexual partners than those of female sex (3 to 2 [or 4 to 2, with the same proviso]). Moreover, those of male sex—Naishi no Kami [M/f] in part I and (Naishi no Kami [M/f] as) Chunagon [F/m] in part III—make all the aggressive moves. No matter what the gender may be, the biological males are active, while the biological females are not merely passive but try, in vain, to resist the sexual overtures of men. No woman here desires sex in the first place, though they apparently get to like it in time. The men have both agency and knowledge; the women don't seem to understand sex and are amazed to find themselves pregnant. Clearly, it is an advantage to have a male sex and/or gender.

As usual, cross-dressing does not indicate same-sex desire. The changelings choose their genders as children and then one day when they grow up find themselves suddenly locked into sexual scenarios they do not want. Chunagon and Naishi no Kami never have sex with people of their biological sex. There are no consummated same-sex acts in this book—beginning with the failure of Naishi no Kami [M/f] to sleep with her wife—but several same-gender acts are consummated, and there is a great deal of unresolved sexual ambivalence. Same-sex relations were attested in Japan before and during this period, though they were not so fully institutionalized as they would become in the Feudal period. The emperor had young boys as lovers, but some people—including, apparently, the author of *The Changelings*—disapproved of sexual acts between adult males. On the other hand, "intense emotional and/or sexual relationships between women were relatively common in palace life."[43] Perhaps this book can be read as a fantasy of the fulfillment of same-gender love within a cross-sex framework. And even though neither of the initial same-gender desires (Saisho for Chunagon [F/m], the imperial princess for Naishi no Kami [M/f]) survives the collapse of the masquerade of genitality, the fantasy may be more real than the reality.

What about the children? When (Naishi no Kami [M/f] as) Chunagon [F/m] has a son with Yon no Kimi, the son is the mirror† image of Chunagon [F/m]:

> This time Chunagon was definitely the father. . . . This time there was no cause for doubt about whose child it was, and the birth ceremonies were held publicly. . . . The child born to Yon no Kimi this time bore no resemblance at all to his elder sisters but looked as though someone had exactly copied Chunagon's face. . . . Chunagon had three sons in a row by Yon no Kimi. (233)

After all the other unusual doubles, this one, finally, *seems* usual, even conventional: the child resembles his putative father. But the family resemblance that brands as the son of Chunagon [F/m] the child that is really the son of (Naishi no Kami [M/f] as) Chunagon [F/m] here again conceals the truth.

It was hard for Chunagon [F/f] to leave the son she had borne to Saisho at Uji, "but perhaps Chunagon had a strength of resolve left to him from the days he was accustomed to being a man." The abandoning mother† is really a man, who renounces not merely her son and husband but her gender. The boy eventually comes to live at court with (Chunagon [F/m] as) Naishi no Kami [M/f] when she is married to the emperor. When the boy grows up, the empress hints to him that she is his mother. "It then occurred to the Uji boy that perhaps she was his mother, and he was suddenly filled with emotion." The emperor sees them and says, "'That boy is the empress's child.' . . . Taking into consideration the boy's age, the emperor had no doubts. For years he had been uneasy. . . . He was happy to have found out" (236). The emperor asks the empress if she knows who the mother of the boy might be, and she does not answer. This is yet another twist of our old friend, the Family Romance.†

What are we to make of this astonishing text? On the one hand, it is saying that gender is purely social, not biological: if you want to live the life of a man, it doesn't matter what genitalia you have. This is supported by the way that Saisho and the princess fall in love with both the male and the female version of the person they love. But, on the other hand, it is saying that sex matters very much: both of the tricksters have to revert to their biological roles, and when the biological male replaces the male-gendered biological female (i.e., when the gender remains the same and the sex changes), the wife does not know the difference (though she certainly suspects). Given the surface homophobia, the same-gender subtext is truly subversive; but the sad ending (Saisho's explicit sadness and, behind it, the implicit sadness of the child and of both Chunagon and Naishi no Kami [M/f]), in which sex triumphs over gender, is not subversive. It shows that people cannot get away with those gender games forever.

When Chunagon [F/m] and Naishi no Kami [M/f] are children, their father recognizes their problem and is sad: "If only I could exchange them, my son for the daughter and my daughter for the son" (16). (This gives the novel its Japanese title, which literally means "if only they could be exchanged.") He gets this wish at the end of the story, which means that they do not get theirs. The biological female would have been happy to remain a boy, and the biological male to remain a girl; though the world (expressed through the judgment of their father) regards this as a masquerade, they see it as the truth. But biology rears its ugly head in the form of the pregnancy of Chunagon [F/m] and forces them to masquerade as their biological selves. To the world, this appears to be simple reality (a biological male playing the role of a male, and a biological female playing the role of a female), but to them the double switchback is a lie, concealing the true middle term of gender: male role concealing female gender concealing male sex, and female role concealing male gender concealing female sex. This is a double-cross-dress-back-play—the quadruple hyphens capturing a quadruple liminality or dualism, two masqueraders each doubling both as their own sex and as another gender and person.

THE MYTH OF GENDER-TRANSCENDING IN REALITY

You can get away with a transvestite masquerade for a long, long time in cultures where gender rather than sex is at issue in courting and where many people are, socially speaking, gender-impaired (which is to say most cultures). And how long does the masquerade have to last? Most of these stories deal not with lifelong identity but with momentary action, with a same-sex union rather than a same-sex nature. Some masquerades, however, do last for a lifetime, like that of the jazz musician Billy Tipton, who was discovered, upon his death, to be a biological woman.[44] As Garber comments, "These are really rather typical cases of what is a relatively widespread phenomenon. In other words, the saga of Billy Tipton is just the tip of an iceberg."[45] Garber goes on to ask the right questions about "lifetime passers": "If they are taken for males (or, in the opposite case, females) throughout their lives, to what gender do they belong? Does the post mortem unmasking of the Phoenix cross-dresser (whose second wife, a chorus girl, wept on learning of his death and declared that the idea of his being a woman was 'nonsense') make him finally a female?"[46] Because of the long-standing homophobic bias of most cultures, there have been many periods and places in which to be gay meant to masquerade as straight—forcing transsexuals to become, from their point of view, transvestites. Many of these stories are, in part, about that masquerade.

Although, on at least one occasion that I have noted, Casanova† could not tell one woman from another, he did tell the difference between a woman and a castrato named Bellino who pretended to be a woman:

Casanova and the Castrato

The masculine attire did not prevent my seeing a certain fullness of bosom, which put it into my head that despite the billing, this must be a girl. In this conviction, I made no resistance to the desires which he aroused in me. . . . I went to bed . . . sorry to leave without having given him proof of the justice I did him in not being hoodwinked by his disguise. . . . I could not take my eyes from this being whom my depraved nature impelled me to love and to believe a member of the sex to which it was necessary to my purposes that she should belong. . . . His gestures, the way he moved his eyes, his gait, his bearing, his manner, his face, his voice, and above all my instinct, which I concluded could not make me feel its power for a castrato, all combined to confirm me in my idea.[47]

Because Casanova desired the castrato, he had to persuade himself that the castrato was a girl; he trusted his groin feeling. (This syllogism† also played a crucial role for Freud,† Barthes,† and the lover of Victor/Victoria.†) Later, however, when Casanova thought he saw a telltale bulge in Bellino's trousers, he became thoroughly confused by what he hoped "was not a monstrous clitoris" and begged Bellino, "All that I ask of you is to let me touch an object which cannot but fill me with disgust!"[48]

The eyes say yes, as usual, though in this case it is the crotch, rather than the mouth,† that says no. But Bellino cuts to the heart of the matter: "Since I am a boy, my duty is not to comply in the least with what you demand, for your passion, which is now only natural, would at once become monstrous. . . . You would finally threaten me with death, if I denied you entrance to an inviolable temple, whose gate wise nature made to open only outward."[49] Absolute homophobia, here as in Balzac's *Sarrasine*† (particularly in Barthes's† interpretation of it), makes the nature of the castrato a Manichean matter—which, given the resolutely ambiguous quality of the castrato's sexuality, can lead to nothing but disappointment. But, luckily, Bellino turned out not to be a castrato after all; Casanova's instincts were right all along. Bellino explained the trick, an elaborate sort of padding, and the reason for it: "My mother thought it a good plan to continue passing me off as a man, for she hoped she could send me to Rome to sing."[50] Both the technical know-how and the "progress narrative"† are stock features in transvestite masquerades, as is the tale of the girl raised as a boy, which is told about Strauss's Zdenka/o,† Amba/Shikhandin and Ila,‡ and a real-life transvestite, the eighteenth-century French chevalier (or chevalière) d'Eon.†[51] This is a myth in the classical sense of the word—a story that has been told, and retold, for many centuries in many cultures, often by men who dress as women and use the story to argue that they are women playing men playing women.

That same myth played a key role in one of the most notorious cases of a successful transvestite bedtrick in recent years, a real-life tragedy on which David Henry Hwang based his tragicomedy† *M. Butterfly.*† The real-life story was reported by Richard Bernstein, in the *New York Times* of May 11, 1986:

"FRANCE JAILS 2 IN ODD CASE OF ESPIONAGE"

Paris, May 10. A former French diplomat and a Chinese opera singer have been sentenced to six years in jail for spying for China after a two-day trial that traced a story of clandestine love and mistaken sexual identity. A member of the French counter-espionage service said at the trial, which ended Tuesday, that the operation to collect information on France was carried out by a Chinese Communist Party intelligence unit that no longer exists. The Chinese Government has denied any involvement in the case. The case has been the talk of Paris lately, not so much because of the charge of spying itself as because of the circumstances. The case centered on a love affair between a young French diplomat, Bernard Boursicot, now 41 years old, who was stationed in Peking two decades ago, and a popular Chinese opera singer, Shi Peipu, 48. Mr. Boursicot was accused of passing information to China after he fell in love with Mr. Shi, whom he believed for 20 years to be a woman. . . .

Apparently, Shi dressed off-stage in public as a man, and Boursicot at first thought Shi was a man. Then Shi told Boursicot that "she" was born a girl but her mother pretended she was a boy to keep an inheritance that followed the traditional male line, or (in another version) that her mother had told this lie to keep her husband from divorcing her after she had produced nothing but girls. And now, Shi argued, "It is far too dangerous, in Mao's China, where men and women are supposed to be equals, to admit that one follows an old, feudal sense of values."[52]

To back up this old chestnut, after they had become lovers Shi also told Boursicot another myth, this one explicitly presented as a myth, the plot of the opera in which he had performed the role that had made him a star in China.[53] The plot of the opera is a variant of an old story from central China that the translator calls "one of the most common Chinese tales, . . . the subject of a great number of theatre plays," some dating from the fourteenth century.[54] It is the story of a girl who, like Yentl,† wants to study and therefore dresses as a boy; eventually, she and the boy she loves die and are transformed into butterflies.[55] After telling Boursicot this story, Shi said, "Look at my hands. Look at my face. That story of the butterfly—it is my story, too."[56]

The plot of this Szechuan story corresponds in its major particulars with the Szechuan opera called *Love under the Willows.*[57] The opera draws upon another tale of star-crossed lovers, who do not cross-dress but who become swallows after their deaths, their human bodies buried in a grave marked by willows (intertwined willows also, sometimes, symbolizing same-sex lovers in China). This is the story illustrated on the most famous of British China patterns—the so-called Willow pattern, in blue and white. Thus, the cross-dressing lovers become rainbows and butterflies and bamboo and an opera; the straight-dressing lovers become swallows and willows and a plate. How appropriate that this Orientalist pattern (somewhat conflated: butterflies, rather than rainbows, plus willows), a classic of what the French call chinoiserie, should supply the lie to confound the French Orientalist Boursicot. Joyce Wadler entitled her article about this incident "The Spy Who Fell in Love with a Shadow." I would have called it "The Spy Who Fell in Love with a Myth."

What Shi's telling leaves out is the frame of the story, the fact that, in the opera, a man would play the part of Zhu, making it yet another story of a boy (though Boursicot does not know this) playing a girl playing a boy. Hwang's play reinterprets the story in terms of these and other

mythological structures: Puccini's opera *Madama Butterfly* (a choice perhaps inspired by the butterflies in the Chinese opera), Balzac's *Sarrasine*,†
and, perhaps, the film *My Geisha*† (1962), about an American actress who
impersonates a geisha impersonating Madama Butterfly.

Why did Boursicot believe this confection of fairy tales? The most
obvious explanation is self-delusion.† The British accounts imply that
Boursicot did know that Shi was a man and was ashamed to admit it.
Hwang later remarked of Gallimard (his fictionalized version of Boursicot): "[I]t's simply an extreme example of the self-delusion any of us go
through when we fall in love." And: "On some level, I think Gallimard
must know his lover's a man, but chooses not to know. It's a situation
we've all been in, waking up one morning and finding that someone
whom you thought you were in love with turns out to be a completely
different person."[58]

In a case reported in 1998, a man became such a successful female
that she appeared as one of the bimbos in a James Bond film and had a
torrid two-year sexual relationship with a man. Only when the man asked
her to marry him was there a problem: "I knew I had to tell him the
truth. He asked me to convert to Judaism and I thought that was the
least I could do."[59] The religious conversion was apparently regarded as
a satisfactory theological† equivalent of the sexual conversion; only when
the groom's (Jewish) mother found out and raised a fuss did the man
break off the engagement.

Modern technology comes to the aid of contemporary transvestite
masqueraders, such as the woman whose story was summed up by a headline in the *Chicago Tribune*: "After 4 months, bride discovers groom isn't.
Excuses followed on-line courtship." The article, remarking, "Not only
was Thorne Wesley Jameson Groves not Mr. Right, he wasn't even a mis-
ter," suggests a number of reasons for the success of the deception. To
begin with, they met through an America Online "chat room," and the
bride's lawyer said, "If you met someone in a bar and he said he had a
Jaguar and you go outside and there's no Jaguar, you might be suspicious.
That cannot happen on-line." Afterward, Groves claimed to have AIDS
in order to avoid intimacy in the bedroom; she was "so concerned about
transmitting AIDS that he restricted intimacy to fondling over his clothes
and went so far as to wear a prosthetic penis to further the ruse, according
to the lawsuit." Moreover, she bound her breasts with elastic bandages
because of what she said were chest injuries suffered in a car accident.

When mail or telephone messages appeared for Holly Groves, Thorne Groves said Holly was his twin sister[60]—an old-fashioned trope at the bottom of all the high-tech tricks.

My favorite newspaper report is this modern update on the mind-body problem in bedtricks, from the highly mythological *Weekly World News* in 1992:

"I Used to Be a Guy"

Cindy Sands (formerly Gordon Sands) lived for three years with a man named Frank Jablonski. Two nights before their wedding she told him, "I used to be a guy." Hopping-mad Frank Jablonski was so shocked and humiliated he stormed out of the apartment they shared in Detroit, Mich., and heartbroken Cindy hasn't seen or heard from him since. "We've been living together for three years," Cindy sobbed. . . . "It's so unfair. I'm all woman now. My only remaining male characteristic is an insatiable sex drive. I'm a bit of a maniac. I want it all the time." . . . Frank knew Cindy was different from other women, but he never guessed her deepest secret. "She was great in bed. She knew how to turn me on and was quite easily aroused herself," he said. "But she had the mentality of a man. I think that's why we got along so well. We communicated on a man's level." Saddened Cindy prays that Frank will return to her waiting arms. "I love Frank very much. I'm a lot more feminine than most women I know. The fact I was born a boy is merely an inconvenient technicality. But I guess my past will always haunt me."[61]

The assumptions that a strong sex drive is a male prerogative and that a woman who communicates like a man must be a man set up the victim of this Cartesian encounter. One would have expected Frank, not Cindy, to have been heartbroken at the loss of this perfect mate (sex drive of a man, mind of a man, body of a woman). As usual, we are told that men are better than women at being women. Cindy, however, is haunted not only by her own past but by the past of the mythmaking world. The title of this article is a milder version of the title supposedly given to the film *The Crying Game* in China: "Oh No! My Girlfriend Has a Penis!"[62]

So much for low comedy. Many of the same techniques were used in a case that had a tragic ending, the case of Teena Brandon, who was raped and murdered in Nebraska on December 31, 1993, by two men whom she had infuriated by her successful impersonation of a man. As Billy or just Brandon, she had slept with a number of women in Falls City and Humboldt, fooling them in the usual ways: "Lisa claimed that she actually had intercourse with Brandon, Aphrodite Jones tells us, although Lisa added the caveat that she was drunk† at the time."[63]

But it was the psychological, rather than the physical, persuasion that carried the day:

TEENA/BRANDON

That Brandon might be a hermaphrodite was a story many of his conquests accepted with few questions, in order to reconcile what they were doing with him in bed. . . . The reality principle seemed not to apply; Heather went on the pill and Daphne claimed that Brandon got her pregnant. . . . Many of these child-women [who loved Brandon] had had experience with domestic abuse and sexual molestation. They resided on a social frontier where women expected to get battered, where violence against their persons was accepted as a clause in the human contract. Brandon's appeal was that he was an unthreatening romantic, a lean and unmuscular quasi-man who offered sex without pregnancy or fisticuffs.[64]

This is the same argument that was made for the castrati,† often said to be superb lovers; in an age, and a country (Italy), in which women were regarded as objects available to be groped by any man who fancied them, "we may well imagine that some women found a castrato's company restful, and some fell in love with him."[65] As one FTM cross-dresser remarked of Brandon, "He made them feel good. And when you start feeling good there's a lot of mental editing that goes on." That editing edited out such glaring discrepancies as "the tampon wrappers someone had discarded into the heating vents at the farmhouse; the wrappers did not come from Lisa's tampons, and her other roommate, Carrie Gross, was pregnant, and not menstruating.† It was a puzzle that Lisa Lambert chose not to address." Moreover, "The sex was good, Lana reported."[66] The power of sexual illusion was stressed in a novel based on the Teena Brandon story, called *The Illusionist,* in which, when the Brandon character kisses one of his women, he tells her, "Take your glasses off"; when she replies, "I can't see without them," he answers, "You don't need to see." Erotic self-delusion was also stressed by the documentary *The Brandon Teena Story* and by a film, *Boys Don't Cry,* in which Lana glimpses Teena's breasts when they are making love but looks away. Janet Maslin remarked that the women in the film "fell in love with Brandon's masculinity, facts notwithstanding."[67] The men who murdered Teena Brandon, however, driven by hate rather than by love, saw through the illusion; even so, just to make sure, they took her into a bathroom and examined her genitals before they raped her. They planned to chop her hands and her head off so that the body couldn't be identified; in this they resembled the men who raped Lavinia in *Titus Andronicus*† and cut off her hands and her tongue. But this time it wasn't a story.

TURNING THE TRANSSEXUAL TRICKS OF THE TRADE

How do transvestite and transsexual masqueraders get away with it? To a certain extent, the same way that cross-sex (heterosexual) masqueraders do—drunkenness,† self-delusion,† and so forth, or by having sex only rarely. Thorne Groves's trick of avoiding intercourse altogether by claiming he had AIDS could be used by any bedtrickster, though the prosthetic penis would be of no use to a straight bedtrickster. Teena Brandon bandaged her breasts (like Thorne Groves), padded her crotch (like Casanova's pseudo-castrato†), and stood up to pee (like the girl in *Bachelor Party*†), but she also improvised some ingenious new tricks:

> He stuffed socks into his shorts to give his groin the appearance of a male basket; later, he would wear a dildo. Billy . . . suggested to Heather that he was a hermaphrodite, or, alternatively, a man trapped inside a woman's body, explanations . . . picked up from "The Montel Williams Show." Billy told Heather that he had undergone sex-change surgery, but as he refined the story over the next years he would claim that the process had only just begun, that there was something down there, it was small, but it would get bigger by the time all the operations were completed. In carnal situations, Brandon smoothly managed to avoid exposing his genitalia; the butch was always the toucher, never the touched, and in time he worked the references to future surgeries into a routine that passed muster with female companions prepared to take it on faith.[68]

Similarly, Shi, the Chinese spy who bedtricked the Frenchman Boursicot,† apparently explained his masculine appearance by saying that "in order to look masculine she has taken hormones."[69] Shi managed the sexual act in various ways, involving the "American know-how" of a " 'faded diva' with a tube of K-Y jelly"[70] and the use of hands and mouth.[71] At the trial, Shi showed the doctors how he could push his testicles up into his body and push his penis back so that it was hidden, creating a small cavity allowing for shallow penetration. Boursicot thought his lover might have "put cream between his thighs," and that he penetrated Shi's closed legs.[72]

Like these real-life transsexual bedtricksters, the fictional bedtrickster in *The Crying Game*† avoided genital intercourse, sidetracking her victim onto other unisex activities such as fellatio. Fellatio functions as a variation on the theme of the magic kiss,† both more and less intimate than full genital intercourse. Like the kiss, fellatio is often welcomed by the victim as something more intimate, more unusual and exciting than sex in the missionary position; but it is also welcomed by the bedtrickster as something less intimate, since less revealing of gender (everyone has a mouth) than the missionary position. (This paradox was hilariously debated in the film *Clerks*† [1995] by a young man and his girlfriend when he did, and she did not, think it necessary to include among the list of her past sexual partners the dozens of men on whom she had performed fellatio.) Other texts come up with more imaginative transvestite tricks; the "war wound" argument for castrati† alleged that the organ in question had been bitten off by pigs. Uncle Tompa,† the Tibetan trickster who dresses like a woman to marry a rich man, uses the lung of a sheep tied between his thighs with a very strong string to cover his penis: "he cut an opening in the lung to make it look just like a vagina. . . . That night [the rich man] came over to sleep with her and had a beautiful sexual experience with the sheep's lung."[73] This is no more fictional than the fantastic tricks and illusions devised by the transsexual tricksters whose stories are recorded in newspapers rather than in folktales and plays.

Queer Theory and the Theater of Deception

CROSS-DRESS REHEARSALS

The theater is a great source of myths of masquerade, and the cinema also provides a happy retirement home for many old myths. On stage and screen, one form of disguise (the actor in character) is ideally designed to express (or, rather, to disguise) the other (the character in disguise). The brilliance of the Shakespearean variants is a result not only of Shakespeare's genius, and his good eye for folklore, but of the genre: all theater being masquerade, plays about masquerades have built into them a surreal double level on which any good playwright can capitalize. Although some plays and operas in which the players cross-dress do not literally depict bedtricks—that is, do not involve a consummated sexual act—we may attribute this to the stage convention and assume that, in other genres, some of the same plots would have entailed, or perhaps only implied, such a consummation. Some plays, films, and operas raise in more censored ways the questions of recognition and identity, love and desire, that related texts, and different variants of the same plots, resolve in the bedroom.

Actors and actresses who doubled for other characters in films were often themselves doubled by a "body double" or stand-in (lie-in?) during dangerous, tedious, or (most relevant to our subject) nude scenes.[74] The "body double" was often a nubile young woman who would substitute for the starring actress in soft-porn films when things started to harden up a bit, to protect the star from embarrassment—either because she no longer had a good body or because, in days of yore, legitimate actresses did not strip for the camera. The ultimate biological reduction of the bedtrick, the "body double" has no head,‡ as she is merely photographed from the neck down; she functions as the female equivalent of the disembodied phallus.† She need not therefore even resemble in any way the actress for whom she doubles, since we never see the actress naked and never see the double with clothes on.

There are deep connections between transsexual masquerade and the theater, as Marjorie Garber argues: "The phenomenon of cross-dressing within theatrical representation. . . . may be not only a commentary on the anxiety of gender roles in modern culture, but also—and perhaps primarily—a back-formation: a return to the problem of representation that underlies theater itself."[75] Goethe wrote about the pleasure of watching cross-dressing on the stage: "Through their able performance a sort of conscious illusion was produced. Thus a double pleasure is given." As Margaret Reynolds points out, "Part of this 'double pleasure' and 'conscious illusion' may also have come from an awareness of the sexual ambiguity that might arise when the audience looks upon women dressed as men or men dressed as women."[76]

Transvestism on the outside of the theatrical frame (men playing the parts of women, and women of men) is matched when men dress as women and women dress as men *within* the frame of the play; and the plot thickens when transvestism takes place in both frames at once, sometimes reinforcing (men playing women both inside and outside the frame) and sometimes producing different, opposite effects in the outer frame (in the casting) and inside the story (in the plot). In either case, the audience experiences a doubling of their already double pleasure; but when the cross-dressing goes one way in the outer frame (say, MTF) and the other way in the inner frame (say, FTM), the result is a kind of double-back-cross-dress:† someone pretending to be the gender s/he really is.

OPERATIC SCENARIOS

Many of the reasons for cross-dressing apply equally well to opera and to theater, but there are also reasons for cross-dressing specific to opera, such as the kind of exaggeration and artificiality that opera has and Shakespeare does not. In some early operas, the parts of some women (as well as of some men) were played by men (often by castrati†), while in others, the parts of men were played by women. (In one performance, a castrato and a woman in breeches met, the woman playing the man and the castrato the girl,[77] in what I would call a double-cross-dress.†) This arrangement might strike a modern efficiency expert as a rather labor-intensive way of going about the casting of operatic roles: why castrate men to sing in high voices and bind the breasts of women to sing tenor roles (known as "trouser roles," "breeches roles," or *Hosen-Rollen*), instead of letting the men sing the lower voices and the women the higher ones? It was particularly difficult to maintain the parts of castrati by the end of the eighteenth century, when the custom of castrating male singers was made illegal, and the castration of those who remained was often said to have been caused by an "accident," such as the bite of a swan or pig (it is challenging to imagine the circumstances under which this could have occurred), or even a fall from a horse[78] (the excuse given in the film

Farinelli [1995]). But audiences were not fooled: the castrato voice came to symbolize "wound and loss"—"Long live the knife," audiences would chant when they heard a good castrato.[79]

One reason for this mutual cross-dressing is that it is much more challenging and enlightening to do it the hard way, enjoying the frisson of "conscious illusion" and "double pleasure" that Goethe spoke of as part of his enjoyment of cross-dressed operas. Moreover, there were, in Europe, cultural taboos, originally against having women perform on the stage (particularly at the Vatican†) and then, later, against having men and women perform together. (In India, too, strolling bands of male players had men play the parts of women, while troupes of temple dancers, or *devadasis*, had to have women play the parts of men.) Finally, the asymmetry in aging† that proved useful in the theater proved even more useful in opera: the unreliability of the voices of young boys on the cusp of manhood, as well as their immaturity and social unreliability, inspired composers to use women instead, while men in their prime can play old women with a vocal power that most old women do not have.

Opera appears as the frame of many masquerades and as an element in the plot of others. (We might stretch the framing genre to include musical comedy: in 1996 alone, musical comedy versions of several bed-tricks—*Victor/Victoria,*† *The House of Martin Guerre,*† and *The Picture of Dorian Gray*†—were playing in New York and London.) E. T. A. Hoffmann and Hugo von Hofmannsthal together supply most of the mythic operatic scenarios in the contemporary repertoire; Hofmannsthal, with Richard Strauss, produced an almost obsessive corpus of stories about double women (*Ariadne auf Naxos, Die Fraue ohne Schatten, Die ägyptische Helena*‡) and bedtricks (*Rosenkavalier,*† *Arabella*†). Mozart (with Da Ponte†), Verdi,† and Wagner† are simply the best known of many operatic composers who depicted bedtricks. Opera also figures as an object, an element of the plot of many nonoperatic sexual masquerades. Both of the separated twin sisters in *The Double Life of Véronique*† (1991) are singers; *Sarrasine*† and *M. Butterfly*† are about transvestite opera singers; and when the hero of *Victor/Victoria*† (1982) goes to the opera with his transvestite lover, the opera is, significantly, *Madama Butterfly.*†

Opera is a bedtrick-friendly medium because opera is about sex and masquerade. As for sex, Reynolds urges us to take seriously the unmentioned but blatant physical act when one woman (in trousers†) makes love to another: "Everyone knows that opera is about sex. It is no accident that the opera house is furnished with velvet plush, gilded mirrors, naked cherubs, and powdered footmen, for these are the trappings of the brothel, and we go to the opera house for sex."[80] Why do lesbians go to the opera? "Because where else can you see two women making love in a public place?"[81] Corinne Blackmer and Patricia Smith see this as one of the paradoxes of opera: "Because the voice, in opera, transcends both sex and gender, the woman *en travesti*, literally 'in travesty' or 'male drag,' sings and looks like, in theory at least, a man, but sounds like—and, we all know, *is*—a woman."[82]

The voice† can function as a sexual organ through an upward displacement† very different from the sort noted by Freud, as we learn from Cyrano de Bergerac,† as well as from everyday Irish blarney. There is an old English folk song about the erotic (and deluding) powers of the voice:

> When I was a-lying across my bed,
> And his hand across my breast,
> He made me believe by the faults of his tongue,
> That the sun rose in the west.[83]

The film *Hear My Song* (1991) is also about the erotic power of the voice, particularly in its relationship with aging and self-deception. A man who claims, falsely, to be a famous aging tenor enchants a woman who had heard the real tenor sing years ago; she says, "You close your eyes and cast your mind back thirty years, and you see and hear what you want to see and hear." The voice trick in this case is doubled by a bedtrick, but by itself the voice casts its sexual spell; "There won't be a dry seat in the house," says the promoter urging the real tenor to return.

SEXUAL OBJECTIVES AND SEXUAL OBJECTS

Our texts suggest many different sorts of ostensible reasons for men and women to cross-dress both in fiction and in real life. The men who act as women in Shakespearean plays and Noh dramas, and who sing as women in operas (not to mention the men who are castrated in order to sing), often say, We did it only for art (or money); the Vatican† made us do it. Thomas Middleton's *Micro-Cynicon* (1599) tells of a transvestite who cross-dresses not in order to rape the victim of his bedtrick but simply to rob him.[84] This amounts to what Garber might discount as a "progress narrative," a self-deceptive or hypocritical excuse in a real-life masquerade. But although the subtext of transvestism is sexual, there are meaningful surface texts, too.

Some of the women in our stories cross-dress so they can move about freely to accomplish a goal (often on behalf of their husbands, like Jessica and Portia in *The Merchant of Venice*†). Others (Yentl,† the sister in *The Changelings*†) do it to get an education; this is what, in the case of Jane Welsh Carlyle, Phyllis Rose wittily calls "pen envy": "In her childhood, she wanted to study Latin, as boys did. Her parents would not allow it. Furtively, Jane consulted a local scholar and managed to teach herself the declension of a Latin noun, choosing—with unerring emphasis—the word *penna*. . . . She said, 'I want to learn Latin; please let me be a boy.' . . . Her pen envy did not diminish with the years."[85] Virginia Woolf's androgynous hero, Orlando,† challenges the sexist assumption—"Love, the poet has said, is woman's whole existence"—and argues that, for many women, writing is more fun than sex.[86]

Yet Garber is right; we do have to look for the bottom line. We may ask why certain men and women choose to play cross-dressing roles instead of others (and surely there are almost always easier ways of making a living than to have yourself castrated); and we can also ask whether these texts have been received and transmitted without awareness of the sexual sub-text. Cross-dressing to murder a *sexual* enemy (as Amba‡ avenges her own rape), whether or not the killing involves a sexual act, might also be construed as a sexual motive. When it does involve a sexual act (as in the killing of Kicaka†), there can be no doubt that it has a sexual motive; the "sweet death" or "little death" of the orgasm or the romantic *Liebestod* becomes a bitter, full-sized, and most real death. Many women cross-dress to avoid being raped, and since rape is an act of sexual violence that is both nonsexual (in its desire to inflict pain and to dominate) and sexual (in its choice of the sexual act to do this), this, too, is a sexual reason to cross-dress.

But by this same logic, a man who cross-dresses (as a woman) might put himself in danger of being raped. One of the Elder Seneca's moot-court cases debates "whether a young man who has dressed up as a woman on a bet and then been gang-raped should suffer the restrictions on civil rights of an *impudicus*, literally an 'unchaste man.'" One orator, arguing against the young man, declaimed, 'He put on womanish cloth-ing, he arranged his hair in a woman's style, he circled his eyes in girlish pimping, he colored his cheeks.' Another: 'Give him girl's clothing, give him night: he'll be raped.'" As Amy Richlin comments on this case: "The speakers assume both the inevitability of the rape of women and the per-meability of a man who could pass as a woman."[87] There are a number of questions one would like to ask of this text: Did the men who gang-raped the young man start out to rape a woman and then, when they found out that she was a man, simply switch from cross-sex to same-sex rape? Was the argument against him that, like all women, he was "asking for it"?

The same questions might be asked of a modern instance in which the victim is not an MTF but an FTM. For rape, or its inverse, sexual security, was also mentioned as a factor, if not the most important factor, by a cross-dressing woman interviewed by Holly Devor:

> I used to hitchhike home from the hospital and the other nurses used to freak out that I'd hitchhike home. But I'd wear a toque and a down jacket and work boots. No man in his right mind would think I was a woman . . . (a woman would never stop to pick me up, unless it was a dyke, which happened twice, which was great), but the men would stop, thinking I'm a man, and sometimes not find out until I got out of the car, sometimes not find out ever. But I believed that if they think I'm a man, and they're stopping to pick up a man, they can't be into that much kinky."[88]

This statement leaves unanswered a number of the same questions that we might also have asked Seneca, such as: Did she think that a man who picked up a man hoping for sex would leave a woman alone? Did the "dykes" know that the hitchhiker was a woman? What did she do when they found out? How kinky is "that much kinky"?

The assumption behind most of our texts, that men will rape women, is not so easily stymied by a "down jacket and work boots." For if women pretend to be men to avoid rape, they can then be accused of rape, at least for a while: "St. Eugenia, who cross-dressed in order to join an all-male religious community and shortly became an abbot, was accused of rape by a rich lady who desired her; to disprove this charge she disrobed to prove that she was a woman."[89] (On the other hand, a man in a dress, the inverse of the transvestite woman—as in Richard Wright's "Man of All Work"†—may also be accused of rape.) A woman in trousers may even be sued for paternity, at least in stories like Mark Twain's "The Girl Who Was Ostensibly a Man."[90]

But to acknowledge that people often (if not always) cross-dress for sexual reasons is not to assert that they cross-dress to have access to sexual partners of different genders. Those who assume that transvestites are "homosexual" are defining sexuality by the object of desire (the "real" other man or woman): a transvestite is a man who wears woman's clothing *in order* to attract a man. Such people would define gender by asking,

"Do you do it with a man or a woman?" But texts such as *The Changelings,* like many actual transvestites and transsexuals, more often define sexuality by the subject than by the object of desire. The man who had a sex change operation in order to become a lesbian and the man who married a lesbian and who plans to undergo a sex change operation to become a woman[91] puzzle us only in the "Who-do-you-do-it-with?" paradigm ("All that trouble just to end up in bed with a woman anyway") but not in terms of the "Who-are-you?" paradigm. And once we factor in the many other variables—distinctions between sexual anatomy and social presentation, or sex and gender; between self-perception and self-delusion; between masquerades intended to fool and masquerades intended to be perceived as masquerades (which is not the same as the distinction between realistic and exaggerated, or "camp," masquerades)—we realize just how difficult it is to know precisely what is going on when someone cross-dresses.

Finally, we must note the many occasions on which what I have called the double-back-cross-dress† enables men to masquerade as men, women as women. Phylerno† and the chevalier d'Eon† were mistaken for women masquerading as men when they were not disguised at all, and the boy who played Rosalind† in Shakespeare's day was a man masquerading as a woman masquerading as a man (masquerading, in one scene, as Rosalind).[92] In 1929, Joan Rivière published her article "Womanliness as Masquerade," arguing in effect that all women masquerade as women, an argument subsequently refined by Judith Butler and Mary Ann Doane, among others.[93] Buddhist tests such as the tale of the Buddha's sister† spell out what is implicit here: that men regard what all women *are* as a masquerade, no matter what they *do*. But the idea of the fake always implies the idea of authenticity: for A not to be B, you have to know what B is; when a woman is being a woman among men she is also masquerading as the man's image of her, as herself, and as her idea of the authentic woman. This is not, however, merely a feminist problem. The same thing can happen, though in different ways and with far less serious consequences, to men. For men, too, may position the depth as the surface—or the surface as the depth as the surface.

N I N E

Incest

INCEST AND THE BEDTRICK

Tolstoy begins *Anna Karenina* with a variant of the paradox† of the same and the different: "All happy families are alike, but every unhappy family is unhappy in a different way." Incestuous families are certainly unhappy, each in its own way, but the Freudian† hypothesis of the universality of the Oedipal complex implies that, though they may all be different, their unhappinesses look alike in the shadow of incest. Our texts provide evidence in support of both Tolstoy (difference) and Freud (sameness); but beyond that, they provide evidence for a close connection between incest and the bedtrick. The demons Andhaka† and Jalandhara,† born of Shiva, try to seduce Shiva's wife Parvati, their stepmother; and Andhaka's son Adi† impersonates his grandmother, Parvati, to seduce and kill his grandfather, Shiva. Viraka, the son of Parvati and Shiva (and hence Andhaka's brother and Adi's uncle), experiences the devastating fallout from Adi's attack, more particularly the wrath of Viraka's mother when she blames him for his failure both to keep his father from other women (his nephew Adi) and to recognize Parvati herself. What would our world be like if Freud had known this myth instead of Sophocles' relatively straightforward tale of Oedipus?

The bedtrickster Samjna's‡ close connection with the incestuous Sandhya has inspired some Indologists to see an incestuous connection between Samjna and her father, Tvashtri;[1] and one of her twin children, Yami, tries unsuccessfully to seduce her brother, Yama.‡[2] In the Hebrew Bible the myth of the levirate in the tales of Tamar and Ruth is used to overcome resistance to the quasi incest that is necessary for the survival of the race, a kind of modified endogamy. And in the Bedouin† story retold by Lila Abu-Lughod, a man mistakes his mother for his wife after a long absence and sleeps with her. Here, too, is grist for Freud's myth.

Incest is often the result of a bedtrick (on the explicit level) but is also its subconscious cause (on an implicit level), making the masquerade necessary in order to overcome the taboo against incest. Like the bedtrick, incest may take place when the partners (parent and child or siblings in the case of incest, unrelated people or husband and wife in the bedtrick) do not recognize one another. Moreover, masquerade may displace the guilt of incest: the forbidden partner often appears in dreams or myths as someone else, often an animal,† in part to deflect fears of becoming an animal or losing control and in part to allow the dreamer to pretend that he or she does not know that the sexual partner in the dream is the parent or sibling. The need to deny the incestuous urge often provides the narrative lie of the bedtrick, false ignorance:† these are the lies of repression,† projection,† and inversion† and also the lies of "not knowing," "not seeing," and "not recognizing" the parent or child or sibling.

Structurally, incest is the shadow, the mirror image, of the bedtrick; more precisely, both incest and the bedtrick are inversions of the sexual act. Mother† and child are originally one and the same, but then they separate into two that are different. Eventually, sexual union reverses the process, mediating between the original unity, lost forever, and the necessary but painful separation: two that are different become one. But incest and sexual betrayal twist this paradigm in two different ways. Incest, in attempting to re-create the original unity literally, denies separation entirely and unacceptably: two that are the same become one. Sexual betrayal, or masquerade, denies, not the separation, but the unity, reversing the paradigmatic union: two that were different but appeared to become one are then revealed to be two (or three or more . . .) in the bedtrick. In this, incest and betrayal are the two ends of the spectrum of the acts that disrupt the natural balance between separation (from the parent) and union (with the sexual partner).

Incest itself embodies a structural paradox for children of both sexes. A son who does not resemble his father inspires the quandary of paternal insecurity,† but a son who resembles his father too much inspires the quandary of incest, for his mother might mistake son for father. As for daughters, in Lévi-Straussian terms they suffer from two sides of the same problem, a no-win situation: either the father has too little regard for his daughter after her mother dies (he gives his love to the wicked stepmother instead of to the dead mother or to his daughter, and he allows that stepmother to mistreat his daughter) or, since the daughter looks too much like her mother, he has too much regard for her (he wants to marry her). Marina Warner explains this riddle:† "The folktale material continues the traditional association of incest and riddling. The dying queen's demand that her husband should never marry anyone who is not her like in beauty and goodness itself constitutes a riddle: this Other he can marry must be her like. The only figure who can collapse this contradiction is the forbidden daughter, the solution which cannot be proposed."[3]

When we combine this incestuous structure with the complementary structure of the bedtrick or betrayal, we move to the next stage of a structural† dialectic. A. K. Ramanujan suggested that incest and adultery "enact and signify the two threats (temptations?) of a family woman. . . . The world is divided into kin/non-kin and further into marriageable/non-marriageable."[4] Or, to put it differently, marriage partners must be chosen from a group bounded on the one side by those defined as too close (incest) and, on the other side, too far (other races or species).[5] The marginalized women in incestuous/foreign categories masquerade to stretch the too-narrow window of sexual opportunity. We would also do well to recall here the relationship between incest and the problem of asymmetrical aging† and the manner in which the antipathy between older and younger women (or older and younger men) may ultimately be assimilated to the competition between mothers and daughters for the father (or of fathers and sons for the mother).

Incestuous bedtricks involve yet another paradox:† according to Freud, every child both wants and does not want to sleep with his or her parent and siblings. Freud argued (in *Totem and Taboo*) that the fact that every society has some sort of incest taboo proves that everyone wants to commit incest, for it is not necessary to have laws forbidding things that no one wants to do anyway. The taboo embodies the paradox: you want to do it (or else there would be no need for the law), but you do not want to do it (for the law teaches you that there will be dreadful consequences for you if you succumb to your desire). This paradox is another driving force behind the myths of the bedtrick.

MOTHERS AND SONS

A paradigmatic bedtrick is the tale of the son whose mother mistakes him, at the very least, for someone who is not her son (as in Sophocles' *Oedipus the King*) or, at the very most, for his father. Though our concern in this chapter will be primarily with humans, there are myths about the gods *en famille*, rather than in contact with mortals, that function in the same way as stories about human families,† and we shall begin with one of these. The Hindu god Indra,‡ the villain in many divine adulteries, is the victim in one of the earliest stories that I know (from about 900 B.C.E.) about a son who is mistaken for his father:

INDRA AND KUTSA

Kutsa Aurava ("Thigh-born") was made out of the two thighs of Indra. Just as Indra was, so was he, precisely as one would be who is made out of his own self. Indra made him his charioteer. He caught him with his wife, and when he asked her, "How could you do this?" she replied, "I could not tell the two of you apart." Indra said, "I will make him bald, and then you will be able to tell the two of us apart." He made him bald, but Kutsa bound a turban around his head and went to her. Indra caught him again, and again she said she could not tell them apart. Indra smeared dirt between his shoulders, but Kutsa covered it up and went to her. Indra caught him again, and again she said she could not tell them apart. Then Indra bound Kutsa and made him a wrestler (a Malla), and the dirt [*mala* or *rajas*] that Kutsa shook off from his shoulders became the rajas.[6]

Kutsa does not masquerade as Indra; he *is* Indra's double by his very birth, "thigh-born" (as we would say, "sprung of his loins"), because he is Indra's son. In the myth, Kutsa plays upon this physical resemblance and impersonates Indra, resisting Indra's attempts to differentiate them; or, rather, the myth implies that this resemblance is the justification that Indra's wife gives for sleeping with Kutsa. (As usual, the woman's state of mind remains ambiguous: does she recognize the imposture and remain silent because she welcomes the lover—which seems likely, given her suspicious failure to become suspicious—or is she genuinely fooled and angered by the deception when she finally discovers it? In any case, *Kutsa* knew very well that he was not his own father.)

By failing to correct his mother's error, Kutsa is masquerading as himself†—for, according to classical Hindu law, he *is* his father. *The Laws of Manu* (9.8) state: "The husband enters the wife, becomes an embryo, and is born here on earth. That is why the wife is called a wife [*jaya*], because he is born [*jayate*] again in her." This is a particularly vivid expression of a widespread conviction; Otto Rank noted "the totemistic belief that the soul of the father or grandfather lives again in the newborn child. The original belief, however, is still apparent in the father's fear that if the child bears too great a resemblance to him he is doomed to die; the idea being that it has taken from him his image or shadow, that is to say, his soul."[7] He often takes his woman, too.

In the course of this myth, Indra *un*doubles his son in order to keep the woman for himself. Making Kutsa bald deprives him of the hair that is so often a symbol of semen, the seed in the head.[8] Smearing him with dust makes explicit the pollution of incest and, through two puns, associates him with both spiritual and social pollution: *rajas* means "dust," "passion" (in contrast with spiritual purity, *sattva*), and "menstrual† blood," whereas *raja* means "king," regarded by this text as spiritually inferior to a Brahmin; and *mala* means "dirt," whereas a Malla is a wrestler, of low caste. The myth of Kutsa is part of a larger corpus of myths that deal not only with the profane Freudian concerns of the nuclear family but with the cosmogonic concerns of humankind as a whole, the creation of classes† of men (such as wrestlers and rajas) and the estrangement not only of sons from fathers but of humans from gods.

In another story from ancient India, it is the father who almost makes the incestuous error: a man returning from a long journey sees a young man sleeping near his wife and, thinking that he is her lover, moves to kill him; restrained by a verse that he happens to see, he discovers that he almost killed his own son.[9] We are left to wonder if the boy's proximity to his mother was innocent; if it was not, the story presents an Oedipal encounter that averts the punishment for incest. Incest is also averted at the last minute in the much retold Greek tale *The Life of Secundus* (as Herschel Levine remarks, "Strange as it may seem to us, this revolting story was very popular in antiquity and in the Middle Ages and was translated into Latin, Syrian, Armenian and Arabic"). Here is the opening of the Greek text, probably composed during the latter half of the second century C.E.:[10]

The Life of Secundus

[To test his assumption that all women are whores, a young man who had left home as a small boy let the hair on his head grow long, grew a beard, returned home, and, unrecognized by his mother, got her to accept his offer of fifty gold pieces if she would sleep with him.]

She told the maid, "At nightfall I will have him enter secretly and I will go to bed with him." Secundus sent provisions for a dinner, and when they had finished dinner and started to go to bed, she was expecting to mingle with him carnally; but he put his arms around her as he would around his own mother, and fixing his eyes upon the breasts that had suckled him, he lay down and slept until early morning. When the first light of dawn appeared Secundus got up to go, but she held him with her hands and asked, "Did you do this in order to convict me?" And he answered, "No, mother dear, I refrained because it is not right for me to defile the place from which I came forth at birth. God forbid." Then she asked him who he was, and he said to her, "I am Secundus, your son." She blamed herself and could not bear the sense of shame, and so she hanged herself. Secundus realized that his own talking had brought about his mother's death, and so he resolved not to say anything for the rest of his life. And he practiced silence to the day of his death.[11]

The passage of time,† rather than the particular disguise of the hair and the beard (whose removal failed to prevent Kutsa's incest with his perhaps complicitous mother), may account for the mother's failure to recognize her son, though not, alas, for her willingness to go to bed with a stranger for pay. The tragic ending is reminiscent of the tale of Oedipus, whose mother also hangs herself, while Oedipus destroys his vision instead of his voice. The tale suggests one of the many reasons why men don't play this trick as often as women,† and sons seldom play it on their mothers.

Sometimes, however, incest is neither averted nor punished. Marguerite de Navarre (1492–1549), in her *Heptaméron,* told such a story:

THE MAN WHO MARRIED HIS DAUGHTER AND SISTER

[A rich widow had one son. When he was between fourteen and fifteen years old he began to desire a young lady who slept in his mother's room. The girl complained to the mother, who at first refused to believe her but then said, "I will find out if what you say is true," vowing to punish the boy if it was true, and the girl if it was not. At the mother's instruction, the girl told the boy to come at midnight to join her in bed, but the mother took her place. She waited in silence until he did something that would prove that his intentions were bad, but] so long did she wait, and so fragile was her nature, that her anger turned to pleasure, a pleasure so abominable, that she forgot she was a mother. [That night she became pregnant, while he still thought he had lain with the young girl. Overcome with remorse, she sent the boy away. She bore the child, a daughter, in secrecy and gave her away to her own bastard brother to raise as his own. When the child was grown, he placed her, on her mother's advice, with Catherine, queen of Navarre. After some time, the son wanted to return, but his mother, fearing that she might repeat her sin, told him to return only when he had his wife with him. He visited the queen of Navarre, fell in love with his own daughter, and married her. When he told his mother who his bride was, she] sank into a state of such utter desperation that she thought her end was near. [But several doctors of theology advised her never to say anything to her children,] for they had acted in ignorance and consequently had not sinned.... The poor lady returned to her house, and not long after that her son and her daughter-in-law arrived. They were very much in love. Never was there such love between husband and wife, never were a husband and wife so close. For she was his daughter, his sister, his wife. And he was her father, brother, and husband. They endured forever in this great love, while the poor lady, their mother, in the extremity of her penitence, could not see them show their love but she would withdraw to weep alone.[12]

The permutations of this tale resemble those of a double-back-cross of a special sort; and the sophisticated author, a woman, applies to incest the Machiavellian coincidental,† and involuted permutations more generally characteristic of nonincestuous bedtricks.

A modern take on the theme of the mother who does not recognize her son in bed is provided by a group of five films released between 1985 and 1988, all dealing with the switching of an adult man and a boy through a magic transformation or time travel.[13] The series begins in *Back to the Future* (1985), in which a boy finds himself in danger of masquerading as his father with his mother when he travels back in time to become the contemporary of his potential parents in high school. The potential mother keeps falling in love with her son, who is far more attractive (and intelligent) than the ineffectual father. This is a powerful fantasy in which the child surpasses his father but nobly rejects the opportunity to take his mother away from him. The son keeps trying to help his blundering future father win her, because he knows that if this does not happen, *he himself will never be born.* This danger is graphically, and mythologically, represented by a photograph of the family that the boy brings with him into the past: every time the mother rejects the father, the image of the boy in the photograph begins to fade away, just as the portrait of Dorian Gray‡ becomes uglier every time he commits an evil act.

The incestuous shadow of the child lover is all but erased in the film *Big* (1988), in which a thirteen-year-old boy named Josh makes a wish to be big and wakes up to find himself encased in the body of a young adult male. The first person he tries to convince of his real identity is his mother, but when he appears in front of her, *wearing his father's clothes,* she panics and screams for the police, treating Josh as if he were a stranger who had come into the house to attack her or rape her. He tries to shout, over her screams, "Mom, it's me, Josh.... I have a birthmark on my left knee." But when he starts to take off his pants to show her his knee, she screams all the more and reaches for the phone, and he runs away.

In *Vice Versa* (1988, a revival of the film by that title made by Peter Ustinov in 1947), the parents are divorced, and when the father (magically transposed into his son's body) realizes that he must now live with his ex-wife, he says, "This is the woman I couldn't live with as a husband, and now I'm supposed to live with her as her son? It's a Freudian nightmare." *Like Father, Like Son* (1987) uses many of the same tropes, as does *18 Again!* (1988), which ups the ante by making it a grandfather, not just a father, who changes bodies with his grandson; or, as the grandfather puts it, "I'm subletting my grandson's body." When the old man switches back to his own body again, he un-disinherits his previously disinherited grandson (perhaps to pay the rent on the sublet of his body).

FATHERS AND DAUGHTERS

Many variants of Beauty and the Beast† begin with a father who chooses for his daughter a man she does not love, while she gladly sacrifices herself because of her love for her father. Father-daughter incest looms large in the bedtricks in the tale of Cinderella, particularly in the locus classicus, Perrault's "Donkeyskin," in which "the king's beautiful and charming wife falls ill, and on her deathbed she asks him to swear that he will only marry again a woman who is more beautiful than she. He does so gladly. Time passes, and he searches high and low. Only one woman meets the conditions of his vow: his daughter."[14] Incest is blatant in a variant recorded in the American South, in which the dying wife specifies that her husband should remarry, not just someone "more beautiful"† than her, but "someone who resembles me." The father searches the world and finally tells his daughter ("Jackskin"), "I'm compelled to marry you." She stalls for a while and finally runs away.[15] Alan Dundes has suggested that these stories reflect "the common fantasy of a girl wishing to literally replace her mother—with respect to being her father's mate."[16] That is, when she flees from her father's desire, she is projecting† her own desire for him onto his desire for her. A variant of this theme from the southern Blue Ridge Mountains of America jettisons even this paper-thin inversion: it is the daughter who initiates and manipulates the incestuous relationship with her father, putting on her dead mother's wedding dress, which the father had put away while saying that whenever he found another woman who looked as nice in that dress, he'd marry again.[17] The eponymous cat skin that she eventually puts on is a fitting punishment for a woman who tried to look like another woman (her mother): *de nuit, tous les chats sont gris.*†

Many other bedtricks turn upon incestuous ties between father and daughter. Ovid, writing at the turn of the common era in Rome, told a story also known to other Greek and Latin sources:

MYRRHA AND HER FATHER

Myrrha fell in love with her father, Cinyras; she knew that stallions would mate with their daughters, and that there were tribes where fathers mated with their daughters, mothers with their sons, but not, alas, her own. When he asked her what sort of man she would like to marry, she replied, "One like you." This pleased him, for he didn't understand its full meaning. Myrrha confessed her forbidden desire to her nurse, who promised to help her. One dark night, when Cinyras' wife, Myrrha's mother, was keeping a vow of nine days' absence from her husband's bed, and Cinyras was drunk and missed his bed-mate, the old nurse told him that a young girl was in love with him, a young girl the same age as Myrrha. Night after night, Myrrha climbed into her father's bed, until at last he brought a lamp to see her, and recognized her. He drew his sword; she fled and turned into a myrrh tree, and her child, Adonis, came out of the tree.[18]

The analogy with horses† (in contradiction of Aristotle's† story of the horse that preferred death to the dishonor of incest with his mother)[19] and with people of other races† defamiliarizes the all-too-familiar familial crime. Drunkenness,† too, is a stock prop for the bedtrick, particularly the incestuous bedtrick, and perhaps provides an alibi for the father, who claims he "didn't understand its full meaning" when his daughter told him that her heart belonged to daddy. But the father sobers up quickly enough to bring a lamp to see the bedmate who has implicitly demanded what Cupid† explicitly demanded of Psyche: stay in the dark. And then the jig is up.

Incest colors the bedtrick in a film that Tom Milne called "the silliest approach to the subject in any medium,"[20] *The Reincarnation of Peter Proud* (1974), in which a reincarnated man meets his daughter, now his own age, and seduces her. In the film *Chances Are* (1989), a reincarnation of *The Reincarnation of Peter Proud,* the reincarnated protagonist over-comes the double incestuous temptations of his former wife (now old enough to be his mother) and the woman his own age (who *is* his daughter, and who masquerades as her mother in her attempt to bed him). The wife explains the problem to her ex-husband (as it were) in terms of the cliché† about the passing of time:† "It's not that I don't love you; I do. But people change. Not as much as you, generally, but we've both changed. You're just not my husband anymore." Magically stopping time short-circuits the natural process of aging and produces the overlapping of the generations that results in incest. But this situation occurs without magic every time that generations cross the incestuous line, as Oedipus noted in horror when he realized that he was both father and grandfather to his own children.

BROTHERS AND SISTERS

Incest is the love of someone who is too much the same as oneself, and this sameness, which blurs the line between generations, is more powerful among siblings of the same generation and most powerful in twins. Although most cultures do not regard sleeping with the spouse of a sibling as incest (and several cultures expressly legislate for it through the levirate†), many regard it as a kind of quasi incest, particularly when it is done surreptitiously. In chapter 4 we considered stories about twin sisters who replace one another in bedtricks, raising gender-specific questions of beauty and aging; in chapter 6, the relatively straightforward case of twin brothers; and in chapter 8, the case of male and female siblings who are mistaken for one another. Here let us consider male and female siblings who commit incest with one another through bedtricks.

The *Rig Veda* associates brother-sister incest with bedtricks and with injury to the resulting child; an incantation to protect an embryo against an incubus† assumes that a woman might expect her brother, as well as her husband and her lover, in her bed: "The one who by changing into your brother or your husband or your lover lies with you, who wishes to kill your offspring—we will drive him away from here."[21] In the ancient Norse *Volsunga Saga,* a woman who has married a king but wishes to conceive a child with her brother perpetrates a bedtrick by means of a magic transformation, so that her brother impregnates her without recognizing her. The child is Siegfried, who goes on to become both perpetrator and victim of another famous bedtrick.[22] Frederico, in Samuel Harding's *Sicily and Naples,*† inadvertently rapes (and murders) his sister in the course of a double-back-cross-play, a double masquerade that blinds him to his incestuous passion to revenge what he believes to have been his sister's rape and murder.

In an Inuit story, published in 1947, incest is the brother's idea:

THE MARK OF INCEST

A brother came to his sister in the night and slept with her when "it was dark and she could not recognize him." When he visited her again, she marked his face under the left eye with soot; and the next day she discovered the telltale mark on her brother. She was so angry that she took a knife and cut off her left breast. He told her to go to the sun, where it is always warm, and he went to the moon, where it is always cold. And when the sun sets, you can see blood from her breast in the sky.[23]

As in the story of Samjna,‡ the sun goddess is implicated in incest; but in that myth the female masquerades and the male is mutilated. The eye and breast marked as signs of incest resonate with other myths in which blindness† is the punishment for a sexual crime or in which a woman's breast† is cut off to punish her for her excessive sexuality.

THE FAMILY ROMANCE AS COMEDY AND TRAGEDY

The Family Romance, analyzed, after Freud, by Otto Rank, Joseph Campbell, and Alan Dundes,[24] is usually happy, or at least triumphant: in the end, the hero finds his real parents and comes into his true legacy as a king. But the plot often involves a bedtrick, and then it may well take a tragic turn. In the hands of Sophocles and Freud, the child, raised by people he mistakes for his parents, is in danger of mistaking his real parents for unrelated legitimate sexual partners. Sometimes, however, as we have just seen, the incest is avoided at the last minute or revealed never to have been a danger after all, as in the tale of Secundus† or the Tamil tale "The Prince Who Almost Slept with His Mother."[25] In such cases, the Family Romance may become a comedy (or farce, when it happens for the second time, as Marx said of history in *The Eighteenth Brumaire*). More precisely, it becomes a tragicomedy or a black comedy, like other forms of the bedtrick (such as *Measure for Measure*†); indeed, the term "tragicomedy" was first coined by Plautus in the prologue to his play *Amphitryon,*† the paradigmatic European bedtrick. The idea of the tragicomedy was well paraphrased (reversing Marx) in a song in a Broadway musical distantly descended from the Plautus play (*A Funny Thing Happened on the Way to the Forum*): "Tragedy tomorrow, comedy tonight."

After depicting a comic version of the Family Romance in *Wise Children,*†
Angela Carter's Dora remarks, "Comedy is tragedy that happens to *other*
people."²⁶ This leaves us with yet another paradox:† the Family Romance
is very sad and very funny.

In the last act of *The Marriage of Figaro,*† Mozart and Da Ponte employ
the tragic theme to comic effect when Figaro foils Marcellina's attempt
to inflict the *diritto della Signora*† on him:

> In order to remove Figaro as a rival for Susanna's love, the count encour-
> aged Marcellina to force Figaro to marry her against his will. But Figaro
> protested that he was of noble birth and had been stolen as a child. When
> asked to supply proof, Figaro replied, "The gold, the jewels, and the em-
> broidered clothes which, in my infancy, the bandits found upon me are
> the true indications of my noble birth, and moreover this mark upon my
> arm." At this, Marcellina asked, "A spatula on your right arm?" And indeed,
> she turned out to be his mother ("Your mother?" "My mother." "His
> mother?" "His mother.").

The discovery that the woman is his mother—the same discovery that
Oedipus made, to his sorrow—frees Figaro from being forced to wed a
woman whom he does not desire at all. This inversion of the Sophoclean
scenario was probably made possible because the myth of the surrogate
mother was, by this time and in this sophisticated context, just a joke,
complete with the traditional trappings of jewelry and birthmark. It is,
however, a very heavy joke, black humor that titillates us with the antino-
mian defiance of our deepest taboo: "Oh, the woman I was unwillingly
going to marry/I have willingly married is really my mom." Ah, what a
difference the tense makes, but also the presence or absence of desire.
This is *Oedipus Rex* as it might have been staged like *Cyrano de Bergerac*†
in the Steve Martin retelling.

Where Figaro was saved when the woman turned out to be his mother,
the heroes of other Family Romances are saved when the woman turns
out *not* to be the mother after all. For example, a medieval Sanskrit text
tells us that Pradyumna, who had always considered Mayavati his mother,
gradually noticed how ardently attached to him she was. When he said,
"Why are you acting like this, instead of acting like a mother?" she replied,
"You are not my son. A terrible demon stole you from your father and
threw you into the ocean, where a fish swallowed you. I took you out of
the fish's belly, but your own mother is still weeping for you."²⁷ Several
versions of the story express Mayavati's qualms; one creates another sur-

rogate, a wet nurse, to spare her the awkwardness of being both mistress and stepmother,[28] and in another the demon catches Mayavati and Pradyumna *flagrante delicto* and says to her, "You crazy whore, have you lost your mind, making love with your son?"[29] This is not a Freudian nightmare but a dream of wish fulfillment. So, too, in the film of Fielding's *Tom Jones* (1963), when Tom learns that the woman he has just spent the night with is his mother, he and she just look at the camera and shrug, grinning idiotically; then we learn that she is not, in fact, his mother, and we can laugh again.

Approach Nine
Sexual Rhetoric

AURAL SEX

One of the questions that these stories are asking is, What is intimacy? Sex or talk? We began by noting that sex and text are alike in that stories, like bedtricksters, both lie and tell the truth.† Now is the moment to ask why, and how, they lie and speak truth, how language and metaphor serve as the instruments of deception and revelation in the mythology of bedtricks. Sex is aural as well as oral, and the telling of the story is, like the sexual act, an event that requires to be told.[30] What Harold Bloom has dubbed "the anxiety of influence" for writers and scholars is the literary version of what the nineteenth century called "the heredity of influence,"[31] expressing the deep paternal anxiety of husbands and fathers fearful of other "authors" of their children.

The speech act recurs in these stories in opposition to the sexual act. We noted in another context that, in ancient Judaism, as in contemporary India, "conversation" is a euphemism for intercourse. (This link was implicitly invoked by the bedtrickster in the film *The Truth about Cats and Dogs*† [1996], who joked that she had gotten pregnant by having phone sex.) The protagonist of Julian Barnes's "Experiment"† remarks, "The truth is that everyone talks about sex in a different way, just as everyone, we naturally assume, does it in a different way." Deborah Garrison argues "that the old maxim that sex and reading have a lot in common is probably true. Both rely on our ability to make up fantasies and believe in them—or at least to suspend disbelief long enough to get something we need."[32] In Oscar Wilde's† *The Importance of Being Ernest*, a woman accidentally switches a baby and a manuscript, a marvelous metaphor for the interleaving of sexual and textual tricks.

It is surely no accident that many languages, including those that we call Indo-European (Sanskrit, Greek, Latin, French, German, etc.), assign genders to their nouns. The French term *genre* refers to both sexual genders and literary styles, so that we may speak of both gender-bending and genre-bending; A. K. Ramanujan said, "genders are genres."[33] The Sanskrit term *varna*† has a very similar range, designating class† (including, most prominently, the four social classes) and, not gender, but species, mortal versus immortal,† family versus nonfamily,† color,† and a vowel or syllable. A related cluster of meanings is blanketed by the Sanskrit word *linga* (according to the standard Sanskrit dictionary of Sir Monier Monier-Williams), primarily "a mark, spot, sign, token, badge, emblem, characteristic" that might be used to distinguish one person from another. It then means "any assumed or *false* badge or mark, guise, disguise." The idea that a sign is, ipso facto, a deception is worth noting. And *linga* also means "proof, evidence; . . . a sign of guilt, corpus delicti." Moreover, in logic, Monier-Williams continues, the *linga* is "the invariable mark which proves the existence of anything in an object" (as in the proposition "Where there is smoke, there is fire," where smoke is the *linga* of fire). But its narrower meaning of "the sign of gender or sex, organ of generation," is further narrowed to "the male organ or Phallus (esp. that of Siva)" or "the image of a god, an idol." The sign of universal sexuality is linked with the sign of a particular god, Shiva, in texts that argue that all human beings are naturally designed to be the worshipers of Shiva and his wife Parvati. The clear proof of this is the fact that all men have the *linga*, and all women the *pinda* (the vagina, the image of Parvati).[34] And, finally, in grammar, *linga* means, "gender." Thus, the ancient Hindus recognized the primacy of sexuality in human life as the distinguishing sign, the physiological equivalent of the signs of grammar, evidence, deception, and, most strikingly, divinity.

It is significant that Indo-European nouns have not just two genders but three, arguing for the reification of bisexuality† on the linguistic and, perhaps, the human level. Marjorie Garber comments wittily upon the relationship between the inversions of transvestism (Shakespearean women masquerading as young male pages) and those of literature: "This 'blank page' is inscribed with a double story, a double 'reality.' . . . 'Turning the page,' as it were, from recto to verso, appears to have been a popular pastime in the Venetian book of love."[35] Claude Lévi-Strauss remarked on another aspect of the similarity between sexual difference and linguistic difference when he asserted that men exchange women in the same way that they exchange words: "That the mediating factor, in this case, should be the *women of the group,* who are *circulated* between clans, lineages, or families, in place of the *words of the group,* which are *circulated* between individuals, does not at all change the fact that the essential aspect of the phenomenon is identical in both cases."[36] And language, like sex, can be treacherous, an insight captured by the old sexist saw that a translation, like a woman, cannot be both beautiful and faithful (the sentiment expressed by Chaucer's Wife of Bath†); or, as the Italians put it, "Traddi-tore, traddutore" (to translate is to betray†).

DIRTY STORIES

The bedtrick is the occasion of a struggle between two people for the power to remain the subjects of their own stories and to have their partners recognize those stories. But since each of them has two identities, each has two stories to tell. The female trickster has both the story she tells to herself and the one she tells the victim, while the female victim has both the story she thinks she has (a story that depends on the identity of the trickster) and the one that the trickster knows the victim has. And this is equally true for male tricksters and victims. Thus, double beds hold not only four people† but four stories being told at the same time, for both the trickster and the victim want to tell their stories as well as to live out their own stories; each refuses to alter the course of his or her story or to accept the truth of the other's story. Eventually, one person becomes a character in the saga of the other; one story is encompassed and absorbed by the other.[37] Occasionally, storytelling reveals a disguised sexual identity: the victims of the double bedtricks in "The Ruins round Pisa"† are set free by hearing their stories told. And occasionally the bed-trickster makes the trick work by luring the victim with a story about the trick; this happens to several victims of cross-dressers† who fall for the old story of the boy raised as a girl† —a story often told as an alibi for a trickster who does *not* cross-dress but merely appears to do so while remaining as he (or she) is.

One reason such a story is effective, able to convince people against their better judgment, is precisely because it is such a cliché.† "Oh," says the victim, "that story." Thus, in John Erskine's novel, the daughter of Helen‡ of Troy tries to get her mother off the hook by making up a story of a bedtrick:

> I could have told more than one lie; I tried to choose the best. The first I thought of wouldn't do—I had it out of old-fashioned poetry—that situation you get so often where the gods deceive the lover by a spell, and he doesn't know who it is he takes in his arms, but afterward his eyes are cleared and he knows he's been tricked. I was so desperate at first, I thought of saying Aphrodite enchanted you, so you thought it was Menelaos, but it turned out to be Paris. Don't smile—I didn't waste much time on that threadbare poetry.[38]

Helen, however, replied that it was not threadbare poetry but the truth, "profound truth!" At the very least, she recognized it as the story of her life.

Terence Cave has argued that recognition stories in general (of which the bedtrick is a subgenre) work because when the victim recognizes the trickster, the audience recognizes the time-worn plot: "The recognition scene is, as it were, the mark or signature of a fiction, so that even if something like it occurs in fact, it still sounds like fiction and will probably be retold as such."[39] This is certainly true of myths in general, which derive much of their power from repetition,[40] and particularly true of stories of bedtricks; the predictable ending is as expected, and as satisfying, when it finally comes, as the resolving cadences at the end of a Mozart symphony. After a series of insanely unlikely coincidences† in the Chinese Family Romance† "Nativity Room,"† the author, Li Yu, comments: "Who would ever have expected the Creator's ingenuity to be a hundred times greater than man's? It's as if he had deliberately combined these events so that they could be turned into a play or a story—uniting the two couples and then separating them, separating them and then uniting them, at a prodigious cost in mental effort!"[41] Thus, the reader's objections are explicitly addressed, even used to argue that the story is not only literally true but revelatory of a deeper, divine truth.

So well known is the film scenario of the good and evil twins that when a real woman impersonated her real (and murdered) sister in 1997, the police chief remarked, "I don't know if bizarre quite describes it; this is the stuff of a Hollywood movie."[42] In reporting a case of a man who pretended to be a woman and was married for three and a half years before his husband found out, the Associated Press found "the deception reminiscent of the Broadway drama 'M. Butterfly.'"[43] The character of Allie in the novel *Single White Female* muses, "This was, in some strange way, more than mere imitation. It made her think of that old science-fiction movie, *The Body Snatchers*.†"[44] So, too, the wife who plots to masquerade as her husband's mistress, in Olivia Goldsmith's *Switcheroo*,† is inspired by "those World War II films" in which someone impersonates the Nazi general, and when her husband tells a friend, "It's not me going to that woman's house," the friend quips, "It's your evil twin?"[45] Even characters *within films* sometimes refer to themselves, self-referentially, as cinematic characters; the double twins in *Big Business* (1988) refer to pod-people (from *Invasion of the Body Snatchers* [1956]).

Thus, bedtricksters (in real life and in stories) often tell bedtrick stories† to persuade their victims. Martin Guerre† had on his side an already existing corpus of stories in his favor: the man who returns to his wife after a long absence, usually in a war, and must prove to her that he is her husband despite the changes wrought by time and suffering was even in his time a classical motif, often simply called "The Return" or the "Nostos" theme. But the real-life event of Martin Guerre's surrogation also became a story, indeed many stories, in various forms (opera, novel, film, and social history); as Terence Cave remarks, "An occurrence which was manifestly deeply disturbing to those who enacted and witnessed it is thus converted into a variety of recognition plots."[46] And so tragedy is translated into comedy† or tragicomedy.†

The success of bedtricks in real life was often cited to justify the realistic truth of stories,† even myths, about successful bedtricks. Thus, the sixteenth-century scholar-printer Henri Estienne used the story of Martin Guerre to show that Herodotus "was not so unbelievable" when he told the story of a successful imposture.[47] Estienne also cited in defense of Herodotus other supporting cases from what he regarded as real life, the transsexual masquerades of Pope Joan (now regarded as pure mythology) and of a French girl who dressed as a man, married a woman, and was burnt at the stake.[48]

But if some stories make the trick persuasive, some written texts unmask the masquerader. Roxane, in *Cyrano de Bergerac*,† finally realizes that Cyrano was the one who had written the love letters to her, and the heroine in *Love Letters*† (1945) realizes not only that her hero wrote the letters but also that she herself wrote the responses. Often, of course, the stories lie: the courtesan† and the nymph in the tale "The Definitive Loincloth"† try in vain to prove their identity by telling stories. The sage who curses Shakuntala† says that her lover will forget her, "just as a drunk does not remember the story that he told before."[49] And although the criteria† for deception are rather different in real bedtricks and in stories about them, they are often confused by characters within the stories; thus, in Verdi's *Don Carlo*, Eboli first tells the story of a bedtrick and then becomes embroiled in one herself.

I noted, in the introduction, that myths, even more than other sorts of stories, swing upon the double ability of storytelling to conceal or reveal. We must also bear in mind that a story often functions as a negative truth: when, for instance, the stories present successful bedtricks, we should conclude not that bedtricks succeed more than they fail but, rather, that *stories* about bedtricks pay far more attention to successful illusions than to failures, precisely because common sense insists that illusion is what has to be justified, and is hard to justify, in a bedtrick. (Similarly, more texts explain why mortal women prefer mortal men‡ than why they prefer immortal men precisely because that is what needs to be explained.) The narrative dice are loaded in favor of bedtricksters because the real-life dice are believed to be loaded against them.

David Shulman has remarked upon the way that myths force us into the logical impasse of doubling and masquerading whenever we try to think about our lives: "In myths, the articulation of major categories of thought or perception is based on their occlusion or disguise; that is, myth is predicated on the listener's not perceiving the primary categories that the story attempts to set out. For that matter, the author too cannot, by definition, see them. Once you know that this story is meant to 'explain' something like, for instance, the difference between gods and mortals, then it's no longer myth."[50] This self-deception,† the withholding of one's knowledge from oneself, false ignorance,† is essential to the bedtrick.

Bedtricksters are not the only ones who lie; all speech is a lie, in the sense that language is intrinsically false to human experience.[51] But sexual language is particularly false. Heinrich Zimmer has illuminated the connection between myths and bedtricks (of the Lovely Lady† variety) through the metaphor of the aging face,† the source of so many bedtricks:

> The mythical content often appears rather like an overpainted, tricked-out old beauty. Beneath all the frippery there is nothing of the reborn freshness of a youthful figure with radiant countenance, but only a shriveled, corrugated old thing with a rewritten face. Nevertheless, just such long-overripe old beauties are often the very ones to tell best the ancient tales of life; they are better at that, by far, than the young and attractive fascinators. The only problem is not to shudder at the look of them while we are listening.[52]

And one reason that we shudder is that we realize that the old lady is telling the truth, despite the lie implicit in her "overpainted" beauty and "rewritten" face. The knowledge that the myth transmits is, in part, self-validating; it transmits the knowledge of its own truth. But these myths also deconstruct their own truth and tell us, using language, that language, in which myths are inscribed, is a lie. Thus, simultaneously they explicitly affirm and implicitly deny the deceptive nature of knowledge itself, both sexual knowledge and the fragile knowledge transmitted by language.

R. Howard Bloch, in *The Scandal of the Fabliaux,* notes that, among the many sexual tricks depicted in the medieval French stories, the dirty story itself is the greatest trick of all. People use tricky speech to accomplish their sexual ends; the genitals and the tongue are conflated, and genitals† (dismembered and animated) often literally tell tales. As Bloch remarks, "It is not the desiring body that generates the tale which merely reflects it, but the tale which produces desire and which can even be held responsible for the desire for narrative. . . . There can be no difference between the desire so often expressed in sexual terms on the level of the theme and the desire for the story itself."[53] In other words, these are not merely stories about sexual tricks; they are stories about stories, which use dirty sexual tricks to say something about the dirty and deceptive tricks of language. The central event is not necessarily the cuckolding but the clever words that the trickster tells to conceal the cuckolding.

The desire for narrative of which Bloch speaks owes a great deal to the idea of the pleasure of the text in the writings of Roland Barthes, particularly *S/Z*.† The Balzac story of Sarrasine† itself, even before Barthes illuminates it for us, is about language; as Sarrasine says to La Zambinella: "You have dragged me down to your level. *To love, to be loved!* are henceforth meaningless words for me, as they are for you."[54] And Barthes comments: "Not only is sex eradicated, but art too is broken (the statue is destroyed), language dies." That is, for Barthes, both Sarrasine and language are castrated† (a phrase we sometimes use in English to refer to heavily censored† texts). The fact that the French hero does not really understand what the Italians are saying, let alone what they are doing, makes the cultural blinders linguistic blinders; his ignorance of the words kills him. Thus, language is not merely castrated; it castrates.

Balzac's story has a frame: Sarrasine's story is told by a would-be lover to a lady who asks for the story ("I want to know now"), to which the storyteller replies, "You haven't yet given me the right to obey you when you say: 'I want to.'" Barthes's gloss of this reply is:

> If you give yourself to me, I will tell you the story: tit for tat: a moment of love in exchange for a good story. . . . A man in love, taking advantage of the curiosity evidenced by his mistress, . . . offers her a contract: the truth in exchange for a night of love, a narrative in exchange for a body. . . . Carried by the narrative itself, this disease [of castration] ends by contaminating the lovely listener and, withdrawing her from love, keeps her from honoring the contract. Caught in his own trap, the lover is rebuffed: a story about castration is not told with impunity.[55]

Thus, Barthes frames Balzac, adding his own layer outside the narrator who frames Sarrasine. The "desire for narrative" appears here as a contract that is the inverse of Scheherazade's: the story is told by a man to a woman, and it causes, rather than prevents, his "death." For the woman who hears about Sarrasine is horrified; the seducer's story backfires. Where Scheherazade's story forestalls her death, the narrator's story forestalls the seduction (by the narrator) but not the death (of Sarrasine).

The pleasure of the text is an old idea in India. In the Valmiki *Ramayana*,† a king who lives with a man who becomes a woman every other month gives her pleasure as she gives pleasure to him (the verb for sexual enjoyment, *ram*, is consistently used in the causative both for him and for her); and when she becomes a man, the king gives him the pleasure of hearing stories, using the same verb, *ram*, for the pleasures of sex and text.‡

D. W. Winnicott argues that bedtime stories are among the child's first transitional objects,† the first things that build a bridge between the self-created world and the created world, the first substitutes for the mother.†[56] François Flahaut sees a slightly different relationship between narrative, sexuality, and the loss of the mother:

> Every human being has two umbilical cords: one, made of flesh, is cut at birth; the other, even before conception, weaves a person into language. But not only can this second cord never make up for the cutting of the first, it is itself an ambiguous, or paradoxical, umbilicus: it connects only by keeping apart; it plunges each person into the immense universe of meaning only at the price of an irrevocable break. . . . Fictional narratives are one of the forms of compromise (sexual life is another, and the most basic) which seek to reduce this paradox.[57]

The paradox of linguistic alienation argues that the original unity of languages (in Eden) was shattered at the time of the tower of Babel; narratives seek to heal that break, when one person tells a story and the other says, "Yes, I understand; that's my story, too." Similarly, the paradox of sexual separation argues that when the umbilical cord is cut, we are separated from our mother; sexual union (and the advent of the father's phallus and, with it, language, according to Lacan†) seeks to heal that break, when one person joins physically with another. When these two paradoxes of linguistic and sexual alienation, the tower of Babel and the separation from the mother/lover, are simultaneously addressed in narratives about sexual life, the form (the narrative) reinforces the content (the image of the sexual act). In myths about bedtricks, the two paradoxes converge in an attempt to heal one another, as narrative and language themselves may emerge as substitutes for the lost object of love. But, the deconstructionists argue, we never do understand another person's story, and we know that lovers, like stories, prove untrue, widening the rift even farther, language tearing away at sexuality and sexuality at language. And yet poets and mythmakers dare to dream that we can somehow experience one another's stories.

Terry Eagleton has remarked on another aspect of the analogy between the loss of the mother and the telling of a story:

> It is an original lost object—the mother's body—which drives forward the narrative of our lives—impelling us to pursue substitutes in an endless metonymic movement of desire. Something must be lost or absent in any narrative for it to unfold. If everything were fixed, there would be no story to tell. Loss is distressing but also exciting. Desire is stimulated by what we cannot have, but we must know that the object will always be restored to us. We can tolerate the object's disappearance because our suspense was all the time shot through with the secret knowledge that it would finally come home.[58]

This secret knowledge, the literary equivalent of false ignorance in the bedtrick,† is what lends power to the cliché plot of the bedtrick. Without the abandoning mother, or the masquerading lover, there would be no story; but without the assurance that a suitable replacement will be found, and the masquerader unmasked, we could not bear to listen to it.

THE DOUBLE ENTENDRE

When people double, they may become masqueraders; when words double, they may become puns and riddles, verbal hiding places. The riddle often turns on the double meaning of a word or a phrase: the trick is to find out what the second meaning is, to identify the surrogate—which is also the point of so many of the stories of bedtricks. Riddling is often erotic, a kind of teasing, verbal foreplay that sets up the bedtrick; in some societies, including India, a woman may have what is called a "joking relationship" with certain men regarded as sexually safe. The term "distinctive feature," used in structural linguistics to distinguish one phoneme† (or, by Lévi-Straussian extension, mytheme†) from another, applies equally well to the narrative clue that enables us to tell one sexual partner from another.

So many bedtricks depend upon the trickiness of words, riddles, puns, and double entendres. The myth of Samjna,‡ first stated in the form of a riddling verse in the *Rig Veda*, turns upon the riddle of the foot‡ that is both a part of a leg and a part of a meter of poetry; and Samjna embodies the riddle of the relationship between the mother and the nonmother, the Text and the Commentary. The Loathly Lady† sometimes solves riddles that other people have posed for the young hero (What do women want?), sometimes poses riddles to the young hero herself, and sometimes herself constitutes a riddle, either the same riddle that she solves for him (What do women want?) or the riddle of her own ugliness and beauty, or beauty and infidelity.

One retelling of the tale of Rachel† and Leah introduces a play on the phrase "Hi leah, hi leah," which is ostensibly an exclamation of joy (like "Hallelujah") but also means "It is Leah, it is Leah!":

> That night they were singing, "Hi leah, hi leah." In the evening they came to lead her [into the bridal chamber] and put out the light. "What is the meaning of this?" he asked. They replied, "Do you think that we are rams [or, in another reading, disgusting people] like you?" All that night he called her "Rachel," and she answered him. In the morning, however, Behold, it was Leah.[59]

Missing the major pun (about Leah), Jacob is bamboozled by the minor pun (about himself as a ram or a boor, for Rachel's name means "ewe" in Akkadian), and so lets himself be talked into making love in the dark.

A vital clue in the film *Prelude to a Kiss*† (1992) consists of a series of linguistic tests about a riddle in Dutch that the real Rita teaches Peter before the switch. The phrase in Dutch means "What white teeth you have," and the response is "The better to eat you with" (also in Dutch). Becker-as-Rita knows the phrase, and for a moment Peter thinks that this proves that s/he really is Rita; but s/he can't remember the response, and later we learn that Becker was born in Amsterdam and so just happens to know Dutch. When Peter finally meets Rita-as-Becker, he says the Dutch phrase, to which s/he replies, "Not any more," showing the yellow teeth that Rita as Rita had worried about. The Dutch riddle comes from a fairy tale about a masquerade in bed (the wolf† with Little Red Riding Hood), but its transformation here ("Not any more") makes it even more appropriate, for the dream of teeth yellowing and falling out is, as Freud noted,[60] the nightmare of aging and dying, the subtext of *Prelude to a Kiss.*

I have noted that words like "betray"† and "deceive"† in English have both a general and a particularly sexual meaning; the word "myth," too, is one of a small but interesting group of words that mean, usually for reasons of historical conflation, both one thing and its opposite (like "cleave"†).[61] Other languages contain similar sorts of double entendres:

in French, *dédoubler* means both to split one thing in half and to double it; Persian uses one word for both "image" and "beloved,"[62] suggestive of myths in which an image stands in for the lost love object; and Tamil uses one word for both "body" and "reality," suggesting a great deal that is relevant to my arguments about mind and body,† reality and illusion. The fact that in German (as in many languages) there is one word (*Mädchen* in German) for both "maiden" and "girl" is the source of a pun that leads to great misunderstandings between Arabella† and Mandryka: where she means to say goodbye to her maiden*hood*, he thinks she has given her maiden*head*† to another man.

Marina Warner has pointed out the particular relevance of riddles to myths of incest:† "A riddle contains negative terms that turn into positives as soon as they are decoded: riddling means to defy logic in peculiar couplings of like and like. . . . Mutually exclusive terms become one in the verbal game. It is a form which abolishes linguistic logic, just as incest cancels kinship law. . . . The language of the imagination . . . acts as the guardian of real bodies, and cerebral logic, encrypted in enigmas, deflects improper conjunctions in the world of sexual relations."[63] The genetic sameness of two family members is the homophonic identity of the two words, the sameness of the signifier; their sexual difference is the difference of the signified. The "improper conjunctions" of bodies in this paradigm are deflected by the improper conjunctions of words.

Yet words often protect the masquerader and make possible the improper conjunction. English-speaking people nowadays usually regard puns or even strong rhymes as humorous, as doggerel; the accepted social reaction to an elaborate pun is a groan. But puns can be deadly earnest in religious texts (as well as in French literary criticism), and riddles are often a matter of life and death. Barthes demonstrates how puns are used to save Sarrasine from admitting the truth to himself:

> The tenor says, *"You have no rival,"* because: (1) you are loved (Sarrasine's understanding); (2) you are wooing a castrato (understanding of the accomplices and perhaps, already, of the reader). According to the first understanding, there is a snare; according to the second, a revelation. . . . The *double understanding*, the basis for a play on words, cannot be analyzed in simple terms of signification (two signifieds for one signifier). . . . If the play on words seems to be addressed to one person only (for example, the reader), this person must be imagined as being divided into two subjects, two cultures, two languages, two zones of listening.[64]

Thus, Barthes returns us to the question of who knows and who does not know,† and of the reader's delicate balance between these shifting worlds.

A Lover by Any Other Name

Language and sexual identity, the word and the personality, merge in one form: the name. Names are the key to many of the stories in this corpus: they conceal and reveal the true nature of the masquerader, they are given to children in curses on or by masquerading mothers or fathers, they are assumed as hints of the truth, and they are to be guessed at the cost of life or love (the Rumpelstiltskin theme). Names are connected with the most basic ideas about doubles, as Otto Rank points out; since the name is "an essential part of the personality," therefore, "if two offspring of the same family bear the same name, one must die"[65] (hence the traditional prohibition in some religions, including Judaism, against naming a child after a living person). And, as Naomi Segal notes, an inherited name that replaces one generation by another "suggests an alternative version of Lacan's† Oedipal acceptance of the 'nom du père' along with the 'non du père,' for here it is the name that gives the child power over the father, the potential to inherit his place rather than share it."[66]

Bedtricksters masquerade behind their names or other people's names and are exposed by their names. Perhaps the most implausible of the many implausible elements of *A Comedy of Errors*† is the fact that, though the twins are expressly said to have been so alike that "they could not be distinguished but by names" (1.1), when they were separated, each was called by the same name, Antipholus—and happened to employ a servant named Dromio; this double device allows the farce to proceed. In *Love Letters*† (1945), the name of Singleton (which means an only child in contrast with a twin, a strange name for a double woman) is a clue the hero misses at first. In *Dead Ringers* (1988),† one of the twin brothers (who are named, androgynously, Beverley and Elliot, nicknamed Bev and Ellie), finding himself alone in a hotel, sends for twin sisters. When they arrive, he tells them, hesitating uncertainly at the first name, "So that I can tell you apart, I want you, Mimsy, to call me El, and you, Coral, to call me Bev." The names of the twin men are thus given the chiasmic twist of allowing the trickster to tell twins apart not by *their* names but by their names for *him*. This logic of a projected† voice corresponds to the logic of the projected gaze,† which made some people in ancient India paint a magic ointment‡ on *their* eyes in order to become invisible to others (and makes children cover their own eyes when they want to become invisible).

The initials of Jupiter's name on Amphitryon's† box or, in other variants, his monogram on a headband provide a vital piece of damning evidence, though this hard proof fails when the gods tamper with it. Kleist's Alcmena‡ worries about this: "If I could not distinguish, dearest Charis, / Between two names like that, could they belong / To two men—is that possible?—between / Whom I could not distinguish any better?"⁶⁷ By contrast, Kleist's Sosia‡ says to his double, Mercury-as-Sosia: "How did you ever get this unheard-of idea: making off thus with my name? Now, if it were my cloak, or if it were My supper . . . But my name! Why, can you wear it?"⁶⁸ We laugh at Kleist's Sosia for being so foolish as to think that a name is a thing that one can steal and applaud Kleist's Alcmena for seeing through this nonsense. But the weight of evidence in the myths goes against Alcmena's apparent sophistication and in favor of Sosia's apparent naiveté: you can indeed steal someone's name.

Javier Marias's paranoid protagonist, Victor, seeing a prostitute who may or may not be his ex-wife, Celia, wonders what would happen "if it was her and she bore the same name—because a face is not enough, it grows old and can change and can be made up to look different." He asks her name. " 'Victoria,' she lied, assuming she was Celia and perhaps even if she wasn't. But if she was Celia, then she lied deliberately, ironically, maliciously, even mockingly, because that is the female version of my own name." So he lies, too, and says his name is Javier, which is actually the author's name: "I would have known that Victoria was Celia if Victoria had replied 'Celia' when I had asked her what her name was, and I might then have answered 'Victor' when she asked me mine. And in that case, we would have recognized each other and perhaps embraced."⁶⁹ Names really do matter.

The name of a king has both a political† aspect (the title) and an individual aspect (the personal name). In *Prisoner of Zenda*,† both the king and Rasendel have the same first name (Rudolph), yet Rasendel urges Flavia to call him not by his title but only by his name (Rudolph), and later he consoles himself with the memory of her chanting *his* name over and over, even though it is also the name of the king, with whom she is now presumably in bed. This doubleness of the private and the public also affects the taboo against knowing the name of the animal lover or the lover from another world, such as Lohengrin:† "Nie sollst du mich befragen . . . noch meine Name und Art." The prohibition against knowing the name is a narrative parallel to the prohibition against Psyche's looking at Cupid at night. Sometimes the lover of the animal lover wants to *see* the animal form, and sometimes she wants to know the lover's *name;* these are two ways of determining identity, through the eye or the ear/mouth.†

One name in particular is critical in many bedtricks: the name cried out at the moment of passion, the moment of truth. And this is often the wrong name (for the false, present situation) but also the right name (for the true, hidden revelation); the words betray the truth, while the physical act lies (in implying a monogamous love). Crying out in the act of love, a naked cry that may at first appear to be as primitive as a speech act can be, is nevertheless a cultural fact; the inarticulate coital cries give way to the name, a culturally constructed entity. The false name called out in bed reveals the fantasized other; or, if you prefer, the true name blurted out in a false bed reveals the fantasized partner to the "real" partner. When the impostor Jack Sommersby† first makes love to "his" wife, he hesitates until she calls him "Jack" and repeats it again and again; the wrong name is the right name.

So often in Indian texts does a person call out the name of one lover when making love to another that Sanskrit poetics has a name for it, *gotraskhalana* ("stumbling on the name"), and many anthologies of poetry, beginning with the earliest collections, devote a separate section to this theme.[70] When King Dushyanta realizes that he has lost Shakuntala,† he speaks politely to the women in the harem but calls them by the wrong names.[71] When Rambha,† the celestial courtesan, in bed with the poet, calls him by the name of her husband, Nalakubara,† she triggers the entire bedtrick. Europeans do this, too. Andersen's mermaid† hears her prince murmur, in his sleep, the name of his bride, the other woman. In Terry Southern's "A Change of Style," the woman realizes that her husband has mistaken her for his mistress when he calls her Elaine instead of Grace. In Olivia Goldsmith's *Switcheroo,*† when the wife, Sylvie, and the mistress, Marla, change places, and Marla-as-Sylvie accidentally remarks, "Sylvie will be furious," she fears the jig is up. But the bedtricked husband just thinks she's Sylvie and is referring to herself in the third person; he psychobabbles in reply, "I think Sylvie is furious right now. . . . Don't dissociate. You can acknowledge your anger. Especially with me, Sylvie." He himself slips up by calling Marla-as-Sylvie by Marla's nickname, Cookie Face, and she objects, "Cookie Face? Who's Cookie Face?" Flustered, he replies, "Nobody. I mean, you are." And in fact she is.[72]

In Rosamond Smith's *Lives of the Twins,* the name torments the woman caught between the two brothers: "She clutches Jonathan in terror of crying out James's name. She would suck Jonathan deep, deep into her, would swallow him up, speaking his name as if he were an incantation *Jonathan Jonathan Jonathan* until she loses all consciousness of what she does, and what she is trying not to do." And "she recalls how, straddling her, James struck her, systematically, dispassionately, whispering obscene names—*her* names."[73] The name in bed is both truth, the name of her true love, and a lie, when the false lover defiles her own name.

People often "stumble on the name" in films. In *Seven Sinners* (1936), Marlene Dietrich, in drag as a navy officer, sings a song about the navy, of which one verse is: "Many men just can't remember / The affair from last September. . . . But when he says, 'I love you Bessie,' / To some girl whose name is Jessie. . . . You know the man is in the Navy." In *Love Letters†* (1945), *Single White Female†* (1992), and *The Truth about Cats and Dogs†* (1996), people stumble on the name in bed. The FBI man masquerading in the face of the terrorist in *Face/Off‡* (1997), in bed with the terrorist's girl, not only calls her by his wife's name but calls "their" child by the name of his own child. In *All of Me* (1984),† there is a veritable orgy of wrong names as Roger tries to make love to a woman named Terry while Edwina's soul is inside him, fantasizing about *Gone with the Wind:* Terry cries out, "O Roger"; Roger cries out, "O Terry"; and the voice of Edwina cries out, "O Clark, Vivian, and Olivia. O Ashley and Butterly." The protagonist in *An Awfully Big Adventure* (1995), in bed with a young woman named Stella, calls out the name of Stella Maris; when the woman asks him who Stella Maris is, he confesses it was a woman he knew years ago, who had given herself that nickname; later we find out that Stella Maris was the mother of the Stella in his bed, to whom she had given her own fantasy name and—unwittingly and incestuously†—her own lover.

It happens in real life, too, as we know perhaps from our own lives and certainly from those of famous people. During World War II, rumors about an affair between General Eisenhower and his driver, Kay Sommersby, circulated widely, and after the war Ike returned to a very suspicious Mamie. To placate her, he took her off on a three-day vacation, just the two of them, but unfortunately he called her Kay—and not once, but twice.[74] In the notorious William Kennedy Smith rape trial in 1991, the defendant testified that the woman who accused him called him "Michael" (significantly, the name of her stepfather),[75] while she testified that he called her "Cathy" (which was not her name). He argued that this, rather than the physical act, pushed her over the edge into the trauma that drove her to indict him for rape.[76]

The names of gods have special power and deceptive roles in divine bedtricks. In Indian Tantra, the participants in the sexual ritual imagine that they and/or their partners are deities and call them by the names of the deities. An interesting twist on this belief may have been inspired by the observed tendency of people to cry out the name of God at the moment of death or orgasm (the latter having the incidental advantage of preventing them from crying out the wrong human name). According to Imam Budhari (who died in A.D. 870), an authority on hadiths about sexual behavior, a man *should*, at the moment of orgasm, pronounce the name of God, because at that moment, a man loses his reason, and by calling out the name of God, he prevents the devil from influencing him. Therefore, as Fatna A. Sabbah remarks, "The licit sexual act in Islam is not a sexual act between a man and a woman, but a sexual act that sets up a relationship between three beings: man, woman, and God."[77] This is yet another testament to the revelatory power of sex: the name stumbled upon in profane sex is replaced by the name deliberately evoked to reveal the divine bedmate.

T E N

Real Sex and
Fantastic Sex

Despite the evidence that sex lies,† our myths present strong testimony for the counterargument, its revelatory power. The sexual litmus test for reality comes in several strengths, best considered one by one. We will start with the industrial strength—the sexual act—and then move on to the postcoital sleep, the kiss, and (in films) the wo/men's room.

THE SEXUAL ACT

Supernatural or magical bedtricksters in myths can often be identified not by any constant criterion, such as their lack of a shadow,‡ but rather by things that they do at certain moments—such as, for instance, the moment of making love. We have noted psychological projections† in the minds of the victims of bedtricks. Literal† projections also occur in myths: a god or demon projects from his mind, like a beam of light from a film projector (or what, in my childhood, we stilled called a "magic lantern"), an illusion that envelops the mind of his victim. Such a trickster is, however, compelled to take his (more rarely her) own true form when he loses mental control and hence inadvertently turns off the current from the magic projector in his head. When the king in a Sanskrit play asks, "How can you find a deity who has concealed herself by her magic powers?" the jester replies, "Sometimes they fail to conjure up the conceal-ment."[1] This happens, according to various texts, when the trickster sleeps, dies, eats, laughs, gets drunk, angry, frightened, very happy, or, in the case of a demoness, gives birth. It also happens when the trickster makes love, when sexual passion strips away the disguise and reveals the true identity. This cluster of beliefs centers upon the intuition that the truth is encased in the subconscious—in sleep, in dream, in bed, in sex.

When Thomas of Erceldoune, the hero of a medieval English romance, makes love with the ravishingly beautiful queen of the fairies, she is re-vealed as a Lovely Lady.† She protests, from the start, that if he should "have his will of her, he would spoil her beauty and marr her." He does have her and mar her; her eyes and her rich clothing vanish, and her body becomes "black as beaten lead."[2] The power of sex turns her into her true self—in this case, an ugly, black† self. This is not a foolproof method; the Hindu demigod and the celestial nymph involved in a double-back-cross-play† in the affair of the loincloth† did *not* lose this control of their illusions in bed. But the demons Adi† and Jalandhara† inadvertently resumed their own forms when they shed their seed. The Buddha is said to have claimed that there are two occasions when a *naga*† (a cobra god, frequently a snake lover†) will reveal his true form (*svabhava*), presumably after assuming a human form: when he engages in sexual intercourse with a female of his own species and when he sleeps thinking that he is safe from detection.[3] The specification of a female of his own species (*sajatiya*) suggests that it is not just the power of sexuality but the pull toward the form corresponding to that of his partner—toward sameness, away from difference—that draws this bedtrickster back to his true self.

Supernatural creatures are well aware of the fact that they may be unmasked by sex. A Hindu bedtrickster in a Sanskrit text from c. 700 C.E. knows that he may reveal his true form when he makes love, and so he takes precautions:

VARUTHINI AND THE DEMIGOD

A Brahmin named Pravara obtained a divine ointment that, when smeared on his feet, enabled him to fly. But he flew to the Himalayas and walked in the snows, which washed off the ointment so that he could no longer fly, though he longed to return home. A celestial courtesan named Varuthini fell in love with him and begged him to stay with her, but he rejected her, saying, "Don't touch me! Go to some other man who is like you." He continued to protest that he desired only his own wife, and that his gurus had told him never to desire the wife of another man, until finally the householders' fire transported him back home.

Now, a demigod [*gandharva*] named Kali was in love with Varuthini and had been rejected by her. He observed Varuthini now and reasoned, "She is in love with a human. If I take on his form, she will suspect nothing and will make love with me." Kali-as-Pravara approached her and said, "You must not look at me during the time of our shared sexual enjoyment [*sambhoga*], but close your eyes and unite with me." She agreed, and when they made love, and her eyes were tightly closed, she thought, because of his hot energy, it was the form of the [Brahmin] suffused with the sacrificial fire. Then, after a while, she conceived an embryo, who came from

the demigod's semen and from (her) thinking about the Brahmin's form.
The demigod went away, still in the form of the Brahmin.[4]

The mortality of the Brahmin, Pravara, in contrast with the special powers
of the demigod Kali (whose name is related to, but different from, the
name of the goddess Kali†—his has two short vowels, hers two long vowels), is underscored by his need to doctor his feet‡ in order to fly. But
the demigod is more human than the Brahmin, in ways that confuse Varuthini; his "hot energy," or semen *(tejas),* is heated by his lust, not (as
she imagines) by his sacrificial power. Her belief that she is making love
with the Brahmin (never dispelled in this episode—the trickster leaves
before he is unmasked) gives the child the Brahmin's form, through parental imprinting.†

A Telugu version of this myth elaborates upon the bedtrickster's quandary:

> They began to make love, but suddenly he remembered that gods take
> their true form when they sleep, eat, or make love (and demons when
> they die, in addition to the first three). He therefore told her that there
> was a convention in his family that she should not open her eyes during
> lovemaking. She agreed and closed her eyes, and they made love for a
> long time, happily.[5]

The celestial lover fears that she will penetrate his disguise even as he
penetrates her, and that is why he insists that she close her eyes.

One Hindu text substitutes joy for sexual passion as the unmasking
emotion:

> A goblin [*yaksha*] who desired a celestial courtesan took the form of a
> demigod. She thought him beautiful and let him make love to her while
> while the other celestial courtesans were watching. When he achieved his
> object, she immediately had a son, who was born of his father's seed but
> had a form like that of his mother. Then the goblin was so overjoyed that
> he assumed his original form, because big goblins and ogres [*rakshasas*]
> regain their own form when dying, asleep, angry, frightened, or very
> happy. When they saw him in his true form, all the courtesans were puz-
> zled, angry, and frightened, and they fled.[6]

Again the child resists the form of the biological father, this time in favor
not of the mother's imagination but of her physical form. It is not the
sex itself that makes the demon reveal himself here but the emotion of
joy that follows—a strong, uncontrollable emotion, like lust, that short-

circuits the magic machine. A variant of the power of joy in the story of the goblin appears in a Chinese Buddhist text about a masquerading Buddha: "Unable to contain himself, our Great Sage broke into loud giggles, which, alas, he should have never permitted himself to do. For once he laughed, his original features also appeared."[7]

But it is also the birth of a son, not just the Hindu goblin's happiness, that unmasks him—the event that, in many Indian narratives about illusion, frees a dreamer from the world of unreality.[8] This is surely relevant for my argument that it is the issue of male lineage,† rather than sexual pleasure, that drives so many of these myths. A Japanese variant of the myth of Mélusine‡ (another snake lover†) demonstrates the sobering effect of the birth of a son: A man fell in love with the daughter of a sea god, and when she was ready to bear him a child, she said, "All persons of other lands, when they bear young, revert to the form of their original land and give birth. Therefore, I too am going to revert to my original form and give birth. Pray do not look upon me!" But he watched in secret as she turned into a giant crocodile, and he was astonished and ran away. When she learned that he had watched, she felt ashamed and, leaving behind the child she had borne, went back into the sea. (Later she sent her younger sister to nurse the child; the sister also married him.)[9]

The revelatory sexual act is a recurrent theme in the American cinema. In *Shattered*† and *Duplicates,*† both made in 1991, the amnesiac victim has access to his hidden self only through the memory† of making love. In *Basic Instinct* (1991), a brunette masquerades as a blonde by wearing a wig. The movie begins with a man first making love with and then being murdered in bed by a (wigged) blonde with an icepick and ends with the (unwigged) blonde making love exactly like the first, murderous blonde. Everything else is lies; only the sexual act, seen first only by the camera and the victim, then by the camera and the hero (perhaps the next victim), claims to tell us the truth. But what is the truth? That the blonde at the end must be the blonde at the beginning (i.e., the murderer)? Or that *all* women behave like that in bed (i.e., that all cats are gray in the dark)? Or, finally, that all (hyper-)sexual women are murderers? Even in this film, which generally equates sex with reality, the cynical heroine remarks, "Do you think I'm going to tell you all my darkest secrets just because I had an orgasm?" To that question, the hero of *American Gigolo* (1980) would have answered, "Yes." When the heroine in that film, all starry-eyed and worshipful in her postcoital glow, says to the hero (if we can call him that), "I want to know all about you," he replies, "We just made

love, didn't we? Then you know all there is to know." Maybe this is meant
to apply only to gigolos, whose meaning is entirely circumscribed by sex.

But it is all that the woman needs to know about her man in Pedro
Almodovar's *Tie Me Up! Tie Me Down!* (1989), in which the heroine is
abducted by a man who claims that he once knew her (carnally and otherwise), which she vehemently denies. When he finally makes love to her,
at the moment when he enters her she says, "Now I know." "What?" "I
remember you now. You told me that we had screwed before. I said I
didn't remember. Well, now I sure do remember." To which he simply
replies, not skipping a beat, "It's about time." The theme can also be used
in reverse. In *Overboard* (1987), a man persuades a woman who suffers
from amnesia that they are married and she has forgotten him. The first
time he makes love to her, she is swept off her feet; breathless, she asks,
"Was it always like this?" To which he replies, "Every time is like the first
time." Thus, he implies, Jesuitically, that the reason she cannot remember
making love with him before is that the one act that a person *cannot*
remember is the sexual act.

Postcoital Sleep

Our texts suggest that, in addition to the change that sex makes in the
trickster, weakening the power of illusion, sex also changes the victim by
strengthening his or her power to resist illusion. *After* making love, when
the mists of lust have been burnt off a bit, the mind clears and the victim
of the bedtrick looks more closely at the other head on the pillow. This
happens even in mythological texts. In most versions of the myth of
Samjna,† when her husband takes the form of a stallion to mate with her
in her mare form, she fears that he might be another male and resists
him; but one version states that this possibility occurs to her only when
she is resting *after* mating with him.[10] The power of this moment for the
victim is also compounded by changes that postcoital sleep brings about
in the trickster, not unlike the changes brought about by the sexual act
itself. Postcoital sleep also overlaps with the mythological themes of the
demon who is revealed when he falls asleep (for any reason) and the
demon, devil, or intergalactic invader† who can possess a mortal who
falls asleep. (Stith Thompson names one of his tale types TT 475, "Sexual
relations in sleep." Both Samjna's daughter, Tapati,† and the transsexual
bedtrickster in the film *Switch* (1991) are unknowingly impregnated in
their sleep.) According to Jewish tradition, the serpent sneaked into Eden
during Adam's postcoital sleep.[11]

Postcoital sleep is what unmasks the bedtrickster in a story told in a Sanskrit text composed in the eleventh century in Kashmir, *The Ocean of the Streams of Story:*

KALINGASENA AND THE MAGICIAN

King Udayana wanted to marry Kalingasena, but Udayana's prime minister opposed the marriage, because he had promised the king's first wife, Vasavadatta, that she would have no co-wife. The minister mentally summoned a demon [*rakshasa*] and told him to watch over Kalingasena night and day in order to catch her doing something that would prove her unfit to wed the king. In particular, he advised, "If she were to have an affair with a celestial magician [*vidyadhara*] or someone like that, that would be very fortunate. And you must observe the divine lover when he is asleep, even if he comes in a different form, for divine beings assume their own forms when they fall asleep."

Now, a celestial magician named Madanavega ["Storm of Passion"] had fallen in love with Kalingasena; he asked Shiva to help him win her, and Shiva said, "She will marry Udayana. But before the marriage takes place, assume the form of Udayana, as if he were impatient for the union, and make her your wife by the *gandharva* ceremony (of mutual desire)." One night, as Kalingasena was thinking about Udayana, Madanavega used his magic to come to her room in the form of the king. Kalingasena's ornaments seemed to warn her, ringing out the sound, "This is not the man." But she was confused by her longing and gradually she came to believe him, because he had the form of the king. Madanavega made her his wife by the *gandharva* ritual. Just then, the demon, invisible, entered and thought he saw Udayana. Sadly he went and informed the minister, who, however, found out that Udayana was with his queen, Vasavadatta. Then, delighted, the demon returned to observe the form of Kalingasena's disguised lover when he was asleep, as the prime minister had advised. He found Madanavega in his own form, asleep on the bed of the sleeping Kalingasena: his foot had no dust on it, for he was a divine man, who had lost his false form because his magic power to assume such a form vanished when he was asleep.

The demon informed the prime minister, who informed the king and Vasavadatta. That night, the minister took the king to Kalingasena's room when everyone was asleep. Unseen, the king entered and saw Kalingasena asleep and Madanavega asleep beside her in his own form. The king wanted to kill him, but just then Madanavega was awakened by his magic and flew away to the sky. In a moment, Kalingasena woke up too; she saw the empty bed and asked, "Why did the king awake before me and leave me here asleep?" Then she saw the two of them and asked,

"Why did you go away a moment ago and come back with your minister?" The minister explained to the king, "She was deceived by someone who took your form," and he explained to Kalingasena, "Someone who took the form of the king magically deluded you and married you; it wasn't the king." Bewildered, Kalingasena said to the king, "Did you marry me by the *gandharva* ritual and then forget me, as Dushyanta forgot Shakuntala long ago?" But the king lowered his head and replied, "Truly, I never married you at all; I just came here now." And they left.

Then Kalingasena, whose maidenhead had been destroyed, looked up at the sky and said, "Whoever it was that took the form of Udayana and married me, let him appear, for he is the husband of my virginity." And Madanavega descended from the sky in his divine form and told her who he was and what he had done: "Shiva gave me a boon so that I could win you; and since you were in love with Udayana, I took his form and married you." Then he consoled her and gave her gold, and she became devoted to her good husband.[12]

In this case the unmasking of the immortal (through his feet‡) takes place after the damage has been done, but the bedtrickster in his own form finally gets the girl. The man whom he impersonates, King Udayana,† is also, himself, both the victim and the instigator of several double-backcrosses.†[13]

Kalingasena gives birth to a daughter, Madanamanchuka ("Couch of Passion"), who also has postcoital problems, according to a later passage in the same text:

MADANAMANCHUKA AND THE MAGICIAN

Madanamanchuka married King Naravahanadatta, the son of King Udayana. One day a celestial magician named Manasavega ["Storm of Thought"] fell in love with Madanamanchuka and carried her off; and his sister, an unmarried celestial magician named Vegavati ["Stormy"], happened to see Madanamanchuka and took her shape. Naravahanadatta's minister found Vegavati-as-Madanamanchuka and brought her to the king, but when Naravahanadatta wanted to embrace her, she insisted that he marry her "again" because, she said, she had forgotten to make certain promised offerings to the goblins [*yakshas*] during the first wedding ceremony, and so they had carried her off. He married her and drank with her in the bedroom, for he liked to drink, and he made love with this shape-changer, experiencing the pleasure of living creatures, just as the Sun did with the shadow [double of Samjna]. But when they were making love, she said to him, "Darling, you must not uncover my face suddenly and look at me while I am asleep." When the king heard this, he was filled with curiosity, and on the very next night he uncovered her face while she was asleep and looked at it. It was not Madanamanchuka, but someone else whose magic power of disguising her appearance was lost when she slept.

When Vegavati woke up, he asked her who she was, and she realized that she was in her own shape and that he had discovered her betrayal. She told him that his wife had been carried off by her brother Manasavega, like Sita by Ravana. She helped him fight her brother Manasavega, and eventually he was reunited with Madanamanchuka.[14]

We may see here an inversion of the story of Shiva and the mountain woman:† where Shiva was tricked into marrying his own wife again, mistaking her for another woman, King Naravahanadatta (a heavy drinker†) is tricked into marrying another woman, mistaking her for his own wife. Vegavati herself sees a parallel with the story of Sita (in which she is playing the role of Shurpanakha‡); she may also recall the episode in the *Ramayana* in which Ravana rapes a woman named Vedavati, who is reborn as Sita. The author sees a parallel with the story of Samjna;‡ and the English editor sees one with the story of Cupid and Psyche.†[15] Closest of all, of course, is the parallel with the story of Kalingasena, told in this same text and kept in play by certain patterns of words for "passion" and "storm" in the names.†

European bedtricksters, too, are sometimes revealed in their sleep, but at other times sleep facilitates the masquerade. Thomas Mann's Jacob,† seeing Leah asleep in the morning, muses: "Are then sisters so mysteriously alike, and show it in their sleep, though no likeness shows itself in their features?" The protagonist of Carin Clevidence's "The Somnambulists"† cuckolds himself in a bedtrick in his sleep. In the film *Half Angel* (1951), the heroine sleepwalks and becomes another, sexier woman, who falls in love with the hero; both Dracula and the pod people in *Invasion of the Body Snatchers*† (1956) possess (the former sexually, the latter politically†) the bodies of those who fall asleep.

Postcoital sleep overlaps with drunkenness† and anesthesia,† which produce the same kind of unmasking (or, as the case may be, masking): mental paralysis and the same morning-after uncertainty as to whether or not something has happened. And sleep's big brother, death, also often puts an end to the masquerade; the demon Adi† takes back his true shape when he dies. Death often reveals the true form not only of the masquerading demon (through the relaxation of his mental control) but of real-life transvestite humans—through the unmasking in the autopsy room, as Marjorie Garber notes: "[I]t is the doctor or mortician as the ultimate agent of discovery, the bed as a deathbed rather than a place of sexuality and procreation, that is a recurrent feature of the cross-dressing story as it is told, not in film or detective fiction, but in biography and the newspaper reports."[16] Thus, our stories suggest that death, like sleep, is the great unmasker.

WHEN A KISS IS NOT JUST A KISS

If we construct the mouth† as the mind (through its connections with speech and the head), in contrast with the genitals as the body, we produce a Cartesian dichotomy that makes kissing more intimate than actual sexual intercourse—an old cliché among whores who refuse to kiss their customers on the mouth. Sometimes a kiss is just a kiss, but sometimes it is a proof or even a revelation. Often a magic kiss awakens the maiden to her truth, another way of saying that it transforms her back into herself, while the "brave kiss"† transforms the apparent hag into the lovely young thing that she really is. Some of these stories demonstrate another double standard:† the prince's kiss brings his beloved to life, but the woman's kiss threatens to kill her lover. Wagner's Siegfried† uses a kiss to awaken Brunhilde† (before engaging in his bedtrick with her),[17] but Wotan, her father (= Zeus, Indra), has already used the kiss for the opposite purpose, to put Brunhilde to sleep and transform her from a deity to a human: "I kiss the godhead from you," he says as he kisses her lingeringly on the eyes and she sinks unconscious into his arms.[18] Yet the kiss can also awaken the hero, as in the tale of the Serpent Tsarevich, whose wife kisses away his enchantment.[19] Sometimes a kiss even has the force of proof that a scar† has: when a woman, cross-dressed as a merchant, demanded a kiss from her unrecognizing husband, she "gave him such kisses that they left a wound behind," a wound that she later uses as proof that she had been the one who had given him "two kisses, the imprints of which even now you bear on your cheek!"[20]

In Iris Murdoch's *The Sea, The Sea,* the narrator meets his childhood sweetheart after many years, after time† has greatly changed her:

> I kissed her gently, briefly, on the familiar mouth, as we used to kiss; and there was an intelligence in her quiet negative reception of the kiss which was itself a communication.
>
> She said, "I've changed so much, I'm a different person, you were so kind in your letter, but it can't be like that—you care about old times, but that's not me—"

> "It is you. I recognized you in the kiss." It was true. The kiss had transfigured her, like a kiss in a fairy tale. I remembered the feel, the texture, the movement of her mouth.[21]

Did the kiss really transform her, or did it transform his memory of her in the past, and his perception of her in the present? Both, surely.

The kiss can not only awaken but bewitch, not only revive memory but destroy it. When Giraudoux's Alcmena‡ begs Jupiter for forgetfulness, he says, "Forget everything, then—except this kiss." He kisses her. As she comes to herself again she says, "What kiss?" and he replies, "Oh, now, let's have no nonsense about the kiss. I took special care to place it well this side of oblivion."[22] In S. N. Behrman's version, Alcmena presents Jupiter with a theoretical case: "In a marriage ideally happy, a husband has been unfaithful through no fault of his own—what can you do for him?" Jupiter replies, "Cause him never to know it." And so she gets the god to erase her husband's memory as well as her own, and Jupiter says, "I will kiss you. Only this way can I grant forgetfulness. It is the conventional ritual. Forget everything you have lived—everything you wish forgotten. [Kisses her.] Except this kiss!" Alcmena: "What kiss?"[23]

In films, too, the old fairy tale metaphor of the magic kiss often takes the place of actual sexual penetration, still in the service of true memory. Censorship makes the kiss into a euphemism for the sexual act in the Doris Day paradigm of the 1950s ("Don't do It until you have the ring on your finger"), the last gasp of a convention that made it possible for the kiss to remain, as in fairy tales, the moment of sexual revelation. The Hollywood cliché† is mocked in the self-referential film *The Day of the Locust* (1975), when a ditsy film star tells a suitor a story about a woman who masquerades as another woman; finally they appear together, "And he has to kiss them both to see which one kisses the way he remembered." She might have been referring to *The Dark Mirror*† (1946), in which Terry, pretending to be Ruth (though the psychologist knows it's really Terry), asks the psychologist how he can tell them apart:

> T: For instance, kiss me. [*She kisses him.*] Now, do you really believe you could tell that from one of Terry's? Or my lips from hers?
> P: I think so.
> T: Have you ever kissed Terry?
> P: No.
> T: Well, then how could you possibly know?
> P: I think I'd know in my heart.

T: Would you really?

P: I think so.

T: Of course, I don't believe it for a second.

(In the 1986 remake, the evil twin simply asks the psychiatrist, "Can you really tell the difference between us? Kiss me." And then, when she has kissed him, she says, "You see there is no difference." His face, however, tells us that there is a difference, though not as much as he would like there to be.) Alfred Hitchcock employed Salvador Dali to create surreal dream imagery for the magic kiss in *Spellbound* (1945), when the two Freudian psychiatrists (Ingrid Bergman and Gregory Peck) kiss for the first time: a door opens to reveal a long corridor, and then behind it another door, and another . . . a *mise en abîme*. So conventional is this cinematic diagnostic or revelatory kiss that Hitchcock was able to invert it, to brilliant effect, in *Vertigo* (1958). When the detective falls in love with the blonde and kisses her, the camera employs the vertigo cliché† generally used to convey sexual excitement (or fainting): the whirling of the sky overhead. But here it takes on a new meaning: his infatuation with her is compounded by his actual vertigo (from which he had suffered before he met her), literally blinding him with sexual passion.

When Greta Garbo, in *Two-Faced Woman*† (1941), masquerades as her sexy twin sister, her husband is uncertain at first, but he knows the truth when he kisses her, as do the victims of the bedtricksters in *The Major and the Minor*† (1942), *Invasion of the Body Snatchers*† (1956), *Some Like It Hot*† (1959), and *Dead Ringer*† (1964). In *Half Angel*† (1951), when the waking woman denies the hero, who knows her sleeping alter ego, his friend suggests, "Maybe it's the wrong girl," to which the hero replies, "I held her in my arms," as if that were the whole answer. Friend: "Maybe you made a mistake." Hero: "How could you make a mistake like that?" Jeanine Basinger remarks: "The twins films demonstrate that whereas a man can be lured by a bad twin and temporarily seduced by her, he senses (usually when he actually kisses her) that something is wrong. Evidently his lips can detect insurrection."[24] The scene in *The Dark Mirror* mirrors one in *Cobra Woman* (1944) when the "bad woman" kisses the hero and asks him if he can really tell the difference. Aren't her lips the same as her sister's, her kisses just as satisfying? As in *The Dark Mirror,* he insists that they're not. Why? Because one sister is sexually aggressive, and hence defined as evil, an evil that he senses only when he kisses them both. Thus, when the twins pretend to be one another in *Twice Blessed* (1945), and each of the two men they have been fooling kisses the "wrong twin," each man suddenly pulls back and rejects the twin he has just kissed: "Until that moment of lip contact, each had believed he had embraced the one he loved. Kissing is the proof." This is what Basinger calls the "By her kisses we shall know her" argument: "The film suggests that it is hilarious that each man couldn't tell the woman he loves from her twin, and equally hilarious that kissing her could be that different."[25]

But men, too, could be recognized by their kisses; the man's kiss that, in fairy tales, transforms the heroine from dead to alive, or from asleep to awake, is also a film cliché. In *My Little Chickadee* (1940), Mae West† has a masked lover (Joseph Calleia), who kisses her; when he kisses her unmasked, she recognizes him and says, "A man's kiss is like his signature, his identification." Later in the film, when W. C. Fields (playing Mae West's husband) masquerades as the bandit, gets into the bedroom, and kisses her, she suspects him immediately and turns on the light to expose him. In *The Corsican Brothers* (1941), when Lucien pretends to be his twin brother, Mario, he fools Mario's girl until he kisses her; then she recognizes him and protests, but he argues, "Maybe you're making another mistake. If your eyes can't tell the difference between my brother and me, how can your heart tell the difference between his love and mine?"

In the Disney version of *The Little Mermaid*† (1989), the sea-witch sets a condition: "If he kisses you, and not just any kiss, but the kiss of true love, within three days, you will remain human forever." (And they sing a Disney song entitled "Kiss the Girl.") But the film kiss more often transforms the heroine from an amnesiac to a woman with a memory, quite literally a woman with a past. In *The Last Time I Saw Paris* (1954), the hero and heroine meet as strangers, thrown together in the crowds in Paris outside the Dingo Café on the day of the Nazi surrender; she kisses everyone in uniform, including him, and they part; when they meet later and fall in love, he says, "We've kissed before." "Where?" she asks. She kisses him and says, "Now I remember. It was near the Dingo Café." In *Chances Are*† (1989), when a man tries to convince a woman that he is a reincarnation of her dead husband, Louie, his knowledge of the most striking particulars about Louie fails to persuade her; then he says, "Remember this?" and kisses her, and she knows, from her own response, that he's Louie. The same thing happens in *The Reincarnation of Peter Proud*† (1974). In *Batman Returns* (1992), Selina Kyle and Bruce Wayne fall in love, while their masked (animal lover) personae, Cat Woman and Bat Man, spar erotically. First the masked doubles kiss and make small talk about kissing under mistletoe; then the humans, unmasked, kiss and make the same small talk, but this time it is she who says what he had said, and as he begins to counter with what she had said, he stops, and each realizes the masked identity of the other—not in the kiss but in the words† about the kiss.

In *Prelude to a Kiss*† (1992), when the minds of an old man and a young woman are exchanged on her wedding day, it is a kiss that allows the first transformation to take place (the old man kisses the bride), and it is a kiss that reveals the truth to the newlywed husband. When the false bride has managed to give all the right answers to the superficial passwords and cooked† the right food (a fairy tale test), the husband is taken in—until he kisses her, and then tears come to his eyes as he realizes that she is not the real woman but the impostor, the old man, who has learned all the "right answers" from diaries and photographs (unreliable "scientific" evidence,† mental evidence in contrast with somatic evidence). The kiss usually functions in this magical way when it is the first intimate sexual contact, or a euphemism for the sexual act. But here, when the husband has made love several times with both his real bride and the impostor, the kiss should not be so surprising. Only the mythology of the motif allows it to keep its shock value.

PENIS ENVY

In a particularly gross set of variants on this theme, the genitals (more often male than female) may function as the sign by which the bedtrickster is recognized. Surprisingly, the genitals per se are not nearly as useful as one might expect in solving dilemmas of sexual identity. This may be in part because they are often displaced upward,† so that the head and eyes and nose and mouth (or, downward, the feet) take on genital symbolism, leaving the genitals relatively silent (with the notable exception of the French *fabliaux*, where both male and female genitalia often have tongues†). But in Hindu mythology, sometimes a *linga*† is just a *linga*,[26] or, as Edmund Leach put it, "The *linga* represents itself."[27] In one of the many myths about the goddess Kali† going on a rampage, killing everything and everyone in sight and lapping up blood with her lolling tongue,‡ Shiva lies down, asleep, in her path: "In her blinded anger she did not see him and stepped on his chest. At that moment, Shiva's *linga* (penis) became erect and entered Kali. At that instant Kali recognized her husband and pulled out her tongue in ecstasy."[28]

The hero of Li Yu's "Nativity Room," born with only one testicle, was identified in this way years later, at the end of a long Family Romance, and given the name of "Singular Yin";[29] the sexual organ that is usually double (testicles) here is single. A single testicle is also the test of identity in the film *While You Were Sleeping* (1995), in which a woman pretends to be the fiancée of a perfect stranger who is in a coma. When he wakes up and doesn't recognize her, she says (she has accidentally found out about this from a friend) that he recently lost a testicle in an accident. His mother checks ("I'm his mother; somebody's got to look") and is (wrongly) persuaded that the woman has slept with him.

The tricksters in Roald Dahl's "The Great Switcheroo"† fear that genitals, particularly too-small genitals, may be a telltale sign: "[Jerry asked,] 'What about some of the other differences?' 'You mean faces?' I said. 'No one's going to see faces in the dark.' 'I'm not talking about faces,' Jerry said. 'What are you talking about, then?' 'I'm talking about their cocks,' Jerry said. 'That's what it's all about, isn't it?' "[30] But they decide that, though "some are enormous and some are titchy . . . ninety percent are normal," as long as both men are circumcised or uncircumcised. And so it would seem, as the event unfolds.

In Plutarch's variant of the myth of Romulus and Remus, the mother of the twins becomes involved in a bizarre bedtrick:

> King Tarchetius, the cruel and dishonest king of the Albans, saw in the middle of his own house a divine phantasm: a phallus arose out of the hearth and stayed there for many days. The oracle said that a virgin must copulate with it and would then give birth to a heroic son. Tarchetius told his daughter to do this; she did not want to, regarding it as an indignity, and sent her servant girl instead. The servant girl gave birth to Romulus and Remus.[31]

The phallus under Tarchetius's direction threatens to consummate a kind of Lacanian droit du seigneur,† but it is unacceptable to the princess, perhaps because it lacks romance. She reacts to it as if it were a human male and, in the familiar pattern, sends her maid† to it in her place. But some penises apparently lead independent and presumably fulfilling lives. The disembodied phallus appears, winged, as the Hermetic *phallos,* and is often detached from the body of the Native American trickster.[32] It rises from the cosmic ocean in Hindu mythology[33] and, later, from the body of the anonymous hero of Erica Jong's "zipless fuck."[34] The unidimensional male presence of the disembodied phallus is the essence of the surrogate husband or surrogate lover, the feminist answer to the male chauvinist "bag over the head";‡ it reduces the man to nothing but a sexual organ.

In films, too, the ultimate reduction of the sexual revelation is the genital revelation. Pedro Almodovar, who also directed *Tie Me Up! Tie Me Down!* (1989), invoked this more brutal variant of the trope of the sexual diagnostic in *High Heels* (1991), in which a young woman makes love with a transvestite entertainer and notes that he has a mole on his penis; when she meets a woman who tells her that her boyfriend has a mole on his penis, she begins to suspect that they are one and the same man. And what else was left of the lover in *Shattered*† (1991), who had lost his face and his memory? Yet his mistress still loved him, only him, like the female praying mantis, who goes on mating for hours with the male when she has devoured almost all of his body but his genitals. The *reductio ad absurdum* of the "genitals as identity" motif occurs among animals,† more precisely flies, whose genitals allow potential mates to make sure the partner is of the right species: "For this double-check flies use an intricate locking system. Their penis is their passport; species which in other respects look precisely the same each have their own model of penis, which like a key in a lock fits only the corresponding model of sexual opening in precisely the right kind of female."[35]

As for humans, in real life, we may recall that when Paula Jones brought a suit against President Bill Clinton in 1997 for sexual harassment, she claimed that he had exposed himself to her and that she could identify certain telltale characteristics of what she had seen: "a distinctly angled bend visible when the penis is erect."[36] Robert Bennett, one of the president's lawyers, insisted that "a thorough medical examination" of the president had shown that "there is absolutely no unique characteristic of any kind" and that "in terms of size, shape, direction, whatever the devious mind wants to concoct, the president is a normal man."[37] The operative phrase in Paula Jones's accusation is, of course, "when the penis is erect." Unlike most of the criteria in our myths (such as having only one testicle), this particular sign is *only* accessible at a moment of sexual intimacy and thus proves not merely *who* the man in the bed was but *what* he did there.

THE WO/MEN'S ROOM

A particular form of quasi-sexual exposure occurs in films about transvestite bedtricks in which the bathroom, or wo/men's room, replaces the bedroom (or the morgue) as the site of transvestite revelation. The need for the wisdom to choose between them (to borrow a prayer from Reinhold Niebuhr and Alcoholics Anonymous) produces here, as so often, a double standard:† where Americans find it permissible for mothers to take their little sons to the ladies' room, it is not so easy for fathers to take their little daughters to the men's room. Nature, more than culture, dictates this: the greater visibility of both male genitalia and male porcelain (urinals) makes the men's room more awkward than the ladies'. For adults, the problems are more subtle, though still asymmetrical: the women's room is problematic for a woman in drag because the women there would be shocked to see her (dressed as a man); but the men's room is problematic for her because *she* would see *them*. The reverse is true for a man in drag: he shocks the men but is shocked by the women. These situations pose very different problems arising out of the male/female gaze, situations that, in a reversal of the quandary of the parents of little boys and girls, are marginally more problematic for women than for men. In either case, however, since the stories under consideration are masquerades, it is far more dangerous for the trickster to be seen than to see. S/he usually goes, therefore, into the bathroom that matches the false outer semblance, not the physical anatomy, submitting to the problem of seeing rather than being seen. But a man's (Victorian) belief that a woman should not see *any* male genitals reinforces his sense of personal embarrassment at the thought of a woman seeing *his* own genitals. (Recall the tale of Parsons' Pleasure.†)

In *Sylvia Scarlett* (1935), *I Was a Male War Bride*† (1949), *Some Like It Hot* (1959),[38] *Victor/Victoria* (1982) (twice), and *Mrs. Doubtfire* (1993), the hero or heroine in drag faces the quandary of the wo/men's room. In *Bachelor Party* (1984), a boy who goes to bed with a girl discovers that she's not a girl only when she gets out of bed, goes to the bathroom, lifts her skirt and pees, standing up, still leering at him invitingly. *Multiplicity*† (1996) varies the formula by having the hero meet his clone in the men's room; as they leave, they inadvertently change places when the wife greets the clone and the clone's girl greets the original (each woman merely commenting that the man seems to have changed his shirt).

Jacques Lacan uses the "twin door" of the wo/men's rooms to explain the way in which "the signifier enters the signified."[39] A more straightforward solution (not only to the pragmatics of the wo/men's room but to the philosophical problem of androgyny) is offered by a dive in Calcutta called Isaiah's: "Like most other civilized establishments, it had a door marked MEN and a door marked WOMEN. What was unusual was that both of these doors led into a single large and tastefully whitetiled common room, appointed with a variety of porcelain furniture."[40] When, in *Victor/Victoria* (1982), Victoria objects that men act differently from women—for example, they pee standing up—her gay friend replies: "Contrary to popular opinion, men act in many different ways." They can, he points out, sit down to pee. (On the other hand, Teena Brandon† "stood up to pee—a modest endorsement of a heterosexual bedfellow.")[41] We may also take this as a wise caution against gender essentialism: neither men nor women are all alike in the bathroom.

THE RETURN OF THE RETURN OF MARTIN GUERRE

On hearing these stories, contemporary listeners often protest, "But, of course, such a thing couldn't really happen" (usually meaning, "such a thing couldn't really happen *to me*"). How could it be possible that someone could sleep with two different people on several occasions and never tell the difference? Or, in the case of one person masquerading as two different people, how could the partner *not* tell the sameness? Let us touch down, for a moment, in soi-disant real life.

Bedtricks, as we have seen, are not confined to the printed page. There have been a number of notorious bedtricks in real life (such as the prototype of *M. Butterfly*†), and there is a law on the books in many of the states against sexual fraud.† Successful transsexual† masqueraders seem to inspire the most shock, and in real life such bedtricksters may be quickly unmasked; some people do notice the difference.[42] But certain bedtricksters carry on for a long, long time before people notice anything wrong. Hindu law books regard the mistaking of another woman for one's own wife as a real possibility. One commentator says that a relatively light punishment for a man who has slept with his guru's wife—the ultimate incest in Hinduism—applies in a certain case if it was done "without premeditation, because he mistook her for his own wife."[43] As for Renaissance England, Marliss C. Desens drily points out, "There is little indication that bed-tricks were part of social practise."[44] But, according to Francis Oxbourn's *Memoires,* the last great Earl of Oxford was tricked into sleeping with his wife under the mistaken impression that it was his mistress,[45] and Natalie Zemon Davis tells us that, in the thirteenth century, the wife of the false Count Baldwin of Flanders "lived with him familiarly for over three years 'without ever perceiving or even suspecting the fraud,' " despite the doubts constantly expressed by the count's daughter.[46]

Davis cites the "real" case of Count Baldwin in defense of the "real" case that she presents far more extensively, and famously: that of Martin Guerre. There is a lot of fiction in the so-called history of Martin Guerre; no court records were kept, and the people who later wrote the documents that Davis used (such as the jurist Coras) also knew stories about bedtricks. Still, let us consider the incident as at least historically based: Arnaud du Tilh, who claimed to be Martin Guerre, successfully persuaded Martin Guerre's wife, Bertrande de Rols, to believe in him. Or did he? As Robert Finlay notes, "While Coras saw the wife as an innocent victim, Davis views her as a knowing actor and, though guilty of adultery and deception, all the more admirable because of the values embodied in her heroic transgression."[47] (In the film that Davis supervised [*Le retour de Martin Guerre*, 1982, directed by Daniel Vigne] before she wrote her book, the judge tells Bertrande, "By nature, women are very easily tricked by the wiles of men. That was why we found you innocent in the end and recognized as legitimate Bernarde, your daughter.") Finlay sides with Coras, and Davis has had to defend and expand her argument that Bertrande knew that Pansette (as Arnaud du Tilh was called) was an impostor.[48] It is not insignificant, I think, that the men (Coras and Finlay) argue that the woman was stupid and duped, while the woman (Davis) argues that she was cunning, for this is the best that one can do in this familiar no-win situation: if Bertrande was really fooled, she was stupid and weak (as the judge says); if she was in on the trick, she was manipulative and dishonest‡ (as Davis says). Davis does not mount an explicitly feminist argument, but her defense of Bertrande's intelligence and what a feminist would call agency, even subversion, is, I think, thoroughly feminist. Terence Cave is more explicitly feminist when he points out, "Any reading of Martin Guerre's story is bound to make Bertrande central to the uncertainty of the recognition (whom did she recognize behind the scenes, in bed?). Central, yet always, in a male-dominated society, peripheral: which is exactly why she is a blind spot."[49]

Certainly at first, Bertrande was suspicious—or, rather, in retrospect, she *said* that at first she had been suspicious: "When she saw him, . . . she recoiled in surprise. Not until he had spoken to her affectionately,

reminding her of things they had done and talked about, specifically men-
tioning the white hosen in the trunk, did she fall upon his neck and kiss
him; it was his beard that had made him hard to recognize."[50] And so he
got away with it, for a while. But Davis argues that even when Bertrande
realized that he was not her true husband, she helped him to persuade
others that he was: "Either by explicit or tacit agreement, she helped him
become her husband. What Bertrande had with the new Martin was her
dream come true, a man she could live with in peace and friendship (to
cite sixteenth-century values) and in passion."[51] Granting that the "impostor could never have shown all the tiny gestures special to the original,"
she cites an eighteenth-century commentator: "Many people will believe
that Bertrande de Rols helped deceive herself because the error pleased
her."[52] Bertrande wanted to believe that the impostor was her husband;
she needed a husband for social respectability and economic security and
to avoid the stigma of adultery. Moreover, she preferred the impostor to
her true husband. Martin Guerre's surrogate was, from the start, a better
man than the original, and he continued to improve as he lived the life
Martin Guerre should have lived.

When Bertrande was forced to acknowledge the real Martin Guerre,
she argued that Pansette *had* fooled her, but the reasons that she gave are
equally valid proofs of her self-deception and even, perhaps, of her knowing collusion: "Out tumbled all the prepared excuses: your sisters believed
him too readily; your uncle accepted him; I wanted to have my husband
back so much that I believed him, especially when he knew such private
things about me."[53] Several very different sorts of arguments are lumped
together here: social pressure, self-deception,† convincing evidence.†
What began as self-deception ended, as usual, with the deception of
others. Or, rather, one sort of deception shades imperceptibly into the
other.

One of the false "proofs" that Pansette and Bertrande attempted to
construct to fool others was a sexual proof (which was actually verbal:
people *talking* about sex):

> Bertrande searched her memory for a sexual episode—perhaps even em-
> broidered it—with which they could surprise the court. . . . The court must
> hear about the impotence of Martin Guerre and how it ended, and about
> an even more private moment between them. They had been at a wedding
> long ago and for lack of marriage beds *(cubilia),* Bertrande had to spend
> the night with her cousin; by agreement, Martin crept into the bed after

the other woman had fallen asleep. (Le Sueur stops his account here, but Bertrande did not, going on to tell "the things they had done before, during, and after the secret act of marriage.")[54]

Thus, it was *his* sexual memory (of the same intimacy that she remembered) rather than *her* sexual memory (of ways in which one man's sexual technique did or did not differ from another's) that the impostor invoked to persuade the judge of his assumed identity; it was Pansette's public rendition of Bertrande's private, "secret act." The event on which they colluded did indeed happen; it was true. But it did not happen to the man who said it had happened to him; it was a lie that he told, with information that Bertrande gave him.

When you recognize someone in bed, do you recognize his body, his size and muscle tone, or his sexual technique, his style? Davis seemed to argue the latter view in her book, but under attack she retreated to the former. In Janet Lewis's novel based on the story, when Bertrande accuses "Martin" of being someone else and asks for proofs, the first thing he says is, "Proof? But why proof? You have seen me. You have felt the touch of my lips."[55] In the film, Bertrande makes her statement to the judge at the very end of the trial; asked how she knew it was her husband, she says, "He knew when I wanted him to make love to me, and the words I wanted to hear, before, during, and after." Not just sex; sex and words,† indeed the words—"before, during, and after"—that, in the book, she uses at the trial to describe the sexual secret of what happened in the *cubilia,* "the things they had done before, during, and after the secret act of marriage."[56] In the film, the real Martin Guerre, when he returns, looks sternly down upon Bertrande at his feet and coldly remarks that a woman would know her lover (note that he does *not* say "her husband").

Davis argues for the revelatory power of sex:

> Was the weakness of the sex really so great that wives could not tell the difference between married love and adultery? The cuckolded Martin Guerre clearly thought not. . . . What of Bertrande de Rols? Did she know that the new Martin was not the man who had abandoned her eight years before? Perhaps not at the very first, when he arrived with all his "signs" and proofs. But the obstinate and honorable Bertrande does not seem a woman so easily fooled, not even by a charmer like Pansette. By the time she had received him in her bed, she must have realized the difference; as any wife of Artigat would have agreed, there is no mistaking "the touch of the man on the woman."[57]

Finlay, in his debate with Davis, focuses on this paragraph and argues that "the claim runs counter to the account Davis herself gives of Bertrande's dismal sexual experience: she was married for some nine years without intercourse, which was finally achieved after a magic spell was lifted . . . hardly the sort of connubial experience making for a 'touch of the man' that was indelible or unmistakable."[58] And he goes on:

> If Bertrande had perceived any difference in sexual manner between her spouse and the man claiming to be her husband, she could reasonably have explained it to herself as a consequence of her years of sexual abstinence, during which the precarious sexuality of her husband evidently gave way to virile confidence, perhaps assisted by the fleshpots of Spain and Picardy, where he soldiered.

This is the "passage of time"† excuse, with a difference; the war changed him, it is implied, and in particular changed him sexually.

War often both necessitates and facilitates bedtricks. "At the end of a war all our portraits are out of date," Graham Greene remarks in *The Tenth Man* (a novel about an impersonation), and Terence Cave remarks: "One of the oddest coincidences† in the case of Martin Guerre is the accidental symbolism of his name.† Together with aberrant voyages and shipwrecks, war is the calamity which most often erases or suspends identity in narratives of recognition."[59] The hero of *Love Letters*† (1945), attempting to explain away the difference between two men who pretended to be one man, says that when a woman loves a man and he goes to war, "The returned soldier is not the man she knew and loved before he went away." The problem of recognition after a war is bitterly captured in the Irish song in which a mother sings, "Johnny, I hardly knew you."[60]

Finlay goes on to challenge the wider implications of the proverb about the "touch of a man":

> Even that proverb is not uniquely pertinent, for, in the conditions of sexual intercourse in peasant households of preindustrial Europe—the couple clothed, in a darkened house, amid the cold and dirt, surrounded by livestock and relatives—any wife of Artigat might equally well have regarded her bedmate with the jaded perspective expressed in the notorious masculine slur, "De nuit tous chats son gris."[61]

But the sexist argument about cats in the dark,† here, as rarely, applied to *male* cats, the argument for sameness, is precisely what the Romantic† paradigm of difference invoked by Davis is designed to counteract. Finlay concludes:

> Surely, the impostor's subsequent sexual habits would have had to be extraordinary for the happy, trusting wife to conclude that she was in error. . . . The assumption, then, that sexual relations must have revealed the imposture to Bertrande is not an interpretation based on the sources. . . .
> . . . There is no need for unfounded hypotheses regarding maneuvering within sexual constraints, the perpetual uniqueness of sexual behavior.[62]

In answering these accusations, Davis invokes several arguments, one of which she refers to as a "sign": "Arnaud du Tilh's body and its touch to Bertrande." "Individuals may indeed have some long-term patterns of sexual behavior and expression, like a sexual fingerprint,† but of course, there is sexual learning. . . . A new kind of kiss from Arnaud du Tilh need not of itself constitute a contrary clue for Bertrande de Rols."[63] What, then, was the "contrary clue"? It was the impostor's body. The real Martin Guerre was taller, darker, and thinner than the impostor: "Thus, when Bertrande finally found herself in the embrace of Arnaud du Tilh, she was feeling a body quite unlike the one she had lain next to and held for nine or ten years." And Davis argues, against Finlay's assertion, that there is good evidence that couples of that period slept "with nightcaps but naked." True, people might have assumed that he had grown fatter with the passage of time, she admits, but surely he would not have grown shorter and developed smaller feet. Therefore, it is more likely "that Bertrande 'knew,' despite the passage of years, that she was not being held by the real Martin Guerre."[64] "Held" (used twice) is a strange euphemism; and unless there is a veiled reference here to another euphemism that uses "feet"† to refer to genitals, are we really being asked to believe that what Bertrande noticed in the dark was the difference in his *feet*? Surely we are talking about sexual style, as well as sexual organs.

Finally, Davis points out, the line about "the touch of the man" is the quotation not of a proverb but of what Martin Guerre himself actually said to Bertrande in the trial: "How is it possible that you have given consent to this abuse? For my uncle and my sisters there is some excuse: but none in the touch of the man on the woman."[65] Thus, in this revised version, Davis is arguing not for sexual knowledge at all but merely for a more banal memory of physical size. What a pity.

Despite his ultimate failure, Martin Guerre is generally regarded as an astonishingly successful bedtrickster. Thus, Marjorie Garber remarks of people who are taken all their lives for people of the opposite sex and are only exposed after their deaths: "We might think of such phallic cross-dressers—and, indeed, of all lifetime 'passers'—as the Martin Guerres of gender."[66] Martin Guerre's bedtrick did not last until his death, but it lasted a surprisingly long time. In addition to the novel by Janet Lewis and the film by Daniel Vigne, the story inspired a play, another novel, an operetta, a musical comedy (*The House of Martin Guerre*), and another film, the double of the French film that doubled the book, *Sommersby* (1993). This telling, about an impostor who claims to be Jack Sommersby returned from the Civil War in America, steals some points of the original Martin Guerre scenario and inverts others. Like Bertrande de Rols, Sommersby's wife is under pressure to legitimate him as the father of her child. If he is an impostor, she is a tainted woman and their child is a bastard, the woman's side of the paternity nightmare.† Thus, she admits to him, "I wanted you to be him as much as they did, because I was worn out from work, I was lonesome, I didn't want my son to grow up without a father." Again, the passage of time† and the devastations of war are invoked as excuses. The impostor says to his wife: "Well, six years in a war would change anybody," and his wife testifies, "At first, he looked some different—but so did everybody coming back from the war." "You're not yourself; what'd them damn Yankees do to you?" asks one of his friends.

A man who had wanted to marry Jack's wife figures out the imposture fairly soon and says to her, "You've known all along, haven't you? He might have fooled us, but he didn't fool you." And when the judge asks her how she knew he was an impostor, she replies: "Well, it was the little things" (feet,† sex,† memory,† little things like that). When the judge asks, "Why did you allow people to believe he was Jack Sommersby?" she adds, "People believe what they want to, sometimes. . . . But there were signs anyone could notice if they had a mind to." Finally she testifies, "When we were together in a private way, I knew it wasn't Jack. A woman would know her own husband, Your Honor." To which the judge replies, "I'm sure most husbands would like to think so, Mrs. Sommersby." And this remark moves the discourse back from the private to the public sphere: "most husbands."

Good sex may, again, have ensured the collusion of the wife, but it is also the key to the unmasking of the impostor Sommersby. His virility, like Martin Guerre's, stands in dramatic contrast with that of the real Sommersby, who didn't sleep with his wife after their child was conceived.

In bed after making love, she remarks drowsily, "You certainly have changed." "For the better?" "So much better, scares me sometimes." As usual, the impostor is nicer (as well as more virile) than the original, but here this film adds a new twist: the man who impersonates Sommersby is no angel (he has gotten a girl pregnant and abandoned her, deserted his battalion in the army, and committed various frauds), but the original, the real Sommersby, has committed a murder (shot a man in a poker game), for which the impostor is now tried. The false Martin Guerre was simply tried for being an impostor and lost his case when the real Guerre showed up (as the real Sommersby could not, having died in the course of some other skulduggery). The Sommersby variant of the trickster tricked†—making him pay for the previously unknown crime of the person he impersonates—may have been inspired by Bette Davis's *Dead Ringer*† (1964), from which at least one other theme was surely borrowed: where Bette Davis purposely injures her right hand (grasping a red-hot poker) so that she will not be expected to produce her usual, right-handed signature, Jack Sommersby's wife testifies, "He couldn't sign like Jack, so he made up a story about a bad hand" (he claimed that a guard in prison had "tromped" on his hand†).

But then the film adds a second twist, this time political.† The impostor Sommersby had sold a lot of his land to freed slaves and other disenfranchised people to whom no one else would sell. If he were proved an impostor, they would all lose their land, and his daughter (named after another trickster, Rachel†) would be a bastard. Naturally, they all testify that he is Sommersby. By claiming to be the real Sommersby, therefore, the impostor is not ignobly claiming another man's land and wife (as Pansette did) but, on the contrary, nobly sacrificing his life for his wife and the freed slaves. A Ku Klux Klansman who testifies that the impostor *isn't* Jack, in order to take away the land from the freed slaves, is exposed as a racist and hauled away to jail for contempt, sentenced by the black judge.

At the trial, therefore, where we might expect his wife to testify that he was the real Sommersby if she loved him and an impostor if she didn't (for the impostor would go to jail), she argues that he is an impostor because she loves him—in order to send him to jail (for the imposture) but to save him from hanging (for the murder). And so she tells the truth: he isn't Jack Sommersby. Here the theme of the superior impostor reaches its crescendo: when "Jack" asks his wife if she knew he was an impostor because he was mean to her, she replies, "No. That's where you went wrong. Jack Sommersby never said a kind word to me in his life." And then she tells him, "A woman knows her own husband. I know how I feel. I know because I never loved him the way that I love you." This proves that he is great guy, though not Sommersby; but since the great guy wants the people to have the land, the judge does what "Jack" wants, not what his wife wants or what the judge knows to be the true ruling: he rules that "Jack" *is* Sommersby and hangs him for the murder. Her final words of encouragement to him, as he mounts the scaffold, are, "It was always you—I knew from the first moment I saw you."

SEXUAL UNREALITY-TESTING

Actual instances of successful (or, even, unsuccessful) bedtricks in real life are so few in comparison with the enormous body of literature about them (real-life twins,† for instance, behave in ways often diametrically opposed to the behavior of twins in stories) that we must find some other explanation for the popularity of the theme in fiction. Certainly bedtricks do not take place nearly often enough to justify the enormous volume of stories about them. And when they do happen they are often clothed in the words and images of fiction.† The bedtrick is not only counterintuitive but counterfactual, yet all of our texts assume that bedtricks can and do happen.

Here it is necessary to distinguish between realism and reality. I will argue that realism is an issue in many of our texts, which try to imagine how, realistically, the trick might be played and won. Even a myth as fantastic as the tale of the demon Adi† masquerading as Parvati shows a concern for both psychological realism (Parvati's stubbornness) and physical realism (her telltale twist of hair) when it comes to the logic of recognition. But reality plays a very small part in this book, which is primarily about fantasy, about the ways in which people regard sex as more real than other human phenomena. Let us return, therefore, to our fictions.

We have seen bedtricks facilitated by magic, by family resemblance, and by legal sanction; but we have also considered the starker case of common or garden variety cuckolding, where no initial resemblance can be assumed, nor divine or legal sanction. And we have seen bedtricks that work despite extreme intimacy (a familiar spouse) or extreme difference (someone of another biological sex). In more realistic texts, people must use natural means of deception (disguise, a twin sibling), in contrast with gods, who can produce perfect replicas at the flick of a magic switch (transformation, the creation of a magical double).

How realistically do stories about bedtricks deal with the problems that might be involved in bringing it off? What realistic explanations do they construct? What excuses have characters in stories made to explain how they could get away with it? What ways are there of perpetrating the deception, fooling someone in bed? This is the problem of unrealistic nonrecognition. Less pressing and less counterfactual concerns inspire the opposite set of questions about failed bedtricks. For we have also encountered many bedtricksters who were quickly exposed, even among the gods, and then we must ask how bedtricks fail, how the victims see through the trick. What ways are there of detecting the deception, telling one person from another in bed? How do you tell the difference? How does the victim of the bedtrick figure it out? More precisely, what are the reasons that the authors imagined for the success or failure of the bedtrick, the sorts of things that authors *thought* might allow a person to see through the sexual tricks to the sexual truth?

In fiction, often stranger than truth, the success or failure of the bedtrick entails another of our underlying paradoxes:† all successful bedtricks are failures. On the one hand, most bedtricks in stories (there are exceptions) work—at least, in the beginning; otherwise there would be no story to tell, for we wouldn't know there had been a bedtrick. Just as most murders go unsolved, so, perhaps, most bedtricks are successful. On the other hand, we learn only about the unsuccessful ones. (Jean Giraudoux's Ondine‡ remarks: "Ondine husbands are never unfaithful, except by some sort of muddle or mistaken identity; you know, a double, or the water being cloudy. But we arrange it so that anyone who does it by mistake never finds out.")[67] Most bedtricks in stories fail—at least, at the end; for we, the readers, always learn the truth at the end, and even a successful trickster usually reveals the trick after the game has been won, though we would hardly call this a failure. One of the great moments in the plot, after all, is the unmasking, and some masqueraders are unmasked before they achieve anything at all. There are relatively few, rather cynical texts in which the victim either figures it out from the very start and goes along with it (the motif of false ignorance†) or, on the other hand, even at the end of the story never finds out that he or she has been tricked. But some stories emphasize the success of the trick, the relatively long period in which it does work, while others emphasize its failure, the manner in which the victim quickly sees through it. Moreover, as we have noted, stories† often argue precisely for the opposite of what is the case in "real life"; that is, *stories* about bedtricks devote far more argument to the successful illusions than to the failures, precisely because the bedtrick seems to be counterintuitive, and this throws down a gauntlet to the sorts of people who demand logical explanations for everything.

The inherent paradoxes† in myths sometimes leave gaping logical holes, but for most traditions the hole becomes part of the story; you tell it that way, note the pothole, and walk around it.[68] That is how it is with the logical flaws in bedtricks: we expect them, wait for them, and then ignore them. But as the years go on, and sensibilities change, suddenly someone will notice the hole and do something to cover it up. Realistic arguments are often used, indeed reused to the point of becoming clichés,† and some texts deal realistically with the problems of deception and recognition, describing elaborate stratagems. But other stories of bedtricks don't bother with these explanations and simply ignore the real problems involved; they are more interested in exploring the effects of the events than in cross-examining their plausibility. These are, after all, not police reports but myths. However, because the mechanics of the trick are precisely what fascinate certain people, some texts try to explain how people got away with it (or, on the other hand, how they were found out). Thus, some stories of bedtricks do, and some do not, acknowledge that we have a problem here.

Each genre has its own conventions that determine the degree of realism; myths and novels handle bedtricks in different ways, as Claire Rosenfield has noted: "The Double or *Doppelgänger* was made initially respectable in romance, fairy tale, and mystery story where repressed† fantasies asserted themselves with particular vengeance in extravagant plots. But the novel requires that the opposing selves submit to the canons of plausibility."[69] It is also useful to distinguish between different cultural and methodological approaches to this problem, for the Hindu myth in which the masquerading demon assumes his true form in bed differs from the Hollywood (and Freudian) myth in which human beings reveal their true forms in bed. Here we are working simultaneously with two variables that might produce other permutations: theology versus psychology, and Hinduism versus Hollywood.

In the English Renaissance, realism was often trumped by convention;† for, according to John Wain, "The conventions of Elizabethan drama do not allow tactile recognition of women."[70] William R. Bowden agrees: "We should emphasize the purely conventional nature of the device [of the bedtrick]. It does not pretend to be credibly realistic. . . . Although we know that among real-life people there is considerable range in size and shape, in the drama doubt does not usually arise in the mind of the person tricked that his bedfellow is not the one he expected to encounter."[71] (Significantly, both of these scholars assume that men will be tricked by women.) Bowden thus accounts for the fact that stories about bedtricks are usually not pornographic or titillating: "Any dwelling on physical details would tend to remind us of the fundamental improbability of the whole business; and whereas a good dramatist may accept and use an improbable convention without apology, he does not flaunt its improbability."[72] These conventions do not prevent Shakespeare, to take an example within the English Renaissance, from exploring the nature of recognition in highly realistic psychological detail; and other works of fiction do so, too. The purely conventional† nature of the bedtrick in most renditions of the theme is wonderfully satirized in Robert Benchley's parody of Wagner's *The Ring* (in which Siegfried and Brunhilde engage in a complex bedtrick): "They do not recognize Immerglück, as she has her hair done differently, and think that she is a beggar girl selling pencils."[73]

Ten Ways Not to Know Your Lover

Let us postpone, for a moment, the ways in which bedtricks are exposed and consider the ones that succeed, the bedtricksters who are never exposed (at least until they choose to reveal themselves). How did they get away with it? What excuses did the bedtricksters devise to account for any apparent inconsistencies between their image and that of the original, and what excuses did those who were duped use to justify being taken in? This is not the place, nor am I the scholar, to review the more general philosophy of recognition, beginning with Aristotle's *Poetics* (chapter 16), where the types of recognition *(anagnorisis)* are ranked, beginning with the worst (signs, congenital and acquired), then proceeding through memory and reasoning (including false reasoning, *paralogismos*), and culminating in plausible interpretations of the incidents themselves (a process from which Aristotle expressly excludes contrived signs).[74] For one thing, where Aristotle was interested in recognition, I am more interested in nonrecognition; and for another, the focus of this book is on sexual recognition, which does not seem to have sparked Aristotle's imagination.

There are more arguments explaining success than failure, more reasons why the victims of the bedtrick might not be able to tell the difference between two partners in bed. It is harder for a victim to prove that the bedtrickster is *not* the original than for a bedtrickster (wrongly) to prove that he or she *is* the original; so, too, while the victim has no infallible ways of unmasking a trickster, the trickster has ways to make the trick work, and these are usually described at much greater length than the reasons for failure. The weight of the evidence is in favor of illusion, the fail-safe position for the human mind.

Natalie Zemon Davis regards the tricksters' track record in these stories as surprisingly good:

> In those frequent comic stories of the time, where one person is substituted for another for lovemaking in the dark of night, it is rare that the tricked person can tell the difference. (I know of only one counterexample: the old knight in the *Cent Nouvelles Nouvelles,* who notes the difference between the serving maid's firm breasts and his wife's mature form.) In all of these the tricked person learns the truth only when it is revealed to her or him later. Stith Thompson gives no reference to a tale with the same type of imposture as that in the story of Martin Guerre; the closest example is a twin who deceives the wife of his brother; K 1915–1917, K 1311.[75]

But here I beg to differ with Davis. In addition to many stories that resemble Martin Guerre in various ways, the counterexample that she herself offers (which I have called "The Old Mistress and the Young Maid"†) is quite typical; the clue that exposes the ruse is, as so often, age† versus youth, precisely things like flabby breasts; for example, Kiviok's† mother-in-law's skinny legs† betray her. By citing Stith Thompson, Davis moves into the arena of world myth and folktale, where not only does Stith Thompson's index provide many, many cases of unsuccessful bedtricks, but stories beyond his scope provide many others. People (including twin brothers†) are caught all the time—in stories. Indeed, what is surprising is that the trick succeeds as often as it does.

There are a number of specific arguments for the success of the bedtrick. Certain criteria, such as family resemblance,† the voice,† and behavior,† may either enable or unmask bedtricks. These tricks of the trade, factors that swing both ways, can destroy or facilitate the bedtrick, appearing as the problem or as the solution. To understand why the sexual criteria alone do (or do not) keep the victim from seeing through the bedtrick, it is useful to consider briefly ways of manipulating other competing criteria that do (or do not) outweigh the sexual ones. Of the following ten ways of obscuring identity that bedtricksters employ, the first four—darkness, drunkenness, intimate scars, and self-delusion—matter most at the moment of truth in bed, while the others are more generally supportive of the trickster's project.

1. Darkness

As long as vision is privileged, which is to say in most of our texts, darkness is a (masquerading) girl's best friend. To take one instance out of thousands, in *The Marriage of Figaro*,† the countess changes clothes with Susanna, "with the help of the night"; when the count urges her into a dark tryst, she asks, "In the dark, my lord?" to which he replies, "That's what I want; you know I don't want to go there to read." The darkness will serve her ends, not his; he may not have to read, but he won't get to commit adultery, either. Once again, the pleasure of the text† competes with the pleasures of sex. Occasionally, darkness that interferes with reading can be revealing rather than concealing: as Cyrano continues to "read" his letter to Roxanne in the growing darkness of nightfall, she realizes that he can no longer see the page—and thus discovers, at last, that he is the author of the letter—"the voice in the dark."

2. Drunkenness

The bedtrickster may prevail by getting the victim drunk, but drunkenness is also an instance of the more general lapse (which includes the primary mind-clouders, lust and sleep†) that might be described as letting down your guard; tricksters who relax get caught. Thus, when Mrs. Doubtfire (in *Mrs. Doubtfire*† [1993]) gets drunk, she begins to act like a man, reverting to her natural state and flirting with a pretty young woman, who recoils with horror.

Drink, however, is used far more often to fool than to unmask. It often absolves the victim of the responsibility to see through the bedtrick; when the victim is drunk or drugged, consciousness is blurred and the bedtrick works. Drunkenness may justify the release of libido at the expense of the superego: even a victim who is not drunk enough not to *know* a bedmate's identity may be too drunk to *care* about it. Drunkenness releases inhibitions, including those against incest,† that may stand in the way of necessary begettings. Drunkenness accounts for blindness† ("double vision" in the literal, as well as metaphorical, sense), loss of memory† (after the episode), and the inability to discriminate between good and bad, or real and false, people.

In *Measure for Measure*† (5.1), when Mariana argues, "I have known my husband; yet my husband knows not that ever he knew me," Lucio replies, "He was drunk then." Tricksters in the Hebrew Bible who use liquor to fog the mind include Leah,† Tamar,† Ruth,† and Lot's daughters. The sage who curses Shakuntala† makes explicit the links between sexual love, drunkenness, and storytelling† when he likens the king's forgetfulness of her to that of "a drunk who does not remember the story that he told before."[76] And drink may be used to trick the victim into believing that a sexual encounter has taken place when in fact it has not, a trick used by Daniel Defoe's heroine Moll Flanders and by the old prioress in Isak Dinesen's "The Monkey."[77] On the other hand, drunkenness may make one forget a sexual episode that *has* happened. A modern legal twist on the role of drunkenness and amnesia in bedtricks was reported in the *New York Times* in 1996: four men were acquitted of charges that they raped a drunken and unconscious twenty-two-year-old woman in a restaurant bar; since the victim said she did not remember the incident and did not approach the authorities until two weeks later, after friends told her the men were boasting of what they had done, the defendants' lawyer argued that if the woman had consumed enough alcohol to be helpless, as she testified, then she could not be sure that she had not consented to sex.[78] *Sommersby†* places a spin on the theme of drunken amnesia when the impostor claims to remember the night he begot his son—a night when, his wife reminds him, he was drunk and therefore could not be expected to remember. The double "forgot" that his drunkenness was an alibi for his forgetfulness.

Many stories suggest other forms of intoxication, offering supernatural or unnatural reasons for the clouding of reason, resorting to religion, *ex machina,* to extricate the plot from a human tangle: a curse, a ring of forgetfulness,[79] a magic potion. In the nineteenth century, when the new therapy that we now call hypnosis, then called Mesmerism or Animal Magnetism, became popular in England, "The operator was almost invariably male, the subject usually female . . . many people worried about the possibilities for sexual abuse."[80] (Fred Astaire, unconvincingly playing a psychoanalyst in *Carefree* [1938], dances with Ginger Rogers both when she is asleep and dreaming of him and when he has hypnotized her—the ultimate Astaire sexual dance, with the woman completely under his control). But the real-life realization of the "worry" about mesmerism comes in lawsuits involving patients who are raped while under anesthesia.[81] Apparently, a so-called date rape drug is now circulating on college campuses, "a substance that, when dropped in alcohol, can make someone faint and ultimately forgetful," according to the *New York Times.*[82] Such lawsuits inspired a 1996 TV film, aptly entitled *She Woke Up Pregnant,* which was advertised in *TV Guide* by a picture of a masked man (a dental mask this time, but a mask is a mask†), saying, "Trust me, this isn't going to hurt."[83]

3. Intimate Scars

A scar† or birthmark† or other immutable physical characteristic is the decisive proof of identity in many stories. So common is this mechanism that Stith Thompson dubs an entire motif "Recognition by scar" (H 51), and Terence Cave remarks, "the claims of knowledge and self-knowledge we make for literature depend on nothing more or less than the triumphant recognition of a casket or a birthmark."[84] When the couple in *Duplicates* (1991)† are trying to figure out who they are, he notices that he doesn't have any of the scars that his memories tell him he should have (a mark on his chin from a bad cut, an appendectomy scar, etc.). He asks her, "Do you have any memories of scars? I don't have the scars I'm supposed to have"; she asks him, "What happened? Did they heal our scars?" Then they realize that their memories have been replaced: "That's why our bodies are different from what our minds remember."

But scars and birthmarks, by virtue of their cliché status as proofs of identity, can—like all forms of scientific evidence—be faked in order to make the trick work. In Plautus's *Amphitryon,*‡ Jupiter-as-Amphitryon discloses that he has a scar on his right arm, but when they examine Amphitryon, an onlooker exclaims, "Oh, great Jupiter, there it is! What do I see? On both right arms, in exactly the same location, they both of them have the selfsame scar, reddish and livid in appearance, a new-made scar. So much for judgment."[85] In *The Invasion of the Body Snatchers*† (1956), one of the hero's friends cuts his hand,† and in an hour the clone has the scar, still freshly bleeding. In Shakespeare's *Cymbeline,* the trickster uses a mole on a woman's left breast as (false) proof not of her identity but of his sexual intimacy with her. The same trick was used by the trickster in *Overboard*† (1987), who claimed intimate knowledge by telling the amnesiac victim that she had a small strawberry mark (a birthmark or tattoo) high up on her left buttock; she went behind a screen to check, found it, and was persuaded that she must be who he said she was. (He had seen the mark by watching her sunbathe in a bikini on her yacht.) And it was tried by a South Indian trickster, too, who noticed a mole on a woman's leg when she forded a river and later cited the mole as (false) proof that he was her husband.[86]

An interesting twist is provided by scars that bedtricksters incur in the line of battle of their bedtricks, scars that later prove not so much their identity but what they did: proof that, whoever they are, they were at the scene of the sexual crime. Such scars identify the trickster not as someone who might have been known, previously, for that scar but as someone who received that scar in the course of the trick itself. The adulterer is often caught in this way, with some other woman's lipstick on his collar (as in Fumiko Enchi's *Masks*†), or the Hindu equivalent: a woman uses her nails to scratch her lover in the heat of passion, and such scratches as she herself cannot account for on her lover's back prove to a woman that he has been unfaithful. This is a convention in Sanskrit court poetry, and a whole chapter of the *Kamasutra* tells you how to do it. In contemporary American law, the matching of scar tissue with tissue found under the nails of a rape victim is often used as evidence.

Purposely inflicted scars are a device by which the passive victim of the deception suddenly becomes active and inflicts upon the bedtrickster a mark that later betrays the trickster's identity, either publicly (when the scar is on his face) or privately (when, since the scar is in an intimate place, knowledge of it proves sexual intimacy). Thus, in the Inuit† story of incest,† the sister marks her seducer's face under the left eye with soot, and the next day discovers the telltale mark on her brother. In several tales told by the Thompson Indians, a woman marks her lover with paint or creates some other sign and in this way discovers that he is an animal lover,† a dog.†[87] In Plautus's *Amphitryon*,‡ Mercury attempts to inflict a scar on his opposite number in the masquerade, precisely in order to identify him later; he beats Sosia, who later remarks, "Now, if only his back is scarred like mine, then really he's my twin."[88] The trickster in Roald Dahl's "The Visitor"† also purposely inflicts a scar on the neck of a woman whom he hopes to identify, in the morning, as his partner in the dark; his efforts prove vain, as both she and the other woman he suspects wear high collars at breakfast.

The scar may show who a person is by indicating what that person has suffered. Often it is painful or even fatal, as when the witch-wife, the mare,† is revealed by her mutilated hands and feet.† These physical mutilations are also the clue to deeper emotional mutilations, testimony that the person has been formed by pain. In the film *Dave*† (1993), the wife realizes that the impostor lacks the "scars" of all their years together; he has had "something that amounts to moral cosmetic surgery." Scars are the body's memory, in a form visible to others, of what the mind may have forgotten. Our scars may be the strongest signs of who we really are:

perhaps, at the final reckoning, the whole body will disappear, and only our scar tissue will be there to testify for us.

4. Self-deception

Self-delusion is explicitly invoked more often in modern texts, which tend to psychologize in ways that ancient texts do not, but it may be silently present in the earlier texts, too. People can be fooled because they want to be fooled, because they want the trick to succeed; their will to believe leads them to ignore glaring inconsistencies and the debunking implications of hard evidence, however blatant. Bedtricks work because the victims do half the work themselves, often projecting† their own desires, or the image of the one they desire, over the actual trickster. There are times when one really does not want to know the truth about one's sexual partner; the victim of the bedtrick may half suspect that the woman (or man) who *seems* to be the wife or the husband is not the legitimate partner. In many myths, the victim prefers the double to the original, particularly but not only in the case of political pretenders,† a scenario reinforced by the fact that people often notice the difference but keep silent out of fear of political repercussions. When people prefer the illusion to the reality, even when they know, or suspect, the truth, they deny it, lying to themselves and, sometimes, to others.

Self-delusion is the bedtrickster's inside man. Harold Bloom remarks that "only the authenticity of Jacob's passion for Rachel† could have compelled him to ignore all the omens that should have warned him against Laban's duplicity."[89] Roland Barthes argues, at great length, that Balzac's Sarrasine† helps the trickster to trick him through what he calls enthymemes and I have called syllogisms,† which Sarrasine uses "[to] ensnare himself (a task upon which he lavishes a vigilant energy). . . . The subject's vital interest is not to hear the truth, just as the vital interest of the discourse is to continue to suspend the answer to the enigma."[90] The bedtrickster in a Robertson Davies novel argues that the victim "is a partner in the deception. He wills his own belief to agree with the desire of the deceiver . . . just as you will your own deception when you watch a conjuror. . . . We are deceived because . . . it is somehow necessary to us."[91] When a man objects, "I don't believe a word of it," a woman who has been the victim of a bedtrick replies, "But I did. Or a very important part of me did. . . . When a man comes into your very dark room, and you can feel your husband's dressing-gown that you know so well, and he takes you so wonderfully that all the doubt and dissatisfaction of weeks past melt away, do you ask him to identify himself?"[92] As the site of repression, forgetting, self-deception, and ambivalence, the victim fails to understand, or to bring to consciousness, the contradictions in which he or she is swimming, the paradox of his or her life. The victim's resilient lack of curiosity is sustained by a dogged but passive perseverance that amounts to a kind of passive resistance to the truth.

It is not always easy to distinguish between someone who pretends to be fooled by a bedtrickster (on the surface, while knowing the truth below) and someone who allows her/himself to be fooled (just below the surface, with the truth still farther below). The cases of Ahalya‡ in India and of Alcmena‡ in Greece and Europe are long debates on this subject. The translator of Molina's tale of Don Juan argues for a cluster of self-deluding factors that account for Isabela's "puzzling" failure to distinguish between her lover, Octavio, and a total stranger, Don Juan: "the thrill and the danger of a clandestine meeting sweep aside all reason; possibly, from the moment of Don Juan's entry and initial embrace, there is no further conversation between them; it is conceivable that Isabela knows the man to be a stranger but, like the other women in the play, finds him irresistible."[93]

The personality dissociation often noted in cases of sexual avoidance and rape‡ leads the woman falsely to assert that there *was* a difference between the two forms of her—the one who was, and the other who was not, raped. But in the opposite situation, where the woman *wants* the union, this deception appears in an inverted form, and she may falsely assert that there was *no* difference between the two different men—her husband and his impersonator—or none that she could see. Thus, the woman is exonerated from the defilement by a stranger: "I could not tell them apart." This is made quite explicit in variants in which she pretends that she thinks it is her husband, to legitimize the episode, while she enjoys it precisely because she knows it is not her husband. This factor, the primary explanation that Natalie Zemon Davis offers for Bertrande's acceptance of the false Martin Guerre,† also applies to Chunagon's wife in *The Changelings*: she may very well know that the biological male is not her original husband but is just relieved to have a man instead of a woman in bed at last.

In a 1999 survey of lie detection, one of the researchers "was surprised to discover that the subjects with the romantic attachment were considerably worse at spotting their partners' lies than were the strangers," even though "the answers revealed that at some level they had picked up the deception, and picked it up better than strangers did."[94] Other scholars are not so surprised: the historian of science Thomas Kuhn speaks of paradigm shifts, while the sociologist Leon Festinger speaks of cognitive dissonance.[95] Festinger is referring to religious desire, and Kuhn to intellectual expectation; together they tell us that people will willingly falsify the details, or ignore them and argue them away, if there is an emotional reason to want to believe; that they will hang on to a cherished belief in the face of massive contradictory evidence. Years ago, Jerome Bruner performed experiments on people who were asked to identify each card in a deck that contained a red ace of spades. Most of them identified it as an ace of hearts or an ace of spades, though some were puzzled and bothered.[96] Someone who looks just like your husband but acts differently (better?) is a red ace of spades.

Marjorie Garber makes this point well with regard to the scene in *The Crying Game*† (1992) in which the woman turns out to have male genitals:

> Innumerable men of my acquaintance—admittedly, straight men, and, as it happens, white men, and, as it happens, middle-aged men—told me that director Neil Jordan had used a body double for this scene. The naked body, the body with the penis, was not, they said, the body of the person who had been on-camera in the previous scenes. In other words, they were in the grip of what Freud would call "disavowal." Their problem was the same as Fergus's: They had come to desire that which, once they "knew" what it was, they "knew" they didn't desire. Or did they? The split between mind and body, or knowledge and desire, was so extreme for these men that they preferred to believe that the trick was in the technology rather than in their own psyche and libido.[97]

Self-delusion of this sort is certainly the most persuasive explanation for the success of the real-life transvestite bedtrick depicted in *M. Butterfly*.† First, as the bedtrickster points out, "Men always believe what they want to hear." (" 'This is my first time' and 'That's the biggest I've ever seen'—or *both*, which, if you really think about it, is not possible in a single lifetime.") Then, "Because when he finally met his fantasy woman, he wanted more than anything to believe that she was, in fact, a woman." The play implies that, after a while, the French diplomat did suspect that his lover was a man and that, after that, he didn't want to see him/her naked. The words of the *Wizard of Oz* (1939) take on new meaning: "Pay no attention to the man behind the curtain."

5. Inattention

The bedtrick doesn't require an active process of self-delusion; people can be fooled simply because they are not paying attention. People are blinded by the superficial, especially by unusual beauty or, at the other end of the continuum, unusual ugliness, such as the disfiguration of scars,† which they look away from. The general theme of inattentiveness to sexual others takes three forms: men do not usually notice *(a)* women,† *(b)* people of other races or classes,† and *(c)* people who simply do not interest them. I have discussed category *a* in the context of feminism† and *b* in the context of race and class.† The last category hardly needs demonstration, but here are a few striking examples from the extreme case of transvestite bedtricks.

In *The Changelings,*† when the boy and girl began to swap places, people "were all of the same mind, musing that though they had heard the child was a girl, they must have been misinformed." And their father remarked, of their changing places: "No one will see anything at all different in you. Anyway, what difference does it make if you do look a bit different? No one will discuss it or argue about it."[98] People do not notice when a man passes as a woman, as Jan Morris reports: "I soon discovered, too, that people see in you what they expect to see: they knew me down there only as a woman, and if I had come down the street wearing flying boots and a crash helmet, woman they would have thought me still."[99] Morris noticed the cultural differences in various people's ways of not noticing her: "Americans generally assumed me to be female. . . . Frenchmen were curious. . . . Scots looked shocked. Germans looked worried. Japanese did not notice."[100] Or is it that Jan Morris did not notice the differences in the reactions of individual Japanese†? Or, perhaps, was politeness mistaken for self-delusion? As one of Angela Carter's characters in *Wise Children*† remarks of an apparently successful bedtrick: "I'll never know if he could tell the difference. If he did, he was too much of a gent to say."[101]

6. Time

Time works for the trickster in various ways. It is usually just a matter of time, after all, before the bedtrickster is unmasked. But how long does the trick have to last? In many myths of this genre, the bedtrick takes place on the first night, and the victim has no time for comparison-sleeping. (As the philandering husband of the Isak Dinesen character in the film *Out of Africa* remarks, justifying his practice of sleeping only with virgins, "I can't stand criticism.") Traditional convention ensured that the other person would be sexually unknown before marriage, and by the time the substitution is discovered, the damage has been irreparably done: the one-night stand is regarded as an irrevocable moment. If the woman loses her maidenhead, gets pregnant, and so forth, all is lost forever, even when the bedtrick is quickly discovered. Thus, Boursicot† was fooled by the Chinese transvestite because, he said, it was the first time he had had sex with a woman.[102] The first night is, like Passover, different from all other nights with the same woman: the fear, the blood, the newness, set it apart from all subsequent engagements. And that first night marks the transition from one relationship to another so entirely different as to justify the oft-expressed folk wisdom that you marry one woman and find yourself married to a different woman, a stranger. As Janet Adelman points out, "In both *All's Well* and *Measure for Measure* the bed tricks are portrayed as one-night stands that the male protagonists have no desire to repeat—and not only, I think, for reasons of dramatic economy and credibility. Both Bertram and Angelo lose their desire for their virgins as soon as they have ravished them."[103] The first time that one makes love with a new partner has a strangeness that may justify the confusion of the bedtrick, as Casanova† himself remarked: "Though the darkness forbade my seeing, and the silence my hearing, my sense of touch should have enlightened me—after the first set-to, at all events, but my imagination was in a state of ecstasy."[104] During the "first set-to" *(le premier assaut),* even the master seducer cannot trust his sense of touch.

On the other hand, differences between the impostor and the original are often accounted for by the passage of time. Short-term memory,† especially of names,† fades as we fade, while the memory of the years of our youth often remains young. Bedtricksters in stories often succeed by appearing on the scene long after the original has left and invoking as their allies time† and the natural disguise of aging.† The false Martin Guerre used the "passage of time" trope in his defense, implicitly evoking the unspoken story of the true husband who returned and was doubted. The translator of one text explains why Samjna† "could not recognize her Lord at the first sight. She met the Sun after a long time, and quite unexpectedly."[105] In the Bedouin† story in which the man's mother pretends to die but actually kills and impersonates his wife during his absence, he does notice the difference when he returns, but his mother sets his doubts at rest simply by saying, "You've been gone a long time."[106]

This same fact is used in Shakespeare's *The Winter's Tale* to explain why Leontes doesn't recognize Hermione when he meets her again years after he thought her dead: thoughtless as always, he exclaims, "Hermione was not so much wrinkled, nothing / So aged as this seems"(5.3). In the *Invasion of the Body Snatchers*† (1956), Becky confesses that she had noticed something different about her father: "I felt something was wrong, but I thought it was me, because I'd been away for so long." In Janet Lewis's novel, the change, not in Martin Guerre's impostor, but in his *wife*, threatens to undo the impostor, who cannot suppress an expression of delight at her unexpected beauty† and hastily accepts the suggestion that she has become *more* beautiful with the passing of the years.[107] Time is the bedtrickster's ally.

When Angela Carter's Nora and Dora are very old and meet a man they have known since childhood (a man who, in fact, has always pretended to be their father), he greets them with the usual cliché:

> "Floradora! You haven't changed one bit!" I was about to say him nay, draw his attention to the crow's feet, the grey hairs and turkey wobblers but I saw by the look in his eye that he meant what he said, that he really, truly loved us and so he saw no difference; he saw the girls we always would be under the scrawny, wizened carapace that time had forced on us for, although promiscuous, he was also faithful, and, where he loved, he never altered, nor saw any alteration. And then I wondered, was I built the same way, too? Did I see the soul of the one I loved when I saw Perry, not his body?[108]

Aye, that is the question. How do we recognize one another, and ourselves, despite the ravages of time?

Time, which ages us and changes us, is the trickster, Time that changes the god that we married into an animal—or the reverse—or changes us in one way or another, so that we end up with the wrong one after all. Time magically transforms the people we love into other people, people we can't stand. Scientists tell us that our bodies are entirely regenerated, cell by cell, every seven years (the period that American folklore regards as the limit for male sexual fidelity, the so-called seven-year-itch). The aging *Marschallin,* in Richard Strauss and Hugo von Hofmannsthal's *Rosenkavalier,*† sensing that she is about to lose her young lover (played by a woman) to a younger woman, confesses that she sometimes gets up in the middle of the night and stops all the clocks. How do we stop the face of the clock—or, rather, the clock of our faces?

7. Naive Testimony: Dogs and Kids

Often, the revelatory proof of identity is offered by an animal.† Orlando's‡ elkhound "threw himself with such ardour upon his mistress that he almost knocked her to the ground," despite the fact that the last time he had seen her she was his master, not his mistress. Virginia Woolf comments, "No one showed an instant's suspicion that Orlando was not the Orlando they had known. If any doubt there was in the human mind the action of the deer and the dogs would have been enough to dispel it, for the dumb creatures, as is well known, are far better judges both of identity and character than we are."[109] Kleist's Alcmena† protests to Amphitryon, "The dogs that wagged their tails about your knees / Would testify about you if they could" (2.2).

In Disney's *The Little Mermaid* (1989), the prince's dog, who had loved the mermaid, growls at the masquerading Ursula. In Japan, wild foxes not only may assume any shape but may make themselves altogether invisible to humans, though not to dogs, who always scent their real nature; that is why transformed foxes are afraid of dogs[110] and flee even from a puppy.[111] But dogs are also a fallible criterion, especially in films. In Peter Sellers's version of *The Prisoner of Zenda*† (1979), the dog growls at the impostor, but the general remarks, "Jasper certainly believes you're the king. He could never stand Rudolph." Sommersby† simply kills the dog when he realizes that it doesn't recognize or accept him (and then, when he turns into a good guy, buys the kid a darling puppy to replace it). At the trial, his wife cites the fact that "his own dog didn't know him" as evidence that he is an impostor, but everyone just laughs. In *The Dark Mirror*† (1946), the psychologist says, "I interviewed a pair of twins one time, so alike that dogs got mixed up about them." And in *A Stolen Life*† (1946), when Pat's dog, named Mike, ignores the call of the impostor, Katy, she just jokes, "Mike seems to have forgotten me for the moment." Then she feeds him treats by hand, and he comes to her by the time the husband returns. Sometimes the dog, like the rest of us, likes the impostor better than the original. In *Dead Ringer*† (1964), the boxer dog, Duke, who hated Maggie, likes the impostor, Edie, who explains this by saying that the dog became lonely after his master's death. *There's Something about Mary* (1998) thoroughly deconstructs the cliché about the dog who knows whether the suitor is good/real.

Sometimes dogs and kids are explicitly compared as witnesses. When

Kobo Abe's protagonist realizes that a retarded child has recognized him in his disguise, he consoles himself at first by reasoning, "I suppose that she had been able to see through me precisely because she was retarded. Just as my mask would not fool a dog. An uninhibited intuition is often far more keen than the analytical eyes of an adult." But then he turns the argument on its head and worries, "Wasn't it a sign that the girl had seen directly through to my real self without being taken in by the outward appearance of the mask or bandage? Such eyes actually existed."[112]

The dog that hates the false duke in *Excalibur*† (1981) is backed up by the child (Morgana/Morgause), who arises from sleep, cries out, "My father is dead," and is ignored—by Igraine, who points to the impostor and insists, "See, your father is there." Since children are not generally respected, their evidence may have no effect. Wise children know not only their own parents but sometimes other people's as well, yet dogs are more often taken seriously as witnesses both of the identity of a masquerading individual and of the reality/goodness of a species (dogs growl at devils and body snatchers); their sense of smell† is more reliable than our sense of sight.

8. Food and Smells

Food often functions as a clue in folktales, while the related olfactory sense takes its place in more sophisticated modern variants of the bedtrick. Food is another somatic memory that, like sex, competes with the memory of the mind: often the trickster is unmasked by the victim's recognition of the particular taste (and smell) of a particular food, like the identifying dishes that Cinderella† prepares. The demigod Kali† included eating, along with making love and dying, among the moments when a bedtrickster might reveal himself. Food and sex, the two great physical sensations, often join together to conjure up a reality; Edmund Leach points out the structural parallels between the continuum of animals† we eat or don't eat and that of the women we marry and don't marry.[113] Proust's *madeleines de Combray,* a single taste of which evoked a lost childhood memory several volumes long, cast their shadow over more adult (even adulterous) memories as well. In the film *Duplicates*† (1991), the memory-altered hero insists, "I hate mushrooms," but realizes, as he taste mushrooms, "My mind tells me no, but my mouth says, oh yes" (a remark reminiscent of the rape mentality in *M. Butterfly*† and elsewhere: the mouth† says no, but the eyes say yes). The old memory (in the body) loves mushrooms, and the new memory (in the head) hates them, and when the mind (bewitched by science, by memory implants) lies, the body (here located in the mouth) tells the truth. (Mushrooms are a good choice, suggesting the ambivalent qualities of the caterpillar's mushroom in Looking-Glass Land ["One side will make you grow . . ."] and the mind-altering qualities of magic mushrooms like the fly agaric.)[114] Often the trickster is recognized by the ability to cook a particular food; this is true of Nala,‡ Kusa,† and Cinderella in several variants.

But smell is employed more often than taste in bedtricks. Smell plays a part in Basile's "The Old Woman Discovered,"† when the king who is tricked into bed with the old woman perfumes himself so heavily that he cannot "smell the stink of her mouth, and the vinegar of her arm-pits, and the mustiness of that ugly thing." Ahalya‡ sometimes recognizes the god Indra by his divine smell. In Thomas Mann's retelling, Jacob thinks (wrongly) that he smells Rachel's† hair (when he is in bed with Leah).[115] In Roald Dahl's "The Great Switcheroo,"† the instigator of the bedtrick resolves to give up cigarettes and take to a pipe so that he will smell the same as the other man, and he insists that both of them start using the same brand of hair oil and aftershave lotion.[116] In Dahl's "The Visitor," the traveler in Palestine who meets the wife and daughter of his Arabian host is misled by their distinctive smell—distinctive from all other women but not from one another; they wear the same perfume, thus canceling out the clue of another, more sinister smell, the stench of leprosy.

In films, too, smell is a vital clue. Even the W. C. Fields character in *My Little Chickadee* (1940) can tell, by the smell, that he is in bed with a goat rather than with Mae West. And the uncle in Julian Barnes's *Experiment*† notes that the two apparently different women wear the same overwhelming perfume but still insists that they are not the same woman. Like the woman who bedtricks the blind man in *Sirens*† (1994), Angela Carter's twin sisters† are careful to switch their distinctive perfumes when they carry out their bedtrick, and the woman who in turn impersonates one of them uses the appropriate perfume. The villain in *Single White Female*† (1992) argues that her victim must have known who she was by her distinctive smell.

Smell can identify not only sexual partners but children and parents, the family resemblance. And children, presumably, know their mothers' smells. But a confusion of smells facilitates a quasi-incestuous† bedtrick in the dark in Gabriel García Márquez's *One Hundred Years of Solitude*: "José Arcadio kept looking for her all night long, for the smell of smoke that she had under her armpits and that had got caught under his skin.

. . . From the moment he entered, sideways and trying not to make a noise, he caught the smell. . . . [They made love] in a bottomless darkness in which his arms were useless, where it no longer smelled of woman but of ammonia."[117] Though the smell is the smell of another woman, even that is diffused in this darkness and ultimately blotted out by the ammonia smell of the narrator's own semen, so that he cannot distinguish one woman from another. Humans differ from most other animals (particularly dogs) in privileging vision over smell in sexual selection; we alone ignore the pheromones, the sexual smells that animals emit and other animals sense. Hindus believe that the traces of our former lives hover over us in the form of perfumes (*vasana*s) that tantalize us with memories that we cannot quite grasp. So, too, we cannot always quite grasp the smells of our elusive partners in bed.

9. Physical and Scientific Evidence

Any unique physical object—like a ring or a shoe—may be used to prove a unique human sexual identity, but objects may be lost or stolen or faked in so many ways. Scientific evidence, too, can swing both ways—to reveal or to conceal the truth. Evidence can be forged and manipulated, and for every instance in which science, or hard evidence, is used to expose an impostor, in another story—especially in films—miscellaneous scientific-sounding excuses make the trick work. When the mother in *Duplicates*† (1991) says, "Fingerprints don't lie," the cop replies, "Sometimes experts make mistakes. . . . I can't vouch for the caliber of this print technician in, what, Cleveland?" In *Wolf* (1994), the heroine has a lab test the trickster's DNA, but the test misfires when the technician throws out the blood because, he says, some canine DNA got into it somehow. The wife in *Face/Off*† (1997), who is a physician, checks the blood type of the impostor—but only after her husband has begged her to do it and said, "I love you"; and even then she doesn't believe the evidence until he tells her the details of their first date. The authenticity of scientific proof often ricochets: because people put such blind faith in "science," they do not use their own common sense to challenge the assertions of the tricksters. In *Killer in the Mirror*† (1986), dental records are subpoenaed to distinguish between the twins—but the dentist has been bribed to switch them.

10. Coincidence and Common Sense

One convention† of the recognition narrative is coincidence, which is often invoked to explain why two different people can look exactly alike.

In *Measure for Measure*† (4.3), when Provost finds a head to substitute for Claudio's, a head that belongs to a man dead of natural causes and conveniently a dead ringer for Claudio ("A man of Claudio's years; his beard and head / Just of his colour"), the duke replies, "O, 'tis an accident that heaven provides." Names† are often subjected to the critique of coincidence. Mandryka wonders how many other girls named Arabella† might be at the ball, and in Euripides' story of the phantom Helen,‡ Menelaus tries to explain away the double by coincidence: he wonders if "some other woman with the same name as my wife has been living in this house. . . . Can it be there is some man who bears the name of Zeus and lives beside the banks of the Nile? . . . I suppose it must be that in the great world a great many have the same name, men named like other men, cities like cities, women like women. Nothing to wonder at in this."[118] So, too, King Dushyanta at first rejoices when the young boy he meets says that his mother is named Shakuntala,† but then he remarks that there arc a lot of similar names. Here again, the triteness of the old story is taken as evidence for, not against, the reality of the trick. Javier Marias's cuckolded husband wavers on this point:

> One moment, I would feel certain that she was Celia . . . and the next I would be sure that it couldn't possibly be her and that it was just one of those extraordinary resemblances which nevertheless do sometimes happen, as if it was Celia but with another life or history, the same person who had been swapped while in her cradle, as occurs in children's stories or in the tragedies of kings, the same physical appearance but with a different memory and a different name and a different past in which I would not have existed, perhaps the past of a gypsy child. . . , Our Lady of the rag-and-bone men.[119]

Modern readers generally do not find coincidence a useful explanation, though we do fall back upon it sometimes in desperation. Even within stories, the argument from coincidence can always be countered by common sense. In *Duplicates* (1991), for instance, the woman's husband is not convinced by the evidence of coincidence—until it happens twice: "One look-alike—that can happen," he says. "But two?" (Here we may recall Lady Bracknell's comment in *The Importance of Being Ernest*:† "To lose one parent might be regarded as unfortunate; to lose both is careless.") This is not merely a modern attitude; common sense challenged the argument from coincidence even in ancient India.[120] But it is tolerated as a convention in recognition stories.

Common sense, reason, the sorts of arguments that might be used in a court of law, constitute the prescientific method of unmasking a trickster, corresponding to the "hard evidence" of science in the modern age. One might think that common sense would function on the side of the victim, and sometimes it does—as when, for instance, the original appears on the scene together with the until-then-successful masquerader, and explanations are demanded. Thus, when the demon thinks he has seen Udayana in bed with Kalingasena,† the prime minister realizes that this can't be so because Udayana is with Vasavadatta.

A down-to-earth, commonsense element often crops up in even the most fantastic magical bedtricks. When a man who has been married for three years notices, one night, that his wife has a fox tail three feet long, "Naturally, he seeks safety in flight and forgets to return home."[121] But common sense, too, is double-edged, for the basic expectation that one's sexual partner *couldn't* be replaced by someone else works in favor of the bedtrickster. Flat-footed excuses may be used to unmask the bedtrick or, on the other hand, to explain away problematic aspects of the bedtrick, objections to the trick. Mrs. Doubtfire (1993), careless in her drunkenness, forgets to remove her perfume and lipstick when she switches into male attire; challenged about this, she thinks for a moment and says, "I just bumped into an old girlfriend who hugged me and kissed me a lot."

Thus, we may conclude that, in general, the same sorts of criteria may be used by a victim to expose an impostor against his/her will or by the trickster to disprove, falsely, his/her falseness; by the genuine original to prove, truly, his/her genuineness, or by an impostor to prove, falsely, the original's falseness. That is, the trickster can manipulate sexual magic, can fake memory, can mimic behavior, can duplicate a scar or birthmark, and can falsify scientific evidence to make the trick work. The steadily escalating technology is effectively inconclusive: it can be used on either side, to unmask or to conceal the identity of the bedtrickster. In any case it is almost always brushed aside when the victim has other reasons to go along with the bedtrick, particularly when reason is swept aside by sexual desire. The so-called hard evidence deconstructs itself, and we are left with the soft evidence: one just knows whom one desires.

In public, out of bed, as it were, it was not easy, in premodern times, to prove who you were not. Carlo Ginzburg notes the problem of identification in the premodern period: "The chances of mistake or of fraudulent impersonation remained high. . . . Even signatures could of course be faked; and above all, they provided no check on the illiterate. . . . In this kind of society it was child's play to cover one's tracks and reappear with a new identity."[122] Natalie Zemon Davis's remarks on this subject could stand as a caveat for all bedtrick victims:

> How, in a time without photographs, with few portraits, without birth certificates, with parish records still irregular if kept at all—how did one establish a person's identity beyond doubt? You could test the man's memory, though there was always the possibility that he had been coached. You could ask witnesses to identify him, and hope that they were accurate and truthful. You could consider special marks on his face and body, but their significance could only be established by witnesses who recollected the earlier person. You could look to see whether he resembled other members of the family. You could check his handwriting, but only if he and the earlier person could both write and you had samples of the latter's work.[123]

Several of these criteria—memory, witnesses, marks, family resemblance, and handwriting—play important roles in our stories, too. They are of course irrelevant during a bedtrick, since people do not usually write or summon witnesses in bed, though they can be used to determine the bedtrickster's identity on other occasions, and indeed we have seen bedtricksters unmasked in these ways. But the point made by Ginzburg and Davis is that these criteria were generally useless in determining identity in public. Their inadequacy therefore ultimately tossed the problem of identity back into bed; for sexual intimacy, subjective though it was and is, was one of the few criteria that one might resort to in premodern times to establish someone's identity.

FANTASTIC SEX

One reason, in so many stories, the victim of the bedtrick cannot tell the true partner from the bedtrickster is that the partner and the bedtrickster are two polarized images of the same person. The myth preserves the fantasy that there are two separate people there. And it works in two different directions at once: the fantasy of the masquerade allows the fantasizer to make the sexual act more intimate, while the fantasy of the double distances it. And since we often want the two at once, intimacy and distance, reality and fantasy, both points of view are often expressed in the same myth.

The bedtrick story is a very real fantasy that may serve either to support or to subvert social reality. The reactionary form maintains the status quo, serving as an opiate (in the Marxist paradigm, or perhaps God's methadone, as it has been called). In the past, "telling stories about run-away wives substituted for wives running away,"[124] and even nowadays, cultures "use their myths of love in much the same way as do individuals their central sexual fantasy: to express their deeper wishes which are utterly at odds with the accepted ideologies of the man-woman relationship."[125] Sexual fantasy may also inspire us to do what the culture does not allow us to do, serving as a stimulus to make the dream come true, to change reality. Negative fantasies may have tragic† or unhappy endings, discouraging the reader or hearer from following a similar path, while happier endings encourage imitation; but either may inspire innovation.

Fantasy is an integral part of the sexual act. Our myths are themselves, of course, the authors' sexual fantasies, but within the narrative frame they often explicitly depict fictional characters having sexual fantasies, as, for instance, when the victim of a bedtrick asks, "Am I dreaming?"[126] The *Kamasutra* acknowledges the prevalence of sexual fantasy when it speaks of the passion that arises "when a man [the commentary says a woman can do this too], placing in his mind another woman who is dear to his heart, interposes her from the moment he begins making love until he achieves a climax."[127] It remarks: "The imaginations and mistaking of one person for another that are fantasized on the spur of the moment in the midst of sexual intercourse—they cannot even be seen in dreams."[128]

The myths say that someone is out to trick us; but we are the ones making the myths, enjoying the fantasy that the person we are in bed with is not the person we are in bed with. Is this paranoia,† projecting onto others what we want them to do for us and then seeing it as a hostile act on their part? Jealousy, as well as paranoia, may be a strong motivation behind sexual fantasies. The pathologically jealous and/or paranoid fantasize that their partners are fantasizing about someone else. According to the theory of parental imprinting,† a child who did not resemble his father was "as a visible image of the mother's hidden passions. . . . the public display of all secret, and at times illegitimate, yearnings. There are no desires, shameful or innocent, that one's progeny does not publicly disclose."[129] Thus, the child reveals the reality of the sexual fantasy. This is an extreme case, but even normal sexual fantasy has a significant effect upon the lives of the people who fantasize.

Our myths serve so many different purposes. We may read these texts as the happy fantasies of a child ("My mother is not really my mother; my real mother is better; this woman here is just a whore"), the sad fantasies of a child ("My life is terrible because my real mother abandoned me

to this evil stepmother, this whore"),† or the fantasies of the theologian†
that that child grows up to be ("The world is full of evil and suffering
because the real god abandoned us, and/or we are the children of the
stepparent"). We may see them as the fantasies of the wife ("This is not
really me in bed with this brute"†) or the husband ("Now I understand
why my wife acts so strangely sometimes; it's someone else there in her
place"†).

Or, through the multivalence of myth, all these purposes can be served
at once.[130] Myths, like people, have multiple personalities and are notorious shape-shifters. Why can't we kick out of bed all those faces and voices
from the past? Why this need to transform reality into fantasy? Is sexual
reality so intolerable? Throughout human history, men and women have
been forced to sleep with people they didn't want to sleep with, and they
have longed to sleep with people who couldn't or wouldn't sleep with
them. It is therefore hardly surprising that people have told stories about
surrogates or doubles for centuries all over the planet. The myth may
imagine the ideal solution, the perfect integration, the infinity in which all
aspects of human sexuality can stretch out without invading one another's
territories, an infinity that can never be achieved in real life. Science can
turn myths into reality, dreams into nightmares, and fantasies into lawsuits. Yet the need to mythologize, to dream, and to fantasize remains an
integral part of human sexuality. When, each for his or her own reason,
two people in bed close their eyes to an intolerable reality, each sees in
the dark the myth that makes the reality tolerable. What is produced by
the fantasy in the head while the bodies are joined? Myths, stories. The
myths are the true love-children of sexual fantasy; the stories are joined
at the hip.

When Dreams Become Nightmares

Why is sexual fantasy both a dream and a nightmare? There are two different sorts of fantasy at play here, desired and feared (or, to use the language
of our texts, white and black†). People masquerade sometimes to avoid
danger, sometimes to exert or subvert power, sometimes just to have fun.
There is a tension in the victim of a masquerade between the terror that
one might be betrayed and the hope that one could be in bed with someone other than the safe, perhaps unloved (or at least undesired) partner—
yet another paradox.† In fantasies of adultery, for instance, there are two
opposing currents, from the man's standpoint: (1) You pretend that
you're with your mistress when you're with your wife, and so you have

the fun but don't get into trouble. (2) You pretend that you're with your wife when you're with your mistress, so you feel safe when you are in danger. Or you can pretend that you are just pretending that the woman is your forbidden mistress (or your wife)—the double-back.† So, too, in incest, to take another example: (1) You pretend that you don't know it's your mother or sister when you are with her, so that you can commit the forbidden act in innocence. (2) You pretend that it *is* your mother or sister when you are not with her, so that you can enjoy the forbidden act without committing it at all. Or you can imagine that you are just imagining that the woman is, or is not, your mother—another double-back. In every case, the reader may sympathize with either the victim or the trickster, or with both; this, too, will determine whether the story is a dream or a nightmare, a joke or a tragedy.†

One sort of bedtrick is playful and useful, a way of expanding your sense of self, your range of sexual options: you're in bed with Marilyn Monroe (or Sean Connery) instead of the woman (or man) you've been married to for thirty years. (Such fantasies may ricochet upon the real people who inspire them; Rita Hayworth, the pin-up girl for the entire U.S. armed forces during World War II, once remarked of her most famous movie character, and of the men she actually slept with, "They go to bed with Gilda and they wake up with me.") These stories highlight human foolishness, erotic fun. But the other sort of bedtrick is frightening and dangerous, subtracting from (or destroying) your sense of self and the courage of your sexuality; you are vulnerable, waiting in bed for a man who may turn out to be Mr. Goodbar[131] or Edward Hyde, a psychopath. These stories highlight violence, terror, cruel lies, and the dehumanizing aspects of sex. The playful fantasy makes illicit sex safe, but the paranoid fantasy makes safe sex seem dangerous. Some of these variations, like the variations in the degree of realism,† are the result of the many different literary genres in which bedtricks occur. There is a world of difference between the naughty promiscuity of the daisy chain in Schnitzler's *La Ronde*, or a double-back-cross-play,† and the sinister, paranoid pyramid of cuckolders† that torments Javier Marias's† protagonist. But bedtricks that are dreams are often found side by side with nightmare bedtricks in the same culture, indeed the same text.

The princess who gazed on a picture of Andromeda† during intercourse accidentally influenced the form of her embryo. The *Gynecology* of Soran, composed in the second century in Rome and Alexandria, tells of a hideous tyrant who did it on purpose, who made his wife look at beautiful statues of gods during intercourse and became the father of well-shaped children.[132] Soran's tale expresses a dream of controlling pregnancy; but the nightmare takes over the story when one man actually impregnates another man's wife, cuckolding the man physically just as his wife cuckolds him psychologically when she fantasizes about another man while she is in bed with her husband. As long as we control the fantasy (no matter what it is, to be perceived as whole or as multiple), it is a dream; when we stumble into someone else's masquerade, or when the double that we make turns upon us and takes on a will of its own, it is a nightmare.

Most active doubles are useful to the person who is doubled: they get you out of a bad situation or into a good one; you make the double yourself, and it extends you. The passive fin de siècle doubles in Germany, Russia, and England, however, are fatal to the doubled person: they diminish, or even kill, the people whom they double. The passive double (as in the *Comedy of Errors*,† in which the hero accidentally encounters his double, or, later, in the body-snatcher films†) feels persecuted. His initial perception is that he knows something that no one else knows or that everyone else is crazy or asleep, but he slips from this position to his paranoid perception that everyone else knows something that he does not know or that everyone believes that he is mad or that he *is* mad. Active doubles generally do not become the victims of their own creations in the traditional texts. But in the late nineteenth century, Oscar Wilde ("The Shadow"), Dostoyevsky (*The Double*), and E. T. A. Hoffmann ("The Doubles"), inspired in part by Mary Shelley's *Frankenstein,* imagined a new synthesis, a kind of active-and-passive double: the hero who actively creates a double who eventually persecutes him. This is a new expression of the ambivalence of the bedtrickster: the hero does and does not want to have the double, and he does and does not want to kill the double and/or to die himself. Jeanine Basinger, commenting on films in which a woman, during sleep† or hypnosis, becomes someone else (*Half Angel,*† *Lady in the Dark, Whirlpool*), suggests that the key question is "Does it control her, or does she control it?"[133] If the former, the film can be either a horror film or a comedy; if the latter, it will be a comedy. Yet we are the ones who imagine both situations; the playful fantasy is glossed for us by Charles Rycroft,[134] the paranoid fantasy by Otto Rank. And the fantasy and the nightmare converge in black comedies or tragicomedies.†

DOUBLE BEDS HOLD THREE OR MORE PEOPLE

Sexual fantasy allows the fantasizer to project the image of one woman over that of another. Many of these myths speak of the power of the eye,† in particular the eye of someone in love, to project fantasies, but the projection† may take place in the heart just as easily as in the eye. This is a recurrent theme in Hindu mythology. Queen Vasavadatta† accuses King Udayana† of being obsessed with a new woman: "You have projected her into your heart, so that you imagine that *everything* seems to be made of her."[135] Ravana,‡ in the Tamil *Ramayana*, sees an image of Sita when she is not there, and his sister Shurpanakha† accuses him of hallucinating. Women like Ahalya,‡ faced with the problem of telling their husbands from gods, may confess that they have imagined the gods in their husbands' places; or, on the other hand, like Alcmena,‡ they may be accused of projecting their images of their husbands over all other men.

When John Erskine's Helen‡ argues that her love for both Menelaus and Paris was an illusion, though she preferred her illusion for Paris, she resists the fabrication of a myth: that Aphrodite made her mistake Paris for Menelaus.[136] Instead, she insists, "You always think it's Menelaos you're embracing, and it turns out to be Paris." For Helen, the epitome of the woman onto whom men have projected their erotic ideals, the lover is real, the husband the fantasy. For most women, it is the other way around—as Helen herself knows, when she consoles a woman whose lover has deserted her. Helen tells the woman that had her lover stayed with her and married her, he would have become "a stranger, with a haunting resemblance to your lover."[137]

Lawrence Durrell at the start of the first volume of his Alexandrian quartet cites one of Freud's most famous remarks: "I am accustoming myself to the idea of regarding every sexual act as a process in which four persons are involved. We shall have a lot to discuss about that." I had always assumed that the four in Durrell's mind were the subjects of the four volumes, and that the other two in Freud's mind were two other real or imaginary people who were desired—given the Oedipal connection, perhaps her father and his mother. But on looking more closely I saw that Freud had said, "You are certainly right about bisexuality. I am also getting used to regarding every sexual act as one between four individuals."[138] So perhaps the other two were her mother and his father? Or his female half and her male half?[139] When I asked a well-known psychoanalyst of my acquaintance who, in his opinion, the other two were, he quipped, "One of them was probably an analyst."[140] The copulating couple makes, therefore, not merely Iago's† "beast with two backs" but a beast with four backs. Apparently it takes not two but four to tango; or we could say that all sex is four-play.

Fantastic sexual doubles tend to form squares. In *Cat on a Hot Tin Roof†* (1958), Maggie tells her husband, Brick, why she had an affair with Skipper, the man that Brick was in love with: "We made love to each other to dream it was you, both of us!" This eternal triangle is the bisexual fantasy of the cuckolding† scenario: both the man and the woman of the original pair are in love with another man, or another woman. (In the classical heterosexual triangle, two men are in love with one woman, or two women with one man.) The protagonist of Kobo Abe's *The Face of Another,* who bedtricks his own wife, constructs a more convoluted geometry to explain to himself what he has done: "This was a triangular relationship with one actor playing two parts. If one were to make a drawing of 'me,' 'the mask, that is, the other me,' and 'you,' it would be a non-Euclidean triangular relationship, existing on a single straight line."[141] Which is to say, a Möbius strip.[142] In the film, when he tells the doctor he's going to seduce his own wife, the doctor replies: "It's a dangerous triangle."

In these instances, there is one extra person (the fantasized third) in bed. But if each of the two original partners fantasizes about a different person (as in Goethe's *Elective Affinities* or Giraudoux's tale of Alcmena and Amphitryon and Jupiter and Leda‡), we have a double-play† or an eternal square dance. (William R. Bowden described the double-play in Thomas Heywood's *The Fair Maid of the West†* [1631] as "reminiscent of a figure in square dancing, the Grand Squares,"[143] and this image fits the Freudian quartet equally well.) And then there is the story of Kunigunde Orlamunde, a widow who wished to remarry and who heard that Albrecht the Fair had said that if "four eyes" were not in the way, he would make her his wife. Misinterpreting his words to mean that her two children were the obstacle to her remarriage, she killed them, only to learn that Albrecht had been referring to her parents, and her act of infanticide so horrified him that he rejected her.[144]

This magic square of four people in the bed has found its way into (or from?) the Talmud and Jewish folklore. "A Yiddish proverb warns us that in a second marriage there are four in the bed: her first husband, his first wife, and the two who really are there."[145] The Babylonian Talmud puts it significantly differently: when a divorced man marries a divorced woman, there are four *minds* in the bed.[146] (These may not be the same four minds that Freud had in mind.) The *Zohar* applies the double standard† and reduces the minds to three: if a man who has a son, and therefore does not qualify for the levirate,† dies, he leaves his spirit (which still "cleaves"† to his wife) not merely in the bed but actually inside the body of his widow; if she remarries, this is what happens when her second husband is in bed with her: "When the second husband's spirit enters into the body of the woman the spirit of the first husband contends with it, and they cannot dwell in peace together, so that the woman is never altogether happy with the second husband, because the spirit of the first one is always pricking her, his memory is always with her, causing her to weep and sigh over him. In fact, his spirit writhes within her like a serpent. And so it goes on for a long time."[147] The two spirits clash within the woman's body like the couple inside the man's head in *All of Me*† and *Being John Malkovich*† or the twins in the wombs of Rebecca† and Tamar.†[148] The first husband writhes within her like a serpent, a vivid sexual image; if he prevails, the second husband dies too, and his spirit roams as a ghost. If, however, the second spirit prevails, the first must leave the woman's body and roam as a ghost.

Why stop at four in the bed? Javier Marias's† cuckolded† husband imagines an infinite pyramid of "co-fuckers," the proliferating web of social partners. Women, too, may be plagued by the multiplicity of their surrogates; the multiple-personality protagonist of *The Three Faces of Eve*† later complained that her husband "had secretly thrived on my illness and gotten excitement from having so many different wives—even the ones who rejected him. Doctor, I now know that the man enjoyed a virtual harem in his bedroom, and the worst part is that *I* created all those women even though I was none of them."[149] On another occasion, she insisted that her husband "never had a monogamous marriage; because of the disorder he could sleep around without ever leaving his bedroom. And I made that bizarre circumstance possible."[150]

Conjoined twins—the literal embodiment of Freud's four in the bed—have always provoked special interest: what did the other twin do when one twin was making love? Didn't the hormones in their shared blood excite the one who wasn't doing it (to say nothing of the soft-porn value of voyeurism)? Apparently not. Some conjoined twins managed their sex lives with surprisingly little ambivalence (except for Christine and Millie, reported by Mark Twain,† twins who narrowly escaped being sued for breach of promise). The Bunker brothers, conjoined twins, slept in a specially built bed, "large enough to accommodate four occupants . . . it is . . . likely that conjugal duties were carried on with all four people in the same bed at the same time." When the physician who attended the widows after their husbands' deaths asked them "how much inhibition and embarrassment was created by the necessity of three [why not four?] persons being in bed at one time," the women spoke of "alternate mastery," "the alleged ability of one twin to become mindless, to 'blank out,' as it were, thus allowing his joined brother to enjoy his wife in what might be termed at least mental privacy."[151]

A similar statement was made by one of the conjoined twins Violet and Daisy Hilton, born in Texas in 1909: "Each of us acquired the ability to blank out the other in romantic moments."[152] And there is more. The girls were literally joined at the hip but turned slightly from each other. They were attractive, interested in men, and could even dance. They were also promiscuous when young. A reporter asked, "How do you make love?" Violet said that when Daisy was engaged, "sometimes I quit paying attention. Sometimes I read and sometimes I just take a nap." From Houdini they learned concentration: "We learnt not to know what the other was doing unless it was our business to know it."[153] These twins were able to preserve precisely the "mental privacy" that is invaded by the two supernumeraries in a joint sexual fantasy. Their mental bracketing produced the inverse of Freud's two people imagining that they are four; here, four imagine that there are just two.

Some of these texts support the assumption that Freud was talking about the object of desire in his remark about the quadruple-bed, the two people desired by each of the present partners; others suggest that he was talking about the subject of desire, the male half of the woman in bed and the female half of the man. If we allow the possibility of both bisexual subjects and bisexual objects, there would be eight in the bed: each partner both *is* two and *desires* two. The assumption that people imagine that they are in bed with other people is demonstrated by the widespread evidence that a person may call his or her bedmate by someone else's name† and pay heavily for the error. People may also call upon the name of God at this moment. Of course, Freud would have argued that having God in your bed is not all that different from having your parents in your bed. In any case, in the myths of bedtricks, the beds get very crowded.

Approach Ten

Structuralism

SPLITTING HARES

The great French structural anthropologist Claude Lévi-Strauss retells a group of stories about bedtricks told among several North and South American tribes: the Tupinambas, the ancient coastal Indians of Brazil (recorded by the French monk André Thevet in the sixteenth century); the Kootenay; and the Salish:

> [A] woman was going to meet the god who would be her husband, and while on her way the Trickster intervenes and makes her believe that *he* is the god; so, she conceives from the Trickster. When she later finds the legitimate husband-to-be, she conceives from him also and later gives birth to twins. And since these false twins had different fathers, they have antithetical features: one is brave, the other a coward; one is the protector of the Indians, the other of the white people. . . .
>
> Among the Kootenay, who live in the Rocky Mountains, there is only one fecundation which has as a consequence the birth of twins, who later on become, one the sun, and the other the moon. And, among some other Indians of British Columbia of the Salish linguistic stock—the Thompson Indians and the Okanagan—there are two sisters who are tricked by apparently two distinct individuals, and they give birth, each one to a son. . . .
>
> There are two sisters who are travelling in order to find, each one, a husband. They were told by a grandmother that they would recognize their husbands by such and such characteristics, and they are then each deluded by the Tricksters they meet on their way into believing that they are the husband whom each is supposed to marry. They spend the night with him, and each of the women will later give birth to a son.
>
> Now, after this unfortunate night spent in the hut of the Trickster, the elder sister leaves her younger sister and goes visiting her grandmother, who is a mountain goat and also a kind of magician; for she knows in advance that her granddaughter is coming, and she sends the hare to welcome her on the road. The hare hides under a log which has fallen in the middle of the road, and when the girl lifts her leg to cross the log, the hare can have a look at her genital parts and make a very inappropriate joke. The girl is furious, and strikes him with her cane and splits his nose.[154]

A series of sexual deceptions results in the birth of twins† to two different fathers.† But the last episode takes a different turn, ending in a series of splittings—the separation of the two sisters, of the legs of the older sister, and of the nose of the hare. We have seen many women in these stories split or double themselves to avoid sexual violence,‡ and I have suggested that the bedtrick is itself a form of sexual violence. In this reading, the violent splittings in the final episode are a displaced† reaction to the sexual deceptions.

Lévi-Strauss's own gloss of this story suggests some of the structural aspects of splitting: "The elder sister starts to split the body of the animal; if this split were carried out to the end—if it did not stop at the nose but continued through the body and to the tail—she would turn an individual into twins, that is, two individuals which are exactly similar or identical because they are both a part of a whole."[155] "Exactly similar or identical" twins are the appropriate product of a sexual act brought about by one individual pretending to be "exactly similar or identical" to another; and the hare (a trickster figure) is split to compensate for the doubling of the sexual trickster.

Minimal and Other Pairs

Lévi-Strauss's method of analysis is both inspired by and designed for stories and problems such as these; it might have been invented precisely to deal with bedtricks. His canonical formula $(a:b::c:a^{-1})$ relates what is the same (the two sets of parallel terms: a and c, and b and a^{-1}) to what is different—more specifically, to what is opposed or inverted (the two sets of compared terms: a and b, and c and a^{-1}).[156] To consider multiple variants simultaneously (which is the genius of the structural method), one must choose variants on the basis of their similarity; but to determine the significant oppositions in the myth, one must isolate factors of difference. These factors are defined by means of minimal pairs, two terms that change the meaning when they replace one another in the same situation, like c and h in "cat" and "hat"—or like the partners in bedtricks, who might well be called "minimal pairs." Minimal pairs are defined by what linguists call distinctive features—another term that serves equally well in structuralism and in the plot of the bedtrick.

What answers do we get if we ask structuralist questions of the myths of the bedtrick? Lévi-Strauss asserts that all mythology is dialectic in its attempt to make cognitive sense out of the chaotic data provided by nature and that this attempt inevitably traps the human imagination in a web of dualisms, which is to say splittings and doublings. We may see a dialectic at work in myths of bedtricks: doubling in situations of pairing. That is, bedtrick myths are about the tension between the desire to remain whole and the desire (or necessity) to split into two, a tension tentatively resolved by having the two become one (the sexual act) while one becomes two (the bedtrick double). The dyad of "integrated" and "split" is itself a basic contrasting unit in mythology; that is, any split image may be used to form one-half of a pair, the other half being the integrated image of which the half is the dissection. The question of whether or not to split something in half may be answered by yes or no. (Most cultures, but not all, have usually answered yes to this question.) On this level, the structure *is* the meaning; the medium is the message.

The doubles of people occur in response to a splitting or doubling of roles. They may also occur in response to other doubles: the wife masquerades when her husband takes another woman, or doubles herself when a man other than the man she loves forces her to his bed. The basic split is between the self and the double of the self, the "I" and the "non-I." To this is then added the particular dualism of the sexual act: "I" and "the other." In most texts, this sexual other is singular at any moment, the person with whom one engages in a single sexual act at any time, though in some texts this lover may then be doubled by another lover (or by a series of lovers). One would merely have to go on doubling the doubles to apply the same sort of analysis to polygamous societies or group orgies. So, too, the human body is often dichotomized, both by the texts and by the scholars looking at the texts. Sometimes the face is all that is seen and is therefore equated with the body, in contrast with the soul or mind,† which is not seen. Sometimes it is the eyes† versus the mouth.† And these dichotomies often attract to themselves polarized moral judgments.

Yuri Lotman has applied a structural theory (more precisely, a semiotic theory of transformational grammar) to literary texts and come up with certain formulations that illuminate the problem of masquerades, particularly in his discussion of what he calls cyclicity. He points out that "a mythological text, because of its exceptional capacity for topological transformation, can boldly make assumptions about the identity and similarity of things which we would be hard pushed to do." He argues that the need to compress a cyclic view of time and the universe into the linear form of a narrative is the reason mythological texts abound with "certain characters identical with each other."[157] When the three dimensions are collapsed into two, things begin to coincide—in fact, to coincide with themselves.

THE STRUCTURE OF THE BEDTRICK

The structural method allows us to make an inventory of the network of dialectical themes that make up a corpus of myths. These themes are roughly equivalent to what Lévi-Strauss called "mythemes," in response to the "phonemes" of his colleague the linguist Roman Jakobson—the atomic building blocks of meaningful sounds that make up words. As I employ them, mythemes are not images or concepts but events, things that happen, plots; each consists of a sentence, with an actor and an action, a noun and a verb.[158] The defining mytheme of the bedtrick might be formulated:

> The victim does not know the identity of the trickster during the sexual act.

The binary opposition or dialectic implicit in this sentence lies in the presence or absence of knowledge:† the trickster knows, and the victim does not. In addition, we might isolate subsidiary but still basic mythemes that have polarized instances, such as:

> The trickster produces a double (to avoid sexual intimacy) or masquerades (to seek sexual intimacy).
> The trickster impersonates someone who exists or someone who does not exist.
> The trickster is the unofficial or the official partner of the victim.
> The trickster is older or younger than the victim.
> The trickster is uglier or better looking than the victim.

Structuralism also enables us to isolate themes polarized only by their presence or absence, such as:

> The trickster is incestuously related to the victim.
> The trickster hates, rejects, or injures the victim.
> The trickster is a twin.
> The trickster or victim dies or is mutilated.
> The trickster or victim rejects a child.
> One of the trickster's or victim's senses is impaired.
> The trickster is of another species, race, class, or order.
> The trick involves art: riddle, story, painting, sculpture.
> An object (usually a ring) is used as proof of identity.
> The trick takes place on the wedding night.
> The trickster is tricked.

These themes do not constitute a structure that can be diagrammed in a family tree, a trunk line from which variants branch off. They form, rather, something that can best be suggested by a Venn diagram: a core of themes that appear in every story in the set is enriched by other themes that appear only in some variants, but in conjunction with other themes in the set.[159] This core is open-ended; other themes could also be accommodated as factors in differentiating story types, such as moral judgments: the trickster is good or evil, or the story has a happy or unhappy ending.

What use is this list? It summarizes the underlying structure that the list-maker uses to draw together many tales of bedtricks, from different times and places, and to argue that they are, in some sense, "the same." It shows us how a few variables, in permutation, can account for the rough outlines of the thousands of variants in our vast corpus. It enables us to identify stories within our corpus and to see their structural patterns. It alerts us to things to look for in each story; it helps us to see the connections, to determine degrees of affinity between the structures of variants. It makes it possible to trace the recurrent themes through the corpus of myths without discussing each theme every time it occurs. And it helps us to see what is missing from some variants. If, for instance, we were to trace the themes through all the myths in this book and list the occurrences of all the themes for male and for female bedtricksters, we would see that the lists are not symmetrical: some themes occur more in one gender than in the other. A comprehensive list shows us all the symmetrical slots of possibility for the themes, but the actual examples of the stories show that some combinations do not seem to occur (perhaps because of the biological or psychological or cultural asymmetry† of men and women). Once we have seen this structure, we may use other methods to inquire after the reasons for these lacunae.

SEXUAL PARADOX

The network of interlacing dichotomies cannot, however, be neatly laid out as a structuralist might wish them to be and paired up tidily like children in the buddy system: goddess/woman, man/woman, permitted/forbidden, maternal/erotic, good/evil, light/dark, Brahmin/Outcaste, integrated/split, and, at base, known/unknown. The binary categories in these stories tend to generate potentially infinite intermediary subcategories, and different cultures find different ways of blurring the lines between sex and gender (two genders or three), mind and body, and so forth. Moreover, through the very nature of the dialectic, the splitting that seems to solve the original problem of conflict or ambivalence is in itself a source of new anxiety. The solution to the problem of doubling is a new integration, with new tensions. Thus, the mytheme of male *or* female may yield a new, paradoxical mytheme of male *and* female, and we are off and running on a new and differently conflicted path of androgyny and bisexuality.

Dualism, the either/ordering of the world, is deeply embedded in European thought. What got Greek philosophy off the ground was the notion that, for any state of affairs, there were only two possibilities, A and not-A, and only one could be true. This is what Parmenides' poetic ravings about the One and the Many are all about, and what makes possible Platonic dialectic, Aristotelian logic, and the Cartesian approach to the mind/body problem.† This aspect of consistency is the essence of what historians of science and philosophy (and modern Greek propagandists) call "the Greek miracle." The Greek paradigm casts its shadow over many myths about binary choices (posed by Loathly Ladies† and animal lovers†), about bisexuality, and about monogamy, myths that cling to the A/not-A logic, animal *or* human, male *or* female, wife *or* mistress, but not both. This is what makes so many of these stories assume, counterintuitively, that you can only love one person.

The problem here is that in mythology (and much of human life), A and not-A are often *simultaneously* true, a position that those miraculous Greeks and their descendants regard as irrational. From the mythological point of view, consistency is the hobgoblin of people who cannot, philosophically speaking, walk and chew gum at the same time. Other mythologies, notably but not only Hindu, flourish within the realm of the both/and,[160] and between the grid lines of bedtrick myths we may discern more complex human implications that arise out of the dualistic structures and seem to emerge as paradoxes. I am using "paradox" here in the broader sense as glossed by the *Shorter Oxford English Dictionary:* "statement contrary to received opinion; seemingly absurd though perhaps really well-founded statement; self-contradictory, essentially absurd, statement. . . ." In this sense, a paradox expresses something closer to ambivalence than to logical self-contradiction, something closer to the word's lexical Greek sense: "against opinion," or, as we would say, "counterintuitive."

The greatest methodological contribution that structuralism makes to our understanding of the myths of bedtricks lies in Lévi-Strauss's insight that every myth is driven by the obsessive need to solve a paradox *that cannot be solved,* to tidy up a mess that cannot be cleaned up.[161] In his view, myths transform the paradox into a narrative that expresses a contradiction; they simultaneously express two opposed paradigms, two major human contradictions, two human truths that are simultaneously true and mutually opposed. (Calvin Klein's perfume called Contradiction, advertised with the slogan "She is always and never the same," would have been called Paradox if it had been made in France.)

The tension between these two paradigms holds us in suspense to the very end of the story, where we often discover that both of them are true. For the bedtrick, the basic paradox—that sexual intimacy is simultaneously revelatory of truth and falsehood—is mediated by a series of other paradoxes.

PARADOX LOST

Different cultures not only view their paradoxes in different ways but also experience different paradoxes. Myths from polytheistic cultures like Hinduism generally differ from those of monotheistic cultures in allowing, or spelling out, the maximum number of paradoxes, in exploiting as many possibilities as possible, maximizing the number of problems (in contrast, for example, with biblical myths, which tend to attempt to solve problems). But many of these formulations are shared by more than one culture.

Jean Giraudoux's Jupiter‡ spells out a veritable jeremiad of human paradoxes about the bedtrick when he tells Mercury what he wants: "Everything a man wants, I'm afraid: a thousand contradictory desires. I want Alcmena to stay faithful to her husband, and I want her to abandon herself rapturously to me. I want her to be chaste when I kiss her, and I want nameless desires to flare up in her at the sight of me. I want her to know nothing of all these manoeuvres, and I want her to approve them utterly."[162] And Kobo Abe's masked protagonist in *The Face of Another* admits to the wife he thinks he bedtricked, "I wanted to get close to you, and at the same time to stay away from you. I wanted to know you, and at the same time I resisted that knowing. I wanted to look at you and at the same time felt ashamed to look."[163] The many variants of the myth approach these paradoxical truths from different angles, each adding its own opinion as to the nature of the indefinable truth beyond words that we sometimes find in bed.

There are so many sorts of selves, and so many ways of knowing them, that the sexual way, for all of its deceptiveness, remains a unique source of something true—indeed, of several sorts of truth. The bedtrick is a paradigmatic expression of the problem of the mind and the body, reality and illusion, compounding the paradox of the double that is both us and non-us and of the story that lies and tells the truth. This paradox makes people tell the story over and over again, using the myth to negotiate the territory carved out by the paradox.

The structural premises of these myths become paradoxical when combined with their opposed forms. The mythology is saying that a sterile or impotent man should let his brother produce a child for him, despite the fact that he hates to imagine his brother sleeping with his wife. It is saying that a barren woman should have her maid produce a child for her, even though she hates that maid. It is saying that women collude together to save the family, even though older women are the enemies of younger women. It is saying that a man commits adultery because he is in love with the wife of another man but also that he commits adultery because he hates the husband whom he cuckolds. It is saying that you want to be in bed with a certain person but also that you don't want to be in bed with that person.

To accommodate all of these tensions and ambivalences, the myth allows you to fantasize that there are two of you, like the two Zen Buddhists that it takes to screw in a light bulb in the joke: one to do it, and one *not* to do it. In this way, both the central ideal and the subversive ideal may be expressed in the same story. We are not dealing here with two different, warring bodies of mythology; in most cases, a single myth is saying both things at once. It can do this because it speaks both for the group (survival, biology) and for the individual (dying for love, romanticism).

To the extent that all great myths are built upon paradox, all myths (including myths about bedtricks) contain their own doubles. A paradox is like the *shlesha* figure of speech in Indian poetics, an "embrace" of two contradictory ideas (what Yigal Bronner has nicely called a "bitextual masquerade").[164] Like a bedtrick, a paradox is a cleaving† in both senses of the word, a cutting away from and a clinging to the self, and a cutting away from and a clinging to the desired and feared other. Salman Rushdie has argued that "all stories are haunted by the ghosts of the stories they might have been" and that "every story . . . has a *shadow self*."[165] Like Rushdie's shadow stories (and like the shadow men and women who people the mythology of bedtricks), paradoxes contain truths and their shadows, their mirror images, their doubles. A lie is the shadow of the truth; a masquerade (to invert a phrase from Richard Nixon) is an operative lie. The power to express both sides of the paradox at once lies in the ambiguity that is the soul of myth. For the paradox itself is a double, like the masqueraders in our myths: it forces the reader to refuse to choose between two mutually exclusive, or not mutually exclusive, alternatives, just as the plot forces the protagonist to refuse to choose between two mutually exclusive, or not mutually exclusive, lovers.

CONCLUSION

Carnal Ignorance and
Carnal Knowledge

❧

CARNAL IGNORANCE

One of Eve White's later personalities remarked of her husband, whom she had inherited, as it were, from an earlier personality, "I had not chosen him. I had not married him. My alter named Jane had made those choices. . . . How could I tell this man that he had loved an *illusion?*"[1] Barbara Walters described the real-life duping of the French diplomat Boursicot by his male Chinese lover as a "sexual illusion that kept their love alive for years."[2] In Spanish, "the aura of romantic love is called illusion *(ilusion),* a word that connotes the feelings of euphoria and well-being when someone believes he or she is the most wonderful person in the world in the eyes of another."[3] The man in the arms of one of the twin sisters in Angela Carter's *Wise Children* creates this illusion for her, as she later recalls: "While we were doing it, everything seemed possible, I must say. But that is the illusion of the act. Now I remember how everything seemed possible when I was doing it, but as soon as I stopped, not, as if fucking itself were the origin of illusion."[4] "The illusion of the act" is what generates the myth of the bedtrick.

If sex gives birth to illusion,† and is born of it, every sexual act is a bedtrick in the weak sense of the word; the strong sense of the bedtrick requires the deliberate attempt to trick (except for inadvertent bed-tricks—as in *A Comedy of Errors*† or *Oedipus Rex*†—which have victims but no conscious tricksters; or, rather, where Fate, or Time, is the trickster). Sex can raise or lower our perception of a partner, moving us (according to later, retrospective judgment) from illusion to truth or from truth to illusion. The permutations are complex, if not infinite, because there are several variables, each of which may prove illusory. Sometimes we are deluded about our partners, over whom we project our own fantasies (before, after, or during the sexual act); sometimes we delude ourselves with fantasies about ourselves, thinking that we are animals seeking animal partners when in fact we are looking for gods, or the reverse; sometimes, all of the above. "Whatever can he see in her?" we ask one another about our friends, and often, when emotion is recollected in tranquility,[5] "Whatever did I see in him?" (*see*, indeed—or rather, project† onto him as a visual image). We all suffer from *bovarysme,* named after the heroine of Flaubert's novel *Madame Bovary,* who deluded herself constantly, especially about sexual love. It is easier to find someone to go to bed with than to find someone to wake up with; we need a different sort of morning-after pill, a mental, rather than physical, retroactive contraceptive.[6]

Lust functions, like drunkenness,† to cloud the mind, to throw a monkey wrench in the rational machine. The antirational power of the genitals was already enshrined in the ancient Greek concept of "hysteria" (literally, the wandering of the womb in such a way as to drive women mad) and is still encoded, for the other gender, in the contemporary phrase that accuses a man of "thinking with his little head" (immortalized in the rock song "Don't Use Your Penis for a Brain"),[7] as well as in the belief, widespread in India and elsewhere, that semen is stored in the head.‡[8] This anatomical fantasy of upward displacement,† conflating the organs of generation and cogitation, implies that both enlightening sexual experience and deluding lust rise to the head, that is, that sex both provides and corrupts knowledge, that sex is, as I argued in the introduction, a source of both truth and lies.

We trick ourselves in bed when we lie about who our partners are and about who we are. Though we may think we are "our real selves" in sex, we may actually be least so. As Lord Henry remarks, in Oscar Wilde's *The Picture of Dorian Gray,*‡ "When one is in love, one always begins by deceiving one's self, and one always ends by deceiving others. That is what the world calls romance."[9] John Donne argued a similar point (in "A Lecture upon the Shadow"):

> So whilst our infant love did grow,
> Disguises did, and shadowes, flow,
> From us, and our cares; but, now 'tis not so.
>
> .   .   .   .
>
> Except our loves at this noone stay,
> We shall new shadowes make the other way.

> As the first were made to blinde
> Others; these which come behinde
> Will worke upon our selves, and blind our eyes.

The story of the sun and the shadows‡ it casts is an ancient myth of a bedtrick; the problem it describes remains thoroughly modern.

The power of sexual illusion is demonstrated in Preston Sturges's film *The Lady Eve* (1941), in which Jean seduces Charles first in her true persona of a cardsharp and then when she masquerades as a titled Englishwoman named Eve. She offers an explanation of how the trick worked: "Do you know why he didn't recognize me? I hardly recognized him myself. He seemed shorter and bonier. It's because we don't love each other anymore. You see, on the boat we had an awful yen for each other, so I saw him as very tall and very handsome, and he probably thought I had big melting eyes and a figure like Miss Longbeach the Dream of the Fleet." Thus, Eve, aptly named, explains her own blinding appeal and that of sexual love in general.

Victims, therefore, lie to themselves, while tricksters lie to their victims and, often, to themselves as well. To seduce is to deceive; although not every masquerade is sexual, every sexual encounter is in a sense a masquerade. So basic is deception to sex—and so tight are the bonds between sex and text—that several languages have a pun† linking sex and deception. In English "deceive" means both to fool someone and to violate a sexual promise, a pun that Robertson Davies puts in the mouth of a man who slept, disguised as a man named Arthur,† with Arthur's wife, Maria: "I know that I deceived Arthur. I can't say if I deceived Maria."[10] By saying that someone who has been sexually unfaithful has "deceived" his or her partner, do we also imply that if you sleep with someone other than your partner, you will lie about it? English abounds in such double entendres; it is only partly an accident of the English language that we lie *to* the people we lie *with*. As Shakespeare puns, in Sonnet 138: "Therefore I lie with her, and she with me,/And in our faults by lies we flattered be"; and, in *A Midsummer Night's Dream*, when Lysander is negotiating how close he will lie to Hermia in the night, "Therefore I am not lying when I lie." Or, as the author of a book about infidelity put it: infidelity isn't about "whom you lie with. It's about whom you lie to."[11] In 1963, long before the Zippergate scandals of President Clinton, the British Profumo affair, involving call girls named Christine Keeler and Mandy Rice-Davies, destroyed a Cabinet and produced one memorable limerick:

"What on earth have you done?" said Christine.
"You have ruined the party machine.
 To lie in the nude
 Is not at all rude,
 But to lie in the House is obscene."[12]

And what is the "trick" implied when a whore "turns a trick"? *Burlador* in Spanish means both "seducer" and "mocker," and the French *trobar* is both a teller of dirty stories and a trickster.

"Betray"† has the same range of meanings as "deceive"; Angela Carter's bedtrickster asks, "Did we betray the innocence of the boy with our deception? Of course we did."[13] But "betray" also has its own overtones of political treachery. Joseph Roth† stretches its meanings to indicate the harm done by the bedtrickster not only to the victim (significantly, in this story, a political† figure) but also to the woman whom the victim thought he was in bed with, someone who was not even aware that the trick had taken place at all: "It crossed his mind to write to Countess W. and ask her forgiveness for betraying her to the Persian."[14] And Zisco, in *Sicily and Naples,*† twists the sense of the word in yet another direction when he offers to destroy the man he thinks raped and murdered his sister: "I'll take him in's cups, / When he's drunk, betray him in a rape, or fouler sin, then kill him in the act" (1.4).

"True" and "false" lovers resonate with both the philosophical connotations of the English words ("Speak the truth") and their moral-sexual connotations ("Be true to me"). The moral-sexual meaning of "false," in normal usage, implies that a woman is "false" to her lover if she sleeps with someone else; its philosophical meaning grows much stronger in narrative texts, where she is "false" to him if she *is* someone else—a bedtrickster. In the first case, the oath of love is a false copy of the true oath; in the second, the person is a false copy of the true lover.

The legal scholar Jane E. Larson points out an underlying assumption of our culture: "lying is integral to the 'dance' of sexual initiation and negotiation. Exaggerated praise, playful suggestions, efforts to impress, and promises intended to reassure and trigger emotion (but not to be strictly believed) are all part of the ritual of escalating erotic fascination that makes up a 'seduction' in the colloquial sense. To lie to a sexual partner is to share a leap of fancy—all very harmless and justifiable." This leads Larson to ask, "[I]s it ever reasonable to believe a lover? Were our grandmothers right in telling us that men always lie for sex, and the woman who listens is a fool? This counsel rests on the presumption that lying for sex is in 'the rules of the game.'"[15] Larson argues that the courts must change the game, but the myths reveal how deeply entrenched a game it is. Indeed, *The Rules of the Game*† *(La règle du jeu)* is the title of Jean Renoir's great film about a bedtrick.

The ancient wisdom of the grandmothers persists in the cynicism with which we regard sociological surveys of sexual behavior. Ned Zeman, reviewing *The Janus Report on Sexual Behavior* (a two-headed report? dedicated to Janus, god of closet doors?), advises us to "remember this one sexual truth: men lie."[16] R. C. Lewontin, reviewing another sex survey, writes:

> Anyway, why should anyone lie on a questionnaire that was answered in a face-to-face interview with a total stranger? After all, complete confidentiality was observed. It is frightening to think that social science is in the hands of professionals who are so deaf to human nuance that they believe that people do not lie to themselves about the most freighted aspects of their own lives, and that they have no interest in manipulating the impression that strangers have of them. . . . In the single case where one can actually test the truth, the investigators themselves think it most likely that people are telling themselves and others enormous lies.[17]

And when the authors tried to defend the veracity of their subjects, Lewontin responded with the last word:

> People do not tell *themselves* the truth about their own lives. . . . Perhaps, as men contemplate their impending mortality, the dread of something after death makes lying about sex seem risky. We must, however, at least consider the alternative that affirming one's continued sexual prowess in great age is a form of whistling in the dark.

And the dark, of course, is where all cats are gray. The consciousness of aging† and impending death is indeed a major motivation for bedtricks.

Anthony Lane, reviewing the same sex survey, put the matter with his characteristic wry humor:

> These books are not about sex. They are not even about dancing. They are about lying. They are constructed with admirable clarity, but they represent the ne plus ultra of fuzziness—the unalterable fuzz of our duplicity, the need to hide the truth from other people in the hope that we will cease to recognize it ourselves. Read a sentence such as, "Men report that they experience fellatio at a far greater rate than women report providing it,"

and you find yourself glancing down a long, shady vista of self-delusion. This is not a question of inefficient research, or of culpable hypocrisy, or even of that much loved villain of the piece, the male boast; it is simply what T. S. Eliot called *bovarysme*, "the human will to see things as they are not," and throughout *The Social Organization of Sexuality* it never once failed to give me a good laugh.[18]

The fellatio ratio is one of many asymmetries† between male and female perceptions of the same act. The American public's reaction to President Clinton's revelation of the fact that he had had a sexual relationship with Monica Lewinsky and had lied about it was simply, "Why make such a fuss? Everyone lies about sex." A 1999 survey of lie detection apparently established, statistically, that "not surprisingly, the most common of such lies were about affairs."[19]

The evidence of our myths, too, indicates that the mating game is one whose rules were designed to be broken. Men lie in sexual situations: Pinocchios all, their noses stretch in resonance with (a Freudian might say upward displacement† from) their lower noses. (In the aftermath of the Clinton scandals, some entrepreneur marketed a Clinton watch, with a picture of the president on the face and a computer mechanism that makes the nose grow, suggestively, longer and then shorter.) Men are particularly inclined to lie in cultures, such as ours, where with one hand (the right hand of the superego) they impose monogamous† constraints that, with the other hand (the left hand of the id), they evade. If tyrants make liars, monogamous societies make sexual liars, and those who are, as it were, maritally challenged often turn bedtricks. In the film *Liar, Liar* (1998), about a man—more precisely, a *lawyer*—magically compelled to tell the truth, the first place the curse manifests itself is where it is most obvious, the place where everyone lies: not in court, but in bed. When his adulterous partner asks him, in postcoital languor, how it was for him, the lawyer responds, to his own shocked dismay and her fury, "I've had better."

It is easier for women than for men to lie physically in some ways, faking orgasms, for example, a widely attested, and debated, skill. But it is more difficult (though by no means impossible) for women to lie about other physical aspects of sex, such as maidenheads.[20] When Isolde† played her bedtrick on King Mark to disguise the fact that she had lost her maidenhead to Tristan, she "devised the best ruse that she could at this juncture, namely that they should simply ask [her maid] Brangane to lie at [her husband] Mark's side during the first night." And the author of this version of the story, Gottfried, remarks, "Thus love instructs honest minds to practice perfidy."[21]

Getting pregnant is a big truth-teller. Pregnancy† may be the problem, proof that adultery has taken place; hence the accusations against Tamar,† Mary† (Matthew 1.18–25), and many other women.[22] But sometimes pregnancy is the solution, proof that the woman is fertile (when barrenness, rather than fertility, is the problem) or that her husband enjoys sleeping with her after all (when rejection,† i.e., *his* barrenness, is the problem). As Carol Thomas Neely has remarked of the bedtrick that impregnates Mariana in *Measure for Measure*,† "Only a pregnancy . . . would provide a sure distinction between the 'imagined' body and the actual one."[23]

Men, on the other hand, lie about other physical aspects of sex, such as desire. Although Pinocchio's nose declared to the world that he was lying, a man can fake[24]—or conceal—an erection; even chimpanzees can conceal it.[25] Thus, there is an asymmetry,† or double standard,† in both the timing and the concealment of the physical lying and truth-telling of men and women: men's physical truth-test comes earlier, with desire, and is relatively easy to fake, while for women, the truth-test comes later, with pregnancy, and is harder (though not impossible) to fake. These differences in the moment, not of truth but of lying, suggest one reason you cannot take the stories about men and tell them about women, or the reverse; different details give them different shapes.‡

It has even been said that lying is not simply something that occasionally happens in the course of our sexual lives but rather its very essence. Janet Adelman reads in the Shakespearean bedtricks "the suggestion that mistrust and deception are at the very root of the sexual act, as though the man is always tricked, defiled, and shamed there."[26] Just as Angela Carter's character imagines that "fucking itself" is "the origin of illusion," Salman Rushdie's narrator suggests that betrayal might be the very heart of sexuality: "What if she made you love her *so that she could betray you*— if betrayal were not the failure of love, but the purpose of the whole exercise from the start?"[27]

Sexual lies, however common, are not cheap; we pay dearly for them. Precisely because sexual truth† is posited as the ultimate truth, sexual betrayal is posited as the ultimate betrayal. The protean quality of sexual passion, unfortunately coupled with our foolish tendency to use sexual love as the rock on which we build the church of our identity,† drives

us to use highly charged words like "betrayal" (with its political† overtones) and "unfaithful" (with its religious† overtones) to describe the
sexual lie. For this is the betrayal and infidelity that cuts closest to the
bone, encompassing within it the other two, the political and the religious.
When we deceive others about our sexual identity, or are deceived by
them, we lose one of the main anchors of our *own* sense of identity, since
we are lying to ourselves when we betray, or are betrayed by, those whom
we desire and/or love. Why, then, do we speak of the sexual act as carnal
knowledge? We would do better to call it carnal ignorance.†

CARNAL KNOWLEDGE

Despite the massive testimony to the power of sexual fantasy† and the
argument that sex is a lie,† our myths present strong evidence for the
counterargument, the revelatory power of sex. "Knowing" is a euphemism
for the sexual act in many languages, deriving from the biblical Hebrew
usage. (Here we may note the power of language:† once someone in ancient Israel used a verb meaning "know" to refer to the sexual act, it
predisposed all Jews, Christians, and Muslims to believe that they would
know the people they slept with.) Zvi Jagendorf relates this biblical usage
to the biblical stories of the bedtrick (Rachel,† Tamar†) and to an even
more basic biblical text:

> The awareness of sexual difference is the fruit of knowledge and after the
> Fall Genesis imagines sex in a new and striking way: "And Adam knew Eve
> his wife." The metaphor of sex as knowing cannot in this context be ac-
> cepted as a euphemism, "modesty of language" as some commentators
> have called it. . . . In the first chapters of Genesis the same verb "YADA"
> means to know and distinguish between moral categories and to be aware
> of one's own and another's physical difference (nakedness). Underlying all
> the first instances of knowing is the concept of distinction rendered physi-
> cally immediate by the image of the opened eyes.[28]

The verb appears in the negative form for the man at the end of the story
of Tamar† and Judah: "And he knew her again no more." Commenting
on this text, Jagendorf says, "Just as lack of knowledge originally made
sex possible so knowledge and discovery finally forbid it."[29]

   Not surprisingly, the gendered usage of this verb is asymmetrical:†
Genesis never says that a woman "knows" a man. "Hebrew, it seems,
could not say that (although it could in the negative as Lot's daughters

are said not to have known man, Gen. 19.8)."[30] When the pun extends into New Testament Greek, even a woman as special as Mary† is still only allowed to use the verb negatively: when the angel tells Mary that she is going to have a baby, she replies, "How can that be, since I do not *know* a man?" (Luke 1.34).[31]

Margaret Miles has argued that the term "carnal knowledge," from medieval canon law, "seems to suggest that embodied knowledge of oneself and another human being can be attained in the intimacy of lovemaking." But this intimacy is merely physical: "the qualifier 'carnal' effectively canceled recognition that either intellectual or spiritual understanding can occur." She goes on to quote Tertullian ("The flesh will still be the thinking place of the soul") and asks: "Is 'carnal knowing,' then, a contradiction in terms? . . . In my usage, 'carnal knowing' suggests minimally (as in Tertullian's description) that the brain in which thinking occurs is a material substance."[32] I would modify this statement; carnal knowledge means that the body transmits to the brain a knowledge that the brain would not otherwise have. Terence Cave has speculated on the nature of such knowledge in tales of recognition, such as the bedtrick: "What emerges if one puts together these different aspects of the idiosyncrasy of recognition is first of all a sense of a means of knowing which is different from rational cognition. It operates surreptitiously, randomly, elliptically and often perversely, seizing on precisely those details that from a rational point of view seem trivial."[33] In these stories, all differences fall apart, trumped by sex, which is irrational and hence cannot be disproved; which is in the body and hence cannot be subjected to mental criteria.

Measure for Measure† climaxes in a wonderful passage of puns and riddles† on "knowing." Mariana argues, "I have known my husband; yet my husband knows not that ever he knew me." (To which Lucio remarks, "He was drunk† then.") Mariana continues by referring to "Angelo, Who thinks he knows that he ne'er knew my body, But knows, he thinks, that he knows Isabel's." When the duke asks Angelo, "Know you this woman?" Lucio again interpolates, "Carnally she says," but Angelo confesses that he does, in fact, "know" the woman, though he denies any but public knowledge, to which Mariana replies, "But Tuesday night last gone, in's garden-house, He knew me as a wife" (5.1).

That the sexual act is the ultimate key to concealed identity is a Freudian assumption, which Michel Foucault (building on the insights of Bachelard) sums up well:

[W]e also admit that it is in the area of sex that we must search for the most secret and profound truths about the individual, that it is there that we can best discover what he is and what determines him. And if it was believed for centuries that it was necessary to hide sexual matters because they were shameful, we now know that it is sex itself which hides the most secret parts of the individual: the structure of his fantasies, the roots of his ego, the forms of his relationship to reality. At the bottom of sex, there is truth.[34]

So, too, the work of the Lacanian feminist Luce Irigaray seems to assume, or imply, that sexual difference is more fundamental than other forms of difference and is not to be understood as articulated through other vectors of power—indeed, that other forms of difference might be *derived* from sexual difference.[35] In the context of the bedtrick, this means that the failure to distinguish sexual difference—by which I mean not only the difference between one sex and another but the difference between the sexuality of one person and another, that is, the difference between partners in bed—creates a vector of power through which other vectors such as race† or class† may be filtered.

But Freud did not invent the belief that sex is where we find the truth about an individual's often masquerading identity; he learned it from the texts of stories from other times and other cultures. These texts insist that the body tells the truth: the real person is the person glimpsed in bed, while the person whom we see at other times is a veneer, a superficial double. The extreme form of this view, which denies individuality and reduces sexuality to animality, is characteristic of pornography, as John Hubner remarked: "Sex strips away identities it takes a lifetime to build. A naked aroused man is not a brain surgeon or a university president or a Methodist bishop. He is an animal with an erection."[36] Javier Marias, in his tale of a man who sleeps with a prostitute who may or may not be his wife, explores this laser-focus power in the sexual act:

What a strange contact that intimate contact is, what strong, non-existent links it instantly forges, even though, afterwards, they fade and unravel and are forgotten, sometimes it's hard to remember that they did exist that one night, or two, or more, after a while it becomes difficult. But not immediately after establishing those links for the first time, then they feel as if they were burned into you, when everything is fresh and your eyes still wear the face of the other person and you can still smell them, a smell for which one becomes, for a while, the repository. . . . I could still smell the smell of Victoria or Celia which was not the same smell as that of Celia when she could only have been Celia. . . . that strange, intimate contact that creates the immediate illusion of some real connection, even through a condom.[37]

Even the most illusory of sexual acts, the bedtrick, holds out the hope of a deeper truth beneath the lying surface. This is what the character of Casanova† in a Schnitzler story thinks when he is in bed with a woman he has bedtricked: "Would not the ineffable bliss of this night transmute into truth what had been conceived in falsehood?"[38]

A number of texts express or imply the view that, in bed, the victim might put his or her finger on the sexual trigger of identity. In Angela Carter's version of the Bluebeard story, the heroine wonders what she might find in the locked and forbidden room: "Perhaps I half-imagined, then, that I might find his real self in his den, waiting there to see if indeed I had obeyed him; that he had sent a moving figure of himself to New York, the enigmatic, self-sustaining carapace of his public person, while the real man, whose face I had glimpsed in the storm of orgasm, occupied himself with pressing private business in the study."[39] Why does she assume that the face "glimpsed in the storm of orgasm" is the face of "the real man"? Why do we all (i.e., we Anglophone readers)? Because of our shared assumption that sex reveals the truth.

In David Lodge's *Small World,* after the hero has slept with one twin whom he mistook for the other (in a story that Cave regards as "a *parody* of romance recognitions"),[40] she chides him: "If you can't be sure whether the girl you just screwed is Angelica or not, how can you be in love with her? You were in love with a dream. . . . because Angie loves somebody else."[41] Milan Kundera's† womanizing hero sought the secret of each woman's minute difference† in bed, and Kundera tells us why: "Why couldn't he find it, say, in a woman's gait or culinary caprices or artistic taste? To be sure, the millionth part dissimilarity is present in all areas of human existence, but in all other areas other than sex it is exposed and needs no one to discover it, no scalpel. . . . Only in sexuality does the millionth part dissimilarity become precious, because, not accessible in public, it must be conquered."[42] Ignoring other signs of identity, such as the gait of the foot,† which distinguishes humans from animals,[43] and tastes in food,† the womanizer wants not only to know a woman, to cut her open like a surgeon (the man in question, Tomas, actually is a brain surgeon), but also to conquer her in her sexuality, in her hiddenness.

Some gay men say that each of the two partners can know simultaneously what both of them experience separately, that they can know what it is to penetrate while being penetrated, or the reverse—the Teiresias‡ paradigm. Daniel Mendelsohn argues, "If the emotional aim of intercourse is a total knowing of the other, gay sex may be, in its way, perfect, because in it a total knowledge of the other's experience is, finally, possible."[44] This is, as Jonathan Lear put it, "a fantasy of the total transparency of the other's experience."[45] It assumes that because your partner is *doing* the same physical act that you have done and will do, s/he is *feeling* what you have felt and will feel. The cross-sex (or heterosexual) fantasy, by contrast, is the challenge of knowing someone who is otherwise opaque to you, someone as different from you as you can imagine or find (not just someone of the other gender but, ultimately, someone of another culture or even another species, as in the tale of Beauty and the Beast). Mendelsohn's assertion that "sex between men dissolves otherness into sameness"[46] makes no allowance for the sexual individuality that applies equally well to same-sex and cross-sex experience: the chance to know the unique qualities revealed both in sexual sameness and in sexual difference, the different ways in which each of us is penetrated or penetrates.

The sadistic aspect of sexual knowledge as power was chillingly depicted by Nicholas Delbanco in his glimpse into the mind of a serial killer named Trip:

> Control: Trip liked the way he kept it and how his partners lost it—the weepers, the screamers, the polite ones swearing shamelessly and then the proud ones begging, stripped of pride. He liked what he learned about women from the way they behaved in the dark. There was nothing else— well, drowning or torture maybe, but he wasn't into drowning—that could teach you so much, and so fast. . . . From the moment he first understood how people change without their clothes, how what they're hiding *matters* and you can get their secrets when you get them into bed, Trip understood the game. And everybody played. He *knew* her, says the Bible, and Eve swallowed knowledge when she ate the apple and offered a piece to Adam and then got dressed and left. . . . The satisfaction was *discovery*—how you never knew beforehand what a person would reveal to you when you had your cock or hand inside them and were bearing down. You never knew till you were trying them how they would respond.[47]

The casual dismissal of drowning, but not torture, as an equivalent to the sexual manipulation of knowledge is one of the minor terrors of this passage.

Annie Dillard balances the assertion that sexual love is the best (and the counterassertion that it is the worst) source of knowledge† of personal identity in her novel, in a passage about a man named Clare:

> Clare knew that common wisdom counseled that love was a malady that blinded lovers' eyes like acid. Love's skewed sight made hard features appear harmonious, and sinners appear saints, and cowards appear heroes. Clare was by no means an original thinker, but on this one point he had reached an opposing view, that lovers alone see what is real. The fear and envy and pride that stain souls are phantoms. The lover does not fancy that the beloved possesses imaginary virtues. He knew June was not especially generous, not especially noble in deportment, not especially tolerant, patient, or self-abasing. The lover is simply enabled to see—as if the heavens busted open to admit a charged light—those virtues the beloved does possess in their purest form. June was a marvel, and she smelled good.[48]

The animal sense of smell,† transmuted into the human seventh sense of sex, simultaneously encapsulates and triggers the boundless, ineffable appreciation of the "marvel" of another living being. And this combination of physical and emotional factors outweighs the intellectual assessment of the object of desire.

FALSE IGNORANCE AND FALSE KNOWLEDGE

But what sort of knowledge is obtained in the sexual act, and by whom? One could answer, knowledge of the body of the other, of course, on the most superficial level, and of the emotional vulnerabilities of the other. Against a rather material view of human identity (the assumption that carnal knowledge is the best knowledge, or even the only knowledge that we have), the criterion of intellectual knowledge asserts itself in many myths. But the range of stories about bedtricks teaches us that when we ask, "Who is being fooled?" different stories will give different answers. As Cave remarks, "Anagnorisis in this sense is the perception of an ineradicable—but also seductive—asymmetry between the recognizer and the recognized."[49] And one aspect of this asymmetry† is gender.

If power is gendered, is knowledge gendered? Can she "know" him as he "knows" her? It may well be that because men have given most of our texts their final form, those texts speak primarily of a woman being entered and known, and of a man as having (carnal) knowledge of the woman. The man is the knower of the woman-as-field (of knowledge and of progeneration). The Hindus speak of the soul as the knower of the body-as-field *(kshetrajna)*, just as they speak of the legitimate son as the one born from the wife's body-as-field *(kshetraja)*.[50] In these texts, the man goes inside the woman's head as well as inside her body,[51] and in this sense he claims to know more about her than she, who does not physically penetrate him in the same way, knows about him.

But the inadequacy of the assertion that men know women sexually is often demonstrated by the very text that makes it in the first place: all that the man learns is a lie. A woman can conceal a number of things, including her very identity, by virtue of that very passivity† that was to give him the advantage in knowing. This asymmetry is compounded by the asymmetry of public knowledge concerning who is the father (uncertain)† or the mother (more certain) of the child, made yet more asymmetrical by the fact that the mother usually knows perfectly well who the father of her child is, though the father may not know what children he has fathered.

Moreover, women can know through being penetrated. Sexual knowledge, like power, can flow both ways, as Yeats pointed out in his poem about the rape of Leda† by Zeus: "Did she take on his knowledge with his power, before the indifferent beak could let her drop?" The Swan's penetration of Leda is a source of Leda's knowledge; women (like Delphic oracles) are possessed and thereby become not only mediums for knowledge but also knowers. Thus, when a man "knows" a woman, he may not know her at all, but she may very well know him. As Jagendorf puts it:

> A man may know a woman (physically) and be mistaken about her identity. He may even know her carnally without any awareness whatsoever; he may be drunk. On the other hand, a woman being possessed in sex, apparently the object, may yet be the subject, the only possessor of the volatile element of awareness. She may know the man who mis-takes her. . . . This striking fusion of body and mind in the verb to know contains the seeds of its own reversal. For there is no way in which this pristine clarity, this strict division into sexual subject and object can withstand the facts of human experience in the world, the deviousness and duplicity, the lies and illusions that mark the relations and especially the sexual relations between people.[52]

This could stand as a summary of the essence of the bedtrick.

There is also such a thing as false knowledge, and there is false ignorance. True ignorance characterizes the victims of most bedtricks, who are simply fooled. It also characterizes unwitting bedtricksters, who do not actively mean to trick anyone but are, passively, mistaken for other people, as is the case in *Oedipus Rex*,† where neither Oedipus nor Iocasta knows that she is his mother, and in *The Comedy of Errors*,† where neither of the twin brothers is aware that the other is there, or in *Twelfth Night*, where Sebastian is mistaken for "Cesario." False ignorance (which is not the same as actually *being* carnally ignorant) is fairly straightforward: the victim of a bedtrickster who impersonated the victim's spouse claims, falsely, not to have recognized the trickster and therefore, falsely, not to be guilty of infidelity. Thus, it is argued that the wife of Martin Guerre† (or Alcmena‡ or Ahalya‡) did know it was someone else in the form of her husband and falsely claimed ignorance because she preferred the impostor. This claim is seldom made against a man, but in the film *Body Language* (1992), an adulterous psychiatrist interviews a man who is brain-damaged; the psychiatrist shows the man a picture of Marilyn Monroe, whom he does not quite recognize. The doctor assures him that this is someone he knows. After a while he says, "Is that my wife?" to which the psychiatrist's colleague remarks, "Hey, that would be a great line. You could cheat on your wife and say, 'I thought she was you.'" False ignorance about bedtricks is also recognized in a song by Lerner and Loewe entitled "I'm Glad I'm Not Young Anymore" (from *Gigi*), in which an old man lists the things he is glad to be rid of,

> **No more confusion,**
> **No morning-after surprise,**
> **No self-delusion,**
> **That when you're telling those lies, she isn't wise.**

Mutual self-deception, so characteristic of sex, is here terminated only by aging; but aging† is more often a sexual problem than a sexual solution.

False knowledge begins as the other side of the same coin, another way out of another sort of adultery, the sort that is exposed through a double-back† bedtrick. The unanswerable argument that the victims of bedtricks can use to bail themselves out when their spouses catch them in bed with people who appear to be other than the spouse is to say, with simple common sense, "I saw through the trick from the start and just pretended to be fooled." Marliss C. Desens argues that "the major drawback to a husband's testing his wife's fidelity by means of a bed-trick [is the fact that] she can always claim to have recognized him."[53] Victims of the bedtrick can foil the trickster in this way even when, in fact, they may have been tricked. Thus, in Thomas Middleton's *The Family of Love*†

(1602), the wife explains away an incriminating ring† by arguing that she knew him "as well as the child knows his own father" and "as well by night as by day.†"[54] In the *Arabian Nights* story "The Wife's Device to Cheat Her Husband,"† the woman whose husband catches her sending out for a lover (who turns out to be her husband) makes a preemptive strike; by pretending that she knew about his infidelity *before* she set out to commit her own, she can argue that she acted merely to entrap him.

But this excuse carries with it a more subtle form of betrayal, vividly depicted in Kobo Abe's *Face of Another*. After the husband has, he thinks, bedtricked his wife, she leaves him, and he finds a letter that says, in part:

> From the very first instant, when, elated with pride, you talked about the distortion of the magnetic field, I . . . saw through you completely. . . .
> . . . Even you knew very well that I had seen through you. You knew and yet demanded that I go on with the play in silence. I considered it a dreadful thing at first, but I soon changed my mind, thinking that perhaps you were acting out of sympathy for me. . . . My insides have almost burst with your ridicule. I shall never be able to get over it, never.[55]

Her assumption that he knew that she knew is not, however, justified, as we learn from his reaction to her letter:

> What a surprise attack. To imagine that you perceived that my mask was a mask and nevertheless went on pretending to be deceived. . . . To imagine that you had seen through everything! It was as if I were putting on a play in which I was the only actor, thinking I was invisible, believing in a fake spell.[56]

Like her, he finds the knowing deception—*her* deception of *him*, her pretense not to know—even more terrible than he had felt her apparent infidelity to be—through *his* deception of *her*.

False knowledge may also come into play when someone asserts falsely that a bedtrick has taken place. Casanova† lies like this when he asserts that he himself was *not* the victim of a bedtrick because he perpetrated his own double-cross.† This might make us wonder about other texts in which characters *say* that a bedtrick has taken place; perhaps they, too, are lying. Was the demigod lying to King Janamejaya† about the substitution of another woman for his queen when Indra substituted himself for the sacrificial stallion? Did the host of "The Visitor" invent the story of a leprous daughter to punish his guest for actually seducing the host's wife or daughter? Did the Brighton† lady lie about her adulteries just to make it possible for her son to go to bed with the neighborhood girls (allegedly begotten by his father)? Did Ruth lie to Boaz in the morning just to get him to marry her? Or, stepping out of the text for a moment, did the authors of certain texts invent bedtricks (in the case of Esther,† for instance) to absolve their heroines of the guilt for inappropriate sexual acts? Certainly this was done for Sita‡ and Helen of Troy.‡ Thus, sometimes you get off the hook by falsely claiming carnal ignorance ("Oh darling, I thought he was you") and sometimes by falsely claiming carnal knowledge ("Oh darling, I knew it was you all along").

The bedtrick is an exercise in epistemology: How could you know? How could you *not* know? The answer to the question "Is it the same person?" will be expressed differently according to the different points of view of several different characters within the story. It has been argued that in *all* narratives there are no events (for an event would imply a narrator with a god's-eye view) but, rather, only the conflicting and intersecting points of view of the characters. Whether or not this is true of all narratives—there are points of view about this, too, after all—it is particularly true of myths[57] and even more particularly true of bedtrick myths, whose very premise is that there are two different points of view about the identity of the masquerader: that of the trickster who plays the bedtrick and knows the true identity of both partners, and that of the victim who is the object of the bedtrick and does not know the identity of the bedtrickster. In the case of inadvertent bedtricks, where neither the trickster nor the victim knows that a bedtrick is taking place, only we, the audience, and the author, know the truth. And sometimes the narrative forces us, the readers or hearers, to change our point of view in midstream, even several times, as we discover that the protagonist (or the author) has been hiding something from us.

Point of view determines subject/object: if you know the trick and the other doesn't, you are the subject and the other is the object. This knowledge is what turns the tables (or beds) in the balance of sexual power. In the bedtrick, for the partner who knows, or who keeps his or her eyes open, sex is a source of knowledge. For the one who is fooled, or who allows lust to dupe him or her, sex is a lie. The bedtrick, like all masquerades, is situated on the cusp between knowing and not knowing, more precisely on the narrow divide between not knowing, knowing while pretending to yourself that you don't know (self-delusion), and knowing while pretending to others that you don't know (lying).

The question is not simply whether one "knows" one's partner in the sexual act but which of the many aspects of the partner one recognizes in this most revealing, and concealing, of human interactions. The theme of "knowing" is particularly crucial to the many incest† myths in this corpus, which ask, each in its own way, "How do you know it is your mother (or father)? Are you let off the hook if you do not know?" But the more pertinent question, coded in the story and relevant not just to incestuous bedtricks but to all bedtricks, is perhaps "How is it that you do not know who is in bed with you?" Or "How is it that you do not know that you do not know who is in bed with you?" Or, better, "Who are you who do not know that you do not know who is in bed with you?" Or, finally, "How is it that you do not know who you are?"

Bedtricks in Stith Thompson's
Motif-Index

Stith Thompson has traced several subthemes (which he calls motifs) that give a general idea of some of the forms that the story traditionally assumes.[1] Such a survey can only be a sketch, not a statistical survey. It is impossible to know all the variants of a theme, for a number of reasons: not all stories are recorded (some are being invented even as you read this line); those that are recorded are subject to the selective biases of scholars and publishers; and no one can know all the stories that have been published. Stith Thompson's lists are, like the old pregnancy tests, useful only for positive, not for negative, information: if he says the story exists in a particular culture, it usually does; but the motifs, and examples of motifs, that he does not mention may also very well exist. The form that his titles take, in quasi-scientific imitation of the atomic periodic tables, was nicely satirized by Salman Rushdie in *Haroun*, whose young, eponymous hero found himself in "Princess Rescue Story Number S/1001/ZHT/420/41(r)xi. . . . unlike . . . Princess Rescue Story G/1001/RIM/777/M(w)i, better known as 'Rapunzel.'"[2]

We might compare Stith Thompson's basic building blocks with some of those on the structural list in chapter 10, but let us settle for a brief survey of the topics in his index that correspond roughly to the plots of the bedtrick, according to the four possible permutations of gender and seeking/avoiding: women, first avoiding, then seeking; and men, first avoiding, then seeking.

1. A woman creates an identical double to avoid a man's bed.

H 38.2.3 Recognition of maidservant substitute by her habitual conversation

K 1223 Mistress deceives lover with a substitute

K 1223.1 Bride leaves goat as substitute in bed (TT 1685)

K 1843 Wife deceives husband with substitute bedmate

K 1843.1 Bride has maid sleep in husband's bed to conceal pregnancy (cf. TT 870, 870A)

T 327.6 Princess assumes loathsome disguise to avoid demon lover

2. A woman masquerades as another woman to sleep with a man.

D 40.2.1 Transformation to resemble a man's mistress so as to be able to kill him

D 659.7 Transformation: wife to mistress

D 2006.1.1 Forgotten fiancée reawakens husband's memory

H 13 Recognition by overheard conversation with animals or objects (see also H 38.2.3 above)

H 151.12 True bride builds house opposite husband and effects recognition

K 1223.2 Mistress sends man's own wife as substitute, without his knowledge (cf. TT 891*D)

K 1814 Woman in disguise wooed by her faithless husband

K 1843.1.1 Wife sends mistress to her husband disguised as herself

K 1843.2 Wife takes mistress's place in husband's bed

K 1911 The false bride; an impostor takes wife's place without detection

K 1911.1 The false bride; an impostor kills (or transforms) the wife (TT 403, 408, 425, 450, 510, 511, 533)

K 1911.3.3.1 False bride's mutilated feet (TT 510)

N 831.1 The mysterious housekeeper

3. A man creates an identical double to avoid a woman's bed.

K 1844 Husband deceives wife with substitute bedmate

K 1844.1 Strong servant for strong wife (TT 519)

K 1844.2 Substitute bridegroom to save husband from poison maiden (TT 507c)

4. A man masquerades as another man to sleep with a woman.

D 658.2 Transformation to husband's (lover's) form to seduce woman

G 303.12.5.7 Devil takes form of girl's lover

K 1300–K 1399 Seduction or deceptive marriage

K 1311 Seduction by masking as woman's husband

K 1311.1 Husband's twin brother mistaken by woman for her husband

K 1315.1 Seduction by posing as a god

K 1321 Seduction by man disguising as woman

K 1321.3 Man disguised as woman courted (married) by another man

K 1321.3.2. Two men fooled in love affair; both men, disguised as women, are locked in the same room; each starts making love to the other

K 1328 Disguise as animal to seduce woman

K 1335 Seduction (or wooing) by stealing clothes of bathing girl

K 1813 Disguised husband visits his wife

K 1813.1.1 Disguised husband shows his wife that he is not repulsive, as she thinks him

K 1918.1 or 1919.2 Ogre imposes on widow by assuming form of dead husband

K 1915 The false bridegroom; takes place of the real bridegroom (TT 1417)

T 161 *Jus primae noctis*

In addition, there are what Aarne and Thompson have classified as full tale types (TT), entire plots: TT 475, Sexual relations in sleep; TT 891*D, The rejected woman as lover; TT 1417, The false bridegroom; TT 870, 870A, Bride has maid sleep in husband's bed to conceal pregnancy; TT 507c, Substitute bridegroom to save husband from poison maiden; TT 1685, Bride leaves goat as substitute in bed. The cluster of TT 403, 408, 425, 450, 510, 511, 533 (An impostor kills or transforms the wife) includes a plot that is basic to the myth of sexual masquerade: TT 403, The black and white bride (with, in particular, TT 408, The three oranges).

Several recurrent subthemes of our stories are listed as distinct motifs:

B 640.1 Marriage to beast by day, man by night

D 732 Loathly Lady

D 735 Disenchantment by kiss

H 51 Recognition by scar

H 94 Recognition by ring

H 94.7 Recognition by ring springing off finger

H 481 Infant picks out his unknown father

H 1578.1 Test of sex of girl masking as man

J 1791.6.1 Ugly woman sees beautiful woman reflected in water and thinks it is herself

TT 706 The maiden without hands

NOTES

PREFACE

1. Doniger, *The Implied Spider*, 35, 93–95, 140–41.

2. I am planning a still narrower focus, on bedtricks about marriage and adultery (a theme treated briefly in chapter 1 of the present volume), in a forthcoming book, tentatively titled *Rings of Rejection and Recollection*, which analyzes Shakespeare's *All's Well That Ends Well* and *Measure for Measure*, Mozart's *Marriage of Figaro*, and Wagner's *Götterdämmerung*, as well as two Indian stories (about Shakuntala and Muladeva). This makes the corpus a trio—or, if you count *The Implied Spider* (which uses some bedtricks for examples) as the introduction to the other three, a quartet.

3. Doniger, *The Implied Spider*, 43–46.

4. Bowden, "The Bed-Trick," 112.

5. Garber, *Vested Interests*, 69–70.

6. Senelick, "The Illusion of Sex," 15.

7. Ibid., 16.

8. The 1998 productions by David Bell in Chicago and by Nicholas Hytner at Lincoln Center.

9. The 1999 Court Theatre production in Chicago.

10. Thus, for psychology, I have drawn more upon Freud and Rank than upon even Winnicott and Lacan, let alone still more contemporary authors; and for feminism and gender studies, Marjorie Garber, Mieke Bal, and Mary Ann Doane, among others, more than Luce Irigaray and Judith Butler.

11. O'Flaherty, *Women, Androgynes*, 5–7; Doniger, *The Implied Spider*, 269–313.

12. William Buckley once gave one of his books to Norman Mailer, signing it, beside Mailer's name in the index, "Hi, Norman." Martin Peretz, "Cape Cod Diarist: I Am a Footnote," *New Republic*, July 29, 1996, 42.

13. Jagendorf, "'In the Morning,'" 57.

14. Fineman, "Fratricide and Cuckoldry," 427.

15. Hodgdon, "The Making of Virgins," 48.

16. Arjun Appadurai, pers. comm., Apr. 7, 1999.

17. Doniger, *The Implied Spider*, 43–46.

18. Cave, *Recognitions*, 15.

19. Tracy, *Pluralism and Ambiguity*, 19–20.

20. Bowden, "The Bed-Trick," 120.

21. Doniger, *The Implied Spider*, 53–60.

22. Desens, *The Bed-Trick*, 16.

23. cummings, *him*, 13.

24. Doniger, "The Sanskrit Maverick."

25. Doniger, "From Great Neck to Swift Hall."

26. I am thinking here of the old remark about Marilyn Monroe, that she had curves in places where other girls didn't even have places.

27. O'Flaherty, *Other Peoples' Myths*, 39, 124, 131–32.

28. I owe this delightful epigram to George Kateb, pers. comm., Princeton, Mar. 2, 1999.

29. Doniger, *The Implied Spider*, 75–79, 138–45.

30. Alan Bennett, "Madness: The Movie," *London Review of Books* 17, no. 3 (Feb. 9, 1995): 3, 6–7.

31. The term was coined by Claude Lévi-Strauss; see Doniger, *The Implied Spider*, 143–51.

32. These recycled elements make it extremely difficult to copyright the plot of a film; see Tad Friend, "Copy Cats," *New Yorker*, Sept. 14, 1998, 51–57.

33. Cave, *Recognitions*, 489.

34. Eliade, *Cosmos and History*.

35. The very different degrees of my intimacy with the various cultures drawn upon in this book are necessarily reflected in different methods of citation. I have translated all the Sanskrit and Greek texts from the original but have not reproduced them verbatim as I did in the translations I made for the Penguin Classics; I have abbreviated them by cutting words and passages that are not essential to the tale I wish to tell, referring readers to the full text and to full English translations where they are available. Other texts I have, in general, quoted verbatim from translations by other scholars and marked with the usual convention of quotation marks or (for long passages) indentation. Where I have summarized and reworded such translations, I have so indicated in the notes. Some stories indented as source texts I have partly summarized and partly cited verbatim; the summaries are bracketed and the verbatim passages unbracketed. In the case of direct speech quoted verbatim, I have simply used quotation marks. The statements of other scholars are cited with the usual conventions. I have given titles to all the stories I have translated and to stories that others translated without giving them a title, but I have kept other translators' titles where they exist (and identified them as such in the notes); titles given by authors writing in European languages have been kept. The ratio between the length of the translated text and of the cited text is an index of the author's transparency, as Michael Wood wisely noted (pers. comm., Princeton, Mar. 4, 1999).

36. "La verità non sta in un solo sogno, ma in molti sogni."

37. Kilgour, *From Communion to Cannibalism*, 18.

38. Cave, *Recognitions*, vii.

39. *Introduction to the Jataka* 1.68 (trans. Warren, *Buddhism in Translation*, 71–72).

40. Doniger, *The Implied Spider*, 29–30.

41. O'Flaherty, *The Origins of Evil*, 321–46.

Acknowledgments

1. O'Flaherty, *Other Peoples' Myths*, 137–39, 55, 62, 164.

Introduction

1. Lawrence, *Shakespeare's Problem Comedies*, 51. The term was coined for *All's Well That Ends Well.*

2. It is often spelled "bed trick" or "bed-trick," but I will use the simpler form, "bedtrick." Some people think a bedtrick consists in putting a frog in someone's camp bunk or folding the sheets over so that the feet only go halfway down when you get in (which is what I was taught to call an "apple-pie bed" or "short-sheeting" or "Frenching" or "double-sheeting" a bed), but this book is about the other kind of bedtrick.

3. Malory, *Morte d'Arthur,* and the *Merlin* and *Lancelot* cycles; see Doniger, *Rings.*

4. Festinger, *A Theory of Cognitive Dissonance.*

5. Doniger, *The Implied Spider,* 79–80.

6. Orrey and Milnes, *Opera,* 107; Dent, *Mozart's Operas,* 190.

7. Quiller-Couch, introduction to *All's Well That Ends Well,* xxx–xxxiv.

8. Desens, *The Bed-Trick,* 31, summarizes and challenges this construction of the bedtrick by scholars of English Renaissance drama.

9. Detmer, "The Politics of Telling," 209.

10. Johnson, *Johnson on Shakespeare,* 404.

11. Terrence Rafferty, "Long, Hot Summer," review of *Multiplicity* (movie), *New Yorker,* July 29, 1996, 75–77.

12. Jagendorf, "'In the Morning,'" 58.

13. Cave, *Recognitions,* 489.

14. Doniger, *The Implied Spider,* 1–5.

15. David Shulman, the Danziger lecture at the University of Chicago, Apr. 8, 1999.

16. Thigpen and Cleckly, *Three Faces,* 167.

17. Lancaster, *The Final Face of Eve,* 117 (italics in original).

18. Thigpen and Cleckley, *Three Faces,* 195–97.

19. Goldenweiser, "The Principle of Limited Possibilities in the Development of Culture," in *History, Psychology, and Culture,* 35–58; Doniger, *The Implied Spider,* 139–45.

20. Goldenweiser, *History, Psychology, and Culture,* 45.

21. I owe this summary to Linda Hess, pers. comm., Mar. 1999.

22. From Lorraine Daston's remarks at the Einstein Forum, Berlin, Dec. 9, 1997.

23. Doniger, *The Implied Spider,* 35, 139, 143.

24. Doniger, "What Did They Name the Dog?"

25. At the traditional Jewish Passover celebration, a child must ask, "Why is this night different from all other nights?"

26. Salman Rushdie uses the image of the hole in the sheet to describe a more extended fragmentation of the object of desire in *Midnight's Children,* 18–23.

27. Cave, *Recognitions,* 495.

28. Ambrose, *The Man Who Turned into Himself,* 58 (italics added).

29. Cadden, *Meanings of Sex Difference in the Middle Ages,* 212–13.

30. Daston and Park, "The Hermaphrodite," 426.

31. Peter Steinfels, "Beliefs," *New York Times,* Aug. 22, 1998, A11.

32. Cave, *Recognitions,* 489.

33. Hegel, *Phänomenologie des Geistes,* 19.

34. Doniger, "Myths and Methods in the Dark"; Doniger, *The Implied Spider,* 29–30.

35. Levinas, *Totality and Infinity*.

36. Doniger, *The Implied Spider*, 75–79, 138–45.

37. Bowden, "The Bed-Trick," 121.

Chapter One

1. Nathalie Davis, *The Return of Martin Guerre*, 39.

2. Rushdie, *The Moor's Last Sigh*, 425–26.

3. Doniger, *Rings*.

4. Fineman, "Fratricide and Cuckoldry," 425.

5. Doniger, *The Implied Spider*, 109–36.

6. Desens, *The Bed-Trick*, 78.

7. Cervantes, *Don Quixote*, pt. 1, chaps. 33–35, "The Story of One Who Was Too Curious for His Own Good."

8. *Kalika Purana*, 46–52; O'Flaherty, *Siva*, 227; *Manasabijay* of Vishnu Pala, cited by Dimock, *The Place of the Hidden Moon*, 58.

9. *Skanda Purana* 1.1.34.1–153, 35.1–62; Shulman and Handelman, *God Inside Out*, 19–20; Doniger, "The Scrapbook of Undeserved Salvation."

10. O'Flaherty, *Siva*, 90–110.

11. *Mahabharata* 3.24.

12. O'Flaherty, *Siva*, 172–209.

13. *The Laws of Manu* 3.34; Doniger, *The Laws of Manu*, 46. See also the application of the term "ghoul" to the rape of Ila when she was suffering from amnesia (*Ramayana* of Valmiki, 7.87–90).

14. Claus, "Playing *Cenne*," 290–93; Shulman and Handelman, *God Inside Out*, 108.

15. This song was given to me by Dr. Meena Rao, who heard it from her grandmother. Aditya Behl translated it for me; pers. comm., Atlanta, Ga., Jan. 1989.

16. *Manasamangal* of Vishnu Pala, 76, cited by Dimock, "Doctrine and Practice," 58.

17. *Kalika Purana* 49.1–58, 50.1–76, 51.1–28; Doniger, *Siva*, 206–7.

18. Garber, *Vice Versa*, 429.

19. Thomas Middleton, *The Family of Love*, 5.3.288–93.

20. Marias, *Tomorrow in the Battle*, 178–79, 206.

21. Ibid., 222.

22. Doniger, *Rings*.

23. Warner, "Stolen Shadows," 50.

24. Richard Neely, *The Plastic Nightmare*, 24.

25. Ibid., 236.

26. Ibid., 237.

27. Ibid., 220.

28. Southern, "A Change of Style."

29. Goldsmith, *Switcheroo*, 159.

30. Morson, *Narrative and Freedom*; Doniger, *The Implied Spider*, 38–39, 85–86.

31. Angela Carter, *Wise Children*, 65.

32. The second section of Judah's† public confession in the *Targum Neofiti* opens with the famous rabbinic dictum "With the measure with which a man measures it will be measured to him," and in a Jewish-Moroccan version of the tale of the Clever Wife, the wife insists, "The measure of woman is two measures and the measure of man is one," until her husband becomes exasperated and throws her down a deep

well (Hasan-Rokem, *Proverbs,* 78–79, IFA 6512). Did Shakespeare take his title, and perhaps some aspects of his bedtrick, from the story of Tamar and Judah?

33. Boccaccio, "Ricciardo and the Wife of Filippello," *Decameron,* 231; see also third day, ninth story, 267, and eighth day, fourth story, 572.

34. Marguerite de Navarre, *Heptameron,* day 1, story 8, 108–14.

35. Desens, *The Bed-Trick,* 100.

36. Gossett, "'Best Men,'" 315.

37. Childs, *Casanova,* 115.

38. *The Memoirs of Jacques Casanova,* trans. Machen, 430, 438.

39. Ibid., 3.15, 469; *Casanova mémoires,* 2.17, 425.

40. *The Memoirs of Jacques Casanova,* trans. Machen, 3.15, 467.

41. Ibid., 485.

42. Ibid., 493.

43. Zweig, *The Adventurer,* 154.

44. Casanova, *History of My Life,* 6.7, 167–68, quoting Virgil's *Georgics* 3.67.

45. Schnitzler, *Casanova's Return to Venice.*

46. Dineson, "The Roads round Pisa."

47. Dahl, "The Visitor," 9.

48. Ibid., 48, 54.

49. *Manasabijay* of Bipradas, 235, cited by Maity, *Historical Studies,* 79. I have changed this text's spelling of the god's name from Siva to Shiva, for consistency. See also *Manasabijay* of Visnu Pala, cited by Dimock, *The Place of the Hidden Moon,* 58; O'Flaherty, *Siva,* 227.

50. Desens, *The Bed-Trick,* 30.

51. Poem attributed to Amaru, in *Subhashitaratnakosha,* no. 617, translated in Ingalls, *Anthology of Sanskrit Court Poetry,* 212.

52. *Gita Govinda* 5.18, translated in Barbara Miller, *Love Song of the Dark Lord,* 94.

53. *Ahalyasankrandanamu* 3.129, translated in Shulman, *Symbols of Substance,* 157.

54. Shulman, *Symbols of Substance,* 157.

55. *The Arabian Nights* 6.152 (trans. Burton; his title). Nobody really knows how to date any of the stories in this collection, but Muhsin Mahdi does not include this one in his edition of the earliest layer.

56. Granoff, *Forest of Thieves,* 360–73. From the Jaina *Upamitabhavaprapancakatha,* chap. 3, composed by Siddharshi in a Jain temple on Billamala; he says he recited it and a nun wrote it down. I have condensed the action somewhat and the sermons a great deal, and simplified some of the names, but kept all the direct quotations and much else unchanged.

57. O'Flaherty, *Dreams,* 114–26.

58. This story is merely a subtext of the main plot of the *Kalapurnodayamu* of Pingali Suranna. I am indebted to V. Narayana Rao for relating the story to me. This is my condensed summary of his retelling, with the help of some clarifications from David Shulman.

59. *Mahabharata* 3.52–54.

60. Harsha, *Naishadiyacarita* 2.26.

61. *Ramayana* of Valmiki, 7.26.8–47.

62. *Mahabharata* 3.52–54.

63. Bowden, "The Bed-Trick," 113; Desens, *The Bed-Trick,* 71.

64. Bowden, "The Bed-Trick," 115.

65. Girard, *Violence and the Sacred*; O'Flaherty, *Other Peoples' Myths*, chap. 3.

66. Schnitzler, "Casanova's Homecoming," 231.

67. Nietzsche, *Beyond Good and Evil*, par. 194.

68. Giraudoux, *Amphitryon*, 33.

69. Krauss, *The Originality of the Avant Garde*, 109.

70. Roddenberry, "Second Chances," 131.

71. Rostand, *Cyrano de Bergerac*, trans. Hooker.

72. Tale 42 from the Sanskrit *Tantrakhyana*, Nepal, dated A.D. 1484; translation by Herman Tull, who generously brought this text to my attention.

73. Bendall, "Originals and Analogues of the Canterbury Tales," 501.

74. Bloch, *The Scandal*, 115–16 (citing *Recueil* 3.55).

75. Ramanujan, "*A Flowering Tree*," 85.

76. *Chandogya Upanishad* 8.7–10.

Approach One

77. The issue of the authentic and the copy in our day is brilliantly argued by Hillel Schwartz in *The Culture of the Copy*.

78. O'Flaherty, *Dreams*, 65–66.

79. Commentary on *Abhidharmakosha* of Vasubandhu, chap. 4, *karma*, 74a–b (my paraphrase).

80. From Lorraine Daston's remarks at the Einstein Forum, Berlin, Dec. 9, 1997.

81. Carol Neely, *Broken Nuptials*, 93

82. Adelman, "Bed Tricks," 167.

83. Basinger, *How Hollywood Spoke to Women*, 86.

84. Ibid., 100.

85. Doniger, "Jewels of Rejection."

86. Lewis, *The Wife of Martin Guerre*, 51.

87. Willig, *The Changelings*, 29.

88. Ibid., 214.

89. Babrius, no. 32.

90. *State of Arizona, Appellee, v. Arnold Ballesteros Navarro, Appellant,* no. 1201, 90 Arizona 185 (Supreme Court of Arizona, en banc, Dec. 13, 1961), in *367 Pacific Reporter*, 2d ser., pp. 227–30.

91. Marias, *Tomorrow in the Battle*, 190 (italics in original).

92. Doniger, "The Masques of Gods and Demons."

93. Kates, *Monsieur d'Eon*, 27.

94. Ibid., 266.

95. *Shrishriramakrishnakathamrita* 1.181, translation by Jeffrey Kripal, pers. comm., May 1993. Tuccham brahmapadam paravadhusangah kutah.

96. Acarya K. V. Raman, pers. comm., Madras, Jan. 1996.

97. *Ramayana*, trans. Buck, 301.

98. Behrman, "*Amphitryon 38*," 95; cf. Giraudoux, "*Amphitryon*," 41.

99. Keillor, "Zeus the Lutheran," 33–34.

100. Andrew Lang, *Harper's Magazine* 85 (1892): 213, cited by Lawrence, *Shakespeare's Problem Comedies*, 36.

101. Wain, *The Living World of Shakespeare*, 120–21.

102. Bowden, "The Bed-Trick," 119.

103. Boswell, *Same-Sex Unions in Premodern Europe*.

104. Gold, "Sexuality," 49.

105. Johnson, "Frame of Reference."

106. From Lorraine Daston's remarks at the Einstein Forum, Berlin, Dec. 9, 1997.

107. Warner, *From the Beast*, 353.

108. Doniger, "Three (or More) Forms."

109. I owe most of the ideas in this paragraph to a conversation with Lorraine Daston, May 1994.

Chapter Two

1. Doniger, *The Implied Spider*, 115–18, 122–24, 128–36.

2. Ibid., 95–103.

3. Shulman and Handelman, *God Inside Out.*

4. *Kalika Purana* 52.105–22. The curse is realized in the story of Shiva as Candrashekhara; see O'Flaherty, *Siva*, 204–9.

5. *Padma Purana* 1.46.1–32, 47–108, 119–21. The same text, with some variations, appears in the *Skanda Purana* 1.2.27–29 (the version translated in O'Flaherty, *Hindu Myths*, 251–61) and in the *Matsya Purana* 154–57 (the version translated by Shulman and Handelman in *God Inside Out*, 156).

6. *Shiva Purana, Dharmasamhita*, 4.4–26; translated in O'Flaherty, *Hindu Myths*, 169.

7. O'Flaherty, *Hindu Myths*, 168–74.

8. Cf. the snakes who penetrate the defenses of Parikshit in the *Mahabharata* (1.36–40) and of Behula in the Bengali tales retold by Dimock in *The Thief of Love.*

9. *Matsya Purana* 156.18–21.

10. Stein, "The Guardian of the Gate."

11. *Skanda Purana* 1.2.27.4.

12. *Matsya Purana* 156.27.

13. *Skanda Purana* 1.2.27.21.

14. This is not as unlikely as it might at first appear; Samjna conceives the Ashvins (Hindu half-horse gods) by mouth and gives birth to them through her nose (Doniger, *Splitting the Difference*, 44–55). It may be, however, that one scribe just naturally put the tooth in the place where he thought it belonged—the mouth.

15. Shulman and Handelman, *God Inside Out*, 157.

16. *Harivamsha* 8.1–48.

17. *Markandeya Purana* 103.27–32.

18. Ibid., 74.31–32.

19. *Matsya Purana* 11.1–39.

20. "Surya," Amar Citra Katha, no. 58.

21. *Mahabharata* 1.104, 3.290–94.

22. Ibid., 5.144.1–9.

23. Desens, *The Bed-Trick*, 17, 142, 153 n.

24. Larson, "'Women Understand,'" 418.

25. Posner, *Sex and Reason*, 392.

26. Larson, "'Women Understand,'" 419.

27. Posner, *Sex and Reason*, 392.

28. Ibid., 392.

29. O'Flaherty, *Tales of Sex and Violence*, 26–28.

30. Hoffmann, "The Doubles," 269.

31. Réage, *Story of O*, 23.

32. Ibsen, *The Vikings at Helgeland*, 3.74; Doniger, *Rings.*

33. Abe, *The Face of Another*, 4.

34. Desens, *The Bed-Trick*, 142.

35. *The Memoirs of Jacques Casanova*, trans. Machen, 3.15, 469; *Casanova mémoires*, 2.17, 425.

36. Schnitzler, *Casanova's Return to Venice*, 159.

37. Desens, *The Bed-Trick*, 131.

38. Dorje, *Tales of Uncle Tompa*, 36–38.

39. "The Party's Over," in *Bells Are Ringing*, lyrics by Betty Comden and Adolph Green.

40. Abe, *The Face of Another*, 187.

41. Ibid., 225.

42. Wadler, "For the First Time."

43. Adelman, "Bed Tricks," 158.

44. Jagendorf, "'In the Morning,'" 57.

45. Carol Neely, *Broken Nuptials*, 92.

46. Allan Bloom, *Love and Friendship*, 339.

47. Desens, *The Bed-Trick*, 61.

48. Nathalie Davis, *The Return of Martin Guerre*, 59, 61.

49. *Sri Venkateca Mahatmiyam* 3.11–12; translation by Norman Cutler. See also Doniger, *Splitting the Difference*, 15–16.

50. Bowden, "The Bed-Trick," 120.

51. Detmer, "The Politics of Telling," 210, citing David Bergeron, Eileen Cohen, and Janet Adelman.

52. Detmer, "The Politics of Telling," 210.

53. Carol Neely, *Broken Nuptials*, 80.

54. Ibid., 94, 81.

55. Karen Bamford uses the term "rape-trick" in "Sexual Assault in Jacobean Drama," her dissertation for the University of Toronto, 1993; cited by Detmer, "The Politics of Telling," 254.

56. Carol Neely, *Broken Nuptials*, 92.

57. Thigpen and Cleckly, *Three Faces;* Doniger, *Splitting the Difference*, 81–84.

58. Lancaster, *The Final Face of Eve*, 201.

59. Ibid., 201–2.

60. Ibid., 201–2, 95.

61. Sizemore and Pittillo, *I'm Eve*, 284.

62. Lancaster, *The Final Face of Eve*, 201–2, 208.

63. Thigpen and Cleckley, *Three Faces*, 202.

64. Detmer, "The Politics of Telling," 243.

65. Ibid., 207, 242, 244.

66. Freud, *Three Essays on a Theory of Sexuality*.

67. Winnicott, *The Family and Individual Development*, 143.

68. Garber, *Dog Love*, 135.

69. Doniger, *The Implied Spider*, 79.

70. *Rig Veda* 10.72.8–9; O'Flaherty, *The Rig Veda*, 37–39.

71. Padel, "Putting the Words into Women's Mouths," 15.

72. Freud, "Family Romances," 74–78.

73. Thigpen and Cleckley, *Three Faces*, 206, 24.

74. Lancaster, *The Final Face of Eve*, 218, 95.

Approach Two

75. Hegel, *Phenomenology of Spirit,* 111.

76. Kleist, *Amphitryon,* 3.11.

77. Nathalie Davis, *The Return of Martin Guerre,* 83.

78. Ibid.

79. Basile, *Pentamerone,* tenth diversion of the third day, 267–76.

80. Kleist, *Amphitryon,* 3.11.

81. Roth, *The Tale of the 1002nd Night,* 258.

82. Garber, *Vice Versa,* 430.

83. Shulman, "On Being Human."

84. Doniger, *The Implied Spider,* 95–103.

85. Slovenko, "The Multiple Personality," 705.

86. Freud, "The Splitting of the Ego in the Defensive Process."

87. Freud, "The Uncanny."

88. Freud, *Three Essays on a Theory of Sexuality.*

89. Freud, *Totem and Taboo,* 20–21.

90. Freud, "A Special Type of Choice of Object Made by Men."

91. Ibid.

92. Klein, *Contributions to Psychoanalysis.*

93. Trawick, *Notes on Love,* 244–45.

94. Freud, "Psycho-analytic Notes on an Autobiographical Account of a Case of Paranoia," 63.

95. Sedgwick, *Epistemology,* 161.

96. Garber, *Vested Interests,* 207.

97. Ibid., 453.

98. Ibid., 207.

99. Ovid, *Metamorphoses* 3.3.341–510.

100. Freud, "A Difficulty in the Path of Psycho-analysis," 139; "Leonardo da Vinci and a Memory of His Childhood," 100.

101. Sedgwick, *Epistemology,* 161.

102. Capgras and Reboul-Lachaux, "L'illusion des 'sosies.'"

103. Mikkelsen and Gutheil, "Communication and Reality," 144.

104. Ibid., 139.

105. Ibid., 143–44.

106. Ibid., 139.

107. Freud, "The Uncanny."

108. See, e.g., Tymms, *Doubles in Literary Psychology;* Rogers, *A Psychoanalytic Study of the Double in Literature;* Karl Miller, *Doubles;* Hawthorn, *Multiple Personality and the Disintegration of Literary Character;* Girard, *Desire, Deceit, and the Novel.*

109. Jameson, "Imaginary and Symbolic," 371.

110. Freud, "The Splitting of the Ego in the Defensive Process."

111. Rank, *The Double,* 11, 15.

112. Ibid., 33.

113. Ibid., 70, 77–78.

114. Ibid., 85.

115. Ibid., 70, 77–78.

116. Pausanias, *Description of Greece,* 9.31.6.

117. Rank, *The Double,* 71–72.

118. Winnicott, "Mirror-Role of the Mother and Family in Child Development."

119. A Rumanian variant, cited by Böklen, *Schneewittchen-Studien,* vol. 7, fasc. 3, p. 51.

120. Abramovitch, "Turning Inside Out," 8.

121. Warner, "Stolen Shadows, Lost Souls," 43.

122. Lacan, "The Mirror Stage as Formative of the Function of the I."

123. Trawick, *Notes on Love,* 145.

124. Segal, "Doubles," 161.

125. Jameson, "Imaginary and Symbolic in Lacan."

126. Moi, *Sexual/Textual Politics,* 99.

127. Lacan, "The Agency of the Letter," 171–72.

128. Hess, *The Bijak of Kabir,* 92.

CHAPTER THREE

1. Leach, "Anthropological Aspects of Language."

2. Warner, *From the Beast,* 273.

3. Aarne and Thompson dubbed it TT 425, "East of the Sun and West of the Moon" or "Rose Red and Rose White."

4. This tale of transformation is part of Apuleius's *Metamorphoses,* also called *The Golden Ass,* 4.28–6.24.

5. Warner, *From the Beast,* 273.

6. Rushdie, *Shame,* 158.

7. Hatto, "The Swan Maiden," 333.

8. *Markandeya Purana* 105.1–13.

9. *Harivamsha* 8.1–48; *Matsya Purana* 11.1–39.

10. Lommel, *Kleine Schriften,* 272–74. Philologists now generally reject this etymology.

11. This etymology too is rejected by European philologists; see Skutsch, "Helen," 189, and Nagy, *Greek Mythology and Poetics,* 92–93. The favored etymology is from *nes,* as in the Greek Nestor, "savior," or in the sense of "returning home," as in *nostos.*

12. *Bhagavata Purana* 8.13.8–10.

13. English translation of the *Matsya Purana,* ed. Akhtar, 1.32–34.

14. Ibid. (italics in original).

15. Leach, "Anthropological Aspects of Language."

16. O'Flaherty, *Women, Androgynes,* 241–54.

17. Doniger, *Splitting the Difference,* 61.

18. Baudis, *Czech Folk Tales,* 191–92; George B. Douglas, *Scottish Fairy and Folk Tales,* 228–30; Doniger, *Splitting the Difference,* 175–85.

19. Randolph, *"The Devil's Pretty Daughter,"* 309.

20. Pindar, *Pythian* 2.21–48.

21. Aristotle, *On the Generation of Animals* 9.47. Cited by Aquinas, question 154, "Of the Parts of Lust," article 9, "Whether Incest is a Determinate Species of Lust," p. 181. I am grateful to Lorraine Daston for this citation. See also Aelian, *On the Characteristics of Animals* 4.7–8: A well-trained horse will go to considerable lengths to maintain sexual conventions, such as the prohibition of incest.

22. For Indra as performer of horse sacrifices and obstructor of horse sacrifices, see O'Flaherty, *Origins of Evil.* For the identification of the horse with the sacrificer and with Prajapati, see *Shatapatha Brahmana* 13.1.1.1, 13.2.1.1. For the many variants of the story of Indra's theft of the sacrificial horse of King Sagara, see *Mahabharata*

3.104–8; *Ramayana* of Valmiki, 1.38–44; *Vishnu Purana* 4.4.1–33, etc. For a discussion of these stories, see O'Flaherty, *Women, Androgynes,* 220–222.

23. *Harivamsha* 118.11–39.

24. O'Flaherty, "Horses and Snakes."

25. O'Flaherty, *Origins of Evil,* 253–58.

26. *Rig Veda* 1.51.13 (cf. 10.111.3, 1.121.2); *Maitrayani Samhita* 2.5.5; *Kathaka Samhita* 13.5; *Jaiminiya Brahmana* 2.70; *Shatapatha Brahmana* 3.3.4.18; O'Flaherty, "The Case of the Stallion's Wife."

27. *Maitrayani Samhita* 2.5.5.

28. Snorri Sturluson, *Edda,* 36 (Gylfaginning 42–43).

29. "The Lay of Thrym," from the *Elder Edda;* cited by Hallmundsson, *An Anthology of Scandinavian Literature,* 187–92; Doniger, *Splitting the Difference,* 262–63.

30. O'Flaherty, *Women, Androgynes,* 180–82.

31. *Rig Veda* 10.95.9; O'Flaherty, *The Rig Veda,* 253–56.

32. Leavy, *In Search.*

33. *Shatapatha Brahmana* 11.5.1.1–17; O'Flaherty, *Women, Androgynes,* 180–81.

34. *Baudhayana Shrauta Sutra* 18.44–45.

35. Libretto by Vladimir Begichev and Vasily Geltser, choreography by Julius Reisinger, later reworked by Lev Ivanov and Marius Petipa in St. Petersburg.

36. Beaumont, *The Ballet Called "Swan Lake,"* 19–40.

37. Arlene Croce, "The Story of O," review of Mikhail Baryshnikov's *Swan Lake, New Yorker,* May 29, 1989, 105–7.

38. Fanger, *"Swan Lake,"* 35.

39. Jaan Parry, "Black or White, They're Birds of a Feather," *New York Times,* Sept. 27, 1998, AR29.

40. In Euripides' play *Helen,* Helen herself expresses her doubts about this story; she mentions her two fathers, Tyndareus and Zeus, and the story of Zeus taking the form of a swan to seduce her mother, Leda, but then adds, quite casually, "if this story [*logos*] is credible" (Euripides, *Helen* 21).

41. Garber, *Vice Versa,* 150.

42. *Mahabharata* 1.92–94.

43. Dijkstra, *Idols of Perversity,* 21.

44. Pseudo-Callisthenes, *Alexander Romance,* trans. Dowden, 650–735.

45. *Pancatantra* 1.23 (trans. Rajan, 159–61, 163).

46. Ramanujan, "Towards a Counter-System," 47–54; I have somewhat condensed and occasionally reworded Ramanujan's text but have not changed the dialogue. The story, though not the analysis, is reprinted in Ramanujan, *'A Flowering Tree.'*

47. Doniger, "Jewels of Rejection."

48. This ingenious construction came to me from Justin Kaplan, pers. comm., July 4, 1995.

49. Ramanujan, "Towards a Counter-System," 53.

50. Kakar, *Intimate Relations,* 59–63.

51. Baring-Gould, *Curious Myths,* 470–79.

52. Leavy, *In Search,* 238.

53. Kramrisch, "Two," 123.

54. Andersen, "The Little Mermaid."

55. de Visser, "The Fox and the Badger," 57.

56. Jacobsen and Leavy, *Ibsen's Forsaken Merman,* 20.

57. Benwell and Waugh, *Sea Enchantress,* 17.

58. Krappe, "Scandinavian Seal Lore," 156.

59. Jacobsen and Leavy, *Ibsen's Forsaken Merman,* 20.

60. *Mahabharata* 1.109.

61. Ibid. 8.20.32–35.

62. *Ramayana* of Valmiki, 1.1–2.

63. Ibid., 2.57–58.

64. The creature is a *jrimbha,* a rare word (related to the verb "to yawn," "expand," or "have an erection") that probably refers to a bird.

65. Ibid., passage rejected by critical edition at 2.32, app. 1, 14, 36–54. Cf. *Jataka* no. 386 (the *Kharaputta Jataka*) about a *nagini* woman and talking animals.

66. Ovid, *Metamorphoses* 7.700–865.

67. *Newsweek,* Mar. 6, 1995, 55.

68. Leavy, *In Search,* 221–22, 235.

69. Warner, *From the Beast,* 354.

70. Leavy, *In Search,* 354–55, 358.

71. Howard Schwartz, "The Beast." From Egypt, IFA 2675, recorded by Z. M. Haimovitch from Shaul Ephraim; AT 934B.

72. Greer, *The Female Eunuch,* 320–21.

73. Bettelheim, *The Uses of Enchantment,* 286.

74. Blackburn, "Coming Out," 68.

75. Bettelheim, *The Uses of Enchantment,* 297.

76. Ibid., 297, 295.

77. Blackburn, "Coming Out," 68.

78. Ramanujan, "Towards a Counter-System." He speaks of what Tamil poets call *akam* and *puram.*

79. Kirin Narayan, pers. comm., July 1997.

80. Ralston, "Beauty and the Beast," 995, citing Müller.

81. Kunos, *Forty-four Turkish Fairy Tales,* 71.

82. Nina Auerbach, *Our Vampires, Ourselves,* 25.

83. Mary Douglas, "Children Consumed and Child Cannibals," 43; Doniger, *The Implied Spider,* 98.

84. Delarue, *The Borzoi Books of French Folk Tales,* 178–79.

85. "Whitebear Whittington," in Chase, *Grandfather Tales,* 52–64.

86. "Dinore citrini, ratire naguni"; Marglin, *Wives of the God-King,* 242.

87. Ramanujan, "Towards a Counter-System," 51.

88. Linda Hess inspired me to ask these questions here; pers. comm., Apr. 1999.

89. Showalter, *Sexual Anarchy,* 106–7.

Approach Three

90. Jones, *On the Nightmare,* 260.

91. *The Nibelungenlied,* trans. Hatto, 117.

92. Here we may recall Freud's† fascination with eagles, rather than cuckoos, whose rejected young are raised by other birds; Doniger, *Splitting the Difference,* 67–70.

93. Hoffmann and Leibowitz, "Molecular Mimicry," 383.

94. Ibid., 390.

95. Ibid., 393, 395.

96. Dekkers, *Dearest Pet,* 21.

97. Ibid., 32.

98. Ibid., 29.

99. Batten, *Sexual Strategies.*

100. Dekkers, *Dearest Pet,* 21.

101. Ibid., 28.

102. Ibid., 67.

103. Crews, "Animal Sexuality," 113–14.

104. Ibid., 114.

105. Lorenz, *King Solomon's Ring.*

106. Dekkers, *Dearest Pet,* 65.

107. Doniger and Spinner, "Misconceptions."

108. Dekkers, *Dearest Pet,* 65.

109. Ibid., 67.

110. David Grene, pers. comm., Jan. 1985.

111. Barbara Smuts, pers. comm., Princeton, Oct. 8, 1997.

112. Freud, *Totem and Taboo,* 20–21.

113. Ginzburg, "Morelli," 28, citing Stendahl on horses.

114. Ginzburg, "Morelli," 21–22.

115. Francis, "Bright White Star," 68: "The markings and whorls had to be carefully drawn onto regulation outline pictures of side, front and rear views of horses."

116. Leavy, *In Search,* 56.

117. Roth, *The Tale of the 1002nd Night,* 34–36.

118. Joel Kraemer, pers. comm., June 1995.

119. *Cornell University College of Veterinary Medicine Animal Health Newsletter* 7, no.1 (Mar. 1989).

120. Molly Haskell, "If You Liked the Movie, You'll Probably Love the Hormones," *New York Times,* June 21, 1998, WH4.

121. Garber, *Vice Versa,* 370.

122. Lorraine Daston, remarks at the Einstein Forum, Berlin, Dec. 9, 1997.

CHAPTER FOUR

1. Rushdie, *Shame,* 159.

2. *Ramayana* of Kamban, 3.2888–91, in Hart and Heifetz, *The Forest Book;* summarized by Shulman, "Sita and Satakantharavana," 12–16. All citations of the Kamban text here are from the Hart and Heifetz translation.

3. *Ramayana* of Kamban, 3.2918.

4. *Adhyatma-ramayana,* cited by Erndl, "The Mutilation of Surpanakha," 76.

5. Erndl, "The Mutilation of Surpanakha," 69.

6. *Ramayana* of Valmiki, 5.12.

7. Ibid., 3.17.

8. Ibid., 3.34.

9. *Ramayana* of Kamban, 3.2857–58. The *kokila* bird is what I have rendered as "cuckoo."

10. Ibid., 3.2961.

11. Ibid., 3.3195.

12. *Radheshyam Ramayana,* cited by Erndl, "The Mutilation of Surpanakha," 80.

13. *Ramayana* of Kamban, 3.2944–47.

14. Ibid., 3.2958.

15. Ashvaghosha, *Buddhacarita* 5.85–86.

16. O'Flaherty, *The Origins of Evil,* 207, 213.

17. Ashvaghosha, *Buddhacarita* 15.13–36.

18. Elizabeth Wilson, *Charming Cadavers,* 131 and 39.

19. "Uccavaca kho purisanam adhippaya."

20. *Samyutta Nikaya* 1.4.3.5. They literally offer him not "old women" but "great women," *mah'itthiyo,* an unusual word for old age, though a commentary on a related text says they have broken teeth and gray hair.

21. *Dhammapadatthakatha* (*The Commentary to the Dhammapada*), 3.114–19, cited and translated by Elizabeth Wilson, *Charming Cadavers,* 159–60; the quotation marks within my citation are Wilson's.

22. O'Flaherty, *Dreams,* 146–57.

23. John Gower, *Confessio amantis,* I, vv. 1396–1861; reproduced by Bartlett J. Whiting, "The Wife of Bath's Tale," 224–35.

24. Cited by Whiting, "The Wife of Bath's Tale," 235–41.

25. Retold here from Laura Sumner's edition as reproduced by Whiting, "The Wife of Bath's Tale," 242–67. See also Zimmer, *The King and the Corpse,* 93–94.

26. Chaucer, *The Canterbury Tales,* lines 857–1265, pp. 180–91.

27. Leavy, *In Search,* 290.

28. The contrast between beauty and fidelity, though not between beauty and youth, is also echoed in the calypso song that advises, "Never marry a pretty woman; marry a woman uglier than you." (Revived by Sam Cook: "If you want to be happy for the rest of your life / Never make a pretty woman your wife.")

29. "Benjamin Franklin Urges a Young Friend to Take an Old Mistress," in Schuster, *A Treasury of the World's Great Letters,* 159–62.

30. Leavy, *In Search,* 290, 241.

31. Shirley, *A Lady of Pleasure* 4.1, 5.1 (ed. Thorssen, 213–19, 266–70).

32. Chailley, *"The Magic Flute," Masonic Opera,* 109.

33. Doniger, *Rings.*

34. Schofield, "Studies on the Libaeus Desconus," 206.

35. Coomaraswamy, "On the Loathly Bride," 399.

36. Maynadier, *The Wife of Bath's Tale,* 51.

37. Basile, *Pentamerone,* tenth diversion of the first day, 79–87 (original title).

38. Nathalie Davis, *The Return of Martin Guerre,* 63.

39. Dahl, "The Visitor."

40. Roheim, "The Garden of Eden," 18.

41. Frazer, *Taboo and the Perils of the Soul,* I.74; Meier, *Mythe und Erzählungen der Küstenbewohner der Gazelle Halbinsel.*

42. Roheim, "The Garden of Eden," 20.

43. Ibid., 21.

44. Millman, *A Kayak Full of Ghosts,* 127; told by Gustav Broberg Kulusak, East Greenland; VFT-1, 170.

45. Kalluak, *How Kablomat Became and Other Legends,* 18–21.

46. Dillard, *Pilgrim at Tinker Creek,* 273, citing Mowat, *People of the Deer,* 159: "He had got wet during the day, and the moisture shrunk the false skin on the old woman's face so that it all split and came off."

47. The Substitute Bride is a sub-subtheme of that subtheme known in French folklore as "The Love of Three Oranges" (which is also a tale type, TT 408, as well as an opera and a ballet) and known in India as "The Belbati Princess" (Bompas, *Folklore of the Santal Parganas,* 462–64).

48. Muhawi and Kanaana, *Speak, Bird,* 60.

49. Abu-Lughod, *Veiled Sentiments*, 138–45.

50. Ibid., 154.

51. Ibid., 161, 163, 164.

52. Doniger, "Transplanting Myths of Organ Transplants."

53. Men can bear children in myths; see Yuvanashva, *Mahabharata* 3.126; O'Flaherty, *Women, Androgynes*, 50, 299–300.

54. *Malleus Maleficarum* 1.3 (trans. Summers, 26).

55. Schweitzer, "My Children, My Grandchildren," 125 ff.

56. Kirin Narayan, *Mondays on the Dark Night of the Moon*, 197.

57. Mann, *Joseph*, 202.

58. *The Complete Grimm's Fairy Tales*, 608–11.

59. Megillah 13b, cited by Rashi on Genesis 29.16–21. Megillah, interestingly, discusses the Rachel and Leah story in the context of the story of Esther, another deceiving Jewish woman. Cf. also Rashi on Genesis 29.16–21; Azulai, *Hesed le-Abraham*, 2.6, cited by Ginzberg, *Legends of the Jews*, 5.294; *Midrash Rabbah* on Genesis 29.18 (Soncino ed.: pp. 111–16 of the Hebrew text, pp. 647–51 of the English translation). According to another text (Azulai, *Hesed le-Abraham*, 2.6, cited by Ginzberg, *Legends of the Jews*, 5.294), "The sign consisted in Rachel's touching Jacob's right toe, right thumb, and right lobe." In Exodus 29.19–25, these are the three parts of his body that the priest, "blinded" by the presence of God, touches with his fingers when he has dipped them in the blood of the animal sacrificed in the Temple. (Here, it might be relevant to ask who or what is being sacrificed in the Jacob, Rachel, Leah triangle.)

60. *Midrash Rabbah*, Lamentations, 24, Petikhta, Eikhah Rabbah 24.

61. Tishby, *The Wisdom of the Zohar*, 2.646–49.

62. At Sota 26b, the legal parameters of adultery are interpreted through the phrasing of Numbers 5.13.

63. Tishby, *The Wisdom of the Zohar*, 3.1401.

64. *Zohar* 1.154–55; Tishby, *The Wisdom of the Zohar*, 3.1402–3. This text rejects the explanation given in Chronicles itself, which states that Reuben "polluted his father's bed," a reference to the time when Reuben got into trouble by sleeping with Bilhah, Rachel's maid, the woman whom Jacob had taken as a substitute for Rachel and on whom he begat two sons "of Rachel"—a tale told in Genesis 30.

65. Jagendorf, "'In the Morning,'" 60.

66. Yehuda Liebes, pers. comm., Jan. 1997.

67. *Midrash Rabbah* on Genesis 29.18 (Soncino ed.: pp. 111–16 of the Hebrew text, pp. 647–51 of the English translation).

68. Ginzberg, *Legends of the Jews*, 5.299.

69. Jeremy Cohen, pers. comm., Chicago, Feb. 1999.

70. Micha Joseph Bin Gorion, *Classical Jewish Folktales*, no. 97, p. 181. The Hebrew source is the *Midrash of the Ten Commandments;* see *Midrash Aseret Hadibrot Verona 1647* and *Midrash Tanhuma, Naso*, par. 6. I am grateful to Galit Hasan-Rokem for this story, which I have retitled.

71. Wright, *Twins*, 33.

72. Ibid., 10.

73. Angela Carter, *Wise Children*, 83.

74. Ibid., 99.

75. Ibid., 102.

76. Basinger, *How Hollywood Spoke to Women*, 85.

77. Ibid., 100.

78. Ibid., 89.

79. Doniger, *Rings.*

80. Adelman, "Bed Tricks," 158.

81. Doniger, *The Implied Spider,* 27–32.

82. *Alphonsus, Emperor of Germany,* 38–39.

83. Beaumarchais, *The Barber of Seville,* act 3, p. 82, my translation. The French text reads: "Mais la nuit, dans l'ombre, / Je vaux encor mon prix; / Et quand il fait sombre, / Les plus beaux chats sont gris." John Wood translates, "'Tis true I am no beauty / But I know a husband's duty. / . . . Though I may not look much of a catch by day / In the dark all cats are grey!"

84. *The Memoirs of Jacques Casanova,* trans. Machen, 3.15, 473; *Casanova mémoires,* 2.17, 429.

85. *The Memoirs of Jacques Casanova,* 2.16, 486; *Casanova mémoires,* 2.18, 440: "Il est façile que vous ayez pris mon domestique pour moi, car la nuit, tous les chats sont gris, . . . à votre haleine et à vos appas décrépits, je vous aurais reconnue a l'instant."

86. Panckoucke, *Dictionnaire des proverbes françois,* 66; cited by Darnton, *The Great Cat Massacre,* 95, 272 n. 32.

87. Freud, "Fragment of an Analysis," 48.

88. Gallop, "Keys to Dora," 209.

89. Freud, "The Question of Lay Analysis," 212.

90. John Heywood, *Proverbs,* pt. 1, chap. 5.

91. Erasmus, *Adage* 3.4.77, in *Opera Omnia* 2.821: "Ego certe antequam Plutarchi locum adiissem, hujusce Graeci adagii sensum a Gallico edoctus eram adagio. De nuici tous chats son gris."

92. Plutarch, *Conjugalia Praecepta* (or *Gamika Paraggelmata*), no. 46 (part of the *Moralia*).

93. Pseudo-Callisthenes, "Alexander Romance," trans. Dowden, 650–735.

94. Kleist, *Amphitryon,* 3.1.

95. Zweig, *The Adventurer,* 151.

96. Herrick, *Selections from the "Hesperides."*

97. Yeats, "The Three Bushes," in *Collected Poems,* 341.

98. Kundera, *The Unbearable Lightness of Being,* 200.

99. Sidney, *The Countess of Pembroke's Arcadia,* 4.2.724–38.

100. Francis, *Straight,* 275.

101. Leavy, *In Search,* 56.

102. Rushdie, "Kipling," 74.

103. Bloch, *Medieval Misogyny,* 5.

104. *Kamasutra* 1.1.9, Jayamangala commentary.

105. Satyacharan Mitra, *Shrishri Ramakrishna Paramahamsa,* 118–19. I am indebted to Jeff Kripal for this text and its translation.

106. Hegel, *Phänomenologie des Geistes,* 19; Doniger, *The Implied Spider,* 29.

107. *Ramayana* of Valmiki, 7.30.17–36.

108. Dijkstra, *Idols of Perversity,* 223.

109. Advertisement for Gyne Lotrimin, *Newsweek,* Feb. 28, 1994.

110. Calvino, "Love Far from Home," 94.

111. Aristotle, *Generation of Animals,* 2.3.

112. Laqueur, *Making Sex.*

113. Rukeyser, "Myth" (1973), in *The Muriel Rukeyser Reader,* 252.

114. It would be good to know whether he said *anthropos,* which includes men

and women, or *aner/andros,* meaning men and excluding women. Sophocles doesn't tell us the riddle, but Apollodorus does—and uses the inclusive term, *anthropos.* Apollodorus, *Library* 3.5.7–9. See also Diodorus Siculus, *Library and History,* 4.64.1–65.1.

115. Gold, *A Carnival of Parting,* 108–35.

116. Ibid., 107.

117. O'Flaherty, *Dreams,* 114–21.

Approach Four

118. The anthropologist Kaveh Safa gave me the witty twist on Lévi-Strauss's famous line "Animals are good to think with" that I have used for the title of this section.

119. Doniger, *The Implied Spider,* 132–35.

120. Ramanujan, *Folktales from India,* xv.

121. Warner, *From the Beast,* 405.

122. *The Laws of Manu* 9.60.

123. Showalter, *Sexual Anarchy,* 181. Here she cites O'Flaherty, *Women, Androgynes,* on Freudian headshrinking. See also Eilberg and Doniger, *Off with Her Head.*

124. *The Changelings,* 157 and 198.

125. Harper, *On Presence,* 31.

126. Ovid, *Metamorphoses* 6.425–675.

127. O'Flaherty, *Siva,* 84–90.

128. Showalter, *Sexual Anarchy,* 136.

129. O'Flaherty, *Siva,* 158–64.

130. Rushdie, *Shame,* 73.

131. Keene, "Feminine Sensibility in the Heian Era," 116.

132. García Márquez, *One Hundred Years,* 32–35.

133. When I was a teenager, there was a song, "Where Is Your Heart?" that contained the lines "When we kiss, do you close your eyes, pretending that I'm someone else?"

134. Dinesen, "The Deluge at Norderney," 73.

135. This is my summary of Oxford lore current in the 1960s.

136. Casanova, *History of My Life,* 2.1, 17–18, 20.

137. Carol Neely, *Broken Nuptials,* 99.

138. From Lorraine Daston's remarks at the Einstein Forum, Berlin, Dec. 9, 1997.

139. Lüthi, *The Fairytale as Art Form,* 13, 20–21, 28, 37.

140. Tracy, "Iris Murdoch and the Many Faces of Platonism," 12–13.

141. Kunio Yanagida, *Japanese Folk Tales,* 90–92 ("52. The Old Woman's Skin").

142. Kunio Yanagida, *Yanagida Kunio no Bunrui niyoru Nihon no Mukashibanashi,* 86–87.

143. Barthes, *S/Z,* 144.

144. Ibid., 72.

145. Freud, "The Theme of the Three Caskets."

146. This formulation is reminiscent of one of the "sayings" of Kosmo-Prutkov, a nineteenth-century Russian satirist: "It's better to be rich and healthy than to be poor and sick."

147. Lévi-Strauss, *Tristes tropiques,* 287.

148. *Lamentations of Matheolus* 1.647–80, cited by Bloch, *Medieval Misogyny,* 50.

149. Cave, *Recognitions,* 492.

150. Phillips, *On Flirtation,* 93.

151. Garber, *Vested Interests,* 44, 168.

152. Reynolds, "Ruggiero's Deceptions," 140.
153. Žižek, "'The Wound is Healed,'" 205–6.
154. Garber, *Vested Interests*, 44, 168.
155. Greer, *The Change*.
156. The most notorious reason, that they are grateful, resurfaced in a recent Mexican joke about Viagra, the drug touted as a cure for male impotence: the name is said to mean "it makes old women grateful," from *vieja* and *agradecida*.
157. Siebert, "The Cuts," 24.
158. Ibid., 45.
159. Garber, *Vested Interests*, 117.
160. Bellow, *The Adventures of Augie March*, 540.
161. Kleist, *Amphitryon*, 1.2.
162. Angela Carter, *Wise Children*, 155–56, 161.

Chapter Five

1. McDermott, "Karma and Rebirth in Early Buddhism," 171–72.
2. *Kamasutra* 1.5.1–21. See Doniger, "Playing the Field"; O'Flaherty, *Textual Sources*, 104–5.
3. The *Cape/North (Fla.) Weekend Shopper*, noted by *New Yorker*, July 13, 1992, 92.
4. *Shiva Purana* 2.5.14.28–29; cf. *Padma Purana* 6.3.1–52.
5. *Shiva Purana* 2.5.13–22; cf. *Padma Purana* 6.97–103.
6. O'Flaherty, *Siva*, 261–62.
7. *Padma Purana* 6.11–17.
8. O'Flaherty, *Siva*, 103–10.
9. O'Flaherty, *Dreams*, 81–88, 132–33.
10. *Skanda Purana* 5.3.67.3–97.
11. *Shiva Purana* 2.5.22.
12. *Padma Purana* 6.102.29.
13. *Padma Purana* 6.4.47–48.
14. *Padma Purana* 6.15–16; cf. *Shiva Purana* 2.5.22–24.
15. There is a double pun here, for the Sanskrit words for both jackal (*shiva*) and lion (*pancha-mukha*, "five-faced") are also names of Shiva. On one level, the demons are telling Jalandhara that he, a jackal, cannot have the wife of Shiva, a lion. But if both of the animals in the metaphor are Shiva, how can Shiva take away Shiva's wife? This implies not only that Vishnu is Shiva (as Vishnu argues elsewhere) but that Jalandhara is Shiva, as is true on a deeply metaphysical level; a demon killed by a god often enters (back into) the body of the god at its death (O'Flaherty, *The Origins of Evil*, 298–99, 308–10).
16. *Padma Purana* 6.17.34.
17. *Ramayana* of Valmiki, 6.68.1–28.
18. *Shiva Purana* 2.5.22; cf. *Padma Purana* 6.97–103.
19. *Padma Purana* 6.19.14–45; cf. *Shiva Purana* 2.5.24.
20. *Ramayana* of Valmiki, 6.31.
21. *Padma Purana* 6.15–16.
22. *Shiva Purana* 2.5.26.46–52; cf. *Padma Purana* 6.105.1–7.
23. *Brahmavaivarta Purana* 2.21.16 (sukhasambhogaad aakarshanavyatikramaat); *Shiva Purana* 2.5.41.29 (sukhasambhaavaakarshanasya vyatikramaat).
24. *Shiva Purana* 2.5.40–41.

25. *Shiva Purana* 2.5.40–41.

26. Tulsi Das, *The Holy Lake,* trans. Prasad, 1.124.

27. Tulsi Das, *Ramacaritamanasa,* trans. Hill, 512.

28. Narayan, "The Tulsi Plant in Kangra."

29. Babb, *Divine Hierarchy,* 107–8.

30. Garber, *Vice Versa,* 448.

31. Marias, *Tomorrow in the Battle,* 174.

32. Ibid., 177, 207.

33. Ibid., 187; see also 205.

34. Ibid., 177.

35. *Shiva Purana, Dharma Samhita,* 10.49–55; O'Flaherty, *Siva,* 189.

36. Boswell, *Same-Sex Unions,* 177. It also appears as the second story in Petrus Alfonsi's *Disciplina clericalis.*

37. Boccaccio, *Decameron,* tenth day, eighth story.

38. Kellet, *A Pocket of Prose and Verse,* 20–22. Original punctuation. I am indebted to Gary Ebersole for furnishing me with this remarkable story.

39. Réage, *Story of O,* 11.

40. Ibid., 105.

41. *The True Trojans,* attributed to Jasper Fisher (1625), 3.6 and 4.3; cited by Desens, *The Bed-Trick,* 109–10.

42. Desens, *The Bed-Trick,* 145.

43. Dahl, "The Great Switcheroo."

44. Rushdie, *The Ground beneath Her Feet,* 58.

45. Enchi, *Masks,* 133.

46. Pam Belluck, "Paternity Testing for Fun and Profit,"*New York Times,* Aug. 3, 1997, 4.1.

47. Hatto, "The Swan Maiden," 336, citing Uno Harva.

48. This much-quoted bon mot appears in *The Importance of Being Ernest.* When Lady Bracknell asks Jack, her prospective son-in-law, "Are your parents living?" and Jack replies, "I have lost both my parents," Lady Bracknell remarks, "To lose one parent might be regarded as unfortunate; to lose both is careless." This is the text as it is most often cited, and as it appears in the Oxford standard edition of Wilde (1990), as well as in the classic film with Michael Redgrave (1952). But in present-day performances it is usually cited as I have it in the text. A shorter version, also widespread, appears in the Vintage edition: Lady Bracknell simply says, "Both? . . . That seems like carelessness" (p. 449).

49. Rushdie, *Shame,* 19.

50. Angela Carter, *Wise Children,* 222–23.

51. *Tapati-Samvaranam,* attributed to Kulashekhara Varman, c. A.D. 1100.

52. *Tapati-Samvaranam,* act 6: snehas tvam jaanaati, na punar aham.

53. Zvelebil, *Two Tamil Folktales,* 44–52 ("The Story of the Prince Who Was About to Sleep with His Mother").

54. Herodotus, *History,* 4.180.

55. Thomas Middleton, *The Family of Love,* 5.3.288–93.

56. Desens, *The Bed-Trick,* 75.

57. Angela Carter, *Wise Children,* 72, 171, 174.

58. Kalidasa, *Abhijnanashakuntalam* 7.19.

59. "The Two Viziers," in the *Arabian Nights,* trans. Haddawy, vol. 1, 157–206.

60. Basile, *Pentamerone,* third diversion of the first day, 24–31.

61. Beaumarchais, *The Marriage of Figaro*, 178.
62. Karl Miller, *Doubles*, 43.
63. Doniger and Spinner, "Misconceptions."
64. Huet, *Monstrous Imagination*, 79–80.
65. Ibid., 80.
66. Ibid., 81.
67. Eric Gerber, "Not-So-Hot a Lover," *Houston Post*, May 21, 1986.

Approach Five

68. Harper, *On Presence*, 107.
69. *Hypostasis of the Archons* 87 and 89.20–30 (ed. Robinson, 163–64).
70. Perkins, "Sophia as Goddess," 110, citing Gedaliahu Stroumsa, *Another Seed*, 42–44.
71. Calasso, *The Marriage of Cadmus and Harmony*, 364.
72. Pagels, "Pursuing the Spiritual Eve," 197.
73. Richer, "The Androgyne."
74. Poimandres, *Corpus Hermeticum* 13 ff.; cf. similar reflections in the *Apocryphon of John* 2.1.4 ff., and *Hypostasis of the Archons* 87 ff.
75. O'Flaherty, *Dreams.*
76. "Pursuing" is the King James euphemism for the much more insulting suggestion of the Hebrew text: "shitting." The Hebrew word, *siyn*, is treated more clearly, though still euphemistically, by the Jewish Publication Society of America: "he is gone aside."
77. Warner, *From the Beast*, 274–75.
78. Margalit and Halbertal, *Idolatry.*
79. Ramanujan et al., *When God Is a Customer*, afterword.
80. Lodge, *The British Museum*, 65.
81. Shringarasankirtanalu of Annamayya, vol. 15, p. 86. Translation by David Shulman and V. Narayana Rao (pers. comm., Nov. 20, 1997).
82. O'Flaherty, *Dreams.*
83. *The Life of St. Theresa of Avila*, 188.
84. Herodotus, *History* 7.15–17 (trans. Grene, 475–77).
85. Pausanias, *Description of Greece* 9.31.6.
86. Gellner, *The Psychoanalytic Movement*, 180.
87. Rosenzweig, *Das neue Denken*, 389. I have rendered his *übersetzt* as "translated," and his *vorgetrieben* as "projected."

Chapter Six

1. Patai, *Sex and the Family*, 45.
2. *Mahabharata* 1.112.30.
3. Lévi-Strauss, *Tristes tropiques*, 356.
4. *Kusa Jataka*, bk. 20, no. 531 (pp. 141–64 of vol. 5 of Pali Text Society translation).
5. Schiefner's translation of the *Kanjur*, cited by Ralston, "Beauty and the Beast," 1011.
6. Zall, *Abe Lincoln Laughing*, 55 (italics in original).
7. Hertz, *The Hidden Lincoln*, 287.
8. B. P. Thomas, *Abraham Lincoln*, 19.
9. Lévi-Strauss, *Myth and Meaning*, 29–30.

10. Rank, *Beyond Psychology*, 13.

11. Libretto by George Abbott; lyrics by Lorenz Hart; music by Richard Rodgers.

12. Lodge, *Small World*, 334–35.

13. Gurney, *"The Perfect Party,"* 49, 53, refering to Luigi Pirandello's *Six Characters in Search of an Author* (1922) and Wilde's *The Importance of Being Ernest*,† in which a man named Jack pretends to be his brother named Ernest.

14. Janet Maslin, "Two Sisters' Beaus Are Just One Guy," *New York Times*, Mar. 15, 1996, B13.

15. "The Two Brothers," in *The Grimms' German Fairy Tales*, 308–11. See Doniger, *Rings*.

16. Doniger, "What Did They Name the Dog?" The project was carried out by David Lykken and Matt McGue.

17. Wright, *Twins*, 108–9.

18. Ibid., citing Lykken and Tellegen.

19. Ibid., 46.

20. Ibid., 109.

21. Ibid., 33.

22. Reported in the *New York Times* in 1975: 20 July, sec. 4, p. 38; 21 July, sec. 3, p. 25; Aug. 1, sec. 1, p. 15; Aug. 15, sec. 5, p. 1; Aug. 16, sec. 5, p. 20; and Aug. 19, sec. 7, p. 1.

23. *Rig Veda* 10.40.2; O'Flaherty, *The Rig Veda*, 292.

24. *The Laws of Manu* 9.60.

25. See, e.g., the story of Uttanka and his guru's wife in *Mahabharata* 1.3.85–90.

26. Bal, *Lethal Love*, 86.

27. Doniger, "Begetting on Margin."

28. A. K. Ramanujan, pers. comm., Dec. 1992.

29. "The Murderous Bride," in Shulman, *Tamil Temple Myths*, 176–91.

30. *Rig Veda* 10.85; O'Flaherty, *The Rig Veda*, 270–73.

31. O'Flaherty, *Siva*, 64–67.

32. *Mahabharata* 1.98.7–33; cf. the telling in the *Brihaddevata* 4.11–15.

33. *Mahabharata* 1.99–100.

34. Ibid., 1.94, 99; O'Flaherty, *Textual Sources*, 46–51.

35. *Shatapatha Brahmana* 13.2.8.1–4; *Taittiriya Samhita* 7.4.19; O'Flaherty, *Women, Androgynes*, 154–61; O'Flaherty, *Textual Sources*, 15–19.

36. *Mahabharata* 1.90, 109.

37. Sullivan, *Krsna Dvaipayana Vyasa and the Mahabharata*.

38. *Mahabharata* 1.104, 3.290–94, 5.144.1–9.

39. "Maksudan's Baby," in Gill, *Turn Northeast at the Tombstone*, 136–45.

40. Gold, "Sexuality, Fertility, and Erotic Imagination."

41. Neufeld, "Levirate Marriage," 36.

42. Sattampillai, *Ruttammavai*, 26, 28. I am indebted to Eliza Kent for bringing this text to my attention and translating it for me.

43. Doniger, *The Implied Spider*, 139–44.

44. Translation by Robert Alter, *The Art of Biblical Narrative*, 7–10.

45. Tikva Frymer-Kensky, pers. comm., Jan. 1999.

46. Bal, *Lethal Love*, 101.

47. Sasson, *Ruth*, 232, citing EBI 5.72.

48. *Bereshit Rabbah* 85.11. See also *Targum Neofiti*, Genesis 38.25–26.

49. *Genesis Rabbah* 85.4.

50. O'Flaherty, *Siva*, 40–63.

51. Pritchard, *Ancient Near Eastern Texts*, 182, par. 33.

52. Ibid., 172.

53. Alter, *The Art of Biblical Narrative*, 7.

54. Harold Bloom, *The Book of J*, 314.

55. Bal, *Lethal Love*, 100.

56. Goldin, "The Youngest Son," 124.

57. *Testament of Judah* 8.1–3; Menn, *Judah and Tamar*, 135.

58. Sasson, *Ruth*, 71–72. I have summarized the parts of the story that I wish to discuss, alternating between my rough paraphrasing, bracketed, and Jack Sasson's more precise translation.

59. Bal, *Lethal Love*, 78.

60. *Midrash Ruth Zutta* 55 (p. 49) and *Legah Tov* on Ruth 4.17: "They said, 'On the same night that he had intercourse with her he died.'" See also Friedman, "Tamar, a Symbol of Life," 44.

61. Fishbane, "Ruth," 303.

62. Adelman, "Bed Tricks," 160.

63. Friedman, "Tamar, a Symbol of Life," 27.

64. Dundes, "The Hero Pattern and the Life of Jesus."

65. Leach, "The Legitimacy of Solomon," 58.

66. Babylonian Talmud, Megillah 14a, 15a.

67. Leach, "The Legitimacy of Solomon," 62.

68. Keats, "Ode to a Nightingale": "Perhaps the self-same song that found a path / Through the sad heart of Ruth, when, sick for home, / She stood in tears amid the alien corn." Cf. the satire in David Lodge's *Changing Places*, where the Berkeley professor stumbles into the strip joints of Soho (in London) and finds himself quite confused, "amid the alien porn."

69. Bal, *Lethal Love*, 80.

70. Lyke, "What Does Ruth Have to Do with Rahab?" 24.

71. On the reference to this legend by the medieval authors, see Zunz, *Synagogale Poesie*, 129; *Kele Yakar*, 1 Samuel 17; Azulai, *Midbar Kedemot*, s.v. yšy [i.e., Jesse], no. 20; R. Elijah Wilna in his commentary on Yoreh De'ah, 157.24.

72. Psalm 51 was often cited in sermons during the Starr prosecutions of the Clinton-Lewinsky affair.

73. *Yalqut Makiri* 2.214; my summary of a translation by Charlotte Elisheva Fonrobert, in "The Handmaid," 8–9.

74. Ginzberg, *Legends of the Jews*, 4.82, citing "an unknown Midrash quoted by Makiri, PS. 118, 214."

75. Bayle, *Historical and Critical Dictionary*, 403, citing Bartolocci. But for a discussion of Pierre Bayle's distortions of Jewish materials, see Manuel, *The Broken Staff*, 207.

76. Doniger, "Jewels of Rejection."

77. Bayle, *Historical and Critical Dictionary*, 403. A strikingly similar argument was offered in the trial of the man who masqueraded as Martin Guerre:† "For a child to be a bastard, both parents had to be conscious of the circumstances; the children of a woman unaware that she had married a priest would be legitimate" (Nathalie Davis, *The Return of Martin Guerre*, 89).

78. Babylonian Talmud, Kiddushin 81b; Doniger, *The Implied Spider*, 99–100; see also Nach, "Freedom and Celibacy."

79. Dinesen, "The Deluge at Norderney," 73.

80. *Toldoth Jeshu* 2.1.1–13 (trans. Schonfield, 35, with excised passage supplied to me by Willis Johnson).

81. Gittin 7, 77A; Neusner, *The Talmud of Babylonia,* 35.

82. *Toldoth Jeshu* 2.1.38–40.

83. Mary Douglas, *In the Wilderness,* 174–78.

84. I am indebted to Mary Douglas for this idea; it appeared in an earlier draft of her book *In the Wilderness,* which she kindly allowed me to see, but it was cut from the final manuscript.

85. Huet, *Monstrous Imagination,* 30.

86. Tracy, *On Naming the Present.*

87. Bowen, *Return to Laughter,* 147–49.

88. Zolani Ngwane, pers. comm., May 1993.

89. Enchi, *Masks,* 119–20, 126, 140; my summary.

90. Marglin, *Wives of the God-King,* 75–76.

91. *Thidrekssaga* and *Nibelungenlied,* cited by Hatto, *The Nibelungenlied,* 376–77; Doniger, *Rings.*

92. *Encyclopaedia Britannica,* 15th ed., 10.610, unsigned article.

93. Giraudoux, *Amphitryon,* 52–55.

94. Christopher Buckley, "Shouts and Murmurs: 1999, The Year in Headlines," *New Yorker,* Jan. 11, 1999, 40.

95. Warner, *From the Beast,* 346.

96. Desens, *The Bed-Trick,* 43.

97. Beaumarchais, *Marriage of Figaro,* 165.

98. Adelman, "Bed Tricks," 166.

99. Angela Carter, "The Tiger's Bride," 65.

100. *The Saga of Tristram and Isond,* trans. Paul Schach, 72.

101. Gottfried von Strassburg, *Tristan,* 208.

102. de Villiers, *Les cent nouvelles nouvelles,* 174–78; "The Thirty-fifth Tale," in Diner, *The One Hundred New Tales,* 151–54.

103. Paulus Diakunnus, *History of the Lombards,* chaps. 28–29, pp. 81–85.

104. Desens, *The Bed-Trick,* 131.

105. Boccaccio, *Decameron,* third day, second story.

106. Handelman, "The Guises of the Goddess."

107. *Kalika Purana* 49.1–58, 50.1–76, 51.1–15; Doniger, *Siva,* 206–7.

108. *Jaiminiya Brahmana* 2.269–70; O'Flaherty, *Tales of Sex and Violence,* 105–7.

109. Insler, "The Shattered Head," 120.

110. Ginzberg, *Legends of the Jews,* 4.387, with nn. 79 and 80, citing Megillah 13a; Septuagint Esther 2.7; *Zohar* III, 275b–276b; *Tikkune Zohar* 20. Ginzberg adds: "Comp. Sanhedrin 74a (Zohar, *loc. cit.,* obviously polemicizes against this statement of the Talmud); WR 5.13."

Approach Six

111. Margaret R. Brown, "Whose Eyes Are These, Whose Nose?" *Newsweek,* Mar. 7, 1994, 12.

112. Posner, *Sex and Reason,* 393.

113. "Fertility Doctor Gets Five Years," *New York Times,* May 9, 1992, 5.

114. *San Francisco Chronicle,* Feb. 3, 1995.

115. *Mathews v. Superior Court of the County of Butte,* 119 Cal. App. 3d 309, 173 Cal. Rep. 820–822 (1981).

116. *In re Childers*, 310 P. 2d 776–7 (Okla. 1957).

117. "Odd Sex Saga of 'Fantasy Man,'" *San Francisco Chronicle*, Feb. 3, 1995.

118. "Sexual Misconduct Count Dismissed in Deception of Twin's Girlfriend," New York Law Publishing Company, New York Law Journal, Jan. 18, 1994, Tuesday. Byline: Martin Fox. Thanks to Judge Richard Posner for bringing this case to my attention. *People v. Hough*, 159 Misc. 2d 997, 607 N.Y.S. 2d 884 (1994) (italics added).

119. *The People of the State of New York v. Lamont Hough*, Index no. 17214/93, District Court of New York, First District, criminal term, Nassau County; Jan. 13, 1994, decided. Judge John Michael Galasso. Edited for publication.

120. *Payne v. State*, 40 Tex. Cr. R. 202, 49 S.W. 604 (Court of Criminal Appeals of Texas, Feb. 15, 1899), in *Southwestern Reporter*, pp. 604–7.

121. *State v. Navarro*, 307 P. 2d 227 (Ariz. 1961); *State of Arizona, Appellee, v. Arnold Ballesteros Navarro, Appellant*, no. 1201, 90 Arizona 185 (Supreme Court of Arizona, en banc, Dec. 13, 1961), in *367 Pacific Reporter*, 2d ser., pp. 227–30.

122. Posner, *Sex and Reason*, 392–93.

123. *People v. Minkowski*, 204 Cal. App. 2d 832, 23 Cal. Rep. 92 (1962).

124. *State v. Ely*, 114 Wash. 185, 194 P. 988 (1921); *People v. Borak*, 13 Ill. App. ed. 815, 301 N.E. 2d 1 (1972); and *Story v. State*, 712 P. 2d 1020 (Wyo. 1986).

125. *State v. Ely*, Wash. 1921; *People v. Borak*, Ill.1972; *Story v. State*, Wyo. 1986.

126. *State v. Atkins*, 292 S.W. 422 (Mo. 1926).

127. Slovenko, "The Multiple Personality," 693.

128. "Multiple-Personality Rape Verdict: Guilty," Associated Press, copyright 1990, Chicago Tribune Company, Friday, Nov. 9, 1990, North Sports Final ed., News section, p. 5.

129. "One Woman Becomes 6 Witnesses at Rape Trial," Cynthia Gorney, *Washington Post* staff writer, Oshkosh, Wis., Nov. 7, 1990, *Washington Post*, Nov. 8, 1990, Thursday, Final ed.

130. Mark Twain, "People and Things," *Buffalo Express*, Sept. 2, 1869; cited by Gillman, *Dark Twins*, 58.

131. *Newsweek*, Nov. 13, 1995, under "Identities" in "Periscope."

132. *Dallas Morning News*, Nov. 27, 1994, Bulldog ed. (byline: Leef Smith, *Washington Post*).

CHAPTER SEVEN

1. *Skanda Purana* 1.2.27.74–84; O'Flaherty, *Hindu Myths*, 253.

2. *Rig Veda* 2.20.7.

3. *Skanda Purana* 1.2.27.58–65; O'Flaherty, *Hindu Myths*, 252.

4. *Harivamsha* 8.1–48.

5. Syrkin, "Chernoye Solntse." Milan Kundera suggests an explanation for the confluence of brilliance and blackness in the sun, perhaps a variant of the realization that gazing at the sun darkens vision: "Seeing is limited by two borders: strong light, which blinds, and total darkness" (*The Unbearable Lightness of Being*, 94).

6. *Vishnu Purana*, trans. Wilson, 215.

7. Ramesan, *Temples and Legends of Andhra Pradesh*, 145–47. This is a version told at the temple of Arsavalli in South India.

8. *The Memoirs of Jacques Casanova*, trans. Machen, 3.15, 469; *Casanova mémoires*, 2.17, 425.

9. Osgood and Luria, "Case Report" (in Thigpen and Cleckley, *Three Faces*, 284).

10. Leavy, *In Search*, 219, 217 n. 91.

11. Ibid., 217 n. 17.

12. Warner, *From the Beast*, 363.

13. Leavy, *In Search*, 217.

14. Li Yu, *The Carnal Prayer Mat*.

15. Desens, *The Bed-Trick*, 69.

16. Ibid., 98.

17. Bowden, "The Bed-Trick," 121.

18. De Murat, "Starlight," 149–87.

19. Ramanujan, "Two Realms of Kannada Folklore," 58–61. I have condensed and paraphrased his telling.

20. *Jataka* 498, *Cittasambhuta*.

21. Assayag, *La colère de la déesse décapitée*, 41–46.

22. Ramanujan, "Two Realms of Kannada Folklore," 61.

23. "In the Court of Destiny," in Kirin Narayan, *Mondays on the Dark Night of the Moon*, 145.

24. Heliodorus, *Aithiopika* 4.8 (trans. Reardon, 432–33).

25. Reardon, "An Ethiopian Story," 433, citing Achilles Tatius 3.7 and Philostratos, *Imagines* 1.29.

26. Jerome, *Hebrew Questions*, on Genesis 33 (trans. Hayward, 67).

27. Doniger and Spinner, "Misconceptions." I owe some of the ideas in this paragraph to a personal communication (Aug. 1999) from Benjamin Braude, who will develop them in a forthcoming book tentatively entitled *Sex, Slavery, and Racism* (New York: Alfred Knopf).

28. Gillman, *Dark Twins*, 79.

29. Larsen, *Passing*, 60.

30. Garber, *Vice Versa*, 444.

31. Doane, *Femmes Fatales*, 235.

32. Ibid., 235.

33. Ibid., 237.

34. "Twins—With Two Fathers," *Newsweek*, July 3, 1995, 38.

35. Jim Yardley, "After Embryo Mix-Up, Couple Say They Will Give Up a Baby," *New York Times*, Mar. 30, 1999, B1, col. 2.

36. Jim Yardley, "Health Officials Investigating to Determine How Woman Got the Embryo of Another," *New York Times*, Mar. 31, 1999, B3, 1.

37. Laurie MacDonald, coproducer of *Men in Black*, cited by Kurt Andersen, "The Origin of Alien Species," *New Yorker*, July 14, 1997, 38–39.

38. Freud, "The Question of Lay Analysis," 212.

39. Gilman, "Black Bodies," 238.

40. Gates, "Editor's Introduction."

41. Doane, *Femmes Fatales*, 246.

42. Richard Wright, "Man of All Work."

43. Garber, *Vested Interests*, 293.

44. Summary by Lewis Jacobs, in Leyda and Musser, *Before Hollywood*, 112.

45. Mayne, "Uncovering the Female Body," 66.

46. Scott, *The Jewel in the Crown*, 242, 269.

47. Doyle, "The Case of Lady Sannox."

48. Showalter, *Sexual Anarchy*, 136.

49. Ibid.

50. Ibid., 134.

51. Speaking at the meeting of the American Council of Learned Societies, in Washington, D.C., on Apr. 26, 1996.

52. Nandy, *The Intimate Enemy,* 7–8; Spivak, "Can the Subaltern Speak?"

53. Hwang, afterword to *M. Butterfly,* 94, 98.

54. Ibid., 94.

55. Ibid., 98.

56. The title of this section, the punch line of an old joke, is the advice allegedly given to Prince Charles on the eve of his marriage to Princess Diana, by a friend who knew that the prince was in love with another woman.

57. Desens, *The Bed-Trick,* 54.

58. Thomas Heywood, *The Fair Maid of the West,* 3.1.5–8, 13–18.

59. *Midrash Rabbah* on Genesis 29.18 (Soncino ed.: pp. 111–16 of the Hebrew text, pp. 647–51 of the English translation).

60. Handelman, "The Guises of the Goddess."

61. Ron Rosenbaum, "The Spy Who Created the Cold," *New York Times Magazine,* July 10, 1954, 30–31.

62. Le Carré, *The Little Drummer Girl,* 376–77.

63. The sexual and political levels combine in another variant of the basic trope: "Put a flag over her face and fuck her for Old Glory!"

64. Levinas, *Totality and Infinity,* 198–99.

65. The classic political film double occurs in *The Great Dictator* (1940), in which Charlie Chaplin impersonates Adolf Hitler. This burlesque was further burlesqued in *To Be or Not to Be* (1942), in which an actor (Jack Benny) and his company masquerades, onstage and then off, as Hitler and an entire Gestapo troop. And that film was burlesqued, in turn, by Mel Brooks in a film by the same title in 1983, which also added a cross-dresser, for good measure: another double to the third degree.

66. David Ansen, in *Newsweek,* May 10, 1993, 59.

67. Terrence Rafferty, "Accept No Substitute," review of *Dave* (movie), *New Yorker,* May 17, 1993, 101–2.

68. Goldsmith, *Switcheroo,* 92.

69. Graham, *Boris Godunof,* 226–57.

70. Robert C. Marsh, "Boris Godunov: The Opera and the Man," pp. 67–71 of the 1994–95 Chicago Lyric Opera program of Mussorgsky's *Boris Godunov.*

71. Other paranoid dictators (including Saddam Hussein) also adopted this technique to draw off attempted assassins.

72. Rushdie, *The Moor's Last Sigh,* 29–32.

73. Treitel, "Stalin, Stalin, and Stalin."

74. Ibid.

75. Alison Lurie, "Bookend: Reading at Escape Velocity," *New York Times Book Review,* May 17, 1998, 51.

76. Doniger, *The Implied Spider,* 105.

77. Sedgwick, *Epistemology of the Closet.*

78. Wagner, *Siegfried,* in *The Ring of the Nibelung,* 218–19: "Du einz'ge hat ihre Angst mich gelehrt."

APPROACH SEVEN

79. Chilli, *Folk-Tales of Hindustan,* 98–108.

80. Ramanujan, "Towards a Counter-System," 52–53.

81. Doniger, *The Implied Spider,* 101–3.

82. Singer, *Enemies, A Love Story*, 247.

83. Radin, *The Trickster*; Dorje, *Tales of Uncle Tompa*.

84. Gillman, *Dark Twins*, 77.

85. James Scott, *Weapons of the Weak*. In *Tender Is the Night*, F. Scott Fitzgerald had written of the "tyranny of the weak," speaking of psychological, rather than political, weakness.

86. Ginzburg, "Morelli," 24.

87. From the *Raleigh (N.C.) News and Observer*, cited in *New Yorker*, July 22, 1996, 73.

88. Foucault, *History of Sexuality*.

89. This line, which was not in the original printed or performed edition of *Travesties*, was later added by Tom Stoppard after the crisis of Gorbachev and Yeltsin in August 1991 and has become part of the stage tradition.

90. Sedgwick, *Epistemology of the Closet*, 4–5.

91. Ibid., 33.

Chapter Eight

1. *Brahmanda Purana* 4.10.41–77; O'Flaherty, *Siva*, 228–29.

2. Shulman, *God Inside Out*, 157–58.

3. *Mahabharata*, bk. 16 *(Mausala Parvan).*

4. *Mahabharata* 4.21.1–67, with a verse omitted from the critical edition after 4.21.46.

5. *Padma Purana, Svarga Khanda*, 16.6–24; O'Flaherty, *Textual Sources*, 98.

6. *Kamasutra* 1.2.36, 1.3.15, apropos of arts nos. 57 and 58 of the list of sixty-four.

7. *Bodhisattvabadanakalpalata* of Kshemendra; I am grateful to Matthew Schmalz for this text and its translation. See also a Sanskrit version, Kshemendra's *Avadanakalpalata*, no. 66.

8. *Harivamsha* 47–48; O'Flaherty, *Hindu Myths*, 205–13.

9. Songling, "Die Rächerin," in *Schmetterlinge fliegen lassen*, 222–26. I am indebted to Paize Keulemans for this passage. See also Zeitlin, *Historian of the Strange*, chap. 4, "Dislocations in Gender."

10. Zeitlin, *Historian of the Strange*, 125.

11. Henry Fielding, *Joseph Andrews*, bk. 4, chap. 14, pp. 298–303.

12. Singer, "Yentl the Yeshiva Boy," 149–69.

13. Senelick, "The Illusion of Sex," 14, in reference to the film *Sylvia Scarlett*.

14. David Ansen, *Newsweek*, July 20, 1992, p. 69.

15. *Victor/Victoria, the Musical*, book by Blake Edwards, music by Henry Mancini, lyrics by Leslie Bricusse, directed by Blake Edwards. With Julie Andrews, Tony Roberts, Michael Nouri, Rachel York.

16. Bell-Metereau, *Hollywood Androgyne*, 114.

17. Peter Marks, "Good Man Hard to Find: Raquel Welch's 'Victor,'" *New York Times*, June 27, 1997.

18. As told in a 1947 *Reader's Digest* story, hence the form of the title.

19. Garber, *Vice Versa*, 135, 138, 147–48.

20. This much-quoted line inverts the utterance attributed to a woman who had just been told that the handsome, multitalented, and prominently married Leonard Bernstein was gay: "Is there nothing that man can't do?"

21. Barthes, *S/Z*, 144.

22. Ibid., 198.

23. Riche, "Phylotus and Emilia."

24. The actual names Shirley uses are as follows: for Alberto, Cornelio; for Phylotus, Rufaldo; for Flanius, Infortunio; for Phylerno, Antonio; for Emelia, Selina; and for Brisilla, Hilaria.

25. Natesa, *Tales of Tennalirama*, 11–14.

26. "The Story of Qamar al-Zaman and His Two Sons," in *The Arabian Nights II*, trans. Haddawy, 165–268. In the Burton translation it is the 216th night, vol. 2, 1150–52. See Doniger, *Rings*.

27. Knowles, "The Young Gambling Merchant," 294–95.

28. Sidney, *The Countess of Pembroke's Arcadia*, 3.4.675, 4.2.724–38.

29. Garber, *Vested Interests*, 412.

30. Woolf, *Orlando*, 252, 258.

31. Twain, "1,002nd Arabian Night"; Doniger, *Rings*.

32. Garber, *Vested Interests*, 4.

33. Shepherd, Kohut, and Sweet, *News of the Weird*, 9.

34. Willig, introduction to *The Changelings;* Miner, *The Princeton Companion*, 250; Doniger, *The Implied Spider*, 133.

35. It is criticized in another work of that date.

36. Pflugfelder, "Strange Fates," 348.

37. Miner, *The Princeton Companion*, 249–50.

38. Obeyesekere, "The Tale of the Demoness Kali."

39. *The Holy Teachings of Vimalakirti*, trans. Thurman, 56, 61–62.

40. Pflugfelder, "Strange Fates," 368.

41. Ibid., 362.

42. Pausanias, *Description of Greece*, 9.31.6.

43. Pflugfelder, "Strange Fates," 367.

44. Middlebrook, *Suits Me;* Kay, *Trumpets*.

45. Garber, *Vested Interests*, 68.

46. Ibid., 47.

47. Casanova, *History of My Life*, 2.1, 5–6, 15, 16.

48. Ibid., 17–18, 20.

49. Ibid., 10–21.

50. Ibid., 17–18, 20.

51. Kates, *Monsieur d'Eon Is a Woman*.

52. Wadler, "The Spy Who Fell in Love with a Shadow."

53. Garber, *Vested Interests*, 238.

54. Eberhard, *Folktales of China*, 204.

55. Ibid., no. 15, pp. 21–24; Eberhard, *Typen*, no. 212, with eleven texts.

56. Wadler, "The Spy Who Fell in Love with a Shadow," 36.

57. Ho, *Liang Shan-po yü Chu Ying-t'ai*.

58. Sid Smith, "An Unconventional Love Story."

59. "Bond 'Girl' Was a Man," in *Luxury Lifestyles of the Rich and Famous*, Apr. 1998, 24. Barry Cossey became Caroline, better known as Tula.

60. Associated Press, reported in the *Chicago Tribune*, Jan. 9, 1997, sec. 1, p. 18.

61. *Weekly World News*, Oct. 20, 1992, 24–25.

62. Cameron Diaz, "Lost, and Gained, in the Translation," *New York Times*, Nov. 15, 1998, Week in Review, p. 2. Though widely reported as fact, this translation was the inspired invention of the Web site www.topfive.com.

63. Dunne, "A Reporter at Large," 53.

64. Ibid., 52.

65. Roselli, *Singers,* 52.

66. Dunne, "A Reporter at Large," 54.

67. Janet Maslin, review of *Boys Don't Cry* (movie), in *New York Times,* Oct. 1, 1999, B10.

68. Dunne, "A Reporter at Large," 50–51.

69. Wadler, "The Spy Who Fell in Love with a Shadow," 37.

70. Garber, *Vested Interests,* 235.

71. Wadler, "The Spy Who Fell in Love with a Shadow," 50.

72. Wadler, "For the First Time."

73. Dorje, *Tales of Uncle Tompa,* 36–38.

Approach Eight

74. Hillel Schwartz, *The Culture of the Copy,* 197–99. According to CBS TV's *Entertainment Tonight,* Feb. 22, 1993, some of the women who were body doubles in nude scenes tried, in vain at that time, to get their names on the credits.

75. Garber, *Vested Interests,* 40.

76. Reynolds, "Ruggiero's Deceptions," 138.

77. Ibid., 137.

78. Poizat, *The Angel's Cry,* 39.

79. Padel, "Putting the Words into Women's Mouths," 13.

80. Reynolds, "Ruggiero's Deceptions," 132.

81. Ibid., 133.

82. Blackmer and Smith, *En Travesti,* 5.

83. Arthur Davis, *More Traditional Ballads of Virginia,* 286.

84. Thomas Middleton, *Micro-Cynicon,* in *Works,* vol. 3, 130–44.

85. Rose, *Parallel Lives,* 26.

86. Woolf, *Orlando,* 269.

87. Richlin, "Making Up a Woman," 204, citing Seneca, *Controversiae,* 5.6.

88. Devor, *Gender Blending,* 132–33.

89. Garber, *Vested Interests,* 213.

90. Mark Twain, "'Feud Story' and 'The Girl Who Was Ostensibly a Man'"; Gillman, *Dark Twins,* 201 n. 25.

91. Paul Smith, thirty-six, married Debi Easterday, forty-one, a lesbian; he plans to undergo a sex change operation (Akron, Ohio, Dec. 12, 1996; reported in a Seattle newspaper). Kate Bornstein's *Gender Outlaw* is the story of a heterosexual male who became a lesbian woman.

92. For this trope in ancient India, see Doniger, "The Dreams and Dramas," "Jewels of Rejection," "The Masques of Gods and Demons," and *Rings.*

93. Butler, "Lacan, Rivière," 47; Doane, *Femmes Fatales,* 38.

Chapter Nine

1. Bloomfield, "Contributions," 181; Adalbert Kuhn, "Saranyu-Erinnus," 448; Bergaigne, *La religion védique,* ii, 318.

2. *Rig Veda* 10.10; O'Flaherty, *The Rig Veda,* 247–50, selected verses. The Ashvins, too, have an incestuous relationship with their sister Suryā, another daughter of the Sun (and, presumably, of Samjna) (*Rig Veda* 10.85.14). Greek texts tell of the parallel incestuous relationship between the Dioscuri—the Greek version of the Ashvins—and their sister Helen, and in Egypt a similar story is told about Isis and Osiris, also part of a solar family.

3. Warner, *From the Beast*, 331–32.

4. Ramanujan, "Hanchi," 267–68.

5. Leach, "Anthropological Aspects of Language."

6. *Jaiminiya Brahmana* 3.199–200; O'Flaherty, *Tales of Sex and Violence*, 75–76.

7. Rank, *The Double*, 99.

8. Obeyesekere, *Medusa's Hair*.

9. Huilgol, *The Panchatantra of Vasubhaga*, 1, "The Valuable Stanza."

10. Levine, "Three Talmudic Tales of Seduction," 469.

11. Perry, *Secundus the Silent Philosopher*, opening of the Greek text, lines 1–15, pp. 68–71. I have used Perry's translation in devising my own.

12. Marguerite de Navarre, *Heptameron*, 317–21 (day 3, story 30).

13. A sixth film about a child who travels back in time to become her parents' contemporary was made during this period, though not involving mother-son incest: *Peggy Sue Got Married* (1986). An earlier film, *Freaky Friday* (1976), weaves much the same plot around a mother and daughter who change places.

14. Warner, *From the Beast*, 323.

15. Fauset, "Negro Folk Tales from the South," 243–44.

16. Dundes, "'To Love My Father All,'" 236.

17. Isabel Carter, "Mountain White Folklore: 361–63.

18. Ovid, *Metamorphoses* 10.295–500.

19. Aristotle, *De Animalium Generatione* 9.47.

20. Halliwell, *Halliwell's Film Guide*, 894.

21. *Rig Veda* 10.162.5; O'Flaherty, *The Rig Veda*, 292.

22. Doniger, *Rings*.

23. Rainey, *The Whale Hunters of Tigara;* cf. Edith Turner, *The Hands Feel It*, 47.

24. Rank, *The Myth of the Birth of the Hero;* Campbell, *The Hero with a Thousand Faces;* Dundes, "The Hero Pattern and the Life of Jesus."

25. Zvelebil, *Two Tamil Folktales*, 44–52.

26. Angela Carter, *Wise Children*, 217.

27. *Vishnu Purana* 5.27.1–31; cf. *Bhagavata Purana* 10.55.1–12; *Harivamsha* 99; O'Flaherty, *Dreams*, 99–100.

28. *Harivamsha*, passage excised from critical edition after 99.7.

29. *Brahmavaivarta Purana, Krishnajanmakhanda* 112.7–23.

Approach Nine

30. See O'Flaherty, *Other Peoples' Myths*, for storytelling as an event.

31. The term was coined in French (*l'hérédité d'influence*) in 1890 by Théodule Ribot, in *L'hérédité psychologique* (Paris, 1890), 205.

32. Deborah Garrison, reviewing Nicholson Baker's *Vox*, in the *New Yorker*, Mar. 9, 1992, 93.

33. Ramanujan, "Towards a Counter-System," 53.

34. *Skanda Purana* 8.18–19.

35. Garber, *Vested Interests*, 87.

36. Lévi-Strauss, "Language and the Analysis of Social Laws," 61. See Dan Sperber's penetrating critique of this formulation in "Claude Lévi-Strauss," 23.

37. The ideas in this paragraph are based upon an essay by Shaina Mander, June 1999.

38. Erskine, *The Private Life of Helen of Troy*, 57.

39. Cave, *Recognitions*, 4.

40. Doniger, *The Implied Spider*, 79–83; Eliade, *Cosmos and History*.

41. Li Yu, "Nativity Room," 245.

42. "Sister Charged with Murder, and Identity Switch," *New York Times*, July 17, 1997, A16.

43. Associated Press, reported in the *Cape Cod Times*, July 14, 1995.

44. Lutz, *Single White Female*, 140.

45. Goldsmith, *Switcheroo*, 92, 159.

46. Cave, *Recognitions*, 397.

47. He is referring to Herodotus's stories of Candaules† and Gyges† (the man hiding behind the door), 1.10–13, and of Croesus and Atys (the young man mistaken for a boar), 1.34–45. Neither is what I would call a bedtrick.

48. Nathalie Davis, *The Return of Martin Guerre*, 116, citing Henri Estienne, *L'introduction au traité de la conformité des merveilles anciennes avec les modernes*, xviii–xix.

49. Kalidasa, *Abhijnanashakuntalam* 4.1; Doniger, "Jewels of Rejection."

50. David Shulman, pers. comm., Mar. 1993.

51. Indeed, it is false to mammalian experience: as soon as chimpanzees learn to speak, they lie.

52. Zimmer, *The King and the Corpse*, 308.

53. Bloch, *The Scandal of the Fabliaux*, 103, 109.

54. Balzac, *Sarrasine*, 200.

55. Barthes, *S/Z*, 86, 212.

56. Winnicott, *The Family and Individual Development*, 143.

57. Flahaut, "Imagination and Mythology," 790.

58. Eagleton, *Literary Theory*, 185–86.

59. *Midrash Rabbah* on Genesis 29.18 (Soncino ed.: pp. 111–16 of the Hebrew text, pp. 647–51 of the English translation).

60. Freud, *Interpretation of Dreams*, 6.E, "Some Further Typical Dreams."

61. Doniger, *The Implied Spider*, 79.

62. I am indebted to Shantanu Phukan for this etymology; pers. comm., Oct. 19, 1996.

63. Warner, *From the Beast*, 330–32.

64. Barthes, *S/Z*, 144.

65. Rank, *The Double*, 53.

66. Segal, "Doubles," 160.

67. Kleist, *Amphitryon*, 2.4.

68. Ibid., 1.2.

69. Marias, *Tomorrow in the Battle*, 174, 182, 191.

70. Ingalls, *An Anthology of Sanskrit Court Poetry*, 217; see *Kamasutra* 2.10.27.

71. Kalidasa, *Abhijnanashakuntalam* 6.5.

72. Goldsmith, *Switcheroo*, 245, 202.

73. Rosamond Smith, *Lives of the Twins*, 144–45, 202.

74. Stephen Ambrose, *Eisenhower*, 1.278.

75. David Margolick, "Smith Lawyers Assail Accuser's Memory," *New York Times*, Dec. 6, 1991.

76. "Smith's Accuser, on TV, Says, 'I'm Not a Blue Blob,'" *New York Times*, Dec. 20, 1991.

77. Sabbah, *Woman in the Muslim Unconscious*, 106. This concept is also recorded in early Jewish sources.

Chapter Ten

1. *Tapati-Samvaranam†* of Kulashekhara Varman: asambhavitatiraskariko 'pi kada cit.

2. *The Romance and Prophecies of Thomas of Erceldoune.*

3. *Vinaya Pitaka, Mahavagga*, 1.63.5.

4. *Markandeya Purana* 58–61.

5. Marana wrote one version of the entire *Markandeya Purana*, and then King Krishnadevaraja's best poet, Allasani Peddana, wrote a poem (called a *prabandha* in Telugu) about the part of the *Purana* about Manu Svarocisha. David Shulman translated and annotated portions of this poem in his essay "The First Man." An unpublished English translation of the poem, the Peddana text, by Hank Heifitz and Narayana Rao, was summarized for me by Narayana Rao. This is my summary of Narayana Rao's summary of Peddana's poem.

6. *Vayu Purana* 2.8.131–40.

7. Yu, *Journey to the West*, 3.75.414.

8. O'Flaherty, *Dreams*, 81–89, 132–57.

9. *Kojiki* 1.45.156–57.

10. *Brahmanda Purana* 2.3.59.75: maithunaantanivishta ca parapumso 'bhishankayaa. This is a variant of the *Harivamsha* reading, 8.27: maithunaaya viceshtantiim parapumso vishankayaa (*she struggled against mating* because she feared that he might be another male).

11. *Genesis Rabbah* 19.2–3.

12. *Kathasaritsagara* 33 [6.7].156–217.

13. Doniger, "Jewels of Rejection"; Doniger, "The Dreams and Dramas."

14. *Kathasaritsagara* 105 [14.21].1–63.

15. Penzer, *Ocean of Story*, 8.25.

16. Garber, *Vested Interests*, 203.

17. Doniger, *Rings*.

18. Wagner, *Valkyries*, in *The Ring of the Nibelung*, 151: "'So küsst er die Gottheit von dir.' Er kusst sie lange auf die Augen. Sie sinkt mit geschlossenen Augen, sanft ermattend, in seinen Armen zurück."

19. Bain, *Cossack Fairy Tales*, 198.

20. Knowles, "The Young Gambling Merchant," 294–95.

21. Murdoch, *The Sea*, 213.

22. Giraudoux, "*Amphitryon*," 88.

23. Behrman, "*Amphitryon 38*," 172.

24. Basinger, *How Hollywood Spoke to Women*, 86.

25. Ibid., 93.

26. Doniger, "When a Lingam Is Just a Good Cigar."

27. Leach, "Magical Hair," 159.

28. Marglin, *Wives of the God-King*, 214–15; the story was told by P. C. Mishra.

29. Li Yu, "Nativity Room."

30. Dahl, "The Great Switcheroo," 62.

31. Plutarch, *Parallel Lives*, Romulus, 2.

32. Radin, *The Trickster*.

33. O'Flaherty, *Siva*, 123.

34. Jong, *Fear of Flying*.

35. Dekkers, *Dearest Pet*, 30.

36. *Washington Times*, Oct. 15, 1997; cited by Stuart Taylor, Jr., "At War in *Jones v. Clinton*," in *Newsweek*, Oct. 27, 1997, 66.

37. Robert Bennett, on CBS's *Face the Nation*, Oct. 12, 1997; cited by Stuart Taylor, Jr., "At War in *Jones v. Clinton*," in *Newsweek*, Oct. 27, 1997, 66.

38. Billy Wilder had Curtis and Lemmon go into a ladies' room to test their drag: no women shrieked, so he declared that they had got the makeup and wigs right, and told them not to change it.

39. Lacan, "The Agency of the Letter in the Unconscious," 151.

40. Dimock, *Mr. Dimock Explores the Mysteries of the East*, 31.

41. Dunne, "A Reporter at Large," 54.

42. Devor, *Gender Blending*, 122.

43. Medhatithi, commenting on *The Laws of Manu* 11.106 (104 in the Dave ed.); Doniger, *The Laws of Manu*, 261.

44. Desens, *The Bed-Trick*, 15.

45. Ibid., 13.

46. Nathalie Davis, *The Return of Martin Guerre*, 109.

47. Finlay, "The Refashioning of Martin Guerre," 556.

48. Nathalie Davis, "On the Lame," 576.

49. Cave, *Recognitions*, 15.

50. Nathalie Davis, *The Return of Martin Guerre*, 42.

51. Ibid., 44.

52. F. Gayot de Pitaval, *Causes célèbres et intéressantes* (Paris 1734), vol. 1, chap. 1, cited by Nathalie Davis, *The Return of Martin Guerre*, 130.

53. Nathalie Davis, *The Return of Martin Guerre*, 86.

54. Ibid., 68–69.

55. Lewis, *The Wife of Martin Guerre*, 51.

56. Nathalie Davis, *The Return of Martin Guerre*, 69.

57. Ibid., 110, 43–44. She cites in her note Etienne Pasquier, *Les recherches de la France* (Paris: L. Sonnius, 1621), 571–72.

58. Finlay, "The Refashioning of Martin Guerre," 558.

59. Cave, *Recognitions*, 397.

60. Doniger, *The Implied Spider*, 102.

61. Finlay, "The Refashioning of Martin Guerre," 559, with footnotes to Plutarch, Erasmus, and Darnton.

62. Ibid., 559, 562.

63. Nathalie Davis, "The Lame," 578.

64. Ibid.

65. Ibid., 579.

66. Garber, *Vested Interests*, 47.

67. Giraudoux, *Ondine*, 235.

68. Doniger, *The Implied Spider*, 95.

69. Rosenfield, "The Shadow Within," 314.

70. Wain, *The Living World of Shakespeare*, 111.

71. Bowden, "The Bed-Trick," 111.

72. Ibid., 121.

73. Benchley, "Opera Synopses," 67.

74. Cave, *Recognitions*, 38.

75. Nathalie Davis, *The Return of Martin Guerre*, 110.

76. Kalidasa, *Abhijnanashakuntalam* 4.1.

77. Defoe, *Moll Flanders*, 75–76; Dinesen, "The Monkey," 127.

78. "Man Is Acquitted in '91 Barroom Rape That Stirred Sex-Abuse Debate," *New York Times*, Mar. 26, 1996, A17.

79. Doniger, "Jewels of Rejection."

80. Rose, *Parallel Lives*, 145.

81. In 1991, a Dr. Sebollena "injected two male patients with the drug Versed, a central-nervous-system depressant that leaves a person conscious but immobile, and performed oral sex on them" (Fredric Dannen, "The G-Man and the Hit Man," *New Yorker*, Dec. 16, 1996, 74). A dentist named Nicholas A. Polito was convicted in 1970 of battery and deviate sexual assault after several women patients said they had been sexually assaulted after he had given them a general anesthetic. He was arrested in 1969 by police who broke down his door and found him sexually assaulting his receptionist, whom he had anesthetized (*Chicago Sun Times*, Feb. 3, 1981).

82. Jacques Steinberg, "As Freshmen Work on Their Timetables, Parents Take a Short Course in Letting Go," *New York Times*, Aug. 21, 1991, A7.

83. *TV Guide*, Apr. 28, 1996.

84. Cave, *Recognitions*, 3.

85. Plautus, *Amphitryon*, "interpolated scenes" composed by Cardinal Hermolaus Barbarus in 1480 in imitation of Plautus; cited by Passage and Mantinband, *Amphitryon*, 98–99.

86. "A Would-Be-Wife-Stealer Foiled," in Ramachandra Rao, *Tales of Mariada Raman*, 40–41.

87. Teit, *Mythology of the Thompson Indians*, 354–55.

88. Plautus, *Amphitryon*, lines 316, 445.

89. Bloom, *The Book of J*, 215.

90. Barthes, *S/Z*, 167, 178.

91. Davies, *The Lyre of Orpheus*, 271, 247–48.

92. Ibid., 249–50.

93. Molina, *The Trickster of Seville*, x.

94. Erica Goode, "To Tell the Truth, It's Awfully Hard to Spot a Liar," *New York Times*, May 11, 1999, D1, D9; reporting on a study by Dr. Bella DePaulo at the University of Virginia.

95. Kuhn, *The Nature of Scientific Revolutions*; Festinger, *A Theory of Cognitive Dissonance*.

96. Bruner and Postman, "On the Perception of Incongruity," 222.

97. Garber, *Vice Versa*, 231.

98. Willig, *The Changelings*, 164.

99. Morris, *Conundrum*, 111.

100. Ibid., 105.

101. Angela Carter, *Wise Children*, 83.

102. Barbara Walters, Oct. 8, 1993, broadcast of an interview with Boursicot and Shi Pei Pu.

103. Adelman, "Bed Tricks," 153.

104. *The Memoirs of Jacques Casanova*, trans. Machen, 3.15, 469; *Casanova mémoires*, 2.17, 425.

105. *The Matsya Purana*, ed. Akhtar, 1.34.

106. Abu-Lughod, *Veiled Sentiments,* 138.

107. Lewis, *The Wife of Martin Guerre,* 44.

108. Angela Carter, *Wise Children,* 208.

109. Woolf, *Orlando,* 169–70.

110. Krappe, "Far Eastern Fox Lore," 136.

111. de Visser, "The Fox and the Badger," 145.

112. Abe, *The Face of Another,* 208.

113. Leach, "Anthropological Aspects of Language."

114. Wasson and O'Flaherty, *Soma.*

115. Mann, *Joseph and His Brothers,* 202.

116. Dahl, "The Great Switcheroo," 67.

117. García Márquez, *One Hundred Years,* 32, 34–35.

118. Euripides, *Helen,* trans. Lattimore, l.500.

119. Marias, *Tomorrow in the Battle,* 183.

120. Doniger, "Jewels of Rejection."

121. Krappe, "Far Eastern Fox Lore," 124.

122. Ginzburg, "Morelli," 25.

123. Nathalie Davis, *The Return of Martin Guerre,* 63.

124. Leavy, *In Search,* 302.

125. Kakar and Ross, *Tales of Love, Sex, and Danger,* 9.

126. O'Flaherty, *Dreams,* 61–80.

127. *Kamasutra* 2.10.21.

128. Ibid., 2.7.32.

129. Huet, *Monstrous Imagination,* 6, 17.

130. Doniger, *The Implied Spider,* 84–88.

131. Rossner, *Looking for Mr. Goodbar.*

132. Soran, *Gynecology* 1, par. 39; Doniger and Spinner, "Misconceptions."

133. Basinger, *How Hollywood Spoke to Women,* 100.

134. Rycroft, *The Innocence of Dreams.*

135. Harsha, *Ratnavali.*

136. Erskine, *The Private Life of Helen of Troy,* 43, 57.

137. Ibid., 235.

138. This remark, which Freud made in a letter to Wilhelm Fliess on Aug. 1, 1899, is cited in footnote 5 on p. 205 of Ernest Jones's biography of Freud, *Book One: The Formative Years, The Fliess Period (1887–1902).* Erich Fromm cites it, quoting Jones (and supplying the date), on p. 44 of his *Sigmund Freud's Mission.* Jeffrey Moussaieff Masson published a translation of it in *Complete Letters of Freud,* p. 364.

139. Letter to Fliess, Jan. 4, 1898: "You yourself said that each of the two halves probably contains both kinds of sex organs. But where, then, is the femininity, for instance, of the left half of a man if it carries testicles (and the corresponding lower male/female sexual organs) just like the right one? Your postulate that for all results male and female must unite is already satisfied, after all, in one half!" (Masson, *Complete Letters of Freud,* 292).

140. Dr. Martin Stein, pers. comm., Oct. 8, 1994. Indeed, it has long been a truism that there are always more than two people in the room during analysis.

141. Abe, *The Face of Another,* 192.

142. O'Flaherty, *Dreams,* 240–44, 258–59.

143. Bowden, "The Bed-Trick," 114.

144. Kirtley, "'La Llorona' and Related Themes," 157–59.

145. Anne Tolstoi Wallach, writing in *New York Times Book Review*, July 7, 1991, 14.

146. *Gemara Pesachim*, b. Pesachim 112a. Thanks to Gregory Spinner for this citation.

147. *Zohar*, Mishpatim (the commentary on Exodus 21.1–24.18), 102a–102b (trans. Sperling, Simon, and Levertoff, 309–12).

148. This happens in Hindu mythology, too: when Brihaspati raped the pregnant wife of his brother, Utathya, the child already in the womb kicked out the intruding penis (*Mahabharata* 1.98.7–17).

149. Sizemore, *A Mind of My Own*, 59.

150. Gary Libman, "A Survivor Savors Living Just One Life," copyright 1989, The Times Mirror Company, *Los Angeles Times*, Oct. 20, 1989, Friday, Home ed., pt. E, p. 1, col. 2.

151. Wallace and Wallace, *The Two*, 180, 183.

152. Ibid., 183.

153. Hugo Williams, *Times Literary Supplement*, Feb. 25, 1994, 14.

APPROACH TEN

154. Lévi-Strauss, *Myth and Meaning*, 29.

155. Ibid., 29–30.

156. Lévi-Strauss, *The Jealous Potter*.

157. Lotman, "The Semiosphere," 152.

158. Doniger, *The Implied Spider*, 88–94.

159. Ibid., 31, 65, 90.

160. Ibid., 157–58.

161. Lévi-Strauss, "The Structural Study of Myth" and "The Story of Asdiwal."

162. Giraudoux, "Amphitryon," 44; cf. Behrman, "Amphitryon 38," 101.

163. Abe, *The Face of Another*, 93.

164. Bronner, "Poetry at Its Extreme."

165. Rushdie, *Shame*, 116; Rushdie, *Haroun and the Sea of Stories*, 160.

CONCLUSION

1. Sizemore, *A Mind of My Own*, 49–50.

2. Barbara Walters, Oct. 8, 1993, broadcast of an interview with Boursicot and Shi Pei Pu.

3. Taggart, *Enchanted Maidens*, 93.

4. Angela Carter, *Wise Children*, 221–22.

5. As William Wordsworth defined the origins of poetry, in his preface to the second edition of his *Lyrical Ballads* (1800).

6. This philosophy is reflected in Norman Mailer's alleged statement that you never really get to know a woman until you confront her in divorce court.

7. Written by Ron Romanovsky in 1985 and recorded by Romanovsky and Philips in an album called *Trouble in Paradise*, in 1986.

8. Obeyesekere, *Medusa's Hair*.

9. Wilde, *The Picture of Dorian Gray*, 200.

10. Davies, *The Lyre of Orpheus*, 273.

11. Dr. Frank Pittman, cited by Jerry Adler, "Adultery: A New Furor over an Old Sin," *Newsweek*, Sept. 30, 1996, 56.

12. P. D. J. Weitzman cited this in a letter, under the heading, "Is it ever acceptable for ministers to lie to Parliament?" in the *Times* (London), Mar. 10, 1994.

13. Angela Carter, *Wise Children,* 102.

14. Roth, *The Tale of the 1002nd Night,* 72.

15. Larson, "'Women Understand So Little,'" 449, 465.

16. Ned Zeman, review of *The Janus Report on Sexual Behavior,* by Samuel S. Janus and Cynthia L. Janus, *Newsweek,* Mar. 8, 1993, 56.

17. Lewontin, "Sex, Lies, and Social Science."

18. Anthony Lane, "Sex in America," review of *The Social Organization of Sexuality, New Yorker,* Dec. 19, 1994, 110–14.

19. Erica Goode, "To Tell the Truth, It's Awfully Hard to Spot a Liar," *New York Times,* May 11, 1999, D1, D9; reporting on a study by Dr. Bella DePaulo at the University of Virginia.

20. Japanese doctors, using a technique invented by the Chinese, are now able to sew up the hymen in a kind of reflowering operation. It is, therefore, possible to fake a maidenhead.

21. Gottfried von Strassburg, *Tristan,* 205.

22. But pregnancy, too, can be concealed. The *New York Times* in Aug. 1997 documented the case of girl who gave birth to a baby in the bathroom at her senior prom, destroyed the baby, and went back to the prom and danced, with no one the wiser; she was convicted in 1998.

23. Neely, *Broken Nuptials,* 101.

24. The widespread marketing of the drug Viagra, which claims to cure impotence, has now made it possible, in a sense, to fake an erection.

25. "Dandy and a female were courting each other surreptitiously. Dandy (a young, subdominant male) began to make advances to the female, at the same time restlessly looking around to see if any of the other males were watching. Male chimpanzees start their advances by sitting with their legs wide apart revealing their erection. Precisely at the point when Dandy was exhibiting his sexual urge in this way, Luit, one of the older males, unexpectedly came around the corner. Dandy immediately dropped his hands over his penis, concealing it from view" (De Waals, *Good Natured,* 77).

26. Adelman, "Bed Tricks," 158.

27. Rushdie, *The Moor's Last Sigh,* 425–26.

28. Jagendorf, "'In the Morning,'" 51.

29. Ibid., 55.

30. Ibid., 52.

31. Pos estai touto, epei andra ou gignosko?

32. Miles, *Carnal Knowing,* 8–9.

33. Cave, *Recognitions,* 3.

34. Foucault, *Hercule Barbin,* x–xi.

35. Luce Irigaray, discussed by Butler, "Passing, Queering," 266.

36. Hubner, *Bottom Feeders,* 62.

37. Marias, *Tomorrow in the Battle,* 203, 205.

38. Schnitzler, "Casanova's Homecoming," 231.

39. Angela Carter, "The Bloody Chamber," 26.

40. Cave, *Recognitions,* 7.

41. Lodge, *Small World,* 369–71.

42. Kundera, *The Unbearable Lightness of Being,* 200.

43. Doniger, "The Mythology of Masquerading Animals."

44. Mendelsohn, *The Elusive Embrace*, 74.

45. Jonathan Lear, review of Mendelsohn, *The Elusive Embrace*, in *New York Times Book Review*, July 4, 1999, 7.

46. Mendelsohn, *The Elusive Embrace*, 73–74.

47. Delbanco, *In the Nature of Mercy*, 230.

48. Dillard, *The Living*, 269–70.

49. Cave, *Recognitions*, 270.

50. Doniger, "Playing the Field."

51. See O'Flaherty, *Other Peoples' Myths*, chap. 1, for the Hindu embodiment of this metaphor, the myth of the sage who goes inside the hunter.

52. Jagendorf, "'In the Morning,'" 52.

53. Desens, *The Bed-Trick*, 75.

54. Thomas Middleton, *The Family of Love*, 5.3.288–93.

55. Abe, *The Face of Another*, 222 and 224.

56. Ibid., 225.

57. Doniger, *The Implied Spider*, 79–83.

Appendix

1. The numbers in the following outline refer to the motifs in Thompson, *Motif-Index* and in Thompson and Balys, *Oral Tales of India;* the tale types (TT) are from Aarne and Thompson, *The Types of the Folk-Tale.*

2. Rushdie, *Haroun*, 73.

BIBLIOGRAPHY

One-time citations from newspapers or magazines occur only in the relevant note, and there in full.

ANCIENT AND MEDIEVAL SOURCES

Works are alphabetized by title or, when known, by author. Where the transliteration of a key word in an edition differs from mine, I have included in brackets the spelling used in the edition.

Aelian. *On the Characteristics of Animals.* Text, with trans. by A. F. Scholfield. Cambridge, Mass.: Loeb Classical Library, 1958.

Alphonsus, Emperor of Germany. (Attributed to George Chapman.) Facsimile reprint of 1664 ed. New York and London: G. P. Putnam's Sons, 1913.

Apocryphon of John. Trans. Frederik Wisse. In *Nag Hammadi Library in English,* 104–23.

Apollodorus. *The Library.* Text, with trans. by J. G. Frazer. 2 vols. Cambridge, Mass.: Loeb Classical Library, 1921.

Apuleius. *The Golden Ass.* Trans. P. G. Walsh. Oxford and New York: Oxford University Press, 1994.

The Arabian Nights. Trans. Richard Burton. 16 vols. Benares: Printed by the Kamashastra Society for Private Subscribers Only, 1885.

The Arabian Nights. Trans. Husain Haddawy, based on the text edited by Muhsin Mahdi. New York: W. W. Norton, 1990.

The Arabian Nights II: Sindbad and Other Popular Stories. Trans. Husain Haddawy. New York: W. W. Norton, 1995.

Aristotle. *Historia Animalium.* Vol. 4 of *The Works of Aristotle,* ed. and trans. J. A. Smith and W. D. Ross. Oxford: At the Clarendon Press, 1919.

———. *On the Generation of Animals (De Animalium Generatione).* Text, with trans. by A. L. Peck. Cambridge, Mass.: Loeb Classical Library, 1953.

———. *Poetics.* Trans. Stephen Halliwell. Chicago: University of Chicago Press, 1998.

Ashvaghosha [Asvaghosa]. *Buddhacarita* [*The Buddhakarita of Asvaghosa*]. Ed. E. B. Cowell. Oxford: Oxford University Press, 1893.

Ashvashastra [*Asvasastra*]. (Attributed to Nakula.) Ed. S. Gopalan. Saraswati Mahal Series, no. 56. Tanjore, 1952.

Babrius and Phaedrus. Text, with trans. by B. E. Perry. Cambridge, Mass.: Loeb Classical Library, 1965.

Babylonian Talmud. For an English translation, see *The Talmud of Babylonia, An American Translation*. Trans. Jacob Neusner. Atlanta, Ga.: Scholars Press, 1992.

Baudhayana Shrauta Sutra of the Taittirya Samhita. Vol. 2. Ed. W. Caland. Calcutta: Asiatic Society, 1913.

Bhagavata Purana. With the commentary of Shridhara. Benares: Pandita Pustakalaya, 1972.

Bible, Septuagint. Greek text, with an English translation by Charles Thomson. *The Septuagint: The Oldest Version of the Old Testament*. Indian Hills, Colo.: Falcon's Wing Press, 1954.

Boccaccio, Giovanni. *Decameron*. Trans. John Payne. Berkeley and Los Angeles: University of California Press, 1982.

Brahma Purana. Gurumandala Series, no. 11. Calcutta, 1954.

Brahmanda Purana. Bombay: Venkateshvara Steam Press, 1857.

Brahmavaivarta Purana. Anandasrama Sanskrit Series no. 102. Poona, 1935.

Brihadaranyaka Upanishad. In *The Early Upanisads*. Trans. Patrick Olivelle. New York and Oxford: Oxford University Press, 1998.

Brihaddevata of Shaunaka. Cambridge: Harvard University Press, 1904.

Les cent nouvelles nouvelles (*The One Hundred New Tales*). Paris: Garnier Frères Libraires-Éditeurs, 1866. See also Diner, *One Hundred New Tales*.

Chandogya Upanishad. In *The Early Upanisads*. Trans. Patrick Olivelle. New York and Oxford: Oxford University Press, 1998.

Chaucer, Geoffrey. *The Canterbury Tales*. Ed. A. C. Cawley. London: Everyman, 1958.

Dhammapadatthakatha (*The Commentary to the Dhammapada*). Ed. H. C. Norman. 4 vols. London: Pali Text Society, 1906–14.

Dhammapadatthakatha. Trans. E. W. Burlingame. 3 vols. Cambridge: Harvard University Press, 1912.

Diodorus Siculus. *Library and History*. Text, with trans. by C. H. Oldfather. 12 vols. Cambridge, Mass.: Loeb Classical Library, 1933–67.

Eschenbach, Wolfram von. *Parzival*. Trans. Jessie Weston. London: D. Nutt, 1894.

Euripides. *Helen*. Text, with trans. by Arthur S. Way. Cambridge, Mass.: Loeb Classical Library, 1912.

———. *Helen*. Trans. Richmond Lattimore. In *The Complete Greek Tragedies*, ed. David Grene and Richmond Lattimore. Chicago: University of Chicago Press, 1959.

Genesis Rabbah. See *Midrash Rabbah*.

Harivamsha. Poona: Bhandarkar Oriental Research Institute, 1969.

Harsha. *Naishadiyacarita*. Bombay: Nirnaya Sagara Press, 1986.

———. *Ratnavali*. Ed. Ashokanath Bhattacharya and Maheshwar Das. Calcutta: Modern Book Agency, 1967.

Heliodorus. *Aithiopika*. In *Collected Ancient Greek Novels*, by B. P. Reardon, 432–34. Berkeley and Los Angeles: University of California Press, 1989.

Herodotus. *History*. Trans. David Grene. Chicago: University of Chicago Press, 1987.

Homer. *Odyssey*. Text, with trans. by A. T. Murray. Cambridge, Mass.: Loeb Classical Library, 1919.

Hypostasis of the Archons. Trans. Bentley Layton. In *Nag Hammadi Library in English*, 161–69.

Introduction to the Jataka. See Warren, *Buddhism.*

Jaiminiya Brahmana. Ed. Raghu Vira and Lokesha Chandra. Sarasvati-vihara Series 31. Nagpur, 1954.

Jatakas [*Jataka Stories*]. Ed. E. B. Cowell. London: Pali Text Society, 1973.

Jayadeva. *Gita Govinda.* Ed. and trans. Barbara Stoler Miller. New York: Columbia University Press, 1977.

Jerome. *Saint Jerome's Hebrew Questions on Genesis.* Trans. C. T. R. Hayward. Oxford: Clarendon Press, 1995.

Jubilees. In *The Old Testament Pseudepigrapha,* vol. 2, ed. James H. Charlesworth. Garden City, N.Y.: Doubleday, 1985.

Kalidasa. *Abhijnanashakuntalam.* With the commentary of Raghava. Bombay: Nirnaya Sagara Press, 1958.

Kalika Purana. Ed. Sri Biswanarayan Sastri. Varanasi: Chowkhamba Sanskrit Series Office, 1972.

Kamasutra of Vatsyayana. With the "Jayamangala" commentary of Shri Yashodhara. Bombay: Lakshmivenkateshvara Steam Press, 1856.

Kathaka Samhita. The standard edition is *Die Samhita der Katha-Sakha.* 3 vols. Leipzig, 1900.

Kathasaritsagara (*The Ocean of the Rivers of Story*). Bombay: Nirnara Sagara Press, 1930. For an English translation, see *The Ocean of Story.* Ed. N. M. Penzer, trans. C. W. Tawney. 10 vols. London: Chas. J. Sawyer, 1924.

"King Kusha: A Jataka Tale." Ed. Anant Pai, retold by Kamala Chadrakant. Amar Citra Katha. Bombay: H. G. Mirchandani for India Book House, Jan. 1980.

Kojiki. Trans. Donald L. Philippi. Tokyo: University of Tokyo Press, 1968.

Kshemendra. *Bodhisattvabadanakalpalata.* Trans. [into Bengali] Saratcandra Dasa. Calcutta: Lipika, 1979.

Lamentations Rabbah. See *Midrash Rabbah.*

The Laws of Manu [*Manavadharmasastra*]. Trans. Wendy Doniger, with Brian K. Smith. Harmondsworth: Penguin Books, 1991. *Manusmriti.* Ed. Harikrishna Jayantakrishna Dave. Bombay: Bharatiya Vidya Bhavan, Bharatiya Vidya Series, vols. 29, 33, 37–40. Bombay, 1972–85.

Legah Tov [Rabbi Tovia b. Eliezer, *Lekach Tob zu Megillat Ruth*]. Ed. S. Bamberger. Mainz, 1887.

Linga Purana. Calcutta: Shri Arunodaraya, 1812.

Mahabharata. Poona: Bhandarkar Oriental Research Institute, 1933–69.

Maitrayani Samhita. Ed. L. von Schroeder. Wiesbaden, 1881.

The Malleus Maleficarum of Heinrich Kramer and James Sprenger. Trans. Montague Summers. New York: Dover, 1971.

Manavadharmasastra. See *The Laws of Manu.*

Marguerite de Navarre [d'Angoulême]. *L'heptaméron.* Paris: Club des Libraires de France, 1964.

———. *Heptameron.* Harmondsworth: Penguin Classics, 1984.

Markandeya Purana. With commentary. Bombay: Venkateshvara Steam Press, 1890.

Matsya Purana. Anandashrama Sanskrit Series, no. 54. Poona, 1907. For an English translation, see *Matsya Purana.* Ed. Jamna Das Akhtar. 2 vols. Delhi: Oriental Publishers, 1972.

Midrash Aseret Hadibrot Verona 1647. Jerusalem: Akademon Jerusalem, 1981.

Midrash of the Ten Commandments. Trans. Joel Rosenberg. *Fiction* 7 (1983), special issue ed. by David Stern.

Midrash Rabbah. Vols. 1–2, *Genesis.* Ed. H. Freedman and M. Simon. London: Soncino, 1939.

Midrash Rabbah. Lamentations. Ed. Salomon Buber. Vilna: Wittwe & Gebruder Romm, 1899.

Midrash Ruth Zutta. Ed. Salomon Buber. Berlin: H. Itzkowski, 1894.

The Nag Hammadi Library in English. Ed. James M. Robinson. 3d, rev. ed. San Francisco: Harper & Row, 1988.

The Nibelungenlied (Das Ring des Nibelungen). Trans. A. T. Hatto. Harmondsworth: Penguin Books, 1965.

Ovid. *Metamorphoses.* Text, with trans. by Frank Justus Miller. Cambridge: Loeb Classical Library, 1977.

Padma Purana. Anandashrama Sanskrit Series, no. 131. Poona, 1893.

Pancatantra of Vishnu Sharma. Trans. Chandra Rajan. Penguin Classics. New Delhi, India, 1993; Harmondsworth, U.K., 1995.

Paulus Diakunnus [Paul the Deacon]. *History of the Lombards (Historia Longobardorum).* Trans. William Dudley Foulke. Philadelphia: University of Pennsylvania Press, 1974.

Pausanias. *Description of Greece.* Text, with trans. by Sir James George Frazer. New York: Biblo & Tannen, 1965.

Perry, Ben Edwin. *Secundus the Silent Philosopher: The Greek Life of Secundus, Critically Edited and Restored so far as Possible, Together with Translations of the Greek and Oriental Versions, the Latin and Oriental Texts, and a Study of the Tradition.* Philological Monographs no. 22. Ithaca: Cornell University Press for the American Philological Association, 1964.

Pindar. *The Odes of Pindar.* Text, with trans. by Sir John Sandys. Cambridge: Loeb Classical Library, 1961.

Plato. *Republic.* Text, with trans. by Paul Shorey. 1930–35. Cambridge: Harvard University Press, 1982.

Plautus. *Amphitryon: Three Plays in New Verse Translation (Plautus, Molière, Kleist), Together with a Comprehensive Account of the Evolution of the Legend and Its Subsequent History on the Stage.* Trans. Charles E. Passage and James H. Mantinband. Chapel Hill: University of North Carolina Press, 1974.

———. *Menaechmi (The Brothers Menaechmus).* Northbrook, Ill.: AHM Publishing Co., 1958.

Plutarch. *Moralia.* Text, with trans. by F. C. Babbitt. Cambridge, Mass.: Loeb Classical Library, 1936.

———. *Parallel Lives (Bioi Paralleloi).* Athens: Papyros, 1953.

Pseudo-Callisthenes. *Alexander Romance.* Trans. Ken Dowden. In *Collected Ancient Greek Novels,* ed. B. P. Reardon, 650–735. Berkeley and Los Angeles: University of California Press, 1989.

Ramacaritamanasa (The Holy Lake of the Acts of Rama). Trans. W. D. P. Hill. London: Oxford University Press, 1952.

Ramacaritamanasa (*The Holy Lake of the Acts of Rama*) of Tulsi Das. Trans. R. C. Prasad. Delhi: Motilal Banarsidass, 1990.

Ramayana. Trans. William Buck. Berkeley and Los Angeles: University of California Press, 1986.

[*Ramayana.*] *The Forest Book of the Ramayana of Kampan.* Trans. George L. Hart and Hank Heifetz. Berkeley and Los Angeles: University of California Press, 1988.

The Ramayana. A shortened modern prose version by R. K. Narayan of the Indian epic, suggested by the Tamil version of Kamban. London: Chatto & Windus, 1973.

Ramayana [Kashmiri] of Divakara Prakasa Bhatta. Calcutta, 1930.

Ramayana of Valmiki. Baroda: Oriental Institute, 1960–75.

Rashi, commentary on the Hebrew Bible. *Chumash, with Rashi's Commentary.* Ed. Rabbi A. M. Silbermann. 5 vols. Jerusalem: Feldheim Publishers, 1934.

Rig Veda. With the commentary of Sayana. 6 vols. London: Oxford University Press, 1890–92.

Samyutta Nikaya of the *Suttapitaka.* Ed. Léon Feer. London: Pali Text Society, 1973–90.

Sattampillai, A. N. *Ruttammavai.* Palamkottah: Church Mission Press, 1884.

Shatapatha Brahmana. Benares: Chowkhamba Sanskrit Series, 1964.

Shivalaya Mahatmya of the *Sahyadrikhanda* of the *Skanda Purana.* MS in the library of the Royal Asiatic Society in Bombay. Trans. Micaela Soar. 1996.

Shiva Purana. Benares: Pandita Pushtakalaya, 1964.

Shiva Purana, Dharma Samhita. Bombay, 1884.

Skanda Purana. Bombay: Shree Venkateshvara Steam Press, 1867.

Snorri Sturluson. *Edda.* Trans. Anthony Faulkes. Everyman's Library. London: J. M. Dent, 1987.

Sophocles. *Oedipus Rex* (*Oedipus the King*). Text, with trans. by F. Storr. Cambridge, Mass.: Loeb Classical Library, 1913.

Soran. *Soranus' Gynecology.* Trans. Oswei Temkin. Baltimore: Johns Hopkins University Press, 1956.

Sri Venkateca Mahatmiyam of N. C. Teyvacikamani. Madras: Pilot Publications, 1976.

"The Story of Sukanya." Retold by Shanta Iyer. Amar Citra Katha, no. 63. Bombay: H. G. Mirchandani for India Book House, n.d.

Sturluson. See Snorri Sturluson.

Subhashitaratnakosha [*Subhasitaratnakosa*] of Vidyakara. Ed. Daniel H. H. Ingalls. Harvard Oriental Series 42. Cambridge, 1957. See also Ingalls, *Anthology of Sanskrit Court Poetry.*

"Surya." Ed. Anant Pai, retold ("from the Markandeya Purana") by Mayah Balse. Amar Citra Katha, no. 58. Reprint, Bombay: H. G. Mirchandani for India Book House, 1987.

The Svarga Khanda of the Skanda Purana. Ed. A. C. Shastri. Varanasi: All-India Kashiraj Trust, 1972. For an English translation of the episode cited, see O'Flaherty, *Textual Sources for the Study of Hinduism,* 98–100.

Taittiriya Samhita of the Black Yajur Veda. With the commentary of Madhava. Calcutta: Bibliotheca Indica, 1860.

Tanhuma. Midrash Tanhuma. Trans. John T. Townsend. Hoboken, N.J.: Kitav, 1989.

Tantrakhyana. Sanskrit text from Cecil Bendall, "The Tantrakhyana." *Journal of the Royal Asiatic Society* (of Great Britain and Ireland), n.s., 20, no. 4 (Oct. 1888): 465–500.

Tapati-Samvaranam: The Sun God's Daughter and King Samvarana. (Attributed to Kulashekhara Varman.) Ed. and trans. N. P. Unni and Bruce M. Sullivan. Delhi: Nag Publishers, 1995.

Tertullian. In *The Ante-Nicene Fathers,* vol. 4, ed. the Reverend Alexander Roberts and James Donaldson. Grand Rapids, Mich.: Wm. B. Eerdmans Publishing Co., 1951.

Testament of Judah. In *The Testaments of the Twelve Patriarchs: A Critical Edition of the Greek Text.* 2 vols. Pseudepigrapha Veteris Testamenti Graecae. Leiden: E. J. Brill, 1978.

Theresa of Avila, Saint. *The Life of St. Theresa of Avila.* Harmondsworth: Penguin Books, 1957.

Thomas Aquinas, Saint. *Summa Theologica.* Vol. 4. Trans. Fathers of the English Dominican Province. Westminster, Md.: Christian Classics, 1981.

Toldoth Jeshu. According to the Hebrews, a New Translation of the "Jewish Life of Jesus" (the Toldoth Jeshu), with an Inquiry into the Nature of Its Sources and Special Relationship to the Lost Gospel according to the Hebrews. By Hugh J. Schonfield. London: Duckworth, 1937.

Tristan of Gottfried von Strassburg. Trans. A. T. Hatto and supplemented with the surviving fragments of the *Tristan* of Thomas. Harmondsworth: Penguin Books, 1960. See also *The Saga of Tristram and Isond.* Trans. Paul Schach. Lincoln: University of Nebraska Press, 1973.

Tulsi Das. See *Ramacaritamanasa.*

Upamitabhavaprapancakatha of Siddharshi. Ed. Peter Peterson. Bibliotheca Indica. Calcutta: Baptist Mission Press, 1899.

Vasubandhu. *Abhidharmakosham; Svopajnabhashyasahitam.* With the Sputartha commentary of Acarya Yasomitra. Ed. Swami Dvarikadasa Sastri. 4 vols. Bauddhabharati Series 5–7, 9. Varanasi, 1970–73.

Vayu Purana. Anandasrama Sanskrit Series 49. Poona, 1860.

Vimalakirti. *The Holy Teachings of Vimalakirti: A Mahayana Scripture.* Trans. Robert A. F. Thurman. University Park and London: Pennsylvania State University Press, 1976.

Vinaya Pitaka. Vol. 1, *The Mahavagga.* Ed. Hermann Oldenberg. Pali Text Society. London: Luzac, 1969.

Vishnu Purana. With the commentary of Shridhara. Calcutta: Sanatana Shastra, 1972.

Vishnu Purana. Trans. Horace Hayman Wilson. London, 1840. 3d ed., Calcutta: Punthi Pustak, 1961.

Volsungasaga (The Saga of the Volsungs). Trans. Jesse Byock. Berkeley and Los Angeles: University of California Press, 1990.

Yalqut Makiri [Jalkut Machiri]. Ed. Salomon Buber. Berdyczew: J. Scheftel, 1899.

Zohar. See Sperling, Simon, and Levertoff, *Zohar;* and Tishby, *Wisdom of the Zohar.*

Modern Sources

Aarne, Antti. *The Types of the Folk-Tale: A Classification and Bibliography.* Folklore Fellows Communications no. 74. Ann Arbor, Mich.: Edwards Brothers, 1928. Translation of *Verzeichnis der Märchentypen.*

Aarne, Antti, and Stith Thompson. *The Types of the Folk-Tale.* Folklore Fellows Communications no. 184. Helsinki: Academia Scientiarum Fennica, 1961.

Abe, Kobo. *The Face of Another.* Trans. E. Dale Saunders. New York: Alfred Knopf, 1966. Reprint, Tokyo: Kodansha International, 1992.

Abel, Elizabeth, Barbara Christian, and Helene Moglen. *Female Subjects in Black and White: Race, Psychoanalysis, Feminism.* Berkeley and Los Angeles: University of California Press, 1997.

Abramovitch, Henry Hanoch. "Turning Inside Out: Disguise as a Transition to Homecoming." Paper presented in Chicago at the meetings of the Jung Association, Aug. 27, 1992.

Abu-Lughod, Lila. *Veiled Sentiments: Honor and Poetry in a Bedouin Society.* Berkeley and Los Angeles: University of California Press, 1988.

Adelman, Janet. "Bed Tricks: On Marriage as the End of Comedy in *All's Well That Ends Well* and *Measure for Measure.*" In *Shakespeare's Personality,* ed. Norman N. Holland, Sidney Homan, and Bernard J. Paris, 151–74. Berkeley and Los Angeles: University of California Press, 1989.

Alter, Robert. *The Art of Biblical Narrative.* New York: Basic Books, 1981.

Ambrose, David. *The Man Who Turned into Himself.* New York: Picador Books, 1993.

Ambrose, Stephen E. *Eisenhower.* Vol. 1, *Soldier of the Army, President Elect, 1889–1952.* New York: Simon & Schuster, 1984.

Andersen, Hans Christian. "The Little Mermaid." In *Hans Christian Andersen: The Complete Fairy Tales and Stories,* trans. Erik Christian Haugaard. New York: Doubleday, 1974.

Assayag, Jackie. *La colère de la déesse décapitée: traditions, cultes, et pouvoir dans le Sud de l'Inde.* Paris: CNRS Éditions, 1992.

Auerbach, Erich. *Mimesis.* Princeton: Princeton University Press, 1968.

Auerbach, Nina. *Our Vampires, Ourselves.* Chicago: University of Chicago Press, 1995.

Babb, Lawrence A. *The Divine Hierarchy: Popular Hinduism in Central India.* New York: Columbia University Press, 1975.

Bain, R. Nisbet. *Cossack Fairy Tales and Folk-Tales.* London: A. H. Bullen, 1902.

Bal, Mieke. *Lethal Love: Feminist Literary Readings of Biblical Love Stories.* Bloomington: Indiana University Press, 1987.

Balzac, *Sarrasine.* See Barthes, *S/Z.*

Baring-Gould, S. *Curious Myths of the Middle Ages.* Ed. Edward Hardy. New York: Oxford University Press, 1978.

Barnes, Julian. "Experiment." *New Yorker,* July 17, 1995, 62–67.

Barthes, Roland. *S/Z: An Essay.* Trans. Richard Miller. New York: Farrar, Straus & Giroux, 1974. Originally published in French as *S/Z* (Paris: Éditions du Seuil, 1970).

Basile, Giovanni Batiste. *Il Pentamerone, or The Tale of Tales.* Trans. Sir Richard Burton. New York: Horace Liveright, 1927.

Basinger, Jeanine. *How Hollywood Spoke to Women, 1930–1960.* New York: Alfred Knopf, 1993.

Batten, Mary. *Sexual Strategies: How Females Choose Their Mates.* New York: G. P. Putnam's Sons, 1992.

Baudis, Josef. *Czech Folk Tales.* London: George Allen & Unwin, 1917.

Bayle, Pierre. *Dictionnaire historique et critique.* Vol. 5. New ed. Paris: Desoer, 1820.

———. *Historical and Critical Dictionary.* Trans. Richard H. Popkin. Indianapolis: Bobbs-Merrill, 1991.

Beach, Joseph Warren. "The Loathly Lady." Ph.D. diss., Harvard University, 1907.

Beaumarchais, Pierre-Auguste Caron de. *The Barber of Seville/The Marriage of Figaro.* Trans. John Wood. Harmondsworth: Penguin Books, 1964.

———. *Théatre de Beaumarchais: "Le barbier de Séville," "Le mariage de Figaro," "La mère coupable."* Ed. Maurice Rat. Paris: Éditions Garnier Frères, 1956.

Beaumont, Cyril W. *The Ballet Called "Swan Lake."* New York: Dance Horizons, 1982.

Behrman, S. N. *"Amphitryon 38": A Comedy in a Prologue and Three Acts.* New York: Random House, 1938.

Bell-Metereau, Rebecca. *Hollywood Androgyne.* 2d ed. New York: Columbia University Press, 1993.

Bellow, Saul. *The Adventures of Augie March.* New York, 1949. Reprint, New York: Avon, 1977.

Benchley, Robert. "Opera Synopses." In *The Benchley Round-up,* 65–72. New York: Delta Books, 1962.

Bendall, Cecil. "The Tantrakhyana." *Journal of the Royal Asiatic Society* (of Great Britain and Ireland), n.s., 20, no. 4 (Oct. 1888): 465–500.

———. "Originals and Analogues of the Canterbury Tales." *Journal of the Royal Asiatic Society* (of Great Britain and Ireland), n.s., 20, no. 4 (Oct. 1888): 501–50.

Benwell, Gwen, and Arthur Waugh. *Sea Enchantress: The Tale of the Mermaid and Her Kind.* New York: Citadel Press, 1965.

Bergaigne, Abel. *La religion védique d'après les hymnes du Rig Veda* [*Abel Bergaigne's Vedic Religion*]. Trans. V. G. Paranjpe. Delhi: Motilal Banarsidass, 1978.

Bergeron, David. "The Structure of Healing in *All's Well That Ends Well.*" *South Atlantic Bulletin* 37 (1972): 25–34.

Bettelheim, Bruno. *The Uses of Enchantment: The Meaning and Importance of Fairy Tales.* New York: Alfred A. Knopf, 1986.

Bin Gorion, Micha Joseph, collector. *Classical Jewish Folktales.* Ed. Emanuel Bin Gorion, trans. I. M. Lask. Bloomington and Indianapolis: Indiana University Press, 1990.

Blackburn, Stuart. "Coming out of His Shell: Animal-Husband Tales from India." In Shulman, ed., *Syllables of Sky,* 43–75.

Blackmer, Corinne E., and Patricia Juliana Smith. *En Travesti: Women, Gender Subversion, Opera.* New York: Columbia University Press, 1995.

Bloch, R. Howard. *Medieval Misogyny and the Invention of Western Romantic Love.* Chicago: University of Chicago Press, 1991.

———. *The Scandal of the Fabliaux*. Chicago: University of Chicago Press, 1990.

Bloom, Allan. *Love and Friendship*. New York: Simon & Schuster, 1993.

Bloom, Amy. "The Body Lies." *New Yorker*, July 18, 1994, 38–49.

Bloom, Harold J. *The Book of J*. New York: Weidenfeld, 1990.

Bloomfield, Maurice. "Contributions to the Interpretation of the Veda. III. The Marriage of Saranyu, Tvastar's Daughter." *Journal of the American Oriental Society* 15 (1893): 172–88.

Bohanan, Laura. See Bowen, Elizabeth Smith.

Böklen, Ernst. *Schneewittchen-Studien*. In *Mythologische Bibliothek*. Leipzig, 1915.

Bompas, Cecil H. *Folklore of the Santal Parganas*. London: David Nutt, 1909.

Bonnefoy, Yves. *Mythologies*. Ed. Wendy Doniger. 2 vols. Chicago: University of Chicago Press, 1991.

Borges, Jorge Luis. "The Double." In *The Book of Imaginary Beings*, 80–81. Harmondsworth: Penguin Books, 1972.

———. "Pierre Menard, Author of the *Quixote*." In *Labyrinths*, 36–44. New York: New Directions, 1962.

Bornstein, Kate. *Gender Outlaw: On Men, Women, and the Rest of Us*. New York: Vintage Books, 1995.

Boswell, John. *Same-Sex Unions in Premodern Europe*. New York: Villard Books, 1994.

Boureau, Alain. *The Lord's First Night*. Chicago: University of Chicago Press, 1998.

Bowden, William R. "The Bed-Trick, 1603–1642: Its Mechanics, Ethics, and Effects." *Shakespeare Studies* 5 (1969): 112–23.

Bowen, Elizabeth Smith [Laura Bohanan]. *Return to Laughter: An Anthropological Novel*. New York: Doubleday, 1954, 1964.

Bronner, Yigal. "Poetry at Its Extreme: The Theory and Practice of *Slesa* in Indian Culture." Ph.D. diss., University of Chicago, 1999.

Brown, Judith C. *Immodest Acts: The Life of a Lesbian Nun in Renaissance Italy*. New York: Oxford University Press, 1986.

Bruner, Jerome, and Leo Postman. "On the Perception of Incongruity." *Journal of Personality* 18 (1949): 204–23.

Butler, Judith. *Gender Trouble: Feminism and the Subversion of Ideas*. New York and London: Routledge, 1990.

———. "Lacan, Rivière, and the Strategies of Masquerade." In *Gender Trouble*, 43–56.

———. "Passing, Queering: Nella Larsen's Psychoanalytic Challenge." In Abel, Christian, and Moglen, *Female Subjects in Black and White*, 266–84.

Cadden, Joan. *Meanings of Sex Difference in the Middle Ages: Medicine, Science, and Culture*. Cambridge: Cambridge University Press, 1993.

Calasso, Roberto. *The Marriage of Cadmus and Harmony*. New York: Alfred Knopf, 1993.

Calvino, Italo. "Love Far from Home." *New Yorker*, June 12, 1995, 94–98.

Campbell, Joseph. *The Hero with a Thousand Faces*. New York: Pantheon, 1949.

Capgras, Joseph, and J. Reboul-Lachaux. "L'illusion des 'sosies' dans un délire systématisé chronique." *Bulletin de la Societé de Médecine Mentale* 11 (1923): 6–16.

Carter, Angela. "The Bloody Chamber" and "The Tiger's Bride." In *The Bloody Chamber and Other Stories*. London: Victor Gollancz, 1979; Harmondsworth, Penguin Books, 1981.

———. *Wise Children*. New York: Farrar, Straus & Giroux, 1991.

Carter, Isabel G. "Mountain White Folklore: Tales from the Southern Blue Ridge." *Journal of American Folklore* 6 (1925): 356–59, 361–63.

Casanova, Giacomo. *Casanova mémoires*. Ed. Robert Abirached. Paris: Gallimard, 1959.

———. *History of My Life*. Vol. 6. Trans. Willard R. Trask. New York: Harcourt, Brace & World, 1966.

———. *The Memoirs of Jacques Casanova de Seingalt*. Trans. Arthur Machen. London: 1894.

Cave, Terence. *Recognitions: A Study in Poetics*. Oxford: Clarendon Press, 1990.

Cervantes, Miguel de. *The Ingenious Gentleman, Don Quixote de la Mancha*. Trans. Samual Putnam. New York: Random House, 1949.

Chailley, Jacques. *"The Magic Flute," Masonic Opera*. Trans. Herbert Weinstock. New York: Alfred Knopf, 1971.

Chapman, George. *The Widow's Tears*. Ed. Ethel M. Smeak. Lincoln: University of Nebraska Press, 1966.

Chase, Richard, ed. *Grandfather Tales: American-English Folk Tales*. Boston: Houghton Mifflin, 1948.

Childs, J. Rives. *Casanova: A New Perspective*. New York: Paragon, 1988.

Chilli, Shaikh. *Folk-Tales of Hindustan*. Bahadurganji, Allahabad: Panini Office, 1913.

Claus, Peter. "Playing *Cenne*: The Meanings of a Folk Game." In *Another Harmony: New Essays on the Folklore of India*, ed. Stuart Blackburn and A. K. Ramanujan, 265–93. Berkeley and Los Angeles: University of California Press, 1986.

Clevidence, Carin. "The Somnambulists." *Story* magazine, autumn 1994, 56–63.

Cohen, Eileen. " 'Virtue Is Bold': The Bed-Trick and Characterization in *All's Well That Ends Well* and *Measure for Measure*." *Philological Quarterly* 65 (1986): 171–86.

Coomaraswamy, Ananda K. "On the Loathly Bride." *Speculum* 20 (Oct. 1945): 391–404.

Cornell University College of Veterinary Medicine Animal Health Newsletter 7, no. 1 (Mar. 1989).

Crews, David. "Animal Sexuality." *Scientific American*, Jan. 1994, 108–14.

cummings, e. e. *him*. New York: Liveright Publishing Corp., 1927.

Dahl, Roald. "The Visitor" and "The Great Switcheroo." In *Switch-Bitch*, pp. 7–54, 55–80. New York: Penguin Books, 1976.

Da Ponte, Lorenzo. *Così fan tutte; Don Giovanni; Marriage of Figaro*. Libretti.

Darnton, Robert. *The Great Cat Massacre and Other Episodes in French Cultural History*. New York: Basic Books, 1984.

Daston, Lorraine, and Katharine Park. "The Hermaphrodite and the Orders of Nature: Sexual Ambiguity in Early Modern France." *GLQ: A Journal of Gay and Lesbian Studies* 1 (1995): 419–38.

Davies, Robertson. *The Lyre of Orpheus.* New York: Penguin Books, 1988.

Davis, Arthur K. *More Traditional Ballads of Virginia.* Chapel Hill: University of North Carolina Press, 1960.

Davis, Natalie Zemon. "On the Lame." Reply to Robert Finlay. *American Historical Review* 93, no. 3 (1988): 572–603.

———. *The Return of Martin Guerre.* Cambridge: Harvard University Press, 1983.

Defoe, Daniel. *Moll Flanders* (1722). Harmondsworth: Penguin, 1978.

Dekkers, Midas. *Dearest Pet: On Bestiality.* Trans. Paul Vincent. London and New York: Verso, 1994.

Delarue, Paul. *The Borzoi Books of French Folk Tales.* New York: Alfred A. Knopf, 1956.

Delbanco, Nicholas. *In the Nature of Mercy.* New York: Warner Books, 1995.

de Murat, Henriette-Julie. "Starlight" (attributed). Trans. Terence Cave. In *Wonder Tales,* ed. Marina Warner, 149–87. London: Chatto & Windus, 1994.

Dent, Edward J. *Mozart's Operas: A Critical Study.* New York: Oxford University Press, 1991.

Desens, Marliss C. *The Bed-Trick in English Renaissance Drama: Explorations in Gender, Sexuality, and Power.* Newark, N.J.: University of Delaware Press, 1994.

Detmer, Emily. "The Politics of Telling: Women's Consent and Accusations of Rape in English Renaissance Drama." Ph.D. diss., Miami University, Ohio, 1997.

de Villiers, Pierre. In *Les cent nouvelles nouvelles.* Paris: Garnier Frères Libraires-Éditeurs, 1866.

de Visser, M. W. "The Fox and the Badger in Japanese Folklore." *Transactions of the Asiatic Society of Japan* 36, pt. 3 (1908): 1–59.

Devor, Holly. *Gender Blending: Confronting the Limits of Duality.* Bloomington: Indiana University Press, 1989.

De Waals, Frans. *Good Natured: The Origins of Right and Wrong in Humans and Other Primates.* Cambridge: Harvard University Press, 1996.

Dijkstra, Bram. *Idols of Perversity: Fantasies of Feminine Evil in Fin-de-Siècle Culture.* New York and Oxford: Oxford University Press, 1986.

Dillard, Annie. *The Living.* New York: Harper Collins, 1992.

———. *Pilgrim at Tinker Creek.* New York: Bantam Books, 1975.

Dimock, Edward Cameron. "Doctrine and Practice among the Vaisnavas of Bengal." In *Krishna: Myths, Rites and Attitudes,* ed. Milton Singer, 41–63. Honolulu: University of Hawaii Press, 1966.

———. *Mr. Dimock Explores the Mysteries of the East.* Chapel Hill, N.C.: Algonquin Books of Chapel Hill, 1999.

———. *The Place of the Hidden Moon: Erotic Mysticism in the Vaisnava Sahajiya Cult of Bengal.* Chicago: University of Chicago Press, 1966.

———. *The Thief of Love: Bengali Tales from Court and Village.* Chicago: University of Chicago Press, 1963.

Diner, Judith Bruskin, trans. *The One Hundred New Tales (Les cent nouvelles nouvelles).* Garland Library of Medieval Literature, vol. 30, ser. B. New York and London: Garland Publishing, 1990.

Dinesen, Isak. "The Deluge at Norderney," "The Monkey," and "The Ruins round Pisa." In *Seven Gothic Tales.* New York: Random House, 1934.

Doane, Mary Ann. *Femmes Fatales: Feminism, Film Theory, Psychoanalysis*. New York and London: Routledge, 1991.

Doniger, Wendy. "Begetting on Margin: Adultery and Surrogate Pseudomarriage in Hinduism." In *From the Margins of Hindu Marriage: Essays on Gender, Religion, and Culture*, ed. Paul Courtright and Lindsey Harlan, 160–83. New York: Oxford University Press, 1995.

———. "The Dreams and Dramas of a Jealous Hindu Queen: Vasavadatta." In *Dream Cultures: Toward a Comparative History of Dreaming*, ed. Guy Stroumsa and David Shulman, 74–84. New York: Oxford University Press, 1999.

———. "From Great Neck to Swift Hall: Confessions of a Reluctant Historian of Religions." In *The Craft of Religious Studies*, ed. Jon R. Stone, 36–51. New York: St. Martin's Press, 1998.

———. *The Implied Spider: Politics and Theology in Myth*. The 1996–97 ACLS-AAR Lectures. New York: Columbia University Press, 1998.

———. "Jewels of Rejection and Recognition in Ancient India." *Journal of Indian Philosophy* 26 (1998): 435–53.

———. "The Masques of Gods and Demons." In *Behind the Mask: Dance, Healing, and Possession in South Indian Ritual*, ed. David Shulman and Deborah Thiagarajan. New York: Oxford University Press, forthcoming.

———. "The Mythology of Masquerading Animals, or Bestiality." In *In the Company of Animals*, ed. Arien Mack. *Social Research, An International Quarterly of the Social Sciences* 62, no. 3 (fall 1995): 751–72.

———. "Myths and Methods in the Dark." *Journal of Religion* 76, no. 4 (Oct. 1996): 531–47.

———. "Playing the Field: Adultery as Claim-Jumping." In *The Sense of Adharma*, by Ariel Glucklich, 169–88. New York: Oxford University Press, 1994.

———. " 'Put a Bag over Her Head': Beheading Mythological Women." In Eilberg-Schwartz and Doniger, *Off with Her Head!* 14–31.

———. *Rings of Rejection and Recollection*. Forthcoming.

———. "The Sanskrit Maverick." *Radcliffe Quarterly*, summer 1997, 15.

———. "The Scrapbook of Undeserved Salvation: The *Kedara Khanda* of the *Skanda Purana*." In *Purana Perennis: Reciprocity and Transformation in Hindu and Jaina Texts*, ed. Wendy Doniger, 59–83. Ithaca: State University of New York Press, 1993.

———. *Splitting the Difference: Gender and Myth in Ancient Greece and India*. Chicago: University of Chicago Press, 1999.

———. "Three (or More) Forms of the Three (or More)–Fold Path in Hinduism." *Graven Images: Studies in Culture, Law and the Sacred* (special issue: *Madness, Melancholy, and the Limits of the Self*) 3 (1996): 201–12.

———. "Transplanting Myths of Organ Transplants." In *Organ Transplantation: Meanings and Realities*, ed. Stuart J. Youngner, Renée Fox, and Laurence J. O'Connell, 194–220. Madison: University of Wisconsin Press, 1996.

———. "What Did They Name the Dog?" Review of Lawrence Wright, *Twins: Genes, Environment, and the Mystery of Identity*. *London Review of Books*, Mar. 19, 1998, 32.

———. "When a Lingam Is Just a Good Cigar: Psychoanalysis and Hindu Sexual Fantasies." In *The Psychoanalytic Study of Society: Essays in Honor of Alan Dundes,* ed. L. Bryce Boyer et al., 81–104. Hillside, N.J.: Analytic Press, 1993.

Doniger, Wendy, and Brian K. Smith. "Sacrifice and Substitution: Ritual Mystification and Mythical Demystification." *Numen* 36, no. 2 (Dec. 1989): 189–224.

Doniger, Wendy, with Brian K. Smith, trans. *The Laws of Manu.* Harmondsworth: Penguin Books, 1991.

Doniger, Wendy, and Gregory Spinner. "Misconceptions: Female Imaginations and Male Fantasies in Parental Imprinting." *Daedalus* 127, no. 1 (winter 1998): 97–130.

Donne, John. *The Poems of John Donne.* Ed. John Hardward. Harmondsworth: Penguin Books, 1950.

Dorje, Rinjing. *Tales of Uncle Tompa, the Legendary Rascal of Tibet.* Barrytown: Station Hill Arts, 1997.

Dostoyevski, Fyodor. *The Double: Two Versions.* Trans. Evelyn Harden. Ann Arbor: Ardis, 1985.

Douglas, George B. *Scottish Fairy and Folk Tales.* New York: A. L. Burt Co., 1903.

Douglas, Mary. "Children Consumed and Child Cannibals." In *Myth and Method,* ed. Laurie Patton and Wendy Doniger, 29–51. Charlottesville: University Press of Virginia, 1996.

———. "The Cloud God and the Shadow Self." *Social Anthropology* 3, no. 2 (1995): 83–94.

———. *In the Wilderness: The Doctrine of Defilement in the Book of Numbers.* Sheffield: JSOT Press, 1993.

———. *Purity and Danger: An Analysis of Concepts of Pollution and Taboo.* London: Routledge & Kegan Paul, 1966.

Doyle, Sir Arthur Conan. "The Case of Lady Sannox." In *The Conan Doyle Stories,* 495–506. London: John Murray, 1929.

Dundes, Alan. *Cinderella: A Casebook.* New York: Wildman Press, 1983.

———. "The Hero Pattern and the Life of Jesus." In *In Quest of the Hero,* ed. Robert Segal, 179–223. Princeton: Princeton University Press, 1990.

———. " 'To Love My Father All': A Psychoanalytic Study of the Folktale Source of *King Lear.*" In Dundes, *Cinderella,* 229–44.

Dunne, John Gregory. "A Reporter at Large: The Humboldt Murders." *New Yorker,* Jan. 13, 1997, 46–62.

Durell, Lawrence. *The Alexandrian Quartet.* Vol. 1, *Justine.* New York: E. P. Dutton, 1957.

Eagleton, Terry. *Literary Theory: An Introduction.* Minneapolis: University of Minnesota Press, 1983.

Eberhard, Wolfram. *Folktales of China.* Chicago: University of Chicago Press, 1965.

———. *Typen chinesicher Volksmärchen.* Helsinki: Suomalainen Tiedeakatemia, Academia Scientiarum Fennica, 1937.

Eilberg-Schwartz, Howard, and Wendy Doniger. *Off with Her Head! The Denial of Women's Identity in Myth, Religion, and Culture.* Berkeley and Los Angeles: University of California Press, 1995.

Eliade, Mircea. *Cosmos and History: The Myth of the Eternal Return.* New York: Pantheon, 1954.

Ellison, Ralph Waldo. *Invisible Man.* New York: Modern Library, 1952.

Enchi, Fumiko. *Masks* (1958). Trans. Juliet Winters Carpenter. New York: Vintage Books, 1983.

Erasmus of Rotterdam. *Opera Omnia.* Leiden, 1703. Reprint, London: Gregg Press, 1962.

Erndl, Kathleen M. "The Mutilation of Surpanakha." In *Many Ramayanas: The Diversity of Narrative Traditions in South Asia,* ed. Paula Richman, 67–88. Berkeley and Los Angeles: University of California Press, 1991.

Erskine, John. *The Private Life of Helen of Troy.* Indianapolis: Bobbs-Merrill, 1925.

Estienne, Henri. *L'introduction au traité de la conformité des merveilles anciennes avec les modernes.* Paris, 1566.

Etcoff, Nancy L. *Survival of the Prettiest: The Science of Beauty.* New York: Doubleday, 1999.

Fanger, Iris M. "*Swan Lake:* Productions outside Russia." In *International Encyclopedia of Dance,* ed. Selma Jeanne Cohen et al., vol. 6, 31–35. New York: Oxford University Press, 1998.

Fass, Barbara F. "*La Belle Dame sans Merci*" and the Aesthetics of Romanticism.* Detroit: Wayne State University Press, 1974.

———. "The Little Mermaid and the Artist's Quest for a Soul." *Comparative Literature Studies* 9, no. 3 (Sept. 1972): 291–301.

Fauset, Arthur Huff. "Negro Folk Tales from the South." *Journal of American Folk-Lore* 40 (1927): 243–45.

Festinger, Leon. *A Theory of Cognitive Dissonance.* Stanford: Stanford University Press, 1957.

Fielding, Henry. *Joseph Andrews [The History of the Adventures of Joseph Andrews . . .].* Ed. Douglas Brooks-Davies. Oxford: Oxford University Press, 1966.

Fineman, Joel. "Fratricide and Cuckoldry: Shakespeare's Doubles." *Psychoanalytic Review* 64 (1977): 409–53.

Finlay, Robert. "The Refashioning of Martin Guerre." In AHA Forum: The Return of Martin Guerre. *American Historical Review* 93, no. 3 (1988): 553–71.

Fishbane, Mona DeKoven. "Ruth: Dilemmas of Loyalty and Connection." In *Reading Ruth: Contemporary Women Reclaim a Sacred Story,* ed. Judith A. Kates and Gail Twersky Reimer, 298–308. New York: Ballantyne Books, 1994.

Flahaut, François. "Imagination and Mythology in Contemporary Literature (Tolkien, Lovecraft) and Science Fiction." In Bonnefoy, *Mythologies,* 2:790.

Fletcher, John [and William Shakespeare]. *The Two Noble Kinsmen.* Ed. Lois Potter. The Arden Shakespeare. London: Thomas Nelson and Sons, 1997.

Fletcher, John, Nathaniel Field, and Philip Massinger. *The Queen of Corinth.* In *The Dramatic Works in the Beaumont and Fletcher Canon,* ed. Robert Kean Turner, vol. 8, ed. Fredson Bowers, 1–112. Cambridge: Cambridge University Press, 1992.

Fonrobert, Charlotte Elisheva. "The Handmaid, the Trickster, and the Birth of the

Messiah." In *Feminist Readings of Classical Jewish Texts,* ed. Susannah Heschel and Rachel Biale. Berkeley and Los Angeles: University of California Press. Forthcoming.

Forsythe, Robert Stanley. *The Relation of Shirley's Plays to the Elizabethan Drama.* New York: Columbia University Press, 1914.

Foucault, Michel. *History of Sexuality.* Trans. Robert Hurley. 3 vols. New York: Vintage, 1990.

———. Introduction to *Hercule Barbin: Being the Recently Discovered Memoirs of a Nineteenth-Century French Hermaphrodite.* Trans. Richard McDougall. New York: Pantheon Books, 1980.

Francis, Dick. "Bright White Star." In *Field of Thirteen,* 65–75. London: Michael Joseph, 1998.

———. *Straight.* New York: Putnam, 1988.

Franklin, Benjamin. "Benjamin Franklin Urges a Young Friend to Take an Old Mistress." In *A Treasury of the World's Great Letters,* ed. M. Lincoln Schuster, 159–62. New York: Simon & Schuster, 1940.

Frazer, James George. *Taboo and the Perils of the Soul.* Vol. 3, pt. 2, of *The Golden Bough.* New York: Macmillan, 1922.

Freud, Sigmund. *Collected Papers.* (Abbreviated as *CP.*) Ed. James Strachey. 5 vols. London: Hogarth Press, 1950.

———. *Standard Edition of the Complete Psychological Works.* (Abbreviated as *SE.*) Ed. James Strachey. London: Hogarth Press, 1958.

———. "A Difficulty in the Path of Psycho-analysis." *SE* 17:135–44.

———. "Family Romances." *CP* 5:74–78.

———. "Femininity." In *New Introductory Lectures on Psychoanalysis,* trans. James Strachey, lecture 33, 112–35. New York: W. W. Norton, 1966.

———. "Fragment of an Analysis of a Case of Hysteria" [Dora]. *SE* 7:1–122.

———. *The Interpretation of Dreams.* Trans. James Strachey. New York: Basic Books, 1965.

———. "Leonardo da Vinci and a Memory of His Childhood." *SE* 11:63–138.

———. *Leonardo da Vinci and a Memory of His Childhood.* Trans. Alan Tyson. Harmondsworth: Penguin, 1963.

———. "Medusa's Head." *CP* 5:105–6.

———. "Psycho-analytic Notes on an Autobiographical Account of a Case of Paranoia (Dementia Paranoides)" ("The Case of Schreber") (1911). *CP* 12:3–84.

———. "The Question of Lay Analysis: Conversations with an Impartial Peson." *SE* 20:183–251.

———. "A Special Type of Choice of Object Made by Men." *SE* 11:163–76.

———. "The Splitting of the Ego in the Defensive Process." *CP* 5:372–75.

———. "The Theme of the Three Caskets." *CP* 4:244–56.

———. *Three Essays on a Theory of Sexuality.* Trans. James Strachey. New York: Basic Books, 1963.

———. *Totem and Taboo.* Trans. A. A. Brill. New York: Vintage, 1918.

———. "The Uncanny." *SE* 17:217–56.

Friedman, Mordecai A. "Tamar, a Symbol of Life: The 'Killer Wife' Superstition in the Bible and Jewish Tradition." *Association for Jewish Studies Review* 15 (spring 1990): 23–61.

Fripp, Edgar. *Shakespeare, Man and Artist.* London: Oxford University Press, 1938.

Fromm, Erich. *Sigmund Freud's Mission: An Analysis of His Personality and Influence.* New York: Harper, 1959.

Fuentes, Carlos. *Aura.* Text, with trans. by Lysander Kemp. New York: Farrar, Straus & Giroux, Noonday Press, 1965.

Gallop, Jane. "Keys to Dora." In *In Dora's Case: Freud—Hysteria—Feminism,* ed. Charles Bernheimer and Claire Kahane, 200–220. 2d ed. New York: Columbia University Press, 1990.

Garber, Marjorie. *Dog Love.* New York: Simon & Schuster, 1996.

———. *Vested Interests: Cross-Dressing and Cultural Anxiety.* New York and London: Routledge, 1992.

———. *Vice Versa: The Bisexuality of Everyday Life.* New York: Simon & Schuster, 1995.

García Márquez, Gabriel. *One Hundred Years of Solitude.* New York: Harper & Row, 1970.

Garver, Joseph C. "Die Macht der Phantasie: Die 'heredity of influence' als literarisches Thema." *Saeculum* 33, nos. 3–4 (1982): 287–311.

Gates, Henry Louis, Jr. "Editor's Introduction: Writing 'Race' and the Difference It Makes." *Critical Inquiry* 12, no. 1 (1985): 4.

Gautier, Théophile. "Avatar." In *Avatar et autres récits fantastiques,* 1–89. Verviers, Belgium: Marabout Géant, 1856–57.

Gellner, Ernest. *The Psychoanalytic Movement, or The Cunning of Unreason.* London: Paladin Grafton Books, 1985.

Gill, Walter. *Turn Northeast at the Tombstone.* Adelaide: Rigby, 1970.

Gillman, Susan. *Dark Twins: Imposture and Identity in Mark Twain's America.* Chicago: University of Chicago Press, 1989.

Gilman, Sander. "Black Bodies, White Bodies: Toward an Iconography of Female Sexuality in Late Nineteenth-Century Art, Medicine, and Literature." *Critical Inquiry* 21, no. 1 (autumn 1985): 204–43.

Ginzberg, Louis. *The Legends of the Jews.* 7 vols. Philadelphia: Jewish Publication Society of America, 1909–37.

Ginzburg, Carlo. "Morelli, Freud, and Sherlock Holmes: Clues and Scientific Method." *History Workshop* 9 (1980): 5–36.

Girard, René. *Desire, Deceit, and the Novel.* Trans. Yvonne Freccero. 1961. Baltimore: Johns Hopkins University Press, 1976.

———. *Violence and the Sacred.* Trans. Patrick Gregory. 1972. Baltimore: Johns Hopkins University Press, 1979.

Giraudoux, Jean. *Three Plays: "Amphitryon," "Intermezzo," "Ondine."* Trans. Roger Gellert. New York: Oxford University Press, 1976.

Goethe, Johann Wolfgang von. *Elective Affinities.* Trans. James Anthony Froude and R. Dillon Boylan. New York: Frederick Ungar, 1962.

Gold, Ann Grodzins. *A Carnival of Parting: The Tales of King Bharthari and King Gopi*

Chand as Sung and Told by Madhu Natisar Nath of Ghatiyali, Rajasthan. Berkeley and Los Angeles: University of California Press, 1992.

———. "Gender and Illusion in a Rajasthani Yogic Tradition." In *Gender, Discourse, and Power in South Asia,* ed. Arjun Appadurai et al., 102–35. Philadelphia: University of Pennsylvania Press, 1991.

———. "Sexuality, Fertility, and Erotic Imagination." In *Listen to the Heron's Words: Reimagining Gender and Kinship in North India,* ed. Gloria Goodwin Raheja and Ann Grodzins Gold, 30–72. Berkeley and Los Angeles: University of California Press, 1994.

Goldenweiser, Alexander. *History, Psychology, and Culture.* London: Kegan Paul, Trench, Trübner & Co., 1933.

Goldin, Judah. "The Youngest Son, or Where Does Genesis 38 Belong?" In *Studies in Midrash and Related Literature,* ed. Barry L. Eichler and Jeffrey H. Tigay, 121–39. Philadelphia: Jewish Publication Society, 1988.

Goldsmith, Olivia. *Switcheroo.* New York: Harper Collins, 1998.

Gossett, Suzanne. " 'Best Men Are Molded out of Faults': Marring the Rapist in Jacobean Drama." *English Literary Renaissance* 14, no. 3 (autumn 1984): 305–27.

Graham, Stephen. *Boris Godunof.* London: Ernest Benn, 1933.

Granoff, Phyllis, trans. *The Forest of Thieves and the Magic Garden: An Anthology of Medieval Jain Stories.* New Delhi: Penguin Books, 1998.

Greene, Graham. *Our Man in Havana, An Entertainment.* Harmondsworth: Penguin Books, 1962.

———. *The Tenth Man.* New York: Simon & Schuster, 1985.

Greer, Germaine. *The Change: Women, Aging, and the Menopause.* London: Hamish Hamilton, 1991.

———. *The Female Eunuch.* New York: McGraw-Hill, 1970.

Gregor, Reverend Walter. *The Folklore of North East of Scotland.* London: Folklore Society, 1881.

Grimm, Brothers. *The Complete Grimm's Fairy Tales.* Trans. Margaret Hunt and James Stern. New York: Pantheon Books, 1944.

Gurney, A. R. *"The Perfect Party": A Comedy in Two Acts.* New York: Dramatists Play Service, 1986.

Halliwell, Leslie. *Halliwell's Film Guide.* Ed. John Walker. New York: Harper, 1995.

Hallmundsson, Hallberg. *An Anthology of Scandinavian Literature.* New York: Collier Books, 1965.

Handelman, Don. "The Guises of the Goddess and the Transformation of the Male: Gangamma's Visit to Tirupati, and the Continuum of Gender." In Shulman, ed., *Syllables of Sky,* 283–337.

Harding, Samuel. *Sicily and Naples, or The Fatal Union, a Tragedy.* New York: Garland Publishing, 1986.

Harper, Ralph. *On Presence: Variations and Reflections.* Philadelphia: Trinity Press International, 1991.

Hasan-Rokem, Galit. *Proverbs in Israeli Folk Narratives: A Structural Semantic Analysis.* Folklore Fellows Communications no. 232. Helsinki: Academia Scientiarum Fennica, 1982.

Hatto, A. T. "The Swan Maiden: A Folk-Tale of North Eurasian Origin." *Bulletin of the School of Oriental and African Studies* 24 (1961): 326–52.

Haughton, William. *Englishmen for My Money*. London: Oxford University Press, 1912.

Hawthorn, Jeremy. *Multiple Personality and the Disintegration of Literary Character*. New York: St. Martin's Press, 1983.

Hegel, W. G. F. *Phänomenologie des Geistes*. Hamburg: Felix Meiner, 1952.

———. *Phenomenology of Spirit*. Oxford: Clarendon Press, 1977.

Henry, O. "The Gift of the Magi." In *The Complete Writings of O. Henry*. Garden City, N.Y.: Doubleday, 1917.

Herrick, Robert. *Selections from the "Hesperides" and "Noble Numbers."* New York: Harper, 1882.

Hertz, Emmanuel. *The Hidden Lincoln: From the Letters and Papers of William H. Herndon*. New York: Viking Press, 1938.

Hess, Linda, and Shukdev Singh, trans. *The Bijak of Kabir*. San Francisco: North Point Press, 1983.

Heywood, John. *A Dialogue of Proverbs*. Ed. Rudolph E. Habenicht. Berkeley and Los Angeles: University of California Press, 1963.

Heywood, Thomas. *The Fair Maid of the West, Part II*. Ed. Robert Turner, Jr. Lincoln: University of Nebraska Press, 1967.

Hill, W. D. P., trans. *The Holy Lake of the Acts of Rama*. London: Oxford University Press, 1952.

Ho, Chan-hao. *Liang Shan-po yü Chu Ying-t'ai*. For an English translation, see *Love under the Willows: A Szechuan Opera*. Trans. Yang Hsien-hi and Gladys Yang. Peking: Foreign Languages Press, 1956.

Hodgdon, Barbara. "The Making of Virgins and Mothers: Sexual Signs, Substitute Scenes and Doubled Presences in *All's Well That Ends Well*." *Philological Quarterly* 66, no. 1 (winter 1987): 47–71.

Hoffmann, E. T. A. "The Doubles" and "The Sandman." In *The Tales of E. T. A. Hoffmann*, trans. Leonard J. Kent and Elizabeth C. Knight, 234–79 and 92–125. Chicago: University of Chicago Press, 1969.

Hoffmann, Roald, and Shira Leibowitz. "Molecular Mimicry, Rachel and Leah, the Israeli Male, and the Inescapable Metaphor of Science." *Michigan Quarterly Review* 30, no. 3 (summer 1991): 383–97.

Hofmannsthal, Hugo von. *Arabella*. Libretto. 1933.

———. *Rosenkavalier*. Libretto. 1911.

Hope, Sir Anthony. *The Prisoner of Zenda*. New York: H. Holt, 1896.

Hubner, John. *Bottom Feeders: From Free Love to Hard Core—The Rise and Fall of Counterculture Heroes Jim and Artie Mitchell*. Garden City, N.Y.: Doubleday, 1993.

Huet, Marie-Hélène. *Monstrous Imagination*. Cambridge: Harvard University Press, 1993.

Huilgol, Varadraj. *The Panchatantra of Vasubhaga: A Critical Study*. Madras: New Era Publications, 1987.

Hwang, David Henry. *M. Butterfly*. New York: Plume, Penguin, 1989.

Ibsen, Henrik. *The Vikings at Helgeland* (1858). Trans. James Walter McFarlane. In *The Oxford Ibsen*, vol. 2, 27–94. London: Oxford University Press, 1962.

Ingalls, Daniel H. H. *An Anthology of Sanskrit Court Poetry: Vidyakara's "Subhasitarat-nakosa."* Harvard Oriental Series no. 44. Cambridge, 1965.

Insler, Stanley. "The Shattered Head Split and the Epic Tale of Sakuntala." *Bulletin d'Études Indiennes* 7–8 (1989–90): 97–139.

Jacobsen, Per S., and Barbara Fass Leavy. *Ibsen's Forsaken Merman: Folklore in the Late Plays.* New York: New York University Press, 1988.

Jagendorf, Zvi. "'In the Morning, Behold It Was Leah': Genesis and the Reversal of Sexual Knowledge." In *Biblical Patterns in Modern Literature,* ed. David H. Hirsch et al., 51–60. Brown Judaic Studies 77. Chico, Calif.: Scholars Press, 1984.

Jameson, Fredric. "Imaginary and Symbolic in Lacan: Marxism, Psychoanalytic Criticism, and the Problem of the Subject." In *Yale French Studies 55/56, Literature and Psychoanalysis, The Question of Reading: Otherwise,* ed. Shoshana Felman, 338–95. New Haven, 1977.

J. D. *Grushenka.* Los Angeles: Holloway House, 1966.

Johnson, Barbara. "The Frame of Reference: Poe, Lacan, Derrida." In *The Purloined Poe: Lacan, Derrida, and Psychoanalytic Reading,* ed. John P. Muller and William J. Richardson, 213–51. Baltimore: Johns Hopkins University Press, 1988.

Johnson, Dr. Samuel. *Johnson on Shakespeare.* Ed. Arthur Sherbo. New Haven: Yale University Press, 1968.

Jones, Ernest. *On the Nightmare.* London: Hogarth Press, 1949.

Jong, Erica. *Fear of Flying: A Novel.* New York: New American Library, 1974.

Kakar, Sudhir. *Intimate Relations: Exploring Indian Sexuality.* Chicago: University of Chicago Press, 1990.

Kakar, Sudhir, and John Munder Ross. *Tales of Love, Sex, and Danger.* New York: Basil Blackwell, 1987.

Kalluak, Mark, ed. *How Kablomat Became and Other Legends.* Canada: Program Development, Dept. of Education, Govt. of Canada, 1974.

Karnad, Girish. *Naga-Mandala: Play with a Cobra.* In *Three Plays: "Naga-Mandala," "Hayavadana," "Tughlaq,"* 19–66. Delhi: Oxford University Press, 1995.

Kates, Gary. *Monsieur d'Eon Is a Woman: A Tale of Political Intrigue and Sexual Masquerade.* New York: Basic Books, 1995.

Kawabata, Yasunari. *The Old Capital.* San Francisco: North Point Press, 1987.

Kay, Jackie. *Trumpets.* London: Picador, 1998.

Keene, Donald. "Feminine Sensibility in the Heian Era." In *Japanese Aesthetics and Culture: A Reader,* ed. Nancy G. Hume, 109–24. Albany: SUNY Press, 1995.

Keillor, Garrison. "Zeus the Lutheran." *New Yorker,* Oct. 29, 1990, 32–37.

Kellet, Alexander. *A Pocket of Prose and Verse: Being a Selection from the Literary Productions of Alexander Kellet, Esq.* Bath: R. Cruttwell, 1778.

Kelly, Walter K. *Curiosities of Indo-European Tradition and Folk-lore.* 1863. Detroit: Singing Tree Press, 1969.

Kemp, William. *A Knack to Know a Knave.* 1594. London: Tudor Facsimile Texts, 1911.

Kilgour, Maggie. *From Communion to Cannibalism.* Princeton: Princeton University Press, 1990.

Kincaid, C. A. *Tales of Old Sind.* London: Oxford University Press, 1922.

King, Karen L., ed. *Images of the Feminine in Gnosticism.* Philadelphia: Fortress Press, 1988.

Kirtley, Basil F. " 'La Llorona' and Related Themes." *Western Folklore* 19 (1960): 155–68.

Klein, Melanie. *Contributions to Psychoanalysis, 1921–45.* London: Hogarth Press, 1948.

Kleist, Heinrich von. *Amphitryon.* Trans. Charles E. Passage. In *Plays,* ed. Walter Hinderer, 91–164. New York: Continuum, 1982.

Knowles, James Hinton. "Shabrang, Prince and Thief," and "The Young Gambling Merchant." In *Folk-Tales of Kashmir,* 104–23, 272–96. London: Kegan Paul, Trench, Trübner & Co., 1893. Jammu Tawi: Jay Kay Book House, 1985.

Kramrisch, Stella. "Two: Its Significance in the Rgveda." In *Indological Studies in Honor of W. Norman Brown,* ed. Ernest Bender, 109–36. New Haven: American Oriental Society, 1962.

Krappe, Alexander H. "Far Eastern Fox Lore." *California Folklore Quarterly* 3 (1944): 124–47.

———. "Scandinavian Seal Lore." *Scandinavian Studies and Notes* 18 (1944): 156–62.

Krauss, Rosalind. *The Originality of the Avant Garde and Other Modernist Myths.* Cambridge: MIT Press, 1987.

Kuhn, Adalbert. "Saranyu-Erinnus." *Zeitschrift für vergleichende Sprachforschung* 1 (1852): 439–70.

Kuhn, Thomas. *The Nature of Scientific Revolutions.* 2d ed. Chicago: University of Chicago Press, 1970.

Kundera, Milan. *The Unbearable Lightness of Being.* New York: Harper & Row, 1984.

Kunos, Ignacz. *Forty-four Turkish Fairy Tales.* London: George G. Harrap & Co., 1885.

Lacan, Jacques. "The Agency of the Letter in the Unconscious, or Reason since Freud." In *Écrits: A Selection,* trans. Alan Sheridan, 146–78. New York: W. W. Norton, 1977.

———. "The Split between the Eye and the Gaze." In *The Four Fundamental Concepts of Psychoanalysis,* trans. Alan Sheridan, 67–78. New York: W. W. Norton, 1978.

———. "The Mirror Stage as Formative of the Function of the I." In *Écrits: A Selection,* 1–7.

Lancaster, Evelyn. See Sizemore, Chris Costner.

Lane, Anthony. "Sex in America." Review of Edward O. Laumann et al., *The Social Organization of Sexuality: Sexual Practices in the United States. New Yorker,* Dec. 19, 1994, 110–14.

Laqueur, Thomas. *Making Sex: Body and Gender from the Greeks to Freud.* Cambridge: Harvard University Press, 1990.

Larsen, Nella. *Passing.* New York: Alfred A. Knopf, 1929. Reprint, New York: Negro Universities Press, 1969.

Larson, Jane E. " 'Women Understand So Little, They Call My Good Nature "Deceit" ': A Feminist Rethinking of Seduction." *Columbia Law Review* (special issue: *Seduction and Sexual Fraud*) 93 (1993): 374–472.

Lawrence, William Witherle. *Shakespeare's Problem Comedies.* 1931. New York: Frederick Ungar, 1960.

Leach, Edmund. "Anthropological Aspects of Language: Animal Categories and Verbal Abuse." In *Reader in Comparative Religion*, ed. William A. Lessa and Evon Z. Vogt, 153–66. 4th ed. New York: Harper & Row, 1979.

———. "The Legitimacy of Solomon." *European Journal of Sociology* 7 (1966): 58–101. Reprinted in *Genesis as Myth and Other Essays* (London, 1969), 25–84.

———. "Magical Hair." *Man: Journal of the Royal Anthropological Institute* 88 (1958): 147–68.

Leavy, Barbara Fass. *In Search of the Swan Maiden: A Narrative on Folklore and Gender.* New York: New York University Press, 1994.

Le Carré, John. *The Little Drummer Girl.* New York: Alfred Knopf, 1983.

Lever, J. W. Introduction to *Measure for Measure.* London: Arden, 1965.

Levinas, Emmanuel. *Totality and Infinity: An Essay on Exteriority.* Trans. Alphonso Lingis. The Hague: Martinus Nijhoff, 1979. Originally published as *Totalité et infini* (1961).

Levine, M. Herschel. "Three Talmudic Tales of Seduction." *Judaism* 36, no. 4 (fall 1978): 466–70.

Lévi-Strauss, Claude. *The Jealous Potter.* Chicago: University of Chicago Press, 1988.

———. "Language and the Analysis of Social Laws." In *Structural Anthropology*, 55–66.

———. *Myth and Meaning.* New York: Schocken Books, 1979.

———. "The Story of Asdiwal." In *The Structural Study of Myth and Totemism*, ed. Edmund Leach, 27–30. London: Tavistock Publications, 1967.

———. *Structural Anthropology.* Trans. Claire Jacobson and Brooke Grundfest Schoepf. Harmondsworth: Penguin Books, 1963.

———. "The Structural Study of Myth." In *Structural Anthropology*, 206–31.

———. *Tristes tropiques.* Trans. John and Doreen Weightman. London: Jonathan Cape, 1973.

Lewis, Janet. *The Wife of Martin Guerre.* Denver: Alan Swallow, 1941.

Lewontin, R. C. "Sex, Lies, and Social Science." A review of Edward O. Laumann et al., *The Social Organization of Sexuality: Sexual Practices in the United States* (Chicago: University of Chicago Press, 1995). *New York Review of Books*, Apr. 20, 1995, 24–29. See also response to Laumann's response, in *New York Review of Books*, May 25, 1995.

Leyda, Jay, and Charles Musser, guest curators. *Before Hollywood: Turn-of-the-Century Film from American Archives.* New York: New York University Press for the American Federation of the Arts, 1986.

Lodge, David. *The British Museum Is Falling Down.* 1965. Harmondsworth: Penguin Books, 1981.

———. *Changing Places: A Tale of Two Campuses.* Harmondsworth: Penguin Books, 1975.

———. *Small World.* London: Macmillan, 1984.

Lommel, Herman. *Kleine Schriften.* Wiesbaden: Steiner, 1978.

Lorenz, Konrad. *King Solomon's Ring.* New York: Crowell, 1952.

Lotman, Yuri M. "The Semiosphere." In *Universe of the Mind: A Semiotic Theory of Culture*, trans. Ann Shukman. Bloomington: Indiana University Press, 1990.

Lurie, Alison. *Foreign Affairs.* New York: Random House, 1984.

Lüthi, Max. *The Fairytale as Art Form and Portrait of Man.* Trans. Jon Erickson. Bloomington: Indiana University Press, 1984.

Lutz, John. *Single White Female Seeks Same.* New York: Pocket Books, 1992.

Lyke, Larry L. "What Does Ruth Have to Do with Rahab?" Paper presented at the annual meeting of the American Academy of Religion, Nov. 1995.

Maity, Pradyot Kumar. *Historical Studies in the Cult of the Goddess Manasa.* Calcutta: Punthi Pustak, 1966.

Malory, Sir Thomas. *Le morte d'Arthur.* New Hyde Park, N.Y.: University Books, 1961.

Mann, Thomas. *Joseph and His Brothers.* Trans. H. T. Lowe-Porter. New York: Alfred Knopf, 1948.

Manuel, Frank E. *The Broken Staff: Judaism through Christian Eyes.* Cambridge: Harvard University Press, 1992.

Marglin, Frédérique Apffel. *Wives of the God-King: The Rituals of the Devadasis of Puri.* Delhi: Oxford University Press, 1985.

Margalit, Avishai, and Moshe Halbertal. *Idolatry.* Trans. Naomi Goldblum. Cambridge: Harvard University Press, 1992.

Marias, Javier. *Tomorrow in the Battle Think on Me.* Trans. Margaret Jull Costa. New York: Harcourt Brace & World, 1996.

Marx, Karl. *The Eighteenth Brumaire.* Peking: Foreign Language Press, 1978.

Masson, Jeffrey Moussaieff. *The Complete Letters of Sigmund Freud to Wilhelm Fliess, 1887–1904.* Cambridge: Harvard University Press, 1985.

Maynadier, G. H. *The Wife of Bath's Tale: Its Sources and Analogues.* London, 1901. Reprint, New York: AMS Press, 1972.

Mayne, Judith. "Uncovering the Female Body." In *Before Hollywood: Turn-of-the-Century Film from American Archives,* by Jay Leyda and Charles Musser, guest curators, 63–67. New York: New York University Press for the American Federation of the Arts, 1986.

McDermott, J. P. "Karma and Rebirth in Early Buddhism." In *Karma and Rebirth in Classical Indian Traditions,* ed. Wendy Doniger O'Flaherty, 165–92. Berkeley and Los Angeles: University of California Press, 1980.

Meier, P. Joseph. *Mythe und Erzählungen der Küstenbewohner der Gazelle Halbinsel.* Berlin: Anthropos Bibliothek, 1909.

Mendelsohn, Daniel. *The Elusive Embrace: Desire and the Riddle of Identity.* New York: Alfred Knopf, 1999.

Menn, Esther Marie. *Judah and Tamar (Genesis 38) in Ancient Jewish Exegesis.* Leiden: Brill, 1997.

Middlebrook, Diane Wood. *Suits Me: The Double Life of Billy Tipton.* Boston and New York: Houghton Mifflin, 1998.

Middleton, John. *Myth and Cosmos: Readings in Mythology and Symbolism.* Austin: University of Texas Press, 1967.

Middleton, Thomas. *The Family of Love* and *Micro-Cynicon.* In *The Works of Thomas Middleton,* vol. 3, ed. A. H. Bullen. Boston: Houghton, Mifflin, 1885–86.

Mikkelsen, Edwin J., and Thomas G. Gutheil. "Communication and Reality in the Capgras Syndrome." *American Journal of Psychotherapy* 30 (1976): 136–45.

Miles, Margaret R. *Carnal Knowing: Female Nakedness and Religious Meaning in the Christian West.* Boston: Beacon Press, 1989.

Miller, Barbara Stoler. *Love Song of the Dark Lord.* New York: Columbia University Press, 1977.

Miller, Karl. *Doubles: Studies in Literary History.* Oxford: Oxford University Press, 1987.

Millman, Lawrence, ed. *A Kayak Full of Ghosts.* Berkeley and Los Angeles: University of California Press, 1987.

Milton. *Paradise Lost.* Ed. Christopher Ricks. New York: Signet, 1968.

Miner, Earl, et al. *The Princeton Companion to Classical Japanese Literature.* Princeton: Princeton University Press, 1985.

Mitra, Satyacharan. *Shrishri Ramakrsna Paramahamsa—Jivana o Upadesa.* Calcutta: Great Indian Press, 1897.

Moi, Toril. *Sexual/Textual Politics: Feminist Literary Theory.* London and New York: Methuen & Co., 1985.

Molina, Tirso de. *The Trickster of Seville and the Stone Guest.* Trans. Gwynne Edwards. Warminster: Aris and Phillips, 1976.

Morris, Jan. *Conundrum.* London: Faber & Faber, 1974.

Morson, Gary Saul. *Narrative and Freedom: The Shadows of Time.* New Haven: Yale University Press, 1994.

Mowat, Farley. *People of the Deer.* Boston: Little, Brown & Co., 1952.

Mozart. *Marriage of Figaro.* See Da Ponte.

Muhawi, Ibrahim, and Sharif Kanaana. *Speak, Bird, Speak Again: Palestinian Arab Folktales.* Berkeley and Los Angeles: University of California Press, 1988.

Murdoch, Iris. *The Sea, the Sea.* New York: Viking Press, 1978.

Murray, James A. H., ed. *The Romance and Prophecies of Thomas of Erceldoune.* Early English Text Society no. 61. London, 1875.

Nach, Shlomo. "Freedom and Celibacy: A Talmudic Variation on Tales of Temptation and Fall in Genesis and Its Syrian Background." In *The Book of Genesis in Jewish and Oriental Christian Interpretation,* ed. Judith Frishman and Lucas van Rompay, 73–89. Louvain: In Aedibus Peeters, 1997.

Nagy, Greg. *Greek Mythology and Poetics.* Ithaca: Cornell University Press, 1990.

Nandy, Ashis. *The Intimate Enemy: Loss and Recovery of Self under Colonialism.* Oxford: Oxford University Press, 1983.

Narayan, Kirin. *Mondays on the Dark Night of the Moon: Himalayan Foothill Folktales told by Urmila Devi.* New York: Oxford University Press, 1997.

———. "The Tulsi Plant in Kangra." Forthcoming.

Natesa, Pandit S. M. Sastri. *Tales of Tennalirama (The Famous Court Jester of South India).* Madras: G. A. Natesan & Co., 1900.

Neely, Carol Thomas. *Broken Nuptials in Shakespeare's Plays.* New Haven: Yale University Press, 1985.

Neely, Richard. *The Plastic Nightmare.* New York: Ace Publishing Corp., 1969. Republished, after the movie (1991), and entitled *Shattered* (New York: Random House, Vintage Crime, 1991).

Neufeld, Ephraim. "Levirate Marriage." In *Ancient Hebrew Marriage Laws with Special*

References to General Semitic Laws and Customs, 26–55. London: Longmans, Green & Co., 1944.

Nietzsche, Friedrich. *Beyond Good and Evil: Prelude to a Philosophy of the Future.* Trans. Walter Kaufmann. New York: Vintage Books, 1966.

Obeyesekere, Gananath. *Medusa's Hair: An Essay on Personal Symbols and Religious Experience.* Chicago: University of Chicago Press, 1981.

Obeyesekere, Ranjini, and Gananath Obeyesekere. "The Tale of the Demoness Kali: A Discourse on Evil." *History of Religions* 29, no. 4 (May 1990): 318–35.

O'Flaherty, Wendy Doniger. "The Case of the Stallion's Wife: Indra and Vrsanasva in the Rg Veda and the Brahmanas." *Journal of the American Oriental Society* 105, no. 3 (1985): 485–98.

———. *Dreams, Illusion, and Other Realities.* Chicago: University of Chicago Press, 1984.

———. *Hindu Myths.* Harmondsworth: Penguin Books, 1975.

———. "Horses and Snakes in the Adi Parvan." In *Aspects of India: Essays in Honor of Edward Cameron Dimock,* ed. Margaret Case and N. Gerald Barrier, 16–44. New Delhi: American Institute of Indian Studies and Manohar, 1986.

———. *The Origins of Evil in Hindu Mythology.* Berkeley and Los Angeles: University of California Press, 1976.

———. *Other Peoples' Myths: The Cave of Echoes.* New York: Macmillan, 1988. Reprint, Chicago: University of Chicago Press, 1995.

———. *The Rig Veda: An Anthology.* Harmondsworth: Penguin Books, 1981.

———. *Siva: The Erotic Ascetic.* London: Oxford University Press, 1973. Formerly entitled *Asceticism and Eroticism in the Mythology of Siva.*

———. *Tales of Sex and Violence: Folklore, Sacrifice, and Danger in the Jaiminiya Brahmana.* Chicago: University of Chicago Press, 1985.

———. *Textual Sources for the Study of Hinduism.* Chicago: University of Chicago Press, 1990.

———. *Women, Androgynes, and Other Mythical Beasts.* Chicago: University of Chicago Press, 1981.

Orrey, Leslie, and Rodney Milnes, eds. *Opera: A Concise History.* New York: Thames & Hudson, 1987.

Osgood, Charles E., and Zella Luria. "Case Report." *Journal of Abnormal and Social Psychology* 49, no. 4 (Oct. 1954). Reprinted as appendix A in Thigpen and Cleckley, *The Three Faces of Eve.*

Padel, Ruth. "Putting the Words into Women's Mouths." *London Review of Books,* Jan. 23, 1997, 12–17.

Pagels, Elaine. "Pursuing the Spiritual Eve: Imagery and Hermeneutics in the *Hypostasis of the Archons* and the *Gospel of Philip.*" In King, *Images of the Feminine,* 187–206.

Paré, Ambrose. *On Monsters and Marvels.* Trans. Janis L. Pallister. Chicago: University of Chicago Press, 1982.

Passage, Charles E., and James H. Mantinband. *Amphitryon: Three Plays in New Verse Translation (Plautus [Mantiband], Molière [Passage], Kleist [Passage]),* Together *with a Comprehensive Account of the Evolution of the Legend and Its Subsequent Hitory on the Stage.* Chapel Hill: University of North Carolina Press, 1974.

Patai, Raphael. *Sex and the Family in the Bible and the Middle East.* New York: Doubleday, 1959.

Perkins, Pheme. "Sophia as Goddess in the Nag Hammadi Codices." In King, *Images of the Feminine,* 96–112.

Pflugfelder, Gregory M. "Strange Fates: Sex, Gender, and Sexuality in *Torikaebaya Monigatari.*" In *Monumenta Nipponica* 17, no. 3 (autumn 1992): 347–68.

Phillips, Adam. *On Flirtation.* Cambridge: Harvard University Press, 1994.

Poizat, Michel. *The Angel's Cry: Beyond the Pleasure Principle in Opera.* Trans. Arthur Denner. Ithaca: Cornell University Press, 1992.

Posner, Richard A. *Sex and Reason.* Cambridge: Harvard University Press, 1992.

Pritchard, James B., ed. *Ancient Near Eastern Texts Relating to the Old Testament.* Princeton: Princeton University Press, 1969.

Proust, Marcel. *Remembrance of Things Past.* Trans. C. K. Scott Moncrieff and Terence Kilmartin. 3 vols. New York: Random House, 1981.

Quiller-Couch, Sir Arthur. Introduction to *All's Well That Ends Well.* Cambridge: Cambridge University Press, 1968.

Radin, Paul. *The Trickster.* New York: Bell Publishing Co., 1956.

Rainey, Froelich. *The Whale Hunters of Tigara.* Anthropological Papers of the American Museum of Natural History, vol. 41, no. 2. New York, 1947.

Ralston, W. R. Shedden. "Beauty and the Beast." *Nineteenth Century* 4 (1878): 990–1012.

———. "Cinderella." In Dundes, *Cinderella,* 30–56.

Ramachandra Rao, P. *Tales of Mariada Raman: 21 Amusing Stories.* London, 1902.

Ramanujan, A. K. *The Collected Essays of A. K. Ramanujan.* New Delhi: Oxford University Press, 1999.

———. *"A Flowering Tree" and Other Oral Tales from India.* Berkeley and Los Angeles: University of California Press, 1997.

———. *Folktales from India.* New York: Pantheon Books, 1992.

———. "Hanchi: A Kannada Cinderella." In *The Collected Essays of A. K. Ramanujan,* 369–76.

———. "The Prince Who Married His Own Left Side." In *The Collected Essays of A. K. Ramanujan,* 398–411.

———. "Towards a Counter-System: Women's Tales." In *The Collected Essays of A. K. Ramanujan,* 429–47.

———. "Two Realms of Kannada Folklore." In *The Collected Essays of A. K. Ramanujan,* 495–512.

Ramanujan, A. K., et al. *When God Is a Customer: Telugu Courtesan Songs by Ksetrayya and Others.* Berkeley and Los Angeles: University of California Press, 1994.

Ramesan, N. *Temples and Legends of Andhra Pradesh.* Bombay: Bharatiya Vidya Bhavan, 1962.

Randolph, Vance. *"The Devil's Pretty Daughter" and Other Ozark Folk Tales.* New York: Columbia University Press, 1955.

Rank, Otto. *Beyond Psychology.* New York: Dover Publications, 1958.

———. *Der Doppelgänger: Eine psychoanalytische Studie.* Leipzig, 1925.

———. *The Double: A Psychoanalytic Study.* Trans. Harry Tucker, Jr. New York: New American Library, 1971.

———. "The Double as Immortal Self." In *Beyond Psychology,* 62–101.

———. *The Myth of the Birth of the Hero.* New York, 1914. Republished in Otto Rank et al., *In Quest of the Hero* (Princeton: Princeton University Press, 1990).

Réage, Pauline [Dominique Aury]. *Story of O.* Trans. Sabine d'Estrée. New York: Ballantine Books, 1973. Originally published in 1954.

Reardon, B. P. "An Ethiopian Story." Trans. J. R. Morgan. In *Collected Ancient Greek Novels,* ed. B. P. Reardon, 349–589. Berkeley and Los Angeles: University of California Press, 1989.

Reynolds, Margaret. "Ruggiero's Deceptions, Cherubino's Distractions." In Blackmer and Smith, *En Travesti,* 132–51.

Riche, Barnabe. "Phylotus and Emilia." In *His Farewell to Military Profession,* ed. Donald Beecher, 291–314. Ottawa: Dovehouse Editions, 1992.

Richer, Jean. "The Androgyne, the Double, and the Reflection: A Few Myths of Romanticism." In Bonnefoy, *Mythologies,* 765–66.

Richlin, Amy. "Making Up a Woman: The Face of Roman Gender." In Eilberg-Schwartz and Doniger, *Off with Her Head!* 185–213.

Rider, William. *The Twins. A tragi-comedy: acted at the private house at Salisbury-Court, with general applause.* London: Printed for Robert Pollard and John Sweeting, 1655.

Rivière, Joan. "Womanliness as a Masquerade." In *Formations of Fantasy,* ed. Victor Burgin, James Donald, and Cora Kaplan, 35–44. New York: Methuen, 1986.

Roddenberry, Gene. "Second Chances." An episode of *Star Trek: The Next Generation.* In *Star Trek: 30 Years Special Collector's Edition,* 131. Ontario: Paramount Pictures Corp., 1996.

Rogers, Robert. *A Psychoanalytic Study of the Double in Literature.* Detroit: Wayne State University Press, 1970.

Roheim, Geza. "The Garden of Eden." *Psychoanalytic Review* 27 (1940): 1–26, 177–99.

Rose, Phyllis. *Parallel Lives: Five Victorian Marriages.* New York: Vintage Books, 1983.

Roselli, John. *Singers of Italian Opera.* Cambridge: Cambridge University Press, 1992.

Rosenfield, Claire. "The Shadow Within: The Conscious and Unconscious Use of the Double." In *Stories of the Double,* ed. Albert J. Guerard, 311–21. Philadelphia and New York: Lippincott, 1967. Originally published in *Daedalus* 96 (spring 1967).

Rosenzweig, Franz. *Das neue Denken.* In *Kleine Schriften.* Berlin: Schocken Verlag, 1937.

Rossner, Judith. *Looking for Mr. Goodbar.* New York: Simon & Schuster, 1975.

Rostand, Edmond. *Cyrano de Bergerac.* Trans. Brian Hooker. New York: Bantam Books, 1950.

Roth, Joseph. *The Tale of the 1002nd Night.* Trans. Michael Hofmann. New York: St. Martin's Press, 1998.

Rukeyser, Muriel. *The Muriel Rukeyser Reader.* Ed. Jan Heller Levi. New York: W. W. Norton, 1994.

Rushdie, Salman. *The Ground beneath Her Feet.* New York: Henry Holt, 1999.

————. *Haroun and the Sea of Stories.* New York: Grant Books, 1990.

————. "Kipling." In *Imaginary Homelands: Essays and New Criticism, 1981–1991,* 74–80. New York: Penguin Books, 1991.

————. *Midnight's Children.* New York: Avon, 1980.

————. *The Moor's Last Sigh.* New York: Pantheon, 1995.

————. *Shame.* London: Jonathan Cape, 1983.

Rycroft, Charles. *The Innocence of Dreams.* New York: Pantheon Books, 1979.

Sabbah, Fatna A. *Woman in the Muslim Unconscious.* New York: Pergamon Press, 1984.

Said, Edward. *Orientalism.* New York: Vintage Books, 1978.

Sasson, Jack. *Ruth: A New Translation, with a Philological Commentary and a Formalist-Folklorist Interpretation.* Baltimore: Johns Hopkins University Press, 1979.

Sattampillai, A. N. *Ruttammavai.* Palamkottah: Church Mission Press, 1884.

von Schiefner, F. Anton. *Tibetan Tales, Translated from the Tibetan of the Kan-Gyur.* London: George Routledge & Sons, 1926.

Schnitzler, Arthur. "Casanova's Homecoming." Trans. Eden Paul and Cedar Paul. In *Plays and Stories,* ed. Ego Schwarz, 153–248. The German Library, vol. 55. New York: Continuum, 1982.

————. *Casanova's Return to Venice.* Trans. Ilsa Barea. London: Pushkin Press, 1998.

Schofield, William Henry. "Studies on the Libaeus Desconus." In *Studies and Notes in Philology and Literature,* vol. 4, 199–208. Boston: Ginn & Co., 1895.

Schuster, M. Lincoln. *A Treasury of the World's Great Letters.* New York: Simon & Schuster, 1940.

Schwartz, Hillel. *The Culture of the Copy: Striking Likenesses, Unreasonable Facsimiles.* New York: Zone Books, 1996.

Schwartz, Howard. "The Beast." In *Lilith's Cave: Jewish Tales of the Supernatural,* 59–61. New York: Oxford University Press, 1988.

Schweitzer, Arlette, with Kathryn Casey. "My Children, My Grandchildren." *Ladies' Home Journal,* Feb. 1992, 125 ff.

Scott, James C. *Weapons of the Weak: Everyday Forms of Peasant Resistance.* New Haven: Yale University Press, 1985.

Scott, Paul. *The Jewel in the Crown.* 1966. Chicago: University of Chicago Press, 1976.

Sedgwick, Eve Kosofsky. *Epistemology of the Closet.* Berkeley and Los Angeles: University of California Press, 1990.

Segal, Naomi. "Doubles." In *The Unintended Reader: Feminism and Manon Lescaut,* 59–193. Cambridge: Cambridge University Press, 1986.

Senelick, Laurence. "The Illusion of Sex." *American Theatre,* Nov. 1995, 12–16.

Shakespeare, William. *The Complete Works.* Ed. David Bevington. Glenview, Ill.: Scott, Foresman, 1980.

Shepherd, Chuck, John J. Kohut, and Roland Sweet. *News of the Weird.* New York: New American Library, 1989.

Sheridan, Richard Brinsley. *The Rivals.* New York: Oxford University Press, 1998.

Shirley, James. *The Lady of Pleasure.* In *A Critical Edition of James Shirley's "A Lady of Pleasure,"* ed. Marilyn J. Thorssen. New York and London: Garland Publishing, 1980.

————. *Love Tricks, or the School of Complements*. London: Thomas Dring, Jr., 1667.

Showalter, Elaine. *Sexual Anarchy: Gender and Culture at the Fin de Siècle*. New York: Penguin Books, 1990.

Shulman, David. "First Man, Forest Mother: Telugu Humanism in the Age of Krsnade-varaya." In *Syllables of Sky*, 133–64.

————. "On Being Human in the Sanskrit Epic: The Riddle of Nala." *Journal of Indian Philosophy* 22 (1994): 1–29.

————. "Sita and Satakantharavana in a Tamil Folk Narrative." *Journal of Indian Folk-loristics* 2 (1979): 1–26.

————. *Tamil Temple Myths*. Princeton: Princeton University Press, 1980.

————, ed. *Syllables of Sky: Studies in South Indian Civilization in Honour of Velcheru Narayana Rao*. Delhi: Oxford University Press, 1995.

Shulman, David, with Don Handelman. *God Inside Out: Siva's Game of Dice*. New York: Oxford University Press, 1997.

Shulman, David, with Velcheru Narayana Rao and Sanjay Subrahmanyam. *Symbols of Substance: Court and State in Nayaka Period Tamil Nadu*. Delhi: Oxford University Press, 1992.

Sidney, Sir Philip. *The Countess of Pembroke's Arcadia*. Middlesex, England: Penguin, 1977.

Siebert, Charles. "The Cuts That Go Deeper." *New York Times Sunday Magazine*, July 7, 1996.

Singer, Isaac Bashevis. *Enemies, a Love Story*. 1966 (in Yiddish). Trans. Aliza Shevrin and Elizabeth Shub. New York: Farrar, Straus & Giroux, 1972.

————. "Yentl the Yeshiva Boy." In *The Collected Stories*, 149–69. New York: Farrar, Straus & Giroux, 1988.

Sizemore, Chris Costner. *A Mind of My Own: The Woman Who Was Known as Eve Tells the Story of Her Triumph over Multiple Personality Disorder*. New York: William Morrow, 1989.

Sizemore, Chris Costner, with Elen Sain Pittillo. *I'm Eve*. New York: Jove, 1978.

Sizemore, Chris Costner [as Evelyn Lancaster], with James Poling. *The Final Face of Eve*. New York: McGraw-Hill, 1958.

Skutsch, Otto. "Helen: Her Name and Nature." *Journal of Hellenic Studies* 102 (1987): 188–93.

Slovenko, Ralph. "The Multiple Personality: A Challenge to Legal Concepts." *Journal of Psychiatry and Law* (winter 1989): 681–719.

Smith, Dinitia. *The Illusionist*. New York: Scribner, 1997.

Smith, Rosamond [Joyce Carol Oates]. *Lives of the Twins*. New York: Simon & Schuster, 1987.

Smith, Sid. "An Unconventional Love Story: What Makes Audiences Flock to 'Butter-fly'?" and "The Odd Couple: 2 Actors Reflect on their Unusual Roles." *Chicago Tribune*, Sunday, Mar. 3, 1991.

Songling, Pu. *Schmetterlinge fliegen lassen: der Bände dreizehn bis fünfzehn aus der Sammlung Liao dschai dschi yi*. Trans. Gottfried Rösel. In *Liao dschai dschi yi*, vol. 4. Zurich: Die Waage, 1992.

Southern, Terry. "A Change of Style." In *Red-Dirt Marijuana and Other Tastes,* 183–86. London: Granada, 1955.

Sperber, Dan. "Claude Lévi-Strauss." In *Structuralism and Since: From Lévi-Strauss to Derrida,* ed. John Sturrock, 19–51. London: Oxford University Press, 1979.

Sperling, Harry, Maurice Simon, and Dr. Paul P. Levertoff, trans. *The Zohar.* Vol. 3. New York: Rebecca Bennet Publications, 1958.

Spivak, Gayatri Chakravorty. "Can the Subaltern Speak?" In *Marxism and Interpretation of Culture,* ed. Cary Nelson and Lawrence Grossman. Urbana: University of Illinis Press, 1988.

Stein, Rolf A. "The Guardian of the Gate: An Example of Buddhist Mythology, from India to Japan." In Bonnefoy, *Mythologies,* vol. 2, 896–910.

Stoker, Bram. *Dracula.* London, 1897; New York: Bantam, 1981.

Stoppard, Tom. *Travesties.* New York: Grove Press, 1975.

Stroumsa, Gedaliahu. *Another Seed: Studies in Gnostic Mythology.* Leiden: E. J. Brill, 1984.

Sullivan, Bruce. *Krsna Dvaipayana Vyasa and the Mahabharata: A New Interpretation.* Leiden: E. J. Brill, 1990.

Syrkin, Alexander. "Chernoye Solntse." *Kratkiye Soobshcheniya Instituta Narodov Azii* 80 (1965): 20–32.

Taggart, James M. *Enchanted Maidens: Gender Relations in Spanish Folktales of Courtship and Marriage.* Princeton: Princeton University Press, 1990.

Tailor, Robert. *The Hogge Hath Lost his Pearl.* 1613. Ed. D. F. McKenzie. Oxford: Malone Society Reprints, 1967, 1972.

Tawney, C. H. *The Ocean of Story.* With notes by M. Penzer. 10 vols. London: Chas. J. Sawyer, 1924.

Teit, James A. *Mythology of the Thompson Indians.* Vol. 12 of *The Jesup North Pacific Expedition, Memoirs of the American Museum of Natural History,* ed. Franz Boas. New York: G. E. Stechert, 1913.

Teyvacikamani, N. C. *Sri Venkateca Makatmiyam.* Cennai, Madras: Pailat paplikesans (Pilot Publications), 1976.

Thigpen, Corbett H., and Hervey M. Cleckly. *The Three Faces of Eve.* New York: McGraw-Hill, 1957.

Thomas, B. P. *Abraham Lincoln.* New York: Knopf, 1954.

Thomas of Erceldoune. *The Romance and Prophecies of Thomas of Erceldoune.* Ed. James A. H. Murray. London: N. Trübner & Co., 1875.

Thompson, Stith. *Motif-Index of Folk Literature.* 6 vols. Bloomington: Indiana University Press, 1955–58.

Thompson, Stith, and Jonas Balys. *The Oral Tales of India.* Bloomington: Indiana University Press, 1958.

Thomson, David. *A Biographical Dictionary of Film.* 3d ed. New York: Alfred Knopf, 1998.

Tishby, Isaiah, ed. *The Wisdom of the Zohar: An Anthology of Texts.* Trans. David Goldstein. 3 vols. New York: Oxford University Press, 1989.

Tracy, David. *Dialogue with the Other: The Inter-religious Dialogue.* Louvain: Eerdmans, Peeters Press, 1990.

———. "Iris Murdoch and the Many Faces of Platonism." In *Iris Murdoch and the Search for Human Goodness*, ed. William Schweiker and Maria Antonoccio, 54–75. Chicago: University of Chicago Press, 1997.

———. *On Naming the Present: Reflections on God, Hermeneutics, and Church*. Maryknoll, N.Y.: Orbis Books, 1994.

———. *Pluralism and Ambiguity: Hermeneutics, Religion, Hope*. Chicago: University of Chicago Press, 1987.

Trawick, Margaret. *Notes on Love in a Tamil Family*. Berkeley and Los Angeles: University of California Press, 1990.

Treitel, Jonathan. "Stalin, Stalin, and Stalin." *New Yorker*, Sept. 21, 1992, 32–34.

Turner, Edith. *The Hands Feel It: Healing and Spirit Presence among a Northern Alaskan People*. DeKalb: Northern Illinois University Press, 1996.

Twain, Mark. "Feud Story and the Girl Who Was Ostensibly a Man." Ed. Robert Sattelmeyer. *Missouri Review* 10 (1987): 97–112.

———. "1,002d Arabian Night." 1883. In *Mark Twain's Satires and Burlesques*, ed. Franklin R. Rogers, 88–133. Berkeley and Los Angeles: University of California Press, 1967.

———. *The Prince and the Pauper: A Tale for Young People of All Ages*. New York: Harper & Brothers, 1903.

———. *Pudd'nhead Wilson and Other Tales*. Ed. R. D. Gooder. London and New York: Oxford University Press, 1992.

Tymms, Ralph. *Doubles in Literary Psychology*. Cambridge: Bowes & Bowes, 1949.

von Strassburg, Gottfried. See *Tristan*.

Wadler, Joyce. "For the First Time, The Real-Life Models for Broadway's *M. Butterfly* Tell of Their Very Strange Romance." *People* 30, no. 6 (Aug. 8, 1988).

———. "The Spy Who Fell in Love with a Shadow." *New York Times Magazine*, Aug. 15, 1993, 30 ff.

Wagner, Richard. *The Art-Work of the Future*. In *The Art-Work of the Future and Other Works*, trans. William Ashton Ellis. Lincoln: University of Nebraska Press, 1993.

———. *The Ring of the Niebelung*. Trans. Andrew Porter. New York: W. W. Norton, 1976.

Wain, John. *The Living World of Shakespeare*. Middlesex, England: Penguin, 1966.

Wallace, Irving, and Amy Wallace. *The Two: A Biography*. New York: Simon & Schuster, 1978.

Warner, Marina. *From the Beast to the Blonde: On Fairy Tales and Their Tellers*. London: Chatto & Windus, 1995.

———. "Stolen Shadows, Lost Souls: Body and Soul in Photography." *Raritan*, 1996, 35–58.

Warren, Henry Clarke. *Buddhism in Translation*. New York: Atheneum, 1969.

Wasson, R. Gordon, and Wendy Doniger O'Flaherty. *Soma, Divine Mushroom of Immortality*. New York: Harcourt Brace, 1968.

White, T. H. *The Once and Future King*. London: Fontana Books, 1958.

Whiting, Bartlett J. "The Wife of Bath's Tale." In *Sources and Analogues of Chaucer's*

Canterbury Tales, ed. W. F. Bryan and Germaine Dempster, 223–64. Chicago: University of Chicago Press, 1941.

Wilde, Oscar. "The Importance of Being Ernest." In *The Portable Oscar Wilde*, 430–507. New York: Viking/Penguin 1946, 1974.

———. *The Picture of Dorian Gray*. London, 1890; 1891. Ed. Donald L. Lawler. New York: Norton, 1988.

Williams, Tennessee. *Cat on a Hot Tin Roof*. In *The Theatre of Tennessee Williams*, vol. 3. New York: New Directions, 1972.

———. *A Streetcar Named Desire*. In *The Theatre of Tennessee Williams*, vol. 1. New York: New Directions, 1972.

Willig, Rosette F. *The Changelings: A Classical Japanese Court Tale (Torikaebaya Monogatari)*. Trans., with an introduction and notes. Stanford: Stanford University Press, 1983.

Wilson, Elizabeth. *Charming Cadavers: Horrific Figurations of the Feminine in Indian Buddhist Hagiographic Literature*. Chicago: University of Chicago Press, 1996.

Wilson, H. H., trans. *The Vishnu Purana*. London, 1840. 3d ed., Calcutta: Punthi Pustak, 1961.

Winnicott, D. W. *The Family and Individual Development*. London: Tavistock, 1965.

———. "Mirror-Role of the Mother and Family in Child Development." In *The Predicament of the Family*, ed. P. Lomas, 26–33. New York: International Universities Press, 1967.

Wolf, Naomi. *The Beauty Myth: How Images Are Used against Women*. New York: William Morrow, 1991.

Woolf, Virginia. *Orlando: A Biography*. New York: Harcourt Brace, 1928.

Wright, Lawrence. "Double Mystery." *New Yorker*, Aug. 7, 1995, 45–62.

———. *Twins: Genes, Environment, and the Mystery of Identity*. London: Weidenfeld & Nicholson, 1997.

Wright, Richard. "Man of All Work." In *Eight Men*. New York: Thunder's Mouth Press, 1987.

Yanagida, Kunio. *Japanese Folk Tales: A Revised Selection*. Trans. Fanny Hagin Mayer. Taiwan: Asian Folklore and Social Life Monographs, 1972.

———. *The Yanagida Kunio Guide to the Japanese Folk Tale*. Trans. Fanny Hagin Mayer. Bloomington: Indiana University Press, 1970.

———. *Yanagida Kunio no Bunrui niyoru Nihon no Mukashibanashi* (Japanese Folk Tales Classified by Kunio Yanagida). Ed. Toshio Iwasaki. Tokyo: Kadokawa, 1977.

Yeats, William Butler. *The Collected Poems of W. B. Yeats*. London: Macmillan & Co., 1965.

Yu, Anthony. *Journey to the West*. Chicago: University of Chicago Press, 1977–83.

Yu, Li. *The Carnal Prayer Mat*. Trans. Patrick Hanan. New York: Ballantine, 1990.

———. "Nativity Room." In *A Tower for the Summer Heat*, trans. Patrick Hanan, 221–49. New York: Ballantine, 1992.

Zall, P. M., ed., *Abe Lincoln Laughing: Humorous Anecdotes from Original Sources by and about Abraham Lincoln*. Berkeley and Los Angeles: University of California Press, 1982.

Zeitlin, Judith. *Historian of the Strange: Pu Songling and the Classical Chinese Tale.* Stanford: Stanford University Press, 1993.

Zimmer, Heinrich. *The King and the Corpse: Tales of the Soul's Conquest of Evil.* Ed. Joseph Campbell. Princeton: Bollingen, 1948.

Žižek, Slavoj. " 'The Wound Is Healed Only by the Spear That Smote You': The Operatic Subject and Its Vicissitudes." In *Opera through Other Eyes,* ed. David J. Levin, 177–214. Stanford: Stanford University Press, 1993.

Zunz, Leopold. *Die synagogale Poesie des Mittelalters.* Berlin: Julius Springer, 1855.

Zvelebil, Kamil. *Two Tamil Folktales: The Story of King Matanakama; The Story of Peacock Ravana.* Delhi: Motilal Banarsidass, 1987.

Zweig, Paul. *The Adventurer.* New York: Basic Books, 1974.

FILMOGRAPHY

DOUBLE FEATURES: BEDTRICKS (AND RELATED PLOTS) ON FILM

w = written by, *d* = directed by, *wd* = written and directed by, *s* = starring

All of Me, 1984, *w* Phil Alden Robinson, from the novel *Me Two,* by Ed Davis; *d* Carl Reiner; s Steve Martin, Lily Tomlin, Victoria Tennant.

American Gigolo, 1980, *wd* Paul Schrader; s Richard Gere, Lauren Hutton.

An Awfully Big Adventure, 1995, *w* Charles Wood, from the novel by Beryl Bainbridge; *d* Mike Newell; *s* Hugh Grant, Alan Rickman, Georgina Cates.

Bachelor Party, 1984, *w* Neal Israel, Pat Profit, from a story by Bob Israel; *d* Neal Israel; *s* Tom Hanks, Tawny Kitaen.

Back to the Future, 1985, *w* Robert Zemeckis, Bob Gale; *d* Robert Zemeckis; *s* Michael J. Fox, Christopher Lloyd.

The Ballad of Little Joe, 1993, *wd* Maggie Greenwald; *s* Suzy Amis, Bo Hopkins, Ian McKelen, David Chung.

Basic Instinct, 1991, *w* Joe Eszterhas; *d* Paul Verhoeven; *s* Michael Douglas, Sharon Stone.

Batman Returns, 1992, *w* Daniel Waters, Sam Hamm; *d* Tim Burton; *s* Michael Keaton, Michelle Pfeiffer.

Being John Malkovich, 1999, *w* Charlie Kaufman; *d* Spike Jonze; *s* John Malkovich, John Cusack, Orson Bean.

La belle et la bête (Beauty and the Beast), 1946, *wd* Jean Cocteau, from a story by Madame LePrince de Beaumont; *s* Jean Marais, Josette Day.

Bells Are Ringing, 1960, *w* Betty Comden and Adolph Green, from their play; *d* Vincente Minnelli; *s* Judy Holliday, Dean Martin.

Big, 1988, *w* Gary Ross, Anne Spielberg; *d* Penny Marshall; *s* Tom Hanks, Elizabeth Perkins.

Big Business, 1988, *w* Dori Pierson, Marc Rudel; *d* Jim Abrahams; *s* Bette Midler, Lily Tomlin.

Bitter Moon, 1992, *w* Roman Polanski, from the novel by Pascal Bruckner; *d* Roman Polanski; *s* Peter Coyote, Hugh Grant.

Blade Runner, 1982, *w* Hampton Fancher, David People, from Philip K. Dick's novel, *Do Androids Dream of Electric Sheep?; d* Ridley Scott; *s* Harrison Ford, Rutger Hauer, Daryl Hannah.

Body Double, 1984, *wd* Brian de Palma; *s* Craig Wasson, Gregg Henry, Melanie Griffith.

Body Heat, 1981, *w* Lawrence Kasdan, from James M. Cain's novel *Double Indemnity*; *d* Lawrence Kasdan; *s* William Hurt, Kathleen Turner.

Body Language, 1992, made for television, *wd* Arthur Allan Seidelman; *s* Heather Locklear, Linda Purl, James Acheson.

Boys Don't Cry, 1999, *w* Kimberly Pierce and Andy Bienen; *d* Kimberly Pierce; *s* Hilary Swank, Cloe Sevigny.

Bringing Up Baby, 1938, *w* Dudley Nichols, Hagar Wilde; *d* Howard Hawks; *s* Katharine Hepburn, Cary Grant.

Butterfield Eight, 1960, *w* Charles Schnee, John Michael Hayes, from the novel by John O'Hara; *d* Daniel Mann; *s* Elizabeth Taylor.

Carefree, 1938, *w* Allan Scott, Ernest Pagano; *d* Mark Sandrich; *s* Fred Astaire, Ginger Rogers.

Casanova's Big Night, 1954, *w* Hal Kanter, Edmund Hartmann; *d* Norman Z. McLeod; *s* Bob Hope, Joan Fontaine.

Cat on a Hot Tin Roof, 1958, *w* Richard Brooks, James Poe, from the play by Tennessee Williams; *d* Richard Brooks; *s* Elizabeth Taylor, Paul Newman, Burl Ives.

Cet obscur object de désir (That Obscure Object of Desire), 1977, *w* Pierre Lary, Juan-Luis Buñuel, based on Pierre Louys's novel *La femme et le pantin;* music by Richard Wagner; *d* Pierre Lary, Juan-Luis Buñuel; *s* Fernando Rey, Carole Bouquet, Angela Molina.

Chances Are, 1989, *w* Perry Howze, Randy Howze; *d* Emile Ardolino; *s* Cybill Shepherd, Robert Downey, Jr., Ryan O'Neal, Mary Stewart Masterson.

China, 1943, *w* Frank Butler, from Reginald Forbes's novel *The Fourth Brother;* *d* John Farrow; *s* Alan Ladd, Loretta Young.

Clerks, 1995, *wd* Kevin Smith, Scott Mosier; *s* Brian O'Halloran, Jeff Anderson, Marilyn Ghigliotti, Lisa Spoonauer, Jason Mewes.

Cobra Woman, 1944, *w* Richard Brooks, Gene Lewis; *d* Robert Siodmak; *s* Maria Montez.

Comrade Stalin's Trip to Africa (Georgia, Russia), 1991, *d* Irakli Kvirikadze.

Consenting Adults, 1992, *w* Matthew Chapman; *d* Alan J. Pakula; *s* Kevin Kline, Kevin Spacey, Mary Elizabeth Mastrantonio, Rebecca Miller.

The Corsican Brothers, 1941, *w* George Bruce, Howard Estabrook, from the Alexander Dumas novel; *d* Gregory Ratoff; *s* Douglas Fairbanks, Jr., Akim Tamiroff, Ruth Warrick. *The Return of the Corsican Brothers*, 1953, *w* Richard Schayer; *d* Ray Nazarro; *s* Richard Greene, Paula Raymond, Raymond Burr.

Cover Girl, 1944, *w* Virginia Van Upp; *d* Charles Vidor; *s* Rita Hayworth, Gene Kelly.

The Crying Game, 1992, *wd* Neil Jordan; *s* Stephen Rea, Miranda Richardson, Forest Whitaker, Jaye Davidson.

Cyrano de Bergerac, 1950, *w* Brian Hooker, from the play by Edmond Rostand; *d* Michael Gordon; *s* Jose Ferrer, Mala Powers.

The Dark Mirror, 1946, *w* Nunnally Johnson, from a story by Vladimir Pozner; *d* Robert Siodmak; *s* Olivia de Havilland, Lew Ayres; remade in 1986.

Dark Victory, 1939, *w* Casey Robinson, from the play by George Brewer, Jr.;

d Edmund Goulding; *s* Bette Davis, George Brent, Humphrey Bogart, Ronald Reagan.

Dave, 1993, *w* Gary Ross; *d* Ivan Reitman; *s* Kevin Kline, Sigourney Weaver.

The Day of the Locust, 1975, *w* Waldo Salt, from the novel by Nathaniel West; *d* John Schlesinger; *s* Donald Sutherland, Burgess Meredith, Geraldine Page.

Dead Again, 1991, *w* Scott Frank; *d* Kenneth Branagh; *s* Kenneth Branagh, Emma Thompson, Derek Jacobi, Robin Williams.

Dead Ringer, 1964, *w* Albert Beich, Oscar Millard, from a story by Rian James; *d* Paul Henreid; *s* Bette Davis, Peter Lawford, Karl Malden.

Dead Ringers, 1988, *w* David Cronenberg from the novel *Twins,* by Bari Wod and Jack Greasland; *d* David Cronenberg; *s* Jeremy Irons, Geneviève Bujold.

Decameron Nights, 1952, *w* George Oppenheimer; *d* Hugo Fregonese; *s* Louis Jordan, Joan Fontaine, Joan Collins.

Destination Tokyo, 1943, *wd* Delmer Daves; *s* Cary Grant, John Garfield.

The Divorce of Lady X, 1938, *w* Lajos Biro, Arthur Wimperis, Ian Dalrymple, from Gilbert Wakefield's play *Counsel's Opinion; d* Tim Whelan; *s* Merle Oberon, Laurence Olivier, Ralph Richardson.

Doña Flor and Her Two Husbands, 1976, *w* David Cronenberg, from the novel by Jorge Amado; *d* David Cronenberg; *s* Sonia Braga.

Double Impact, 1991, *wd* Sheldon Lettich, Jean-Claude Van Damme; *s* Jean-Claude Van Damme.

Double Indemnity, 1944, *w* Billy Wilder, Raymond Chandler, from the novel by James M. Cain; *d* Billy Wilder; *s* Fred MacMurray, Barbara Stanwyck, Edward G. Robinson.

The Double Life of Véronique, 1991, *wd* Krzysztof Kieslowski; *s* Irène Jacob.

Double Threat, 1992, *wd* David A. Prior; *s* Sally Kirland, Andrew Steves, Sherrie Rose, Chick Vennera, Gary Swanson, Richard Lynch, Anthony Franciosa.

Dream Lover, 1994, *wd* Nicholas Kazan; *s* James Spader, Madchen Amick.

Dressed to Kill, 1980, *wd* Brian de Palma; *s* Michael Caine, Angie Dickinson.

Duck Soup, 1933, *w* Bert Kalmar et al.; *d* Leo McCarey; *s* the four Marx brothers, Margaret Dumont.

Duplicates, 1991, made for cable; *w* Sandor Stern; *d* Andrew Neiderman; *s* Cicely Tyson, Kevin McCarthy, Gregory Harrison, Kim Greist.

The Eagle Has Landed, 1977, *w* Tom Mankiewicz, from the novel by Jack Higgins; *d* John Surges; *s* Michael Caine, Donald Sutherland, Robert Duvall, Donald Pleasence.

18 Again! 1988, *w* Josh Goldstein, Jonathan Price; *d* Paul Flaherty; *d* George Burns, Charlie Schlatter.

Enemies, a Love Story, 1989, *w* Roger L. Simon, Paul Mazursky, from the novel by Isaac Bashevis Singer; *d* Paul Mazursky; *s* Anjelica Huston, Ron Silver, Lena Olin.

Europa, Europa, 1991, *w* Agnieszka Holland, from the book by Salomon Perel; *d* Agnieszka Holland; *s* Marco Hofschneider.

Everyone Says I Love You, 1997, *wd* Woody Allen; *s* Woody Allen, Goldie Hawn, Alan Alda, Julia Roberts.

Excalibur, 1981, *w* Rospo Pallenberg, John Boorman; *d* John Booman; *s* Nigel
  Terry, Helen Mirren, Nicol Williamson.
Eyes Wide Shut, 1999, *w* Stanley Kubrick, from a novella by Arthur Schnitzler;
  d Stanley Kubrick; *s* Nicole Kidman, Tom Cruise.
Face of Another, 1966, *w* Hiroshi Teshigahara, Kobo Abe, from the novel by Kobo
  Abe; *d* Hiroshi Teshigahara, Kobo Abe; *s* Tatsuyu Nakadai, Machiko Kyo.
Face/Off, 1997, *w* Mike Werb and Michael Colleary; *d* John Woo; *s* Nicholas Cage,
  John Travolta.
A Face to Die For, 1996, *w* Marvin Welin, Mark Welin; *d* Jack Bender; *s* Yasmine
  Bleeth, James Wilder.
Farinelli, 1995, *w* Walther Vanden Ende; *d* Gérard Corbiau; *s* Stefano Dionisi,
  Enrico L. Verso, Elsa Zylberstein.
The File on Thelma Jordan, 1949, *w* Ketti Frings; *d* Robert Slodmak; *s* Barbara Stan-
  wyck, Wendell Corey.
The Flame of New Orleans, 1941, *w* Norman Krasna; *d* René Clair; *s* Marlene Die-
  trich, Bruce Cabot, Roland Young.
The Forbidden Street, 1948, *w* Ring Lardner, Jr., from Margery Sharp's novel *Britan-
  nia Mews* (also the British title of the film); *d* Jean Negulesco; *s* Dana Andrews,
  Maureen O'Hara, Sybil Thorndike.
Freaky Friday, 1976, *w* Mary Rodgers, from her novel; *d* Gary Nelson; *s* Jodie Fos-
  ter, Barbara Harris, John Astin.
The Front, 1976, *w* Walter Bernstein; *d* Martin Ritt; *s* Woody Allen, Zero Mostel,
  Herschel Bernardi, Andrea Marcovicci, Michael Murphy.
A Funny Thing Happened on the Way to the Forum, 1987, *w* Melvin Frank, Michael
  Pertwee, from the play by Burt Shevelove and Larry Gelbart, with additional lyr-
  ics by Stephen Sondheim; *d* Richard Lester; *s* Zero Mostel, Phil Silvers, Jack Gil-
  ford, Buster Keaton.
Goddess of Love, 1988, *d* Tim Drake; *s* Vanna White, David Naughton, Amanda
  Bearse.
Gone with the Wind, 1939, *w* Sidney Howard et al., from the novel by Margaret
  Mitchell; *d* Victor Fleming, George Cukor, Sam Wood; *s* Clark Gable, Vivien
  Leigh, Leslie Howard, Olivia de Havilland.
Goodbye, Charlie, 1964, *w* Harry Kurnitz from George Axelrod's play; *d* Vincente
  Minnelli; *s* Debbie Reynolds, Pat Boone, Walter Matthau, Tony Curtis.
The Great Dictator, 1940, *wds* Charlie Chaplin.
The Great White Hope, 1970, *w* Howard Sackler, from his play; *d* Martin Ritt;
  s James Earl Jones, Jane Alexander.
Groundhog Day, 1993, *w* Danny Rubin, Harold Harmis; *d* Harold Ramis; *s* Bill Mur-
  ray, Andie MacDowell.
Guys and Dolls, 1955, *w* Joseph L. Mankiewicz, from the musical by Jo Swerling,
  Abe Burrows; lyrics by Frank Loesser; *d* Joseph L. Mankiewicz; *s* Frank Sinatra,
  Marlon Brando, Jean Simmons, Vivian Blaine, Stubby Kaye.
Half Angel, 1951, *w* Robert Riskin; *d* Richard Sale; *s* Loretta Young, Joseph Cotten.
Hear My Song, 1991, *w* Peter Chelsom, Adrian Dunbar; *d* Peter Chelsom; *s* Ned
  Beatty, Adrian Dunbar, Shirley Anne Field.

Heaven Can Wait, 1978, *w* Warren Beatty, Elaine May, from the play by Harry Seg-
all (and the 1941 film *Here Comes Mr. Jordan*); *d* Warren Beatty, Buck Henry;
s Warren Beatty, Julie Christie, James Mason, Jack Warden.

Hello Again, 1987, *w* Susan Isaacs; *d* Frank Perry; *s* Shelly Long, Judith Ivey, Gabriel
Byrne.

Henry and June, 1990, *w* Philip Kaufman, Rose Kaufman, from the book by Anaïs
Nin; *d* Philip Kaufman; *s* Fred Ward, Uma Thurman.

Here Come the Waves, 1944, *w* Allen Scott et al.; *d* Mark Sandrich; *s* Betty Hutton,
Bing Crosby.

High Heels, 1991, *wd* Pedro Almodóvar; *s* Victoria Abril, Marisa Paredes, Miguel
Bosé.

Imitation of Life, 1934, *w* William Hurlbut, from the novel by Fannie Hurst; *d* John
Stahl; *s* Claudette Colbert, Warren William, Louise Beavers, Rochelle Hudson;
1959, *w* Eleanore Griffin; *d* Douglas Sirk; *s* Lana Turner, Juanita Moore, Susan
Kohner.

The Importance of Being Ernest, 1952, *w* Anthony Asquith, from the play by Oscar
Wilde; *d* Anthony Asquith; *s* Michael Redgrave, Edith Evans, Margaret Ruther-
ford, Joan Greenwood, Dorothy Tutin.

In This Our Life, 1942, *w* Howard Koch, from the novel by Ellen Glasgow; *d* John
Huston; *s* Bette Davis, Olivia de Havilland, George Brent, Dennis Morgan, Walter Huston.

Invasion of the Body Snatchers, 1956, *w* Daniel Mainwaring, from the novel by Jack
Finney; *d* Don Siegel; *s* Kevin McCarthy, Dana Wynter; 1978, *w* W. D. Richter;
d Philip Kaufman; *s* Donald Sutherland, Brooke Adams, Leonard Nimoy, Jeff
Goldblum, Kevin McCarthy.

The Iron Mask, 1929, *w* Elton Thomas (Douglas Fairbanks); *d* Allan Dwan, from
Alexandre Dumas's novel *Ten Years After;* *s* Douglas Fairbanks, Belle Bennett,
Ullrich Haupt.

I Was a Male War Bride, 1949, *w* Charles Lederer et al., from a 1947 *Reader's
Digest* story; *d* Howard Hawks; *s* Cary Grant, Ann Sheridan.

Killer in the Mirror, 1986, made for television, *wd* Frank De Felitta; *s* Ann Jillian,
Len Cariou, Max Gail.

The Lady Eve, 1941, *w* Preston Sturges from the play by Monckton Hoffe; *d* Preston Sturges; *s* Barbara Stanwyck, Henry Fonda, William Demarest.

Ladyhawke, 1985, *w* Edward Khmara et al.; *d* Richard Donner; *s* Rutger Hauer,
Michelle Pfeiffer, Matthew Broderick, Leo McKern.

The Last Time I Saw Paris, 1954, *w* Julius J. Epstein, Philip G. Epstein, Richard
Brooks; *d* Richard Brooks; *s* Van Johnson, Elizabeth Taylor.

Let's Make Love, 1960, *w* Norman Krasna; *d* George Cukar; *s* Yves Montand, Marilyn Monroe.

Liar, Liar, 1997, *w* Paul Guay, Stephen Mazur; *d* Tom Shadyac; *s* Jim Carey.

Like Father, Like Son, 1987, *w* Lorne Cameron, Steven L. Bloom; *d* Rod Daniel;
s Dudley Moore, Kirk Cameron.

The Little Drummer Girl, 1984, *w* Loring Mandel, from the novel by John Le Carré;
d George Roy Hill; *s* Diane Keaton, Yorgo Voyagis.

The Little Mermaid, 1989, *w* John Musker, Ron Clements, from the story by Hans Christian Andersen; *d* John Musker, Ron Clements.

Love Letters, 1945, *w* Ayne Rand, from Chris Massie's book *Pity My Simplicity; d* William Dieterle; *s* Joseph Cotton, Jennifer Jones.

Magnificent Obsession, 1935, *w* George O'Neil et al., from the novel by Lloyd C. Douglas; *d* John M. Stahl; *s* Irene Dunne, Robert Taylor; 1954, *w* Robert Blees; *d* Douglas Sirk; *s* Jane Wyman, Rock Hudson.

The Major and the Minor, 1942, *w* Charles Brackett, Billy Wilder; *d* Billy Wilder; *s* Ginger Rogers, Ray Milland, Diana Lynn.

The Man in the Iron Mask, 1939, *w* George Brent; *d* James Whale; *s* Louis Hayward, Joan Bennett; 1977, *d* Mike Newell; *s* Richard Chamberlain.

The Man Who Never Was, 1955, *w* Nigel Balchin, from the book by Ewen Montagu; *d* Ronald Neame; *s* Clifton Webb, Robert Fleming, Gloria Grahame.

Maxie, 1985, *w* Patrick Resnick, from Jack Finney's novel *Marion's Wall; d* Paul Aaron; *s* Glenn Close, Mandy Patinkin, Ruth Gordon.

Men in Black, 1997, *wd* Barry Sonnenfeld; *s* Tommy Lee Jones, Will Smith.

Metropolis, 1926, *w* Thea von Harbou; *d* Fritz Lang; *s* Brigitte Helm, Alfred Abel.

Mighty Aphrodite, 1996, *wd* Woody Allen; *s* Woody Allen, Mira Sorvino, Helen Bonham-Carter.

Mirror Images, 1991, made for television; *w* Georges des Esseintes; *d* Alexander Gregory Hippolyte; *s* Delia Sheppard, Jeff Conaway.

Mission: Impossible, 1996, *wd* Brian de Palma; *s* Tom Cruise, Jon Voight, Vanessa Redgrave.

Moon over Parador, 1988, *w* Leon Capetanos, Paul Mazursky, from a story by Charles G. Booth; *d* Paul Mazursky; *s* Richard Dreyfuss, Raul Julia, Sonia Braga.

Mrs. Doubtfire, 1993, *w* Randi Mayem Singer, Leslie Dixon, from Anne Fine's novel *Alias Madam Doubtfire; d* Chris Columbis; *s* Robin Williams, Sally Field, Sidney Walker.

Multiplicity, 1996, *w* Chris Miller, Mary Hale, Lowell Ganz, Babaloo Mandel, based on a short story by Chris Miller; *d* Harold Ramis; *s* Michael Keaton, Andie MacDowell.

My Geisha, 1962, *w* Norman Krasna; *d* Jack Cardiff; *s* Shirley Maclaine, Yves Montand, Robert Cummings, Edward G. Tobinson, Yoko Tani.

My Little Chickadee, 1940, *w* Mae West, W. C. Fields; *d* Edward Cline; *s* Mae West, W. C. Fields, Joseph Calleia.

My Twentieth Century, 1990, *wd* Ildiko Enyeko; *s* Dorotha Segda, Oleg Jankovskij, Paulius Manker.

National Velvet, 1945, *w* Theodore Reeves, Helen Deutsch, from the novel by Enid Bagnold; *d* Clarence Brown; *s* Elizabeth Taylor, Mickey Rooney, Anne Revere.

Night Song, 1947, *w* Frank Fenton et al.; *d* John Cromwell; *s* Dana Andrews, Merle Oberon.

Ninotchka, 1939, *w* Charles Brackett, Billy Wilder, Walter Reisch, from a story by Melchior Lengyel; *d* Ernst Lubitsch; *s* Greta Garbo, Melvyn Douglas.

North by Northwest, 1959, *w* Ernest Lehman; *d* Alfred Hitchcock; *s* Cary Grant, Eva Marie Saint.

Nudo di Donna, 1984, *w* Nino Manfredi, Paolo Levi; *d* Nino Manfredi; *s* Eleanora Giorgi, Carlo Bagno.

Olivier, Olivier, 1992, *w* Agnieszka Holland et al.; *d* Agnieszka Holland; *s* Françoise Cluzet, Brigitte Rouan, Jean-Françoise Stévenin.

On the Double, 1961, *w* Jack Rose, Melville Shavelson; *d* Melville Shavelson; *s* Danny Kaye, Dana Wynter, Diana Dors.

On the Riviera, 1951, *w* Valentine Davies, Phoebe Ephron, Henry Ephron; *d* Walter Lang; *s* Danny Kaye.

Our Man in Havana, 1959, *w* Graham Greene, from his novel; *d* Carol Reed; *s* Alec Guinness, Noel Coward.

Overboard, 1987, *w* Leslie Dixon; *d* Garry Marshal; *s* Goldie Hawn, Kurt Russell.

Peggy Sue Got Married, 1986, *w* Jerry Leichtling, Arlene Sarner; *d* Francis Coppola; *s* Kathleen Turner, Nicholas Cage.

The Picture of Dorian Gray, 1945, *wd* Albert Lewin; *s* George Sanders, Hurd Hatfield, Donna Reed, Angela Lansbury, Peter Lawford.

Pinky, 1949, *w* Philip Dunne, Dudley Nichols, from Cid Ricketts Summer's novel *Quality; d* Elia Kazan; *s* Jeanne Crain, Ethel Barrymore, Ethel Waters.

Pleasantville, 1998, *w* Don Knotts; *d* Gary Ross; *s* William Macey, Joan Allen.

Portrait of Jenny, 1948, *w* Peter Bernais et al., from the novel by Robert Nathan; *d* William Dieterle; *s* Jennifer Jones, Joseph Cotton.

Prelude to a Kiss, 1992, *w* Craig Lucas, from his play; *d* Norman René; *s* Alec Baldwin, Meg Ryan, Sydney Walker.

The Prisoner of Zenda, 1937, *w* John Balderston, Wills Root, Donald Ogden Stewart, from the novel by Anthony Hope; *d* John Cromwell; *s* Ronald Colman, Douglas Fairbanks, Jr., Madeleine Carroll.

The Prisoner of Zenda, 1952, *w* John Balderston, Noel Langley; *d* Richard Thorpe; *s* Stewart Granger, James Mason, Deborah Kerr, Robert Coote.

The Prisoner of Zenda, 1979, *w* Dick Clement, Ian La Frenais; *d* Richard Quine; *s* Peter Sellers, Lionel Jeffries, Elke Sommer.

Psycho, 1960, *w* Joseph Stefano, from the novel by Robert Bloch; *d* Alfred Hitchcock; *s* Anthony Perkins, Vera Miles, Janet Leigh.

Queen Christina, 1933, *w* Salk Viertel, H. M. Harwood, S. N. Behrman; *d* Rouben Mamoulian; *s* Greta Garbo, John Gilbert.

Rebecca, 1940, *w* Robert E. Sherwood, Joan Harrison, from the novel by Daphne du Maurier; *d* Alfred Hitchcock; *s* Laurence Olivier, Joan Fontaine.

La règle du jeu (The Rules of the Game), 1939, *w* Jean Renoir, Carl Koch; *d* Jean Renoir; *s* Marcel Dalio, Nora Gregor, Jean Renoir.

The Reincarnation of Peter Proud, 1974, *w* Max Ehrlich, from his novel; *d* J. Lee-Thompson; *s* Michael Sarrazin, Margot Kidder, Jennifer O'Neill.

Le retour de Martin Guerre, 1982, *w* Jean-Claude Carrière, Daniel Vigne; *d* Daniel Vigne; *s* Gérard Depardieu, Nathalie Baye.

Return from the Ashes, 1965, *w* Julius J. Epstein, from the novel by Hubert Monteilhet; *d* J. Lee-Thompson; *s* Ingrid Thulin, Maximillian Schell, Samantha Eggar, Herbert Lom.

Revenge of the Nerds, 1984, *d* Jeff Kanew; *s* Robert Carradine, Anthony Edwards, Timothy Busfield, Andrew Casses.

The Richest Girl in the World, 1934, *w* Norman Krasna; *d* William A. Seiter; remade, in 1944, as *Bride by Mistake*, with Laraine Day.

Roxanne, 1987, *w* Steve Martin; *d* Fred Schepisi; *s* Steve Martin, Daryl Hannah.

The Scar, 1948, *w* Daniel Fuchs, from a novel by Murray Forbes; *d* Steve Sekely; *s* Joan Bennett, Paul Henreid, Leslie Brooks, Mabel Page. (Formerly called *Hollow Triumph*.)

"Second Chances," in *Star Trek: The Next Generation*, week of May 24, 1993, no. 250; *w* René Echevarria, from a story by Michael A. Medlock; *d* LeVar Burton; *s* Jonathan Frakes, Marina Sirtis.

Seven Sinners, 1936, *w* John Meehan, Harry Tugend; lyrics by Frank Loesser; *d* Tay Garnett; *s* Marlene Dietrich, John Wayne.

Shattered, 1991, *w* Wolfgang Petersen, from Richard Neely's novel *The Plastic Nightmare*; *d* Wolfgang Petersen; *s* Tom Berenger, Greta Scacchi, Bob Hoskins.

She Woke Up Pregnant, 1996, made for television; *w* Michael O'Hara; *d* James A. Cotner; *s* Michele Greene, Joy Penny, Linda Carter.

Showboat, 1936, *w* Oscar Hammerstein II, from the novel by Edna Ferber; *d* James Whale; *s* Helen Morgan, Irene Dunne, Paul Robeson; 1951, *w* John Lee Mahin; *d* George Sidney; *s* Ava Gardner, Kathryn Grayson, William Warfield, Joe E. Brown.

Single White Female, 1992, *w* Don Roos, from John Lutz's novel *Single White Female Seeks Same*; *d* Barbet Shroeder; *s* Bridget Fonda, Jennifer Jason Leigh.

Sirens, 1994, *wd* John Duigan; *s* Hugh Grant, Tara Fitzgerald, Sam Neill, Elle Macpherson.

Sleeper, 1973, *w* Woody Allen, Marshall Brickman; *d* Woody Allen; *s* Woody Allen, Diane Keaton.

Snow White and the Seven Dwarfs, 1937, *w* Ted Sears et al., from the fairy tale by the Brothers Grimm.

Some Like It Hot, 1959, *w* Billy Wilder, I. A. L. Diamond; *d* Billy Wilder; *s* Jack Lemmon, Tony Curtis, Marilyn Monroe, Joe E. Brown, George Raft.

Sommersby, 1993, *w* Nicholas Meyer, Sarah Kernochan; *d* Jon Amiel; *s* Richard Gere, Jodie Foster, James Earl Jones, Bill Pullman.

Spellbound, 1945, *w* Ben Hecht, from Francis Beeding's novel *The House of Dr. Edwares; d* Alfred Hitchcock, with dream sequences by Salvador Dali; *s* Ingrid Bergman, Gregory Peck, Leo G. Carroll.

Splash, 1984, *w* Lowell Ganz et al.; *d* Ron Howard; *s* Tom Hanks, Daryl Hannah.

The Stepford Wives, 1974, *w* William Goldman, from the novel by Ira Levin; *d* Bryan Forbes; *s* Katharine Ross, Paula Prentiss, Patrick O'Neal.

A Stolen Life, 1946, *w* Catherine Turney; *d* Curtis Bernhardt; *s* Bette Davis, Glenn Ford. (Also 1939, *w* Marget Kennedy, George Barraud, from the novel by Karel J. Benes; *d* Paul Czinner; *s* Elizabeth Bergner, Michael Redgrave.)

A Streetcar Named Desire, 1951, *w* Tennessee Williams from his play; *d* Elia Kazan; *s* Marlon Brando, Vivien Leigh, Kim Hunter, Karl Malden.

Switch, 1991, *wd* Blake Edwards; *s* Ellen Barkin.

Sylvia Scarlett, 1935, *w* Gladys Unger et al., from the novel by Compton Mackenzie; *d* George Cukor; *s* Katharine Hepburn, Cary Grant.

The Tales of Hoffmann, 1951, *wd* Michael Powell, Emeric Pressburger; *s* Robert Rounseville, Robert Helpmann, Pamela Brown, Moira Shearer, Ludmilla Tcherina.

There's Something about Mary, 1998, *wd* Peter Farrelly, Bobby Farrelly; *s* Cameron Diaz, Matt Dillon, Ben Stiller, Lee Evans, Chris Elliott.

They Live, 1988, *w* Frank Armitage, from the story "Eight O'Clock in the Morning" by Ray Nelson; *d* John Carpenter; *s* Roddy Piper, Keith David, Meg Foster, George "Buck" Flower, Jason Robards III.

The Three Faces of Eve, 1957, *w* Nunnally Johnson, from the book by Corbett H. Thigpen and Hervey M. Cleckley; *d* Nunnally Johnson; *s* Joanne Woodward, Lee J. Cobb, David Wayne.

Tie Me Up! Tie Me Down!, 1989, *wd* Pedro Almodóvar; *s* Victoria Abril, Antonio Banderas.

To Be or Not to Be, 1942, *w* Edwin Justus Mayer, from a story by Ernst Lubitsch and Melchior Lengyel; *d* Ernst Lubitsch; *s* Jack Benny, Carole Lombard; 1983, *w* Thomas Meehan, Ronnie Graham; *d* Alan Johnson; *s* Mel Brooks, Anne Bancroft, Charles Durning, Christopher Lloyd.

Tom Jones, 1963, *w* John Osborne, from the novel by Henry Fielding; *d* Tony Richardson; *s* Albert Finney, Susannah York, Hugh Griffith, Diane Cilento.

Tootsie, 1982, *w* Larry Gelbart, Murray Shisgal; *d* Sidney Pollack; *s* Dustin Hoffman, Jessica Lange, Teri Garr, Dabney Coleman, Charles Durning, Sidney Pollack.

Trading Places, 1983, *w* Timohy Harris, Herschel Weingrod; *d* John Landis; *s* Dan Aykroyd, Eddie Murphy.

True Lies, 1994, *wd* James Cameron; *s* Arnold Schwarzenegger, Jamie Lee Curtis.

The Truth about Cats and Dogs, 1996, *w* Audrey Wells; *d* Michael Lehmann; *s* Uma Thurman, Janeane Garofalo, Ben Chaplin.

Turnabout, 1940, *w* Mickell Novak, Berne Giler, John McLain, from the novel by Thorne Smith; *d* Hal Roach; *s* Adolphe Menjou, John Hubbard, Carole Landis.

Twice Blessed, 1945, *w* Ethel Hill; *d* Harry Beaumont; *s* Preston Foster, Gail Patrick.

Two-Faced Woman, 1941, *w* S. N. Behrman, Salka Viertel, George Oppenheimer, from the play by Ludwig Fulda; *d* George Cukor; *s* Greta Garbo, Melvyn Douglas.

Two Much, 1996, *w* Fernando Trueba, David Trueba, based on the novel by Donald E. Westlake; *d* Fernando Trueba; *s* Antonio Banderas, Melanie Griffith, Daryl Hannah.

The Unbearable Lightness of Being, 1987, *w* Jean-Claude Carrière, Philip Kaufman, from the novel by Milan Kundera; *d* Philip Kaufman; *s* Daniel Day-Lewis, Juliette Binoche, Lena Olin.

Vertigo, 1958, *w* Alec Coppel, Samuel Taylor, from the novel *D'entre les morts,* by

Pierre Boileau and Thomas Narcejac; *d* Alfred Hitchcock; *s* James Stewart, Kim Novak, Barbara Bel Geddes.

Vice Versa, 1947, *w* Peter Ustinov, from the novel by F. Anstey; *d* Peter Ustinov; *s* Roger Livesey, Kay Walsh, Anthony Newley.

Vice Versa, 1988, *w* Dick Clement, Ian La Frenais; *d* Brian Gilbert; *s* Judge Reinhold, Fred Savage.

Victor/Victoria, 1982, *w* Blake Edwards, from the German film of 1933, *Viktor und Viktoria* (*wd* Reinhold Schunzel); *d* Blake Edwards; *s* Julie Andrews, James Garner, Robert Preston.

Watermelon Man, 1970, *w* Herman Raucher; *d* Melvin Van Peebles; *s* Godfrey Cambridge, Estelle Parsons.

What Happened in the Tunnel, 1903, *d* Thomas Edison.

While You Were Sleeping, 1995, *w* Daniel G. Sullivan, Fredric Lebow; *d* Jon Turteltaub; *s* Sandra Bullock, Bill Pullman.

White, 1995, *w* Krzysztof Piesiewicz, Krzysztof Kieslowski; *d* Krzysztof Kieslowski; *s* Zbigniew Zamachowski, Julie Delpy.

The Wizard of Oz, 1939, *w* L. Frank Baum, Jr., Leon Lee, Larry Semon, from the novel by L. Frank Baum; *d* Victor Fleming; *s* Judy Garland, Bert Lahr, and Ray Bolger.

Wolf, 1994, *w* Jim Harrison; *d* Mike Nichols; *s* Jack Nicholson, Michelle Pfeiffer.

Wonder Man, 1945, *w* Don Hartman et al.; *d* Bruce Humberstone; *s* Danny Kaye, Vera Ellen.

Yentl, 1983, *w* Jack Rosenthal, Barbra Streisand, from the story by Isaac Bashevis Singer; *d* Barbra Streisand; *s* Barbra Streisand, Mandy Patinkin, Amy Irving, Nehemiah Persoff.

You're Never Too Young, 1955, *w* Sidney Sheldon; *d* Norman Taurog; *s* Dean Martin, Jerry Lewis, Diana Lynn, Nina Foch.

Zelig, 1983, *wd* Woody Allen; *s* Woody Allen, Mia Farrow.

INDEX AND GLOSSARY